JOHN HOWARD
Lazarus Rising

JOHN HOWARD

Lazarus Rising

A PERSONAL AND POLITICAL AUTOBIOGRAPHY

HarperCollins*Publishers*

HarperCollins*Publishers*

First published in Australia in 2010
by HarperCollins*Publishers* Australia Pty Limited
ABN 36 009 913 517
harpercollins.com.au

HarperCollins*Publishers*
25 Ryde Road, Pymble, Sydney, NSW 2073, Australia
31 View Road, Glenfield, Auckland 0627, New Zealand
A 53, Sector 57, Noida, UP, India
77–85 Fulham Palace Road, London, W6 8JB, United Kingdom
2 Bloor Street East, 20th floor, Toronto, Ontario M4W 1A8, Canada
10 East 53rd Street, New York NY 10022, USA

National Library of Australia Cataloguing-in-Publication data:

Howard, John, 1939–
    Lazarus rising / John Howard.
    ISBN: 978 0 7322 8995 9 (hbk.)
    Includes index.
    Howard, John, 1939-
    Liberal Party of Australia.
    Prime ministers – Australia – Biography.
    Politicians – Australia – Biography.
    Political leadership – Australia.
    Australia – Politics and government – 1996–
994.066092

Cover design by Philip Campbell Design
Front cover image © Sam Mooy/Newspix
Back cover image: The Hon. John W. Howard AC, 2009 by Jiawei Shen (1948–) courtesy of the
Historic Memorials Collection, Department of Parliamentary Services, Canberra, ACT
Flap pictures courtesy Auspic
Index by Alan Walker
Picture sections design, Alicia Freile, Tango Media
Typeset in 10.5/14pt Minion by Kirby Jones
70gsm Bulky Book Ivory used by HarperCollins*Publishers* is a natural, recyclable product made from
wood grown in sustainable forests. The manufacturing processes conform to the environmental
regulations in the country of origin, New Zealand.

9 8 7 6 5   10 11 12 13

*To my parents, who gave me the values and
determination I took into public life*

*To John Carrick, my mentor,
from whom I learned more about politics than anyone else*

*To my family,
whose love and support sustained me through my years
in parliament and government*

CONTENTS

PART 1

EARLY LIFE AND THE FRASER GOVERNMENT

1

THE SOURCE

Towards the bottom of William Street, Earlwood, in the 1940s there was a paddock; it was next to a baby health centre. Later, the paddock disappeared when a library and new baby health centre were built. Near the end of 1949 that paddock was a hive of activity as the nerve centre of the local efforts to re-elect Daniel Mulcahy as Labor member for the division of Lang, in the federal parliament. The Howard household, at 25 William Street, lay diagonally opposite this paddock. Mulcahy was the first member of parliament I had consciously set eyes on. He wore a three-piece suit and smoked a pipe.

The Labor campaign team for Lang had put up a temporary shed on the paddock. Plenty of people, mainly men, came and went, picking up leaflets and generally looking very busy. This was my first contact with local grassroots election campaigning. Although the suburb of Earlwood then produced a Liberal vote of about 45 to 50 per cent, the Labor Party never had much trouble in holding the seat; the other suburbs in Lang, like Campsie, Canterbury and Belmore, were very solidly Labor.

I knew nothing about Mulcahy other than what my mother told me: he lived in Darling Point, in Sydney's wealthy eastern suburbs, owned a number of hotels and by reputation was one of the most affluent MPs in the parliament.

I once saw him speaking outside the Earlwood Hotel. Later I heard Liberal supporters say that he only turned up at election time, shouted the bar and on the strength of that got re-elected. I am sure that this was quite unfair, and that he was probably a conscientious member, but that was the typecasting of political opponents.

That Labor shed really interested me. I would stand on the edge of the paddock looking at it and the campaign workers milling around. They gave the impression of doing something important. Observing it began a lifelong fascination of mine with politics. This book is my story of that fascination, my career in Australian and world politics and a commentary on the changes in Australian society and national life during the 60 years which have passed since I first gazed at that shed.

Any narrative of politics must include the shaping and implementation of policies which influence the direction of a nation and as well the constant interaction of personalities, particularly within political parties. The regular swirl of ideas, ambition and egos inevitably produces rivalries and, in some instances, alienation.

In this book I explore the public policy issues I grappled with as a member of parliament for more than 33 years. In addition, I endeavour to deal objectively with the key relationships of my years in politics, the difficulties in them as well as the generosity, loyalty and decency which they involved.

Mum and Dad were born at the tail end of the 19th century, my father in 1896 and my mother in 1899. As such, their lives were forever shaped by the three historic tragedies of the 20th century — World War I, the Great Depression and World War II. To this day I marvel at the stoicism of a generation which coped with the trauma, deprivation and sadness of those epic events, but still kept intact the cohesive and optimistic society which later generations were to inherit.

The American journalist Tom Brokaw called the generation which came of age during the Great Depression and World War II the Greatest Generation, and that phrase has resonated powerfully amongst Americans. That same generation of Australians also is owed an immense debt of gratitude by mine and later generations for what they endured for Australia. In Australia, however, the description of the Greatest Generation would have to belong to the generation before the one of which Brokaw wrote. That was my parents' generation, because it directly experienced the impact of World War I.

Although America joined the Great War in 1917, its effect on that nation was nothing like it was for Australia. For our nation, no tragedy has matched that of World War I. The loss of life was on a scale that today's generation would find impossible to come to terms with. Many small country towns never recovered from the staggering losses of their young manhood. To lose more than 60,000 dead, with tens of thousands more blinded and crippled, from a male population of no more than 2.5 million, was a terrible depletion of our precious human resources. Les Carlyon, in his book *The Great War*, wrote, 'There were so many of them, and we never really, saw them.'[1]

Both of my parents left school at the age of 14, as did most children of that era. It was their children's generation that completed secondary education in large numbers, and often went on to university.

My father, Lyall Falconer Howard, was born at Cowper, near Maclean on the Clarence River in northern New South Wales, the eldest of nine children. He attended Maclean Public School. His parents had very little money, and shortly after leaving school he secured an apprenticeship as a fitter and turner at the Harwood Island Mill, on the Clarence River, owned by Colonial Sugar Refinery (CSR). He enlisted in the Australian Imperial Force (AIF) on 27 January 1916 at the age of 19. His first attempt to join up had been unsuccessful because he did not meet the height requirements. He became a signaller with C Company of the 3rd Pioneer Battalion of the 3rd Division.

After several months training in both Brisbane and Melbourne his unit sailed for England on the *Wandilla* on 6 June 1916. His youngest sibling, Ian, was barely a year old when my father left on the troopship for Europe. The 3rd Division was commanded by Sir John Monash, certainly the best field commander Australia has ever produced. Many rank him and Sir Arthur Currie of Canada as the most talented commanders of World War I. Monash insisted that his men undergo extensive training in England before being sent to the front.

Dad's unit spent several months encamped on Salisbury Plain, in Wiltshire, undergoing rigorous training. It left for France late in November. My father spent his first day in the horrible trenches of the Western Front on 1 December 1916, near Armentières.

While my father was at the war, his parents and the remaining eight children moved from Maclean to the suburb of Petersham, in Sydney. My grandfather, who was a marine engineer, had a number of very different jobs in his working life, from harbourmaster at Coffs Harbour to starting what was believed to be the first motion picture show in northern New South Wales, at the Caledonian Hall in Maclean. I suspect that the reason for the family leaving the Clarence during the war was that my grandfather would have found it easier to obtain work in Sydney.

In July 1917, and at the age of 44, my grandfather, Walter Herbert Howard, also enlisted in the 1st AIF. He wound up in the 56th Battalion of the 5th Division, arriving in France during the early part of 1918. Meanwhile, my father had been gassed during a German attack near Messine Ridge, in Belgium, in July 1917; he returned to the front after a brief hospitalisation. For the rest of his life he would experience the after-effects of the mustard gas he ingested, in the form of weakened lungs and recurring bouts of dermatitis.

The Australian divisions to which my father and grandfather were attached both took part in the Battle of Villers-Bretonneux in April 1918. The gratitude of the villagers from there to *les Australiens*, who halted a major German advance during the liberation of the town, persists to this day. Villers-Bretonneux is the site of the giant Australian War Memorial to those who perished on the Western Front, and the place where a special Anzac Day ceremony is now held.

Later that year, by a remarkable coincidence, my father and grandfather met near the French village of Clery on 30 August 1918, on the eve of the battle of Mont St Quentin, in which my father's unit participated. Just three days later my grandfather was wounded in the stomach, evacuated and took no further part in the war.

Eighty-two years later, as Prime Minister of Australia, and with the assistance of the very helpful army defence attaché, Colonel Chris Galvin, from the Australian Embassy in Paris, I was able to establish roughly where my father and grandfather had met up all those years ago.

One of the journalists who accompanied me on that visit, Tony Wright of the *Age*, described the scene thus:

> On Friday, at the village of Clery, between a farmhouse and the great marshes and ponds and swiftly-flowing streams of the Upper Somme River, those experts found for him the most likely spot where his father and grandfather had met. Howard carried with him excerpts from his father's wartime diary. The entry for August 30 1918, reads simply 'Met dad at Clery'. Here in Clery, close to the slopes of Mont St Quentin, the site of one of the great battles of World War I, Howard experienced a sort of coming home of the heart. You could see it in his face as he peered intently at the map laid out before him, not heeding the rain falling or the small crowd milling about him.[2]

Wright had captured the emotion of the occasion for me.

I had attended the 85th anniversary of the landing at Gallipoli, at Anzac Cove, and then called to see President Chirac in Paris before visiting the battlefields. French gratitude for the huge sacrifice of Australia in defence of France, so many years before, was not forgotten. At the beginning of our discussion, the President expressed the thanks of his nation for the war service of my father and grandfather.

It was fairly unusual to have father and son fight in the same war. My grandfather died when I was only nine, and it was only occasionally that I talked to my father about his wartime experiences. His generation were a reticent lot. Who could blame them? They had lived through unimaginable horrors, and to come home alive and intact would have been a miracle to celebrate in itself. All those years ago, veterans were encouraged to forget about things, and not talk about their experiences. That was thought to be the right therapy. There weren't too many counsellors then, but returned soldiers were welcomed home as heroes, and in addition to repatriation benefits a variety of special schemes were set up to help them.

My father usually marched on Anzac Day, in Sydney, and the family would go and watch the march. The last Anzac Day that he was alive was in 1955. He hadn't been very well that year so didn't march. Instead he stayed at home, propped himself up on the couch in our back room, and reminisced with me, his youngest son, about his time on the Western Front 40 years earlier.

He told me of being detailed to escort an Australian officer back from the front, towards the end of the war. When they came under heavy attack the other man panicked, telling my father that he had been at the front for three years and was going on extended leave, and feared he would get hit before he made it to safety. There would have been numerous stories of men who had dodged bullets for several years, only to be hit minutes from the relative safety of being away from the front. I recall the story so vividly because Dad rarely spoke about the war. Like most Australians who served in that conflict, he thought that Australian soldiers were the equal of, or superior to, any others. Dad had no hostility towards the Germans who had been his enemies.

When my father came back from the war, he resumed his apprenticeship with CSR, only this time it was at Pyrmont, in inner Sydney, as his family had decamped there. According to my mother, he was retrenched in the early 1920s, during a slump, when the company had a policy of giving preference to the retention of married employees. My father was then still single.

After my mother left school she was employed doing office work with Nock & Kirby's, then a well-known Sydney department store, which disappeared as a separate entity in the 1980s. Two of Dad's sisters also worked in the office at N&K, and it was through them that my parents met.

I took a part-time job with that store in the late 1950s whilst going through university. I was in the pet section for a time, which resulted in Bill Hayden as Opposition leader, years later, dubbing me a budgerigar salesman. The description amused me.

My parents married at the Presbyterian church, Marrickville, on 11 July 1925 and honeymooned at the still-standing Clarendon Guesthouse, Katoomba, in the Blue Mountains west of Sydney.

My mother, born Mona Jane Kell in 1899 in Smith Street, Summer Hill, an inner suburb of Sydney, always found immense security in the familiarity of her home environment. She would often say to me that if she started early in the morning, she could walk to all of the locations in which she had lived and be back at home by lunchtime. Whilst a bit of a stretch, the point being made said a lot about my mother. Mum did not like straying far from her roots, either geographically or the value system by which she lived.

To my mother, family was everything. From her immediate family of husband and four sons to the very large extended Howard family, my mother's life was all about the welfare and, importantly, the stability of her family. Her early family life had been far from happy: losing her mother to a brain tumour at age eight, and having a father whom she clearly adored, but who was a heavy drinker, she plainly found in my responsible and sober father a source of security and dependability.

The heavy drinking of my grandfather had a lasting impact on my mother. She retained throughout her life a real dread of alcoholism and virtually anything associated with drinking. I enjoy a drink but realised, as the years went by, how deep and understandable had been my mother's reaction.

Many years ago, drinking habits were different; women drank a lot less. It was very much a male pursuit. Men got drunk at hotels and staggered home, often to the great public embarrassment of their families. There was much less drinking at home than is the case today. For many women and children, the local hotel was anything but a place associated with warm conviviality.

Something else was to touch Mum's younger years: that was sectarianism. She was a child of what was once called a 'mixed marriage'; that is, her father was a Protestant and her mother a Catholic. After her mother's death, although Mum had been baptised a Catholic, her father sent her to a Church of England Sunday school. There was subsequent estrangement with her mother's family and, given the Catholic/Protestant divide of the time, that action of my grandfather had likely been a cause.

Mum was a good Christian, totally lacking any pretensions in her dealings with others. She was privately devout. Every night she would kneel at her bedside to say her prayers. Sadly, however, she was always self-conscious about the fact that she had been born Catholic, but raised Protestant. For people of her generation, regrettably, those differences mattered much more than would later become the case. For all of her life she retained what I thought to be an unreasonable suspicion of Catholicism. Then I was of a generation which, in the 1960s, would experience the welcome disintegration of sectarianism.

Mum had a sister, May, and a brother, Charlie, and after her father's remarriage following her mother's death, two half-brothers, Ted and Arthur. She spoke frequently of her affection for her stepmother, and how fortunate she had been in having her after losing her mother at such an early age.

Premature death returned to Mum's family in a particularly tragic way, several months before I was born. Ted, who had been diagnosed with epilepsy at the age of 16, suffered a seizure while standing on Newtown Railway Station, in inner Sydney, and fell under an oncoming train. He died from the terrible injuries he sustained. To add to the family's grief, May, Mum's sister, was a passenger on the train.

Mum's family never owned their own home, and always lived in rented accommodation in and around Petersham and Lewisham, inner suburbs of Sydney. I suspect that my grandfather was an unsuccessful punter, and that his gambling habits were strongly disapproved of by both his wife and his elder daughter. Whenever I visited their home as a young child there was a sad atmosphere. As I grew older, and learned more of the background, I understood why.

Grandfather Joe Kell was a great walker. When over 80 he would regularly walk from his home in New Canterbury Road, Petersham, to his daughter May's place in Wardell Road, Earlwood, a distance of almost 4 kilometres. That is something he passed on to one of his grandsons.

Mum's brothers, Charlie and Arthur, had both fought in World War II, Charlie in the army, and Arthur in the Royal Australian Air Force (RAAF). Charlie had been part of an army unit guarding the Cowra prisoner of war camp when the Japanese breakout occurred The experience permanently clouded his attitude towards the Japanese because of their behaviour during the breakout.

Charlie's marriage had broken up by the time I was in my teens, and his only close family were his two sisters. Charlie had always drunk heavily, and his failed marriage only made this worse. I respected the way in which Mum tried to help him, having him home regularly, despite Charlie often being the worse for wear. Her tense reaction whenever he was affected by drink showed just how strongly her childhood experiences of alcoholism had affected her. She often told me that she thought Charlie had had a tough life, frequently mentioning the fact that he had spent the night of his 21st birthday sleeping under a bridge, whilst on the track for work in the Shepparton area of Victoria in the mid-1920s.

My mother and her sister May (Roberts) were very close. May did not marry until her early 40s and had no children. She lived in the same suburb as us and saw a great deal of our family, especially me. We formed a very close bond, as she also did with my brother Bob, when we were all a good deal older. May had a genuinely sunny and positive disposition. To employ a phrase typical of her generation, her life had been no 'bed of roses', yet she always seemed happy with her lot. She was a wonderful woman, and like my wife's mother, Beryl Parker, had an extraordinary capacity always to see the best in people. She was a special person and I remember her with very deep love and affection.

Lyall and Mona Howard had four sons: Walter (Wal), born in 1926, Stanley (Stan) in 1930, Robert (Bob) in 1936 and me in 1939. The Great Depression had its impact on family planning.

As best I could describe it, I grew up in a stable, lower middle-class home. When Dad went into business, establishing a garage with his father, he was able to make a reasonably comfortable living for our family. Mum was a full-time homemaker, who dedicated her life to the care and upbringing of her four sons. Mum and Dad were both conservative, patriotic Australians.

The house I grew up in was a Californian bungalow, built in the early 1920s. Earlwood, in Sydney's inner southwest, was full of them. It was heavily settled after the Great War. Street names such as Flers, Hamilton, Dellwood, Kitchener and Fricourt were testament to that. It was a three-bedroom home, so until I was well into my teens I shared a bedroom with Bob. About my earliest memory was looking at the blackout paper which my parents had placed over the small casement window in the loungeroom. That must have been in 1942, when there were frequent blackouts in Sydney through fear of possible air raids.

Politics was talked a lot at home. From a very early age I listened to discussions about world events, as well as particular issues affecting Sydney and Australia. Being the youngest in the family, it was natural that I imbibed much from my parents and elder brothers.

Towards the end of 1949, I knew that there was an election coming up from the talk at home, seeing the newspapers and listening to the Australian Broadcasting Commission (ABC) news. Mum and Dad were both strong Liberals and had plenty of good things to say about Bob Menzies, then Leader of the Opposition, but soon to become prime minister and to stay in that position longer than any other person in Australian history.

Owning a garage, or service station, my father had been bedevilled from the war years onwards by petrol rationing. Dad would bring home the ration tickets and my brother Bob would join me in counting them on the breakfast-room table. I thought this was a lot of fun, and I missed it when it ended. My parents didn't. Menzies' 1949 election promise to remove petrol rationing attracted them greatly, and they were delighted when it was abolished.

Petrol rationing had been an understandable wartime measure, but in peacetime it was a real bugbear for anyone in my father's business, and motorists generally. It was abolished for a period and then brought back shortly before the 1949 election.

The Labor PM at the time, Ben Chifley, was well liked. To his credit, his Government began the great postwar migration surge — then overseen by his Immigration Minister Arthur Calwell — which helped shape the modern Australia. He also launched the Snowy Mountains Hydro-Electric Scheme, which remains a national development icon.

But when it came to economics, the Chifley Labor Government, in the late '40s, remained locked in the wartime mindset of controls and micro-management of the economy.

Chifley led a government which tried to nationalise the private trading banks. This move galvanised into action many supporters of free enterprise, and not just the banks. Everything had gone wrong for Chifley following his Government's re-election in 1946. His attempt to nationalise the banks had been rejected as unconstitutional by both the High Court of Australia and the Privy Council. Massive strikes on the NSW coalfields in 1949 produced prolonged blackouts in Sydney. In the end Chifley had to embrace what for a Labor man like him must have been a nightmare: the use of troops on the coalfields to keep essential supplies moving.

The times were clearly right for a man and a party preaching the gospel of competition and fewer government controls. Bob Menzies and the Liberal Party neatly filled the bill. Anyhow, that was what my parents, Lyall and Mona Howard, thought. So did my eldest brother, Wal, the only one of their children then to have a vote.

My parents were part of the 'forgotten people' who Menzies had defined in his famous radio broadcast in 1942: they neither belonged to organised labour, nor were rich and powerful. He called them middle class, with the description of 'salary-earners, shopkeepers, skilled artisans, professional men and women, farmers, and so on'. Mum and Dad aimed to give their four sons more security and more opportunities than they themselves had had. In that, they were successful, for which I and my brothers are eternally grateful.

Several days before the election took place a newspaper I bought carried the headline 'Final Gallup Poll Predicts Coalition Victory'. On election night, my brother Bob and I had gone to a local picture theatre with our parents. During the screening of the second film, the theatre management displayed a slide which showed that the Coalition had taken an early lead. In those days polling booths remained open until 8 pm.

When we got home, we found my brother Wal sitting on the floor in front of the radio. He said that Menzies had won and that the biggest swing had been in Queensland. On that latter score at least, nothing much has changed in almost 60 years. When the Coalition won government in 1996, Labor was routed in the Sunshine State, and in 2007 the Labor Party achieved a greater swing in that state than in any other part of Australia. Everyone in our household was very happy with the result. Daniel Mulcahy was comfortably returned as the Labor member for Lang. Those shed workers across the road had done their job.

For as long as I can remember, I was a regular listener to sport on ABC Radio, mainly cricket and rugby league. Cricket always came first. I knew the names of Bradman, Miller and Lindwall before I learned the name Menzies. My father took me to the Sydney Cricket Ground on 28 February

1949 to see Don Bradman play for the last time at that ground, in the Kippax-Oldfield Testimonial. It was the only occasion on which I saw the great man play.

I also had a keen interest in boxing. I could recite, in order, all of the heavyweight champions of the world from James J. Corbett onwards. Controversies in boxing, such as the famous long count in the bout between Jack Dempsey and Gene Tunney, enthralled me. I was fascinated when I read that Sydney had hosted a fight for the heavyweight title in 1909 between Tommy Burns and Jack Johnson. In my late teens I went to Sydney Stadium, in Rushcutters Bay, to see several bouts. Years later, when I was in politics, some of my friends were horrified when I confessed to my boyhood interest in boxing. As I grew older I lost interest in it, in part because I realised the terrible damage people suffered, but I had been quite taken by it in my youth.

From a young age I was an avid reader of the Biggles books, authored by Captain W.E. Johns, which told the story of a group of British airmen who not only fought heroically in the Battle of Britain but did other great things in defence of liberty. A little later I devoured books such as *Reach for the Sky*, by Paul Brickhill, an Australian, which covered the amazing war service of Douglas Bader, who lost both legs but resumed flying in the Royal Air Force (RAF); *The Dambusters*, the saga of the RAF bombing raids on the dams of the Ruhr Valley; and Nicholas Monsarrat's classic *The Cruel Sea*. This book, which like the other two led to a film of the same name, covered the perils and heavy human losses involved in keeping open the sea lanes from Britain to Russia through the North Sea. Barely a decade had passed since the end of World War II and books and films about aspects of that huge conflict abounded.

I read a lot of sporting books, naturally starting with cricket. Two which I still have in the sports section of my bookshelves at home are *Straight Hit*, co-written by Keith Miller, one of Australia's greatest-ever all-rounders, and R.S. Whitington. It told of the West Indies' tour of Australia in 1951–52. I read it again and again over a period of years. The other was *A Century of Cricketers*, by A.G. 'Johnny' Moyes. He had compiled the stories of one hundred famous cricketers, ending in about 1950. Moyes was an accomplished analyst. It was a different era and a vastly different medium, but he was something of a Richie Benaud of radio.

As I grew older my reading tastes expanded to include history as well as biographies. To this day I maintain a marked preference for books in these two categories. My father subscribed to the *Saturday Evening Post*, a well-illustrated American periodical, which I read thoroughly. It gave me an early feel for some of the differences in both American culture and politics. This was the early 1950s, and hostility to communism came through strongly in the pages of the magazine.

We always had a dog. For almost 14 years we had a marvellous Irish setter named Caesar. He went everywhere with me, even to church, where he would position himself in the back vestibule. Nobody seemed to mind; it was, after all, his home territory. He had to be put down not long before I turned 21. I took him to the vet, and I cried as he died in my arms.

The 1950s, when I grew up, was probably the most stable, secure and prosperous decade Australia had yet experienced in the 20th century. There are many now who belittle 1950s Australia. In the process they do their country and an earlier generation much disservice. True, the Australia I was raised in was far from perfect. Women were denied many opportunities; the white Australia policy was still in place; and the plight of Indigenous Australians had yet to stir the national consciousness.

But it is beyond churlish to deny the achievement of an era when so many struggling Australian families secured a modest level of material comfort, sent children to university for the first time and laid the economic and social foundations of modern Australia.

Television arrived in 1956, the year that I did my Leaving Certificate. For most of the decade, and before television changed forever the leisure habits of Australians, going to the pictures was a major social pursuit. It certainly was for the Howards, and going to the pictures for us meant on Saturday nights. Saturday afternoon matinees were off limits. That was when young men were meant to be in the open air, playing sport.

This was Hollywood's golden era, years before the renaissance of the Australian film industry. American films dominated the screen, although there was a reasonable stream of British productions featuring such talented actors as Alec Guinness. The familiarity I felt with both London and New York, especially the latter, when I first saw those cities in the 1960s was a mark of the cultural deposit left by Hollywood in its hey-day.

We four boys and our mother attended and were involved in the activities of the local Methodist church, which stood opposite our home at 25 William Street. The church played a big part in the lives of all of us, but in different ways. For my eldest brothers, Wal and Stan, it was in their teen years a large part of their social life, more so than for Bob and me. I maintained regular attendance at the church until I left Earlwood in my late 20s. My brothers and I indulged our sporting passions through the church.

Earlwood Methodist Church had a large congregation, and was able to field several teams in the very extensive Protestant church cricket and soccer competitions. At one stage the four of us, and one of our uncles, making five Howards in all, played in the church cricket team. I have fond memories of many Saturday afternoons in the sun, playing cricket for Earlwood Meths at grounds such as Rudd Park in Belmore, and Tempe Reserve and Steele Park in Undercliffe. This cricket competition proudly boasts Bob Simpson and Brian Booth, both Australian Test Cricket captains, amongst those who played for their local church teams at a very young age.

Although our lives revolved very much around the church, religion and theology were rarely discussed at home. My father was a very infrequent churchgoer. He was a believer, but not a participant. My parents belonged to a generation of Australians which did not talk a lot about religion, even if they held to their faith. Then again, it was an era in which personal feelings generally, and not just about religion, tended to be internalised. The willingness of today's generation, especially men, to speak more openly about their feelings is something to be welcomed. This is an area where the good old days were definitely not better.

We grew up at a time when church attendance was much higher, and when a moral consensus flowing from the Judaeo-Christian ethic held a largely unchallenged place in Australian society. The influence of the Christian religion, even amongst those who privately repudiated it, was both strong and pervasive.

The fundamentals of Christian belief and practice which I learned at the Earlwood Methodist Church have stayed with me to this day, although I would not pretend to be other than an imperfect adherent to them. I now attend a local Anglican church, denominational labels within Christianity meaning nothing to me. Any religious belief requires a large act of faith. To many people, believing in something that cannot be proved is simply a step too far. To me, by contrast, human life seems so complex and hard to explain yet so extraordinary that the existence of God has always seemed to offer a better explanation of its meaning than any other.

The extended Howard family, given that Dad had been one of nine children, was quite large. My paternal grandmother, Jane Falconer Howard, lived with one or other of her daughters for the last years of her life. Most Sunday afternoons involved visits to my grandmother. She was a stoic woman, confined to a wheelchair from the age of 62 as a result of rheumatoid arthritis. Deeply religious, she was in every way the matriarch of the family until her death in 1953, when I was aged 14. I have quite happy recollections of extended Howard family gatherings for special occasions, which brought me in touch with my numerous cousins.

A great Howard family ritual was observance of Bonfire Night, strictly speaking Empire Day, 24 May, that date being marked because it had been Queen Victoria's birthday. We always had large amounts of fireworks, built huge bonfires, had a half-day school holiday and enjoyed ourselves immensely. Like all Western societies Australia has become a nanny state on activities such as this. As a consequence today's children are denied much innocent fun. I think that fireworks prohibitions are ridiculous.

My parents were quiet, even shy people whose total focus was the care and upbringing of their four children. They wanted us to have better educational opportunities than they had enjoyed. Doing homework or studying for university exams took precedence over everything else at home. My mother and father would frequently forgo listening to the radio — after the ABC news of course — so that one or more of their children could study undistracted. Often Stan would be at his desk in his bedroom, and Bob and I would be working on the dining-room table. They wanted their children to succeed, and did all in their power to bring that about.

There was nothing self-important or pompous about either of my parents. They actively discouraged such character traits in their children and were scornful of anyone who exhibited what their generation called 'side'. We were taught to be polite to people doing menial tasks. My mother rebuked me at the pictures one night because I had used my foot to push a sweet wrapper towards a cleaning lady who was collecting rubbish during interval. She said that I should have picked it up and handed it to her.

Due to the age difference, I had a minor form of hero worship towards my two eldest brothers, Wal and Stan. At the age of 15, I was absolutely devastated when Wal was not elected captain of the church cricket team. This was because he took it for granted, owing to his seniority, that he would be elected. He had not bothered to organise his numbers. I thought the decision of the team was most unfair, and it left me feeling upset and angry for weeks. I found it hard to accept that the other members of the team would not all want Wal as captain. It also taught me a lesson about ballots, which I have never forgotten.

I attended Earlwood Public School, the local primary school, and won admission to Canterbury Boys' High School, then one of the nine selective high schools in Sydney. Its catchment area was the St George and Canterbury-Bankstown districts, a large chunk of southwestern Sydney.

Earlwood Primary School reflected the locality which it serviced. About half of my final-year class had fathers who were tradesmen, and in most other cases they worked in banks, insurance companies or utilities, with just two or three in small business.

In my last year at Earlwood, I had a wonderful teacher, Jack Doherty. He constantly fed my interest in current affairs and conducted plenty of additional question periods on the news of the time. A very fine ABC Radio program called *The World We Live In*, narrated by H.D. Black (later Sir Hermann and Chancellor of Sydney University) and which extensively covered world affairs, was a regular part of our class work. This was in 1951, and the Korean War was still raging. One of the hotly debated issues then was the sacking of General Douglas MacArthur by President Harry Truman. This was a big call by Truman. MacArthur was an iconic World War II figure who had established his headquarters in Brisbane after being pushed out of the Philippines by the Japanese. From there he led the Allied fightback, which ended in victory. When the Korean War started in June 1950 with communist North Korea invading South Korea, MacArthur was the Supreme Allied Commander in the Pacific.

He clashed with Truman over the conduct of the Korean War, wanting to carry the fight against the Chinese, who had come in on the side of the North, over the North Korean border into China itself. Truman opposed this and when their differences could not be resolved, Truman, as Commander-in-Chief, sacked him. I followed these developments avidly.

At the end of primary school, when I was 12, I made my first public speech, at the school presentation day at the local Mayfair Theatre in Earlwood. The headmaster was retiring, and I gave a short speech of thanks on behalf of the teachers and pupils, and presented him with a watch. I was nervous, but it seemed to go well. My father and mother were both there and appeared very proud. Dad was so pleased he gave me my first fountain pen to mark the occasion. I needed one for high school.

My interest in politics mounted during my years at Canterbury Boys' High School, where my active participation in school debates and as a member of the school's debating team in the Combined High Schools' (CHS) competition laid the groundwork for such speaking skills as I was able to bring with me into public life years later. I learned then the great value of speaking 'off the cuff', because a significant part of the debating curriculum required me to speak in an impromptu fashion on subjects of which I had no prior notice. It was marvellous training. It was invaluable during my early years in parliament when, at a moment's notice, I was able to respond to the whip's call and jump into a debate.

The immense merit of formal debating is the discipline of having to articulate the reasons for holding a particular opinion. Years later, in public life, I learned that it was not enough simply to assert a strongly held view. Logically arranged arguments, explaining why that view was held, were crucial. My friend and long-time advisor Grahame Morris would often say to me, when discussing an announcement, 'Boss, what's the why?' In other words, he wanted to hear my explanation.

Perhaps my love of debating, or the chronological memory gifted to me by my mother, or both of them, meant that I never felt comfortable reading a prepared speech. In senior office, it was essential, on certain occasions, to do so. Nonetheless, less than 10 per cent of the speeches I gave as Prime Minister were read from a prepared text. I feel that I always give my best speeches when, having thought about what I will say, I then eyeball the audience, and speak directly to the people in it. Never in my life have I used an autocue or teleprompter. I hold them in contempt as rhetorical crutches.

Canterbury High wasn't all debating though. I played both cricket and rugby in the school's second XI and second XV respectively, in the CHS competition. History and English were far and away the subjects I enjoyed and excelled in most. History fascinated me. One of my real educational regrets was that I never did an arts or economics degree as a precursor to law. Amongst other benefits, it would have allowed me to further indulge my passion for history.

My Leaving Certificate exams, in 1956, were sat against the backdrop of the brutal Soviet invasion of Hungary and the controversial Anglo-French Suez operation. On the happier side there was the great excitement of the Olympic Games coming to Melbourne. It was also a time when Robert Menzies appeared to have established a stranglehold on Australian politics, courtesy of the bitter Labor split of 1955 and the ultimate emergence of the

Democratic Labor Party (DLP), initially called the Labor Party (Anti-Communist), which in 1961 would save Menzies from otherwise certain defeat.

Both of my parents were fierce believers in private enterprise. This was barely surprising, given that my father had worked incredibly long hours for more than 20 years in building up his garage business in Dulwich Hill, an inner suburb of Sydney. He was a qualified motor mechanic, and the garage he ran provided the full range: not only did he serve petrol, but he also serviced and repaired cars. In my lifetime, Dad always opened the garage on Saturday and Sunday mornings. Only on Christmas Day, Good Friday and Anzac Day was the garage closed all day. Years earlier it had been even tougher, with Dad not getting home until about 10 o'clock at night, after he had closed.

If you ran a small business, there was nothing particularly strange about this. Both then and now, running a small business of the sole trader or sole owner type entails a total commitment of time and energy. There are no guaranteed market shares, and no penalty rates or overtime for effort beyond normal working hours. The qualitative difference between owning and operating a genuinely small business and working, even at a senior executive level, in a large corporation is immense and rarely understood by those not involved in it.

My father was always very tired when he came home from the garage, particularly on Saturdays, when he would often spend most of the afternoon resting. The business was discussed over the dinner table. My brothers had helped out, serving petrol and doing other tasks at the garage. I couldn't wait until I was old enough so I could have a go as well. I started when I was about 14. I loved it. It was a real buzz serving petrol, checking oil levels, pumping up tyres and trying to sell a few 'sundries', such as new spark plugs. Years later Paul Keating would sneeringly refer to the 'bowser boy from Canterbury' (sic). To me it was a badge of honour.

I enjoyed meeting the customers, who, my father reminded me, were always right. I had quite an argument with one customer, who insisted on smoking a cigarette as he stood beside me while I pumped petrol into the tank of his car. In the end I pulled the nozzle of the pump out of the tank. Then he put out his cigarette. I hope he stayed as a customer.

Like all service stations of that time, my father's sold all different brands of petrol. Unlike many others, though, Dad owned the freehold of his garage. From the early 1950s onwards, the major oil companies began an aggressive 'one brand' service station expansion policy of either building new service stations or doing deals, of various kinds, with existing operators, so that only one brand of fuel was sold at a site. This intensified competition as the number of sites expanded rapidly, with new operators often being obliged to open for longer hours. It was hard for someone in my father's position to match this. The inevitable business pressure affected Dad's health. Although he didn't want to go one-brand, it became a commercial necessity as there was a small rebate per gallon paid to owners who sold only one brand. He signed up with Mobilgas in 1954.

The one-brand switch badly affected Dad's business, but it had to be accepted as a tough but unavoidable competitive development which could occur in any market. What could not, however, be viewed in the same light was an arbitrary edict delivered by the local Marrickville Council later in the year.

The council told him to remove his petrol bowsers from the kerbside in front of his service station, as it wanted traffic lights installed on the street corner where the garage stood. This was tantamount to telling Dad to close down his business. Neither the council nor the NSW Government authority, at whose instigation the council would have acted, offered any compensation for the potential destruction of my father's business. It dealt a real body blow to my father and, coming on top of the market-related setbacks he had suffered, left Dad deeply dispirited and worsened his health.

As a 15-year-old boy, I thought that my father had been treated outrageously by an insensitive, high-handed council, against which he had no redress. This edict hung over my father and was still there when he died at the end of 1955. Exchanges went on for some time after that, and it was not until the early '60s that traffic lights were finally installed on the corner.

This incident reinforced the feeling in my family that governments, generally speaking, weren't all that sympathetic to small business; that if you had one, you were very much on your own. Big companies could look after themselves and unions were strong, but the little bloke got squeezed. Such attitudes weren't entirely logical, and in government I always emphasised the common interests of businesses, large and small. Yet, when on-balance judgements were called for, I confess to usually siding with the small operator, even if some violation of free-market principles might be involved; my support for newsagents and pharmacies come readily to mind.

*   *   *

As I've said, politics and current affairs were frequently discussed, not only around the dinner table, but also in direct conversation between my mother and father. There was no particular starting point for the discussion of politics at home. I can remember it always being there. My eldest brothers usually joined the discussions quite freely.

Occasionally, my father would listen to important parliamentary broadcasts on the ABC. We all followed the events leading up to the double dissolution of federal parliament obtained by Bob Menzies in 1951. It was the first time that a double dissolution had been sought since World War I, and — particularly given the political antecedents of the Governor-General, Sir William McKell, who had been the Labor Premier of New South Wales — there was much conjecture as to whether he would agree with the advice offered by Menzies supporting the request for a double dissolution.

In the end, McKell did the right thing and granted the dissolution. For doing his sworn duty he incurred the lifelong hostility of some Labor people, who simply believed that he should have done the bidding of his old political party rather than discharge his constitutional responsibility. This was a precursor to a much more savage application of the Labor belief that the party always owned the man, irrespective of the circumstances, some 25 years later.

Although my parents were united in their commitment to the Liberal Party, I suspect that they voted differently on one important occasion, and that was the referendum, held on 22 September 1951, to ban the Communist Party of Australia.

At that time the Cold War was intense, the communists had taken over in China only two years before, and Soviet communism was seen as a real threat to the peace of the world. On top of this, communist officials held many senior positions in Australian trade unions. The Communist Party in Australia was regarded by many as a subversive organisation because it sought the overthrow of the economic and social order under which Australians then lived. Menzies had secured passage of a law which declared the Communist Party an illegal organisation.

The validity of that law was challenged, and the High Court of Australia declared the law unconstitutional, as being beyond the power of the federal parliament to enact. Menzies' response had been to propose a referendum asking the people to agree to change the Constitution of the Commonwealth to give the federal parliament the power to pass the law which had previously been ruled invalid. The referendum campaign provoked intense debate and division. Menzies and his followers argued that the free world was engaged in a life-and-death struggle against communism, and Australia should not tolerate what he believed amounted to a fifth column in our country. Against that, many argued that the proposal violated free speech, and that it was never desirable to drive political movements underground.

This debate spilled over into the kitchen of our household. I recall quite clearly my mother's strong reservations about the additional power being sought by Menzies. One night she said, 'Menzies would be a bit of a dictator, if he had his way.' My father would have none of this. This was the one particularly short and sharp exchange on the subject, and after that I heard nothing more. Knowing my mother's determination once she had made up her mind, I am sure that she ended up voting against the proposal. If such loyal Liberals as my mother had reservations, then it is not surprising that the referendum went down.

This incident said a lot about my parents. They were both politically and socially conservative, but that was the result of their separate convictions. In no way did my mother automatically embrace the views of my father. Although in so many ways Mum fulfilled the traditional homemaker role typical of the times, she was a woman who held fiercely to her own independent opinions. Like my father, she had a well-developed interest in politics, and for years after Dad's death she and I would have quite lengthy discussions about political events in Australia in the 1920s and '30s.

I became totally absorbed in the Petrov Affair. Vladimir Petrov had been the third secretary in the Soviet Embassy in Canberra (but in reality a low-level spy) when suddenly, in April 1954, he defected and sought political asylum in Australia, which was granted in return for Petrov providing details of Soviet spying in Australia. It was a dramatic event, complete with KGB agents arriving to take Mrs Petrov back to Moscow. There were wild scenes at Sydney Airport as, seemingly against her will, she was taken on board an aircraft, Soviet-bound. On instructions from the Government, police intervened when the plane stopped for refuelling at Darwin, and having satisfied themselves that she did not wish to return to Moscow, relieved her KGB escort. The agents returned empty-handed to an uncertain welcome in Russia, and Mrs Petrov rejoined her husband. They spent the rest of their lives in Australia.

Menzies swiftly established a Royal Commission to examine the extent of Soviet espionage in Australia. This happened on the eve of the 1954 federal election. When the ALP lost that election quite narrowly, its leader, Dr Bert Evatt, convinced himself that the whole Petrov Affair had been a giant conspiracy, orchestrated by Bob Menzies to damage the ALP by raising the communist issue on the eve of the election. As a barrister, Evatt had appeared before the commission, representing people who had previously worked for him. He attacked the Royal Commissioners who, ultimately, withdrew his right to appear.

Dad and I both listened in astonishment as Evatt told parliament that he had written to the Soviet Foreign Minister, Molotov, asking whether or not Petrov had been a Russian spy. Molotov had written back denying that Petrov had spied for the Soviet Union. Evatt actually believed Molotov. This extraordinary incident did immense damage to Evatt's credibility, and was a clear sign of the paranoia that he had developed as a result of losing the 1954 election. It was a forewarning to many in his party of the erratic behaviour of his which was to come, and which contributed so much to the momentous split in the Labor Party in 1955.

My parents held conservative foreign policy views. They were staunchly anti-communist and saw Britain and America, in that order, as our real friends. Whenever we talked history, and this would have been in the 1950s, when memories of World War II were still relatively fresh, I was left in no doubt that my parents felt that the appeasement policies of the '30s, espoused by Neville Chamberlain and supported, to varying degrees, by most Australian leaders, including Robert Menzies and John Curtin, had been wrong.

Mum and Dad, especially the latter, were ardent admirers of Winston Churchill. I was born on 26 July 1939, at a time when Churchill was still out of favour, regarded as too belligerent and scorned by many in the British Establishment as temperamentally unsuited for leading the nation. Few thought that just 10 months later the House of Commons would, in desperation, turn to him. My parents gave me Winston as a second Christian name because my father had strongly supported Churchill's opposition to appeasement and shared his forebodings about its consequences. All my life, I have taken quiet pride in the fact that my own father was on the side of history in his attitudes to the 1930s, and I have a second name and a birth date to prove it.

I have often wondered how it was that I developed such an intense interest in politics so early, and why it was that it became such a lifelong passion. A big reason was that politics was talked about at home from as long as I can remember. Being the youngest, I was exposed to politics from an early age, with my parents being willing to explain issues and never hustling me away because I was too young. My parents often disagreed with actions of governments, but were not cynical about them and always encouraged in their children respect for society's institutions. I was brought up to believe that governments could do good things, if only they were comprised of the right people.

These were all influences which meant that I saw politics as good public service, as a way in which change could be achieved. That was important, but not as crucial as my seeing politics as an arena in which ideas and values could be debated, contested and adopted. That was the foundation of my lifelong view that politics is, more than anything else, a battle of ideas. Not only did I enthuse about the contest of ideas, I revelled in the experience of the contest itself. Debating, arguing, testing ideas about how society could be improved energised me.

The influence of parents on their children's political views is a fascinating study. I embraced most of my parents' political attitudes, particularly their support for private enterprise and especially of the small-business variety. Mum and Dad were often quite tough on people who worked for the Government. They thought that people in the private sector did all the work. In politics, I encountered numerous public servants who worked very hard indeed.

Dad had been a heavy smoker all his life, which no doubt aggravated his lungs, already damaged by the gassing he had suffered close to 40 years earlier during his war service. With all that is now known of the harmful consequences of smoking, we tend to shake our heads at the foolishness of a generation which so extensively embraced the habit, often, as in my father's case, worsening a war-caused condition.

Yet, given the older belief that smoking calmed the nerves, and the horrors which these men had experienced, their nicotine addiction was entirely understandable. With none of the reasons my father had, I smoked from the age of 21 until I was 39, finally kicking the habit while I was Treasurer in the Fraser Government. I didn't find it easy, and given what Dad had experienced in war, I could understand why he kept smoking until a few months before his death.

1954 was the last year that my father enjoyed reasonably good health. A combination of the chronic bronchitis which afflicted him as well as intense worrying about his business exacted its toll. The following year saw his health collapse dramatically: he suffered in rapid succession from pleurisy and an attack of double pneumonia. Dad spent a large part of 1955 resting at home, away from his business. He would be there when I returned from school. We would often talk politics or play chess. It was, despite Dad's ill-health, a wonderful conjunction in our lives which drew us much closer together in the space of just a few months. Regrettably it was not to last.

Towards the end of the year he made arrangements to lease the business to a trusted associate who had operated the workshop in the garage for close to a decade. Sadly, on the very day, 30 November, that he was to hand over he died suddenly of a cerebral haemorrhage, at the age of 59. When it happened I was playing cricket for my school at Blick Oval, Canterbury. My brother Wal arrived and told me that Dad had suffered a stroke, and that I should come home. When we were both in his car he put his arm around me and simply said, 'He's gone.'

I missed my father intensely. We had really got to know each other so much better during the last two years of his life; we had found a great common point of interest in politics. On many occasions, years later, I would think to myself how much pride Dad would have derived from my political career. Those last months in 1955, when we spent much more time with each other, I recall even to this day.

Understandably, my life changed enormously after the death of my father. My two eldest brothers had both married only months before his death, Bob had left school and gone to teachers' college and, as a result, I was thrown even more into the company of my mother. We talked endlessly about family history, current events and, of course, the need for me to succeed at school and go on to university.

2

INDULGING
THE TASTE

Although undecided until my last year at school, I enrolled at Sydney University for a law degree. There is no doubt that I was influenced by my brother Stan having become a lawyer. He became a partner in one of Sydney's best-known firms, Stephen Jaques and Stephen (much later Mallesons), aged only 27, and would be a most successful and highly regarded corporate lawyer as the years went by.

Thanks to Stan I had a great experience for eight weeks between school and university. He arranged a job for me as an assistant to a barrister's clerk in Denman Chambers in Phillip Street, Sydney. In Phillip Street, each floor of barristers was looked after by a clerk; the really good ones were invaluable, such as Jack Craig, with whom Stan had arranged my job. The barristers looked after by Jack Craig were some of the best and most colourful then at the Sydney bar. They included Clive Evatt QC, brother of Bert, then still federal Labor leader. The latter often turned up and used the chambers for some of his meetings. The brothers were a big contrast. Clive was likeable and amusing. Bert was sullen and unfriendly. John Kerr was another cared for by Jack Craig. Kerr was friendly and stylish. Amongst other things, I did his banking. He had a good practice.

Another prominent one in the group was Ken Asprey QC, who became a judge, and who in the 1970s would write a report for the federal government recommending major taxation reform. I was just the office boy but, given the personalities involved and the taste of the legal profession I was able to indulge, it was a heady experience. I was very grateful to Stan for setting it up. It was my first paying job. When I served petrol in my father's garage I was paid son's rates!

When aged about nine, I had been identified with a hearing problem, during a routine health check conducted at my school. It was an affliction that I had been born with and, whilst something of a nuisance during my younger days, it was not until I entered my later teens that it became a real hindrance. It worsened quite markedly during my first year at university, and by my second year I had to wear a large and not particularly effective hearing aid.

Deafness made it very difficult for me at lectures. I would sit as close as possible to the lecturer with my hearing aid turned up, but still missed a lot. I owed much to some of my law school friends, who generously lent me their notes. Although I was reluctant to admit it to myself at the time, my bad hearing really meant that I could never become a barrister, something which I had had at the back of my mind for a long time. In 1960, I underwent an operation which gave me back some hearing in my right ear, and in 1963 there was a similar operation on my left ear. These two operations gave me about 60 per cent of normal hearing. This was a huge improvement, and I felt very grateful to the surgeon, the late Sir George Halliday.

Despite a restorative operation on my right ear in 1985, my hearing continued to deteriorate, but fortunately the development of modern and inconspicuous hearing aids meant that I have been able to retain reasonably serviceable hearing.

Directly enrolling for a law degree meant that all of my university time was spent at the law school in Phillip Street, Sydney. I only ever went to the main university campus to sit for exams, or attend Union Night debates, which I did fairly frequently. Lectures in Phillip Street were spread amongst the main law school building, the old Phillip Street Theatre and the Teachers Federation Building.

Some 250 enrolled in the first year, of which fewer than 20 were women. Thirty-five years later, when my daughter, Melanie, enrolled at Sydney University Law School, more than 50 per cent of the first-year intake were women.

Like all academic years the class of '57 had its share of students who achieved eminence in their chosen profession. It included Terry Cole, later a Supreme Court judge, a Building Industry Royal Commissioner and the man who conducted the Australian Wheat Board Inquiry. There was also Roger Gyles QC, who became a Federal Court judge and had previously been a Special Prosecutor pursuing illegally evaded tax. Murray Gleeson and Michael Kirby, later Chief Justice and a justice, respectively, of the High Court were in the class of '58.

My first two years were full-time, and then I commenced three years of articles with a solicitor, attending lectures early in the day and late in the afternoon. With the law school in easy walking distance, such a daily schedule worked smoothly.

My lecturers were a mixture of academics and practising lawyers. The doyen of the academics was Professor Julius Stone, Challis Professor of Jurisprudence and International Law. Julius Stone had a formidable intellect. An erudite English Jew, he had written a landmark textbook on international law. He was a lecturer of mine in 1960, the year in which the Israelis snatched Adolf Eichmann from Argentina and flew him to Israel for trial for his alleged major role in the Holocaust. There was much debate about the legality of what the Israelis had done. Stone held a public lecture on the legality of the Israeli action at the old Assembly Hall in Margaret Street, Sydney. I went to the lecture with three of my law school friends, Marcus Einfeld, Peter Strasser and Murray Tobias, all of whom were Jewish.

It was an emotional issue for them, especially for Peter, whose family had been directly touched by the Holocaust. After the lecture, the four of us stood on the steps of the hall, locked in furious argument about what Stone had said. Despite his understandable sympathy with the Jewish cause, Stone had applied his customary juridical objectivity to the issue. I fully agreed with what Israel had done. Eichmann, who played a key role in implementing the Nazis' 'Final Solution' for the extermination of the Jewish people, decided upon in 1942, was convicted and hanged in Israel.

A relatively young Bill Deane tutored me in the subject of succession (probate and death duties). He became a judge of the High Court, and was appointed Governor-General, on the recommendation of Paul Keating, taking up that position just before the change of government in 1996. Deane's first major duty as Governor-General was to swear me in as Prime Minister, on 11 March 1996.

I had graduated from the Sydney University Law School in early 1961, and in June 1962, having completed my articles, was admitted to practise as a solicitor of the Supreme Court of New South Wales. My articles were served with one of the most colourful and remarkable people I have ever known, Myer Rosenblum. As a youngster Myer had emigrated from South Africa with his family, who settled in Marrickville, not far from my father's garage. Myer's father became a regular customer at the garage. When Myer qualified as a solicitor and commenced his own practice, my father returned the compliment and engaged him as his solicitor.

Myer Rosenblum had very diverse tastes and talents. He had represented Australia at rugby union, having played breakaway (flanker) for the 1928 Waratahs; was a hurdler at the 1932 NSW Championships; represented Australia as a hammer thrower in the 1938 Empire Games in Sydney; and held the NSW hammer throw record for something like 20 years. A cultivated person, he played the bassoon in the Sydney Conservatorium Orchestra, spoke fluent German and Yiddish, and began to teach himself Italian when in his 50s.

My becoming articled to Myer Rosenblum followed the making of close friendships with a number of Jewish students at law school. One of them, Peter Strasser, remains a very close friend. Thus began, for me, a long association with members of the Jewish community in Australia. Those early friendships, and the experience I gained from working with much of the Jewish clientele which Myer's firm attracted, created within me a deep respect, and in many ways affection, for the Jewish people.

As Prime Minister, I saw to it that Australia remained a staunch ally and friend of Israel. This was more than just a projection onto the international stage of my home-grown regard for Jewish people. I admired the remarkable struggle of the people of Israel against hostile Arab neighbours, and the democratic character of that country.

In 2006, Australia and the United States, almost alone amongst Western democracies, backed Israel in opposing a UN resolution condemning the latter for constructing a wall to protect its people against terrorists. I was staggered at the level of international hostility towards Israel over her action, which seemed to me to be a clear-cut case of self-defence.

Although I had joined the Earlwood branch of the Young Liberals when I was 18, participated in general campaigning for the 1958 federal election in the local area where I lived, and was briefly a member of the Sydney University Liberal Club, it was not until I had left university that I became really active in politics.

Largely due to my hearing problem, I found university quite taxing. I was reluctant to get too heavily involved in other activities until I knew that I would qualify as a lawyer. As a result, my experience was very different from that of many of my colleagues, who cut their teeth on university politics.

Once out of university, I hurled myself into Liberal Party activities, both at a local and NSW level. I took over the presidency of the local Young Liberal branch and became very active in the Youth Council, which comprised delegates from the various Young Liberal branches in the Sydney metropolitan area.

It was easy for cynics to dismiss Young Liberal activities as being entirely social and lacking in political gravitas. That was a superficial judgement. Sure there was plenty of social activity — and of course, why not? — but to those who were so inclined there were ample opportunities for political involvement. The Youth Council was a great forum for debate on contemporary political issues, and the physical participation of young people in local campaigns was especially welcome.

In those days members of parliament (MPs) did not have postal allowances; we were years away from direct-mail campaigns. Hand delivery of pamphlets to individual letterboxes, usually at night, was the staple way of getting the local candidate's message across.

My first experience of serious organisational politics was my election, in 1962, as the Young Liberal representative on the state executive of the NSW division of the Liberal Party. This body was the power centre of the party in NSW and included the leader and deputy leader of the state parliamentary party as well as the most senior member from New South Wales of the Menzies Government. I was now involved in genuine politics.

It was then that I first really got to know John Carrick, the general secretary of the party in New South Wales, a person who would influence me enormously over the years. He was to become my political mentor. I learned more about politics from John than from any other person I have known.

He had become the party's general secretary, the chief executive officer, in 1948 at the age of 29. During World War II, when a member of the Sparrow Force in Timor, he was captured by the Japanese and as a prisoner of war spent time working on the infamous Burma–Thailand railway. John would hold the position of general secretary for 23 years, until his election to the Senate in 1971. He became a senior minister in the Fraser Government, and served as Leader of the Government in the Senate, until that government was defeated in 1983.

Possessed of abundant energy, as well as immense organisational skills, John always realised that politics was a battle of ideas — a philosophical contest — and not merely a public relations competition. He drew many people to his orbit through the force of his intellect and his indefatigable commitment to the political cause of the Liberal Party. To him, one of the roles of a general secretary was to act as a constant talent scout for people who might contribute as members of parliament, irrespective of whether they were members of the party.

He formed a close relationship with Menzies, who much admired his tactical and strategic abilities. To my mind, one of John Carrick's immense contributions to the continuing political success of the Liberal Party was the role he played along with others in persuading the Prime Minister to embrace a policy of direct government assistance to independent (principally Catholic) schools. This change was an important factor in the Liberal victory, federally, in 1963. Thus began the most enduring demographic shift in Australian politics in the past generation, namely the change in allegiance of a whole swag of middle-class Catholic voters, who hitherto had remained loyal to the Labor Party for none other than tribal reasons.

Until the 1960s the ALP was the party of choice for the majority of Australian Catholics. Theology played no part in this; it was driven by socioeconomic factors, with Irish Catholics being predominantly of a working-class background. The sectarianism of earlier generations served to reinforce this alignment. Although the warming of Catholics towards the Liberal Party had begun in earnest with Menzies' state aid gesture in 1963, the first Fraser cabinet of 1975 still included only one Catholic, Phillip Lynch. Over the coming years the dam would really burst on this old divide. One-half of the final Howard cabinet in 2007 were Catholics. Once again this had nothing to do with religion, it being the inevitable consequence of a socioeconomic realignment.

When education became 'free, compulsory and secular' in the 1860s, Australian Catholics resolved to maintain their own school system, at enormous ongoing cost both to parents and the faithful. There was no government help for them. The prevailing view, in a much more sectarian age, was that those who sent their children to Catholic schools should bear the full cost of that choice: the free public system was available to Catholics and Protestants alike. As the decades rolled on, Catholic resentment grew, especially as, there being 20 per cent or so of the school-age population in Catholic schools, the state was relieved of a large financial burden.

By the 1960s attitudes had changed. There was more recognition of the immense sacrifice made by Catholics to keep their education system;

sectarianism had begun to crumble and there was a realisation that state schools would not cope if the Catholic system collapsed.

Menzies, the self-styled 'simply Presbyterian', became persuaded of the justice of the Catholic argument. In the 1963 election campaign he promised money for all schools in Australia to construct science blocks. Inspired politics, it was also cultural balm, and aided the decline of sectarianism. This symbolic breakthrough led over time to extensive funding of independent schools in Australia, with the greatest help going to those who were in most need.

The Menzies thrust was not easily accepted throughout the Liberal Party and internal debate continued to rage. Early in 1964 I pushed a pro-state aid motion through the Youth Council, which struck real turbulence. The Liberal leader in New South Wales (later premier), Bob Askin, remained very sensitive about opposition to the policy within the party and was still to summon the courage to assert the merits of it at a state level in the way that Menzies had federally. During a telephone conversation with me, Askin remonstrated about the pro-state aid position of the Young Liberals, even musing that perhaps the Young Liberals might have to be closed down if they continued to cause trouble. That did not change the Youth Council's view.

Askin was an earthy and instinctive politician who loved horseracing, rugby league and card playing. He won four elections for the NSW Liberals, far ahead of any other Liberal leader in that state.

The 1963 election was a real triumph for Menzies. He called it a year early and increased his slender majority of two to 22. For me, the personal high of that election was the victory of Tom Hughes QC in the electorate of Parkes. I was still living in Earlwood, which was in this electorate, and was Tom's campaign director. He needed a swing of some 6 to 7 per cent, something he did not believe that he would achieve. It was a classic grassroots campaign, attracting much high-profile attention.

Tom Hughes came from a well-known family of Sydney's eastern suburbs. He had served in the RAAF in World War II. He was intelligent and engaging. I took an instant liking to him, and we have remained friends ever since. His Bellevue Hill address did not bother the Liberal locals in Parkes. They liked the way in which he quickly adapted his speaking style from the courtroom to the back of a truck.

Tom had close links with the Packer family, which led to him being dubbed 'Packer's pea for Parkes'. He enlisted their help to produce a local campaign newspaper, called the *Parkes Examiner*. I spent several hours, a week out from the election, in the office of the now defunct magazine the *Bulletin*, with Clyde Packer, elder brother of Kerry, Tom Hughes and Tom's younger brother, Robert, working on the newspaper. Robert was at that time quite an accomplished cartoonist. Clyde Packer's editorial skill did wonders with the copy written by Tom and me.

The incumbent Labor member for Parkes, Leslie Haylen, had a left-wing reputation. He had visited China, and we decided on a cartoon which depicted Haylen dancing arm in arm with the Chinese leader, Mao Zedong. They were doing the 'Peking two-step'. This was 1963 after all; the Cold War was still in full swing, and consorting with the Chinese communist leadership was not calculated to impress middle Australia.

The 1963 election took place under the shadow of the assassination of President John F. Kennedy. 'Where were you when Kennedy was assassinated?' forever and a day would become a question asked of my generation. I was at home in Earlwood, about to leave and meet Tom Hughes in the Campsie shopping centre for some campaigning. My brother Bob telephoned me at about 8.30 am, and said simply, 'Kennedy has been shot dead in Dallas.' What more could be said! When I arrived at the campaign headquarters on the way to the Campsie shopping centre, volunteers had already assembled to help with pamphlet distribution. One of them, Roddy Meagher, a brilliant barrister who went on to become a much-admired judge of the Court of Appeal in New South Wales, speculated about the possibility of the Russians taking advantage of the situation.

Whatever one's politics, and whatever one's opinion of the quality of Kennedy's presidency at that time, it was impossible to shake the view that a remarkably talented and attractive young president, offering much hope for the future, had been cut down before he really had a chance to prove himself.

In 1964, as NSW Young Liberal leader, I was a delegate to the federal council meeting of the party in Canberra in April. It was a memorable event for me, as it included my one and only meeting with Sir Robert Menzies. It was at the traditional cocktail party for federal council delegates at the Lodge hosted by the Prime Minister. He was a big man, with a commanding presence, who chatted amiably with the six Young Liberals present. The great man demonstrated his reputed passion for martinis by mixing some for his guests.

Thirty-two years later, on my first weekend at the Lodge as Prime Minister, Janette and I invited Menzies' daughter, Heather Henderson, and her husband, Peter, over for a drink. We mixed and drank martinis in memory and honour of her late father. I have not had one since; I don't like them, shaken or stirred, but proper respect had been paid.

There was an unhealthy air of smug self-satisfaction at that 1964 Federal Council meeting. Several speeches, including one from Menzies himself, suggested that the Liberal Party would remain in office indefinitely. As things turned out it was to be more than eight years before the party finally lost, but nonetheless the tone seemed wrong. Perhaps I was not sufficiently attuned to the 'natural party of government' sentiment amongst Liberals from Victoria. Henry Bolte had been Premier since 1955 and the Liberals would hold office in that state for a further 18 years.

By contrast, Labor seemed to have an iron grip on power in New South Wales. Moreover, there had been a very heavy swing against the Liberal Party in New South Wales at the 1961 federal election, prior to the 1963 resurgence. By contrast, again despite the recession, the Liberal Party had given no ground to Labor at the 1961 election in Victoria. This had been due, overwhelmingly, to the great bulk of DLP preferences flowing to Menzies.

The DLP emerged from the great Labor split of the mid-1950s, which played a major role in keeping Labor from office until 1972. The split was caused by a clash between, on the one hand, Labor trade unionists and branch members worried about communist influence in the unions and, on the other hand, the rest of the ALP, who regarded the activities of those worried about communist influence as having ulterior motives, subversive to the true interests of the Labor Party.

Those concerned about communist influence banded together in what were called industrial groups, in turn strongly supported by a Catholic lay organisation known as the Movement, led by B.A. (Bob) Santamaria, certainly the most influential person in post-World War II politics never to serve in parliament. Possessed of high intelligence and strong Catholic beliefs, he was a compelling and articulate critic of communism within both the ALP and elsewhere. He was a person for whom I developed enormous respect.

In 1955 the ALP's National Conference declared membership of the industrial groups as out of bounds for ALP members. Many rank-and-file branch members, especially in Victoria, reacted against this and left the

Labor Party. Seven federal Labor MPs resigned to form a new parliamentary Party, later called the DLP. As most Catholics then supported the Labor party, the split caused huge tension within the Church. Senior prelates took different positions: Archbishop Daniel Mannix of Melbourne backed the DLP, whereas his Sydney counterpart, Cardinal Norman Gilroy, urged Catholics to 'stay in [the ALP] and fight'.

The new party, at first called the Labor Party (Anti-Communist) made a crucial decision to give its second preferences to the Coalition ahead of the ALP when Menzies called an early election for late in 1955, in part to capitalise on the ALP split. Menzies had already seen the split destroy Victoria's Cain Labor Government; this catapulted Henry Bolte to office, with the help of Labor Party (Anti-Communist) preferences in May 1955. This preference decision was largely justified by the belief of the new party that the ALP's foreign policy was not sufficiently anti-communist. Even though all of the seven MPs who had resigned from the ALP lost their seats to the Labor Party in the 1955 poll, that preference decision had far-reaching consequences. It conferred a huge advantage on the Liberal Party in marginal seats, not only in 1955 but also in subsequent elections. Normally 90 per cent of DLP preferences flowed to Liberals.

Many Liberals hung on in circumstances where they would otherwise have lost. This made the decisive difference in the 1961 election, which saw a huge swing against the Menzies Government, resulting in its majority being reduced from 32 at the 1958 election, to just two. Amazingly, in Victoria, where the DLP presence was greatest, the Liberal Party did not lose a single seat. In other states, Coalition seats tumbled. The DLP had saved Bob Menzies. He and other Liberals, such as Malcolm Fraser, never forgot this.

In July of 1964 I gave up the leadership of the Young Liberals and went overseas, following the familiar Australian pattern of the time. Go to London, work for a while, then 'do Europe', return home. Although I added, atypically then, visits to India and Israel on the way across and a period of weeks in Canada and the United States on the way home. In London I worked for solicitors at Ilford, Essex. This frequently took me to the Stratford Magistrates Court, in East London, putting me in touch with a cross-section of Londoners. Representing people charged with all manner of offences was a huge experience, one that I would like to have pursued for longer.

My time in London coincided with the election of the Labour Government led by Harold Wilson, in October 1964. The Conservatives had been in power for 13 years, having been returned to office under Winston Churchill in 1951. Naturally, I volunteered my services to the Conservative Party, and helped out in a very narrowly held Tory constituency in London, Holborn and St Pancras. Polling day was a cultural shock for an Australian. It was all about getting people out to vote, not handing out how-to-vote tickets at polling booths. Voting in Britain is not compulsory. I spent hours running up and down flights of stairs of council flats in inner London, knocking on the doors of people believed to be Conservative voters, reminding them to vote. I was still on this round at 9.30 pm, and given that the polling booths closed at 10 pm, I developed a diminishing belief that the assurances I would receive that 'She'll be right, gov' meant anything. The Tories lost Holborn and St Pancras.

Winston Churchill died whilst I was living in London, and I watched his funeral procession from Ludgate Hill with an English girlfriend. Returning to her home, I then, with her family, viewed a marvellous speech by our own Prime Minister, Sir Robert Menzies, delivered from the crypt of St Paul's Cathedral. Menzies' eloquence and sense of history deeply impressed this small English gathering, and left an Australian supporter feeling very proud.

The Britain I experienced was a nation in clear economic decline; worse than that, it had begun to lose that priceless quality of self-belief. I would not return to Britain for another 13 years when, as a junior minister in the Fraser Government, I paid a short visit. The process that I had sensed in 1964 was much further advanced in 1977.

It was to take that remarkable woman Margaret Thatcher to turn around her nation. I don't remember her promising any revolutions during her 1979 election campaign. She did, however, deliver one in many areas of British life. The most important one was that of self-belief. She restored Britain's pride and sense of achievement, as well as her economy.

My brief visit to the United States, on the way home from Europe, had me staying at Columbia University in New York with my cousin Glenda Felton (later Adams), who years later would win the Miles Franklin award with her book *Dancing on Coral*. It was well into 1965 by the time of my visit, and already mounting opposition to American involvement in Vietnam could be felt on university campuses. Not long before, the civil rights movement, led by Martin Luther King, Jr, had grabbed national consciousness. The enthusiasm of student bodies for the civil rights cause was strong and widespread.

When I returned to Australia I found that a full-scale debate was under way, not only about Australia's involvement, side by side with the United

States, in the war in Vietnam, but also about the decision of the Menzies Government, early in 1965, to bring in conscription to obtain the necessary numbers of troops to meet our country's commitment. This debate was to continue for another seven years, until all of Australia's combat troops had been withdrawn from South Vietnam. In that time a huge shift in public opinion took place.

Although the introduction of conscription was always a touchy subject, the Australian public began by endorsing the sending of troops to fight with the Americans. Support for the American alliance was strong; in addition, most Australians broadly accepted the so-called domino theory, namely that if one Southeast Asian country fell to communism, then others might follow, and this could bring potential aggressors closer to Australia.

In 1966 Lyndon Johnson became the first serving American President to visit Australia. He received an enthusiastic reception, and at the federal election at the end of the year the Coalition, led by Harold Holt (who had replaced Menzies as Liberal leader in January 1966), won with a significantly increased majority. Although there remained controversy over conscription, the war itself still attracted support; Holt benefited from that. Over time that would change. As the conflict dragged on, seemingly without end, domestic support for Australia's commitment declined, and with a spitefulness of which this country should be ashamed, many of those opposed to our military support of South Vietnam vented their hostility towards our soldiers.

Labor's defeat brought Arthur Calwell's leadership of the Labor Party to an end and delivered stewardship of the opposition to Gough Whitlam, whose intellect, energy and modernity were to transform the Labor Party and make it an election-winning force.

After my return to Australia I re-entered Liberal Party activities wholeheartedly, and within a few months was back on the state executive, not as a Young Liberal but as a representative of the full membership of the party; this was a big step forward, once again putting me at the centre of the party's affairs in New South Wales. My association with John Carrick strengthened, as it did with Eric Willis, deputy Liberal leader and, by then, a senior minister in the newly elected Askin Government.

From 1967 onwards, I began to participate in debates on Australia's involvement in Vietnam. Before long they included opponents such as Jim Cairns, the federal Labor MP and future deputy prime minister, who was a relentless critic of the Australian commitment. These were tough encounters, before large and normally hostile audiences, but the political experience was priceless. Many of them were at universities, and they were sometimes euphemistically called 'teach-ins'.

The bulk of the audiences were strongly opposed to our being in Vietnam. Many academics were active in their criticism of the war. Often they comprised the most vocal part of an audience, asking hostile but effective questions. It is impossible to exaggerate the extent to which this experience hardened me for later political life. Being booed and cat-called by hundreds of students in my late 20s, and receiving abuse delivered without a skerrick of good humour, was not only rigorous training for later public life, it also forced me to confront and be satisfied of the strength of my own beliefs on issues. By 1968 Vietnam had begun to deeply divide the Australian community. There were bitter feelings on the conflict which would only intensify as time passed.

3

DRUMMOYNE

During 1967 I decided to seek the Liberal Party's nomination for the state seat of Drummoyne. A redistribution of electoral boundaries carried out in 1966 had made the seat winnable for the Liberal Party. A very pro-Labor slice had been removed from the electorate, leaving a small but useful Liberal majority, based on the results obtained in the 1965 election. The electorate was comprised of the suburbs of Drummoyne, Five Dock, Abbotsford, Haberfield and Croydon, all inner-western suburbs of Sydney.

Although my real goal was federal politics, I had the naïve belief that a seat in state parliament was a stepping stone to Canberra. It might have been so in the earlier days of Federation, but it became increasingly less so from the '60s onwards.

Also at that time, I saw a superficial connection between most of the law I was practising, such as dealing with commercial leases, other property transactions and common law matters, and state politics. State parliaments enacted most of the laws on which I gave advice.

I was encouraged to seek the Drummoyne nomination by both John Carrick and Eric Willis, who had held the seat of Earlwood since 1950. Through my activities in the local Young Liberals and ordinary party branches in the area, I had come to know Willis extremely well. I liked him a lot. He became something of a public patron of mine, and openly encouraged me to run for Drummoyne. He was Askin's deputy and heir apparent for nine years. In 1976 he served briefly as premier, then lost narrowly to Neville Wran, after having called an election way too early.

I won the preselection for Drummoyne and set about campaigning for the seat. What I had not taken into calculation was the immense popularity and appeal of the sitting Labor member for Drummoyne, Reg Coady. He was a likeable, knockabout and hard-working local member. Partly crippled with polio at an early age, he continued, as a bachelor, to live in the old family home in Leichhardt. He had been an official in the union representing brewery workers and was a classic example of the committed Irish-Catholic working-class member of the Labor Party.

Whenever we met, he killed me with kindness, never saying anything critical of me. On the upcoming election his standard public lament was that because of the redistribution he had no hope of winning. It worked a treat. After a few months it was obvious to me that I'd face a real uphill battle to win the seat.

There was a lot of local resentment within the Liberal Party at my having won the preselection. Most of it came from a number of aldermen on the local council who had contested the preselection. Although I moved into the area, I continued to be regarded as an outsider, and a young, inexperienced one at that. Everywhere I went I was told what a decent, hard-working man Reg Coady was. This came back to me even from hardened Liberals.

I sensed that many people thought it unfair Coady might be removed as the member. And even some strong Liberals thought that they could have both a state Liberal Government and Reg Coady as their local member. The local Liberal Party branches were small, but willing to help. Many of my friends and family members came to assist in the campaign, but at no stage did I feel that I had gained any traction. I would comfort myself by regularly looking at the figures from the 1965 election, which showed that I should win.

The election was scheduled for 28 February 1968. It had been just under three years since the election of the Askin Government, and there was a widespread belief that the Government would gain ground against Labor at the election. Three seats, including Drummoyne, were generally regarded as near-certain wins for the Government. It had performed well during its first three years. Having been in office for almost 25 years before its defeat, the Labor Party was seen as tired and needing fresh blood at the top.

One of the other seats thought to be an easy Liberal win was the newly created seat of Fuller, which adjoined Drummoyne, and for which Peter Coleman, the journalist and former editor of the *Bulletin* magazine, had been chosen. I could not know it at the time, but both Coleman and the seat of Fuller would touch my life considerably in the future. Fuller included suburbs such as Gladesville, Hunters Hill and East Ryde, all within the federal electorate of Bennelong.

Reg Coady achieved a swing of about 3 per cent, which was contrary to a state-wide movement to the Liberals elsewhere, and held Drummoyne by 839 votes. Given the general result, it was a remarkable performance and a tribute to his hard work and popularity as a local member. It was a grim night for me and my supporters. When the first tally came in from a booth in Haberfield, then a pro-Liberal area, the sign was ominous. Malcolm Mackay, the federal member for the area, was with me that night and flinched at that first result. He lived in Haberfield, and would himself face the voters within a year or 18 months.

I was devastated by the outcome. In a climate which had been favourable to the Liberal Party, there had been a swing against me. There could be no excuses; I had been beaten by a much better man in a seat to which he had become deeply attached. Certainly I was young, not inexperienced in a political sense, but still very raw when it came to community activism, particularly when pitted against a sitting member who knew his electorate intimately. Coady had tentacles which reached into every organisation of any moment in the area.

The outcome was an early and hard lesson for me about the maturity of the voting public in Australia. Despite the condescending attitude of many commentators, the voters are very deliberate, and know what they are doing. In Drummoyne, on 28 February 1968, sufficient numbers of them knew that they could hang onto their well-loved Reg Coady and still keep the Askin Government, and as for that young fellow Howard, he was a bit of a blow-in anyway and could wait his turn.

When the result was known on the night, and quite on impulse, I went to the Labor campaign headquarters to congratulate Coady. The civic centre in Great North Road, Five Dock, was jam-packed with people celebrating a stunning victory. I made a short speech, paying tribute to him and the decency of his campaign. Not surprisingly, they liked that, and the mayor of Drummoyne, a Labor stalwart, Peg Armitage, who still possessed the rich brogue of her native Belfast, pulled me aside and said, 'I hope you get a safe Liberal seat.' It was the sort of generous remark, no doubt well meant, which the luxury of a political triumph encourages. Several years later, and after I had entered parliament as the member for Bennelong, which at that stage was a fairly safe Liberal electorate, I ran into Peg and reminded her of that comment. She seemed pleased for me; by that time she had become very disillusioned with the Labor Party.

The range of people who had come to the civic centre that night bore testament to the pull of a very popular local member. Many were staunch Labor people, proud of what they had brought off, but quite a lot were there because of Reg Coady, and would, in other circumstances, have voted Liberal. Local sporting and community leaders were thick on the ground.

It had been a big mistake going for Drummoyne, but I didn't think so when I nominated. Even more importantly, it was a blessing that I had lost — I certainly didn't think that then! I thought that I had let down the party and had blown a golden opportunity to get into parliament at the age of only 28. Moreover, I felt the loss had put paid to my future prospects of preselection, federal or state. I went through the miseries for quite a while. Amongst other things, I had failed all those family and friends who had toiled for me. My mother had upended her life by moving house with me to Drummoyne, and had then worked incredibly hard in the campaign.

That was the jumble of thoughts that consumed me in the wake of the Drummoyne defeat. It became crystal clear later, after I had won preselection for Bennelong, that my loss in Drummoyne had been a huge stroke of good fortune. If I had won Drummoyne it would have only been by the narrowest of margins, the demographics of the area were to move for some years against the Liberals, and with the natural swing of the pendulum I might have had no more than two terms and then lost.

Perfect field evidence for this piece of ex post facto rationalisation was, ironically, provided by my marginal-seat candidate in arms from 1968, Peter Coleman. He succeeded in Fuller where I had failed in Drummoyne. Sir John Cramer, the member for Bennelong, which enveloped Fuller, announced in 1973 that he would not fight the next federal election, and predictably Peter Coleman sought Liberal endorsement for Bennelong. So did I, and I was successful, beating him in the final ballot. So the 1968 state election failure had defeated a 1968 success, for a much greater prize than either had been aiming for in 1968. Apart from again demonstrating the vagaries of politics, it illustrated the difficulty of transferring from state to federal politics, particularly when any degree of marginality is involved.

Drummoyne had one marvellous human interest story which was a reminder of the often conflicting loyalties in politics. For many years Bill Brown had been the superintendent of the Sunday school at Earlwood Methodist Church, which I attended from early childhood. He was a

Geordie, having come from Newcastle-on-Tyne as a young man to work with Dorman Long, the company that built the Sydney Harbour Bridge. He was a staunch unionist and Labor supporter. Bill typified the strong link there had always been between the organised labour movement and the Methodist Church in Great Britain. One wouldn't meet a finer practical Christian. For a number of years I had helped him in running the Sunday school at Earlwood.

Bill and his wife had moved to Drummoyne to live, and I caught up with them when I began attending the Drummoyne Methodist Church. As the election approached, he sought me out to discuss the voting intentions of him and his wife. He said that in other circumstances both of them would have followed their normal loyalty and voted Labor. My being the Liberal candidate had complicated things. Bill told me that, after a lot of soul-searching, they had decided that one of them would vote for me and the other, as usual, vote Labor. I didn't ask which would be which. I was pleased to know that I would receive at least one vote from the Brown household. I was quite touched by their gesture.

4

REGROUPING AND REBUILDING

I stayed in Drummoyne after my 1968 loss, even though I knew that I would never run for the seat again. It was a question of regrouping, and working out where I went next in politics. Besides, I had more or less agreed to be Malcolm Mackay's campaign director, in the federal seat of Evans, at the election due at the end of 1969. It was going to be a tough fight for him; Gough Whitlam had given the Labor Party a new edge, and at least some movement back to Labor from the devastating loss of 1966 seemed likely. Evans would need a lot of work to hold. Mackay was a good local member. He listened well to people's concerns, and both he and his wife, Ruth, had established close links with key organisations.

We had become good friends. The Mackays welcomed me into their home and we swapped thoughts on all political issues. I was in constant touch with Malcolm through the drama-packed days which followed Harold Holt's drowning on 17 December 1967. In fact I had been at his home in Haberfield when news that Holt was missing came through. It was such an Australian tragedy. The Prime Minister had apparently drowned after plunging into a rough surf at Cheviot Beach near Portsea in Victoria. His body was never found.

John McEwen, Deputy Prime Minister and Leader of the Country Party, announced that the Country Party would not serve in a government led by Holt's Liberal Party deputy and Treasurer, Bill McMahon. That complicated the imminent leadership stoush within the party. Due to the McEwen veto,

McMahon ruled himself out of contention. Mackay started out as a supporter of 64-year-old Paul Hasluck, but over time, I watched him shift to John Gorton, who was energetic in pursuit of his leadership ambitions. This contrasted with Hasluck's 'merit unheralded' approach, which shunned overt convassing for support.

The real clincher for Gorton, however, was his appearances on television in the lead-up to the leadership vote. His relaxed laconic manner, coupled with his crumpled war-hero face, really appealed to viewers. He was new. Most Australians had not previously noticed him. On first blush they liked him a lot; he gave direct answers and clearly wanted the job. He was the first person to win the leadership of a major political party in Australia largely through the force of his television appearances.

I remained on the party's state executive and, therefore, heavily involved in the party's organisational affairs. This was also the time when I went into partnership with Peter Truman, and the following year we were joined by John Nelson to form the firm Truman, Nelson and Howard. Although my passion for politics never receded, this was a period when I derived considerable satisfaction from the practice of law. The firm had offices in Pitt Street, Sydney.

There was nothing quite like having a direct stake in the business. It was a mixed practice, and I handled any variety of work. I had carriage of any litigation which came the firm's way, including divorce work. I didn't like doing divorce work very much, but it was part of the practice and someone had to look after it. Time and time again I was reminded of how irrational people would become when a formerly close relationship had broken down altogether. Levels of intelligence or wealth made no difference to the degrees of irrationality.

I drew much professional encouragement from a personal injury case I ran on behalf of a man called Bozanic. He was an immigrant from the old Yugoslavia, and had been injured whilst working on the Snowy Mountains Hydro-Electric Scheme. The injuries he sustained resulted from his being thrown from a loader. Bozanic had tried a number of solicitors who, after a while, told him he did not have a strong enough case. I felt sorry for him and took his case on, essentially on a speculative basis.

It took a long time for a hearing date to be fixed, and at times I wondered about the wisdom of having taken on the matter in the first place. The poor man had been referred to me by a friend in the Liberal Party who felt that because of his age and poor language skills Bozanic had been pushed around. The date of the court hearing finally arrived; the case went extremely well, and Bozanic was awarded $40,000 plus costs. In 1969, given the nature of his injuries, this was a terrific outcome. To me this was a good example of how the law could be used to help someone who really needed assistance.

The 1969 election saw Harold Holt's 1966 majority of 38 reduced to seven. Whitlam outperformed Gorton during the campaign. At one stage, there had been real concern that Gorton might lose. He came to Mackay's electorate, where I presided at a Liberal Party dinner held at the Western Suburbs Leagues Club, in Ashfield. He was late for the dinner because he had detoured to the members' room of the club to have a game of darts and a beer with local club members. Some at the dinner were aggravated by this, but next morning a marvellous photo appeared in the *Sydney Morning Herald* showing the Prime Minister throwing darts. This kind of behaviour now by prime ministers would be regarded as quite commonplace and natural, but 40 years ago it was seen by some as unconventional.

John Gorton made no secret of his liking for parties and conviviality. This would not have mattered if he had applied more discipline and routine hard work to the job of being prime minister. He had an appealing personality, a direct style and was extremely intelligent. It was his lack of general discipline over such things as punctuality that did him damage. I had not been attracted to him when he was chosen as the party's leader and would have preferred Paul Hasluck, but several people close to me, such as Tom Hughes, were strong Gorton supporters, and suffered in their own careers when Gorton was later removed as prime minister. I maintained my scepticism throughout his time in office. In later years, however, I changed my mind about Gorton.

The experience of government led me to identify more strongly with Gorton's nationalistic views. During the last few years of his life I saw him and his wife, Nancy, often, and I felt that we had become quite good friends, overcoming earlier estrangement on account, firstly, of my closeness to Malcolm Fraser, whom he loathed, and my rivalry with Andrew Peacock, who had been a Gorton supporter. I spoke at a wonderful dinner to mark Gorton's 90th birthday on 7 September 2001 and felt honoured to launch his biography, written by Ian Hancock.

Although he won the 1969 election, Gorton lost a lot of seats and had to beat off leadership challenges from both David Fairbairn, a senior minister from New South Wales, and Bill McMahon, then still deputy Liberal leader.

By this time, John McEwen had dropped his veto of McMahon, a sure sign that the Country Party had grown uneasy with Gorton's governing style.

It was an inauspicious start to a new term of government, having an incumbent prime minister challenged by two of his ministers. Gough Whitlam's impressive performance in the campaign added to the list of ominous signs. Yet so lengthy had been the Coalition's grip on power that the possibility of being defeated by Labor was still not seriously entertained by many people.

About this time, my brother Bob began to question his earlier support for the Liberals, and by the early 1970s he had joined the ALP. I respected his right to change his opinion and his political allegiance and, for that reason, I never asked him exactly why he had shifted. Over the years I divined that it had been a case of two people growing up in the same environment ultimately having a different take on events and society. For example, where I responded positively to people defeating disadvantage by personal initiative, Bob was repelled by the disadvantage and the fact that not all people could overcome it. That is where he saw a larger role for government. He opposed Australia's involvement in the Vietnam War, but that was a companion to his change of political heart, not the main driver.

For several years Bob had been a Liberal Party member. Like me, he is an activist, and he became quite heavily involved in the local branches in the Earlwood area. He and his wife were living there. Later, and after they had moved to Armidale so that Bob could continue his studies at New England University, his political leanings shifted.

Although her personal commitment to the Liberal cause never faltered, our mother worried that politics would divide Bob from the rest of the family. Sometimes she asked that we steer clear of too many political discussions when all of us were together. Mum was especially anxious about our traditional family gathering on Christmas night, 1975. Bob, by then a staunch Labor man, was in high dudgeon about the dismissal of the Whitlam Government, and had been shattered by the electoral rout of his party. To cap it all, his young brother had just been made a minister by the dreaded Malcolm Fraser. It was a bit tense, but we made it.

Both of us were determined not to allow our political differences to come between us and, although we had plenty of intense arguments, particularly over the 1975 dismissal of Whitlam, this did not happen. By contrast Wal and Stan, my other brothers, who had always been Liberal followers, increased their active involvement and support, particularly after I entered parliament. Wal had been an enthusiastic branch office-bearer for years, and Stan would help out in a variety of ways, including with fund-raising.

In the 33 years that I was in parliament, including some of those difficult opposition years, Wal and Stan were loyal and consistent backers. They were the ultimate in true believers. And it was not just the loyalty that I valued. As a small businessman for much of his working life, Wal was a constant window into a world so important to the Liberal Party's base of support. Stan was a senior partner for many years in one of Australia's largest legal firms (Mallesons) and his professional activities gave him insights into the thinking of corporate Australia. In different ways they were both great sources of counsel and advice.

During the years that I was Prime Minister, Wal, Stan and their families joined Janette, me and our children in election-night celebrations (commiserations on one occasion), as well as other landmark events. Naturally Bob did not. He did, however, find personal ways of marking my success, consistent with his ongoing Labor convictions. When I was sworn in as Prime Minister on 11 March 1996, Bob came to the first part of the ceremony, when I took my oath of office alongside Tim Fischer as Deputy Prime Minister. Bob gave the rest a miss; that involved the swearing in of the remainder of the new Government. 'You've got to draw the line somewhere,' he joked. Likewise, he didn't come to a large Liberal Party celebration of my 30 years in parliament in 2004, but instead asked me and my family to his home for a dinner to mark the occasion. Today we continue to discuss politics in an avid fashion, but with a sense of detachment.

My mother left me with a fount of old aphorisms and sayings, some of which endure today, others having slipped out of usage. 'It's a long road that has no turning' is one that has largely disappeared. 'Blood is thicker than water', though, remains a reasonably commonplace expression. It most certainly applied to the way my family handled political differences within.

5

'THE ONLY GAME IN TOWN'

The year 1970 was to be, for me, at a personal level, momentous. On 14 February I met Janette Parker, and was immediately smitten. She was a fantastic mix of brains and good looks. Fittingly, I suppose, the meeting had a political context. There was a by-election that day for the seat of Randwick, in the NSW Legislative Assembly. The previous incumbent, Lionel Bowen, had been elected as the federal Labor member for the seat of Kingsford Smith at the election late in 1969. The Labor candidate for Randwick was a very youthful Laurie Brereton, who became a senior minister both in state and federal Labor governments.

Janette had agreed to hand out how-to-vote tickets for the Liberal candidate, John McLaughlin, who, by coincidence, had been a law school colleague of mine a decade earlier. He had no chance of winning, and the Liberal campaign was very much a flag-flying exercise.

I had played cricket in the afternoon, but arrived in the electorate to help with scrutineering after the close of the polls at 8 pm. When the count had been completed, Liberal workers gathered at the Centennial Park home of a barrister, Malcolm Broun, to engage in the obligatory wake. It was there that Janette and I met.

From then on, we saw each other constantly. Janette was a high school teacher. She taught English and history at St Catherine's Girls School, at Waverley, in Sydney. Before and after being at St Catherine's Janette also taught, respectively, at Randwick Girls High School and at Killarney Heights

High School. Though Janette never harboured a desire to enter the political arena herself, she was fascinated by the ongoing nature of the political contest. Over the years we have often agreed that politics is 'the only game in town'.

Our views were similar on many issues, and she was a natural Liberal supporter, but her assessments were always self-generated. Like me, Janette had grown up in a household where both of her parents discussed politics. Her father, Charles Parker, had worked for the NSW railways, having joined the railway workshop in Newcastle as a young man prior to World War II. By the time of his retirement in 1973, he had risen to the position of Chief Civil Engineer. Although he held conservative views on most issues, because he had always been a public servant, he came at them often from a different perspective to mine.

Janette's support and counsel throughout my career has been invaluable. To share a common interest in one's vocation with one's life's partner is a real blessing. I know many politicians whose wives or husbands simply do not like politics and are constantly urging them, in one fashion or another, to leave the political arena. That never happened to me. From the start of our relationship Janette knew that my heart was set on a political career.

We became engaged in January 1971, and married on 4 April 1971 at St Peter's Anglican Church, Watsons Bay, the local parish church attended by Janette and her mother. It is a beautiful church, perched on a cliff right beside the ocean, and close to the lighthouse at Watsons Bay. My best man was Alan Plumb, a fellow Young Liberal, who remains a close friend.

After we married, Janette and I rented a home unit in north Lane Cove, in the electorate of Bennelong. The Bennelong Liberal MP Sir John Cramer was 75 and would likely retire in the near future. I had firmly fixed my sights on winning preselection for that seat when Cramer went.

1970 ended poorly for both John Gorton and the Liberal Party. The Coalition fared very badly at a half-Senate election held in November. His detractors quickly blamed Gorton for the result. This added to the pressure on the Prime Minister.

The legendary political journalist Alan Reid had a colourful saying to describe a situation within a political party where an event, coming from nowhere, could bring about sudden change, usually of leadership. He would speak of there being 'plenty of dry grass around', meaning that the leader's position was inherently unstable, and all that was needed was for someone to throw a match to the dry grass. That was the position for John Gorton early in 1971. The person who threw the match was Malcolm Fraser.

Fraser had been one of John Gorton's principal backers in 1968, when Gorton secured the leadership to succeed Holt and became PM. Yet it was Fraser quitting the Government, followed by a searing resignation speech, which triggered the events producing Gorton's removal. Fraser had resigned because of what he regarded as Gorton's disloyalty to him as Defence Minister, concerning press reports damaging to Fraser of army activities in Vietnam. He believed that Gorton could easily have stopped the story appearing, but had been content to let it go ahead — to Fraser's embarrassment. In his speech Fraser went way beyond the immediate cause of his resignation, delivering a general broadside against Gorton's style of government. This provoked the moving of a motion of confidence in Gorton in the party room which was sensationally tied — 33 each. Gorton used his casting vote to oust himself, thus surrendering the prime ministership.

The totally chaotic, and hopelessly compromised, way in which the Liberals changed from Gorton to McMahon was a symptom and not the cause of the party's malaise after so long in office. Contested leadership changes should only occur where a majority clearly believe that an alternative to the incumbent can do a better job. In 1971, McMahon was not the preferred choice over Gorton. Rather, half the party room, for a whole variety of reasons, could no longer stomach Gorton. This was as much a reflection on their lack of foresight as it was on Gorton's failings as a leader. They must have known that McMahon was the only alternative to Gorton.

The personal animosity which flowed from the manner of Gorton's removal as prime minister was the most intense that I have ever seen in politics. Gorton never forgave Fraser for his perceived betrayal. In March 1975, when Malcolm Fraser was elected Leader of the Liberal Party, Gorton, who had voted for Snedden, immediately the result of the ballot was announced, walked out of the party room, slamming the door behind him, and never returned to the room again. In the 1975 election, sadly, the former Liberal Prime Minister contested a Senate seat from the ACT as an independent.

On two occasions I witnessed the refusal, some 30 years after the events of early 1971, of John Gorton to speak to Malcolm Fraser. One was at a Liberal Party dinner in the Great Hall of Parliament House to mark the 50th anniversary of the election of the Menzies Government, when

Malcolm Fraser, John Gorton and I, with our wives, were left together as the last entrants to the dinner. Janette looked after the Gortons; I entertained Malcolm and Tamie. The other occasion was a formal dinner hosted by the Queen and Prince Philip at Buckingham Palace, where the six of us plus Gough Whitlam and Bob Hawke and their wives, Margaret and Blanche respectively, were also present. This dinner was one of a series of events honouring the centenary of the passage through the British Parliament of the Australian Constitution Act. With typical Buckingham Palace efficiency, the seating arrangements made appropriate allowance for all sensitivities, and no difficulties arose. I have reflected since that Her Majesty would not have minded Gorton's intransigence, because he was the only one of her former Australian prime ministers who would have voted for her in the republic referendum in October 1999![1]

Thirty-one years after Gorton's deposing as leader, Tom Hughes, his former Attorney General, delivered the eulogy at Gorton's state memorial service in Sydney. It consisted, largely, of a blow-by-blow account of what he saw as Malcolm Fraser's dishonourable role in Gorton's downfall. In the eulogy Hughes traversed many of the points of criticism of Gorton contained in Fraser's resignation speech, rebutting all of them. It was an amazing performance, and largely reflected Hughes' loyalty towards Gorton.

Towards the end of 1971, Tom Hughes presented me with an unexpected opportunity to obtain preselection for a safe seat in federal parliament. Disillusioned with federal politics, he had decided to retire from parliament and return full-time to the Sydney bar. McMahon had sacked him as Attorney General. Few people saw this as anything other than a pay-off to Gorton's opponents within the party. It was an unwise and spiteful act. Hughes had been an extremely good Attorney General; on merit he should have been left there. His seat of Berowra was very safe and attracted a huge field. I lived a fair distance from the area, however had lots of Liberal Party contacts there, including my eldest brother, Wal, who was the president of one of the local branches.

Several people encouraged me to stand, including some who wished me out of the way of their own ambitions in other seats they believed would become vacant through retirements within the next few years. The party was fast reaching a stage when there would be a batch of sitting members retiring in seats like Bennelong, North Sydney, Mackellar, Bradfield and Wentworth. These were safe Liberal seats, and a once-in-a-generation cornucopia of opportunity for those wanting to get into federal parliament.

The fact that I did not live in Berowra at the time was not a problem. I had not long married and it would be quite easy for Janette and me to move to the electorate. My pitch to the preselectors was very much that, although young, I had a lot of political experience on my side. Preselection campaigns then were not as 'full on' as they are now. Too much overt campaigning could be counter-productive. Making sure that, on the day, the speech delivered and answers to questions were the best possible meant everything — even more so than now.

I didn't win the preselection; it went to a local resident, Dr Harry Edwards, who was a professor of economics at Macquarie University. It became apparent prior to the ballot that many local branch members wanted somebody strongly identified with the electorate. I did, however, poll much better than anyone expected. I finished third behind Edwards and the local state member, Jim Cameron.

This surprised a lot of people, particularly given the high profile of other aspirants, such as the Commonwealth Solicitor General, Bob Ellicott QC, and Dr Peter Baume, a highly respected consultant physician. They both won seats in parliament at the 1974 federal election. The outcome boosted my stocks in the party. Incidentally, my brother Wal was precluded by party rules from sitting on the preselection committee. The Liberal Party in New South Wales, to its credit, is a lot stricter about family influences than is the Labor Party.

My morale-boosting performance in Berowra was followed by an unexpected request to assist the Prime Minister, Bill McMahon, in the two months immediately prior to the 1972 election. By that time I was metropolitan vice-president of the party in New South Wales. I was asked to go full-time onto his staff, to assist with liaison between his office and the party organisation as well as provide some campaign advice and help out with speechwriting. After some arm-twisting by my two partners (one of them kept saying, 'John, it's time'), I secured the necessary leave from my practice and hurled myself into what turned out to be the final weeks of 23 years of Coalition Government in Australia.

I travelled around Australia with McMahon and, despite some hilarious and erratic moments, took from the experience a healthy respect for the dignified manner in which he accepted defeat on 2 December 1972. Janette and I were both with him at his home in Drumalbyn Road, Bellevue Hill, and he showed a lot of grace under pressure. Later, we drowned our sorrows with those great Liberal stalwarts John and Sue Atwill, at their nearby

Woollahra home. Whitlam, despite the length of time the Coalition had been in office and the skill of Labor's advertising campaign, won by only nine seats. As was the case in 2007, the swing in Western Australia was to the Coalition and not to Labor.

Having spent so long in the wilderness, it was natural that Whitlam and his colleagues would luxuriate in the very experience of being in government. Yet shrewder political heads would have detected warning signs in the narrowness of his victory. It was not the clear rejection of the Coalition that the Fraser defeat represented in 1983, and it was narrower than Kevin Rudd's victory in 2007. And on the other side, of course, it was nothing like the thumping victories achieved by the Coalition in 1975 and 1996. The truth is, despite all the hype and mythmaking of a generation, the Australian public barely thought that it was time in 1972.

The obverse of this was that a narrow defeat for the Coalition left it with a false sense of complacency about the need for fundamental policy reassessment. Both the ALP and the Coalition went to the watershed election of 1972 on the assumption that the good economic times would continue to roll on. In his Blacktown policy speech, Gough Whitlam declared that Labor would fund its vast public sector expansion from 'the huge and automatic increase in Commonwealth revenue'.[2] He fantasised about annual growth rates of 6 or 7 per cent a year, displaying fearful ignorance of the economic task ahead. When the economic upheaval flowing from the quadrupling of oil prices and the collapse of the old Bretton Woods-inspired fixed exchange system hit Australia, the responses of the ALP Government would massively aggravate rather than mitigate their effects. Labor would be hounded from office in 1975, with its economic reputation in tatters.

The early 1970s were a period of huge global economic change and turmoil, yet the two major political parties in Australia contrived in their different ways to ignore this. Whitlam had no coherent economic plan for government; that is why he proved completely unable to handle economic adversity when it confronted him.

Most in the Coalition felt that having only just lost, there was no need for a full policy appraisal. There were plenty of reviews, but there was no fundamental examination of such things as the heavy regulation of the Australian economy, our high tariffs or our increasingly out-of-date taxation system. As for any questioning of centralised wage fixation, that was not even thought to be a problem.

Like most people, I assumed that Whitlam would govern uninterrupted for three years. There was no perception of what lay ahead, or what Labor had in store for the Australian people.

The story of the disintegration of the Whitlam Government has been told in much detail many times. Labor inherited a strong economy, with low unemployment and apparently good prospects for growth. Whitlam assumed that the benign economic conditions, which he had seen as the natural order of things in Australia, would simply go on. From the start he was uninterested in economic issues and paid little attention to mounting inflationary pressures. By October 1973 when OPEC countries quadrupled the price of oil, with all the inflationary consequences that entailed, inflation in Australia already stood at 10 per cent — well above what it had been less than 12 months earlier. Worldwide inflation became the big problem, and national governments were required to manage their economies with imagination and flexibility and take hard decisions which courted short-term unpopularity, not lazily assume that the good times would always be there.

Whitlam found economics irksome, far less exciting than the foreign excursions and progressive social posturing that he had been elected to champion. This disconnection between the needs of the nation and the disposition of its leader was to prove very damaging to the former and fatal to the latter. Although the chaos of 1975 is seen as basic to Labor's annihilation at the end of that year, the Government's fate was really sealed in 1973 when, in the face of a clear need for a fresh policy direction, Whitlam ploughed on regardless.

He never once confronted the Australian people with the reality of the times and, therefore, the need for a different approach. He may well have been surprised with the response he would have received.

Australians are pragmatic, worldly people who respond well to governments which ask of them difficult things, provided they are taken into the confidence of the Government, and the nature of the national interest is laid out.

If Whitlam had told the people very directly in 1973 that the altered world circumstances meant that many parts of his electoral platform must either be put to one side or at least deferred, the popularity he still then enjoyed as the first Labor prime minister in a generation would have carried the day.

When the people decide to change their government, they cut the new man a lot of slack. They are slow to admit to themselves that they may have made a mistake. As a consequence, the public will accept a change in the direction of a fresh government early in its new term, provided a proper explanation is given. Gough Whitlam seemed oblivious to these political realities. He received an early warning from the electorate that they were not all that enchanted with the beginnings of his Government when Labor suffered a swing of 7 per cent against it in the Parramatta by-election held in September 1973. The seat was won by Philip Ruddock. He became a close and trusted colleague in my Government. Philip was an excellent Immigration Minister and Attorney General. In March of 2010 he became the third-longest-serving member of the House of Representatives since Federation.

The swing in the by-election was much larger than might have been expected for a newly elected government after less than 12 months in office. A lot of this was due to growing unease about the economy; some to the already apparent erraticism in the new Government's style; and, as a local issue, Gough Whitlam's arrogant declaration that the people of western Sydney would have the city's second airport at Galston (which was close to the Parramatta electorate) didn't help matters for Labor.

The by-election should have been a real warning for Whitlam, but it wasn't. If anything, he pushed even harder on the accelerator. It gave Bill Snedden, the Opposition leader, a huge boost, perhaps engendering some of the false optimism which led the opposition to threaten the blocking of supply some months later.

The Liberal Party of late 1973 was static, policy-wise. Its personnel were beginning to change, but only gradually and not at the top. Certainly McMahon had gone from the leadership, but not from parliament. Nigel Bowen had gone to the Bench, but other big names from government days, such as Snedden, Lynch, Fraser, Peacock and Chipp remained, as did the National Country Party trio of Doug Anthony, Ian Sinclair and Peter Nixon. In fact, given the length of time the Coalition had been in power prior to 1972, there was remarkably little turnover. That was because those occupying senior positions were still relatively young themselves. Those on the backbench tended to be older, and it was there that generational change would begin in 1974.

Meanwhile, Janette and I had scraped together enough money to buy a home unit near Wollstonecraft station, in Sydney. It is the suburb in which we lived until I became Prime Minister, and the suburb to which we returned after the end of my parliamentary career. One of our happy recollections of living at the unit was to wake up on Sunday mornings to the sound of tennis being played on the grass court in a large home next door. That home was owned by the L'Estrange family. Dr Jim L'Estrange was one of Sydney's most respected paediatricians. He was highly regarded in the Catholic Church, which conferred on him the honour of a papal knighthood. One of his sons, Michael, would become one of my closest advisors as PM.

6

A SAFE SEAT

As 1973 drew to a close, Australians had begun to feel nervous about Whitlam's lack of interest in economic matters. They were also troubled by Lionel Murphy's provocative 'raid' on the Australian Security Intelligence Organisation (ASIO), when, accompanied by federal police, he marched unannounced on the agency's headquarters demanding access to papers. The Attorney General did not usually behave like this. ASIO may not have been everyone's cup of tea, but it was pledged to protect the national interest. Murphy also tried to radically change the divorce laws by regulation, rather than legislation. Inevitably this was blocked by the Senate. The new Government was beginning to unsettle people.

Ensconced in our unit in Wollstonecraft, Janette and I were blissfully enjoying the early years of married life. Politics remained the main preoccupation. From almost the moment we had met, it was common ground between us that I would go into politics. I wanted it, and Janette wanted it for me. I had standing and respect in Liberal circles, but the challenge was to realise my ambition.

In the second half of 1973, the NSW division of the Liberal Party decided to call nominations for the preselection of candidates for safe seats in the federal parliament. I knew the moment of truth had arrived. It was inevitable that there would be a number of retirements, and possibly serious challenges to other sitting members of long standing. Both John Cramer in Bennelong and Harry Turner in Bradfield announced that they would retire. Naturally, I nominated for Bennelong, where we lived. I knew that I faced a tough battle.

My principal rival was Peter Coleman, the state MLA for the electorate of Fuller, which was entirely enclosed within Bennelong.

Coleman had a lot of support. Cramer backed him quite strongly, regarding me as a bit of an interloper, and because I was metropolitan vice-president of the division, he saw me as the head-office candidate. That was not entirely accurate. Although I had a close association with John Carrick and, as well, had developed a good friendship with Jim Carlton, the new general secretary, both of them had a high regard for Peter Coleman.

The committee to choose a candidate then comprised 50 people. Thirty were from the local branches in Bennelong, broadly according to the membership size of each branch, and the remainder from the membership of the state executive and the state council of the party. The logic of this approach was that a mixture of locals and others, with the locals having a majority, would more often than not produce the right result.

It will sound self-serving but, at that time, I thought this was a very balanced way to choose candidates. Some years ago I became a strong supporter of the branch plebiscite system, in which every financial member of the party in a given electorate, perhaps subject to some minimum membership time, has a vote. I have more to say about this at the conclusion of the book.

I knew virtually all of the 50 people who were to make the choice in Bennelong; some well, others only casually. Apart from Coleman and me, there were 21 other candidates. It was a very strong field. Although not absolutely blue-ribbon, Bennelong at that time was regarded as a safe Liberal seat.

Campaigning for the preselection meant some personal visits — but not too many, because the culture of the party at that time deprecated the hard sell — as well as participating in various branch forums with question-and-answer sessions. I had a good idea how the 20 people from state executive/state council would vote, but was less certain about how the locals would go. Bennelong was exactly composed of the two state electorates: Fuller, held by Coleman, and Lane Cove, held by Ken McCaw, Attorney General in the Askin Government, who pretty well kept out of local party political matters. The branches in Fuller were loyal to Coleman, but those from the Lane Cove end were up for grabs.

There was a bit of drama the day before the preselection. Whitlam had called a referendum to secure Commonwealth power to control both prices and wages. It was an unworkable notion, and despite public concern about inflation, the proposal was doomed to defeat. Liberal workers in Bennelong, including most of the preselectors, manned polling booths in support of the 'no' case. John Cramer, as the sitting member, visited all of the booths in his electorate, and lobbied hard for Coleman.

Some of Coleman's supporters alleged that I had not done enough to keep the polling places in my part of the electorate adequately staffed with volunteers. These were signs that I was seen as a big threat to Coleman, who many observers originally had assumed would walk it in because he was already a local state member. My mood was far from good the night before the fateful day, which had been appointed for Sunday 9 December 1973 at the Menzies Hotel in Sydney. I was very nervous about what had happened during Saturday, and Janette had to keep telling me to concentrate on my speech and forget about other things.

There was a lot at stake for me. This would be my third preselection. I had won the first, for Drummoyne, but had failed to win the seat. I had lost the second, Berowra, but had done better than expected. If I missed out on Bennelong, the view might form that perhaps I wouldn't end up making it. This was, after all, where Janette and I had made our home. If the Liberals of Bennelong knocked me back, what particular appeal might I have to those in other Sydney electorates? Bradfield was no longer available. Its preselection had been held the previous Friday and had been won by David Connolly, a serving diplomat. A preselection was scheduled for Wentworth within a few days and, although I could have flowed on to it under the party's rules, that would have looked like an afterthought. The sitting member, Leslie Bury, a former Treasurer, was facing a strong challenge from Bob Ellicott, the Commonwealth Solicitor General, and there wouldn't have been many spare votes around for a latecomer whose first choice had been another seat.

A lot hung on the Bennelong outcome, and it was a gruelling day. All of the candidates were assembled in front of the preselection committee, and the rules explained. Voting was by secret exhaustive ballot. That meant, in the absence of a tie, preselectors were always asked to write on a ballot paper the name of the candidate they wanted to be the Liberal representative in the electorate concerned.

Each candidate was to address the preselection committee for a maximum of eight minutes and then a period of seven minutes was allowed for questions. With large fields of candidates, such as in Bennelong in 1973, the field was reduced to six (unless of course a candidate had secured an absolute majority), who were invited to address the committee again for a shortened period, with an equally truncated time for questions. After this, the balloting resumed until a candidate was chosen.

The tension during the day was extraordinary. Candidates could not listen in on any of their opponents. There was a candidates' room, and although we were free to come and go, no fraternising with preselectors was allowed. There was plenty of false bonhomie, but the whole day seemed to go on for an eternity.

I expected to make the final six. The real question was what happened after that. There is no rule of thumb about the type of speech which will appeal to a preselection committee. It depends entirely on the man or woman seeking selection, the character of the electorate and the political circumstances of the time. In my case I decided that, because the best quality I thought I could bring to the Liberals of Bennelong was a political appreciation of the circumstances in which the Liberals found themselves in 1973, I would focus on what was needed for the Liberal Party to win back political support in the Australian community.

Quite a lot of new, youngish business and professional people had joined branches in Bennelong, especially in the Lane Cove and Longueville areas. They were already angry with the economic policies of the Whitlam Government, and wanted a road map for a return to Liberal government. That was the pitch I took. The mood amongst many Liberal supporters was that while, in a very short period of time, the economy had begun to deteriorate, they were not at all sure that the Liberal Party had either the policies or the political strategy to offer an effective alternative. I intended to tell the preselectors of Bennelong what those policies and that strategy should be. Australia needed to stop spending recklessly, get on top of inflation, understand how the world economy had changed and stop insulting our traditional friends, such as the United States.

As I expected, I made the final six and was called to make my second speech and answer more questions. During my second appearance I sensed an interest in what I was saying beyond what I had experienced earlier in the day. It could have been imagination, but I nonetheless felt that. When the final six had made their speeches and answered further questions, the balloting recommenced, and finally Jim Carlton, who was returning officer, came to the candidates' room and said that there was a result and that all of the candidates should join the preselectors for the announcement of the winner.

Back in the meeting room, Carlton was asked to declare the ballot. I shall never forget this moment. He announced that the ballot had been properly conducted and that 'Mr J.W. Howard has been chosen as the candidate for Bennelong.' In the final ballot I had defeated Coleman by 28 to 20. Two members of the committee had not turned up. At least one of them, I felt, would have been a certain supporter of mine. It's as well he wasn't needed.

It is impossible to exaggerate the significance of this moment in the life of someone who had dedicated his career to the profession of representative politics. I had achieved something that I had wanted for most of my adult life. I now knew that, all things being equal, I would be a member of the House of Representatives after the next federal election. I also knew that if I worked hard and was available to, and regularly communicated with, the Liberal Party branches in Bennelong, I would remain in parliament for a long time.

There was absolutely no doubt about my intention, or indeed ability, to both work hard and look after my Liberal Party branches. Already Janette and I had immersed ourselves in the activities of the Liberal Party in Bennelong. We had made, even at this early stage, some new and close friendships, particularly with people who had come into the party in reaction to the policies of the Whitlam Government.

As soon as I could decently escape the aftermath of the ballot result I rang Janette, who was overjoyed with the result. She came into the Menzies Hotel to collect me, and we invited plenty of people to the unit at Wollstonecraft for a celebration. It was a day that I would never forget, for the simple reason that it had launched me on a parliamentary career, which would be as secure as any in that uncertain profession could be. To say this is to put into context the real significance, in a parliamentary system, of winning the endorsement of one's party for a seat in parliament. I have never forgotten my Liberal Party roots. I would never have been a member of parliament without the Liberal Party, nor a minister, and certainly not prime minister.

The evening of 9 December 1973 had been a high point, career-wise. The next day that experience was trumped by Janette informing me that she was pregnant. That was fantastic news. She had known for a few days, but had held back from telling me until after the preselection. It was one of many examples, throughout our life together, of the care and sensitivity she displayed towards my political career.

In the space of a few days my life had been irrevocably changed. We were thrilled at the prospect of having children. They have been not only the joy but, equally, the great success of our lives. To watch one's children grow to adulthood, to see their professional and other achievements, but most preciously of all maintain a close and loving relationship with each of them, and also observe their obvious affection for each other, is the most rewarding experience imaginable. For me it dwarfs anything I may have realised in public life. I don't say that lightly; I am proud of what I did in politics, but I am even prouder of what my family represents.

The Bennelong branches were very accepting of the result. Peter Coleman was most friendly; we both realised that we would need to work closely together looking after our common constituents. Eight years later, and after he had lost his state seat to the Neville Wran juggernaut of 1978, Peter entered federal parliament as the member for Wentworth. His daughter Tanya married Peter Costello in 1982. I continued working in my practice, expecting it to be some two years before my partners and I would need to work out arrangements once I entered parliament.

Janette and I indulged in some desultory house hunting, feeling that much as we liked our unit, we should have a house for our children to grow up in. Nine months later we bought a Federation-era house in a nearby street in Wollstonecraft. It needed a lot of work, but was by far the best investment we ever made. It was renovated and extended through the years, with a whole storey being added in the early 1980s. It was the house in which our children were raised; it remained vacant for almost 12 years whilst I was Prime Minister, and it was the home to which Janette and I returned after the election loss in November 2007. Incredibly, by the time we bought the house, in October 1974, I had already been a member of parliament for five months.

Despite Whitlam winning government in 1972, the Coalition, the DLP and independents controlled the Senate. As a result, many of the Whitlam Government's initiatives in sensitive areas were blocked by the Senate. There were constant allegations that the Coalition was behaving in a negative fashion, although most of those who made those allegations ignored the frequent declarations made by both Gough Whitlam and Lionel Murphy, in earlier years, that it was the role of the Senate to oppose government legislation with which it disagreed.

Despite being aware, from closely following events in Canberra, that a lot of government legislation had been blocked, it came as a surprise to me when the opposition threatened to block supply in April 1974.

The catalyst had been Whitlam's appointment of the DLP senator and former Queensland Premier Vince Gair as Australian Ambassador to Ireland. This appointment was designed to ensure there would be a sixth Senate vacancy from Queensland in the half-Senate election which Whitlam had called for 18 May 1974. If six vacancies were being filled from Queensland, there was a chance that the ALP could win control of the Senate. But Whitlam would be outsmarted in this ploy by the Premier of Queensland, Joh Bjelke-Petersen, who advised the Queensland Governor to issue the writs for the five Senate vacancies from that state normally up for election, separately from the vacancy caused by Gair's appointment to Ireland. This meant that the Gair vacancy would be treated as a casual one; under the Constitution, casual Senate vacancies are filled by state parliaments.

There was plenty of Coalition outrage over the Gair Affair, and a lot of Liberal supporters wanted an early poll, but in the broader community, although there was growing disillusionment with the Whitlam Government, there was still a fundamental sense that the Government should be given a fair go. After all, Vince Gair had not been the first politically expedient diplomatic appointment. To my mind, the most reprehensible feature of the whole affair was Gair's betrayal of his own party, the DLP, by doing the political bidding of the ALP for personal advancement. He was deservedly expelled from the DLP. It was the beginning of the end for the party. Its remaining senators would lose their seats in the coming election.

Whitlam responded to the Coalition threat by seeking and obtaining from the Governor-General, Sir Paul Hasluck, a double dissolution based on previous Senate rejection of several government bills. The election was to be on the same date, 18 May, originally chosen for a quiet half-Senate poll. In a double dissolution election, every Senate seat is vacant, so the original shenanigans about the Gair vacancy became academic.

Personally, I was pleased at the prospect of an early election. Within the space of a week, I went from being an endorsed Liberal candidate for an election still at least 18 months away to being someone who should start campaigning immediately. At long last I could get my teeth into the real business of winning a seat in parliament.

Naturally I campaigned entirely in Bennelong. My campaign was opened at St Mark's Anglican Church hall in Hunters Hill by Andrew Peacock, shadow minister for Foreign Affairs. He was destined in the years ahead to play a major role in my political life. The local campaign attracted plenty of helpers.

Local branches of the ALP voted to install the left-wing legal activist Jim Staples as their Bennelong candidate. The Labor Party head office, however, would not have a bar of Staples, so they imposed the writer, and Whitlam confidant, Richard Hall as the ALP candidate.

Although I had nervous moments, particularly on the night of the election before the first results came in, deep down I expected to win Bennelong. I was far from sure, however, about the overall result. Whitlam campaigned extremely well, and was able to exploit the claim that his government had not been given a fair go. On the face of it this was a good argument. There had been a Coalition Government for 23 years, yet after less than 18 months the newly elected Labor Government had been forced to go back to the people by the non-Labor majority in the Senate.

One of the problems the Coalition had was that it had not really completed serious policy work when the election was called. This made it easier for Whitlam to claim that we were not ready for government. Much play was made of an intensive policy weekend which produced the Coalition's manifesto 'The Way Ahead'. Policy written in the pressure cooker of a weekend, in the shadow of an election which has already been called, is unlikely to be well thought through.

For my campaign we had established an office in Lane Cove Plaza. Although she was five months pregnant, Janette worked very hard and thoroughly enjoyed the campaign. She is a meticulous organiser and kept me and many others up to the mark with campaign tasks. I treated it as a marginal seat campaign.

Bennelong had scores of active community groups, particularly in areas of nature conservation. It also had, in 1974, an active Women's Electoral Lobby, which played a particularly prominent role in the campaign with candidates' forums, questionnaires and the like. The convener of the Bennelong WEL was Janelle Kidman, mother of Nicole. She, her husband, Antony, and children lived in the electorate at Longueville. They were strong Labor supporters.

They were cordial to me but I had no doubt that the majority of WEL's members were sympathetic to Labor's social agenda. The main WEL meeting was held at the Lane Cove Town Hall, attended by hundreds of people. I was asked my opinion about abortion; not surprisingly my rather conservative response caused an audible intake of breath from most of those in the audience. I hadn't tried to sugar-coat the reply; that wins no one's respect. On sensitive social issues it is always desirable to be direct and clear.

On polling day, 18 May 1974, it rained heavily all day, and must have been a nightmare for the booth workers. There were a record number of candidates for the Senate, and as a consequence the large how-to-vote papers became very sodden and cumbersome. It was a long day as I worked my way around each of the 34 polling booths in the electorate.

I went home to our unit in Wollstonecraft for dinner at 7 pm. I didn't eat a lot, as I was very nervous. Janette's parents came over for dinner and drove up to the campaign office with us. I had arranged for my mother to come to the office with one of my brothers. Wal and Stan had worked on polling booths during the day. We all waited in the campaign rooms, the arrangement being that as soon as a booth count had been completed, a scrutineer would ring through the result.

The first result was rung through at about 8.38 pm, and it was from the Congregational hall in Lane Cove. They were good figures, showing a lift in the Liberal vote of about 6 per cent. Figures then came in rapidly, and it became very apparent that not only had I won, but I had increased the majority won by Cramer in 1972. I had no reason to get delusions of grandeur, but it had been a good outcome. Nonetheless, Bennelong was not as blue-ribbon as Bradfield or North Sydney. The two-party-preferred Liberal vote was only 53–54 per cent. I would need to work hard. Having, at the age of 34, achieved my longstanding ambition to be a member of the national parliament, I had every intention of doing just that.

There had been a small swing against the Labor Government nationwide, its majority falling from nine to five seats. The Senate count took six weeks to complete, with the ALP picking up an extra three seats in the upper house. The initial reaction had been that Snedden had fought a good campaign and there was little doubt that he would be re-elected unopposed as leader. Nevertheless there remained, amongst many, real doubts about him as leader in the longer term. I shared those doubts. Even then I was attracted to Malcolm Fraser as a possible leader of the party. It was a tough judgement to make, but to me Bill Snedden seemed out of his depth as leader against Whitlam. There was too much bluster and not enough substance. He did not have strong philosophical positions on anything. I barely knew Fraser, but he seemed to have policy substance and clear attitudes on certain foreign policy issues.

Ironically, given his later change of heart on the issue, I had first been drawn to Fraser several years earlier when he had strongly and effectively argued the case for Australia's involvement in Vietnam. He did a much better job than any other minister, or either Holt or Gorton. Fraser had presence and seemed to possess that streak of toughness and ruthlessness needed in a political leader. Although economic policy would dominate so much of my political thinking and action in the years ahead, at the time I entered parliament, foreign affairs was uppermost in my mind. It seemed that Malcolm Fraser's attitudes on this subject were very close to mine.

After the election I remained a partner in my firm. There was no conflict of interest and I wanted to retain as much contact with the law as possible, feeling that this added to my usefulness as a member of parliament. Naturally I was not able to do as much work.

John Cramer had maintained his electorate office in the Commonwealth Bank building in Martin Place. So I decided, for the time being, to follow suit. Many of my federal colleagues from New South Wales, such as John Carrick and Bob Cotton, also had their offices there. It is a stylish old building and was used for cabinet, ministerial and parliamentary purposes up until the mid-1980s, when the Hawke Government finally agreed to the repeated urgings of the bank and shifted the last of the cabinet and ministerial facilities to the current Commonwealth Parliamentary Office in 70 Phillip Street, where they remain to this day.

7

THE HONOURABLE
MEMBER FOR
BENNELONG

When I took my seat in federal parliament in 1974, Islamic extremism was unknown to the world. International politics was still shaped by the Cold War; the Berlin Wall stood as a metaphor for all that divided East and West. Australian politics reflected that mindset; our nation was still in the slipstream of the fierce and divisive debate regarding our involvement in the Vietnam War.

There was still a serious constituency within Australia for the state having a larger share of the economic pie. In his budget speech on 17 September 1974, the Treasurer, Frank Crean, said, 'The relatively subdued conditions in prospect in the private sector provide the first real opportunity we have had to transfer resources to the public sector.'[1] He saw the private sector's adversity as the public sector's opportunity. Thirty-five years later, another Labor Treasurer would justify spending a large budget surplus in the name of shoring up, not replacing, the private sector.

The new parliament, to which I had been elected as the member for Bennelong, assembled for the first time on 9 July 1974. It was an unforgettable day for me. The sheer awe of entering the House of Representatives for the first time as an elected member is a feeling which has stayed with me ever since. Although I was a member of parliament for more than 33 years, I never lost my sense of respect, indeed a nervous edge, at being in that House of Representatives chamber.

As a new boy I soaked it all up. With Janette, by then heavily pregnant, I drove to Canberra for the opening ceremonies. My brother Bob sat in the public gallery with Janette to watch the swearing-in ceremony. The older hands were immensely courteous to the new members. David Fairbairn and his wife, Ruth, took Janette and me to lunch, making us feel very much at home. David had a distinguished war record in the Royal Australian Air Force: he had been awarded a Distinguished Flying Cross (DFC); and was an old-school gentleman. That evening there was a formal reception in Kings Hall in Parliament House, a building richly steeped in Australian history.

There was a party meeting at which the new members were welcomed. Bill Snedden and Phillip Lynch were re-elected unopposed as leader and deputy leader, but not before some jousting over whether or not the ballots should then proceed, given that the Senate count had not been completed, and the final composition of the parliamentary party not determined. This suggested to me that, even at this very early stage after an election, there was some unease within the parliamentary party about the direction in which it was heading.

After the week of the swearing-in, we next assembled at the historic joint sitting of the two houses of parliament, on 18 July, to consider and pass the legislation blocked by the Senate in the previous parliament, and on which the double dissolution of 18 May 1974 had been granted. It was historic because on the two previous occasions when a double dissolution had been granted, the Government had either been defeated at the polls (1914) or had won control of the Senate (1951), in which latter event no joint sitting was needed, as it had the numbers in both houses to pass the bills on which the double dissolution had been granted.

The Constitutional provisions covering double dissolutions had been inserted to provide a mechanism to resolve deadlocks between the two houses. They therefore allow a joint sitting of the two houses when a government has been returned at a double-dissolution election, but without a majority in the Senate. That was Whitlam's position in 1974.

In the course of that week, I got to know many of my new parliamentary colleagues, and found that I was to share an office in a remote part of the house with my fellow NSW MPs David Connolly from Bradfield and Alan Cadman from Mitchell. They had also been elected for the first time at the 1974 poll.

The room was very crowded. At that time I smoked cigarettes, and so did Alan Cadman. It must have been stifling for David Connolly, a non-smoker, but he displayed considerable forbearance.

Unquestionably the larger New Parliament House has given excellent office facilities to the ordinary member and senator. Everyone now has some staff, and working conditions are a world away from what they were in the old building. Something has, however, been lost in the process. There is far less camaraderie. In the old building not only did the average member and senator have to share a room with one or two other colleagues, but this very fact resulted in many of the members and senators spending a lot more time in the party room. It functioned as a common room. It was immediately adjacent to a side entrance to the parliamentary chamber, and a frequent occurrence, after a division had occurred, was for members to wander into the party room to talk, make telephone calls or read newspapers. I know that this sounds faintly nostalgic, but it does have a real impact on the atmosphere of a parliament. It can dramatically change the group dynamic of a political party, especially during times of internal crisis.

Several long-serving members, such as Jim Forbes, Bert Kelly and Duke Bonnett, went out of their way to make new members welcome. We spent some relaxed time in the parliamentary bar, listening to the veterans. Jim and Duke were veterans of war as well. Jim Forbes had won a Military Cross in World War II, and Duke had served in the airborne units, or paras. They were generous with their time and friendship, teaching me a great deal about both good political representation and human nature.

During my very first days in parliament, Malcolm Fraser, shadow minister for industrial relations, saw to it that I joined him and several other colleagues for afternoon tea. He wasn't overtly touting for support, but had taken the trouble to demonstrate an interest in new members. I already had a good view of his abilities and I listened keenly to what he had to say. He argued that the Coalition had to produce policy alternatives, not just oppose the Government.

For a brand-new member, the joint sitting was an amazing experience. All members and senators were seated in the House of Representatives chamber; there were special rules of procedure for the sitting, which was fully televised. Bill Snedden wisely used it as a forum to continue his general attack on the Government's handling of the economy. Economic conditions were deteriorating quite rapidly, and further debate on the substance of the bills which had been blocked in the previous parliament was largely academic. Those bills were going to be passed at the joint sitting. I was placed at the joint sitting with John Carrick and Margaret Guilfoyle from the Senate, and one of my fellow new members, Alan Cadman. John and Margaret were very helpful.

Being a new member who was yet to make his maiden speech, I naturally did not participate in any of the debates at the joint sitting. I was pleased about this, as it was, uniquely, an opportunity to listen to speakers from both sides, and for the first time make my own assessments of their respective abilities. I was tremendously impressed with Kim Beazley (father of the subsequent Opposition leader), the Labor Education Minister, who was a very powerful orator.

I joined several parliamentary and party committees and became secretary of the opposition's education committee. The shadow minister for education was Jim Killen, and our main line of attack against Labor was its ambiguous policy towards helping independent schools. After the joint sitting, parliament resumed a more normal pattern, and I had my first opportunity of witnessing Whitlam's performance at question time. He was a fine parliamentarian, much better than Snedden. With his sharp wit and rhetorical flourishes he was superior to anyone on our side. That, of course, was not enough. The economic situation was worsening, and already the Labor caucus was behaving in a completely undisciplined fashion.

Frank Crean was Treasurer at the time and had an unenviable task. The economy was sliding rapidly and he had a Prime Minister who would never back him on really major issues and was himself often responsible for unjustified increases in government spending. On top of this the Labor caucus reserved the right to overrule the cabinet on the detail of economic policy. This was precisely what happened to a statement announcing certain economic measures, deemed necessary by the Government, which Frank Crean had planned to make on 23 July 1974.

Most of those measures were rejected by the Labor caucus immediately before the statement was due to be delivered. It was too late to alter the statement, so Frank Crean was left with the highly embarrassing predicament of delivering a statement full of rhetoric about the Government's determination to take control of a difficult situation, but without any announcements of substance to support it. It was hard not to feel sorry for him.

After this incident, it was obvious that Frank Crean's days as Treasurer were numbered. Crean was no great believer in fiscal restraint, but he did have some idea of how difficult the Government's challenge had become, due to changed international and domestic economic conditions. Inflation had become a big problem and unemployment had begun to rise. By contrast, Gough Whitlam not only failed or was unwilling to acknowledge the new realities, but appeared hurt by them, as if such diversions had no right to interfere with his grand plan for Australia.

My real induction into parliamentary life was my maiden speech. Our first child, Melanie, was only a few weeks old, so Janette could not come to the maiden speech. Melanie had been born on 1 August, and I had been present at the birth, as would be the case with our two sons. It has been common practice for a long time now for fathers to be present at the births of their children, but it was not so common more than 30 years ago. I am so glad that I was, as it was an added link in our lives, and I am sure of help to Janette.

My mother was able to attend and sit in the Speaker's Gallery during my speech. I was very grateful for that. Mum was a shy person, but she took an enormous pride in what I had achieved by being elected to the national parliament. I was nervous, which was natural, but I was well satisfied with the speech. Delivered on 26 September 1974, it emphasised the importance I attached to individual effort, the need to combat loneliness in big cities, the value of the coalition between the Liberals and the Country Party, freedom of choice in education and, very importantly, it contained a strong attack on the big increase in government spending contained in the recent budget. I did not read my speech, but delivered it from headings. That was to be the pattern for the long years I spent in parliament. Almost all of the other maiden speeches were read in their entirety.

Within days I was called upon at short notice to support Jim Killen, the shadow Education minister, in a matter-of-public-importance debate concerning the Whitlam Government's policies towards independent schools. This is a traditional debate, which occurs after question time each day, when the opposition has a go at the Government on some current issue, and because I was able, at short notice, to participate in this debate I won some brownie points in the whip's office. All that impromptu high school debating practice was now being put to good use.

*   *   *

The Family Law Bill, which was designed fundamentally to restructure Australia's divorce law, had been introduced into parliament (in the Senate) on 1 August 1974. The bill was the brainchild of Lionel Murphy, Gough Whitlam's Attorney General. It had Whitlam's enthusiastic support, and directly mirrored progressive thinking at the time that Australia should embrace no-fault divorce. There was strong support in the community for overthrowing the existing framework, which only permitted divorce on specific grounds, such as adultery, desertion or cruelty.

Having done some divorce work as a lawyer, I was familiar with the rancour usually surrounding marriage breakdown, and believed that big changes were needed. I felt that where a marriage had completely broken down, no good purpose was served by barriers being placed in the way of legally dissolving that marriage, provided that proper regard was paid to the welfare of any children.

A particularly distasteful aspect of the old law was the frequent practice of private investigators, at the instigation of an aggrieved husband or wife, conducting divorce raids to obtain photographs of people in compromising circumstances. In many hours of debate on the Family Law Bill there was general agreement about the need for significant change. The question was, how far the changes should go. There was concern, which I shared, that the bill might tip the balance too far in the direction of diminishing the value of marriage through making it too easy to obtain a divorce.

The strongest push for change came from the more strident feminist groups, who saw easier divorce laws as a way of obtaining greater equality of treatment for women.

There was no more important piece of social legislation debated in the time that I was in federal parliament than the Family Law Bill. All parties allowed their members a free vote, and this exposed real fissures and bitterness within the Labor Party. The divide was between its more conservative members, the majority having an Irish Catholic heritage, who had worries about the bill, as opposed to the growing number of progressive and socially libertarian MPs in Labor ranks, who saw the measure as a test of the Labor Party's modernist virility.

Lionel Murphy had a barely disguised contempt for the influence of the Judaeo-Christian ethic on Australian society. When he died, the historian Manning Clark said that one of Murphy's aims had been to dismantle the influence of the ethic on Australian life. To some people, the Family Law Bill was a bite-sized attempt to do just that.

I experienced, first-hand, the depth of rancour and personal hostility the bill had brought forth in Labor ranks. Frank Stewart, Minister for Tourism and Recreation, strongly opposed the bill, despised Murphy and was scornful of Whitlam's encouragement of Murphy. Stewart was a strong Catholic, one of those Labor men in New South Wales who had heeded the injunction of Cardinal Gilroy and Archbishop James Carroll, the leaders of the Sydney Catholic hierarchy, to 'stay in [the Labor Party] and fight' rather than join the DLP at the time of the great Labor split in the 1950s.

Stewart had waited a long time to taste government, having in fact succeeded Dan Mulcahy in the seat of Lang way back in 1953, in a by-election following Mulcahy's death. But the party he now belonged to was drifting further away from the party he had decided to stay in and fight to preserve from communist influence. It was people like Lionel Murphy who were pushing it even further away from the party of his youth. He was a decent, straightforward man who never hid his feelings.

He gave vent to those feelings about the Family Law Bill, and the roles of Whitlam and Murphy relating to it, in no uncertain terms. It was late one night, in a discussion also involving Ralph Hunt, the Country Party MP for Gwydir, who had similar reservations about the effects of the bill to mine. The three of us met in Stewart's office to discuss a tactical approach to the debate on the measure. Stewart was deeply angered by Whitlam's open support for the bill, being particularly incensed that the PM had himself introduced the bill into the house, instead of leaving it to Murphy's representative, Kep Enderby. Sarcastically, he declared that Whitlam had even done the introduction 'in a dinner suit'. No doubt Whitlam was dressed for a formal occasion, but I could see the point Stewart was getting at: the PM had an eye for the theatre of things, and would not have minded one bit being in formal wear when introducing this controversial bill.

The bellwether vote on the bill was a committee amendment moved by Bob Ellicott, the Liberal MP for Wentworth, which effectively aimed to increase the period of separation as the sole ground of divorce from one year to two. There were other changes proposed, some of which succeeded, including one from Malcolm Fraser which sought to protect a woman who wished only to continue her role as a wife and mother. But the Ellicott amendment symbolised the divide between those who thought that the bill went too far and those who did not. I voted for the Ellicott amendment. So did Paul Keating and Malcolm Fraser. Naturally Whitlam voted against it, as did the two former PMs still in the house, John Gorton and Bill McMahon.

It was defeated by just one vote: 60 to 59. Thus came to pass a huge change to our divorce laws, untrammelled even by quite moderate concerns not to change too much too quickly.

A two-year period of separation as the sole ground for divorce, replacing the old multiple-fault provisions, would have constituted a profound modernisation, without the signal the bare 12-month period sent, that marriage mattered somewhat less than used to be the case. More than 30 years later, it is hard to dispute the fact that marriage has been weakened as the bedrock institution of our society. It is at least arguable that the Family Law Act has played a part in this process.

8

FRASER TAKES OVER

As 1974 wore on, the grass around Bill Snedden, the Opposition leader, had become drier and drier. There was natural loyalty to him. We all saw him as the good bloke, and wanted desperately for him to succeed. Yet, especially amongst the more recent arrivals as MPs, there were mounting doubts that he could effectively exploit growing concern in the community regarding the economy, and fix Whitlam with the necessary degree of responsibility for it. Snedden's strongest support came from amongst longer-serving members and senators, who had gone through the pro- and anti-Gorton upheaval three years earlier. Many of them had had enough of leadership stoushes, and in the absence of a Messiah were content to stay with Snedden.

To me, and many others, Malcolm Fraser was the logical alternative to Snedden, but he was a deeply divisive figure, largely because of the part he had played in Gorton's downfall. There were still plenty of Gorton supporters whose organising principle was not the return of Gorton to the leadership, but to keep it away from Fraser. There were some ideological drivers: people like Andrew Peacock and Don Chipp, identified as progressives, labelled Fraser too conservative and backed Snedden. That also kept open Peacock's own aspirations for the leadership, should Snedden fall over.

Snedden's support base also included people with very conservative stances on issues such as South Africa and Rhodesia (now Zimbabwe); John McLeay and Don Jessop, both South Australians, were firmly in this group. It was another reminder that one should not over-simplify the use of philosophical labels when it comes to the choice of a leader. In the end the dominant influence is always who is more likely to deliver victory. Ultimately, that led to Snedden's replacement by Fraser.

Tony Staley, a Victorian MP, was Malcolm Fraser's principal spear carrier. In his first attempt to topple Snedden, in October 1974, he was joined by Eric Robinson, MP for the Gold Coast seat of McPherson; John Bourchier, MP for Bendigo; and Peter Drummond, a farmer MP from Western Australia. Staley and his group were ridiculed for the tactics they employed. They openly waited on Snedden and told him that he should stand down in the interests of the party. There were strenuous denials of any involvement by Fraser in the actions of Staley's group. It was easy to accept that Staley was the prime mover; he had been actively touting for Fraser for some time. It seems implausible that Fraser knew nothing at all of what was to happen when Staley's group went to see Snedden.

Although there were predictable cries of treachery and disloyalty about the behaviour of Staley's group, it was quite the reverse. They had been very open, having directly confronted Snedden with their concerns and asking him to resign. Naïve it might have been, but it was not treasonable.

At a party meeting late in November 1974, Staley moved a motion to declare the party leadership vacant. A clumsy attempt was made by some of Snedden's supporters to prevent a secret ballot. One of them even called out, 'Let's see the dogs.' The spill motion was lost, but the figures were not announced. I understand that this was the last time that the practice of not publicly disclosing numbers was employed by the Liberal Party. It was open to all sorts of mischief. Snedden's supporters put around the story that he had won overwhelmingly. He had not. The vote was probably 36 to 26 in support of Snedden. I deduced from widespread discussion with colleagues in both houses that a majority of the Liberal members in the house had voted for a spill, a very clear sign that Bill Snedden's days were numbered. I voted for Staley's spill motion.

From then on the leadership issue was never far below the surface. The grass didn't get green again until the change to Fraser in March 1975. It had remained tinder-dry over Christmas of 1974, which was dominated by the devastating Cyclone Tracy, which flattened Darwin and claimed 71 lives.

Whitlam's breathtaking arrogance was on full display. He was on an extended overseas trip when the cyclone hit. He came home, went to

Darwin and announced the Government's response and then resumed his overseas visit, as if nothing had happened.

During this time, some absurd attempts were made by some of Snedden's supporters to obtain a public undertaking from Fraser that he would not challenge for the leadership. The ridiculous word game further weakened Snedden. Fraser owed it to the party to be available, if it wanted him.

Snedden was also weakened by his dismal parliamentary performances. One of them involved him calling out 'woof woof' to Whitlam, to which the Prime Minister replied, 'The Leader of the Opposition is going ga ga.' It was one of those parliamentary moments when a short exchange alters the whole dynamic of the chamber, and is perceived to have wider significance.

But it was Andrew Peacock who struck the match that set that dry grass alight. Asked one of those interminable questions about the leadership at Adelaide Airport on 14 March 1975, Peacock flicked back the response that, 'Rumours and divisive speculation about the leadership are doing great damage to the Party. Mr Snedden should call a meeting and ask for a vote of confidence so that speculation can be ended.'[1] Peacock's intervention surprised many. He was a Snedden man. Fraser's camp was ecstatic. Another vote for the leadership now had to be held.

Facing the inevitable, Snedden called a party meeting for 21 March.

The motion to declare the leadership of the party vacant was carried by 36 to 28, and Fraser was elected leader by 37 to 27. It was the right decision, as events over coming months were to show. During that time, Fraser was to demonstrate a steadfast pursuit of a given objective unmatched at any other time in his career. He also changed the mood of the party immediately. Although there was plenty of residual affection for Bill Snedden, and continuing lack of warmth towards Fraser from many colleagues, the mainstream of the Liberal Party knew that it had done the right thing by going for Fraser. He sounded strong and looked like a winner.

Although Fraser and I talked regularly, both of us believed the opposition should have sharper policies, and I had made some impact as a debater in the house, I had no expectation of promotion under Fraser. It was a complete surprise when he asked me to be opposition whip. It took me all of two seconds to say yes. I was bowled over to have any job, knowing that if I did it well, other things could follow.

Politics is a very competitive profession. The golden rule, if you want promotion, is always says yes when the leader offers you a job. If you don't then the leader is entitled to, and will, move on to someone else.

In 1997 as Prime Minister, when doing a reshuffle, I offered Petro Georgiou, the MP for Kooyong, a position as a parliamentary secretary. He knocked it back, implying that it was beneath his dignity, saying 'I'm too old and ugly to be a parliamentary secretary.' This was several years before refugee and asylum-seeker issues were under debate, so Petro did not reject the job on policy principle. Whatever his motives, it was a foolish response. I never offered him another job. Brendan Nelson, Malcolm Turnbull and Tony Abbott all started off as parliamentary secretaries; each was made a cabinet minister by me. All of them would ultimately lead the party. Who did Petro imagine he was?

My surprise at being offered the whip's responsibility was exceeded just two days later when Fraser rang to say that he now wanted me to be the shadow minister for consumers affairs and commerce. The reason was that Bob Ellicott, to whom he had offered the job, had refused Fraser's edict that shadow ministers not do any non-parliamentary work. Ellicott had wanted to keep his hand in at the bar with a small amount of legal work. His position was quite reasonable. I certainly reserved the right, in opposition, to keep my hand in at the law. There was a double standard here. Apparently it was in order for people like Fraser and Tony Street and many others to own farms, or for Eric Robinson to maintain a string of sports equipment stores throughout Queensland, but Ellicott couldn't do some legal work.

The distinction drawn at the time was that there was a manager in charge of the farm or the business. Of course, the principal had no contact with the manager, nor did he take any interest in what happened to the asset!

In any event, Ellicott had the most eloquent precedent of all on his side. Menzies had kept taking briefs, even as Leader of the Opposition, maintaining that it kept him in touch with changes in the law. He was also not ashamed to admit that he needed the money. Before too long Ellicott had made his point; he and Fraser cobbled together some formula and he came back to the shadow ministry.

Nevertheless, Ellicott's temporary absence from the Coalition frontbench was a huge stroke of good fortune for me. Not only was I to speak for the opposition on a wide range of business issues, including competition law, but also to represent the shadow attorney general, Ivor Greenwood, in the lower house. At the time there was an avalanche of legislation in the AG's area, and I would, within a little over 12 months of entering parliament in the lower house, have carriage on behalf of the opposition of some of the most complicated bills of the Whitlam Government's second term. It was a fortuitous opportunity, which I relished.

9

THE DISMISSAL

When Fraser became leader, he cancelled the standing threat Snedden had made to block supply, at the first appropriate opportunity. He said that the Government should not be forced to an early election unless there were 'extraordinary and reprehensible circumstances'. In the light of what unfolded later in 1975, there was some scepticism about how genuine Fraser had been in withdrawing the early-election spectre. It was generally well received, as there continued to be a strong sense in the community that whatever doubts there might be about the competence of Whitlam and his team, they were entitled to a fair go, and that the threat to block supply which had precipitated the May 1974 double dissolution had been unreasonable.

Whatever his motives, and I believed that Fraser was genuine, his decision was clever politics. The consequence was to put the spotlight more sharply on Whitlam and his crew, precisely when their decline into chaos began to gather momentum.

The disintegration of Gough Whitlam's Government was very public. Disunity in government is usually caused by perceived or real challenges to its leadership, or arguments over policy direction or a combination of the two. Neither was the case in 1975.

Whitlam remained a messianic figure to the Labor faithful; he had brought them to the Promised Land, and no matter what political disasters befell the Government, he would remain in charge.

Gough Whitlam, though, did have a vicious streak, which was demonstrated when he cut down the speaker, Jim Cope, on the floor of the house. Cope had named Clyde Cameron, the Labour and Immigration Minister, for defying the chair. Whitlam delivered a humiliating vote of no confidence in Cope by refusing to support the removal of Cameron after he had been named. Cope resigned on the spot. It was dishonourable treatment of a man who had given years of service to his party.

Cope had a keen sense of humour. Ballots for a new speaker are secret, with each member writing on a voting slip the name of the candidate for whom they intend to vote. The Liberal candidate in the ballot following Cope's removal was Geoff Giles, the MP for Angas in South Australia. He had no hope against the ALP nominee, Gordon Scholes, and in the course of the ballot Jim Cope called out, in his piercing voice, 'How do you spell Giles?' It broke up the whole place.

The public beheading of Cope was but one example of Labor's progressive fragmentation through 1975. When Whitlam reshuffled his team mid-year, Clyde Cameron noisily resisted removal from his beloved Labour and Immigration post. During a division on a bill I was handling in the Attorney General's area, a very agitated Cameron worked on a document as he sat beside the Attorney General at the table. The Attorney said to him, 'Think of the party, Clyde'. Cameron's salty reply made it plain that all he wanted to do was pay out on Whitlam. It was impossible for us not to notice such unhappy division. They no longer seemed to care.

Not only was Whitlam's big-spending and permissive approach to public-service wages growth aggravating the rising inflation and higher unemployment which had become a feature of the Australian economy, but the suspicion grew that there was something irregular, even improper, about the Government's efforts to borrow money abroad for national development purposes.

The genesis of that suspicion was a meeting of the Federal Executive Council at the Lodge on 13 December 1974. It was an ad hoc meeting which emerged from a ministerial discussion involving Whitlam; the Deputy PM and Treasurer, Jim Cairns; the AG, Lionel Murphy; and Rex Connor, Minister for Minerals and Energy. The meeting authorised Connor to borrow up to $4 billion. The Governor-General was not at the meeting and did not know of it until the next day, itself highly unusual; the loan was described as being for temporary purposes when so clearly it was not. Under the financial agreement, overseas borrowings other than for defence and temporary purposes required the approval of the states through the loan council. It was also unusual that authority was given to Connor to undertake the borrowing;

Treasury normally handled such matters through well-established and reputable channels.

The Government was never able to shake the impression of irregularity, especially when evidence emerged of dealings with fringe international financiers such as Tirath Khemlani, a Pakistani commodities dealer. When Australia had borrowed before, Morgan Stanley, a solid Wall Street bank, had usually done the work. Treasury could not understand why such a reliable path would not be followed again.

Labor's new Treasurer, Bill Hayden, was an outpost of sanity: bright and economically sensible. If he had been there from the beginning, things might have been different. Hayden's tragedy was that Labor was beyond the point of no return when he brought down his budget in August 1975. Its principal legacy was that of Hayden's reputation. He came out of 1975 as by far the most credible figure in the Labor Party.

There was a steady drip of press stories, keeping alive the sense of chaos, even scandal, which surrounded the Government. Hayden's budget was well received, but could not disperse the fog enveloping Whitlam's team. By September the mood in Liberal ranks had hardened. Many began to argue that the Government was so bad that we had an obligation to force an early election. Remembering what Fraser had said in March, they claimed that the continuing loans saga amounted to 'reprehensible circumstances' and that the Coalition would be justified in blocking supply to force an early election.

The Loans Affair, as it became known, ultimately claimed the scalps of both Cairns and Connor. Cairns finally went in July, when it emerged that, despite having denied it to parliament, he had signed a commission letter to a Melbourne businessman. Connor's resignation on 14 October was the final straw for the opposition; he had continued negotiations with Khemlani after his authority to do so was revoked.

Media pressure grew — typical being a front-page editorial from the Sydney Morning Herald, on 15 October, headed, 'Fraser Must Act'. He did. That very day Fraser announced that the Coalition in the Senate would vote to defer a decision on the supply bills until Whitlam agreed to have an election. The next day the opposition used its numbers in the Senate to achieve this. The bills deferred were routine ones authorising the spending of moneys on the ordinary annual services of government. If the bills were delayed indefinitely, the Government would run out of legally available funds and the business of government would grind to a halt. In political and constitutional terms, it was the nuclear option. Supply had never been refused or delayed before; there had only been the threat of it in 1974. Then, Whitlam countered with an election. He would not do this in 1975.

Just before his announcement, Fraser assembled the entire shadow ministry, tabled his recommendation that the opposition vote to defer supply, and one by one he asked each shadow his or her view. Along with every other shadow present, I supported Fraser's recommendation.

This should be recalled, as revisionism about 1975 has included suggestions that Malcolm Fraser had acted unilaterally on the supply issue. There was no dissent in the shadow cabinet ranks. Don Chipp, later to resign from the Liberal Party, form the Democrats and denounce the blocking of supply by Fraser, was one of those present at the meeting who strongly backed his leader's position. There was enthusiastic support for Fraser's push at the full Coalition party meeting, immediately following shadow cabinet. The late Alan Missen, a Victorian senator, was the only person to express concern. He stood and said, 'Leader, you know I have qualms about this.' Phillip Lynch, the Liberal deputy, replied, saying, 'Alan, let's have a talk about it.' They left the room together. A short while later Lynch came back and said that 'Everything [would] be okay'. Missen voted with the rest of his colleagues to defer supply.

Labor was understandably bitter at the failure of the Bjelke-Petersen Government to follow normal custom and replace the deceased Queensland ALP senator Bert Milliner with his chosen Labor replacement, Mal Colston. The Labor Party was foolishly stubborn in rejecting the initial request of the Queensland Premier to submit three names from which a choice would be made.

The upshot was that Whitlam was left with only 29 senators supporting him against 30 from the Coalition when the crucial Senate vote to defer supply was taken in mid October. Patrick Field, Bjelke-Petersen's chosen replacement for Milliner, did not participate in the vote, but this did not alter the fact that if normal practice had been followed, the vote would have been tied at 30 each and supply blocked rather than deferred.

Several months earlier, the NSW Coalition Government had likewise chosen Cleaver Bunton, an Independent, to replace Lionel Murphy, who had been appointed to the High Court. This did not have the same consequences as the Queensland appointment because Bunton voted with Whitlam on the supply issue.

In 1977 the Australian people voted overwhelmingly for a constitutional change, effectively guaranteeing that when a casual vacancy occurred in the

Senate the replacement would come from the same Party as the former senator.

Unlike May 1974, Whitlam did not call an election. He was determined to prevail, asserting that as governments were formed by the party having a majority in the lower house, the Senate had no right prematurely to terminate a government so formed by forcing an early election. Politically, he had no option. He would face annihilation at an early poll. Fraser's biggest challenge was to hold the Coalition together as the weeks of deadlock dragged on.

His argument was as simple as Whitlam's. Our Constitution gives co-extensive powers to the Senate and House of Representatives, so the government of the day needs the approval of both houses to spend money. As the Senate had not given that approval, the Government could not continue to function and should call an election to resolve the issue. Politically, Fraser had to maintain his position. He knew that he would win an early poll, just as Whitlam knew he would lose it. Stripped of rhetorical excesses, it was a titanic clash of political wills between two determined men. A compromise was never likely once the Senate had deferred supply. Fraser did offer to pass supply if Whitlam agreed to hold an election the following May. This was rejected.

Once the two protagonists had staked out their ground, interest focused on who might blink first, and increasingly, as the weeks passed, how or when might the Governor-General act. Whitlam's operating assumption was that Kerr would always do as he was told. He badly misread his choice as Australia's effective Head of State. Kerr would be no cipher. No one understood this better than John Carrick. In the days that followed the deferral of supply, he said to me several times, 'John Kerr will want the judgement of history. He will do the right thing by the office.' Carrick had known Kerr for a number of years, and well enough to divine that he was not in any way beholden to the Labor Party.

John Kerr was called 'Old Silver' at the Sydney bar because of his impressive mane of white hair. Bob Ellicott knew him well. They had been barristers together. He shared Carrick's opinion that Kerr would want to be seen as having done his Constitutional duty. On 16 October, Ellicott published a prescient legal opinion of what Kerr might have to do; in it he raised the option of dismissal of Whitlam and his ministers as a way through. In a drama which involved many lawyers (mostly from the Sydney University Law School), Ellicott emerged, courtesy of this opinion, as the real star.

Tirath Khemlani, the Pakistani commodities dealer who had been put in touch with the former Minerals and Energy Minister Rex Connor when the latter was on the hunt for overseas loan moneys, landed in Canberra in the middle of the imbroglio, wanting to see the opposition. Ellicott and I were given the job of talking to him and getting details of his contact with Connor. It was disconcerting; if Australia wanted to borrow large amounts of money for development purposes, it beggared belief that it would not act through traditional banking channels. Khemlani was at most a fringe operator, and Connor's behaviour had made Australia look foolish. Bob Ellicott and I found Khemlani a likeable man when interviewed at the Wellington Hotel, Canberra, but we didn't see him and Australia borrowing abroad as a natural fit.

Canberra had a beautiful sunny day on 11 November, not a cloud in the sky. The view down from the War Memorial (surely the most impressive monument of its kind in the world) must have been as spectacular as ever, so ordered and serene. Sir John Kerr must have felt anything but serene as he attended the Remembrance Day service, having already resolved upon a course of action which would result, almost certainly, in him being the only Governor-General in Australia's history to dismiss an incumbent Prime Minister.

What followed is central to the political folklore of Australia. Judgements made are set in cement. It had been a defining political clash between two implacable foes. It fell to John Kerr to find a solution which referred that clash to the Australian people for resolution. He did just that, at immense personal cost.

The money was fast running out; Whitlam wanted a half-Senate election, which would resolve nothing; Fraser would not relent. So Kerr, recognising that it was, above all, a political stalemate, remitted that stalemate to the people for adjudication. It was a thoroughly democratic solution.

When Whitlam called on him to advise a half-Senate election, Kerr asked Whitlam if he would advise a general election, that being the only action which would secure Senate passage of the supply bills, thus resolving the deadlock. Whitlam refused to give that advice, whereupon the Governor-General withdrew Whitlam's commission as PM, handing him written reasons for his decision.

Kerr immediately commissioned Fraser as caretaker PM, on condition that he advised a general election; secured passage of the supply bills; and made no appointments or conducted any inquiries into activities of the Labor Government. Fraser naturally agreed with these conditions.

Earlier in the day, none of us knew this was coming when the scheduled joint party meeting took place, although most sensed that time was running out and something would soon give. Phillip Lynch said, 'Keep patient; I think things are coming to a head.' He had just participated in a meeting of party leaders, convened by the PM to see if common ground to solve the impasse could be found. The meeting was a public-relations prelude to Whitlam advising Kerr to call a half-Senate election.

When the house met, a debate on the supply issue ensued. I continued my normal routine. Leaving the library, I ran into journalists in Kings Hall, who informed me that there would be a half-Senate election, because that is what Whitlam had told his caucus.

The house rose for lunch at 12.55 pm. After eating I went for a walk. As I returned through the front door of Parliament House, Frank Crean, Deputy PM, hurried, and I mean hurried, past me. We exchanged brief greetings. Later I would learn that he was on his way to a hastily convened meeting at the Lodge to talk to the just-dismissed Prime Minister.

I also encountered Tony Eggleton, the Federal Director of the Liberal Party. He appeared to be waiting for someone. It was Malcolm Fraser, who was on his way back from Government House, having just been sworn in as caretaker prime minister. Tony gave nothing away, and I did not then know what had happened. Only minutes later I was in the opposition lobby, and the door from Kings Hall swung open and in strode Malcolm Fraser followed by Tony Eggleton; they both disappeared inside the Opposition leader's office. Fraser and I exchanged greetings on the way through. I noticed that he was holding something in his right hand. I realised later that it was the Bible on which he had just been sworn in.

The bells rang for the resumption of the house at 2 pm. I went straight to the chamber, and whilst the bells were still ringing Vic Garland, a shadow minister from Western Australia, came up to me and some other MPs and simply said, 'Kerr's sacked Gough.' I was stunned. Moments later Fraser entered the chamber as the bells stopped sounding. I knew that Garland had not been kidding when the speaker, Gordon Scholes, who knew the procedures precisely, called Fraser, not by his customary title of Leader of the Opposition, but by the title 'Honourable member for Wannon'. By then Fraser was no longer the Leader of the Opposition.

Fraser then told the house that he had been commissioned to form a caretaker government and that a double dissolution election would be held on 13 December 1975.

My lasting memory of the debate which followed — on a Labor no-confidence motion against the new caretaker Prime Minister — was the remarkable control that Scholes, the speaker, kept over the emotionally charged, angry Labor MPs. Only a few hours earlier, they had been told by their Prime Minister that there was to be a half-Senate election. They now faced an election for the whole parliament, which they knew in their hearts they could not win. That election would be fought on the record in office of the Whitlam Government.

The no-confidence moved by the Labor Party was carried on party lines, with little debate. The sitting was then suspended so that the speaker could call on the Governor-General with the motion, seeking the reinstatement of Whitlam as Prime Minister. Meanwhile, the Senate had met and passed the appropriation bills, thus guaranteeing supply, one of the conditions of Fraser's appointment as caretaker PM. Incredibly, Labor's Senate leader, Ken Wriedt, had not been informed of the dismissal and believed that the Coalition had capitulated when it agreed to pass the bills. This was a huge blunder by Whitlam. Armed with knowledge of the dismissal, the Labor Senate president could have delayed the sitting and at least given his party room for a tactical response.

After our sitting had been suspended, I mingled with a large crowd of angry Labor MPs, staffers and public servants that had gathered outside Parliament House. I ran into Clyde Cameron, who railed to me against what had happened. He predicted an anti-Fraser backlash and said, 'You won't win, and even if you do the country will be ungovernable.' He was wrong on both counts. It was this crowd which, later, gave such a hostile reception to David Smith, the Official Secretary to the Governor-General, when, as tradition required, he read from the steps of Parliament House the proclamation of the Governor-General dissolving the two houses of parliament. Watching over Smith's shoulder was Gough Whitlam, who then delivered his well-reported declaration, 'Well may we say "God save the Queen", because nothing will save the Governor-General.'[1]

All of us felt shock and disbelief at what had happened. It troubled me that Kerr had had to intervene. I knew that he would cop intense abuse from Labor supporters. Yet he had been left with no alternative. Only he, exercising the reserve powers of the Crown vested in him under the Constitution, could sever the Gordian knot.

Opposition MPs gathered in small groups, discussing the day's events, speculating about the campaign ahead and expressing just a tinge of apprehension about the reaction of the Australia public to such a momentous event.

That evening Bob Ellicott and I walked together through Kings Hall and came across Jim McClelland, Minister for Labour and Immigration in the Whitlam Government. Known in the Sydney legal profession as 'Diamond Jim' on account of his immaculate dressing, McClelland had, as a solicitor, briefed Kerr to appear in disputes involving the Federated Ironworkers' Association. They had been bitter encounters, and Kerr and McClelland had become good friends. McClelland was very irate and said, 'You had the Queen's man in the bag right from the beginning.' It was a revealing remark. It was untrue but, importantly, betrayed the fact that Labor had operated all along with the belief that because Kerr had been appointed by Whitlam, he would, when the crunch came, do what Labor wanted. It was a monumental miscalculation, for which McClelland, given his long association with Kerr, no doubt felt a special responsibility.

The next morning, the political analyst Malcolm Mackerras dropped into my office and boldly said, 'You realise that you are now enjoying your last weeks as member for Bennelong. There will be a massive reaction against Kerr sacking Whitlam, and even a safe seat like yours will be lost by the Liberal Party.' I both thought and hoped that he was wrong, which of course he was. Thirty-one years were to pass before Malcolm, in 2006 and following a redistribution which made my seat even more marginal, again predicted that I would lose Bennelong. This time his forecast proved accurate. In that three-decade period, both Australia and Bennelong had undergone much change.

10

A MINISTER

After 11 November I did not see or speak to Malcolm Fraser until the triumphant party meeting following his massive victory on 13 December 1975. The Coalition's majority of 55 was by far the largest in Australia's political history. There had been almost a clean sweep of seats in Queensland; only Bill Hayden's Oxley was narrowly held by the Labor Party. Even the staunchly pro-Labor city of Canberra had returned a Liberal in one of its two seats.

It had been a bitter campaign, before a deeply polarised electorate. The 35 per cent who habitually voted Labor exhibited their hostility over the dismissal by heaping enormous personal invective on Sir John Kerr, and in this they were aided and abetted by Whitlam and his former ministers. The remainder of the electorate, consisting of habitual Coalition supporters and those in the middle, were grateful for the opportunity of voting out what they regarded as the most incompetent government Australia had had, at least since World War II.

Once an election had been called, debate about the merits or otherwise of the Governor-General's actions receded into the background, except for those who would resentfully feed on this for the rest of their political lives. The election became a referendum on the performance of the Whitlam Government, and once this was the case, Fraser's victory was assured.

Naturally Malcolm Fraser and Phillip Lynch were unanimously re-elected to their respective positions at the start of the Liberal Party meeting following our victory. It was an amazing gathering, full of elation, with a sizeable chunk of the party room comprised of people I had never met before. Not only were our ranks swollen by people who had won seats from Labor, but also by those replacing a number of former members who had retired voluntarily.

As a shadow minister, I had some hope of becoming a very junior minister in the new government. I guess, like all other shadow ministers, I had done all sorts of calculations in my head about my prospects, and I knew that Fraser wanted a smaller cabinet than the 32 or 33 which made up the shadow ministry. So I was not overly optimistic.

Just after the meeting ended, John Bourchier, the chief whip, said that the Prime Minister wanted to see me in his office, and I got the clear impression that Bourchier knew I was to become a minister. I felt a keen sense of anticipation and my best hopes were realised when, a short while later, in the Prime Minister's office, Malcolm Fraser told me that he wanted me to become Minister for Business and Consumer Affairs. I was tremendously excited and couldn't wait to tell Janette.

Whilst I thought that I had done a good job as a shadow minister, I knew that it was a fine judgement for a leader when choosing younger members in a new ministry. Malcolm Fraser and I have had our differences over the years and our relationship became very distant after I became Prime Minister, but I will always be grateful for the opportunity he gave me back in December 1975. It was a generous promotion at a critical time.

Business and Consumer Affairs was a new portfolio arrangement which brought together many of the business regulatory functions of the federal government, including responsibility for the Trade Practices Act, the Prices Justification Act, and the Industries Assistance Commission and also, potentially, for the national regulation of companies and securities. Also included was the Customs Bureau, of which the Narcotics Bureau, carrying the federal fight against drugs, was part. The business community applauded this new grouping of responsibilities. The cluster of duties I had been given attracted intense scrutiny from the business media.

The Fraser Government inherited a fragile economy. Inflation had soared to 14.4 per cent; unemployment stood at 5.4 per cent; the budget deficit had blown out to a projected 1.8 per cent of gross domestic product (GDP). Federal government spending had risen by a staggering 46 per cent over the two-year period of 1973–74. The Whitlam Government had been an incompetent economic manager; there was a near universal judgement that it would be a long time before Labor would again be trusted with the purse strings.

Most of the senior members of the incoming Government — Fraser, Lynch, Anthony, Sinclair, Nixon, Bob Cotton, Peacock and Greenwood — had been prominent in earlier Coalition governments, and were heirs of the Menzies years, which had been ones of stability and prosperity. They had been, also, years of government regulation, an inward-looking Australian economy, high levels of tariff protection and a centralised wage-fixation system. This regulatory, activist role for government had seemed to work during that time. There had been much activity and full employment. Why then should that approach be changed?

Maintenance of the status quo might have been justified if the world had not changed. The world, however, had changed quite dramatically in the early 1970s. The challenges for the Australian economy were quite different from what they had been previously; different responses were needed. The Whitlam Government had failed totally to realise this. The new Coalition Government would now have the opportunity of doing things differently, and better.

From the perspective of my portfolio responsibilities, I felt that we needed to restore business confidence by cutting government spending, pruning business regulation, providing more incentives for investment, and tackling some of the excesses of union power.

I appointed Paul McClintock, a Sydney lawyer and former president of the Liberal Club at the University of Sydney, as my principal private secretary. Paul had impressed me with his political courage in keeping the Liberal banner flying on a university campus during the early 1970s when, in the wake of debate over Vietnam and other issues, that was a particularly difficult task. Paul would later return when I was Prime Minister as head of the Cabinet Policy Unit.

Quite early, I established the Swanson Committee of Review into the Trade Practices Act. I wanted the act loosened and made more business-friendly; one of the reasons the Australian economy was performing badly was that too much red tape and regulation had been imposed on the business community. Malcolm Fraser strongly supported the review.

He did, however, backtrack on a promise to abolish the Prices Justification Tribunal. It was set up by Whitlam, and required large companies to obtain approval for price increases. It was impractical and a hindrance for business. Shortly after I became minister, Fraser rang and said it might be necessary to 'give Hawke a win by going soft on our pre-election promise to get rid of the

Prices Justification Tribunal'. Although it ran against our deregulatory thrust, I didn't, at this early stage, question Fraser's judgement, and we eased away from our commitment to abolish the tribunal. In those early months of government I believe that Malcolm Fraser thought that, with the odd gesture, he might win the grudging cooperation of the union movement.

At that time the Trade Practices Act penalised secondary boycotts by companies, but not by unions. I thought that this was a double standard, and therefore wrong. Unions were, for example, placing boycotts on petrol deliveries by certain tanker drivers, which forced up the price of petrol for some motorists. If a company did something like that it would be penalised, yet the unions were not.

I asked Thomas Swanson to look at this. Perhaps influenced by the conventional thinking, Swanson's review did not recommend applying the secondary boycott law to unions. He did, however, suggest other changes which reduced the regulatory load on business, which we largely adopted. With Malcolm Fraser's support I persuaded cabinet to bring unions within the secondary boycott reach of the Trade Practices Act, despite Swanson's recommendation otherwise.

Thus was born what became Sections 45(D) and (E) of the Trade Practices Act, which imposed substantial penalties on unions similar to those for companies that engaged in secondary boycott conduct. It was removed from the Trade Practices Act for a period of time under the Keating Government, only to be returned to the legislation when I became Prime Minister. It survives to this day.

This was an historic change in the law affecting unions. It outraged the union leadership, particularly Bob Hawke. When the legislation was published I agreed to talk both to business groups and the unions regarding its provisions. At a meeting in Parliament House attended by Hawke as president of the Australian Council of Trade Unions (ACTU), as well as leaders of the public sector unions, Hawke glared at me across the committee room table and said, 'If this goes through there will be blood in the streets.' It was a nonsensical threat and one which was counterproductive. It confirmed my view that the proposal struck at the heart of the privileged position of the union movement, and I was more determined than ever that it should become law.

As Minister for Business and Consumer Affairs I had administrative responsibility for the Industries Assistance Commission. Tariff policy was, therefore, another issue I confronted. Up until then I had supported the prevailing orthodoxy.

This issue came to prominence after the Fraser Government, on 28 November 1976, devalued the Australian dollar by 17.5 per cent. Being a member of the economics committee of cabinet, I attended the cabinet discussion on devaluation. I strongly supported the decision, believing, as did Fraser, that Australian industry needed the competitive boost that the devaluation would confer on Australian exporters, because it would make their products cheaper on world markets. Likewise, it would help local manufacturers because the devaluation made imported products dearer and therefore less competitive.

It was that last point which brought in tariffs. Existing tariffs on imported goods already made them dearer for Australian consumers, therefore it was argued that unless some of those tariffs were cut following the devaluation, an unfair additional burden would be placed on consumers and importers. The contrary argument, which I supported, was that it would be self-defeating to reduce tariffs significantly, as one of the reasons for the devaluation had been to help local manufacturers.

Those who attacked our decision not to cut tariffs said that the higher prices of imported goods produced by devaluation would drive up inflation. This did not happen as fierce competition amongst retailers, in a still-recessed economy, meant that price increases were kept to a minimum.

In the early days of the Fraser Government, there was no stauncher high protectionist than Bob Hawke. He frequently invoked a cheap jibe against the Industries Assistance Commission, that it was really the Industries Assassination Commission. It would take the relative safety of government, and security in the knowledge that the Coalition opposition would support him, before Bob Hawke became a supporter of tariff reform.

Shortly after the devaluation, Fraser split the Treasury into two departments: Treasury and the Department of Finance. It made sense as Finance could focus more heavily on expenditure control. Fraser believed that Treasury had been responsible for a damaging press report of an earlier devaluation discussion in cabinet; this could have influenced at least the timing of his split of the Treasury. The circumstances provoked Treasury resentment, which was a pity because of the intrinsic worth of the change.

*　　*　　*

Malcolm Fraser frequently encouraged me to appear in the media and talk generally on economic issues, provided that I kept in line with government policy. My profile received a huge boost when, following a Premiers' Conference proposal, Fraser announced that there would be a price-wage freeze for a period of three months from 13 April 1977. The Prices Justification Tribunal was charged with monitoring the freeze. Whilst it had a certain popular, limited appeal, it was economically unrealistic and could not last long. I was put in charge of the freeze, not even knowing anything about it until the announcement was about to be made.

The public liked the idea because it appeared that the Government was 'doing something' about inflation. The serious media ridiculed the approach, whilst more popular media took an enormous interest in the issue. I had immediate contact with all of the major employer groups and for a period of time it looked, against all expectations, as if the proposal might do some good. After several weeks it was accepted that it could not be continued because of its longer-term unworkability. There is some evidence it may have had a short-lived constraining influence on some price increases.

In May 1977 Malcolm Fraser appointed me as Minister Assisting the Prime Minister, which involved helping with the PM's correspondence and lower-order decision-making. I continued my full duties as Minister for Business and Consumer Affairs. It was a strong endorsement by the Prime Minister of the work that I had done there. I was happy with the promotion, but conscious of some resentment building amongst colleagues that my rise had been rather too rapid.

As a minister I worked closely with the National Country Party (later National Party) trio of Doug Anthony, Peter Nixon and Ian Sinclair. I liked them a lot. Anthony was strong and open, an ideal Deputy PM to Fraser. His languid, country style masked immense political shrewdness. Nixon was a tough political operator who defended country interests whilst recognising that electoral arithmetic was inexorably moving against his party. He gave me good early advice about being a minister. Sinclair was one of the most naturally gifted politicians I have known. He was intelligent, could absorb a brief rapidly — I don't think that he read any submissions until after cabinet meetings had started — and was versatile and talented on his feet.

In July 1977 I paid my first overseas visit as a minister and, accompanied by Janette, visited Washington, London and Ottawa. There was a shock when I returned. Fraser told me that he intended to appoint me as Minister for Special Trade Negotiations, with a specific brief to spend as much time as possible in Europe trying to extract a better trade deal for Australian exporters, particularly farmers.

Earlier, when visiting Europe, the Prime Minister had a stormy session with the European Common Market chieftains, particularly Roy Jenkins, a former British Labour Chancellor of the Exchequer, with whom Fraser had clashed in a very heated fashion. He came back convinced that the only way we would make real progress would be, effectively, to have a resident minister in Europe banging on doors the entire time.

This was a novel concept, involving the creation of a new department. I was not enthusiastic about the appointment, because Janette was several months pregnant with our second child, and I knew that I would be away for lengthy periods of time. Also, I really enjoyed the job I had. But it was a promotion, and would give an international dimension to my ministerial experience.

I assembled a small task group; it could not realistically be described as a department. Philip Flood, whom I had met only a few weeks earlier when I visited Washington, became head of the group. After receiving numerous briefings and meeting industry groups, my team and I set out for Europe in September. For the next seven weeks we traipsed around various European capitals putting our case, railing against high levels of European protection, particularly for agriculture, and not making a great deal of progress. Thirty-three years on, the essential elements of the Common Agricultural Policy, the main protective mechanism for agriculture in Europe, remain in place.

Australian and New Zealand farmers have been given a raw deal by the Europeans. By any measure, our primary producers are extremely efficient and do not receive high levels of protection from their respective governments, particularly when compared with the hefty support given to farmers in Europe, Japan and the United States.

Before I left for Europe, Phillip Lynch had brought down, in August, the second budget of the Fraser Government. For reasons I was not to know then, this budget would have a very significant impact on my political career over the following two years. Surprisingly, the budget contained significant tax cuts. I did not think that the tax cuts were necessary, nor had I thought the budget could afford them, but they would be popular.

Unfortunately, the budget had other problems: the revenue estimates on which it was put together would begin to come apart in only a few months. I learned later that there had been quite an argument between Treasury and the Department of Prime Minister and Cabinet regarding the wages growth figure: Treasury had estimated 7 per cent, the Department of Prime Minister and Cabinet had said it could be as high as 7.5 per cent. The Budget Committee of Cabinet had opted for the higher figure; it produced more revenue, thus making the tax cuts more supportable. The Treasury estimate turned out to be more accurate.

Whilst I was in Europe, speculation grew that Fraser would call an election towards the end of 1977. There was a strong case for an election before 30 June 1978, otherwise the double-dissolution election of 1975 would oblige a separate half-Senate election well before the middle of 1978. Fraser's thinking, no doubt, was that if there were to be an early election then it was better to have it at the end of the calendar year so as to restore the more normal pattern in Australian politics. The speculation was in full swing when I returned to Australia towards the end of October.

On 27 October 1977, Fraser announced an election for 10 December. It was to be the fourth general election in five years. A rather lacklustre campaign commenced. With the benefit of hindsight, the result of the election was never really going to be in doubt. There was no way that the Australian public was going to re-elect Gough Whitlam, having so totally banished him from office just two years earlier. On the other hand, however, there was a bit of suspicion about the early election, despite the strong reasons for having simultaneous elections for the two houses, and a lack of interest in the campaign. Until late in the piece, the opinion polls were very equivocal. There was the further complication of the Australian Democrats.

Some months earlier, Don Chipp had resigned from the Liberal Party and launched the Australian Democrats. He ran as somebody seeking to occupy the centre ground of Australian politics. Chipp had been a discontented soul since Fraser excluded him from the government he formed after the 1975 election. This was a major influence in his decision to form the Democrats. Don Chipp was an engaging personality who was a traditional 'small l' Liberal of the Victorian mould. Our worry was that the Democrats would rip votes from the Liberal Party and, through the preferential system, too many would wind up in Labor hands.

11

'MAY I SPEAK TO THE TREASURER?'

Immediately after Malcolm Fraser called the 1977 election, there were unexpected and dramatic developments involving the Treasurer, Phillip Lynch, which derailed the campaign for three weeks. This was to have amazing consequences for me. The day before Fraser called the election, Peter Leake, a land developer, told a judicial inquiry in Victoria that he had been involved in local land speculation with his friend Phillip Lynch. Whitlam pursued the matter in parliament the day that Fraser called the election. The location of the investment was called Stumpy Gully, a colourful description which added to some of the drama. There were also questions raised about property Lynch had acquired. The press went ballistic.

Lynch had not done anything improper or illegal, but he had been politically indiscreet. It is never a good thing for a senior minister, particularly a Treasurer, to involve himself in anything that can be regarded as financial speculation. The country was still in the economic doldrums, and it was so easy for the Government's opponents to allege double standards.

When the matter was raised in parliament, he had no immediate answer and, from the start, was on the defensive. Only a short time afterwards, the Treasurer became ill and, on 10 November, he entered Peninsula Private Hospital suffering severe kidney pains. It was at this point that I was caught up with the problems that had engulfed Phillip Lynch.

I was having dinner at home with my family on 10 November when Fraser rang and calmly told me that Lynch had gone into hospital and, therefore, had to stand aside as Treasurer, and that he wanted me to 'become the Government's spokesman on Treasury matters'. He didn't say exactly that I was being appointed as acting Treasurer, although that was the case. Totally surprised, I relished the challenge; it would put me back in the mainstream of the political debate. But, at that stage, I did not imagine that this would be anything other than a temporary responsibility.

However, developments were to change that. Lynch went under the knife the next day, and five days later, convinced that it had an issue damaging to the Fraser Government, the ALP went for the jugular. Using parliamentary privilege, two Victorian upper-house MPs made sweeping allegations against Lynch. The issue ran strongly. The media and the Labor Party would not let it rest. They wanted the scalp of the Treasurer.

Fraser was unhappy with the explanations given by Lynch regarding his financial affairs and angry that every day was dominated by an issue which involved, at root, a bad judgement call by his deputy.

At a news conference called by Fraser and me, ostensibly to talk about Whitlam's policy-speech highlight to abolish payroll tax, virtually every question focused on Lynch, and the news conference was a total wipe-out for the Government. Fraser walked from the conference with a stony face, and I knew that Phillip Lynch would not remain as Treasurer through to the election. Unless the Lynch issue was contained, it would overwhelm the entire election campaign.

Fraser correctly concluded that Lynch had to stand aside as Treasurer, leaving his future to be resolved after the election in the event of the Government being returned. But the way in which he achieved this disclosed real flaws in Fraser's handling of people.

Sensibly Fraser should have gone to see Lynch in hospital and talked to him directly in the presence of the party president and federal director. Instead he sent Peter Nixon, a senior National Party man, to do the job. Nixon was close to Fraser, tough, honest and skilful, but here Fraser was dealing with his own deputy. He should have been personally engaged.

On Friday 18 November 1977, after a rather tortured six- or seven-hour period of negotiations between Malcolm Fraser, who was in the Commonwealth Parliamentary Offices in Martin Place in Sydney, and Phillip Lynch, who was in hospital on the Mornington Peninsula, Lynch agreed, reluctantly, to stand aside as Treasurer, though he would stay as Deputy Leader.

Almost all of Fraser's messages to Phillip Lynch were delivered by other people. Resentment against Fraser by Lynch's many followers, such as Fred

Chaney and John Hyde, grew out of his mishandling of this situation. He would display similar clumsiness in handling a problem with Reg Withers a few months later, resulting in Withers leaving the Government and a lasting estrangement between the two men.

As acting Treasurer I thought that I might end up as Treasurer, albeit on a temporary basis, in the event of Lynch standing aside. That was the press speculation, although Fraser never canvassed the matter with me. It wasn't until Alan Carmody, Secretary of the Department of Prime Minister and Cabinet, said to me, after Lynch had agreed to go as Treasurer, 'The swearing in will be at Admiralty House on Saturday at 4 pm' that I realised that I would replace Lynch as Treasurer.

It had been an amazing day, indeed a series of amazing days. During the weekend, Janette told me that late on Friday afternoon, Sir Frederick Wheeler, the Secretary of the Treasury, had rung our home saying, 'May I speak to the Treasurer?' Janette deflected his enquiry by telling him that he wasn't at home. This incident validates a long-held view in Australian politics that public servants and Commonwealth car drivers always know important things well in advance of the politicians.

I was excited about what had happened, but I didn't believe that I was Treasurer for other than an interim period. I assumed that after the election, the Phillip Lynch issue would be resolved and I would return to some other, lesser, portfolio.

Meanwhile, my main concern was not to drop the ball on economic issues during the campaign. At that stage, despite our enormous majority, the Government was travelling badly, having been diverted by the Lynch Affair for several weeks and facing a public quite apathetic towards what we regarded as important campaign issues.

There was a further complication for me personally. Our second child, our elder son, Tim, was actually due on the very day that I was sworn in as Treasurer. He took his time, not arriving until 25 November. The events of these hectic weeks, coming on top of my prolonged absence overseas during the latter stages of Janette's pregnancy, had put a lot of pressure on her, which she handled quite remarkably. I was sworn in as Treasurer at Admiralty House in Sydney by the Governor-General, Sir John Kerr. Afterwards, Malcolm Fraser and I went on what was reported as a pub crawl, although from recollection we visited only one hotel, namely the Kirribilli local. Fraser was relaxed, and engaged in easy chit-chat with the locals. These were pre-mobile phone days, and the best that I could do to keep in touch with Janette was for my Commonwealth car driver, Bob Jenkins, who was at the hotel, to ring Janette periodically to check on her condition and report to me.

With the Lynch issue out of the way the campaign returned to what it always should have been about, namely whether or not Australians would re-elect a Whitlam Government. Once this became the principal issue, it was only a matter of time before the polls turned, and ultimately the Government won.

I had two major one-on-one debates during the campaign. The first was an ABC *Monday Conference* interview chaired by the late Bob Moore, immediately following Malcolm Fraser's policy speech in Melbourne. My opponent was Tom Uren, the Deputy Leader of the Opposition. The second debate was against Bill Hayden, who had been Whitlam's Treasurer. This was an appearance on the ABC's *This Day Tonight* program, and it was chaired by George Negus. These two debates were regarded as key events in the campaign, and the fact that I was judged to have won them convincingly did my reputation no harm at all.

The Fraser Government was returned on 10 December 1977 with a majority of 48 seats, only a fraction less than the record margin of 55 achieved two years before. It was an impressive result given the size of the 1975 majority. In retrospect, of course, there was never a chance that Whitlam would get re-elected. He gave a dignified speech on the night of the election, which ended his remarkable career at the top of the Labor Party.

To this day, Whitlam remains a legendary figure to devoted followers of the Labor Party and others in the community. Nobody can doubt his flair and style, his considerable sense of humour and his erudition. He did something for the Labor Party which seemed for so many years unattainable. He won government. Having won government, he proved to be a very poor Prime Minister. Sentimentality towards him should not smother that reality.

After the election Fraser did what I suspected might happen. Having made some positive comments about my efforts during the campaign, he kept me as Treasurer but gave the finance portfolio to a separate minister. Like Phillip Lynch, I had administered both portfolios from the time of my appointment as Treasurer.

Before any of this occurred, he had to resolve Phillip Lynch's position. Phillip's health had been restored, and he had easily retained his seat of Flinders. Stephen Charles, a well-regarded Melbourne silk, had prepared a report on Lynch's financial affairs, clearing him of any wrongdoing. Fraser called an ad hoc meeting, including Charles, Reg Withers, government leader in the Senate, Senator Fred Chaney and me. Although Charles had given Lynch a clean bill of health, Fraser was querulous at the meeting. He questioned one particular transaction, which, to me, seemed quite normal. When asked my opinion I said so. Reg Withers had the same view. That seemed to end the matter.

Lynch remained as deputy leader, but opted to become Minister for Industry and Commerce, specifically ringing and telling me that this is what he wanted. Thus, at the age of 38 years and 4 months, I became, unconditionally, Treasurer of the Commonwealth.

Again, I had every reason to be grateful to Malcolm Fraser for giving me what was a huge promotion.

Being Treasurer gave me access to the best concentration of brains in the federal bureaucracy. There are plenty of other departments with extremely talented people, but for concentration of brain power, the Treasury is hard to beat. The dominant figures in the Treasury at that time were Sir Frederick Wheeler as secretary and John Stone, the deputy secretary (economic). Wheeler was, with Sir Arthur Tange, Secretary of the Department of Defence, the last of the traditional mandarins of the federal public service. I liked Wheeler a lot.

I admired the way in which he had stood up for due process at the time of the Khemlani Affair, in the Whitlam years. He was tough and cunning and a firm believer in the independent sanctity, if I can put it that way, of the federal bureaucracy and most particularly the Treasury. His minutes were succinctly and strongly written. For all that he no doubt had the view that Treasurers came and went but the Treasury went on forever, I always thought he would give me advice that he believed was in the national interest. He was also a heavy smoker, and that suited me at the time because I was still addicted to the habit.

John Stone, who took over from Wheeler in 1979, was the brightest public servant with whom I ever dealt. That did not automatically make him the best, because, on occasions, his judgements did not match the purity of his intellectual arguments. He nevertheless held resolutely to all of the conclusions that he reached, and was quite uncompromising in the advice which he offered to his minister. Some ministers were nervous when I proposed appointing Stone head of Treasury, because they thought he was too doctrinaire in his economic thinking. My attitude was that people should be appointed to senior public service positions on merit. Passing over Stone would have been to deny that fundamental principle.

Early in April 1979, not long after Stone had been appointed secretary, Fraser asked Stone if he would prepare a memorandum of advice for an incoming Conservative Government in Britain, as to what should be done to fix their ailing economy. Fraser wanted to give it to Lord Peter Carrington, who was to see Fraser in Canberra. He was an old friend of Australia, and became Thatcher's first Foreign Secretary, staying in the post until the Falklands War.

Thirty years on, the Stone memo makes fascinating reading. For example, he wrote, 'Meanwhile union power has become a threat not merely to economic stability, but to civil liberties and the very concept of the rule of law upon which the British society has been founded and of which it has been for so long such a notable exemplar.'[1] The full memo appears as an appendix to this book.

Thatcher visited Canberra, very briefly, not long after her election in May 1979. She had been at a G7 meeting in Tokyo and came to Australia, ostensibly to discuss the situation in Rhodesia in advance of the Commonwealth Heads of Government (CHOGM) meeting in Lusaka. During her brief visit Mrs Thatcher attended a cabinet meeting, giving an uncompromising outline of what she intended to do in her own country. After she had left, quite a number of my colleagues were rather sceptical about some of her intentions, asserting that she was unrealistic. They had underestimated her.

I had badly needed expert advice on economic issues during the election campaign, as the Treasury had to maintain a certain distance during the caretaker period embracing the campaign.

This is when I met John Hewson. Already a professor of economics although only in his early 30s, John Hewson had had an impressive career at the Reserve Bank and the International Monetary Fund (IMF). He had joined Phillip Lynch's staff on a part-time basis, and worked closely with another economics professor, John Rose, who worked, also on a part-time basis, in Fraser's office. They were a real tandem. They provided joint advice to the Prime Minister and the Treasurer, especially on monetary policy issues. I liked John a lot. He gave good advice on most economic issues and was taken by the political atmosphere. In the changeover from Lynch to me, he had glided almost effortlessly from one office to the other.

Tension would develop between the senior people in the department and John early on. The top officials in the Treasury resented the degree to which both Fraser and I listened to private office advisors.

At this time the relationship between the minister, his private office advisors and his department was undergoing significant change. Ten years earlier, somebody like John Hewson would not have existed in the Australian political system. All of the principal policy advisors in a minister's office came from the relevant department. If non-departmental advice were taken, it was overtly taken from someone who was not on the minister's staff.

My five years as federal Treasurer were to change profoundly my opinions on many aspects of managing the Australian economy. When I became Treasurer I was unaware of the extent to which the Australian financial system was in need of deregulation, and although generally aware of the negative impact of across-the-board wage rises granted by the Conciliation and Arbitration Commission, I did not see the issue as one requiring freeing of the labour market. Rather I adhered to the conventional view at the time that the commission should be encouraged to deliver different wage judgements. I did not then realise that fundamental change to the system was required.

I believed that the Whitlam Government had spent far too much and that a big part of my responsibility as Treasurer was to reduce the rate of growth in government spending. I also thought the Australian taxation system needed to be reformed. However, I underestimated the enormity of the task involved in bringing about change in that area.

I was to have successes and failures. In 1978 the idea I floated of introducing a retail turnover tax collapsed, as a policy initiative, fairly quickly after an onslaught from Australian retailers and some very unhelpful comments from one of my colleagues, Bob Ellicott. He used the platform of a Sunday evening address at the Wayside Chapel in Sydney to say that the Government should abandon the whole idea because it was causing disquiet in sections of the business community. Although I had been right, in a pure policy sense, to raise the issue, I had been extremely naïve in the way in which I had gone about it. As I learned from that, you need time to build the case for change by explaining, in detail, the shortcomings of the existing system.

*   *   *

Decisions and promises from the first term of the Fraser Government preoccupied my early months as Treasurer. Treasury told me, shortly after the election, that the 1977 budget revenue estimates would not be realised. This was due to the average weekly earnings issue, already mentioned, as well as early predictions of expenditure over-runs. So from the beginning of 1978, it became increasingly apparent that my first budget would be extremely difficult. Australia still had a large budget deficit, although Lynch had made an impact on this in his first two budgets, and inflation, despite having fallen, was still quite high. Very unpopular decisions would be required if a significant reduction in the budget deficit were to be achieved.

Then there were the interest-rate predictions made by both Malcolm Fraser and Doug Anthony during the election campaign. Interest rates in Australia at that time were high, and financial institutions within the traditional banking sector were still tightly regulated. Fraser and Anthony predicted during the campaign that interest rates would fall by 2 per cent during the next term of office. Fraser said in the campaign, 'Falls in important interest rates could add up to a total of 2 per cent within 12 months.' Doug Anthony said that if interest rates did not fall by 2 per cent he would eat his hat. The statements were not only wildly optimistic, but also politically unnecessary.

At that time, bank lending and borrowing rates were subject to controls administered by the Reserve Bank. All savings bank housing loans and overdraft or business loans under $100,000 were caught by the controls. But the Government effectively decided those rates because, in administering the controls, the Reserve Bank normally reflected the views of the Monetary Policy Committee of cabinet. That committee met regularly, was chaired by Fraser, and as well as me as Treasurer, included Doug Anthony, Ian Sinclair and Peter Nixon plus Phillip Lynch and Reg Withers. The secretary of the Treasury and the Reserve Bank governor normally attended its meetings.

Thirty years on, this may sound an interventionist system, but it was not until the election of my Government in 1996 that the bank was given full independence to set interest rates. Although there was some early success on the interest-rate front in 1978, with a small reduction, there was never any hope that that 2 per cent prediction could be realised. Increasingly, monetary conditions ran in the opposite direction.

From the beginning, the interest-rate issue caused a lot of tension between the PM, the RBA and me. Fraser felt that the bank was dragging its feet on cutting rates. This was nonsense. He should never have made such a specific prediction in the campaign. I was caught in the middle. The Monetary Policy Committee once talked about invoking section 11 of the Banking Act, which enables the Government to direct a monetary policy move by the bank, provided the reasons for the direction and the RBA's contrary view are tabled in parliament. I thought that such a move would be extremely damaging for the Government, because on the economic merits there was no justification for a further cut in interest rates. As part of the debate with the bank, I was asked by the Monetary Policy Committee to meet the RBA board and argue the case for a rate reduction. I felt uncomfortable carrying this brief, and simply went through the motions. Quite justifiably, the RBA did not shift. My discomfort was increased by the presence, as an RBA board member, of Bob Hawke. Fortunately, my senior colleagues thought better of invoking section 11.

Within a few months of becoming Treasurer, it was clear to me that far from interest-rate controls keeping interest rates low, they were having the opposite effect. Banks could not attract enough money to lend for housing because the controls to which they were subject prevented them from offering sufficiently attractive interest rates to attract funds in the first place. Increasingly, as time went by, the solution seemed to me to be the removal of those controls.

The winter of 1978 was consumed with preparing the budget, and I knew it would be extremely unpopular. The expenditure-cutting process was made even more difficult because Eric Robinson, the Finance Minister, was sidelined because of a Royal Commission. I carried both portfolios. It was a lonely exercise.

I was determined to cut the deficit, but at every turn I met solid resistance from colleagues defending their patches. There would be no last-minute revenue surge to relieve the pain. The early forecasts were that, for the first time in 20 years, the Government faced a reduction of revenue receipts in real terms.

The main purpose of the budget, delivered in August 1978, was to cut the deficit, preferably through spending cuts, although some tax increases were needed to achieve the desired result. There was a temporary income-tax surcharge, steep increases in excise duties on spirits and cigarettes, taxation for the first time of certain lump-sum payments, the introduction of an airport departure tax, the elimination of home-loan interest deductibility (which had only been re-introduced by the Fraser Government in 1976), and the tightening of conditions relating to estimating provisional tax.

The big long-term policy announcement in the budget was that Australian crude oil would, in future, be sold domestically at the higher world market price. It was not popular because it pushed up the petrol price by 3.5 cents a litre, but it was good policy. It priced a wasting resource at its market value — surely sound conservation policy. The price increase for crude oil meant that, overnight, oil companies would potentially enjoy a windfall profit gain, so the Government increased the production levy imposed on oil companies to the level necessary to ensure that all of the windfall gain went to the Treasury as revenue, and not to the companies.

The budget was seen as mean and nasty, although some grudging commentary indicated that the Government was at least trying to hold onto its economic fundamentals. The problem was that it was the kind of budget that should have been introduced (with some modifications) in 1976, not two years later. The public thought that the Government was taking back things which should never have been given in the 1977 budget.

Malcolm Fraser was very unhappy about having to take back any of the personal income tax cuts. He had been the real author of them in the 1977 budget. The initial decisions we had taken for the 1978 budget did not include the temporary income tax surcharge. Fraser had wanted a range of increases in indirect taxation, so as to preserve the 1977 tax reductions. At the last moment I persuaded him that we should substitute an income tax surcharge, as the indirect tax increases would have a very negative impact on the consumer price index, thus blunting the impact of our 'fight inflation first' strategy.

Thirty years later, reading through the budget speech of 1978, I was struck by how big an emphasis I placed on the wage-fixing decisions of the Conciliation and Arbitration Commission. It was a reminder of the distance Australia had travelled concerning industrial relations — until Julia Gillard's Fair Work Act reversed much of the progress of the past 25 years — and how all-pervasive, and therefore inimical, a centralised wage-fixation system had been for the Australian economy.

Nasty and unpopular though it was, the 1978 budget did lay the foundation for the next two budgets and was, therefore, important in setting up our economic credentials for the 1980 election. If delivering an unpopular budget is a measure of economic responsibility, then this had been a most responsible budget. Later, whenever I heard Kevin Rudd boast about all the 'tough' economic decisions he had taken, I rolled my eyes and thought of my first budget, more than 30 years ago.

In his 1977 budget speech, Phillip Lynch gave a general warning that he would 'crack down hard' on artificial tax avoidance schemes. In April 1978 I was informed by the Commissioner of Taxation, Bill O'Reilly, that a particular tax avoidance scheme, called the Curran Scheme, was eroding revenue conservatively to the tune of $400 to $500 million a year, with some estimates putting the revenue loss well over $1 billion; O'Reilly recommended that the Government take immediate action to proscribe it.

Cabinet authorised me to outlaw the scheme with effect from budget night 1977. Thus began my long and often very bitter campaign against the tax-avoidance industry, which lasted whilst ever I was Treasurer. At times it poisoned my relations with a large section of the WA Liberal Party; some of its major donors had been involved in tax-avoidance schemes. Some of my anti-tax avoidance activities helped fuel the Joh for PM campaign.

Banning the Curran Scheme caused some anguish amongst Coalition MPs because, strictly speaking, it did have retrospective effect. Many in the Liberal Party held to the purist line that, irrespective of the revenue at stake, the principle of non-retrospectivity should never be violated. Others argued that there was a clear difference between reaching backwards to prevent people from avoiding an obligation parliament had always intended to impose on them as compared with imposing, with retroactive effect, a completely new obligation, previously not intended.

Price, Waterhouse & Co., one of Australia's leading firms of accountants, wrote to me, strongly supporting the stand I had taken. This reflected the fact that many reputable legal and accounting firms did not wish to advise their clients to go into artificial schemes, but as time went by, with no action being taken against those schemes, that position became increasingly difficult to sustain. There were always others in the two professions willing and eager to gain new clientele by advising how taxation obligations could be artificially avoided.

I enjoyed working with the commissioner and his senior people, who had their own distinctive style. On tax avoidance, I found them quite demoralised, and I understood why. Much as I admired the late Sir Garfield Barwick, there was little doubt that the Barwick High Court, in applying a very literal interpretation to the taxation laws, had rendered the general anti-avoidance section of the Taxation Act, namely section 260, largely inoperative.

That section had been in the Tax Act for decades, and stated that if an arrangement were entered into by a taxpayer with the purpose of avoiding taxation, then to the extent of that avoidance, the arrangement was void against the commissioner. For a long time the section had been applied effectively to protect the revenue against blatant and artificial schemes, but from the late 1960s and into the '70s, however, the High Court began applying the section differently. By the time of Cridland's case, decided on 30 November 1977, it was the view of Bill O'Reilly and his colleagues that section 260 was useless.

My response was to instruct the Tax Office to draft a new anti-avoidance section to replace (or update) section 260. The commissioner and his colleagues thought this a waste of time, telling me that no matter what parliament said, the courts would find a way of watering it down in favour of the taxpayer. I persevered and ultimately a new anti-avoidance section, known as part IVA of the Income Tax Assessment Act, was introduced, coming into operation in May 1981. Part IVA has worked very effectively. According to the commissioner, it put a stop to new tax-avoidance schemes of a totally contrived nature.

The controversy following my axing of the Curran Scheme was as nothing to the conflagration which occurred almost five years later when the Government enacted tax recoupment legislation to collect the proceeds of tax evaded through the use of bottom-of-the-harbour schemes. The bottom-of-the-harbour scheme involved a practice which effectively denuded a company of any assets, meaning it was unable to meet its tax obligations. It was different from an artificial tax-avoidance scheme, where the arrangement was such that there was no legal obligation to pay the tax. With bottom-of-the-harbour schemes the legal obligation remained, but the company had no assets with which to meet the obligation. The disposal of the company's assets was a fraud on the revenue because its only purpose was the evasion of the tax. Why 'bottom of the harbour'? In some cases disposal of the assets was accompanied, literally, by the records being thrown into Sydney Harbour.

The legal advice then was that, because fraud was involved, the scheme could not be banished under existing law or a specific prohibition, as with Curran. The only remedy was to make the fraudulent disposal of assets a crime. This caused me to swallow hard. It was one thing to adopt a no-holds-barred approach to outlawing artificial tax schemes; it was entirely another to threaten people, for the first time, with the criminal law if they engaged in certain behaviour. A lot of citizens deplored tax minimisation, but even they may have baulked at making the minimisers criminals.

After a lot of agonising, I recommended to the Government that it use the criminal law to stamp out bottom-of-the-harbour schemes. The Crimes (Taxation Offences) Act came into operation early in December 1980 and ended the practice. I thought that I would hear little more of bottom-of-the-harbour schemes. I was, however, wrong, although it would be two years before this became apparent.

In September 1980, Malcolm Fraser and the Victorian Liberal Government had appointed Frank Costigan QC, a Melbourne lawyer, to conduct a Royal Commission into the activities of the Federated Ship Painters and Dockers Union. This group was notoriously linked to alleged criminal activity on the wharves and elsewhere. The aim was to expose any corrupt or illegal behaviour. But it also could embarrass, politically, the Labor Party, because of its associations with the union, especially in Victoria.

During his investigations, Costigan uncovered the involvement of some officials and affiliates of the union with people who had promoted bottom-of-the-harbour tax schemes. He included this material in his findings, which became a blockbuster report, and along with the separate McCabe/Lafranchi report, tabled in the Victorian Parliament, it ended up damaging the Fraser Government. Names, amounts and shady practices were detailed. This heightened public outrage. The Victorian report cited 'very serious errors and omissions and resigned attitudes on the part of the Australian Taxation Office'.[2] Both reports gave colourful and dramatic descriptions of what had gone on in some bottom-of-the-harbour activities.

Regrettably for the Government, the perception was that a vast amount of tax had been evaded before the criminal law had been invoked, and nothing had been done to recover it. The fact that the Government had taken steps to ensure that even more tax would not be evaded in the future made no impact on the public.

The issue was on our minds as we prepared the 1982 budget. With the country rapidly falling into recession, that budget was proving very difficult to put together. The Taxation Office and the Treasury urged the passage of special legislation to recover tax evaded under bottom-of-the-harbour schemes prior to the passage of the special criminal legislation in November 1980; so did Peter Durack, the Attorney General.

The attraction of collecting the tax to help with the budget, combined with the apparent value of quietening public concern regarding the evasion of so much taxation, proved an irresistible combination. On 25 July 1982 I announced that we would legislate.

This caused uproar in many sections of the Liberal Party and the business community, particularly in Western Australia and Queensland. Elsewhere, there was a lot of support for what the Government had decided to do. The gathering recession had slashed revenue forecasts and, as a consequence, collecting this unpaid tax would avoid some less palatable imposts on honest taxpayers.

The legislation, however, wreaked havoc on Coalition unity. No fewer than 14 members of the Liberal and National parties crossed the floor to vote against it.

The decision to enact the recoupment legislation did not kill the issue. Critics alleged that if the Government and the Taxation Office had not been negligent in the first place, this special legislation would not have been needed. This issue put me under great pressure from the Labor Party and the press. To defuse the situation I tabled in parliament all of the advice I had received from the Tax Office on the subject. It became known as the 'telephone book' because of the large number of documents involved.

There were rough patches for me, particularly some of the delays between Tax Office advice and action in response. The quite radical transparency I had adopted — the bureaucracy was horrified, so were a few of my ministerial colleagues — took a lot of steam out of Labor's attack. In addition, the opposition then scored a spectacular own goal, which effectively took the heat off the Government.

At the time Hayden was under pressure, having just beaten off a challenge from Hawke. He overreached, in the hope of landing a leadership-boosting blow on the Government, with his allegations of tax avoidance against the respected businessman John Reid. Reid had been a director of a company subsequently sold in a bottom-of-the-harbour scheme. Foolishly, Hayden named him in the house on the strength only of a company search showing Reid as a director. At Reid's request, the commissioner quickly looked at his affairs and was able to certify that he had not been involved in any improper conduct. This blew Hayden out of the water. He had gone too far.

Although it was no longer on the back foot, the Fraser Government had been hurt by the whole episode, because there was a lot of disunity and bad blood in our own ranks.

After all the drama I have described, Murray Gleeson QC, the clear leader of the bar, later Chief Justice of New South Wales and then Australia, delivered an opinion that section 260 could, after all, be used to recover tax evaded through bottom-of-the-harbour schemes, and that special recoupment legislation had not been needed. Several years later, the Federal Court agreed with Gleeson. It was a frustrating finale to a distracting revenue and political saga.

Fraser had committed the Coalition to an inquiry into the financial system at the 1977 election, and early in 1979 I established the Committee of Inquiry into Australia's Financial System, to be chaired by Keith Campbell, the boss of LJ Hooker Limited, the leading real-estate developer; other committee members also had impeccable credentials for the task.

It produced a landmark report which reshaped, fundamentally, Australia's financial system. I doubt that any major inquiry in past decades saw as many of its key recommendations adopted by governments as did the Campbell Inquiry. All of the members I appointed to the committee shared my view that the financial system should be deregulated. Therein lay its great strength — philosophical consistency. I ignored the urgings of some to appoint a token regulator. Sadly, Keith Campbell would not live to see the full implementation of his blueprint for modernisation. He died in 1983, shortly after the change of government.

The financial press may have welcomed the Campbell Inquiry, but such things meant little to the average citizen, who was still hoping for some reduction in interest rates. The general economic news, however, was slowly getting better. Unemployment finally began to fall, and something of a mining boom was gathering pace, especially in Western Australia and Queensland.

12

'YOUR INDIRECT TAX
IS DEAD, COBBER'

As Treasurer I worked in close collaboration with the Prime Minister. Malcolm Fraser was a highly intelligent person with prodigious energy and a total preoccupation with the responsibilities of his high office. He was always the best informed on the widest range of subjects within cabinet. Having previously been a minister in both a major domestic portfolio (Education) and one with national security emphasis (Defence), he could bring perspectives to cabinet discussions lacking in others.

But he held too many cabinet meetings, and they went on for too long. Moreover, too many of them were called at very short notice, thus causing chaos with arrangements made to address gatherings in different parts of the country. On several occasions, I had to pull out of speeches or events to which several hundred people had committed themselves, in order to attend a Fraser meeting.

Malcolm Fraser made great demands of the public service. He was entitled to. Any prime minister is. They must, however, be prioritised demands. It is the worst possible administrative style to treat every request made of the public service as urgent. It is not the case. Nothing saps the willingness of public servants more than having to work over a weekend preparing a paper for ministers, only to have ministerial consideration delayed or, at the best, consisting of a cursory glance and a scrawled 'noted' on the paper.

There were regular clashes between Treasury and the Department of Prime Minister and Cabinet over economic policy. Fraser's department mistrusted the Treasury, and Treasury elite were resentful that their advice should in any way be questioned or qualified. Tension could reach absurd dimensions. For one premiers' conference, two completely separate working documents were produced for the discussion between the Prime Minister, me, and our respective advisors. Clearly there should have been agreement on one set of figures.

Having wanted the financial system inquiry, Fraser seemed to go cold on the idea of financial deregulation as Campbell's work proceeded. His own utterances increasingly ran counter to what I expected the inquiry would recommend. At monetary policy meetings he would frequently criticise banks, and talk of the desirability of greater, not less, control of financial institutions. On several occasions he asked that consideration be given to proclaiming part IV of the Financial Corporations Act. That would have further extended financial regulation.

I arranged for Keith Campbell to brief Fraser on the work of his committee to date. As I sat through the briefing, it became clear that Fraser was uncomfortable, even irritated, by the direction the briefing was taking. Campbell made no attempt to disguise his view that significant deregulation of the financial system was essential.

John Hewson and the financial community, especially in Sydney, were enthusiastic about Campbell's work and eagerly anticipated wide-ranging plans to shake up the system. Treasury was unenthusiastic, with the Reserve Bank being more supportive of deregulation. I did not think that the Monetary Policy Committee would be champing at the bit to adopt Campbell's recommendations.

None of this affected Malcolm Fraser and me working together closely on the immediate economic goals: to keep the budget under control; reduce the deficit; and hopefully make room for further taxation relief. The deficit had fallen significantly over a two-year period, and by the time the 1980 election arrived we had a good story to tell on the expenditure-restraint front.

Malcolm Fraser rightly saw me as a close political ally within the Liberal Party. I was conscious of an underlying tension between him and 'the young man', as he called Andrew Peacock. In part it was a product of their former rivalry regarding John Gorton, and the understandable ambitions which Peacock himself entertained about the leadership of the Liberal Party. To some degree I probably filled a gap left by the fracturing of Fraser's relationship with Phillip Lynch, and the complete termination of it with Reg Withers. These two had been very close to Fraser through the Constitutional crisis of 1975, and in the early months of the new Government. Whilst Lynch and he continued to work together, I do not believe that trust was ever fully restored to the relationship following the events on the eve of the 1977 election.

I remained ambitious about my future, but it would have been a grand delusion to have imagined that, by 1978, I had developed any hard core of people who saw me as having a future beyond continuing as Treasurer. The economic dries remained supportive of Lynch. Those unhappy with Fraser, or still, for one reason or another, carrying lingering resentments about earlier disputes, tended to coalesce around Reg Withers and Andrew Peacock. Overwhelmingly, however, Fraser commanded the loyalty and support of the parliamentary party. He had won two massive victories, and had a demeanour which transmitted commitment and toughness.

On the other side of politics Hayden had replaced Whitlam after the 1977 election. He was respected within the political class for having done a good job as Treasurer in quite impossible circumstances. Deciding to stay out of the leadership for the first two years had been a sensible move. He had a Herculean task to restore his party's credibility on financial matters.

Bob Hawke was by this point strutting across the national political stage as president of the ACTU, openly ambitious about winning a seat in federal parliament. It now seems incredible that it should have taken the Labor Party so long to find an electorate for him. Once he did win the prime ministership, he would demonstrate a connection with the Australian electorate stronger than any Labor leader, before or since. That, of course, was still several years into the future.

The other Labor figure outside the federal parliament who continued to make an impact was Neville Wran, the Premier of New South Wales. In my view, Wran joins Bob Hawke as one of the two most significant Labor figures of that generation. Wran gave Labor victory, and also competence in government, at a time when national morale for the party had hit rock bottom. Remember that Whitlam was routed in December 1975, and having waited 23 years in opposition to see their dream of a viable Labor alternative in government destroyed so quickly, Labor people despaired of the future. Winning government in New South Wales in May 1976 gave Labor new heart. Wran was a polished media performer — as good as any I have seen on TV news bulletins — got on well with what he called 'the big end of town', and provided something of a role model for future state Labor governments around the country.

*   *   *

The 1980 budget will chiefly be remembered as the one which was almost fully leaked by Laurie Oakes, then with Channel 10. Oakes got hold of one of the close-to-final drafts of my budget speech, and its leaking a few nights before the budget was a huge embarrassment for the Government. I later thought that the leak had come from a public service source.

The leak completely overshadowed the fact that for the first time in years Australia was projected to record a domestic budget surplus. After five years of grind, it was a significant achievement but its symbolism was completely lost in the bigger story of the budget's premature disclosure.

The 1980 election and its immediate aftermath would markedly change my relationship with Malcolm Fraser on policy issues. I had retained my enthusiasm for taxation reform involving the introduction of a broad-based indirect tax accompanied by reductions in personal income tax. After the election had been called I reached an understanding with the Prime Minister, which he honoured in full, that neither of us, nor indeed the Deputy Prime Minister, Doug Anthony, would, during the course of the campaign, rule out future taxation reform. I wanted to keep open the option of moving on this issue if the Government were returned.

Hayden exceeded expectations in the campaign but Labor still fell short, with the Government winning with a reduced majority of 23 seats. Bob Hawke entered parliament via the safe Labor seat of Wills, in Victoria. There was a big swing against the Liberal Party in Victoria, although we held up better in New South Wales. Most people attributed this to the effective fear campaign waged by the Government on the capital gains tax issue during the dying days of the campaign. Peter Walsh, who became Finance Minister in the Hawke Government, had raised the possibility of a capital gains tax. Fraser grabbed hold of this with an impressive ferocity, reminding all of us what a formidable campaigner he could be. Walsh should have known that Fraser would hurt Labor with a claim it would tax the family home.

When the remarks were made by Walsh, the Government was struggling in the polls, and although Labor had a huge leeway to make up there was considerable nervousness in the Liberal camp. Property values in Sydney were higher than in any other part of the country, and the capital gains tax issue resonated in the nation's biggest city more than anywhere else. Ten days out from the election, Fraser rang me at home and said that 'our polling says that Labor is in a clear winning position'. I had spent most of my time in New South Wales, and told him that the mood in that state was still strong for the Government.

As a measure of Fraser's nervousness, he rang me on the Tuesday before polling, when I was campaigning for Michael Baume at the Moss Vale Golf Club in his electorate of Macarthur. Fraser told me that he had a number of ministers, mainly Victorians, gathered in his office discussing the state of the campaign. They were canvassing the possibility of the Prime Minister announcing that the Government would boost family allowances if it were returned. I said I thought that would be regarded as a panic move by the electorate, and might backfire. He asked me to seek Michael Baume's view, given that Michael held a marginal seat. Michael replied, 'Tell the big bastard to calm down and focus on the Government's record.'

The 1980 election result was a real shock for Malcolm Fraser. It should not have been. The 1977 result simply reflected the unwillingness of the electorate to seriously contemplate Whitlam again. Once Whitlam had gone, things were bound to return to a more normal political situation.

When Malcolm Fraser and I discussed the election outcome, he said that part of the reason why the Government had lost so many seats was that he had not been able to give people lower taxes. He said that his Government had been elected on a smaller-government, lower-tax platform and more had to be done on this front, and that he intended to do something about it. This was encouraging, because I had to agree with him that that was part of the problem. Now that Whitlam himself was gone, it was no longer tenable to hark back to the Whitlam days too much.

He established what became known as the 'razor gang', under the chairmanship of Phillip Lynch. This group of ministers was charged with trawling through all areas of government, to find expenditure savings to form the basis of a major statement about the size and direction of the Government. This was quite separate from my earlier understanding with Fraser to reform the taxation system.

As well as Phillip Lynch as chairman, the committee included me, Margaret Guilfoyle, the newly appointed Finance Minister, Peter Nixon, and Ian Viner. Fraser wanted the committee to start work immediately and have only minimal time off over the Christmas period, with a view to the major statement being made early in 1981.

Margaret Guilfoyle had replaced Eric Robinson as Finance Minister. Fraser demoted Robinson from cabinet to the outer ministry — for no good reason — and Robinson refused to serve in the lesser post. He died suddenly only weeks later (from a congenital heart condition). Robinson had been Queensland Liberal president, and the Nationals in that state unreasonably resented his continued, aggressive advocacy of the Liberal cause in Queensland. The friction this produced would have heavily influenced Fraser's decision to treat Robinson as he did.

In keeping with our understanding, I announced that the Government would immediately start an examination of the taxation system, including the possibility of introducing a broad-based indirect tax, accompanied by reductions in personal income tax. Once again I felt quite excited, as this was a reform I was convinced was needed. There had been a false start two years earlier. There was only a six-month window of opportunity, as the Government would lose control of the Senate by 1 July 1981. There was not a moment to be lost, and I was keen to get to work on the tax proposal immediately.

On 3 December, the Monetary Policy Committee of cabinet, on my recommendation, decided that interest rates paid on deposits taken by banks from customers be deregulated. I had also argued for deregulation of lending rates, but this change was rejected. This was a significant decision and set the ball rolling on interest-rate deregulation, which would emerge a year later as one of Campbell's major recommendations. Once rates offered by banks were deregulated, it was only a matter of time before the rates charged by banks had to be deregulated. Nonetheless, the ball rolled very slowly, as it was not until early 1986 that the Hawke Government moved to phased deregulation of lending rates by removing the ceiling for new loans, thus adopting a policy I had advocated as Opposition leader.

When announcing the 3 December decision to parliament, I challenged decades of orthodoxy on interest-rate controls, from both sides of the house, by pointing out that, in particular, they had resulted in small borrowers being denied access to funds. Today such comments would be accepted as a statement of the obvious; in 1981 they were anything but.

After a gruelling year, I was relieved when I arrived at Hawks Nest, on the Central Coast of New South Wales, for a family holiday late in January. This would be the first of many holidays at Hawks Nest for our youngest child, Richard, who had been born the previous September. It went extremely well until I received a message from the motel owner asking me to ring Michelle Grattan, chief political correspondent of the *Age*. There was nothing strange in this of itself. Michelle was never one to be deterred by the fact that somebody was on holidays. When I rang back, she said, 'Your indirect tax is dead, cobber.' I asked her what she meant, and she told me that Malcolm Fraser had been on Melbourne radio a short while before, pointing out some of the difficulties in broadening the indirect tax base, including the time taken to put the proposal together, and its inflationary impact. The *Age* quoted him on 10 February as having said on radio the previous day that it would cost $3.5 million to cut the standard rate of tax from 32 to 25 cents in the dollar. He was reported as saying, 'If you were going to raise the same amount of revenue by indirect tax you would add about 5 to 7 per cent to Australia's inflation rate.'[1] Fraser gave me no warning of his intervention.

This was very bad news for me. I knew instinctively that he would not have gone public with these reservations unless he had made up his mind to oppose taxation reform. To make matters worse he had not given me any advance warning about his comments. I spoke to him subsequently, and his response was, 'Well, John, there are difficulties, and they need to be considered, but you should continue your work.' I resolved that I would but I knew then that we were not going to achieve taxation reform because the PM was against it.

I, nonetheless, went ahead and put forward a submission proposing a modest broadening of the indirect tax base, including, for the first time, a tax on services, with compensating personal tax cuts. It was a proposal which could be implemented in the remaining six months of government control of the Senate, and could be further expanded once the principle of a broadened indirect tax base had been accepted. It would have begun easing the heavy burden of personal tax in the Australian taxation system, and shifting some of it to the indirect tax base. Cabinet rejected my proposal, as I knew it would once the Prime Minister had disclosed his hand, although I was not without a number of supporters, including Ian Viner, Fred Chaney and Peter Durack.

I made a major statement to parliament, explaining why we had decided not to broaden the indirect tax base, on 12 March 1981. Although the statement contained that explanation, it really put on record my arguments for long-term restructuring of the taxation system.

This episode affected my attitude towards the Prime Minister. We still remained close colleagues, and I was a staunch supporter of his within the parliamentary party, but I felt badly let down on an important policy issue and sensed that when it came to big reforms, he would not chance his arm. This had implications for the durability of the Government. We had lost quite a lot of seats at the just-concluded election, and the immediate summation had been that the Government had not been adventurous enough.

The razor gang proved to be anything but adventurous and was one of the great damp squibs of the Fraser Government. For example, there was a strong view amongst its members that we should privatise government-owned businesses such as Qantas, Australian Airlines and the Commonwealth Bank. There was no point in pursuing this unless we had the support of the Prime Minister. We deputed Phillip Lynch to obtain Fraser's views. Unsurprisingly to me, he was very negative. He held the economically conservative view that government enterprises kept the private ones honest.

Meanwhile, the dynamic within the Liberal Party itself was changing, and a challenge, of sorts, from Andrew Peacock to Malcolm Fraser had begun to brew. Perhaps it was one of the reasons why he got cold feet over taxation reform. Immediately after the election there was the customary party meeting. Naturally there would be no contest for the leadership, and it was assumed by most the same would apply to Phillip Lynch's position as deputy. Peacock nominated for the position, and mustered a very respectable 35 votes against 47 for Lynch. This outcome was interpreted by many as a virtual nomination of Peacock as Fraser's logical successor.

Peacock's strong showing in this ballot had unsettled Fraser a lot, and had injected a new element into the internal mood of the Liberal Party. After the election, Peacock voluntarily gave up the Foreign Affairs portfolio and moved to Industrial Relations. He had been Foreign Minister for five years and before that shadowed in the area. It was thought that his good interpersonal skills would work well with many trade union leaders.

Andrew Peacock lasted just six months as Minister for Industrial Relations before he resigned. There was obvious tension between him and the Prime Minister from the beginning. He complained that the PM interfered too much in the running of his portfolio, but I don't think that he received any rougher treatment than other senior ministers. He was on stronger ground in his dispute with Fraser over the continuing recognition of the Pol Pot regime in Cambodia (then Kampuchea), when he argued that Fraser had broken a promise to deny a false report about his threatened resignation on the Pol Pot issue.

Many colleagues saw Peacock's resignation as the first step in a tilt at the leadership and although he was the likely next leader, that was down the track; there was little belief that Fraser should or would be replaced by

Peacock before the next election. As a consequence, his resignation lacked justification, hurt the Government and was resented by many colleagues.

1981 also saw a major development in the internal debate on economic policy within the Coalition. As Minister for Industry and Commerce, Phillip Lynch took to cabinet a proposal which effectively would continue quite high levels of protection for the car industry in Australia. I, along with a number of other colleagues, opposed the Lynch package but Lynch and Fraser had the numbers.

As a prelude to cabinet's discussion, no fewer than 33 members of the Coalition party room addressed a letter to the Prime Minister and Phillip Lynch calling for lower tariffs and a less protectionist policy. It was a remarkable rebellion on fundamental economic policy. It received wide publicity, but in the final analysis fell on deaf cabinet ears. John Hyde, the Liberal member for Moore in Western Australia, and acknowledged leader of the economic dries within the Coalition, had spearheaded the letter-writing effort, and he had gathered much more support than many had expected.

Lynch lost the support of the dries following the policy decision taken by cabinet on the motor vehicle industry. It also had implications for me. Having been disappointed by Lynch, Hyde and others close to him began to talk more regularly to me, not only about economic policy but also my future within the Liberal Party. This group had become frustrated with Fraser.

The dries were a group of MPs largely elected in 1975, enthusiastically committed to smaller government and more market-oriented economic policies. They had become increasingly disillusioned with the Government's direction because they felt that decisions often failed to reflect the economic principles in which they believed — the motor vehicle one being the most egregious example. John Hyde had come in with me in 1974, but 1975 had brought in Ross McLean from Western Australia, James Porter from South Australia, and Murray Sainsbury from New South Wales as examples of this line of thinking. In 1977 Jim Carlton joined their ranks. To their credit they maintained intellectual consistency, irrespective of political circumstances, in the arguments they put to me both in private and in the party room. They were quite an impressive bunch who wanted the Government to practise as well as preach the values of the free market. All of the dries paid homage to Bert Kelly, Liberal member for Wakefield in South Australia, as the parliamentary trailblazer of their economic values. In an era of high tariff protection, Kelly's had been a lonely voice.

Signs developed through 1981 that the economy was beginning to cool. The impact of the 1979 second oil shock had been masked in Australia by the revenue surge it gave the Government flowing from the parity pricing of crude oil. There could be little doubt, however, that the rest of the world was suffering from the impact of another rise in crude oil prices, with recession spreading in many countries. This was bound to have an impact on Australia.

In the lead-up to the 1981 budget I had a meeting with Hugh Morgan, managing director of Western Mining, and other mining industry leaders where they gave me a very sober assessment of where they saw the Australian economy heading. They were gloomy about the prospects for the mining industry. This was particularly daunting, as the wave of investment in mining over the previous year or two had been the source of a lot of hope concerning the future of the Australian economy.

Having earlier in the year rejected my plea for a broadening of the indirect tax base, accompanied by reductions in personal income tax, perversely, senior ministers agreed to include in the 1981 budget some broadening of the indirect tax base (although not as much as I had earlier proposed), but with no personal tax cuts to smooth the acceptance of the indirect tax changes. The extra revenue from the broadening of the indirect tax base was used to further cut the deficit, so as to take pressure off interest rates.

The Government had lost control of the Senate on 1 July 1981, and, as a consequence, never really had a hope of getting the indirect tax changes in the budget passed. The folly of not acting at the beginning of the year, when there were still the numbers in the Senate to achieve reform and change, was there for all to see. It was immensely frustrating.

For decades the Metal Trades Award had been the benchmark for wage fixation in the Australian industrial relations system. In 1981 pressure mounted for a big increase under this award. While some firms could afford to pay increases, many could not. This was always the inherent contradiction, indeed flaw, in a centralised wage-fixation system. It formed the basis of the intellectual argument that I and many others mounted against the system through the 1980s.

After strike action which caused significant industrial dislocation, there was a settlement which conceded much of what the unions had wanted. On 18 December 1981 the Arbitration Commission ratified an agreement between the Amalgamated Metal Workers and Shipwrights' Union (AMWSU) and the

Metal Trades Industry Association (MTIA), the relevant peak employer group, for a wage rise of $41 a week and a 38-hour week.

Before long the implications were clear. The December 1981 agreement flowed through to all of the other awards, and before long firms unable to pay the higher wages began retrenching staff.

That was how a centralised wage-fixing system worked. For me it was a political, as well as economic, nightmare. The Government was left marooned without a policy response, other than the highly unattractive one of increasing interest rates to restrict the capacity of firms to pay higher wages. That was no response at all, because it would result in still higher unemployment. What our side of politics needed, and did not have at that point, was a totally different approach to wages policy.

Federal Labor was the political beneficiary of the wages explosion, but it also recognised the implications of what had happened. Some years later, Paul Keating would famously say to George Campbell, the Federal Secretary of the Amalgamated Metal Workers' Union (AMWU) at the time of the explosion and later a Labor senator, that he and his associates 'carry the jobs of the dead men' around their neck, a reference to the widespread unemployment caused by the wages breakout. Labor's political argument was that the Liberal Party had no way of controlling wages, except by the blunt instrument of tightening monetary policy through much higher interest rates, thus squeezing firms, which in turn laid off more staff.

This argument would remain valid if a centralised wage-fixing system continued, whereby across-the-board wage increases were delivered irrespective of individual capacity to pay. It would be an entirely different matter if that approach were abandoned, and a system of workplace or enterprise bargaining were introduced. That was the system for which I was to campaign for years. If there were to be a change to such a system, then union power, most particularly the monopoly the unions held over the bargaining system, would need to be rolled back. This was to become the real battleground in a debate which is yet to be fully resolved and remains intensely relevant to Australia's economic future.

13

FOOLED BY FLINDERS

The year 1982 opened amidst a deepening world recession, which Australia did not escape. Stagflation, the economic disease of the 1970s and '80s, afflicted most developed economies. In the United States, interest rates remained very high; for this and other reasons, they were also high in Australia. In 1979 Paul Volcker, a dedicated inflation fighter, had become Chairman of the Federal Reserve in America and signalled that he would push interest rates up to the level necessary to squeeze inflation out of the system. This approach worked. In 1980 annual inflation in the United States was 13.5 per cent. By 1983 it had fallen to a little over 3 per cent.

This year was made worse by one of the most severe droughts of the 20th century, which afflicted large parts of eastern Australia. It threatened the survival of breeding stock as well as producing the usual debilitating effects on farmers and communities of all bad droughts. The response of the Fraser Government was comprehensive and effective, with interest-rate subsidies helping preserve breeding stock, so vital to Australian pastoralists.

On 4 January, the former prime minister Bill McMahon retired from the Sydney seat of Lowe, which he had held since 1949. This would prove to be a bad by-election for the Government. There was a swing of more than 7 per cent and, on 13 March, Labor won the seat from the Liberal Party for the first time since its creation, at the 1948 redistribution.

1982 was also to become a watershed year for Victoria politically. After 27 years of Liberal government, inaugurated by Henry Bolte in 1955, the Labor Party won office under John Cain on 3 April. The psychological impact of this on Liberals from Victoria was immense. Intellectually they had prepared for defeat, but the jewel-in-the-crown sentiment ran deep in this Liberal division.

With the Victorian election out of the way, Fraser acted to bring the long-simmering stand-off between himself and Andrew Peacock to a head. It had become a constant distraction for the Government and a regular signal to the community that the Liberal house was divided. Fraser called a party meeting for 8 April and indicated that he would resign the leadership, thus providing Peacock with the opportunity of challenging for the top job. I never thought that Peacock had a chance of toppling Fraser. The only issue was the size of Fraser's victory.

In the weeks preceding Fraser's initiative, a group of Liberal MPs, led by John Hyde and Ross McLean, had come to me with the proposition that, if there were to be a spill of leadership positions, then I should contest the party leadership. They said they had lost faith in Fraser's economic direction, but that Peacock was not committed to the type of economic policies they thought Australia needed in the years ahead.

I was flattered by their offer of support but, nonetheless, made it very clear that I did not think it was in the best interests of the Liberal Party for me to stand, that I would support Fraser and campaign for him, and I urged them to do likewise. They were not entirely surprised by my response. But their approach had told me that in the year or more which had passed since the 1980 election, the dries had not only transferred their support from Lynch to me, but had well and truly given up on Fraser.

Phillip Lynch decided that he would give up the deputy leadership at the same time as the ballot for the leadership. After a quick assessment of support, I decided to nominate for that position. I had Fraser's support. He promoted the advantages of a deputy coming from Sydney, as against his Melbourne attachment. This was my first experience of a contested party room ballot, and I did the only thing that seemed logical. I directly approached people for their votes, naturally excluding some who I felt intuitively would never vote for me. Michael MacKellar, a fellow New South Welshman and the Health Minister, also stood. It seemed pretty clear that the great bulk of those who were going to side with Peacock against Fraser would also support MacKellar against me.

Fraser defeated Peacock by a neat margin of 2 to 1: 54 votes to 27. In the contest for deputy, I won 45 to 27 on the second ballot against MacKellar. After eight years in parliament I was both Treasurer and Deputy Leader of the parliamentary Liberal Party.

My sense of achievement was heavily qualified. Although it was not a poisoned chalice, I had come to the deputy leadership at a very difficult time. The Government had been in office for over six years, was performing poorly in the polls, had been through a bruising leadership contest, and the economy was slowing rapidly.

I did not see elevation to the deputy leadership as necessarily indicating that I would become the leader after Fraser. The Prime Minister was then only about to turn 52, so issues of longer-term succession were not on the agenda. My total political focus was the re-election of the Fraser Government.

Late in 1981, the Campbell Inquiry reported. It had met all of the expectations. Campbell recommended widespread deregulation of the financial system, including: floating the Australian dollar and the abolition of exchange controls; admitting foreign banks; and the removal of controls on interest rates. It went too far for the comfort of the Prime Minister and some of his senior colleagues.

I had a difficult negotiating session with Fraser over the contents of my statement welcoming the publication of the report. I wanted to be as positive as possible. He did not want the Government locked in too much to supporting the main recommendations.

Doug Anthony wasted no time in saying, publicly, that he was against removing interest-rate controls. Fraser and other senior members of the Government made clear their complete opposition to floating the dollar. As I mention later, Doug Anthony maintained this attitude in opposition, and Fraser, by then out of parliament, attacked the Hawke float.

When the Campbell Report landed with a thud on the cabinet table, interest rates were still high, and there was acute concern in the Government about the cost and availability of finance for housing and small business. The controlled ceiling for housing interest rates was then 12.5 per cent, and there was little finance available at that rate because the banks were losing deposits to other financial institutions offering higher rates. A typical arrangement then was for a borrower to receive a relatively small portion of the required loan at 12.5 per cent and the rest from a finance company, often a trading bank affiliate, at a much higher rate. These 'cocktail' loans usually produced an average rate of 17 to 18 per cent for the whole loan. It was, therefore, easy to see that interest-rate controls were not delivering cheaper loans for homebuyers. That was Campbell's conclusion, which I endorsed.

I therefore recommended in a submission to the Monetary Policy Committee in February 1982 that we commence the process of deregulating interest rates on housing loans of less than $100,000 — average loans in high-priced Sydney were less than $50,000. My submission spelled out how controls were failing their intended objective, and I advocated lifting the controls through a process of negotiating with the banks for phased deregulation. I could not obtain authority to do this; rather, there began weeks of negotiations with banks to secure extra housing finance through a combination of a 1 per cent increase in the interest-rate ceiling and the removal of some restrictions on the banks, as recommended by Campbell. These changes were helpful and produced promises of increased lending, but fell well short of the change needed to break free of counterproductive regulation — and that was removing interest-rate controls altogether on future housing loans. In one stroke, that would have lifted permanently the flow of money into housing.

There was also a time-consuming examination of other quite nonsensical proposals to boost the flow of money to housing, including the unsound idea of the RBA releasing some of the Statutory Reserve Deposits (SRDs) it held from the trading banks to augment the pool of money for housing. One of the reasons it was unsound was because the SRDs were subject to short-term variations, whereas housing finance was for long periods. Another equally flawed idea was to extend the old 30/20 rule whereby life offices and superannuation funds paid higher taxes if they did not invest a portion of their funds in government bonds to housing finance. The life offices and superannuation funds would pay higher taxes if they did not commit a specified level of funds to housing. Campbell had recommended abolition of the 30/20 rule, let alone its extension.

Both proposals ultimately bit the dust, but it was only the combined opposition of me and the RBA governor which stopped the SRD proposal appearing in the 1982 budget speech. These proposals ignored the central reality that interest-rate controls aggravated, rather than ameliorated, the shortage of housing finance at a time of generally high interest rates. That was the view of Campbell. If that was the view of Malcolm Fraser in 1982 he did not act upon it.

With Fraser's support, early in 1983 I announced that the Government would allow in approximately ten foreign banks. They would provide much-needed competition for the existing domestic banks. This decision was applauded by the business community, but criticised by the shadow Treasurer, Paul Keating. In a statement on 26 January 1983, Keating said, 'By allowing foreign bank entry in Australia the nation is being subjected again to ad hoc decision-making which in this case will effectively change by stealth the whole structure of the Australian financial sector.'[1]

Also the Fraser Government had taken the obscure-sounding decision to bring in a tender system for the sale of Treasury bonds. This change meant that demand would determine interest rates on government bonds; as a consequence, there would be less printing of money to finance deficits. In his 2006 Boyer Lecture, Ian Macfarlane, the former governor of the Reserve Bank, said that this had been a major reform not accorded the recognition it deserved — second only in importance to the floating of the dollar. It was a change that Fraser himself strongly advocated.

I knew that putting together the 1982 budget would be a daunting task, even more difficult than my first in 1978. With the economy slowing rapidly and revenues falling away, there was a gruelling tussle between me and the Prime Minister about the direction of policy. He favoured an expansionary budget. By contrast, I argued that the inflationary pressures in the community were still so strong that any large increase in the budget deficit would add to those pressures and be damaging to the economy. Unemployment had begun to increase, and large parts of the country were still racked by drought. All of the options were bleak. I wanted our economic policy to remain consistent. For years we had preached the virtues of fighting inflation, reducing the budget deficit and avoiding the easy resort of spending our way out of difficulties. The way things started, it looked as if this budget would turn all of that on its head.

The budget cabinet deliberations became acrimonious. The differences between me and the Prime Minister were out in the open. Our colleagues must have been dismayed as the Prime Minister and his Treasurer argued and sniped at each other about the shape of the budget as the country headed towards recession.

I became alarmed that early spending decisions were so extravagant that there would be a huge increase in the budget deficit. To me, this was untenable, and I talked about resigning with my wife, John Hewson and Michael Baume, my parliamentary secretary and close friend, later a NSW senator. I put it aside as an option. It would be seen as disloyalty to the Government, only worsen its political difficulties and not necessarily result in a better economic outcome.

Fortunately, Fraser responded to my concern, acknowledging that too many expenditure decisions had been taken which added to the budget deficit. We met in his office and he immediately suggested changes to decisions already taken, and some other measures which would help bring the prospective deficit back to more manageable limits. We would still end up with a very expansionary budget, but it would not be as bad as had seemed likely a short while before.

I brought down the budget on 17 August 1982. It was attacked as too expansionary, and breaking with the economic doctrine the Government had been enunciating for many years. This was the central political dilemma we faced. For years we had preached the virtue of expenditure restraint and reduced deficits, yet all of a sudden we were saying that the solution to the nation's economic problems lay in more government spending. It confused the public.

So much for economic and political theory; the public was more interested in the human consequences of the worsening recession. On several occasions, over coming months, it became necessary to revise upwards, the unemployment predictions. This not only reflected the reality of a collapsing labour market, but unavoidably conveyed the impression that the Government was powerless to do anything about it.

Due partly to his having come to the prime ministership through an early election, Malcolm Fraser was always attended by early election speculation. I felt sure that he wanted, if possible, to have an early election at the end of 1982. I was against this. My principal reason was that the public had grown sick and tired of elections being called to accommodate what they saw as the political interests of the incumbent government. The Liberal Party organisation was in no mood to fight an early election. Fraser was both stunned and angry at opposition to an early election.

Suddenly, in October 1982, Phillip Lynch announced that, because of ill-health, he would retire from parliament, leaving a vacancy in his seat of Flinders to be filled at a by-election before the end of the year. Within a few days there was a real bombshell. Malcolm Fraser developed severe back problems and had to enter hospital for surgery which would sideline him for up to two months. This put paid to any possibility of an election at the end of the year.

It also meant that I would lead the Liberal campaign effort in the by-election, as acting party leader in Fraser's absence. What is more, I was left with most of the responsibility for a wages pause, which Fraser had initiated only a few weeks earlier. It had struck a chord with Australians. By now, employment was falling like a stone, and even some of the more difficult elements of the trade union movement embraced the idea of holding down wages as a trade-off for some others keeping their jobs. As part of the healing process, Andrew Peacock was able to return to cabinet in November, taking the place of the retiring Phillip Lynch.

Bob Hawke had entered parliament in 1980. From that moment onwards there was constant speculation about his replacing Hayden. On 16 July 1982, with the open support of the NSW right, led by Keating, Hawke challenged Hayden. The result was the best possible for the Government. Hayden defeated Hawke by a margin of only five votes: 42 to 37. It left Hayden debilitated and Hawke, despite his wordy protestations, as an untamed predator. Hayden needed a good result in Flinders to consolidate his leadership.

Lynch had held Flinders at the 1980 election with a margin of 5 per cent, and with a by-election in the depths of a recession, it seemed ripe for the taking by Labor. The ALP got off to an atrocious start by choosing a very poor candidate, a local real-estate agent by the name of Rogan Ward. He was uninspiring on the campaign trail. In by-elections, particularly high-profile ones, and Flinders was certainly one of these, there is constant publicity surrounding the candidate. A bad candidate can get lost in a general election. He or she can't hide in a by-election.

The Liberal Party's candidate was a local solicitor, Peter Reith. I opened his campaign with a rally at Mornington High School on 12 November. My travel to the event attracted more than the usual publicity. I had burst an eardrum and had medical advice not to fly. I therefore took the Riverina Express from Central Station in Sydney to Spencer Street Station in Melbourne. It had been a long time since a senior political figure had travelled between Sydney and Melbourne by rail, and there was quite a bit of interest in this.

The Liberal Party's one campaign theme was the wage pause. We said to the people of Flinders that the country was in a recession, unemployment was rising and one way which meshed with the Australian notion of mateship, of helping those whose jobs were at risk, was for those who had jobs to forgo wage increases to help their fellow Australians who were at risk. It seemed to catch on. But I didn't imagine for a moment that it would be sufficient to prevent the seat falling to the Labor Party. Reith was a very good candidate, and he and his wife, with their then young family, presented a good image of a local family, strongly identified with the aspirations and the future of the electorate.

The Labor Party was knocked sideways, three days out from the election, by an article appearing in the Melbourne *Age* suggesting that the Labor candidate, Ward, had been involved in some shady real-estate deals. Rogan Ward denied the allegations. It was manna from heaven for the Liberal campaign. I stayed in Sydney the day of the by-election, 4 December, and rather nervously awaited the result. Finally, I rang Grahame Morris, who had been 'minding' Peter Reith throughout the campaign, and to my great delight he said, 'I am about to go in and tell Peter that he has been elected as the member for Flinders. It has been a great result. The swing against us was only 3 per cent.' This was an amazing outcome, the deficiencies of Rogan Ward notwithstanding. It had huge implications for both the Government and the opposition.

Labor's dismay was palpable. How could it be, that, in the middle of a recession, with unemployment heading towards 10 per cent and the incumbent government having been there for seven years, it was not possible to achieve a swing of 5 per cent? It defied all political reasoning. Inside the Labor Party, the near-universal judgement was that Hayden was the problem. The media hounded Hawke for a response. He had one of his celebrated temper outbursts, telling some television journalists to 'get a grip of yourselves!' This kind of response only reinforced his appeal to the Australian public.

The Flinders by-election came to occupy a special place in Australian political history. It crippled Bill Hayden's leadership, thus creating the eventual circumstances for Hawke to take the Labor leadership in a most remarkable way in February 1983. It also produced, in Peter Keaston Reith, the only person who won a seat in federal parliament, but was never sworn in, because the parliament to which he had been elected did not sit again after the poll in the by-election had been formally declared, and lost the seat at a subsequent general election.

Parliament resumed for a week immediately after the by-election, and there was relief and mild hope at the Christmas drinks in my office for colleagues. It proved to be a false dawn, for the by-election outcome had been precisely the wake-up call which the Labor Party required to galvanise the forces needed to change its leadership.

For me, the beginning of 1983 was a sad one. My mother died on 9 January, just a few weeks after her 83rd birthday. Mum had survived my father by more than 27 years, and had lived for most of that time with extremely good health. She had taken a quiet pleasure out of my political success, but with the typical caution of a person of her generation, who felt that success for themselves or their family was always somewhat unexpected. Mum's tenacity and single-minded fidelity to things in which she believed had left its mark on me.

My parents' lives had been a world away from my own, and even more so from those of my children. My mother was buried from the Earlwood Methodist (by then Uniting) Church, which had been such an important part of our earlier lives. My three brothers had each married there, and my father also had been buried from there.

It soon became obvious that Malcolm Fraser had not lost his desire to have an early election. He believed it was only a matter of time before Hawke replaced Hayden as Labor leader, and was determined that the poll should take place before this occurred, leaving him facing a much stronger opponent. During his convalescence he had developed a campaign theme, based on the belief that Australia could not wait for the rest of the world to deliver it economic recovery. It was something he pounded home to me when I visited him on holiday in January. The election slogan became 'We're not waiting for the world', complete with lyrics sung by the popular Colleen Hewitt.

Our January holiday at Hawks Nest was interrupted by my having to go to Canberra on 2 February for a meeting with the major banks to discuss issues relating to the proposed entry of foreign banks into Australia. That was a useful blind for a meeting with the Prime Minister, Tony Eggleton, the party's federal director, and Peter Nixon, whose advice Fraser always respected. Fraser wanted a poll on 5 March. He remained preoccupied with the possibility of Hawke replacing Hayden and intensely pessimistic about rural Australia, speaking as if he believed that the drought would never break. The mood at that point was optimistic about our prospects, due to the Flinders result and the belief that Fraser would face Hayden. Eggleton said to both Nixon and me, 'I think we should win.'

I returned to Hawks Nest that evening, and over dinner I disclosed our plans to Janette, including that Fraser would announce the election the following day. In response she said, 'Are you sure that they won't change leaders on you?' I said that that was highly unlikely. Janette's assessment had been based on a most equivocal response she had heard Lionel Bowen, the then deputy Labor leader, give to a question about the leadership on radio earlier that day.

The very next day, 3 February, Janette's prophecy was realised, as we learned listening to the radio on a drive to the beautiful Myall Lakes, not far from Hawks Nest. In a highly dramatic turn of events, Hayden, that morning, had succumbed to the pressure of his colleagues and stood down from the leadership in favour of Hawke. What it meant to the political landscape was best summarised by a remark of another Hawks Nest holidaymaker who ran a small business. Passing me outside our unit that evening he simply said, 'So we've got an election. Now you've blown it.' He was a Liberal supporter, concerned that the change to Hawke had made it very likely that the Government would be defeated.

I spoke to Fraser after he had held his news conference and knew that he would face Hawke and not Hayden. He sounded upbeat and remarked that we would be knocking off two Labor leaders at the same time. Yet, he, most of all, must have been totally unsettled by what the Labor Party had done. The truth was that in the space of just 24 hours Fraser had lost control of events. Labor had struck with remarkable boldness, and the dynamic of Australian politics had been turned on its head.

Janette and I both knew how much Hawke's accession had changed things and it was very likely curtains for the Government. Australia was in recession, and Bob Hawke had strong public support. We pinned our hopes on the possibility of Hawke blowing up under the pressure of a campaign, with the Australian people deciding that he was too volatile to be entrusted with the prime ministership. He had already obliged with his bad-tempered response to Richard Carleton's question on *Nationwide*: 'Mr Hawke, could I ask you whether you feel a little embarrassed tonight at the blood that's on your hands?'[2] That proved to be wishful thinking. Apart from that intemperate outburst on the day that Hayden had quit, Hawke was a model of balance and restraint during the campaign. He gathered strength as the days went by. The switch had a near-euphoric effect on large sections of the public.

It was impossible not to feel sorry for Hayden. I sent him a personal note expressing the empathy of a political rival who guessed the agony through which he would be passing. There was one especially poignant TV image of Hayden looking on as a quite adoring crowd of people mobbed Hawke at some public gathering.

Despite this, it took a while into the campaign before I accepted the strong likelihood of defeat. As a political competitor, that, after all, is a natural state. One keeps hoping and fighting until the end. If nothing else,

Australian politics had proved to be remarkably unpredictable during the previous year. A lot of my mood flowed from my respect for Fraser's campaigning abilities. He had won three elections and, up until then, had been the most successful Liberal leader since Menzies.

In an election campaign, there are two ways of testing public opinion. There are the published and private polls and then there is what I call the field evidence. The published polls were bad, having strengthened for Labor once Hawke took over. I learned, after the election, that Gary Morgan had done some private polling for Fraser two weeks out from the election which showed that the Government was in a hopeless position.

The field evidence was uniformly bad. The day after the campaign launch in Melbourne, I flew to Brisbane for a small business luncheon in support of Don Cameron, the member for Fadden. It was a poorly attended event; there was a marked lack of enthusiasm, which troubled me, given that small business was part of our traditional base. Later, passing through Tullamarine Airport, I was stopped by a party activist from Casey, a Melbourne electorate held by Peter Falconer. He was in small business and told me how badly we were doing and that high interest rates had done great damage with small-business proprietors. Grant Chapman, the Liberal member for Kingston in South Australia, invited me to address a public meeting in his electorate, which three people attended. Whilst public meetings at 8 o'clock on a weekday night had long since ceased to be flavour of the month, this was ominous. Cameron, Falconer and Chapman all lost their seats in the 1983 election.

Both Doug Anthony and I wanted Fraser to take up an offer from Rupert Murdoch, who then owned the Ten Network, for a debate with Hawke. The three of us thought that it could help Malcolm, but he refused.

I spent election day visiting polling booths in Bennelong, thanking my helpers for their support, but sensing by then that the election was gone. We gathered at our Wollstonecraft home to watch the results. Once the result was clear, I rang Fraser, who was plainly shattered by the outcome. It was a difficult conversation. He was the fallen giant, who had for so long seemed invincible.

Hawke's win in 1983 has been the best of any Labor leader at a change of government. He won a majority of 25 in a house of only 125. During the campaign, Hawke had captured the imagination of many Australians with his talk of bringing people together. In contrast, Malcolm Fraser often sounded shrill, with exaggerated claims that Australians should put their money under the bed if Labor won.

Overwhelmingly, though, the Coalition lost because Australia was in deep recession, and Labor was led by a person in Bob Hawke whose blend of larrikinism and intelligence had long appealed to lots of Australians. The fates had conspired to deliver Hawke the leadership at the optimum time for him. He never had to face Fraser in parliament, where he could well have fared poorly.

Following the chaos of the Whitlam years, Fraser had restored calm and order to the nation's government. The budget was brought under control. It was being steadily returned to surplus until the recession of the early '80s hit, and this had happened through a time of subdued world economic growth.

To properly assess Malcolm Fraser's economic stewardship is to understand that, first and foremost, he was a creature of the Menzies–McEwen period of economic management, when plenty of benign and protective government intervention appeared to work. There was strong growth and low unemployment to show for it. Why, therefore, should those policies not be continued? Fraser, and many around him, brought that attitude back to government in 1975.

For the seven-and-a-half years that we had worked together, the relationship between Malcolm Fraser and me had been politically close. I was an advocate for Fraser within the parliamentary party, as I always believed that he was the right person to lead the party through the time that we were in government. I also had a strong sense of loyalty towards him, reinforced by his generous promotion of me. Our relationship, although friendly, was very much a professional political one, which was never likely to continue once he left parliament in 1983.

My differences with Fraser, in government, were confined to certain economic issues. It was during my prime ministership that we really parted company, with Fraser attacking many of my stances on social and foreign policy as well: the handling of Pauline Hanson, asylum-seekers, a formal apology to Indigenous people and involvement in Iraq. His quite unfounded allegation that I played the race card ignored, for example, the fact that during the time I was PM my Government maintained a non-discriminatory immigration policy. I deny the claim in Fraser's memoirs, co-authored with Margaret Simons, that in 1977 I said to him, in a corridor conversation, that we should not take too many Vietnamese refugees.

In 1993 Malcolm Fraser announced that he would seek the federal presidency of the Liberal Party, but pulled out when it was obvious that he would not be elected. His withdrawal speech vehemently attacked free-market economics. He said that a small group had pushed our policies further to the right, and that the Liberal Party had become a right-wing conservative one. This was an ideological distortion, but one he would increasingly invoke to explain the growing gulf between him and the party he once led. In truth, the 1980s saw a major shift in the centre of gravity of the economic debate towards a more free-market approach. Attitudes within the Coalition parties as well as the ALP reflected this change.

For Malcolm Fraser, the harsh reality was that legions of Liberals felt that he had not used the massive mandates of 1975 and 1977 to effect sufficient change. Moreover, as time passed, many staunch Liberals who had gone to the barricades for him in 1975 deeply resented his regular attacks on my Government during our time in office.

Although I had commenced my ministerial career with anything but a strong commitment to economic rationalism, I had, by the time of the Fraser Government's defeat in 1983, gone through something of an epiphany. The influences on me had been many and varied, most particularly the experience of administering the Treasury portfolio. In opposition I was to develop my views even further, especially in respect of industrial relations policy.

In retrospect it was clear during the 1980s that Australia needed broad economic reforms to taxation, the labour market, industry protection and the financial system. As well, governments had to be taken out of the ownership of business undertakings. The economic story of the ensuing 25 years was how both Coalition and Labor governments contributed to that reform task, and how in opposition the Coalition also gave crucial support to ALP reforms — a gesture never reciprocated when the ALP was in opposition. I was a major player in that saga, from both government and opposition, and many of the pages which follow contain a detailed account of that economic journey which did so much to ensure that when the global financial crisis of 2008 hit, our nation was better placed than most to withstand its ravages.

PART 2

THE
OPPOSITION
YEARS

14

PEACOCK *vs* HOWARD

In March 1983, the Liberal and National parties commenced 13 years of opposition. We would lose five elections in a row, and pass through some of the most despairing years since the Liberal Party's foundation in 1944. The most traumatic episode would be the split in the federal coalition in 1987, forced by the overwhelming influence, within the National Party, of the Queensland Nationals, led by Joh Bjelke-Petersen, who was, for 19 years, premier of that state.

During this period we would have four leaders: Andrew Peacock (twice), John Hewson, Alexander Downer and me (twice). At the end of this long period of political exile, the party would, in coalition with the Nationals, regain office under my leadership and stay in power for almost 12 years.

Through those opposition years, I experienced just about all that could come the way of a long-serving participant in Australian politics. Yet I always retained a total commitment and sustained enthusiasm for political life. Irrespective of the position I held, I kept an unflagging interest in what I was doing. The experience of those years told me that, beyond argument, politics was my life and vocation. Some of the most productive policy work that I did in the whole time that I was a member of parliament occurred between 1990 and 1993, when I was spokesman on industrial relations for the Coalition, and my only expectation was to hold that portfolio in a Hewson Government.

Being bundled from office is a humbling experience — not that I was unprepared. The campaign had delivered a mounting realisation that there would be a change of government. The adversarial nature of politics requires one to change, almost overnight, from a reasoned decision-maker to a vigorous and informed critic of those now making the decisions. That was virtually impossible. I felt tired, both mentally and physically. What I wanted in March 1983 was a six-month sabbatical. But there was no hope of that; politics was my life.

I decided on the night of the election to stand for the leadership of the Liberal Party, made vacant by Fraser's resignation. I knew that my only opponent would be Andrew Peacock, and that he would almost certainly win. He did, comfortably, by 36 votes to 20. As Treasurer, I was far more closely linked to the policies of the just-defeated government than Peacock. That made him a more appealing choice. I was re-elected deputy leader, and wanted a shadow portfolio away from Treasury. Doug Anthony persuaded me to stick with my old area because of my by-then-vast experience with economic issues. Fraser quietly lobbied for Andrew Peacock in the leadership contest. He did not attend the meeting at which the ballot took place, and later explained this to me on the grounds that it would not have been in my interests if I had won only narrowly, implying, unconvincingly, that he would have supported me if he had been there. I had not sought his support and, strangely perhaps, did not feel particularly offended by his attitude. Many of my friends, however, saw his behaviour as poor repayment of the loyalty I had shown to him over a long period of time.

The early weeks in opposition were very hard for me because I had to beat off claims that I had misled the public about the true state of the deficit. It was right on the eve of the election that I was given a figure of $9.6 billion as the likely deficit for the following year, which was much higher than the stab-in-the-dark figure I had casually mentioned to some journalists. Moreover, the $9.6 billion was only a starting point, and would be reduced in the normal budget process. This did not stop Bob Hawke and Paul Keating, his new Treasurer, making a huge issue of it. This was their honeymoon; the press swallowed their lines and I took quite a shellacking.

Andrew Peacock and I were rivals for the leadership of the Liberal Party for some years, but this did not, as many have argued, completely paralyse the Liberal Party in opposition. Rivalry between key figures in political parties is commonplace. From 1986 onwards, the rivalry between Keating and Hawke within the governing Labor Party was barely disguised, periodically spilling into the public arena. Nonetheless, Andrew's and my rivalry was real, both as personalities and on policy issues.

In the culture of the Liberal Party, Andrew and I were almost born to be rivals. We were only a few months apart in age. When it seemed, to many people, to matter a lot more, he came from Melbourne and I came from Sydney. He had taken over the seat of Kooyong from Sir Robert Menzies, the great hero of our party. We were of different personalities and styles. Andrew's urbanity and very considerable personal charm had won him early notice as a future leader of the Liberal Party. He had been a very effective minister in the McMahon Government, and had won a lot of deserved praise for the relationships he established with key figures in the newly independent Papua New Guinea. It was so easy, given our contrasting styles and personalities, for commentators to paint him as emblematic of the progressive side of the Liberal Party, and me as a dull, dogged conservative.

I respected Andrew Peacock's diplomatic and public relations skills, but I never thought that he had deeply held policy views on more important economic issues. That influenced my attitude towards him, especially after he became party leader.

There was fault on both sides. I don't think Andrew ever understood the depth of feeling about his resignation in 1981 and the damage that many of his colleagues believe it inflicted on the Fraser Government. As for me, I don't think I fully understood the extent to which my continuing ambition to be leader of the Liberal Party was so apparent to colleagues, and others, from the time that Peacock defeated me for the leadership after the 1983 election.

I suspect that the last thing Andrew Peacock wanted in early opposition days was an intense debate about the philosophical direction of the Liberal Party on economic policy, especially industrial relations. Yet that is what he got, because of my determination that the Coalition should take a more consistent pro-market approach. It was, even more importantly, an unavoidable debate because the Hawke Government threw off its old Labor garb and, on issues such as financial deregulation, surprised many by going further than would ever have been expected from a Labor Government.

I never lost my ambition to lead but decided to put it on hold, and resolved to do everything I could to argue the policy positions which I held. I would perform as well as I could as deputy leader and essentially through the prism of my strongly held economic opinions.

Having been frustrated by Fraser's opposition to certain economic reforms in government, such as taxation, I was determined not to go quietly in opposition. When the opportunity presented itself, I took a strong market-centred economic position. Sometimes this was in advance of the party's position and annoyed Andrew Peacock and others who, for a combination of political and other reasons, might have thought that a quieter approach was appropriate.

The quiet approach was not really an option. The dynamic had changed quite rapidly since the election of the Hawke Government. The Liberal Party was under a double pressure to have a clear position on economic issues. Not only did altered world economic circumstances require different responses, but the new ALP Government was not behaving like the Whitlam Government, or indeed consistent with the commitments it had made in opposition. It had assumed the mantle of economic responsibility. This put real heat on the opposition.

Many of the Coalition's traditional supporters in the business community began to like what they saw of the new Government, particularly when it floated the dollar and decided to admit foreign banks. Comments such as 'the best free enterprise government we've had' began to be uttered at boardroom lunches attended by opposition spokesmen. The Liberal and National parties ran the risk of being left behind if the Coalition did not sharpen its thinking on some key economic issues.

In some cases this meant agreeing strongly with what the Hawke Government had announced. In other cases it involved adopting a new policy position likely to win business support, and which the ALP would be unable to match. This made my campaign to change our industrial relations policy so important. Here, I felt, was a policy change which would win wide, but by no means unanimous, business support and which Labor, with its trade union base, could never match.

The farmers, the miners and, crucially, small business would support a new industrial relations system. Many manufacturers, however, were still wedded to the old centralised system. They felt they could live with it. In any event I was told they could 'talk to Hawke' if things got out of hand. The corporate state, Australian-style, was already in full bloom.

My aggressive push for policy change aggravated some colleagues. They didn't share my sense of urgency about the need for policy revision; they thought that some of my prescriptions were too edgy, and I thought they were altogether too complacent about the solidity of our political base. A party needs more votes than its base can deliver so as to win an election, but unless its base is energised, as distinct from just mildly supportive, it has no hope of victory. Big business had been partly mesmerised by Hawke, so I saw the preservation of our small-business base as absolutely critical to our longer-term hopes of revival. Internally difficult though it was, I believed that we had to confront hard policy choices early on.

I loudly supported the Hawke Government when the dollar was floated and exchange controls abolished in December 1983. This was overwhelmingly the right policy response for the future benefit of the Australian economy.

On the morning of the day the decision was taken, the Treasurer announced the closure of our foreign exchange markets, a clear signal that the Government intended to float the dollar. That morning, Liam Bathgate, Doug Anthony's chief of staff, showed me a press statement Doug proposed issuing, strongly attacking the floating of the Australian dollar. Liam knew that Doug's views and mine were different, and he did not want public disagreement between us. I immediately raised the matter with Doug and we had a heated debate, totally disagreeing on the desirability of the float. In the end he acceded to my view and did not issue the statement. Floating the dollar was the 'big bang' of financial deregulation. Our differences on the issue symbolised a deep divide in Coalition thinking on economic policy. Fraser later attacked the float.

The Coalition's clear support for such a huge policy decision was critical to winning acceptance for the change in the general community. It meant that as time went by and fluctuations in the value of the dollar inevitably occurred, hurting some and rewarding others, a cheap fear campaign blaming the float could not have been credibly mounted. In sharp contrast, such unconditional bipartisan support on a big policy issue was never forthcoming from the ALP during the years of the Howard Government.

Floating the dollar had more influence than any other decision taken by either the Hawke or Keating governments. Although Paul Keating is often given the credit for floating the dollar, his timidity on the issue was over-ridden by the Prime Minister, with the strong support of the governor of the Reserve Bank, Bob Johnson.

In its first budget the Hawke Government brought in an assets test for the payment of the aged pension. I thought this was good policy, although politically unpopular. I was absent on a brief holiday with my family in the snowfields when the shadow cabinet discussed the Coalition's attitude to the proposal. The following day I read in the newspapers that the opposition would oppose the assets test.

If I had been present at the shadow cabinet meeting I would have argued that we support the Government. I wasn't there and, by coincidence or not, a decision on this issue was taken. I had no alternative to going along with it, even though I felt uncomfortable.

Politically, it turned out that Peacock's judgement on this issue was absolutely correct. His opposition to the assets test was a major reason why the opposition performed much better in the premature 1984 election than many expected. He developed a fine line of rhetoric, and it resonated with many older voters. It was a very good example of successfully applying the politics of consolidating one's base of support, albeit in a different manner from what I was endeavouring to do with small business.

On 19 June 1984, Phillip Lynch died at the very early age of 50. Some time before, he had been diagnosed with stomach cancer. Lynch had been a hardworking servant of the Liberal Party, and had carried much of the grinding work of building the case of economic mismanagement against the Whitlam Government throughout 1975. We had been close as colleagues, and I felt for his wife, Leah, and their three sons. I called to see him at his home on the Mornington Peninsula only a few weeks before his death. He knew his fate, but was sustained by his strong Catholic beliefs. I admired his fortitude. He did not seek pity; rather he remained deeply engaged about the challenges then facing the Liberal Party.

The opposition languished in the opinion polls all through 1984. Six days before the election was called, the Morgan Poll in the *Bulletin* showed Hawke at 73 per cent against Peacock's 15 per cent on the preferred prime minister rating. This probably encouraged Bob Hawke to call an election for December that year, only 20 months after his win in March 1983. He was to get a rude shock. He entered the election campaign with supreme confidence, believing that the Labor Party would win seats from the Coalition, particularly in Victoria. As a measure of his hubris, he programmed a 55-day campaign, which was ridiculously long, especially as the election was being held so soon after the change of government.

Before the election there was speculation, both amongst some colleagues and in the press, that if the Coalition performed badly, and many expected this, then I would replace Peacock as Leader of the Opposition. My own stocks within the party had been bolstered unexpectedly by a very successful parliamentary speech on race issues in August 1984. I effectively attacked a speech by Hayden, the Foreign Minister, in which he had clumsily attempted to smear people in the opposition as racist. I drew attention to the Labor Party's long historic support for the White Australia policy and managed to capture the moment. For immediate impact, it was probably as good a speech as any I delivered during my 33 years in parliament.

The campaign for the December 1984 election turned into something of a tour de force for Andrew Peacock. Undaunted by his poll deficit, he hammered away very effectively on two issues: the assets test on the aged pension, and altered taxation arrangements for lump-sum superannuation payments.

For the first time in Australian political history there was a televised debate between the Prime Minister and the Leader of the Opposition. Peacock won the debate quite convincingly. As Hawke and others were to learn, the expectations of these debates are such that, as there is an assumed ascendency for the incumbent, a reasonably good performance by the Leader of the Opposition exceeds expectations, and he often ends up 'winning' the debate. That is not to take anything away from Andrew Peacock's extremely polished performance. He put in more than a reasonably good performance; he outclassed Hawke with an engaging, direct style of presentation. Such was the impact of this debate on Bob Hawke that at the next election, in 1987, he refused to debate me as Opposition leader. An overly compliant media allowed him to get away with this piece of dismissive arrogance. Leaders' debates returned in 1990 when Peacock was again against Hawke and have been a permanent fixture ever since.

At the election the Labor Party was returned with a reduced majority of only 16 seats. Peacock and the Liberal Party had performed beyond all expectations. There was a wide feeling within the party, and elsewhere, that we would be back in government at the following election. This result put paid to any idea of a leadership change, and both Peacock and I were unanimously re-elected to our respective positions at the post-election party meeting.

At the news conference following the party meeting, I gave an answer to the question, 'Will you rule out a leadership challenge to Mr Peacock during the term of this parliament?', which was to be the source of intense irritation to Andrew Peacock and his close supporters. My response was, 'I think somebody who has had the track record of loyalty that I've had for the cause of the Liberal Party is not really required to answer that question.'[1]

I took the position that no person could ever be expected to rule out a leadership challenge.

Peacock's leadership had been consolidated by his election performance, and it was my expectation that he would lead the party to the next election. However, politics is always unpredictable, and I saw no reason why I should not, in an upfront fashion, keep my options open. I understood why my response irritated Peacock. In return, he should have accepted that it was a perfectly legitimate stance for me to take.

One other incident concerning the leadership of the party in those months is worth recounting. Andrew Peacock, Malcolm Fraser and I, with our wives, attended a function staged by the Victorian division of the Liberal Party in October 1984, just before the election, to mark the 40th anniversary of the party's foundation. After the function, Malcolm, his wife, Tamie, Janette and I, together with Tom Austin, deputy leader of the Victorian Liberals, and his wife, Judith, adjourned to Austin's hotel room for a drink. In the course of discussion Malcolm lambasted Peacock's leadership, asserting that he had no policies, and said that the party was headed for ruin at the next election and that I had an obligation 'to put my hand up'. Both Janette and I were rather taken aback at this outburst, and afterwards confided to each other that maybe Malcolm had in mind two leaders being knocked off for the price of one election. There had, for some time, been low-level chatter that perhaps Fraser might be recalled to lead the Liberal Party. It should be remembered that he had left the prime ministership at a very young age, 52. Hawke, in fact, was six months older than Fraser when he defeated him for the top job.

Whatever may have been the former Prime Minister's motives, he left me with the unmistakable impression that I should seek the leadership, and quickly do so. I had no intention of doing this and made that clear to him. The very next morning Janette and I ran into him at the airport. Robin Gray, the Premier of Tasmania, was also there and we chatted inconsequentially. As Malcolm left to get his plane, he raised his arm and repeated the words 'Put your arm up.' According to the media, when asked about the whole incident, Fraser denied that it had taken place.

Some months later, after the election, Malcolm Fraser rang me and said that in light of changed circumstances, I should ignore the advice he had given me back in October 1984.

The changed circumstances to which Fraser referred were not only the unexpectedly good election outcome, but also the extraordinary way in which Bob Hawke had handled a national security issue involving the US Alliance. There had been an understanding between the Australian and US governments, concluded under the Fraser Government, whereby Australian facilities would be available to help monitor splash-down trials of the MX missile, then under production in the United States. As the time of the trials approached, this became a sensitive issue within the Labor Party because the missile would be capable of carrying a nuclear warhead.

The 1984 election had seen a surge in support for the Nuclear Disarmament Party (NDP), and Palm Sunday peace rallies had attracted large crowds. Hawke's natural instincts were to honour the agreement with the Americans but, remarkably, he caved in to the left wing. Keating, to his credit, had commented before Hawke's capitulation that the Government should not take any notice of 'fifth-graders'. If he is to be believed, Graham Richardson is the person who finally persuaded Hawke to give in to the left. By chance I ran into Richardson in the lobby of the Imperial Hotel in Tokyo just after the decision had been announced. He was quite happy to confide in me that, having canvassed opinion within the parliamentary party, he had offered Hawke the advice to compromise with those who were nervous about being too close to the Americans. There were never any flies on that fixer.

Hawke's back-flip caused something of a run on the Australian dollar, and coming on top of the worse-than-expected election result, this helped create the impression that the Government had begun to lose its way.

After the 1984 election, which saw the return of Peter Shack to federal parliament as member for Tangney, Peacock made Shack spokesman on industrial relations. This created an interesting position. Shack was very close to Andrew Peacock, having worked on his staff between the 1983 election, when Shack lost his seat, and his return to parliament. On the other hand, he was a strong supporter of a freer labour market. His views on industrial relations were much closer to mine than had been those of Ian Macphee, the previous spokesman, who, prior to entering parliament, had been director of the Victorian Chamber of Manufacturers, which was quite a supporter of the traditional industrial relations order.

1985 gave me an opportunity to give vent to my long-suppressed interest in defence and foreign policy issues. I had some very strong things to say about the Labor Party's capitulation to the left on the MX missile issue. The strategic defence initiative, which involved the creation of a missile shield against a possible nuclear attack, then in its embryonic phase and receiving active support from the Reagan Administration, was something which I openly supported.

At this stage Paul Keating and I enjoyed an easy personal relationship. He had even sought my advice about moving his young family to Canberra. Our links attracted some media interest because the Canberra gallery appreciated the support I extended when the Hawke Government adopted good policy.

For months the Treasurer had been working on an elaborate plan for taxation reform, to be presented to a taxation summit promised by Hawke in the 1984 campaign and due to take place in July 1985. The centrepiece of Keating's plan was the introduction of a broad-based consumption tax, at a rate of 12.5 per cent, accompanied by reductions in personal income tax, the introduction of a capital gains tax and a fringe benefits tax. It was a huge and ambitious proposal that mirrored changes for which I had argued when Treasurer, most particularly the proposal to broaden the indirect tax base and reduce personal income tax.

On the day his tax blueprint was released, he asked me round to his office and gave me a copy of the document, saying how important certain reforms were to the future of the country. Mindful of my past support for taxation reform, he was appealing to me for bipartisan help.

Keating's taxation proposals led to a renewal of tension within the Coalition between those who wanted to oppose it outright for popular political reasons, and those like me, who believed that the national interest required a completely different taxation system. Its foundation was a new broad-based indirect tax in exchange for much lower income tax, something I had advocated for years. How could I oppose it? I made it clear that I backed these parts of the Keating plan.

Due to those tensions, the opposition appeared to want it both ways. It favoured reform, but not this one. In the end this did not matter because the unions heavied Bob Hawke into pulling the rug on his Treasurer over the whole plan. The consumption tax was dumped, leaving a compromise which did not embody such far-reaching reform. The opposition could readily oppose this.

15

LEADER BY ACCIDENT

In the weeks which followed the collapse of the tax summit, three things caused Andrew Peacock to confront me on the leadership issue. The first of these was my being guest host on the Nine Network's *Midday Show*. This program had an enormous audience, and Andrew Peacock had been invited to host it but declined the invitation. My appearance attracted a lot of interest as I was able to nominate people to be interviewed, and amongst those I selected was Bill O'Reilly, the legendary Australian Test cricketer. Secondly, a chance encounter with David Morgan, a senior Treasury official but later to be chief executive of Westpac, led to an embarrassing moment for both me and Jim Carlton, the Liberal MP for MacKellar. In casual discussion Morgan said to me, 'Hypothetically, if you were Leader of the Opposition, who would you have as your shadow Treasurer?' and I replied, 'Jim Carlton'. It was foolish and indiscreet of me and no doubt fuelled the impression, when the story got out, that I was preparing a list of shadow ministers. This was not the case.

The final straw was at the National Press Club on 28 August 1985 when I gave the traditional shadow Treasurer's response to the budget speech. I spoke broadly and passionately about the need for reform in numerous areas, including the maintenance of my commitment to taxation reform. It was widely reported as the speech of somebody who had a policy agenda for the opposition.

My view was that there was nothing disloyal in performing well as a spokesman for one's party, even if, on occasions, that performance might outshine the contribution of the leader. At one point a member of Peacock's staff told my chief of staff, Gerard Henderson, that I should tone down my media appearances because they were overshadowing the leader's contributions. I thought that rather missed the point.

I was away on a short skiing holiday with my family, at Berridale at the foot of the Snowy Mountains, when Andrew Peacock telephoned me on 2 September and asked that I return to Canberra the following day to discuss the leadership issue. He made what I thought to be an absurd and naïve request that I rule out challenging him for the leadership.

Peacock's action was ill-advised. The party did not want him to be removed as leader, and the last thing that colleagues wanted was a public scrap between Andrew and me. Yet that is what they got because of his decision to require what I was unwilling to commit to. I had not been plotting to depose him, I was not gathering any numbers, and I wished to continue working with him as deputy leader of the Liberal Party.

When I refused to give a commitment not to challenge, Andrew called a special meeting of the parliamentary Liberal Party to try and oust me as deputy leader. His planning had been poor. Rather haphazardly, he had settled on John Moore, MP for the Queensland seat of Ryan, to be his candidate for the deputy leadership. It was reported that he approached Jim Carlton and Wal Fife, but they had refused to nominate against me. Maybe he was advised that I would capitulate, but of course I didn't, and set about fighting to retain my position as deputy leader.

I continued to do media appearances, restating my support for him as leader and my willingness to continue working as his deputy. My media appearances also included continued attacks on Labor's economic management; some colleagues were impressed by the fact that I kept a focus on the main battle, despite the pressure I was under. I carefully telephoned just about every person in the parliamentary party with the simple plea that I be retained as deputy on the basis of my experience and my willingness to work with Andrew as leader.

Clearly the Peacock camp had not done a systematic job of canvassing for the numbers. I gave a crucial indication that if I lost the deputy leadership I would go to the backbench. Apart from people strongly committed to Andrew and hostile to me, the colleagues to whom I spoke clearly wanted the status quo. Many were quite embarrassed by the public stand-off, and none to whom I spoke expressed a view that I had been disloyal.

I received a lot of support from close colleagues and friends. Between midnight and 1 am the night before the ballot, Kerry Packer telephoned me from his property near Scone and asked, 'Sport, is there anything I can do to help you?' Loyalty and remembrance of past support was always a strong Packer virtue. During the so-called 'Goanna' accusations surrounding Kerry Packer in 1984, when many people shunned him, I had made a point of identifying with him, simply because I did not believe for a moment the allegations raised about him. He never forgot this expression of friendship.

On the morning of the ballot, I expected to lose. I travelled in a Commonwealth car from the Commonwealth Club to Parliament House, with Pru Goward interviewing me for ABC Radio current affairs. Her first question was, 'Mr Howard, what does it feel like to be in the last day of your time as deputy leader?' That turned out to be an accurate prediction, but not in the way that she and most others expected. Although the motion to remove me as deputy was carried, when John Moore and I nominated for the vacant position, I defeated Moore by 38 votes to 32. The outcome stunned me and many others. To this day, I believe a number of people who voted for me as deputy leader did so in the belief that I would continue working for Andrew Peacock as leader. They did not contemplate what was to follow immediately after this ballot.

Peacock asked me and the other members of the leadership group, Fred Chaney and Peter Durack, to his office. He told us that he was in an impossible position and that he would resign. He then returned to the party meeting, informed those present of his decision, to cries of 'No, don't', and some of 'Grow up', and called immediately for nominations to fill the vacancy in the leadership of the party. The only other person to nominate was Jim Carlton, and I defeated him by 59 votes to six. There were seven informal votes. After several ballots, Neil Brown from Victoria was elected as deputy leader.

The outcome was nothing short of extraordinary. It was a case of a party changing its leader by accident, not by deliberation. Whilst I was naturally happy, indeed exhilarated, to have the leadership, I had not been campaigning for it. True it was that I was ready to parade my policy credentials and to argue publicly for the things in which I believed, but I had not been organising a challenge, and would not have challenged Andrew Peacock in the circumstances then prevailing within the parliamentary party. If Andrew had not lost his nerve and sought to remove me as deputy leader, I am sure that he would have continued as leader until the subsequent election.

The sudden change in leadership was greeted with much enthusiasm within the party and in many sections of the community. There was widespread press endorsement of me, largely on the grounds that I had been prominent in arguing policy substance. Andrew Peacock gave a gracious and light-hearted press conference in which he rather humorously said that he didn't know if he had ever wanted to be prime minister. The immediate reaction was one of surging public support for the Coalition and me.

My honeymoon was very short-lived, however. Starting with the leaking of a shadow cabinet strategy paper prepared by Tony Messner, my newly appointed Finance spokesman, the Coalition leaked like a sieve, until a temporary cessation for the 1987 election. The parliamentary party entered a difficult and divisive phase.

The poll resurgence did not last long, and some tactical mistakes of mine did not help. For example, I maintained the rather rigid policy position that there should be an immediate deregulation of housing interest rates. This was economically sensible but politically very dangerous. It presented the Labor Party in the South Australian state election held on 7 December 1985 with a real gift. Although the Liberal Party opposition distanced itself from the federal policy, it was easy for Labor to make the link. I should have anticipated this and embraced a gradual approach on deregulation of housing interest rates — which I was to advocate early in 1986 and which was copied by the Hawke Government several months later.

Although there were flaws in my leadership style, the larger problem was that I was being targeted from within through a torrent of leaks which undermined my authority, almost on a daily basis. The Coalition ended the year in a very weak political position. The early excitement about my securing the leadership had turned to a sense of puzzlement and drift. The great momentum of September 1985 had dissipated.

For much of 1986 the party struggled. My poll ratings against Hawke were dismal, and until the latter part of the year the Coalition itself was well behind the Labor Party. Polls became the nightmare of my existence, as is inevitably the fate of any Opposition leader who does not keep himself and his party reasonably competitive with the Government and the Prime Minister. Not only did I rate poorly against Hawke but, as time went by, popularity polls were conducted between me and Peacock; predictably, Andrew Peacock began to move ahead on these measurements.

One particularly damaging poll, conducted by the Quantum research group, commissioned from Western Australia, was leaked extensively to the *Australian Financial Review*, which gave it extraordinarily heavy coverage, way beyond what could have been justified by ordinary reporting principles. This included extensive reporting on the morning of a nationally televised address by me. This poll was paid for by a group angry over my anti-tax avoidance action as Treasurer.

The party was in a real bind. By accident it had changed its leader and a substantial section of the party remained profoundly unhappy about this. For some of them, the honourable thing was to grin and bear it and do their best to be an effective opposition. For a much smaller group, the answer was to embark on regular bouts of destructive destabilisation, which of course had a disastrous impact on my leadership authority and badly damaged the opposition.

Despite the instability and leadership problems, I was determined to push ahead on the policy front. Thus the Coalition's new and quite radical industrial relations policy was released by Neil Brown on 11 May 1986. For the first time it provided for individual contracts and made very significant changes to the old centralised wage-fixing system. Getting the policy out and winning wide acceptance for it was quite an achievement given the turmoil within the Coalition parties.

In the first half of 1986, Paul Keating made his widely reported comment on the John Laws radio program that if Australia did not rectify its terms-of-trade problem, it would end up a 'banana republic', which I thought at the time was no more than a throwaway line, not the considered warning to the public it was later claimed to be. The terms-of-trade challenge led to an address to the nation from the Prime Minister, with a response from me, in which I laid out an alternative approach. Despite the fog of leadership speculation, my response won considerable praise from the commentariat.

The Liberal Party held a most successful federal council in Adelaide, in September of that year. Its conclusion coincided with the publication of a Morgan Poll which showed the Coalition ahead of Labor by six points. For a leader who had been under siege from the opinion polls for close to nine months, this was a welcome relief. Generally favourable publicity coming out of the meeting boosted the spirits of the Coalition as the year moved on.

Notwithstanding our internal problems, the Coalition had had some notable parliamentary successes. It severely embarrassed Paul Keating over his failure to lodge an income tax return for the previous year. This hurt Keating a lot with ordinary voters. When the document suggesting that Keating had not filed his return came into my hands, I found it hard to believe. So I asked Jim Carlton, the shadow Treasurer, to call on Keating, confront him with what we had and indicate that if the information were bogus then the matter would not be further pursued. It was clear from Keating's reaction that the information was spot-on. I am glad that I had taken the precaution of checking. That precaution did not for a moment dilute the intense public embarrassment Keating suffered.

Incredibly, Wilson Tuckey, who was a loud barracker for Peacock, criticised me for such caution, and that criticism found its way into the papers.

The ongoing controversy regarding the position of Lionel Murphy on the High Court also provided the opposition with the chance to wrong-foot the Government for an entire week in the parliament. Although spasmodic, these events continued to give Coalition members hope and to remind all of us that we had a real show of getting on top of the Government, if only our own difficulties could be put behind us. That remained our principal challenge.

16

JOH FOR PM

On 2 June 1987 I arrived back at our home in Wollstonecraft close to 8.30 in the evening. Janette met me at the door and said, 'They're in the lounge room'. She was referring to the delegation from the Queensland National Party. This was the end of a quite remarkable day in the distracting saga of the 'Joh for PM' campaign, which did such immense damage to our prospects of winning the 1987 election. The delegation had come to signal an unapologetic surrender in a campaign which had engulfed and enfeebled the federal coalition for close to a year.

The events of the early days of June 1987 may have ended the 'Joh for PM' push, but its ramifications would haunt the Liberal and National parties for some years into the future.

How did it all come about in the first place? As the Coalition in Canberra, and the Liberal Party in particular, struggled through the early part of 1986, there were murmurs out of Queensland that Joh Bjelke-Petersen, that state's long-serving Premier, might take a tilt at Canberra.

Disunity within the Liberal Party and the constant speculation about my leadership encouraged anti-Labor people to believe that an alternative to the orthodox Coalition approach in Canberra was needed. Importantly, Andrew Peacock and Joh Bjelke-Petersen had a warm regard for each other. It stemmed from Peacock's heavy involvement, as Foreign Minister, in negotiating with the Indonesian Government on border issues affecting Queensland. Joh liked Andrew, who was always ready to sing the Premier's praises in public. There was also the Russell Hinze factor. Hinze, a senior Queensland minister, wanted to be state Premier, and to do that he had to get rid of Joh. How better to achieve this goal than to have Joh launch himself in a bid for Canberra, irrespective of the outcome?

Peacock and Hinze had a mutual love of horses, which brought them together. Hinze would frequently deride my standing in the polls, largely in private, but from time to time publicly. There is little doubt that through these difficult days Andrew Peacock was in communication with Joh and Hinze.

The Fraser years had also provided a hangover. At the beginning Fraser worked closely with the Queensland Nationals and incurred the enmity of Queensland Liberals such as Eric Robinson for being too close to them. This friendship soured. Bjelke-Petersen resented the Fraser ban on sand mining on Fraser Island. He thought Fraser was too friendly with Robert Mugabe and had little time for Fraser's strong anti-South African stance.

Then there was the bottom-of-the-harbour tax legislation, which wounded many in Queensland's so-called white shoe brigade. I learned this from comments made to me years later by people who were in a position to know. Many of them were strong financial backers of the Nationals in Queensland, and the Premier frequently mentioned this issue amongst his litany of complaints about the Fraser Government.

Also, by virtue of his intervention in federal politics regarding his Gair manoeuvre and the appointment of Patrick Field to the Senate, both of which hurt Whitlam, Bjelke-Petersen always felt that the federal Coalition owed him a lot.

One of the active proponents of Joh's Canberra campaign was the developer Mike Gore, a fierce critic of my 1982 bottom-of-the-harbour laws. Many believe that Gore paid for research in 1986 by the Canadian company Decima, which allegedly showed that Joh being part of the anti-Labor push would add considerable value to the conservative cause across Australia. Gore had obtained special legislation from the Queensland Government for his Sanctuary Cove development. To Mike Gore, Joh could walk on water. Lake Burley Griffin would be no problem.

Joh Bjelke-Petersen was a rural populist. He placed a premium on development, often without too much regard for competition considerations. When it came to investment in Queensland and the economic growth of the state, he was a corner cutter. This approach achieved results and produced a buoyant Queensland economy, which lasted long after he had gone. Sometimes people were unreasonably enriched in the process, yet the state prospered. As Treasurer, I had several heated discussions with him about my insistence on Australian equity being involved in large coal projects.

Sometimes his preference was that the entirety of the projects should be owned by Japanese investors. His priority was investment in Queensland. I supported that too, but I wanted Australians to participate in that investment where Australian equity was available.

Like all premiers, particularly Queensland premiers, he was happy to beat the anti-Canberra drum. Finishing one very cranky telephone conversation with me regarding a foreign investment decision of mine, he said, 'Why don't you just leave us alone and let us run Queensland?'

The *Australian* newspaper became a prominent vehicle for the propagation of the Joh cause. The editor at the time, the late Les Hollings, gave huge coverage to anything that Bjelke-Petersen said or did. The paper's editorial pages championed the causes of lower taxes and reduced union power. That was fine by me, but the underlying theme from contributors like Katherine West and Des Keegan was that I wasn't quite up to the task and a person with the heft of Joh was needed.

These were all ingredients which led to the 'Joh for PM' campaign. They were not, however, the overriding reasons why it happened. In the end it happened because Joh Bjelke-Petersen himself believed that he could become prime minister. It was not rational, but it was real.

By 1987 he had been Premier of Queensland for 19 years. Australia had a federal Labor Government, and Labor was in power in all other states except Tasmania. Joh was a hero to people on the right and centre-right of politics, not only in his own state but elsewhere. He spoke with the authority of being in government. I spoke with the limitations of being an Opposition leader, and one who was under pressure within his own party.

Bjelke-Petersen had beaten Labor on numerous occasions. He had demoralised the Liberals in Queensland with his remarkable win in November 1986. Although some former National Party insiders say that Joh had resolved to tilt for Canberra before the 1986 election, his amazing victory removed serious doubts in his mind. Until then the possibility of the 'Joh for PM' campaign gathering traction was remote.

To win 49 out of the 89 seats in the Queensland parliament was a huge accomplishment for the National Party. A week out from that election a deadlocked parliament looked likely. The all-out National Party assault during the final week shifted many people who traditionally might have voted Liberal towards Bjelke-Petersen, in the name of having a stable, conservative government in Queensland. This victory persuaded him, and many around him, that he had broad vote-winning appeal, including amongst blue-collar Labor voters.

There was another simple reason why he turned his gaze to Canberra. 1986, despite the triumph it was, was his last state election. It became, therefore, a question of why not have a go for Canberra. In the atmosphere of Queensland politics after the election, such issues as the unlikelihood of his state popularity translating fully into the federal arena never occurred to his spruikers. There have been very few successful translations of successful state political figures into positions of equal power and prominence federally. Behaviour deemed popular, even loveable, at a state level becomes quirky and even embarrassing at a national level.

There was also the reality that many Liberals who happily declared their regard and support for Bjelke-Petersen whilst he was Queensland Premier had a completely different attitude towards the prospect that he might be the alternative to Bob Hawke as prime minister. As Christmas 1986 drew near, none of this seemed to matter. The victory in November had converted a fanciful dream into a tantalising possibility.

Until Bjelke-Petersen's Queensland election victory, I did not judge that the 'Joh for PM' campaign, although distracting, would become a reality. Watching Joh's victory speech that night in November 1986, my concern deepened. I said to Janette, who had watched it with me, 'This is going to create terrible trouble for us.'

My concerns were realised almost immediately. In a post-election interview with the *Australian* on 3 November he said, 'This time I won't be working through them. They'll work with the policies I set or I will work against them, and I've told them that.'[1] Hinze had been even more direct: 'We need a type of leader like Sir Joh in the nation,' he said. 'Howard tried to help Knox [the Queensland Liberal leader] and was not accepted. It's a problem for the conservative parties in Australia, we have to find a new leader,' he continued.[2] When pressed, he said that Andrew Peacock was one of the politicians capable of saving Australia.

Bjelke-Petersen was unresponsive to any personal overtures. I rang him on Christmas Eve 1986. He was polite in response but decidedly distant. It was plain that he had no intention of sitting down with me to plan a joint strategy to defeat Hawke.

The Bjelke-Petersen push had precious little to do with philosophy. It was driven by the desire to achieve and wield power. The Queensland Premier and I were close on some issues. We were both socially conservative and shared similar views on industrial relations, although we differed on other economic policies. He frequently railed against 'trendies' in the Liberal Party — hardly applicable to me. But our similarities meant nothing.

Although, as fellow premiers, Sir Charles Court, of Western Australia, and Sir Joh Bjelke-Petersen often made common cause against Canberra, Court was dismayed by the Joh for PM campaign. He thought it ill-advised, doomed to fail and damaging to the Liberal cause. He tried in various ways to persuade his former premier-in-arms against it, and expressed concern to me about some of the people around Bjelke-Petersen.

Joh used the Christmas/New Year period to keep the speculation going. He held a major rally in Wagga Wagga on 31 January and announced his strong support for a 25 per cent flat tax policy. He spoke of 'starting a bushfire that will spread across Australia'.[3] That meeting was addressed by Des Keegan of the *Australian* and the activist leader of Australia's surgeons, Bruce Shepherd. He personified the type of person who caused me difficulties with Joh. A very conservative man, he professed support for me and had actually told me in advance what he proposed saying at the Wagga Wagga rally, but also told me what a great man Joh was. Shepherd railed against the so-called trendies in my party such as Ian Macphee and Peter Baume. I told him that the Liberal Party was a broad church and that it was the final policies which emerged that really mattered.

In January 1987 I went to Perth for some America's Cup activities and had breakfast with Ian McLachlan, still president of the National Farmers Federation (NFF) but there for a meeting of the Elders board. He was an impressive figure who I liked and really wanted as a Liberal candidate at the next election. Then one of Australia's largest woolgrowers, his leadership of the NFF had made him a real poster boy for industrial relations reform on issues such as the Mudginberri abattoir. Whilst being friendly, he was unwilling to commit. Shortly afterwards, John Carrick, who had been a NSW senator since 1971, told me that he would resign his Senate seat in favour of Ian McLachlan, if that would help. I rang and told McLachlan of this. He was non-committal. Carrick had made a huge gesture, but I don't think that Ian was fully seized by this. A few weeks later I called to see McLachlan when in Adelaide. We had a long and friendly talk, but it was of little avail. He said that he did not wish to commit specifically to either the Liberal Party or the Nationals. He kept referring to the right-hand side of politics. McLachlan said that he had been in touch with Bjelke-Petersen. He said, 'You know, he

really thinks he can do it. I am going to take a detailed look at his proposals.'
He also said that the NFF was resolutely opposed to a consumption tax and
would campaign hard against it if it became Liberal policy. The farmers
wanted fuel excise abolished. I left that meeting feeling dispirited.

A huge complication throughout was the poor relations between Bjelke-
Petersen and the Nationals' federal leader, Ian Sinclair. The Queensland
Premier had no interest in getting closer to his federal colleague, and Ian
Sinclair struggled to find the right modus operandi for handling Joh.
Relations between Joh and the federal Nationals had always been
problematic. In the Fraser Government days, Peter Nixon had been the man
to deal with Joh. Nixon was neither in awe of Joh nor insensitive to his raw
populism. He was a straight shooter, and on many occasions both Malcolm
Fraser and Doug Anthony would ask Peter Nixon to 'deal with Joh'.

Tension built as parliament prepared to resume in February 1987.
Tactically, Bjelke-Petersen's first objective was to break the federal coalition.
My aim was to preserve it. I knew that if the federal coalition held, there was
no real prospect of a 'Joh for PM' campaign getting off the ground. Crucial
to maintaining the federal coalition was the determination and leadership
authority of Ian Sinclair.

We held a joint party meeting on 2 February, after which I called on
Bjelke-Petersen to be either supportive or to keep out of the federal scene.
On the same day, at a news conference, Ian Sinclair reiterated his
commitment to the Coalition and said that no individual premier or leader
of any state parliamentary party 'will have a direct role in determining any
other course'. That was the right attitude.

The agitation from the Queenslanders continued, and attention shifted
to a separate meeting of the federal parliamentary National Party, set for
16 February. This shaped as a test of Ian Sinclair's authority to hold the
federal Nationals in the Coalition. Before the meeting, I spoke to him about
the need to reaffirm the commitment of the Nationals to the Coalition.

The outcome of that National Party meeting could not have been worse.
Instead of a clear statement of support for the Coalition, what was
described to me by Peter McGauran, a National MP, as 'an olive branch to
Bjelke-Petersen' emanated. It said nothing about the Coalition. Rather, it
welcomed the thrust of what the Premier of Queensland had been seeking
to achieve and expressed support for his general philosophy. This outcome
told me that, when push came to shove, Bjelke-Petersen had enough
influence to break the federal coalition. The Queenslanders were in mortal

fear of their party endorsements. Not only could Bjelke-Petersen corral them but also at least two from other states.

This was anything but an endorsement of the federal coalition. The following day, I told Ian Sinclair that I would not preside at a joint party meeting, scheduled for later that day, unless he was willing to have his National Party colleagues join in an affirmation of the Coalition, to be publicly made after the meeting of the two parties. After consulting his colleagues, Ian said he would do as I wished. The joint party meeting was held, and the statement I wanted was issued.

The statement said that Ian Sinclair had informed the joint party meeting of the desire of the National Party to continue in coalition with the Liberals. It also reaffirmed that the maintenance of the Coalition was the most effective instrument to defeat the Hawke Government. Cracks were being papered over.

The shove came from the central council of the Queensland National Party meeting at Hervey Bay on 27 February. Effectively, that meeting called on the parliamentary members of the federal National Party to withdraw from the Coalition. The 'Joh for PM' campaign came out of the closet at that meeting. 'Joh for PM' T-shirts were distributed and ostentatiously donned by people such as the Deputy Premier of Queensland, Bill Gunn. I attached significance to him as my colleague Wal Fife, who had been a fellow Education Minister with Gunn some years earlier, had conveyed to me assurances from Gunn: 'Don't worry, Wal. It won't happen.' The bandwagon was well and truly gathering pace. Ian Sinclair had attended the meeting and rang me afterwards sounding deeply depressed about the outcome, but assured me he would continue to resist any breaking of the federal coalition.

Sinclair publicly ignored the Hervey Bay resolution. The Queensland members of the National Party decided to wait until a meeting of the federal council of the National Party, due at the end of March, before deciding whether or not to bail out. Meanwhile, the central executive of the NSW party reaffirmed its strong support for Ian Sinclair as leader, and the maintenance of the federal coalition.

Separately, the federal member for Groom in Queensland, Tom McVeigh, withdrew from the federal parliamentary National Party. There were rumours at the time that McVeigh had been offered a job by Bjelke-Petersen in return for vacating his very safe Darling Downs electorate in favour of the Premier.

In directing the parliamentary Nationals to leave the Coalition, and threatening their endorsements if they did not do so, the Queensland Nationals were doing something which for decades both the Liberal and National parties had publicly held against the Labor Party. Dictation from unelected party bosses had been a characteristic of the Australian Labor Party in the 1950s and '60s.

To people such as Doug Anthony, this thuggish behaviour by the unelected central council of the Queensland National Party was contrary to fundamental beliefs of the two coalition parties.

Speaking at the Sydney Rotary Club on 2 March, Doug Anthony said, 'I cannot stomach the intimidatory (sic) action against sitting members of parliament. Threatening them with their preselection if they don't obey the organisation is political blackmail … For 60 years, the party was proud of its parliamentary freedom and goodwill. For the Queensland organisation to direct and threaten elected members of parliament smacks of those features of the Labor Party we have always deplored.' He went on to say that if the federal coalition were broken, 'the mantle of blame would fall fairly and squarely on the Queensland National Party'.[4] He said it was absurd of the Queensland National Party to imagine it could ever win seats in metropolitan Sydney or Melbourne and that all that would occur would be the re-election of the Hawke Government. Doug Anthony understood precisely what was at stake.

The federal council met in Canberra on 27 March 1987. It resolved that it be left to the parliamentary Nationals to determine when they would withdraw from the Coalition. Many, me included, saw this as a real breakthrough, and perceived that the Queenslanders had backed off. We were wrong. All they had done was to embrace a tactical retreat. Time had been bought, so it was later claimed by Sparkes, the Queensland Nationals president, and others, to deny Hawke the option of an early election. If that was the reason then clearly it did not work.

The Queenslanders did not waste much time. The State Management Committee of the Queensland National Party met on 10 April and ordered its remaining 11 federal parliamentarians to leave the Coalition. This, of course, ignored the decision of the federal council to leave the timing of Coalition withdrawal to the parliamentary party. It was yet another illustration of how the Queenslanders held the National Party in the rest of the country in contempt. It was poetic justice that, in the end, this contemptuous indifference was the undoing of the whole Queensland enterprise.

I sensed that it would probably be short-lived, but I tried the tactic of holding together a remnant coalition. This was to consist of Nationals who remained committed to the Coalition, namely non-Queenslanders and Liberals. I announced a reshuffled shadow ministry with fewer National Party representatives.

Meeting on 28 April, the full parliamentary National Party rejected two of the stipulations I had made relating to meetings of the parliamentary Nationals as part of the deal I had concluded with Sinclair to keep a remnant coalition going. They regarded them as inconsistent with the continuation of their party as a separate parliamentary entity. Their reaction was understandable, but so had been mine: to do all in my power to preserve as much unity as possible between the two parties.

It was the Nationals who had broken the coalition. It had been the unwillingness of the parliamentary collective of National Party members in Canberra to defy the Queensland organisation which had brought about the crisis. If the Queenslanders in the federal parliamentary National Party had stood together and defied their party organisation and stayed in the coalition, there is no way that all of them would have lost their endorsements. If they had all displayed the fortitude of Stan Collard, who defended the right of the parliamentary members to decide these things, history would have been different. Instead they let him be picked off, and he alone lost his preselection.

At 8.30 pm on 28 April 1987, in Canberra, feeling very sad about it, I announced the end of the federal coalition. I said:

> Mr Sinclair and I reached an agreement which was an honourable agreement. But because a few Queensland National Party members did not have the guts to stand up to the maverick Premier of Queensland, the National Party has broken that agreement and thus the National Party has brought an end to the Coalition. Therefore, the Liberal Party will now go all out to win government in its own right. If we fall short by a few seats of achieving that goal at the next election I will negotiate a new coalition agreement with the National Party so that we can get rid of the Hawke Government, form a new Coalition Government, and implement policies which will benefit all Australians.[5]

They were brave words, uttered with much passion, but I knew in my heart just how difficult our predicament had become.

We were a spectacle of disunity and weakness. Labor could not have believed its extraordinary good fortune. The 'Joh for PM' push had sucked all the oxygen out of the air for me, my party and those parliamentary National Party members who were genuinely trying to concentrate on our main job, and that was to oppose and hopefully defeat the Hawke Government. Ian Sinclair had done his level best to save the Coalition.

It was an immensely dispiriting time for our supporters throughout the country. Constant preoccupation with the threat to the Coalition posed by the Queensland Nationals had rendered serious policy work virtually impossible. Not only was an enormous amount of my time, and that of other senior colleagues, focused on the Bjelke-Petersen issue, but the totally compromised independence of the parliamentary Nationals meant that they were in no mood to focus on, let alone commit to, particular policies.

The Queensland Nationals had achieved their negative objectives. They had wrecked the federal coalition and completely undermined Ian Sinclair's leadership. They had gravely weakened my own position as alternative Prime Minister. Yet, with the exception of John Stone, the former Treasury secretary, they had not recruited any star or high-profile candidates willing to run under the Joh banner. None of the other prominent potential recruits mentioned from time to time materialised. Some made it plain they would not sign up with Bjelke-Petersen. One was Greg Chappell, the cricket great, who in a telephone conversation with me firmly ruled out any possibility of becoming a candidate for the Queensland Premier. The negative part had been accomplished fairly easily. The more difficult part of presenting as a credible alternative conservative force had not been achieved.

By contrast, Hawke continued to govern decisively. On 13 May the Treasurer delivered a major economic statement outlining a reduction of $4 billion in the prospective budget deficit. It gave the appearance of a government dealing directly with the economic challenges then facing Australia.

Hawke had been presented with the irresistible temptation to call an early election. He readily succumbed, and announced it at 5 pm on 27 May. It was a double dissolution, obtained on the strength of Senate rejection of the Australia Card legislation.

Not since its formation in 1944 had the Liberal Party of Australia faced a federal election in less propitious circumstances. Its 40-year coalition with the Nationals had been brutally broken. It had, for months, been racked by leadership speculation and, due in no small measure to these two factors themselves, had not completed enough policy work to go to the people with a comprehensive program, credibly costed.

Early on 2 June 1987, Ian McLachlan telephoned me in Canberra to say that he was having absolutely nothing further to do with the Joh campaign. McLachlan's flirtation with Joh had hurt us a lot. He was a credible figure. No end of effort had been made to encourage him to endorse the federal coalition. Yet he had stubbornly refused, saying that he didn't think that we had the bottle to take the tough decisions needed if we got into government.

Alexander Downer, who had only been elected in 1984, had three months earlier publicly offered to vacate his very safe seat of Mayo to make way for McLachlan as a Liberal candidate. It was a big thing for Downer to do. He had his heart set on a long political career but was motivated by his deep affection for the Liberal Party and driven by his alarm at the spectacle of disunity presented by the Liberal and National parties. There had also been the Carrick offer.

Whatever had been his prevarication in the past, by 2 June McLachlan had become quite angry. He told me, after a meeting with them, that the Queenslanders had done no serious work. They had no policies to speak of. His disillusionment gave me some hope. It was sorely needed.

The Queensland Premier had been in California when Hawke announced the election and was thus caught quite unprepared.

John Stone also telephoned me that same day. He had secured a spot on the Nationals' Senate ticket for Queensland. John would be the main architect of Joh's taxation policy and was the one person who gave some nationwide credibility to the Queensland push. John had always been quite an admirer of Bjelke-Petersen. In his call he hinted that the Queenslanders knew that the 'Joh for PM' campaign could not succeed. He said that they wanted to see me as soon as possible, to discuss ways of working together to defeat the Hawke Government.

So it was agreed that Joh and his senior National Party people would see me at my home in Sydney later that evening. They had been in Melbourne during the day, where the abortive meeting with Ian McLachlan had taken place.

Accompanied by Tony Eggleton, Liberal federal director, and Grahame Morris, my chief of staff, I went to Sydney for one of the more remarkable political meetings of my entire life. 'They', to whom Janette referred, did not include the man himself. At the last minute Bjelke-Petersen, who had come to Sydney, had decided to sit it out, either at the airport or at some hotel. In the lounge room of my home, I found three emissaries from the north. They were Sir Robert Sparkes, the formidable president of the Queensland Nationals, his likeable and friendly deputy, Charlie Holm, and the state director, an advertising man called Fred Maybury. They hurriedly tried to explain Joh's absence. Then we began our discussion about what was to happen.

They were an interesting trio. Holm was a traditional Country Party man from rural Queensland. 'He's the sort of man you would buy a horse from,' remarked my wife later. He was seen by most people as an honest broker. Sparkes had played a major role in building the National Party organisation and had a good political brain. He had never been enthusiastic about the 'Joh for PM' campaign and only signed up quite late in the piece, when he realised that the momentum had gathered so strongly that it could not be ignored. Fred Maybury, given his advertising background, was completely obsessed with market research. He had been an enthusiast for the Canberra push by Bjelke-Petersen from way back.

They hadn't come to apologise but to acknowledge, grudgingly, that the game was up. They accepted that the Liberal and National parties, facing an election on 11 July, needed to cobble together as much unity as possible, even though it was the 11th hour.

Maybury had brought an armful of research material with him. He plonked it on the lounge room floor. Given that the die was already cast, I didn't quite see the point of this. The bizarre feature of the evening was that he kept telling all of us that it would have been possible for Joh to have made it, if it hadn't been for what he saw to be the perfidy of the NSW Nationals.

He was right, but I was the last person to think that the NSW Nationals had done the wrong thing. To me, they had been heroes. For all the political skills and strategic planning of which the Queensland Nationals were alleged to have been capable, they had ignored the most fundamental step needed to achieve their goal. They had not enlisted the support of the National Party organisation throughout Australia for the 'Joh for PM' campaign. Without this they never had any hope. Doug Moppett and his colleagues had outsmarted them.

The real rabbit killer to the 'Joh for PM' campaign had been delivered at a meeting in my office in Canberra just a few weeks earlier. Then an agreement was struck, not only to maintain the decades-old joint Senate ticket between the Liberal Party and the National Party in New South Wales, but to implement a strategy that would cripple Joh in New South Wales.

That meeting was attended by Doug Moppett, the chairman of the NSW Nationals, his state director, Jenny Gardiner, Bronwyn Bishop, president of the NSW division of the Liberal Party, Dr Graeme Starr, the state director of the Liberals, as well as Tony Eggleton, Ian Sinclair and me.

Moppett had shown genuine strength in the face of the Queensland push. From the beginning he had been scathing about what his northern confrères had in mind, and contemptuous of the way in which they had undermined his federal leader, Ian Sinclair. He and Jenny Gardiner shared the historic warmth of the NSW Nationals towards cooperation with the Liberals.

I had always strongly supported close cooperation with the Nationals. The reaffirmation of the joint NSW Senate ticket was very important. Equally important was our agreement that if any 'Joh for PM' Nationals stood against sitting Liberals, then the NSW Nationals would campaign against the Joh Nationals in support of sitting Liberal candidates. In similar vein, the Liberal Party would support sitting Nationals and Nationals endorsed by the party organisation in New South Wales against any 'Joh for PM' Nationals. This tight electoral pact was designed to shut out the Queenslanders. It succeeded.

Although Sparkes and Holm said very little, Maybury bitterly complained about what the NSW Nationals had done. It was quite extraordinary, because he was venting his spleen to someone who thought that the NSW Nationals had behaved honourably and in the best traditions of close coalition harmony. I thought that Doug Moppett, in particular, had displayed tenacity and strength where many others melted away.

We talked at our Wollstonecraft home for about an hour and a half. The message out of the meeting was clear. The 'Joh for PM' campaign was finished, but they thought it had all been rather unfair, because if the rest of the National Party had come on board it might have been successful!

Given all that had happened over the preceding few months, I felt considerable relief. There still remained the awkward issue of a meeting between the Queensland Premier and me. We all knew that without that meeting and a declaration from the two of us that we would work together, there was no hope of stitching up even a façade of unity for the election campaign. They wanted me to go and see Joh in Brisbane in the next few days.

After Sparkes, Holm and Maybury left, I held a council of war with my two Canberra colleagues and Janette. Despite all the rough edges, and the possibility that I would be criticised for going cap in hand to someone I had called a 'wrecker', we all agreed that it was more important to achieve the public outcome we wanted than worry about personal dignity. To have any hope at all in the election we needed to put as much of the Coalition disunity behind us as possible. We could not even begin to do this unless Bjelke-Petersen and I had been seen to have mended fences.

I went back to Canberra that night with Grahame Morris and Tony Eggleton. The following day was devoted to a series of phone calls between me, Sparkes and Stone.

In my discussions, I told both Stone and Sparkes that whilst I accepted that a visit to Brisbane was necessary I would not undertake it in the absence of a guarantee that Joh would come good on acknowledging that his Canberra fantasy was over. They gave me those guarantees. I remained dubious but arranged to fly to Brisbane the next day.

There was a lot of fog at Canberra Airport the following morning, but that was not the real reason for my delayed departure on the RAAF jet. Maybury had rung Eggleton very early to say that Joh was having second thoughts — more likely that Maybury had persuaded Joh to have those second thoughts. At one point Maybury rang my home looking for me. He spoke to Janette and told her that the whole thing was off. Agonising phone calls followed, with my speaking to Sparkes, Maybury and finally Joh. I obtained Joh's word. His press secretary, Ken Crook, even read out the news release Joh would issue.

I finally left for Brisbane. The meeting with the Queensland Premier was awkward but it achieved its purpose. A statement was issued which declared our determination to work together to defeat the Hawke Government. Deference was paid to the Queensland Nationals' views on taxation, without compromising anything which the Liberal Party might say on the subject during the election campaign. Bjelke-Petersen's demeanour was of a man who knew that his great dream would not be realised.

When I returned to Canberra, the house was still sitting. There were predictable cries of derision from the Labor side of the house that I had behaved weakly towards Bjelke-Petersen. I was happy to wear all of that. Hawke even moved a censure motion against me; that was going too far. He sounded rather foolish. A week earlier I would not have thought anything like what had been achieved in the previous 48 hours was remotely possible. Against all the odds of recent months, I now gave the Liberal Party just a faint chance of winning the election racing towards us. But the odds against us were colossal.

*   *   *

The really fatal blow to our 1987 election campaign was the discovery by the Labor Government of a double counting error in the Liberal tax policy after that policy had been released on 10 June at Box Hill in Melbourne.

Savings from cutting expenditure on certain programs were also included in savings from reducing payments to the states which, in turn, had included some payments under those same programs. The mistake involved several hundred million dollars. The tax policy document had been largely prepared in my office but also with the involvement of the relevant shadow ministers. All had been working under near impossible conditions, but when parties make mistakes of this kind, they have to carry the blame. No excuses are permitted. It was our mistake, and when it was exposed, it did us irreparable damage. If the policy had been prepared under different conditions, then adequate time would have been available for further checking, and I am sure that the mistake would not have arisen.

I had to go through the painful experience of calling a press conference, admitting the error and endeavouring to explain that the tax commitments we had made elsewhere in the policy could be properly funded in another manner. I did the best I could but the damage had already been done. Although he did not tell me at the time, Tony Eggleton later let me know that a private poll conducted for the party by Gary Morgan not long after the tax error was discovered showed that the Coalition was 18 points behind Labor.

Although it was of little ultimate consolation, the rest of the campaign went remarkably well for the Liberal Party. Bob Hawke refused to debate me, which barely earned a rebuke from the press.

The Liberal and National parties achieved a nationwide swing of 1 per cent. The final result on a two-party-preferred basis was 50.8 per cent for Labor to 49.2 per cent for the Coalition; we had actually shaded the ALP on the primary vote. Unfortunately for the opposition parties, the swing had not been evenly distributed, and despite the nationwide swing in its favour, the Coalition suffered a net loss of seats to the ALP. The Liberals won the suburban seats of Lowe in Sydney and Chisholm in Melbourne, but lost Michael Hodgman's seat of Denison in Tasmania as well as the Queensland seats of Forde, Petrie, Hinkler and Fisher. Labor also captured the Northern Territory from the Country Liberal Party. Hawke increased his majority from 16 to 24 seats.

The cumulative leadership difficulties within the Liberal Party, the broken coalition as well as the policy mistakes had severely damaged our chances. It was, nonetheless, clear from a regional analysis of the poll that electors had especially punished the Queensland Nationals. Not only did both parties lose seats in Queensland but the loss of the Northern Territory could also be attributed in no small part to the Queensland connection.

The 'Joh for PM' push destroyed more than the Coalition's prospects in the 1987 election. It began the Queensland Premier's own political decline. Not only had he been unsuccessful in his bid for Canberra but, in the process, had done much gratuitous harm to what was still seen as his side of politics in its bid to unseat the Hawke Government.

In a few short months he went from being a political Messiah to someone whose best years were behind him. To all but his most ardent followers Joh increasingly became a political liability.

For all the damage he had done to our prospects in the 1987 election, I recognised the huge contribution he made to his state as Premier. At his state memorial service in Kingaroy, some 18 years later, on 3 May 2005, I said, 'The reality nonetheless is that he made a massive contribution, a defining contribution, to the growth and the expansion of the state of Queensland.'

The 'Joh for PM' campaign had wrecked our chances of winning in 1987. I must acknowledge though that disunity in the Liberal Party helped create a vacuum on the anti-Labor side of politics. This encouraged Joh and his supporters to think that they could successfully indulge their ludicrous political fantasy. A completely united, strongly performing Liberal Party would not necessarily have aborted the Joh push but at the very least it would have given its architects greater pause to think.

17

THE COUP

After the election Andrew Peacock stood for the leadership against me and I defeated him by 41 to 28. He was then easily elected as deputy leader and immediately became shadow Treasurer. Thus began a period of time in which we worked together in quite close professional harmony.

There was a strong feeling within the party that I should be given a fair go. Most accepted that the period leading up to the election campaign, particularly the rupture of the federal coalition, had presented me with an impossible task at the 1987 election and although we had lost seats, the Liberal vote had held up better than might have been expected. Also, due in part to the influx of new MPs from both the 1984 and 1987 elections, there was greater support for my brand of economic policy. Peter Reith, Alexander Downer and Julian Beale had entered in 1984; John Hewson in 1987.

The period from the 1987 election until the end of 1988 was one of calm and unity within the Coalition, with one exception. That was the debate on Asian immigration. After the 1987 election the leaks stopped, and gradually the Liberal Party assumed the appearance of unity. The federal coalition was re-formed, and the federal influence of the Queensland Nationals greatly diminished.

The double-dissolution election had not given the Hawke Government control of the Senate, so the opposition was able to kill off the Australia Card by threatening to block any regulations made under Australia Card legislation, using its majority in the Senate. The Australia Card needed regulations to operate. Bob Hawke did not mourn the loss of the Australia Card.

1988 was significant for the heavy defeats inflicted by the Liberal Party or Coalition whenever there was an electoral contest. Yet in overall terms, the Coalition still finished the year without clear political dominance over the Government. This was because it proved impossible for me to break completely free of doubts regarding my leadership tenure.

There were four by-elections federally. On 6 February Michael Pratt won the seat of Adelaide from Labor, with a two-party-preferred swing of 8.5 per cent. The following month there was a 9 per cent two-party swing to the opposition in the safe Labor seat of Port Adelaide. On 9 April, the conservative voters of Queensland in the Darling Downs electorate of Groom showed what they thought of the antics of the Queensland National Party the previous year. The Liberal Party captured the seat with a 21 per cent swing in its favour away from the Nationals. There was a solid 5.2 per cent drift from Labor. In October of the same year in the seat of Oxley, vacated by the newly appointed Governor-General, Bill Hayden, there was an 11 per cent primary swing against the Labor Party, although it retained the seat. It would take the disendorsed Liberal Pauline Hanson, in 1996, to claim this Labor stronghold from the ALP.

On top of the federal swings there was the Liberal victory in New South Wales, with Nick Greiner ending almost 12 years of Labor Party government.

With Andrew Peacock and me working together, the new leadership flash-point became John Elliott. He had become the federal president of the Liberal Party just after the 1987 election and immediately set about making plenty of statements on policy matters. This was difficult for me and indeed for Andrew Peacock as most of the statements Elliott made were about economics. He regularly advocated the introduction of a broad-based consumption tax. That was something that had never been completely taken off the table, but the timing and political handling of it was entirely a matter for me and the parliamentary leadership.

Media interest in Elliott was huge. He was a boisterous, larger-than-life character, and there was a naïve, even childish, belief within some journalistic and business circles that what the country needed was a key business figure to have a 'sabbatical from the boardroom', go into parliament for a couple of terms, fix the country and then return to business. To these simplistic souls, it was all as easy as that. The two people who fitted this bill and who were most frequently touted were John Elliott and Ian McLachlan. The interface between business and politics is both frequent and very important. Understanding business is a crucial ingredient to being a successful politician in government, particularly at a senior level. Likewise a pragmatic understanding of the political process will always serve a businessman well. My experience, however, has been that an easy exchange from business life to the political and vice versa is often elusive. Understanding another's craft is one thing; practising it successfully is something entirely different.

None of these considerations in any way inhibited John Elliott and his backers, either inside or outside parliament. They saw him as the answer. I was regarded as shop-soiled and 'too political'. I may have had good policy ideas, most of which Elliott agreed with, but I had no 'charisma'. Andrew Peacock, on the other hand, had urbane communication skills but was seen as a policy lightweight. Elliott was the natural alternative, as he could boast both success and high profile. Whenever he made speeches they attracted enormous publicity and plainly stated slogans gained wide coverage. The fact that he appeared to have a lot of money also did not escape attention. Ironically, given the outcome of the election, the Liberal Party had ended the 1987 campaign with a surplus. During the last two weeks of the campaign our fortunes had improved sharply, and applying the age-old insurance principle, a number of business donors had come good right at the end when, regrettably, their donations could not be prudently spent. So John Elliott began his presidency of the Liberal Party by investing heavily in staff recruitment and other activities designed to build the organisation. This endeared him to many at Menzies House, the Canberra headquarters of the party.

In the public's eye the Howard–Peacock rivalry was replaced by the Elliott–Howard rivalry. Elliott and I had a difficult, and quite public, stand-off at the federal council meeting in April 1988. Miraculously this difficulty was overshadowed by the emphatic victory achieved by Bill Taylor, the Liberal candidate in Groom, on the Saturday of the federal council meeting.

In July of 1988 I visited Israel, Italy and Britain. In London I saw the British Prime Minister Margaret Thatcher, who had reached the zenith of her power and influence among centre-right adherents around the world. There was great value in the visit for me. I returned to Australia via the west in order to address the state conference of the WA division of the Liberal Party at Esperance. It was here that I made the first of my 'One Australia' speeches.

For some time I had been ruminating about the policy of multiculturalism. Inaugurated by Whitlam, embellished by Fraser, continued by Hawke, it was a policy with which I had never felt comfortable. Leaving aside for a moment the separate issue of the White Australia policy, Australia's post-World War II immigration policy had been built on the principle of assimilation. We would draw people from many countries, but when they came here they would become Australians. They would be assimilated into the host culture; they were then called New Australians.

That was a term with which I had grown up, and which I had always imagined accurately described the process. They were to become Australians and were new to our country; hence the term seemed to me to make good sense. I never believed that people who used the term did so in a patronising or offensive fashion. As time passed, however, and subsequent generations were born in Australia to those original 'New' Australians, the term was no longer appropriate.

Sensing the political power of individual ethnic groups, Whitlam embraced multiculturalism. There was to be more emphasis under the policy of multiculturalism on the individual characteristics of different ethnic groups. Assimilation was discarded as a term, it being described as too patronising and Anglo-Celtic-centric. It was one of those areas where nuance and degrees of emphasis mattered a lot. If multiculturalism simply meant that there should be a greater emphasis on honouring the culture and land of one's birth, then nobody could possibly object. By contrast, if it meant entrenching differences of culture without acknowledging the mainstream character of the host culture, then more difficult considerations were raised.

My view was that Australia should emphasise the common characteristics of the Australian identity. We should emphasise our unifying points rather than our areas of difference. I extended this thinking to our approach to Indigenous policy issues, where I disagreed with Bob Hawke's flirtation with the notion of a treaty. These were considerations I had in mind when I gave my speech in Esperance.

At the time of my Esperance speech, there was separate debate in Australia about the pace of Asian immigration. Clearly there were some people totally, and wrongly, opposed to any migration from Asia. There were others who were simply concerned about the speed of change in particular localities. My response to several questions on this issue, during two radio interviews, was to state simply that if it were in the interests of social cohesion to slow the pace of Asian immigration a little then that should occur.

The initial reaction of the public was supportive of what they saw, not as a racial outburst, but a commonsense remark about the rapidity of change. That had been my intention. I should have realised that my political opponents, and critics elsewhere, would seize on the comments and use them to attack me, as introducing racial considerations into debate on Australia's migration program. Bob Hawke exploited the situation very cleverly by introducing a motion into the parliament declaring that considerations of race should never be used as a criterion to determine flows of immigration to Australia.

When this motion was discussed in our party room, some, including Ian Macphee and others, argued that we should simply support Hawke's resolution and the matter would then disappear. I argued against this, believing that, if we were to do this, it would be seen as a repudiation of my earlier statements. I had got myself into a bind and was certain to be damaged regardless of how the matter was handled. In the final analysis the party resolved to vote against the resolution. Four of our number, including Philip Ruddock, crossed the floor to support the resolution.

The whole issue had done me considerable damage. It had divided the Liberal Party and diverted attention from the original issue of substance I had introduced during my speech in Western Australia, namely the real doubts I had about multiculturalism. It was a case of having antagonised everybody. Those who supported multiculturalism disagreed strongly with me. Those who may have agreed with my views on multiculturalism lost track of the debate as the Asian-immigration issue intruded, and those who might have agreed, on careful analysis, with what I had said about the pace of Asian immigration, felt that having raised the issue I had then gone quiet on it. I had been wrong to make the original statements on the pace of Asian immigration.

My handling of the issue lost me the support of some press columnists such as the *Australian*'s Greg Sheridan, with whom I had had a good relationship and who over the years had voiced support for many of my positions on other matters. The whole episode weakened my leadership authority within the Liberal Party.

In December 1988 I launched Future Directions, a policy and philosophical manifesto to which Graham Wynn of the Liberal secretariat made a major contribution. In time it would be seen as the document which foretold much of the philosophical direction of the government I would lead from

1996. Its themes were consistent and its policy content strong. It was a classic statement of the economic liberalism and social conservatism which would guide my years as Prime Minister. It depicted the traditional family in front of a white picket fence. There was much initial derision towards the manifesto, but a great deal of that receded as its thrust struck a real chord with middle Australia. I had tapped into something with a subliminal appeal to traditional Australian notions of stability and security in their family and national life.

Months later, and after I had been removed as Liberal leader in May 1989, Rod Cameron of Australian National Opinion Polls (ANOP), the long-time ALP pollster, and a real professional in his business, told me that Future Directions had really begun to bite, that I was 'onto something' and that, by implication, the Labor Party was mightily relieved that I had been removed. The value of this document was not only in what it said but also its easy identification with its author. No political leader can convincingly advocate a policy or a set of values unless he or she genuinely believes in them. I believed in every element of Future Directions. It told Australians that I was very much a conviction politician.

Although the Hawke Government remained in a strong political position, my own leadership appeared more secure in the early part of 1989. Unbeknown to me, John Elliott had quietly put his leadership hopes on hold at the end of the previous year, and the coming together of his supporters and those who wanted Peacock to replace me had begun.

Emboldened by the strong reception received by Future Directions, I became more assertive on a range of issues. I persuaded the NSW division not to field a Liberal candidate against the National Party for the Gwydir by-election made necessary by the retirement of Ralph Hunt. The by-election brought into parliament John Anderson, who was to become my longest-serving deputy prime minister. His maiden speech was that of a person with very strong values and a deep and practical Christianity, who would apply what he believed to the daily business of politics. I liked him from the start. John remains one of the most genuinely decent people I have met in public life.

Disunity between the Liberal and National parties had been such a negative for us at the 1987 election that I felt it essential, where possible, to overcompensate when it came to the two parties working together. I therefore set myself the task of achieving a joint Senate ticket between the Liberal and National parties in Victoria, feeling that if it could be brought about, thus emulating the situation in New South Wales, it would not only achieve the beneficial outcome of removing the need for three-cornered contests involving sitting members of each party, it would also be a symbol of unity.

Having directly lobbied the Victorian executive, and with the enthusiastic backing of Michael Kroger, the new and most effective Victorian president, I carried the day with the Liberals, many of whom had been reluctant, and, with Ian Sinclair's assistance, the leadership of the parliamentary National Party and organisation also came on board.

Jeff Kennett, the Liberal Opposition leader in Victoria, was sceptical, but in the end the push I started produced not only a joint Senate ticket but also a rebirth of the state coalition in Victoria. The formal consummation of these new arrangements took place after I had been removed as leader, but the decisive votes had been taken by the party's governing bodies in Victoria while I was still at the helm.

A difficult and sensitive policy then emerged — deregulation of the domestic wheat market. At that time a single desk operated, both in relation to wheat sales abroad and also sales on the domestic market. The Government indicated that it wished to deregulate the domestic wheat market, and the Coalition was required to form a view. Unless the Coalition adopted the same position as the Government, it would reflect poorly on our economic credentials. Once again it would look as if the Labor Party were more market oriented than, in particular, the Liberals. I made it very clear to both Ian Sinclair and Bruce Lloyd, the two National Party leaders, that I wanted a change in policy, knowing full well that the overwhelming bulk of the joint party room, who were Liberals, would support my position. I suspected that privately several Nationals were also on side. Ian Sinclair knew the pressure this would put on the National Party, and Bruce Lloyd was explosive in his response. To him it represented a fundamental repudiation of something the National Party had always stood for. It was a challenge to the McEwenite orderly marketing tradition still very much in the ascendancy amongst Nationals.

The Coalition decided to support deregulation of the domestic market while reaffirming the maintenance of the single desk for export sales. The Coalition held together, but only just. Despite his deep personal feelings, Bruce Lloyd pulled back from the brink of resigning as deputy leader of his party. At heart he was a good Coalition man.

On both the issue of the joint Senate ticket and wheat marketing policy I had achieved results. There was no dramatic change in the polls, although the Coalition remained reasonably competitive. There was, however, growing confidence in opposition ranks. We had tackled and resolved difficult issues. Parties paralysed by leadership doubts don't normally do that.

It was through Michael Kroger that I first met Peter Costello. They had been friends since university days and were close allies within the Victorian division. Early in 1989 Michael led a push to strengthen the federal representation from Victoria in the parliament by encouraging challenges against sitting MPs who were not perceived as performing well. One of those readily within his sights was Roger Shipton, MP for Higgins, who had followed John Gorton in the seat after the latter's departure from the Liberal Party in 1975. Shipton was a hardworking member, but not likely to make it to senior office in government or opposition. When John Elliott had been hankering after a seat, Higgins was always the one mentioned.

Elliott had never publicly declared an intention of standing for Higgins, so when his parliamentary ambitions went on ice in late 1988, nothing was said. It remained the case, however, that Shipton was still highly vulnerable to a challenge. This created a perfect opening for Costello. He was young, very articulate, and with a well-developed reputation for political toughness. His career at the Bar had been successful, with his appearance on behalf of Fred Stauder in the Dollar Sweets case an industrial relations landmark, winning much praise. Costello had Kroger's strong support. He lived very close to Higgins. Not surprisingly, he nominated against Shipton for the seat.

Interest in Higgins was as nothing compared with the stoush which was developing in the nearby seat of Goldstein, held by Ian Macphee. He had been challenged by David Kemp, former close advisor to Malcolm Fraser when he was PM and also until very recently director of the Victorian division of the Liberal Party. Kemp was close to Kroger, but it was an over-simplification to describe his nomination as a Kroger-inspired head office push to throw out Macphee.

The Canberra press gallery virtually demanded that I intervene in Goldstein to save Macphee. Being a 'small l' Liberal, he was one of their favourites. This was all about stopping the dark reactionary forces of Michael Kroger taking over the Liberal Party in Victoria, although nothing of the kind was occurring. As it happened, one of the key Liberals of local influence in Goldstein, who had encouraged Kemp to stand, was Sir John 'Bill' Anderson, a veteran of World War II and former president of the Victorian division. A party grandee, Anderson was also a man who Malcolm

Fraser greatly respected, although they disagreed about the Goldstein preselection. The former PM strongly backed Macphee.

Given the pressure I was under over Goldstein, not only from the press but also from a growing number of MPs, who always feel nervous and experience an extra charge of collegiality when one of their number is under challenge — after all, I could be next — I decided to do some research of my own. I rang Anderson and was politely but bluntly told to stay out of Goldstein. According to him there was a lot of unhappiness with Macphee within Goldstein branches and influential locals had invited Kemp's nomination; there would be deep grassroots resentment if I poked my nose into the preselection. He confirmed what Kroger had told me all along.

Kroger and I had built a solid relationship. He had been a huge help in my drive for a joint Senate ticket, kept me informed of what was going on in Victoria and strongly supported my leadership. He had lifted the morale of the party in his state. It is a lasting loss for the party that he has never entered parliament. He would have gone a very long way.

Events were moving to a weekend of preselections, commencing with the Higgins ballot on 5 May, which Costello won easily. Kroger rang me that evening, simply saying, 'Peter Howard Costello', which was the future Treasurer's full name. The next day saw the drama of Goldstein, with media coverage at absurd levels. Kemp won comfortably, it clearly being the case that local Liberals wanted someone else. Then on Sunday, Julian Beale, who held the seat of Deakin, defeated Ken Aldred for the safer electorate of Bruce. There had been a redistribution which had touched both seats. Aldred later defeated Macphee for the nomination in Deakin, despite the latter's endorsement by Andrew Peacock, by then the freshly reminted Opposition leader.

These preselections, especially the one in Goldstein, were an important backdrop to the sudden leadership change which occurred the following Tuesday, 9 May. Although each was a good outcome in its own right, the combined impact played into the hands of my critics. When an MP loses his or her preselection, it is so easy for remarks such as 'the boss could have done more to help you', to gain currency. Peacock knew what buttons to push, and he pushed them. In the ABC *Four Corners* program which I mention shortly, John Moore cited my handling of the Victorian preselections (meaning Goldstein) as delivering the final impetus to the push to get rid of me as leader.

*   *   *

The coup against me had been well planned to take place at a routine party meeting. I did not know about it until confronted by Andrew Peacock, Fred Chaney and Austin Lewis (leader and deputy Senate leader respectively) in my office the night before, and was therefore denied any chance to organise in my own defence. Peacock won convincingly by a vote of 44 to 27. I was devastated, as I felt that I had really begun to turn the corner with strong leadership on hard issues. I was angry with Chaney for not having warned me of what was coming. He was entitled to switch support to Peacock but, given our past friendship, should not have been part of the ambush. I felt that it was the end of my dream to be PM. At a subsequent news conference I replied, 'Like Lazarus with a triple bypass', to a question about my returning to the leadership. The best lines are never scripted.

The post-coup atmosphere in the party turned ugly after the hubristic performance of Peacock's numbers men on a *Four Corners* program when four of them, Wilson Tuckey, Chris Puplick, John Moore and Peter Shack, boasted about how clever and secretive they had been in planning and executing the plot to remove me as leader. That program alienated many traditional Liberal people, who felt that the change in leadership had been conducted in the 'wrong' way. There was a protocol to all of these things, and plotting in secret was not meant to be part of an open process of deciding just who could better lead the party.

The Liberal Party made a mistake changing leaders just as I was consolidating my position within the electorate. Momentum had developed out of Future Directions and the strong and successful positions I had taken on the joint Senate ticket in Victoria and wheat policy. That was to be of no avail.

Sudden changes in the leadership of the two Coalition parties occurred on the same day, with Ian Sinclair being replaced by Charles Blunt at the helm of the Nationals. A new and uncertain era for the Coalition had commenced.

Quite apart from the negative impact of the *Four Corners* program, the problem Peacock and his backers had was that the rationale for the leadership change was never established in the minds of the Australian public. It did not signal a sharply different course on policy substance. To the average voter, the change in leadership was nothing more than the product of an internal power struggle.

Andrew Peacock did not handle the transition well. He must have known that I would react angrily to such an ambush. Peacock offered me the shadow Education portfolio which, important though it was, felt to me like rubbing salt into the wound. Defence was an area of potential interest to me, had status and would have allowed me to range fairly broadly, and I would have happily taken it, but Peacock had decided to give it to Jim Carlton.

In the wake of the *Four Corners* program, I said that I would not serve on the front bench whilst Tuckey and Moore were there. Some saw this as petulance; others saw it as perfectly understandable. A coup that was meant to unify and strengthen the party left it looking more divided than it had at any time since the 1987 election.

For the first time in 14 years, I went to the backbench and commenced, almost immediately, writing a weekly column for the *Australian*. I loved doing this and enjoyed immensely my association with Frank Devine, the editor of that paper. It was a friendship which continued until Frank's death in 2009. I wrote about politics, but also about other issues as well. One memorable piece which I enjoyed penning, and which attracted some complimentary reviews, was about the heroic status of Allan Border, who led the Australian cricket team to an Ashes retrieval victory in August 1989 at Old Trafford.

Although I never set out to attack the Coalition's position on issues, I strongly defended the policies I had developed. A notable case was the pilots' dispute, which involved Bob Hawke backing both the ACTU and the airlines against the pilots in a pay dispute. I argued that it was something that should be resolved in the marketplace. This was closer to the real effect of Hawke's strategy than Andrew Peacock's.

In November 1989, Peacock sacked Wilson Tuckey and offered me a front-bench position as spokesman on Manufacturing Industry. I felt that insisting on my original condition that Moore be sacked as well would have seemed petty, but I didn't particularly enjoy going back to the front bench. I lost a fair bit of money as Frank Devine sacked me immediately as a columnist. My several months back in the shadow cabinet were quite dismal. I did not think the Coalition's policies were convincing, although to be fair the economic action plan, which contained detailed tax rebates and family benefits and which had been put together by John Hewson and John Stone, won a lot of support. It gave Andrew Peacock a document to argue for and a set of policies to advocate. He was no policy innovator but he had a capacity to absorb a brief and argue publicly for policies, once they had been carefully formulated.

The Coalition should have won the 1990 election. The Australian economy was in recession, unemployment was over 9 per cent, housing interest rates were at 17 per cent or more and the Hawke Government had been in power for seven years. The polls were quite unclear, and it was obvious that preferences from the Democrats and the Greens would be crucial.

There are always a number of reasons why a party loses an election. In 1990 a significant, but not the only, reason for our loss was an assessment the electorate made about the economic competence of the opposition and its leader. The public knew that the Australian economy was in an appalling condition, and they asked themselves whether the Coalition could do a better job of managing it than the incumbent Labor Party. In the end, sufficient people in the right places for Labor decided in favour of the devil they knew.

The policy credibility of the Coalition was mortally wounded by the failure of the opposition to produce a health policy. I had only recently returned to the shadow cabinet when I learned that there was no policy and the plan was merely to outline some principles about health. When I expressed alarm about the political impact of this, I was promptly told by John Stone and several others that I hadn't been around for some of the earlier discussions and that there was frankly no alternative, given that our expenditure and tax policies had already been put to bed.

Peter Shack, our spokesman, held a news conference revealing that there would not be a detailed health policy and then drove a nail into the Liberal Party's coffin by saying that the Coalition did not have a particularly good record when it came to health policy. How could we really expect people to vote for us?

It was a very uneven election outcome. Due largely to the economic wreckage which Victoria had become under the Cain/Kirner regime, the Liberal Party won no fewer than nine seats in that state. Sharing the ABC's election night commentary with the Foreign Minister Gareth Evans, I heard him describe it to one of his colleagues on the phone as the 'slaughter of the innocents'. I had never known him to sound so solicitous towards members of the Victorian socialist left before. In other parts of the country, most particularly in Queensland and New South Wales, the swing went in the opposite direction.

The result was formally in doubt for some days, but it was obvious to me on the night that the Coalition had fallen short. The Coalition had outpolled Labor on the primary vote by some 4 per cent, but the strong flow of preferences on green issues had saved Hawke's bacon. Hawke and Graham Richardson's strategy of courting Greens preferences had found no counter at all from the Coalition. Naturally, I thought that if the party had not changed leaders in May 1989 the Coalition would have had a better chance of winning. Most of the campaign was about the economy, and I was seen as having better economic management credentials to those of Andrew Peacock. Those musings were, however, not only academic but quite pointless.

Politics is always about today's reality, not that great realm of what might have been. The party had decided to rid itself of my leadership and reinstate Andrew Peacock. That change having failed, it had no intention of revisiting its decision of May 1989. Whatever feelings I may have had on election night that the party might look again to me as a leader, I was quickly to learn that there was no appetite, even among some of my closest supporters, for a reprise of the Howard leadership. The overwhelming mood in the party was that it should move on from the Howard/Peacock years.

My loyal but blunt friend Peter Reith told me during an overnight stay at his home just after the election, that I should forget about any prospect of returning to the leadership. As he put it very candidly, 'You are entitled to feel that you have been badly treated; the party made a huge mistake getting rid of you as you would almost certainly have won the election if you had still been leader, but that is all in the past. The Australian public want the Coalition to look at fresh faces for leadership positions, and not go back to the past.' He encapsulated the mood then prevailing. I hated hearing this but came to respect the candour Reith had displayed.

Andrew Peacock and his followers wanted John Hewson to succeed him as leader. Peacock had wisely made Hewson the shadow Treasurer when he replaced me as leader. Hewson had impressed from the moment he took over as shadow Treasurer. He was a skilled economist, understood the political context of the economic debate, and had developed something of an appetite for political life.

Ready for it or not, John Hewson's time had arrived. There was a surge of support for him within the parliamentary party and also in the broader community. Peter Reith nominated for the leadership as well. He laid out a detailed program in support of his candidature, including a commitment to the introduction of a broad-based indirect tax as part of overall taxation reform. Reith never had any prospect of winning, and sections of the press heaped derision on his enthusiastic campaigning. But his behaviour demonstrated a competitive streak in a man who would come to be a most effective minister. I voted for Hewson out of a combination of past loyalties and a belief that he was seen as the man of the moment, but I had reservations about him.

During a brief discussion in Sydney just before the ballot, I told Hewson that I thought he was making a mistake accepting what had effectively become a draft for the leadership, that he had no idea how difficult it was to lead a political party, and that he ought to continue as shadow Treasurer and gain more political experience. His response was mild but clearly indicated that he saw my remarks as largely self-serving and not to be taken seriously. This was partly true, but my fears proved well founded.

Hewson won the ballot overwhelmingly, by 62 to 13. Peter Reith was elected deputy leader by a comfortable margin and became shadow Treasurer. We didn't know it at the time, but the party was on the road to Fightback!

18

THE 'UNLOSABLE'
ELECTION

As leader, John Hewson looked and sounded fresh, new, bright and quite different. Almost from the beginning he asserted that he was a non-politician, implying his lack of familiarity with politics was a virtue rather than a potential liability. For a long time this seemed to work. The Australian public was attracted to a person who clearly knew a lot about economic issues and seemed intent on fixing the nation's problems, not scoring political points.

Within a short period Hewson moved ahead of Hawke in the opinion polls, and before long stories were being written about how, and not if, John and Carolyn Hewson would inherit the Lodge. Hewson was given extraordinary authority within the parliamentary party and the Liberal organisation. He required and received both support and acclaim for everything he wanted. For a long period of time it ran smoothly. The party was united with two new faces at the top. Also, in the National Party Tim Fischer had scored an upset victory over John Sharp and Peter McGauran to become leader.

Andrew Peacock and I were both part of the shadow cabinet, with Andrew being shadow Attorney General. Hewson had given me the shadow portfolio of Employment, Industrial Relations and Training. I could not have asked for more. It gave me responsibility for an area with which I was identified and about which I had strong convictions. It would be centre stage in the political/economic debate between 1990 and the next election.

Although I still felt a lingering disappointment at the unfair frustration of my own leadership ambitions, I saw in this shadow portfolio a real opportunity to pursue issues in which I was deeply interested. I had been arguing the case for reform for six or seven years, and the economic circumstances of 1990 required more than ever, in my judgement, fundamental reform of Australia's labour markets.

In the middle of 1991, the leadership volcano erupted for Labor with the disclosure of the infamous Kirribilli House agreement whereby Hawke and Keating had entered into a secret undertaking, witnessed only by Peter Abeles, a close friend of the PM, and Bill Kelty, the secretary of the ACTU, that if Labor were successful at that poll, Hawke would hand the prime ministership to Keating after the 1990 election. By any measure it had been a monstrous fraud on the Australian people. They went to the polls in 1990 in complete ignorance of this secret deal.

By mid-1991 Keating had grown tired of waiting and, realising that Hawke would not honour the deal, had it disclosed to the public and challenged for the leadership. His first lunge at Hawke, on 3 June 1991, failed; Hawke received 66 votes and Keating 44. It ended their long and successful partnership, with Keating going to the backbench and John Kerin becoming Treasurer. Hawke never recovered from the damage inflicted by this first challenge.

Late in 1990, after a thorough debate, the Coalition had decided, in principle, to embrace a broad-based indirect tax with compensating reductions in personal income tax as policy for the upcoming election. Peter Reith, as shadow Treasurer, was put in charge of drafting the details of what ultimately became Fightback! although John Hewson was heavily involved and its real architect.

The key to successfully advocating this huge policy initiative was directly linking the introduction of a broad-based goods and services tax (GST) to major reductions in personal income tax. Promoted as an aggregate reform proposal, it had appeal. If the change were seen as introducing a new tax, it was politically dangerous. A sign of this came from the NSW state election, held on 25 May 1991. Labor's Bob Carr did better than expected, in part due to his constant campaigning against the introduction of a GST, which he associated with his state Liberal opponents.

All of the internal resources of the Coalition were devoted to the preparation of the Fightback! manifesto, which would ultimately embrace not only the introduction of a GST of 15 per cent and big income tax cuts, but also the abolition of wholesale sales tax, payroll tax levied by the states as well as other state taxes, plus major reforms to health and social security policies. For good measure, fuel excise was also to be dropped. As 1991 wore on, pressure built for publication of the detailed policy. This was understandable, but for good reasons the Coalition was determined that the policy be bulletproof. It remained haunted by the Box Hill disaster of 1987 and the absent health policy fiasco of 1990.

Finally, on 21 November 1991, Fightback! was released and received nothing short of a rapturous reception, further boosting the Coalition's poll position. Australia was in the throes of a deep recession, with a sense amongst Australians that there was something fundamentally wrong with how the nation was functioning. There was willingness, at a time of despair, to accept big changes. John Hewson appeared to have a plan to fix the nation's problems, and that was immensely attractive. Fightback! was not forced down the throats of reluctant parliamentary Liberals by a bullying leadership. Hewson took his party with him: wet and dry, right and left, all Liberals backed the manifesto.

Bob Hawke's inability to respond effectively to Fightback! finally destroyed his prime ministership. He had no cut-through answer to such a sweeping blueprint. Nor indeed did his increasingly hapless Treasurer, John Kerin. The end for him came after an embarrassing press conference when Kerin was unable to recall the full description of the acronym GOS (gross operating surplus) in describing some economic terms. Hawke sacked Kerin and replaced him with Ralph Willis, who had long coveted the job of Treasurer. His first tenure in the position was to be short-lived.

Hawke's political impotence in the face of Fightback! was the final straw for sufficient Labor members to desert him and back Keating. High farce intervened when a group of Hawke's cabinet colleagues, comprising Kim Beazley, Gareth Evans, Robert Ray, Nick Bolkus, Michael Duffy and Gerry Hand, all of whom were committed Hawke men, had gone to the Prime Minister urging him to stand aside. He had listened to them and responded that he had no intention of standing aside for Paul Keating. As their appointed spokesman, Kim Beazley had then fronted the media, described the nature of their waiting upon Hawke, and declared that they all accepted his decision to stay on and fight and would support him in the ballot. It was extraordinary but, in a sense, understandable. They had no desire to destroy Labor's most successful leader ever.

The pressure forced the holding of another ballot, on 19 December 1991, and this time Keating triumphed by 56 to 51.

Hawke's downfall was a dramatic occasion at Parliament House. We in the Coalition simply watched as the Labor Party pulled down a man who had won four successive elections. There was plenty of bad blood in Parliament House on that December night and it was all on the Labor side.

An emotional Hawke made a statement to the parliament which John Hewson responded to, with me, Andrew Peacock and others making contributions which, in the proper tradition of a parliamentary system, contained laudatory remarks about Hawke's contribution to Australian political life. Bob Hawke had been a good Labor Prime Minister. His early years had been committed and reformist and at that time he established a real bond with the Australian public, which impressed me.

Immediately afterwards, I called to see Hawke in his by then bare prime ministerial office. A strange atmosphere prevailed. The office was already bereft of paper and seemingly of staff. The only people who appeared to be there with the Prime Minister were his personal security detail. I offered some words of commiseration to Hawke. It was the end of a particular Labor era. It was the first and only time that I would visit the PM's office in the New Parliament House until I was sworn in as prime minister almost five years later.

As the recession continued, with all its gloom, the new Prime Minister, Paul Keating, embarked on a round of consultation with business and community leaders. I am certain that from the beginning he had in mind a comprehensive economic statement, but understandably went through the motions of widespread consultations. Hawke quit parliament immediately after the visit of President George H.W. Bush, from 31 December to 3 January, was over. The by-election in Hawke's old seat, Wills, was to be a disaster for the Labor Party, but also a setback for the Liberal Party and the first danger signal for John Hewson.

The electorate of Wills had always been a safe Labor one in the inner suburbs of Melbourne. No doubt its good burghers were irked at having to traipse back to the polls long before a general election, but the tribal instincts of Labor voters were normally much stronger than Liberals'. Labor was expected to win the seat comfortably.

Both parties made errors in their candidate selections. The chosen Labor candidate was Bill Kardamitsis, a Greek community activist within the electorate. The Liberal Party chose a businessman, John Delacretaz, of Swiss-Italian background, whose command of English was poor. The bolter and ultimate victor was something of a local football legend named Phil Cleary, who was a regular ABC football commentator. His politics were Labor or to the left of Labor. In time, he became a very attractive choice for the mainstream of Wills voters. They had no intention of electing a Liberal; they didn't want Kardamitsis because he seemed too identified with a particular ethnic group, so the Independent, Cleary, proved to be the easy alternative.

As the 1982 by-election in Flinders had demonstrated quite dramatically, there is huge focus on individual candidates in by-elections. Every utterance of Kardamitsis and Delacretaz was recorded and analysed by the media. It was said that one wag was asked who he was voting for and he replied, 'The Australian'. This was an irreverent reference to the fact that both Kardamitsis and Delacretaz spoke with strong accents.

John Hewson made the mistake of visiting the electorate no fewer than 13 times during the campaign. This was overkill and would magnify the focus on him if the Liberals did not enjoy a big swing.

Cleary won the seat easily. Superficial media reaction was that it had been a huge reverse for Labor. Calmer analysis suggested that there was no comfort to be derived by the Liberal Party from this by-election either.

In March 1992, Paul Keating produced his One Nation statement in response not only to Fightback! but also the continuing recession. He offered personal tax cuts equivalent to those contained in Fightback! but, of course, without the broad-based goods and services tax. The arithmetic on which the personal tax cuts were based was highly questionable. The Treasury was largely shut out, and there were too many economic projections made in the PM's office alone for the sake of good policy making. This issue received insufficient attention from a parliamentary press gallery which was increasingly obsessed with the personal contest between Paul Keating and John Hewson.

Paul Keating was always far more popular with the parliamentary press gallery than he was with the Australian public. He and they had a mutual fascination with each other. It was a classic case of what the Americans might call 'beltway infatuation'. His rhetorical performances at question time, involving fierce invective and heavy attacks on leading members of the opposition, commanded rave reviews from the gallery, but they left the average citizen, worried about his or her job or mortgage, cold and uninterested.

His One Nation statement enabled Keating to argue that he too had a plan, but it was less harsh than Fightback! It gave him some lift but did not alter the fundamentals. Hewson still appeared well on track to win the election, due in the early part of 1993.

Having produced a policy manifesto of sorts, Keating then set about building his political narrative that John Hewson was an extremist. He used the vehicle of question time to pursue his assault. Relatively innocuous remarks made by Hewson about the involvement of the private sector in relation to social security were grabbed by Keating, shamefully exaggerated and turned into dire warnings that even pensions were at risk if the Liberals won. On one occasion he claimed that pensions would be paid through accountants.

However exaggerated they may have been, these attacks began to unnerve Hewson, and some of his responses and rhetoric became clumsy. At the end of August, John Hewson said that one could always tell which houses in a street were rented; it sounded patronising to poorer people and was badly received. Some weeks later he attacked the NSW Opposition leader Bob Carr for not having a driver's licence, and also left the impression that he was critical of Carr for not having any children. He may not have intended any offence, and did in fact apologise to Carr, but the cumulative impact of these incidents unsettled his supporters.

Then, out of the blue, in the parliament on 5 November, Keating declared that if the Coalition won the upcoming election, then it would have complete freedom to implement the GST proposed in Fightback! Labor would not try to block it in the Senate. Foolishly, Hewson, Reith and others saw this as capitulation by the Labor Party. They even ostentatiously shook hands with each other, loudly declaring that Labor had surrendered. I had a very different view. What Keating had done was to crystallise the principal issue of the coming election around a goods and services tax, making it very clear that the only way to stop a goods and services tax was to re-elect him as Prime Minister. Keating said, 'I want it made totally clear that a vote for Hewson is a vote for the GST. No Democrats or any other group will save Australia from that.'[1] Politically, it was a good tactic.

Along with other colleagues I had begun to hear complaints from business figures, particularly in the car industry, that Hewson would not listen to their legitimate concerns about some of his policies. Andrew Peacock and I compared notes and sought the views, in my case of Robert Johnston, the head of Toyota, and in Andrew's case, Jacques Nasser, head of Ford (later chairman of BHP-Billiton).

Both of them said that the policy embraced by the opposition was far too hardline. They were fearful of any further tariff reductions but accepted that the old days of high protection had gone. They did not ask that the next scheduled tariff reduction be postponed, only that there be a further Industry Commission inquiry about the state of the car industry before it occurred.

That seemed reasonable to both Andrew and me, especially to a party still in opposition. We put it to John, but he was dismissive, implying, as he often did, that the old thinking in the Liberal Party about industry protection was creeping back. He showed no political touch at all, and only encouraged the view in sections of the business community that he was an economic zealot.

Nonetheless, cracks were to appear in the Hewson façade. The Victorian division had conducted its own polling in individual seats. Its president and director began pressuring Hewson to water down the GST. They claimed that the polling showed a drift away from the Coalition and that Hewson's radical economic manifesto was the problem.

Michael Kroger, no longer the Victorian Liberal president but someone with whom I maintained close links, buttonholed me in Melbourne one night and said that the party was in real trouble. 'People don't want a GST. Why are we inflicting a GST on the public? Why don't we just focus on the weakness of the economy and the hostility of Australians towards Keating?' he said. He told me about the Victorian polling, and the line he and other Victorians ran was that food should be taken out of the reach of the GST. Hewson's first reaction was to resist this; so was mine. I bought the argument that 'the broader the base, the lower the rate' was the immutable rule when it came to indirect taxes. Food was covered by the GST I took to the people in 1998.

I did not think that Hewson would shift. Before long, however, he called a meeting of senior colleagues, including me, and sought our views. It was obvious that he intended to soften the GST.

The shift was announced on the kerbside of a Brisbane street after a discussion he had held with Archbishop Peter Hollingworth, head of the Anglican Church in Brisbane. He subsequently announced the details of the change in an address to the National Press Club on 18 December 1992. He excluded food and childcare expenses from the GST. John Hewson also pointed to an additional tax on luxury cars to cancel out an otherwise big fall in their prices following the introduction of the GST.

In retrospect, this had been a psychological victory for Keating. Although in the short term softening the GST might win some public support, in the medium to longer term it represented a major breach in the defences of Fort Hewson. Until then he had been the uncompromising face of hardline long-term economic reform which the dire state of the nation demanded. Now he looked for the all the world like any other political leader, tempering his policies and his rhetoric to win votes. There was nothing wrong with that; the problem for John Hewson was that in the past he had publicly derided such political impulses.

A further complication for the federal coalition was the strong industrial relations reform drive of the new Kennett Government in Victoria. Kennett was elected with a mandate to change industrial relations law, but in announcing the abolition of the 17.5 per cent leave loading, he went beyond his election policy. There was a severe backlash, and we feared there would be adverse federal consequences. So on Saturday 12 December, John Hewson, Peter Reith, Andrew Peacock and I called to see Kennett, his deputy and Treasurer Alan Stockdale, and Phil Gude, Victorian Industrial Relations minister. We asked Kennett to postpone the implementation of some of his industrial relations legislation until after the federal election, due in only a few months time. He completely rejected our entreaties. Jeff Kennett had no intention of accommodating his federal colleagues.

Despite all this, we remained confident that Keating would be defeated when the election was held. The polls had softened for the Coalition, but there remained deep hostility to the Prime Minister, and the 'It's time' factor, combined with the continuing severity of the recession, meant that the omens for the Liberal Party remained very positive. At the end of 1992, unemployment stood at 10.9 per cent, and the budget remained deeply in the red. Due to the recession, interest rates had fallen. It was an abysmal economic scorecard. Many Australians remained resentful about the recession the Prime Minister said they 'had to have' and were determined to reap vengeance on the person they blamed for that recession: Paul John Keating.

The Prime Minister called the election for 13 March 1993 and started a campaign which many believed would be his one and only as Labor leader. Instead the campaign turned into a disaster for John Hewson and the

Liberal Party. The accumulated strain of dealing with an opponent whom he could never match politically caught up with Hewson and resulted in a defeat which left the party spent and demoralised.

Sadly, John Hewson was unable to sell Fightback! in a politically convincing fashion. That manifesto was a very courageous political document in the proper sense of that expression. It identified Australia's economic problems and provided a comprehensive response. One might argue with some of the policy prescriptions but what could not be contested was the willingness of the Coalition to deal with every aspect of Australia's economic malaise. There was no political timidity about Fightback!, or its author, John Hewson.

The debacle involving the birthday cake, when in an interview he could not explain, in simple language, the impact of the GST on the cake, came to symbolise the complications John Hewson encountered in the campaign. Having spent some of his time as Opposition leader deriding the old, and to him, darker political arts such as repetition of clear principles and statements on radio and television, he learned all too late that these skills were essential to winning government.

I watched his debate on Channel Nine against Paul Keating, anchored by Mike Willesee. Those who viewed the program with me sneered at Keating's crass, almost gutter-snipe tactics. He did not behave like a prime minister. Perhaps because he knew that if he behaved like a prime minister he would lose the election. Keating's goal was to make Hewson the issue, not — as should have been the case — allow his government's economic competence or otherwise to be the main campaign focus. That particular debate put the GST, which Keating repeatedly described as a 'monster new tax' or a 'monster' and 'a lifestyle change', front and centre of the campaign. Keating's tactic succeeded, and from then on the election campaign was very much a referendum on the GST.

The Liberal campaign was dealt a psychological blow with the announcement during the campaign by Brian Mulroney, the Progressive Conservative Prime Minister of Canada, that he was resigning. His party had fraternal links with our Liberal Party and it was widely reported that he had decided to quit because of the unpopularity of his government, due in turn to the botched introduction of a broad-based consumption tax in Canada. Whatever the real merits, the loud and clear message was that Canadians had rejected the equivalent of the GST being proposed by the Liberals in Australia.

In my opinion the Coalition's health policy proved to be a very heavy liability, particularly amongst women voters. The severe restrictions proposed for bulk billing and other elements of the policy, which combined to significantly weaken Medicare, were immensely unpopular. Bob Woods, the Liberal health spokesman, lost his seat of Lowe, which he had won in 1987. 1993 would be the last time that the Liberal Party would propose major changes to Medicare.

Hewson's campaign tactics were poor; his rallies were unsettling for people. They were not the forum in which to explain intricate policies. He failed to appear on all the major television programs in the final week of the campaign delivering the reassuring messages about his radical manifesto which Australians desperately wanted to hear. It cost him very dearly in the final analysis. The polls had shown that Australians wanted to change their government, but Keating was able to raise sufficient doubts about Hewson and his program to scare enough people into believing that Hewson would be a dangerous option.

The field evidence was less encouraging than the polls. Three weeks out from the election, I addressed a small gathering of people at the Cumberland Business Club in the electorate of Parramatta in Sydney. People of this type were part of our support base. To my dismay, I was peppered with questions about the detail of how the tax plan would work. It was obvious that these small businessmen had real concerns about the complexities that might be visited upon their activities. That this was the case just three weeks before the election, despite the fact that Fightback! had been in the public domain for some 15 months, really concerned me.

My electorate office was inundated with requests for explanations, and examples of how the new system would work, all indicating a hunger for detail based on growing doubts about the workability of the policy. During the leader debates, Keating probably shaded Hewson. To most observers, including me, the ABC host of the debates, Kerry O'Brien, appeared to go in to bat for Keating in the second debate.

Despite the final Newspoll showing a dramatic contraction in the Coalition's lead over Labor, I still expected a victory. Like so many others, I found it virtually impossible to believe that a government which had been in power for 10 years could possibly get re-elected with such high levels of unemployment and the economy still severely recessed. Yet I was to be proved wrong. It was quite clear after the results had been posted that the Coalition had comprehensively lost the election during the campaign.

Doubts about the Coalition's policies became the issue, rather than the dire state of the economy. With a final rush Keating actually achieved a positive swing over the 1990 result.

It was a remarkable political achievement for Keating. He spoke the truth when he described it as 'the sweetest victory of all'.[2] Politically he had completely overwhelmed John Hewson and despite being surrounded by appalling economic figures, had managed to make the radical nature of Hewson's agenda the issue and frightened enough swinging voters back to the Labor fold.

I had spent election day thanking supporters on polling booths in my electorate and invited the campaign team back to our home in Wollstonecraft for drinks. Tasmania had already moved from daylight saving, so early results came through from that state at approximately 6 pm. They were a real shock, showing a significant swing to the Labor Party in all seats. I knew then that the Liberal Party could not win as there was nothing in the campaign suggesting that Tasmania would vote differently from the remainder of the country. The rest of the evening was dismal, and within a fairly short period of time it was clear that we had lost.

John Hewson had implied before the campaign that this was his one shot at the prime ministership, and that if he failed he would give up the leadership. This was of a piece with his style. He would give his all to one go at the nation's top job, with a no-holds-barred agenda to reform the country, and if that agenda were rejected then he would retire from the scene. The very next day we were to learn that this was not to be the case. He not only made it clear that he wanted to continue as leader but announced, to the amazement of many people, that he intended to abandon the GST.

This was done without any consultation with his colleagues and was greeted with incredulity. Fran Bailey, the member for McEwen, who had won her seat in 1990 and was defeated in 1993, remarked acidly to me several days later, 'It is a great pity that he hadn't abandoned the GST on Thursday instead of leaving it until Sunday. I might then have held my seat.' Thankfully Fran returned to the parliament in 1996 and gallantly held that marginal seat until retiring from parliament at the 2010 election.

In immediately dumping the GST, Hewson diminished his status in the eyes of many in the party. It was one thing to lose an election after toiling to win acceptance of a radical, but courageous, economic platform. It made matters worse to forthwith jettison the central element of that platform after the loss of the election. Many colleagues had gone to the barricades, and some had lost their seats, believing in and supporting the Hewson prescription. To have that prescription arbitrarily put aside without party consultation, within 24 hours of the election defeat, left them feeling badly used.

So for the second time in a row, the Liberal Party had failed to win government in severe economic circumstances with high unemployment and other negatives. It was only human of me to think immediately of how things might have been different in both 1990 and 1993 if I had been in charge. I began, on election night, to contemplate whether or not the party might finally look back to me as the experienced hand, the one with both political skills and economic credibility. Several colleagues telephoned and raised that possibility.

Within a few days I decided that I would again seek the leadership. It seemed to me inconceivable that the Liberal Party would re-elect Hewson. The party had invested him with enormous support, yet he had lost an election in circumstances where victory should have been assured. There was no one else. Peacock had lost twice: in 1984 and 1990. Reith was heavily identified with the GST, which had been summarily dumped, and did not in any event command a lot of support in the parliamentary party. At that stage Alexander Downer was not seen as being 'foreman material'. To me and quite a number around me, it seemed logical, indeed obvious, that the sensible thing for the party to do was to bring me back. I was to be proved completely wrong.

I had not calculated that more time and another failed leadership was needed before the Liberal Party turned back to me. Those with long memories, like Andrew Peacock, rallied behind Hewson. So did John Elliott and Ron Walker. One exception to this, interestingly enough, was John Moore, who made it clear to me that he would support my return.

In the ballot, Peter Costello ran as deputy leader, effectively partnering me. John Hewson defeated me by 47 to 30. Michael Wooldridge was elected deputy leader over Peter Costello by a slightly smaller margin.

I was completely deflated by the result. The scale of Hewson's win told me in no uncertain terms that there was still huge resistance within the party to my return and that at that stage, even in the wake of the shock defeat, a sizeable chunk of Liberal MPs would not have a bar of my again leading them. For some of them, it was a continuation of old animosity. For others, it was a simple unwillingness to go back in time to find a new leader for the party. They held the view that once someone had led the party and had been removed, then it was untenable to bring that person back. The absurdity of Hewson's re-election was that virtually no one saw him as a viable leader in other than the short term. Having lost in 1993, very few people thought that he could win in 1996. Most assumed that he would be replaced by someone else well before then. The question was — who?

Reith went to the backbench after the 1993 election and Hewson had therefore need of a new shadow Treasurer. He was not going to give the job to me and opted for Alexander Downer. This was the move that would deliver Downer the leadership of the party just over a year later. Usually in opposition the only prominent position other than that of leader is that of shadow Treasurer. An intelligent, energetic media-savvy shadow Treasurer can obtain constant, and often saturation, coverage in the media. Downer was all of these things and he did an excellent job in 12 months or more in the position. Hewson returned me to essentially my previous position and added the responsibility of manager of opposition business in the house.

Postmortems on the 1993 election frequently attributed the Coalition's loss to the radical nature of Fightback! That was never a balanced judgement. John Hewson will always deserve credit for directly confronting the nation's economic ills in the early 1990s with a comprehensive plan. The tragedy for him was that, having knee-capped Bob Hawke with policy boldness, he could not match Paul Keating as a political scrapper.

Keating's better political skills proved decisive. In the process, however, he surrendered policy credibility by deriding Hewson's GST, a likeness of which, namely a 12.5 per cent consumption tax, had been the centrepiece of his grand vision for Australia's taxation system eight years earlier.

19

LAZARUS HAS HIS
TRIPLE BYPASS

There was a widespread assumption that John Hewson had been retained as leader after the 1993 election as a stop-gap measure and would not lead the party to the next election. There was still reasonable public support for me, but the parliamentary party had knocked me back quite emphatically. If there were any hope of my ever returning to the leadership, it would have to be by way of a draft and not an orthodox challenge. I still thought about it, despite the setbacks. This was because Hewson's position seemed unsustainable and there appeared no other alternative.

As some years had now passed since the May 1989 coup, I increasingly felt the need to bury the hatchet with Andrew Peacock. I had a mixture of motives. It was because Andrew had been my open competitor for the party's top job that I did not feel any strong sense of grievance against him. Andrew's ambition I could understand all too well, as I shared it.

I also knew that if there were to be any hope, however remote, that I might return to the leadership, then at least to have the acquiescence of Andrew Peacock would be crucial. So I began to take what opportunities I could to engage Andrew in friendly conversation and safe reminiscences about shared political experiences. He responded in a friendly manner. This process had begun before the 1993 election. His attitude to me had not altered by the time of the 1993 election, as he supported Hewson being re-elected as leader.

Although I had an interest in reconciliation with Andrew Peacock, I nonetheless believed that it should happen. We had each committed our active adult years to the Liberal Party, loved politics and wanted a federal Liberal Government returned to office. Both of us were becoming more than a little weary with almost reflex blame being fixed on our rivalry whenever the party had a problem. We had had furious differences and been fierce rivals, hurting the party in the process, but through all of that had maintained a certain civility towards each other. By the beginning of 1994, a good deal of the old tension in our relationship had begun to dissipate.

Then there was the Bronwyn Bishop phenomenon. Vacuums in politics are always filled, and in the case of the leadership of the Liberal Party, the public began to fill that vacuum with its support for Bronwyn Bishop. She had been a Liberal senator from New South Wales since 1987 and had a high media profile of a populist kind. For close to 12 months she was never out of the headlines as a potential leadership rival to John Hewson. She enjoyed a short-term but quite intense popularity spurt with the Australian public.

This was understandable. There was a novelty about her. She was the first woman to be seriously debated as a potential leader of the Liberal Party. She had appeal to conservative voters. Bronwyn made simple, straightforward statements on nationalism and foreign policy. Quite assiduously, she cultivated comparisons between herself and Margaret Thatcher. The fact that she was still a senator at that stage was no more than a minor technical detail. Ironically, attending to that minor technical detail played a major role in the unravelling of the Bronwyn Bishop public phenomenon.

Bronwyn's biggest problem was that no more than a handful of her parliamentary colleagues took seriously the proposition that she could ever become leader of the parliamentary party. She was seen as strong on simple slogans but lacking policy substance and depth. This did not in any way impede her public progress. Polls showed her not only doing well against her Liberal rivals but also Paul Keating.

In the middle of 1993 Paul Keating turned up the heat in the debate about Australia becoming a republic. He had committed to a republican referendum at the 1993 poll and shortly afterwards appointed an advisory committee chaired by Malcolm Turnbull, which included a group of hand-picked Australians with obvious republican sympathies. It was a classic committee stitch-up. He did not want a range of views. He wanted a republic, had a clear idea of what kind of presidency Australia should have, and appointed the people who would give him the advice that he sought.

Keating knew that the republican issue would divide the Liberal Party. Whilst a majority of Liberals supported the constitutional monarchy, there was a significant minority who favoured change.

I was strongly against a republic. To me it was an instinctive issue, and my Burkean conservatism drove my thinking. I was somewhat contemptuous of the equivocal response of so many of my parliamentary colleagues. I accepted that a number of them were republican by conviction but believed a lot of the other lukewarm republicans were merely adopting that attitude because it appeared the fashionable thing to do.

John Hewson seemed undecided. At that time Costello came out against change. Downer shared my views, as did Bronwyn Bishop. Andrew Peacock remained silent on the subject, although I suspect that deep down he was a constitutional monarchist.

Tony Abbott, later Opposition leader, had been John Hewson's press secretary between 1990 and the 1993 election. It had been on my recommendation that Hewson engaged Abbott. A former seminarian, later a journalist with the *Bulletin* and the *Australian*, Tony Abbott had once thought of joining my staff when I was Opposition leader but took what he thought to be a better offer from the *Bulletin*. We had established an instant rapport and kept in touch. I liked his intellectual rigour and gregarious manner. He revelled in the battle of ideas, which he saw to be the stuff of real politics. I admired the fact that he was prepared to argue his case no matter its unpopularity. Abbott's personality was engaging; he had a good sense of humour, and I came to respect his capacity to quickly bounce back from a reversal.

Abbott and Hewson fell out before the 1993 election, and the former was in search of a new job after the Keating Government was re-elected. When the republican issue came into focus Abbott was approached by a number of people to become the executive director of Australians for a Constitutional Monarchy (ACM), the main organising group representing support for the status quo. At that time there was a media frenzy supporting a republic, and people willing to put their hand up for the monarchy were few and far between. Being by instinct a monarchist, Abbott wanted to take the job, but many of his family and friends counselled him against it. He sought my opinion and I told him to take it. I thought he would throw his great energy and communications skills into the task. The group needed an effective executive director.

There was another reason why I thought he should take the job. I told him that a very large number of people with whom he would have contact were active members of the Liberal Party. Branch members of the Liberal Party were overwhelmingly of a monarchist bent. Given that I knew Tony wanted to obtain preselection for a Liberal seat at some time in the future, favourable exposure to Liberal Party branch members would do him no harm. Much earlier than he expected, Tony would have good reason to thank me for this advice.

Keating had appointed John Dawkins as Treasurer after he toppled Hawke. The Dawkins budget of August 1993 was an outrageous repudiation of Keating's campaign against Hewson in March of that year. It contained swingeing increases in existing indirect taxes, cancellation of the by-now-infamous 'l-a-w — law' tax cuts and just about every other budget nasty imaginable. The 'l-a-w — law' description derived from Keating having literally spelled out the word 'law' to emphasise that income-tax cuts in his 1992 One Nation statement had been legislated. To most people, it was beyond the pale that Keating had defeated Hewson on the grounds that the latter was to introduce a monster new tax, and now he was presiding over widespread indirect tax hikes for which he had no mandate.

The Keating Government's poll position slumped. But this did not automatically translate into a consolidation of John Hewson's position. Doubts about the durability of his leadership persisted.

Early in 1994, two long-serving NSW Liberals, Michael MacKellar and Jim Carlton, in the neighbouring seats of Warringah and Mackellar, both safe Liberal fiefdoms on the North Shore of Sydney, announced that they were retiring from parliament. This opened the way for Bronwyn Bishop to move into the lower house. She secured Liberal preselection for Mackellar, with all the attendant publicity and drama that this inevitably entailed, given her clear leadership ambitions and the support she continued to enjoy in the opinion polls.

When I heard of the vacancy in Warringah I telephoned Tony Abbott, who was holidaying at Port Macquarie, and told him that he should nominate immediately for the seat. He lived on the North Shore of Sydney and I felt this was his opportunity. He took my advice and, in part with the assistance of a glowing reference I provided for him, won the preselection. Those who attended the preselection said his presentation had been outstanding and grabbed the attention and the emotions of those sitting on the committee. The stage was therefore set for two by-elections on the same day, 26 March 1994. As both were safe Liberal seats, the Labor Party did not run candidates. The main interest centred on the respective sizes of the Liberal vote in the two seats. It proved to be a defining result for Bronwyn Bishop. Her principal rival was the ALP sympathiser, but Independent, writer Bob Ellis. She suffered a 4.5 per cent decline in her primary vote, whereas Tony Abbott's seat saw his primary vote fall by less than 1 per cent. Unfortunately for Bishop, the enormous focus on her leadership aspirations, which she had regularly encouraged, meant that this decline in her vote, which in other circumstances might not have attracted much attention, damaged her leadership prospects. She never recovered momentum from that time onwards.

Throughout 1994 I would remain active in talking about the party's values and beliefs. In an article in *Quadrant* magazine, I articulated my strong view that the Liberal Party was a broad church, being the custodian of classical liberal as well as conservative beliefs. I also wrote, 'Liberals should become the party of the Australian achievement', pointing to the latent sentiment in the Australian community that legitimate expressions of pride about the past had been suppressed through fear of offending minorities.

As the weeks passed it became clear that it was only a matter of time before a spark ignited the dry grass surrounding John Hewson.

Comment, both in the press and amongst MPs, about Hewson's leadership increased sharply in May. In a pre-emptive strike, Hewson called a party meeting for 23 May at which the positions of leader and deputy leader would be declared vacant. That afternoon Downer and Costello announced that they would run, in that order, for the two positions. They had calculated that I would not nominate and agreed on their course of action before consulting me. Their actions reflected the mood of the party. Colleagues were determined to move on in finding a replacement for Hewson. Although I was full of self-recrimination about not running, my initial instinct to stay out of the ballot was absolutely correct. I would have performed poorly.

The day before the ballot, there was an extraordinary public intervention by the federal president, Tony Staley, who called for Hewson's removal. Hewson himself, although he had lived on borrowed time since his re-election just over a year earlier, would have felt a bruised and angry person. To make matters worse, he was ambushed on the ABC *Lateline* program when Kerry O'Brien confronted him with the details of some internal Liberal Party polling. The leaking of such material by party insiders, although regrettably commonplace, is never forgivable. It breaches every professional principle of private political counsel.

I told John Hewson that I would vote for Downer, who defeated him 43 to 36. Costello became Deputy Leader unopposed after Downer's win. I would have voted for him in a contested ballot. The change was seen as the beginning of a new, younger, fresher opportunity for the Liberal Party.

The dream team of Alexander Downer and Peter Costello got off to a flying start. Alexander had impressed as shadow Treasurer and he was steeped in politics; his father had been a Menzies minister. Liberal supporters were given new heart, and the opinion polls recorded strong support for both Downer and the Coalition.

For me, the election of Downer and Costello had a real air of finality about it. That was it, so far as any lingering leadership hopes of mine were concerned. As a reflection of my mood, I wrote in my diary at the time: 'On Friday 20 May 1994 I was given my last ever chance to reclaim the Leadership of the Liberal Party and again seek the Prime Ministership of my country. I didn't know it at the time and I passed up the opportunity. It will never come again. I think I now feel that.'

I felt and acted as if a completely new era had arrived for the Liberal Party. My role was to stay around and help. Downer and I had a good relationship and he consulted me from time to time about issues. That relationship grew even closer in government.

For the first time in more than 15 years I felt that I was no longer at the centre of the affairs of the Liberal Party. Even though the party had re-elected Hewson after the 1993 poll, there was a strong sense that the leadership issue was unresolved and would be looked at again. The party had looked at it again and gone to the next generation. I had a lot of experience, and there continued to be much goodwill towards me, but the Liberal Party could really get on without me if it had to.

That was how Liberal supporters thought too. In July I was admitted to the Mater Hospital in Sydney for a knee reconstruction operation made necessary following a skiing spill, in turn caused by trying to keep pace with my 18-year-old son, Tim. The anaesthetist, who I sensed and (remembering Ronald Reagan's famous remark before undergoing surgery, 'I hope he's a Republican') hoped was a Liberal, chatted approvingly about the change to younger leaders and said how right I had been to stand aside for them. As I drifted into relaxed slumber, I drowsily agreed.

That was in July. By November, a bare four months later, Alexander Downer's leadership had collapsed and I had begun to believe, as distinct from hope, that the leadership of the Liberal Party would finally come back to me.

Alexander Downer's slide commenced during a public relations disaster he created during a visit to the Northern Territory. At an earlier meeting of the WA Liberals he had raised the possibility, rather surprisingly, of repealing aspects of the Native Title legislation. This had come out of the blue and seemed at odds with what was then the party's policy. He then went to the Northern Territory and in a succession of interviews appeared both to contradict party policy and some of his earlier statements on Indigenous issues. When taxed with the contradictions he blamed them on the emotional impact he felt watching a corroboree. It was an unnerving performance and precipitated a big fall of 17 per cent in his approval rating. Coming as early as it did in his leadership, such a turnaround was magnified in its political significance by the commentators.

The Northern Territory incident undid his confidence and from then on he handled difficult situations with a very unsure touch. John Hewson had cut up rough since his removal from the leadership. Instead of ignoring him, which would have been the right response, Alexander overreacted by sacking Hewson from the shadow cabinet.

The pretext had been some correspondence between Hewson and Chris Miles MP, a parliamentary secretary, over proposals of the federal Government to give effect to a decision of the United Nations Human Rights Committee that laws in Tasmania which still treated homosexual relations between consenting adults as criminal conduct were inconsistent with Australia's obligations under the International Covenant on Civil and Political Rights.

A Tasmanian and a strong believer in states' rights, Chris Miles had reservations about the legislation. I had long thought it wrong to treat homosexual conduct involving adults as criminal, and felt that the laws of Australia should reflect this. The Coalition rightly decided not to oppose the bill.

When the perception of a slide in a leader's support takes hold, it contaminates the reporting of subsequent events. This was the case when it was revealed that Downer had apparently addressed what might loosely be regarded as a League of Rights meeting in 1987. The Labor Party created a huge fuss about it. Downer's explanation that he thought it was a Christian group sounded unconvincing, but the press were in a 'get Downer' mood and pretty well painted it in the darkest manner possible for Alexander.

Shortly after assuming the leadership, Alexander Downer and his staff had begun preparing a policy manifesto which would outline in broad detail the approach of a future Coalition Government. It was not meant to be completely prescriptive but would go beyond banal superficialities. It was to strike a sensible balance between the extensive details in Fightback! as opposed to going to a poll with a public perception that the party stood for nothing other than winning government. It was a good product, being released under the commonsense title of The Things That Matter. That title captured the mood of the public. Many Australians felt that the Keating Government had become obsessed with symbolic issues to the detriment of those things that really mattered to men and women in their daily lives.

Tragically for Alexander Downer, his mishandling of the launch of the document, on 5 September 1994, not only destroyed its impact but was also the real death knell of his leadership. Alexander has always had an engaging self-deprecatory tone. On most occasions this works extremely well and is something that people like. He can, however, go too far and sometimes his humour backfires badly. This happened with his policy manifesto. In describing individual sections of the document, he gave them titles which rhymed with the main title of the document. For example, the section dealing with children was dubbed 'the things that patter', family policy was dubbed 'the flings that matter'. Unfortunately, and with great insensitivity, he described the section on domestic violence as 'the things that batter'. He should have known that domestic violence is never a laughing matter. Not only did he receive enormous criticism for his insensitivity but he had also made fun of his own document. The reaction was one of terrible embarrassment and disbelief. It caused a further nosedive in his poll ratings.

If all of this wasn't enough, the sudden announcement by Andrew Peacock in September that he would retire from politics added a new dimension. I first heard about Andrew from Peter Reith, who telephoned me from China. He knew instinctively that there would not be a Peacock veto on me if the leadership were once again in play. As always, Reith was the pragmatist and not the dreamer. He was a close friend of Downer's but knew that Alexander was in deep trouble. He wasn't being disloyal to Downer, but was making sure that his communication with me remained open.

Within the space of only three months, confidence in Downer had disintegrated and the party was, once again, facing a leadership crisis. All of the 'future' options had been tried and had failed. From all sections of the party, almost spontaneously, the view began to emerge that the best way forward might be my recall as leader. Given attitudes of past years, this was hard to believe, yet, looked at rationally, it made sense. Downer and Costello had been the experiment with a new generation, and Downer's poll position had collapsed, time was moving on and Liberal supporters desperately craved an effective alternative to Keating. It had been an amazing turnaround, and impossible to reconcile with my mood and that of the party just four months earlier.

By October 1994 there was a strongly held view within the party that if Alexander Downer had not noticeably recovered by Christmas then I would replace him. It was largely unspoken but confirmed by my close friends Allan Rocher, the MP for Curtin in Western Australia, and Senator Michael Baume. People as diverse as David MacGibbon, who had been a strong Peacock man, and Rod Atkinson told me directly. Atkinson, a Vietnam veteran, had been John Hewson's whip. I was told by his closest friend in the parliament that Michael Wooldridge would support me in place of Downer.

At the end of November, what I thought had been beyond all hope a few months earlier was now more within reach than ever before. The leader polls had gone heavily against Alexander Downer and I had become the preferred Liberal leader. Increasing numbers of MPs told me that they would support me. Even journalists long hostile to me began to write differently. Typical was Geoff Kitney of the *Sydney Morning Herald*, who captioned his regular Friday column of 11 November 1994: 'Howard hovers ever nearer the leadership'. This piece was still quite grudging, but noteworthy for accepting that I was closer to getting back the leadership than at any time since I had lost it in 1989.

Some of my supporters wanted a leadership challenge before Christmas, but I remained firmly against this. I wanted to be drafted or elected unopposed, because that would be the most effective way of unifying the party behind me. At that point, there were still a few colleagues strongly against my recall. It was clear to me before Christmas that moderates in the party, such as Warwick Smith, Michael Wooldridge and Trish Worth, had decided that I should replace Downer.

People close to Peter Costello, such as Michael Kroger and Ian McLachlan, then shadow minister for the Environment, told me that Peter

Costello would not or could not, because of the age of his youngest child, run for the leadership. The reality was that once it had become accepted that Downer's leadership was finished, and with Andrew Peacock out of the equation, there was no way that Peter Costello could have gathered the numbers to win a leadership ballot against me. The experiment with the next generation had failed with Alexander Downer, so why try another member of that generation in Peter Costello? Moreover, the majority of those who saw themselves as moderates or 'small l' Liberals regarded Peter Costello as being more right-wing than I was. Robert Hill, the most senior of this group, would be reluctant to specifically endorse me, but I knew that he would favour me ahead of Costello.

My 1988 remarks about Asian immigration still bothered some of my close friends. Tony Abbott was one of them. From his university and other days, he was a friend of Greg Sheridan of the *Australian*, who had been highly critical of my controversial remarks seven years earlier. On 30 November, Sheridan had returned to the issue with a column in which he attacked me for not having fully repudiated the 1988 remarks. He at least implied that my failure to do so could be a reason for my not being restored as leader.

Tony took up the issue in December and urged me to go further in disowning the offending remarks. He suggested that I talk to Sheridan about it. I was reluctant at first. I felt that I had dealt quite comprehensively with the matter in May at a dinner in Sydney attended by many Chinese community groups; it had been the day Downer was made leader. I did not think that it needed revisiting. Abbott pressed me on the subject and, on the basis of leaving no stone unturned, I had an interview over lunch at the Buono Gusto restaurant in Chippendale with Sheridan. Not only did it cover Asian immigration, I also roamed over national identity, the republic and other matters. The *Australian* gave it a big run. Splashing with the lead: 'I was wrong on Asians, says Howard',[1] it certainly attracted plenty of attention. I had gone as far as I could be expected to in order to erase any lingering hurt feelings over my serious error of judgement back in 1988. It put the issue to bed for Sheridan and, I suspect, many others.

Ian McLachlan and I met Peter Costello in his office in Canberra on 5 December 1994. We had a wide-ranging discussion about the leadership. As usual, Peter Costello gave nothing away. McLachlan was dismissive of Downer. During the discussion, I said that it would be in the party's interests for me to be elected unopposed in place of Downer; that there was a big age difference between Costello and me; and that he (Costello) could expect, if we were successful in government, to become prime minister after me.

Costello pressed me heavily on the issue of how long I might serve as prime minister, and I said that I would only serve one to two terms. He did not offer me anything in return. We reached no understanding; at no stage during the discussion did Peter say that in return he would help me to become leader unopposed. I left that meeting with no clear indication from Peter Costello as to where he stood on the leadership. I never discussed the leadership again with McLachlan before I was re-elected, unopposed, as Leader of the Liberal Party at the end of January 1995. That meeting on 5 December 1994 was but one of many meetings I had about the leadership at that time.

In the early weeks of December, I had been briefed by Ron Walker, the party's honorary federal treasurer, on what he claimed to be private party research. He said the research showed that we would lose 30 seats under Downer's leadership. He further claimed it showed that I could win, and that Peter Costello was not widely known outside Victoria. According to Walker, Peter Costello, Robert Hill and Richard Alston, the other members of the leadership group, as well as Downer, had been briefed on this research. Alston I spoke to before Christmas. Whilst being very guarded, he acknowledged that 'we have big problems'. Richard was covering his bases. In private discussions, both Tony Staley and Ron Walker, for some weeks, had been saying that the party had to install me in place of Downer.

In mid-December, at Alexander Downer's request, he, Peter Costello and I met at the Adelaide Club. There he said that he would hand the leadership to me without a fight if the Government called an election in January for the following March. There had been some speculation about a snap early election, and that was unnerving a lot of our colleagues. Beyond that, he said that the three of us should keep the matter under review, and if at any time in the future he thought there should be a change for the sake of the party, in my favour, that would be facilitated. In return for these commitments from him, I was to agree that I would not challenge for the leadership. I told him that I could not agree not to challenge.

My recollection of that Adelaide meeting, which I wrote down shortly afterwards, is at odds with the version provided by Peter Costello in his memoirs. He claimed that the three of us had agreed that Downer should be given one last opportunity to pick himself up in the polls, but if his position had not improved by Australia Day, he would stand down, I would be elected unopposed and Costello would continue as deputy leader.

On 28 December I had lunch with Peter Costello near his electorate office in Melbourne. It was clear to me from that meeting that, in the end, he would not seek the leadership but was not in a hurry to tell me that or to reach any understanding to facilitate a peaceful leadership transition from Downer to me. Part of this was a genuine desire not to appear a disloyal deputy. He said that Downer could not win a party ballot against me, but if I challenged him, he would be obliged to support Downer but could well 'dial the phone slowly'.

Costello said he thought that Downer could be persuaded to go and, if the position had not moved in that direction, he might inform Downer after he had returned from a trip to Britain late in January that Downer should resign. Costello reserved the right to nominate for the position himself, which I entirely accepted. He said that he thought a bloodless transfer would be the best outcome for me. We agreed that nothing was likely to change in relation to Downer's support over the holiday period. I made a detailed note of that discussion shortly afterwards.

That evening I spoke to Michael Kroger, who indicated he had also spoken to Costello, and that the latter had told him that nothing should happen in relation to the leadership during January. We agreed that Costello's true position was that he was not going to do anything to precipitate or facilitate a change of leadership, but would not run himself or actively oppose a change. In any contested ballot he would vote for Downer, and make that known publicly. Michael said to me that we had to 'plan around Costello'. I agreed with this.

None of these discussions were consistent with the claim, which I have always disputed, that Costello and I, in McLachlan's presence, did a succession deal about the leadership at the meeting on 5 December 1994. As the year ended, the matter remained unresolved. Peter Costello had not promised me anything. He never did.

The Howard family repaired on what by now had become an annual trek to Hawks Nest. I knew by then that one way or the other the leadership would be mine within a matter of weeks.

Another straw in the wind was a meeting during January with Richard Court, Premier of Western Australia, and his indomitable father, Sir Charles Court. They made a special visit to Sydney to see me. The unspoken background to the meeting was that I was likely to return to the federal leadership, that they were broadly supportive of that, but there were some particular issues they wanted to put on the table for future reference. In so many ways we were natural allies within the Liberal Party. I liked them both, but I sensed a looming problem with the seat of Curtin, our safest in Perth, where Richard's brother, Ken, was likely to successfully oppose my close friend Allan Rocher for Liberal endorsement. Like true-born West Australians, Sir Charles and Richard thought that I was a bit of a centralist.

The parliamentary party was due to have its first meeting in 1995 on 30 January, in Canberra. A shadow cabinet meeting had been arranged for the Dandenongs, just out of Melbourne, for 24 January. I knew that the matter had to be brought to a head and that although Alexander Downer's position had not improved at all over the holiday break, the situation could still drift for weeks, doing further damage to the party's position. The threat of an early election had receded. I had made up my mind to challenge for the leadership if Alexander had not indicated a willingness to resign at the party meeting on 30 January.

The shadow cabinet meeting was conducted in a surreal atmosphere. I had arranged to have dinner with Alexander at the Athenaeum Club that evening. Given the circumstances in which we found ourselves, it was a remarkably civilised dinner. I told him that his position was beyond retrieval, that there had been a very significant shift away from him over the previous two months, and that I would easily win a ballot. He was reluctant to accept this immediately; that was understandable, but he undertook to test the position with his advisors and colleagues and let me know his response the following day. I arranged to call on him at 11 am the next day, in the Opposition leader's temporary office in Melbourne.

It was Grahame Morris who first gave me the news. This remarkably durable political warrior, who has been at the centre of so many Liberal Party dramas — successes and failures — over the last 25 years, had joined Alexander's staff but retained very close friendships with many others, including me. Just before I was to see Downer, Grahame told me that his boss would agree to a leadership transition without a ballot, but wanted to discuss issues relating to personnel and timing.

My meeting with Downer was emotional but controlled. It was a big thing for him to do, and it was a huge moment for me. He told me directly that he would resign the leadership at the party meeting, and make it clear that he supported an uncontested transfer of the leadership to me. I told him that I would appoint him shadow Foreign Minister, with the expectation implied that he would be Foreign Minister if we won power. He asked if he could retain one of his valued staff, Greg Hunt, who had a specialty in foreign affairs. I readily agreed. Hunt went on to become the Liberal MP for Flinders in Victoria. Downer also asked that no comment be made until the following day so that he could make the announcement with his family in Adelaide, in a manner and in a setting of his choosing. I readily agreed to this.

I thanked Alexander Downer for the sacrifice he was making for the good of the Liberal Party. His position was beyond recovery, but that state is often far from clear to those who are directly confronted by it. I know from my own experience that it is a very hard thing to accept that your party has completely turned against you as leader. In agreeing to an uncontested transfer of leadership, Alexander Downer won himself a permanent place of respect in the Liberal pantheon. I have never forgotten that gesture to the Liberal Party and to me, and repaid it as best I could with years of collegiality, support and loyalty as we worked together as Prime Minister and Foreign Minister for almost 12 years.

On Australia Day, surrounded by his family, Alexander Downer would make a gracious speech indicating that he was giving up the leadership because it was in the interests of the Liberal Party to do so. It had been a difficult nine months for him and had ended on a sad personal note. But he had displayed great dignity, which won him many friends and admirers throughout the party and the wider community.

For me, I could only feel a sense of suppressed elation and anticipation. I returned home and quietly reflected with my wife and children on the rollercoaster nature of political life. They had shared so much with me and had borne the brunt of disappointment and sustained me through the difficulties of political life to date. Janette and our three children were united in their enthusiasm and eagerness for what lay ahead. They knew it would be very hard, but they also knew that I had had plenty of preparation for the task which was at hand. Having been through so much, I had no trepidation about the future.

On Australia Day 1995, I attended a citizenship ceremony in my electorate of Bennelong and after the ceremony and on the steps of the City of Ryde Civic Centre, I announced that I would be a candidate for the leadership of the Liberal Party when it met a few days later.

The party assembled in an atmosphere of relief and anticipation on 30 January. Alexander Downer was impeccable. Just before the party meeting was due to start, he walked from the Leader of the Opposition's suite to my office and together we headed for the party room. He announced his intention to resign the leadership, thanked the party for its loyalty and forbearance and called for nominations to fill the vacant position. I was the only nominee and was elected unopposed, with acclamation. The deputy leadership was not in contention, and after a short speech from me, paying special tribute to Alexander, the party meeting ended.

Shortly afterwards, I held a news conference and set out the goals of my leadership and the principles which would guide a Coalition Government if we were to win the next election. I remain intensely proud of how close our behaviour in government reflected the goals I put down in that first news conference of my renewed leadership of the Liberal Party. I said:

> I've always believed in an Australia built on reward for individual effort, with a special place of honour for small business as the engine room of our economy. I've always believed in a safety net for those amongst us who don't make it. I've always believed in the family as the stabilising and cohering unit of our society. And, I believe very passionately in an Australia drawn from the four corners of the earth, but united behind a common set of Australian values.

In those simple direct sentences I had set out so much of what would guide me and my colleagues in government.

Against all expectations, after both April 1993 and May 1994, Lazarus had had his triple bypass. Many people saw my return to the leadership as a case of the last man left standing. There was truth in this because the party only came back to me after three alternatives — Peacock, Hewson and Downer — had failed, but there were more substantial reasons. That I had been prepared to stick it out despite several rejections told my colleagues of my resilience and determination. They knew me as a conviction politician. To them, and, by extension, the Australian public, I stood for certain things. They may not always agree with those things, but at least I had convictions. At a time when the public was feeling just a little tired of packaged politics and spin, this was seen as an asset.

I had become more inclusive. More than they thought I had during my first stint as leader, I would embrace the Liberal Party for what it really was

— a broad church. It was the party of Mill as well as Burke. I would not abandon or seriously compromise strongly held views and values, and my colleagues did not want me to do that. What they wanted, however, and they sensed I would now do, was allow all viewpoints to be fully heard before decisions were taken. My colleagues also knew that I could match Paul Keating in the rough-and-tumble of political combat.

There were millions of my fellow Australians literally aching for a change of government. I was keen to get to the task of delivering this and absolutely determined not to let them down.

20

THE ROAD TO
THE LODGE

On the evening of Friday, 1 March 1996, the day before the federal election which swept away Paul Keating's Government and at which I became Australia's 25th prime minister, I took my staff to the Café Stivelle in Hunters Hill, in my electorate of Bennelong, for an end-of-campaign thank you dinner. This had been a mammoth journey for most of us, with the 33-day intensive part of the campaign merely the culmination of more than 12 months of unceasing hard work and dedication. My staff had been magnificent.

It was a beautiful balmy evening, and I wandered to the open-air part of the restaurant as I had spotted Paul Kelly, editor-in-chief of the *Australian* newspaper with his wife, Margaret. They had come across from their nearby residence for a late dinner. Paul told me that he had the latest Newspoll results, which would appear as the main story in the *Australian* on election day. The poll showed the Coalition with a two-party-preferred vote of almost 54 per cent against 46 per cent for Labor. If repeated in the election, it would give the Coalition a strong win.

I was a little nervous about the poll being run heavily by the newspaper, because in my pre-election state of nerves, I thought it might scare people back into voting Labor. I reflected to Paul Kelly that those poll numbers were almost identical to the Newspoll about a month after I had returned to the leadership, and that through the 12 months which had followed, a virtual straight line could be drawn through the polls showing consistent relative levels of support for the Coalition and the Labor Party. The Australian public had been ready for a change of government for a long time but had been waiting for the Coalition to give it a strong enough reason to vote for that change.

For the previous 13 months, the Coalition had put sustained pressure on the Keating Government. Displaying impressive unity, our team had achieved the right blend of aggression and policy direction. The Australian people knew what a Howard Government would be like, but I was determined that the election would be a referendum on the Keating Government.

I knew that from the time the party took me back as leader, the Coalition's political fortunes would stand or fall on my capacity to nail Paul Keating. That is what I set out to do from the very beginning, both in the parliament and elsewhere.

As if on cue, parliament had re-assembled in February 1995 surrounded by a huge blockade of trucks established by timber industry workers and contractors who were protesting against the Keating Government's forestry policies, especially in Tasmania, which they saw as too accommodating to the greenies. This blockade was a potent symbol of where a party will find itself if it plays opportunistic, interest-group politics devoid of long-term policy consistency. For years Labor had chased the green vote, yet it continued its pretence to be the true friend of the blue-collar worker. The two had collided over forest policy, and the truckies wanted to know whose side the Prime Minister was really on. They had good reason to think it was the greenies, and that is why they had come to Canberra with their trucks.

In the first sitting week I led a most effective parliamentary censure against Keating, which reminded the Australian public, and more particularly our colleagues, that he could be matched — indeed bested — in the parliament, and that we should not feel intimidated by his rhetoric and capacity for verbal abuse. My line that the Australian people had enjoyed 'a bare five minutes of economic sunlight' before returning to recession really resonated with the public. It was exactly how people felt, especially in the wake of the savage increases in interest rates late in 1994.

The March Canberra by-election was a real gift. As Sports Minister, Ros Kelly had been wounded by the 'Whiteboard Affair', with its allegations of political favouritism in the awarding of sports grants, and obviously wanted to leave politics as soon as possible. The Government, nonetheless, was within a year of an election and it was a foolhardy indulgence at such a time for a by-election to take place. It was a sign that Paul Keating's arrogance had really got the better of him. Canberra is a Labor town just as Washington DC is a Democratic Party stronghold. Whatever the explanation might be, except in very atypical circumstances, such as December 1975 and the by-election of 1995, Canberra votes solidly for the Australian Labor Party. That political aphorism 'Looks like Killara but votes like Cessnock' is normally true of the national capital.

Predictably, Canberra returned to the ALP at the general election. The by-election swing to the Coalition in Canberra was a fantastic 16 per cent, way beyond what both the Labor and Liberal parties expected, and delivered the seat to the Liberal candidate, Brendan Smyth. Getting such a huge boost so early in my leadership was invigorating. It hurt Keating a lot as it raised serious doubts about his political judgement. Hard heads in the Labor Party could not understand why he had permitted the by-election to take place. For the Liberal Party, the victory was muted by it occurring on the same day that the Fahey Government in New South Wales lost to Bob Carr.

Throughout 1995 I was heartened by the ineptitude Paul Keating displayed in relation to certain people. Carmen Lawrence was the prime example. Political commonsense suggested that she should stand down until questions relating to whether or not she had committed perjury, and other issues coming out of the Marks Royal Commission, had been disposed of. In keeping her, he violated an important principle of the Westminster system: a minister should resign or stand aside when his or her continued membership of the cabinet is damaging the government. If Paul Keating had applied that principle to Carmen Lawrence in 1995, she would have been gone early in the year and a great deal of prime ministerial energy would have been conserved for other pursuits.

Another example was his pursuit of Kerry Packer. They had fallen out, but it was foolish of Keating to conduct a personal vendetta against the owner of the most powerful TV network and also, courtesy of his knockabout style, quite a popular figure with many Australians. Packer had enraged Keating with the complimentary remarks he had made about me during an interview on his own network. I was grateful for the comments. Keating's obsession with Packer reached absurd proportions when he devoted a large chunk of a news conference he gave in Germany to attacking Packer and alleging some secret deal he had made with me regarding the repeal of the cross-ownership media prohibitions. This was a ludicrous charge. I had been publicly opposed to the cross-media prohibitions from as far back as 1987.

The Republican Advisory Committee, chaired by Malcolm Turnbull, had reported in 1994, and mid-way through 1995 Keating intended to tell parliament of the Government's proposals to convert Australia into a federal republic. Alexander Downer had proposed the holding of a constitutional convention to debate the issue. I confirmed this sensible and pragmatic policy. It allowed the Coalition to appear responsive to discussion of a republic without in any way selling the pass on the substance. It also laid the groundwork for my being able to declare, when the referendum of 1999 was approaching, that the Liberal Party would allow its members a free vote, which was the only feasible approach.

Keating's statement to parliament on 7 June proposed the establishment of an Australian republic, with a president effectively chosen by the government of the day. It was an emotional moment for the Prime Minister, and for most of his parliamentary colleagues.

Virtually all of the Australian media were lyrical in their praise of the Prime Minister, not only for his proposal but the substance and delivery of his speech as well. I knew that I faced a considerable challenge in responding. Many of my colleagues were very discomforted by this issue. Whatever their own feelings might be, they had been savagely spooked by the level of media support for a republic and the polls, which up until then had shown majority, if not overwhelming, support for dumping the monarchy.

Only when the debate crystallised around the retention or rejection of a fundamental element of our system of government would proper perspective be brought to the issue. What many of my somewhat nervous colleagues did not appreciate was the innate conservatism of the Australian electorate, and its highly commendable instinct to resist change unless a convincing case had been made.

Responding to the Prime Minister, I said that I personally opposed change, but if the Coalition were to win the next election it would establish a constitutional convention to debate the issue. My speech, predictably, was dealt with critically in most of the Australian media. The truth was that most journalists wanted a republic, were quite excited with Keating's speech and loathed the conservative position that I had taken.

The day after my reply I lunched with the management and senior editorial staff of the Fairfax newspaper group in Sydney. Fairfax was completely gung-ho for the republic, and one by one they sneered at the position that I had taken. The only exception was Ross Gittins, Fairfax's economics editor, who declared that he was an agnostic on the subject, largely because he did not think it important. On this issue I had the unmistakable impression that most journalists, holding the strongly republican views that they did, decided that it was one of those occasions when they could go their hardest, without any real regard for balance.

The wall of opposition to my position on the republic from the Australian media was unnerving. I waited for the polls conducted after Keating's speech and my response with some trepidation. To my immense relief they had not shifted. Despite several weeks of press criticism of my position and comment pieces which overwhelmingly praised Keating's republican blueprint, support for the Coalition had not fallen. This vindicated my judgement that, to most Australians, the republic was a diversionary second-order issue. It also meant that there was latent support in the Australian community for maintenance of the constitutional status quo.

Health policy had proved, over the years, to be a bugbear for the Liberal Party. The Fraser Government had made numerous changes to its health policy, which had been both unsettling and politically damaging. Returned to office in 1983, the Labor Party under Bob Hawke had introduced Medicare, which largely reprised the Hayden Medibank policy of 1975 with a number of refinements, including the introduction of a 1 per cent Medicare levy. In 1990 the Coalition's position on health had been a shambles. We had no policy. The Coalition's policy, in 1993, proposed big cuts to bulk billing and a paring back of the Medicare rebate. It was quite easy for the Labor Party to depict this as taking a scalpel to Medicare.

After the 1993 election I concluded that the Coalition's health policy had played a much bigger role in our defeat than was commonly acknowledged. Back as leader, I knew that the Coalition must accept Medicare as a reality. We had to renounce any intention of making major changes to it. Michael Wooldridge, my shadow Health minister, had the same view. So, during an interview with Laurie Oakes on 4 June on the *Sunday* program, I lanced the Medicare boil. I said, 'We absolutely guarantee the retention of Medicare; we guarantee the retention of bulk billing; we guarantee the maintenance of community rating.' I could not have been more explicit. I went on to say that the Liberal and National parties were committed to helping people with their private health insurance costs, and would lay out, probably during the campaign, how that help would be given. In government, we kept our word. We not only preserved Medicare, we made it better.

Given the outcome of the 1993 election, there was an understanding within the party that a GST was off the agenda, at least for the next election. On 1 May 1995, I spoke to a business gathering in Sydney and, answering a question, made it plain that a GST would not be policy for the next election. I was vague about what would happen 'some years into the future'. The Labor Party and the media seized on my comments as evidence of some secret agenda, and the following day I was emphatic that we would not introduce a GST. I said that we would 'never ever' bring in a GST. In government we did revisit the GST, but had the political honesty to present it in full detail to the electorate at the 1998 election, thus giving the Australian people the opportunity of voting us from office if they were unwilling to support our plan and change of heart.

In two areas the Coalition moved to neutralise attacks from the Government. It had been long-standing Coalition policy to privatise the near-monopoly telecommunications provider, Telstra. Recognising some of the public sensitivities regarding this issue, the Coalition resolved that, in its first term, it would offer for sale only one-third of Telstra. This was seen as a reassuring compromise. It did not retreat from our previously held position, but moved at a pace that was less likely to alarm people who had real reservations about Telstra passing from public ownership.

The other area was industrial relations. I decided that, in order to bullet-proof the Coalition against attacks from the Labor Party and the unions, we should provide what I described as a 'rock-solid guarantee' that in negotiating a contract outside the award system, no worker could be paid or receive less than the value of the aggregate award conditions. This became enshrined in the 1996 legislation as the 'no-disadvantage test'. It meant that during the campaign I could always answer criticism that we were stripping away people's conditions by saying that if somebody went into a contract of their own volition without the involvement of a union, then that person must receive, as a minimum, the value of the award conditions. I announced this commitment in a major speech at the beginning of 1996. It took the wind out of union and Labor sails.

As the year wore on there was continued pressure from the Government and numerous journalists that the Coalition should release more details of its policies. For good reasons I resisted.

Unlike other Opposition leaders before and since, my principal policies and values were already well known. Peter Reith once told me that I was 'a walking policy'. I could never be a small target. There would, of course, be specific additional policies released during the campaign. I did, however, deliver a series of what I called 'headland' speeches, five in number, which dealt in general and philosophical terms with the way in which the Coalition would govern.

In one of those speeches, to the Australian Council of Social Services, delivered on 13 October, I took head-on the constant claim from the Labor Party, and some of its acolytes in certain welfare groups, that a Howard Government would weaken the social security safety net. I had already directly addressed the Medicare issue but I wanted to go further. The genuinely needy deserved an assurance from me that they would not be out in the cold under a Coalition Government.

I gave specific assurances that a Howard Government would not force workers off awards; would not put a time limit on the receipt of unemployment benefits; would maintain existing sole-parent arrangements; would maintain the real value of pensions and other social security benefits; and in addition I repeated the pledge on Medicare. This was an important speech. Even some of those most cynical about us were willing to adopt a 'wait-and-see' attitude as a result of my address to ACOSS. During our years in government the really vulnerable were looked after.

From the moment I returned to the leadership, I had established a good relationship between my office and the federal secretariat of the Liberal Party, which meant that a smooth Liberal election campaign was in prospect. Nicole Feeley, who had been with me for several years when I was shadow minister for Industrial Relations, headed up my office. I was delighted when Arthur Sinodinos, who had been with me in my previous turnout as Opposition leader, agreed to come back as principal economic advisor and general policy counsellor early in 1995. Later, in government, he would be my chief of staff for nine years of my prime ministership. His work in that position was outstanding. He gave superb leadership to my office. Grahame Morris, an old friend and trusted confidant, transferred from Alexander Downer's staff to mine. I also hired Tony O'Leary, a press gallery veteran. Collectively they represented an effective group and we also had the great resource of Michael L'Estrange's advice. Michael had worked on both Hewson's and Downer's staffs as a policy advisor, but had agreed to serve as executive director of the Menzies Research Centre in 1995. This did not prevent him helping out with some speech drafting and other political counselling.

I was also determined that the 'small l' Liberal section of the party felt fully included. Robert Hill, by virtue of his being Leader of the Opposition in the Senate, as well as his intellectual capacity, was always the most influential figure in this group. He had been very reluctant about my return to the leadership. Like everyone else, though, he wanted to make it work. I set out, over time, to build a closer relationship with him, taking the opportunity, even when it was not strictly necessary, to consult him on policy and other matters. I am sure that Hill sensed what I was doing, and in his own way he responded positively. This process continued after we won government. The trust built between the two of us was an important ingredient in the remarkable cohesion of the party during our years in government.

I had seen the Liberal Party lose too many state elections despite a big swing its way, because we had poor candidates in the marginal seats that mattered. Accordingly, I set out, especially in New South Wales, to overturn some original candidate selections to ensure we had the best possible people; there was too much at stake. The gutsy and likeable Bill Heffernan, NSW Liberal president (later a senator), a good and loyal friend of mine, was of huge help. The new candidates installed included Bob Baldwin and Joanna Gash, who remain MPs. We also ensured that John Fahey, the former NSW Premier, became the candidate in the winnable seat of Macarthur. Charlie Lynn, originally chosen in that seat, is a Liberal stalwart in the NSW Legislative Council.

Paul Keating allowed his animosity towards me to cloud his judgement when he refused me a lift on his VIP plane to the funeral of the assassinated Israeli Prime Minister Yitzhak Rabin. It was a time for bipartisan expression of grief. Rabin's murder, on 4 November 1995, was a tragic event, taking the life of a courageous man who, whilst defending his country's interests, had worked very hard for a long-term peace settlement in the Middle East. Keating thought that he was being clever keeping me off the plane. The public thought him petty. Travelling with Keating on the VIP flight was the only way I could have got to the funeral in time.

The election had to be held early in 1996, but the actual date, which almost certainly was going to be in March or April, was naturally at the discretion of Paul Keating. The Howard family journeyed to Hawks Nest once again, knowing that its holiday would be interrupted on this occasion, for certain, by the need to return to Sydney and learn our son Tim's Higher School Certificate results. They turned out to be extremely good, and the family celebrated Tim achieving all that he had wanted, in the knowledge that he would gain admission to the university course which was his first preference.

Literally, it was whilst walking along Hawks Nest beach that I developed the idea of earmarking part of the proceeds of the Telstra sale towards the environment. I knew that we had to work a little harder on our environmental credentials to counter the ALP in this area. The federal director, Andrew Robb, had collaborated with various environmental groups to secure a better preference deal come the poll. To me, and also the Coalition's environmental spokesman, Senator Rod Kemp, committing some $1 billion of the proceeds of the one-third sale of Telstra shares towards establishing a natural heritage trust would attract a lot of support. When I announced the $1 billion fund in the campaign, it received accolades from the Wilderness Society and others. It also made our Telstra policy more appealing.

On 27 January, Paul Keating announced that the election would be held on 2 March 1996. The announcement of an election date, when you are in opposition, is a huge moment of relief. Finally, there is something definite. For many years now, election campaigns in Australia have been very presidential, and I knew that from that moment on, most of the responsibility for the Coalition's fortunes would rest with me.

We were well prepared. Over previous weeks, we had spent days locked in my Sydney office, constantly ordering in pizza, putting together a detailed economic manifesto in which we had carefully costed all of our individual commitments. Eight of us, comprising the senior parliamentary leadership, plus key advisors, had toiled well together, and I was extremely proud of the watertight nature of our financial documents. Peter Costello had done an excellent job, carefully tabulating the cost of everything and making sure that we had an explanation for every dollar that we were committed to spend.

I wanted a big initiative on taxation assistance for families as the popular centrepiece of my campaign launch. I felt strongly that the taxation system had become increasingly mean in the support it provided to Australian parents towards the cost of raising their children. Our policy involved an increase in the tax-free threshold for each child in a taxpayer's family, with a further proviso that if a family were a single-income one, the tax-free threshold for the breadwinner would be lifted by an extra $2500. The objective was to give extra help to all families with children, and some further help to single-income families, which I believed had been poorly treated over the years.

There would be two head-to-head debates between Paul Keating and me, with a minor skirmish over who would moderate these debates. I flatly refused to have Kerry O'Brien of the ABC, because of the way he had handled the second Keating–Hewson debate in 1993. I plumped for the debates to be held at the Channel Nine studios in Sydney and to be moderated by Ray Martin. On my calculation the first debate was a draw, with the advantage for me being that I had been seen to match the Prime Minister. By contrast I felt that, using a good deal more aggression, I beat Keating in the second debate. I believed that my success in that debate resulted in the final box being ticked for some undecided voters. My son Tim gave me good advice which helped in the second debate. He told me to control the twitch which sometimes developed in my right shoulder when I was under pressure. I did.

We had some campaign glitches, including two successive stumbles (literally) by me at a women's policy launch. For one horrible moment I thought that I had badly sprained my right ankle. Also, on the John Laws radio program, I wasn't sufficiently across the fine detail of an aspect of our tax policy.

I was supplied with the nightly tracking research, which showed that the Coalition started the campaign in a strong position and, although there were fluctuations, maintained a healthy lead in the key marginal seats throughout.

Once again, for me there was field evidence. On this occasion it was found in the electorate of Leichhardt, in far north Queensland, based on the city of Cairns. That seat had fallen to Labor in 1983 and had been held thus ever since. The Liberal candidate was a colourful crocodile farmer, Warren Entsch, whose unconventional habits and larrikin style appealed to many uncommitted voters. His campaign had organised a small-business breakfast at the Cairns International Hotel on 13 February. There was a huge turnout, and the sense of excitement and enthusiasm was quite infectious. Those present just could not wait for election day. I felt for the first time in more than a decade the Liberal Party had really reclaimed its natural small-business base. Small business is the absolute economic backbone of rural and provincial cities, and for our prospects in Leichhardt this breakfast was most encouraging.

Such campaign glitches as the Coalition had were minor compared with two big tactical mistakes made by Labor. Towards the end of the campaign there was a major rally for Keating in Melbourne, sponsored by the ACTU and addressed by Keating's good friend Bill Kelty. No doubt carried away by their political and personal regard for each other, rhetoric overtook the occasion. Kelty's firebrand, traditional-union-leader-type speech attracted plenty of headlines, but of the wrong kind. He made it clear that if the Coalition won the election, there would be a no-holds-barred wages campaign by the unions, irrespective of the economic consequences. This may have pleased the assembled throng, and the Prime Minister, but it was poison to the Australian public. It was precisely the kind of irresponsible union behaviour which middle Australia disliked. Kelty had done his friend no service, although I doubt that Keating himself realised it.

The Treasurer, Ralph Willis, was responsible for a big blunder right at the end of the campaign. Anonymously, he received copies of letters purportedly written by Jeff Kennett to Peter Costello objecting to plans by the Coalition to cut payments to the states. We had no such plans, and the letters were fakes. His decision to punt on the veracity of this material badly damaged Labor right on the death knock. It smacked of a desperate government clutching at anything. It was out of character for Ralph Willis, and I remain completely mystified about the source of those fraudulent documents. I was furious as I entered a news conference to denounce the letters as fakes. Michelle Grattan of the *Age* said to Grahame Morris, who accompanied me, 'You're dead, cobber.' After hearing my angry denial, she said to him on the way out, 'You're still alive, cobber.'

Years of disappointment and successive defeats had robbed me of the capacity to expect other than a narrow victory. Despite the polls and the enthusiasm of our supporters, I kept calculating in my mind, as I visited booth after booth in my electorate of Bennelong on 2 March, the handful of seats we would probably just win in New South Wales and Queensland in order to get us across the line. On election day, I did not imagine the scale of the Coalition's victory. We had thought that we would win comfortably in 1993 and didn't. Why would that not happen again? When so much hangs on an event, the natural defence mechanisms of one's emotions come into play.

Janette and I had taken a suite at the Inter-Continental hotel in Sydney. The plan was to watch the TV coverage there in a small group and then go to the nearby Wentworth Hotel for the formal speech. Tony Staley, the federal president, Nick Minchin, who had travelled for much of the campaign with my party, and of course Grahame Morris were all there with me to analyse the results as soon as they began trickling in. Janette, in another room within the suite, was entertaining a small group of friends, who we had invited to share what we hoped would be a very special occasion.

I was told, before the results started coming in, of the party's exit polls, which indicated that we would have a big win. I did not take much notice of this, as we were too close to getting the real thing for it to matter.

There were two officials with computers from the Australian Electoral Commission (AEC) at the Inter-Continental hotel suite, and they began feeding us small-booth returns from about 6.25 pm. Famously, the very first result we spotted was from a booth near Portland, in rural New South Wales, in the electorate of Macquarie. It showed a swing of some 16 per cent to the Liberal Party, which cheered me hugely. Grahame Morris put a dampener on that by pointing out that the booth had only about 80 voters. It was not long, however, before this trend began to be repeated all over those parts of eastern Australia where counting had commenced at 6 pm Eastern Standard Summer Time. South Australia and Queensland would respectively be half-an-hour and an hour behind. Some time shortly after 7 pm, it was apparent that the Coalition had won, although the size of its victory would grow as the evening wore on. The swing in Queensland was massive, with the Coalition recording 60.2 per cent of the two-party-preferred vote. On neither side of politics has that been bettered since Federation, although it was matched by the Coalition in 1975.

As the counting continued I wandered to the larger room, where our guests had assembled and were, by then, in a state of high excitement. I kept going to a television set to check on the count, and was struck by two results which dramatised the scale of our victory. The first was in the Sutherland Shire-based Sydney seat of Hughes, where the Liberal Danna Vale had secured an 11.3 per cent swing to unseat the sitting Labor member and Minister for Indigenous Affairs, Robert Tickner. This was an especially pleasing result as Tickner epitomised the politically correct left of the Labor Party. Whenever the Coalition disagreed with his proposals for Indigenous people, he would suggest that our position was based on prejudice or discrimination.

The other remarkable result, also in Sydney, was the 11.8 per cent swing which Jackie Kelly secured in the outer-western-suburbs seat of Lindsay. As someone who had spent all of his life in Sydney, I found it extraordinary to contemplate that Penrith and St Marys would be represented in the national parliament by a Liberal.

We were to claim victory with a majority of 45 seats over the ALP in a house of 148, a truly amazing result and way beyond my best hopes and certainly any of my rational expectations. Five independents had been elected, three of whom — Pauline Hanson, Allan Rocher and Paul Filing — were former Liberals. At 9.30 pm we all watched Keating's concession speech and our guests then departed for the nearby Wentworth Hotel. I sat alone for a moment to compose some remarks for my victory speech.

I was overwhelmed with exhilaration and pride. My hand shook as I jotted down some notes. It was an immensely satisfying moment, and one for which I had been well prepared. True it was that as a political warrior I felt gratitude that at long last the Labor Party, which had won several elections it did not deserve, had been bundled out of office in a thumping fashion. I was, however, immediately aware that I had become the nation's 25th prime minister — a special privilege of which I remain conscious to this day. I thought of all those people who had stayed with me with through thick and thin and continued to believe that I could make it to the top. Janette and our three children and broader family, of course, were first amongst these. As well there were so many close friends and staff who had toiled for this day and I hoped would be with me for some years into the future in the great experience of governing Australia.

I had not given any thought to what I might say in my victory speech until just before I left to travel to the Wentworth Hotel. I knew innately that, if we were successful, I would not find it hard to make the speech.

It was a simple speech in which I thanked the people of Australia for the privilege they had given me, paid appropriate tribute to Paul Keating, and thanked everyone who had supported our campaign. I promised to govern for all Australians, but made it clear that we would not be a pale imitation of our predecessors and would make the changes which we believed Australia needed.

I had not received a private telephone call from Paul Keating conceding defeat before he made his speech, nor did I receive one from Kim Beazley in 1998. This well-mannered habit, in my experience, did not commence until 2001 when Beazley telephoned me. Latham repeated the gesture in 2004, and in 2007 I telephoned Rudd, conceding defeat.

After my victory speech in 1996, I mingled with the hundreds of delirious supporters who had gathered in the Wentworth Hotel to savour this long-overdue victory for the Liberal and National parties. Following a congratulatory call from the New Zealand Prime Minister, Jim Bolger, I and my family went back to the Inter-Continental, where we partied with close friends and supporters until 2.30 on Sunday morning. It was very hard to sleep after all of that. In any event, Janette and I rose early and went to church at the family place of worship, St Giles' Anglican Church in Greenwich, where our three children had been confirmed. The closing hymn was 'Be Thou My Vision O Lord of My Life'.

With the benefit of hindsight, it was so clear that once the Liberal Party stabilised its leadership, defeat of the Keating Government was as inevitable as anything in politics can ever be. In contemporary times, any term of office for a national government beyond a decade is very hard to secure. Labor received an unexpected bonus with its victory in 1993, and many believe that it should have been defeated in 1990, given the state of the Australian economy.

Paul Keating had contributed very directly to his government's defeat. On the economic front, his scorecard was dismal. At the time of the election, unemployment was still at 8.2 per cent; interest rates, although having begun to fall, were still very high; and many small businesses felt that the recession had never really lifted. Beyond this, though, he was, to many Australians, remote from and uninterested in their routine concerns. His preoccupation with converting Australia into a republic, his version of reconciliation with Indigenous Australia, which struck so many Australians as being an abject apology for white civilisation rather than a genuine desire to include Indigenous people in the mainstream of the nation, and his total preoccupation with Asia were discordant priorities, and completely removed from the needs of their daily lives.

A metaphor for Keating's attitude to Asia, and in particular Indonesia, had been his febrile excitement when he concluded secret negotiations for a security treaty with Indonesia just before Christmas 1995. He really believed that this would be seen by the Australian public as a masterstroke of diplomacy. I took an excited, indeed breathless, phone call from Gareth Evans, who informed me, in utmost secrecy, of course, that the treaty had been concluded and was about to be announced.

It did no harm to relations between the two countries, and the opposition backed it, but many Australians were puzzled as to why something like this should have been negotiated in secret. Important treaties between Australia and other nations had not been handled in that fashion. The treaty did not shift a vote towards the Labor Party. Yet one felt the Prime Minister believed it was a real opinion shaper with the Australian people.

Overwhelmingly it had become time for a change; long past it in the view of many millions of Australians. Keating was a far less popular figure than Bob Hawke had been. He had unexpectedly defeated John Hewson in 1993, and there was a sense, almost immediately after that election, that many people regretted having voted for him. Once, therefore, the Coalition stabilised, Keating's defeat became very likely.

I came to the prime ministership with a long experience in politics. Serving as federal Treasurer is a great training ground for the top position. In addition I had been tested and tempered by the turbulence of 13 years in opposition. I had known years of rejection by my own party as well as experiencing defeat at the polls in 1987. I came to the job as a known quantity, with not all of the Australian people liking what they knew. For the duration of my prime ministership, the Australian community knew where I stood on issues and that there was a consistency of belief on certain things, according to which I would govern. From the moment of my return to the leadership on 30 January 1995, the Coalition had presented as a unified cohesive force. The old animosities dissolved almost overnight, and every section of the two parties united in a determination to make certain of victory.

There were many touching moments and gestures made to me on the night of the election; one that I shall always remember and which, literally, brought tears to my eyes, came from my brother Wal and his wife, Gwen. They gave me a caricature of Winston Churchill in the form of a mug, into which Gwen had deposited a note in her own handwriting, repeating a recollection of Churchill's which recorded his emotions when he finally became Prime Minister of Great Britain in the dark times of World War II. It read as follows:

> I was conscious of a profound sense of relief. At last I had the authority to give directions over the whole scene. I felt as if I was walking with destiny, and that all my past life had been but a preparation for this hour, and for this trial … I thought I knew a good deal about it all and was sure I would not fail. Therefore, although impatient for the morning I slept soundly and had no need of cheering dreams — facts are better than dreams.

PART 3

THE HOWARD GOVERNMENT

21

SHAPING THE
GOVERNMENT

Paul Keating and I didn't agree on a lot. One view we did share was that to change the Government was to change the country. This has been true of all of the changes of government in Australia since World War II. It was to be true of the decision taken by the Australian people to emphatically change their government on 2 March 1996.

A wonderful aspect of democracy in Australia is the peaceful but also relatively civilised power transition which takes place. In the United States the transition is far too long, especially when the political colour of the Administration alters. Not only is an outgoing president nearing the end of his second term something of a lame duck, he is an ultralame duck in the period between early November and Inauguration Day, usually 20 January the following year. In the United Kingdom the process can verge on the uncivilised and vulgar, so rapid must be the change in residential arrangements from one prime minister to another. There were some pathetic press pictures of Edward Heath's belongings sitting, literally, on a London street the day after he lost power to Harold Wilson in 1974.

We do things in a better, more balanced way than that in Australia. Although Paul Keating did not speak to me on the night of the election, he did telephone me two or three days later, and in the meantime there had been discussion between our respective chiefs of staff about transition arrangements. I told him that he could have as much time as he reasonably required in leaving the Lodge. He volunteered that Kirribilli House would be available within a matter of days. I was content enough with the victory and I had no desire to engage unseemly haste in taking possession of the trappings of office and power.

The day after the election was one of mixed emotions, physical exhaustion and rapid realisation of the task ahead. I was determined that the Australian people would see a difference and I knew that the impact of the early weeks and months of the Government would shape the perceptions of the nation towards us.

At 11 am on Sunday, 3 March, in the Commonwealth Offices in Phillip Street in Sydney, I met the Secretary of the Prime Minister's Department, Michael Keating; Bill Blick, a very senior official in the department; and Martin Bonsey, another senior official, who later became Official Secretary to the Governor-General, Sir William Deane. They gave me the two red books. One of these set out what might be called the formal structure of the Government, official obligations and the pay and rations provisions applying to myself and the future members of my ministry. The second book was a policy compendium. It brought to my attention all of the major policy issues which the department believed confronted Australia in March of 1996. Most importantly, it revealed the true state of the nation's finances.

So it was I learned within hours of winning office that the budget was headed towards a deficit of approximately $10.5 billion without policy change. Both Paul Keating and Kim Beazley must have known this before the election. In my view they had both been guilty of deliberate deception. From the very beginning, I knew that we faced a daunting budgetary task and that how we responded and whether or not we did so with our very first budget would shape the direction of the Australian economy, and attitudes towards our capacity to manage it, over the next few years.

I did not come to office resolved to turn the nation on its head. I did not see deep flaws in Australian society or the character of the Australian people. I wanted to have a vigorous debate about the need for change and improvement in those areas where old attitudes were holding the nation back, but my starting point was one of optimism about the condition of the Australian spirit, and much pride in the Australian achievement.

I had a project for government, but I was not so arrogant as to presume that I should inflict on the Australian people a new vision for the nation. Successive generations had given Australia a good enough vision and a sense of her identity, and I believed in the fundamentals of what I saw around me. Good leadership interprets and applies the received values of a nation. In many ways the changes I wished to bring about would more directly echo the instincts of the Australian people, rather than impose on them something new, and about which they would feel uncomfortable.

How did I want to change Australia? I wanted to rescue Australia from debt and deficit and implement those specific economic policies on which we had been elected, including significant deregulation of the labour market, the partial privatisation of Telstra, and the introduction of a tax system which more adequately rewarded parents for the cost of having children. I intended that small business should have an economic and regulatory environment allowing it to prosper and expand.

I wanted to rebalance the narrative about Australia's past. I did not want the blemishes and failures ignored, but I wanted Australians to feel legitimate pride in their history and the distinctive quality of the Australian character as something worth defending and asserting. I wanted an end to the perpetual navel-gazing about our cultural identity. The constant seminar about national identity which Paul Keating had orchestrated over the previous few years challenged the scale of the Australian achievement. There had been too great a premium placed on shame and guilt and too little on enterprise and individualism.

To me Australia was and remains an extension of Western civilisation in our part of the world, driven by the values we had imbibed from our history, our background and our experience as a nation. Although I would respect the secular traditions of our society, I would never shrink from the belief that Australia had been moulded by the Judaeo-Christian ethic, and that this was an asset worth preserving. Many of our institutions were of British origin, but had been shaped and changed to meet the circumstances of our part of the world, and to reflect the egalitarian nature of the Australian people. We embraced the values of liberal democracy and the Enlightenment. I would say on numerous occasions that Australia occupied a unique intersection of history and geography. We were a nation of Western European origin with strong links with North America and forever living cheek by jowl with the nations of Asia.

We were also a nation which owed it to the first Australians to understand that the greatest blemish on Australia's history had been its indifferent treatment of Indigenous people. I did not, however, believe that the response to the Indigenous dilemma of Australia lay in separate development, but through pursuing a policy of including the Aboriginal people in the mainstream of the Australian community, whilst always respecting their special status as the first Australians and the pride they drew from their own culture and traditions.

I wanted to change Paul Keating's seemingly Asia-only foreign policy focus. To me Asia was the first and most important region of political and economic interaction, but it was not the only one. Australia's foreign relations needed to be rebalanced as, over recent years, we had allowed our traditional links with the United States and the United Kingdom to be taken for granted.

Australia needed an immigration policy which drew new settlers from all parts of the world, without discrimination on race, religion or nationality but with a composition designed to best promote the interests of Australia. I intended to end the divisive features of multiculturalism and place a greater emphasis on those things which united us as Australians and not those which divided us.

I also wanted an approach to social security which reaffirmed the importance of the safety net for those Australians who, through no fault of their own, couldn't work. However, welfare policy should encourage self-reliance and not state-dependency. I wanted to resurrect the conventional wisdom of welfare policy in Australia which saw our nation avoiding the harsh excesses of the American welfare system as well as the over-paternalistic approach of many European nations.

Finally, and very importantly, I intended to give a higher priority to Defence. Expenditure on Defence had been woefully neglected by the Keating Government. From the beginning I made it clear that there would be no cuts to the Defence budget as we commenced the task of rescuing the budget from deficit and debt. As the years went by, spending by the Howard Government on Defence would increase greatly.

I intended to lead a government which was a blend of economic liberalism and social conservatism.

To do all of these things I needed to pick the best people available for cabinet and other ministerial posts. Peter Costello suggested that the Leader of the National Party might not be the Deputy Prime Minister. If this were to be so then he, as Deputy Leader of the Liberal Party, would have been Deputy Prime Minister. I told him this was out of the question.

We were going into coalition with the National Party, and in furtherance of longstanding practice the Leader of the National Party would become the

Deputy Prime Minister. There were a few exuberant Liberals around at the time who thought that as the Liberal Party could have, theoretically, governed in its own right due to the huge number of Liberal gains at the election, then we should put the Nationals to one side. This was ludicrous thinking, and I knew that, come the next election or the one after at the very least, we would be heavily dependent on the Nationals to form a government. I was right about that, even though subsequent elections ate away at the number of Nationals in the House of Representatives.

I was a staunch coalitionist. My negative experience in 1987 at the hands of the Queensland Nationals had left me more rather than less determined to preserve our partnership with the National Party. The disunity of those years had cost us dearly. The unity between our two parties over more than a decade was one of the major reasons we stayed in office for so long. The Coalition covered the broad spectrum of centre-right politics in Australia, absent some of the extremist fringes which we certainly did not want. That was why it was so effective.

All modern political parties are, in one form or another, coalitions. The challenge is to keep the different elements of the coalition together. The key to our success was my recognition that in return for National Party acceptance on broad policy issues that Liberal Party attitudes would hold sway, the Nationals would win acceptance of their point of view on matters especially important to their followers. This was not hard. The economic views of Tim Fischer, John Anderson and Mark Vaile were very similar to those of Peter Costello and me. The old divisions of earlier years had gone. The National Party of the Howard years would not have the interventionist instincts of its predecessors.

Choosing a cabinet is the hardest people-oriented task that any prime minister has. I was determined not to squib my first attempt at putting together a government for the Commonwealth of Australia as I knew that many of the people I would choose would heavily influence public attitudes to me and to my Government in the months and years ahead. Many of the senior positions were quite obvious. Peter Costello would become Treasurer and Alexander Downer would become Foreign Minister. As Leader of the National Party, Tim Fischer wanted the Trade portfolio. As by far the most highly qualified lawyer on the Coalition front bench, I chose Daryl Williams as Attorney General. Michael Wooldridge had done a very good job as shadow minister for Health and transitioned to that portfolio quite naturally. The same could be said of Peter Reith, who had handled the

Industrial Relations brief very well in opposition, so he became a very senior member of the cabinet.

One of the consequences of the election had been a major increase in the number of MPs from New South Wales and Queensland and a relative decline in the proportion of Victorians within the parliamentary Liberal Party. Cabinets should never mathematically reflect state balances, but nor should they be ignored. It is a foolish prime minister who takes a cavalier attitude to the inevitable jealousies between the various states. One of many reasons why the voters of Queensland had so brutally mauled Paul Keating was a feeling that their state had no serious players at the cabinet table in his Government, and that it was a Sydney-centric operation. His gratuitous throwaway lines about the superiority of living in Sydney did nothing to mollify this grievance.

As a consequence of these considerations, many Victorians felt that their state's representation in my first cabinet was lower than ought to have been the case. This was nonsense as the final line-up included no fewer than four Victorians within the cabinet itself. It was simply a case of recognising that other parts of the country deserved, not only on numerical but also talent grounds, senior spots in the main team.

A prime example of this was my decision to make John Fahey, the former Premier of New South Wales, Minister for Finance and thus a member of cabinet. This upset Peter Costello, as he had expected his fellow Victorian Jim Short, to whom I gave the junior assistant Treasurer job, to be the Finance Minister. Such objections were absurd. John Fahey had had more experience in government than any other person in our ranks, outside me. Being premier of the largest state in the country does provide a lot of experience at a high level of government decision-making. Fahey proved to be an excellent Finance Minister, and also became a very close colleague of Peter Costello.

Another of my appointments which ruffled a few feathers was that of Amanda Vanstone to the post of Education and Employment. This shocked a lot of people, but I rather liked her independent attitude and sensed that she would not be frightened to take some tough decisions. This proved to be the case in respect of both university funding and the massive reform involved in dismantling the old Commonwealth Employment Service (CES) and replacing it with the new, privatised Job Network.

The other senior appointment which surprised a number of people was that of Ian McLachlan to Defence. I was conscious that this greatly disappointed Jocelyn Newman, who really loved the shadow Defence portfolio and did have her heart set on being the minister. McLachlan had a lot of ability and I felt very strongly that his style and people skills would be very useful in that difficult portfolio. I felt that we had a similar world-view about national security issues. I was not to ignore Jocelyn Newman's talents. She was appointed to run the giant Social Security portfolio and also be minister assisting me on the Status of Women. She was a minister of enormous tenacity and ability, who in her personal life had struggled with and overcome serious health problems.

Two of the prime activists in my downfall in May 1989, John Moore and David Jull, were both included, with John occupying the senior cabinet post of Minister for Industry, Science and Tourism and David Jull the outer ministry of Administrative Services. Moore did a good job as Minister for Industry. His business background and contacts gave him a store of personal knowledge against which he tested departmental advice. He was also a valuable general contributor to cabinet.

Now we were back in government, I decided to follow the practice of Menzies and Fraser of personally appointing government leaders in the Senate. In opposition they had been elected by the Liberal senators. Robert Hill and Richard Alston had been elected respectively as leader and deputy leader in the Senate, and I told them I would reappoint them to those positions. I continued this appointment process throughout our time in government.

Remembering my experience in the Fraser years with the operation of the cabinet system as well as my observation of what had gone on under Keating, I was determined that the system would function productively and properly in my Government. The key to this was to restore a fully functioning and orderly system of cabinet government, with all of the major decisions of the Government being made by the cabinet or its properly functioning committees. The Government I led proved well disciplined. That was because cabinet ministers were fully involved in all major decisions and MPs generally were regularly consulted. Circumstances sometimes precluded this but, because this was the understandable exception and not the rule, discipline held.

I set up a cabinet policy unit whose head was to be the secretary of cabinet. This body interacted with the political and bureaucratic arms of government. It was physically located adjacent to my office, and as its first head I appointed Michael L'Estrange. He was to become one of my most valuable and trusted advisors in the whole time that I was Prime Minister. A Rhodes scholar, he studied at Oxford University before returning to Australia and joining the public service. He had a disciplined and enquiring intellect and an enormous capacity for hard work. Michael won the confidence of senior ministers very quickly and, as someone who had worked in the public service, he started with a measure of respect from the bureaucracy.

As promised, I established a National Security Committee of cabinet, which was to have the task of dealing with all Foreign Affairs and Defence issues, subject to really major decisions being referred to the full cabinet for final endorsement. It was to prove one of the most successful administrative decisions I took.

The consistency and discipline the Howard Government displayed regarding Foreign Policy and Defence was due overwhelmingly to the effective way in which this committee operated. It comprised, as well as the Prime Minister and Deputy Prime Minister, the Treasurer, the ministers for Foreign Affairs and Defence, and the Attorney General. It was attended on a full-time basis by the head of the Prime Minister's Department and the secretaries of Foreign Affairs and Defence, the Chief of the Defence Force, the Director-General of the Office of National Assessments (ONA) and the Director-General of ASIO. Other senior officials such as the Commissioner of the Australian Federal Police (AFP) and the Secretary of the Attorney General's Department were invited to attend on an ad hoc basis. It worked remarkably well as a group and there were no occasions when any information of any consequence leaked from this body. Crucially this arrangement guaranteed that there would be a whole-of-government consistency on Foreign Affairs and Defence matters. I felt that governments in other parts of the world could have profited from copying the Australian model.

Controversially, I did not re-appoint six secretaries who had served in the Keating administration, including the Secretary of the Department of Prime Minister and Cabinet, Michael Keating.

He almost certainly would have stayed, for a time at least, if I had asked him, but Michael Keating fully expected that I would want somebody else, and volunteered this to me. He helped me with the initial stages of the transition in a very positive way. Before he left he gave me two pieces of advice about the running of cabinet, which I found very easy to accept because they reflected my own instincts. He said that I should always start cabinet on time, and that I should make sure that all of the major decisions of the Government were owned by the full cabinet. I sensed that although he may have proffered that advice in the past, it had not always been followed.

For the position of secretary of my department I chose Max Moore-Wilton, colloquially known in the trade as 'Max the Axe', which reflected some of his cost-cutting activities in the NSW bureaucracy. I chose Max because he had a mix of public service and business experience. I recalled his days in the Department of Trade, years earlier in the Fraser Government; also his vigorous attempts to reform the Australian National Line (ANL), which ultimately led to the Labor Government not reappointing him as chief executive of that body. He then did a number of jobs in the NSW public service and won good reviews from senior ministers in the Greiner and Fahey governments.

Max did not disappoint. He brought the right combination of commonsense, administrative skill and good humour to a very difficult job. He returned to the private sector in 2003 and was succeeded by Peter Shergold; different in stye but equally as effective. Peter had a wonderfully creative policy mind and was a consummate public service networker. I was fortunate with both of them.

Nicole Feeley stayed on as my chief of staff with Grahame Morris occupying a new parallel position as chief political advisor. Arthur Sinodinos remained not only as principal economic advisor but also somebody with a general policy brief. Some months later, Nicole recommended a number of senior advisor appointments to my staff. One of these was John Perrin, who assumed responsibility for Social Security and related issues, including Health. His thoughtful and constructive advice played a big role in shaping the social policies of my Government.

My critics frequently accused me of ignoring symbolism. Nothing could be more wrong. Their problem was that they have never liked a lot of my symbols. Symbols are important. That is why I always took a strong position, either positive or negative, when urged to embrace a symbolic act. My first symbolic act was to resume the practice followed by most recent prime ministers of flying the Australian flag on the bonnet of my car. In an act of contempt for Australia's principal national symbol, Paul Keating had discontinued this practice. That had not been the wont of Bob Hawke, who made no bones about his respect for the Australian flag. Nor did Kevin Rudd or Julia Gillard make Keating's mistake.

I also restored an oath of allegiance to the Queen in the oath to be taken by ministers. Unless and until Australia became a republic, it was right that ministers swear an oath of loyalty to the Queen. I did slightly alter the oath to include a commitment to serve the people of Australia ahead of the swearing of allegiance to the Queen, and, in deference to the fact that at some time in the next few years there would be a referendum on whether or not Australia became a republic, ministers were only asked to swear allegiance to Queen Elizabeth II and not her heirs and successors.

Despite urging from a number of people, I did not restore knighthoods. It would have been possible to have done this within the Order of Australia, and without partially resuming the awarding of imperial honours, which had been formally abandoned as a result of a Commonwealth–state agreement in the early 1990s. For me this was an on-balance decision as in some respects the knighthood system, properly applied, was a way of giving special recognition to certain people. I knew, however, that I had other fish to fry, and as a strong supporter of the constitutional monarchy continuing in Australia, I did not wish to be seen to be reviving an honour which to many, even conservative Australians, was somewhat anachronistic.

There was nothing symbolic about the economic task faced by the new government. Peter Costello and I knew that the first budget would be crucial, not only in changing the financial and economic direction of the country but also in shaping perceptions of how strong the Government would be in dealing with the necessity of economic reform. A new government has a lot of political credit in the bank. There is almost an expectation that it will do tough, unpopular things during the early months of its stewardship. The people knew that Australia had a big deficit and too much debt. They were prepared for change, and I judged that if the pain were fairly spread, the community would accept some tough decisions to get the economy back on its feet.

That was the path we took; we publicly embraced a goal of bringing the budget back into balance within three years. This was quite a challenge, as at that time growth, although improving, was still quite sluggish. Having publicly committed to the goal, the Treasurer and I knew that we would be harshly judged if we didn't reach it.

On 12 March, the day after the new government had been sworn in, Peter Costello announced that our aim was to return the budget to an underlying balance by 1997–98. He said that we would achieve that by cutting the deficit by $4 billion in 1996–97 and a further $4 billion the following year; thereafter we would keep the budget in surplus during periods of economic growth. It was an audacious promise, but it was delivered. From the very moment that Peter Costello became Treasurer, he was unambiguously committed to putting Australia's budget back into surplus and keeping it that way. It was an objective that we shared. Having restored the budget balance, it was common ground between us that we would never by design go back into deficit.

Despite the huge majority the Coalition had won in the House of Representatives, it did not control the Senate. The Labor Party did not believe in the mandate theory of government, especially when it was in opposition. Our mandate for industrial relations reform was clear. It was spelled out in great detail before the election and had been the subject of extensive debate over many years prior to 1996. The Australian public knew that a Liberal Government wanted to change unfair dismissal laws and give workers and employers the option of making their own contracts outside the award system, subject to the value of the award being the bedrock on which negotiations for those agreements took place. These were crystal-clear alternatives at the time of the election, and the Coalition won with a huge majority.

Despite this the Labor Party simply opposed every single change we wanted for industrial relations. Our way forward was with the Democrats. The independent Tasmanian senator Brian Harradine, although supportive of many of the Government's positions on social issues, remained at heart a real Labor man when it came to industrial relations. It was in other areas that I was to find Brian Harradine not only a genuine negotiator and helper of the Government in office, but on particular issues a strong supporter.

In May 1996, a bare two months after the change of government, Peter Reith introduced his workplace relations legislation. It was immediately opposed by the Labor Party, and Reith commenced a long and, ultimately, reasonably successful negotiation with Andrew Murray, the Democrats' spokesman on industrial relations, and Cheryl Kernot, the Leader of the Australian Democrats. Reith was a good negotiator. He knew that he had to give something in order to obtain the support of the Democrats. They were willing to go half-way or even a little more with the Coalition. They accepted the desirability of having Australian workplace agreements outside the award system but subject to a strict no-disadvantage test, which was our campaign promise anyway — but in the negotiations they insisted on a further tweaking of the test.

The real sticking point and the biggest disappointment was that we were not able, ever, to shift the Democrats on unfair dismissal laws. Not only was this frustrating but it ran completely counter to the pro-small business opinions of the Democrats' founder, Don Chipp. He frequently criticised the unfair dismissal laws and understood their impact on small business. Over the years that followed, the Coalition would try on more than 40 occasions to get amendments loosening the impact of these laws through the Senate, but could never garner the support of the Democrats. Increasingly the Democrats were falling into the hands of new class politicians, who were often to the left of the Labor Party. The one conspicuous exception to this proved to be the leadership which Meg Lees showed over tax reform.

Some of my colleagues agitated for a Senate confrontation on workplace relations, with a view to having a double-dissolution election. I never thought that this was worth the candle, with no guarantee that a double dissolution would give us control of the Senate. Although I was unhappy with many of the compromises hammered out with the Democrats, we were nonetheless able to achieve a substantial part of our workplace agenda.

Reith won deserved praise for his capacity to negotiate with the Democrats. One of the major elements of the new legislation was, of course, the creation of Australian workplace agreements. They remained an option and, in the case of many industries, including the mining industry, an extremely valuable one for more than 11 years until their abolition immediately after the Rudd Government was elected. No evidence had been produced showing that workers had been disadvantaged under the Australian workplace agreements legislated in 1996, and which contained the no-disadvantage test.

In winning a lot of plaudits from his colleagues for negotiating an arrangement with the Democrats, Peter Reith attracted some fleeting attention as a potential leadership successor, some years into the future. Some stories even began appearing that I was promoting Reith as a rival to Peter Costello. I was not. Reith was, however, attentive to colleagues on the backbench and understood, from the beginning, the importance of senior cabinet ministers visiting electorates, particularly marginal ones.

Another major election promise was kept when, with the support of Brian Harradine, we obtained Senate approval for the sale of one-third of Telstra. Both the Labor Party and the Democrats had campaigned against the sale of any part of Telstra, so Harradine's support was crucial. With this bill through, we were able to establish the Natural Heritage Trust and continue to keep faith with the pro-environmental stance taken during the election campaign.

I was very grateful to Brian Harradine for the support he gave in the Senate for our New Schools policy. Under the previous government, it was extremely difficult for a new independent school started in an area already serviced by a government and a Catholic parish school — which was the case in most areas — to attract federal government funding. In response to urgings from Sydney Anglicans, who wanted to establish a system of low-fee Anglican schools, I announced a policy change to achieve this.

We legislated for the change, and predictably the Labor Party, still cornered by the education unions, opposed it. So did the Australian Democrats. To his great credit, Brian Harradine saw the virtue in what we were proposing to do. He was a true believer in freedom of choice in education. When the Labor Party moved a Senate amendment which would have severely undermined our proposal, Harradine voted with the Government, as did Senator Mal Colston, to whom I will return later, and the Labor Party abandoned its tactics, lest it be seen as being too opposed to more independent schools. I remain intensely proud of this change as it has resulted in a rapid expansion in the number of low- to moderate-fee-level independent schools. The Anglicans have been active but so have others, and this of course is an area where, subject to the requisite educational standards being met, the assistance is available irrespective of religious affiliation or to a group that has no religious identification at all.

Early in my prime ministership I had also decided on an important diplomatic appointment. That was to invite Andrew Peacock to serve as Australian ambassador to the United States. He accepted with grace, and the opportunity of this appointment pleased me immensely. Andrew had unmatched political contacts on both sides of the American political divide and he would go on to fill the position for three years with effortless skill. Andrew's wife, Penne, is a Texan, and they currently divide their time between the two nations.

I have described some of the early political and policy challenges of my newly won office. There was also a massive adjustment for my family. Janette had left the paid workforce when I was elected to parliament, with our daughter, Melanie, being born just a few months later. She never returned to teaching, at which she excelled, because with my being away on a regular basis with parliamentary sittings and other commitments, the intensive parental care and attention we wanted our children to have would not have been possible. That was our choice; neither of us has ever regretted it. I have always been conscious of the professional sacrifice that Janette made, and although she did it freely, I could not have achieved what I did in politics without it.

In every way imaginable, I was lucky to meet Janette. Not only did I love her enough to want to spend my life with her, but from the beginning we enjoyed talking to each other on all conceivable subjects; 40 years later we are still at it, including politics. Janette is a highly intelligent, independent, opinionated woman who was never reluctant to express her views to me on the issues of the day, even if they were at odds with mine. We had some lively arguments. But once I had taken a decision that was it, not because she accepted that I was right, but I was the elected person. She was highly critical of those husbands, wives and others who exploited their positions to publicly air their thoughts, knowing full well they would attract attention because of who they were related to. She frequently said that if she wanted to inflict her views on the public, she would run for parliament herself. This was one of the reasons she never did many press interviews. I was fortunate that Janette enjoyed politics, was never at me to leave and has kept her intense interest beyond my active participation. In part because she was an only child, Janette is self-reliant, something she was keen to pass on to our three children.

The pattern of our life as a family was well settled before I became Prime Minister; by then our youngest was 16. There had been many stressful times for Janette. I have never forgotten arriving home from Canberra one Friday evening in October 1981, when I was Treasurer, to find her in the midst of the chaos of an almost totally dismembered house, which was in the throes of having a storey added. She was calmly handling three children, the youngest of whom, Richard, was then 14 months, as well as caring for her mother, Beryl Parker, who was staying with us as her husband had died just two weeks earlier. She had set up a makeshift bed for her mother in the partially built stairwell area. I marvelled at her capacity to keep it all together.

Janette's mother was a big part of our lives. She bought a home unit immediately behind our Wollstonecraft home, moving there in early 1982, only a few months after Janette's father died. It was the ideal arrangement, as she had the security of living near us but the independence of her own home. She watched her three grandchildren grow up, influencing them in different and always positive ways.

When I became PM we looked at the possibility of staying at Wollstonecraft, but it was soon apparent that the costs involved in extra security, which in turn would inconvenience our neighbours, meant it was not realistic. As Richard still had two more years at the nearby Shore school, and Melanie and Tim were at university, both in Sydney, we decided to base the family at Kirribilli House, knowing full well that I would spend as much if not more time at the Lodge. Janette did not wish to move too far from her mother, who continued in her Wollstonecraft unit.

It didn't add to the taxpayers' burden. There are fixed running costs for official residences, irrespective of how frequently they are used; the overall staff establishment of the two residences was lower than for my predecessor, and the earlier practice of overseas visitors staying at Kirribilli had largely been abandoned before I became PM. Our children lived with us at Kirribilli until going their different ways, quite a few years later. It was a very happy time in our family life.

Early in July 1996, Janette was diagnosed with cervical cancer. It shocked us both, with the strain and anguish for her being enormous. She underwent a major operation on 28 July, and after weeks of convalescence was able to resume what might loosely be called her 'public duties' in October. She was an amazing example of strength in handling a huge personal medical problem. She never lost her hope and optimism and continued to be totally involved with me in the challenge of my still-very-new responsibilities. Her illness, quite literally, immobilised me for a few days. Although the exact nature of Janette's illness was not made public at the time, most assumed that it was cancer. Paul Keating rang to express his concern. The greatest inspiration I drew from this traumatic time was the profound unity and affection of our family. My three children rallied behind their mother in a way that must have contributed to her sense of optimism. Their love would have steeled her survival instincts. They were terrific.

All five of us remain grateful to God and to good surgeons that Janette emerged from her illness and operation with a very positive prognosis. Like so many others who have passed through such an experience, she came out of it with altered priorities. To her the future was about focusing even more on the welfare of her children and our relationship with them, in recognition that those relationships are the most important and enduring ones that life delivers. She also committed herself to an active level of involvement in helping organisations involved in cancer, particularly forms of cancer affecting women.

Economic issues had dominated our early months in government but two events, completely uneconomic ones, were to interrupt the early focus and themselves become intertwined in the aftershocks from each event.

22

SEIZING THE DAY
ON GUNS

On 28 April 1996, Martin Bryant, a psychologically disturbed man, using two weapons — a semiautomatic Armalite rifle and a semiautomatic SKS assault weapon — killed 35 people on a murderous rampage in remote and eerie Port Arthur, Tasmania. Formerly a desolate penal colony in the early years of the nation, it was a popular tourist destination. The murders on that quiet Sunday shocked Australia and the world. It was the largest number of people who had died in a single series of incidents at the hands of one person. The whole nation reeled in disbelief for weeks afterwards.

The Tasmanian Government and police had the primary responsibility for dealing with the aftermath of the shooting, although there was no doubt as to where the ultimate responsibility would lie. The scale of the massacre gave it a national dimension. Tony Rundle, the Tasmanian Premier, rang me at Kirribilli House a few hours after the slaughter had occurred and asked that I come to Tasmania as soon as possible, visit the scene of the mass murder and associate myself with his government's response. Even at that preliminary stage, we briefly discussed the adequacy of Tasmania's gun laws. Although banned in some states, the weapons used by Bryant were not banned in Tasmania. Gun laws in Australia were then a hodge-podge, lacking both consistency and uniformity.

In one of my headland speeches, on 6 June 1995, I had argued for tougher gun laws in Australia, having for some time believed that we should do all we could to avoid going down the terrible American path, where the ready availability of firearms of all descriptions was directly responsible for the very high murder rate in that country. Although I knew that laws on the availability and use of firearms were exclusively state responsibilities, except in relation to imports, the scale of the massacre gave me pause to reflect. I began to give thought to the possibility of a national initiative to tighten those laws.

On Wednesday, 1 May I visited Port Arthur with Tony Rundle; Kim Beazley, the new Opposition leader; and Cheryl Kernot, the Leader of the Australian Democrats. It was a time for full bipartisanship. It was a bleak experience, the sheer loneliness of the place emphasising the horror of what had occurred. I then attended an emotional memorial service at St David's Cathedral in Hobart. After it had finished I met many of those who had been involved in helping the victims, including a Dr Bryan Walpole, who had attended to the most seriously wounded. He broke down when speaking to me and, spontaneously, I embraced him. As a public figure, the most helpful response one can provide is the natural spontaneous one. Hesitancy and awkwardness only aggravate the grief of the person who is looking to you for support.

These experiences in Tasmania strengthened my instinct that the moment should be seized, and something done at a national level to toughen our gun laws. After returning from the memorial service, I spoke to the media and indicated that I was prepared to look at significant tightening of the laws, including a prohibition on automatic and semiautomatic weapons, which would cover the weapons used by Bryant. That evening I met advisors and senior staff at the Lodge to discuss this and other matters. At one point my chief advisor, Grahame Morris, pulled me aside and said that there had been press enquiries as to the extent of my commitment to prohibition. 'Are you really serious about the semiautomatics?' Morris asked. 'Because if you are not, now is the time to make that clear, on a background basis.' I told him that I was and that the press should understand my willingness to use the authority of my office to bring about a really big change.

Stricter gun control was not an easy issue, especially for the Coalition side of politics. There was plenty of support from the Labor Party. The NSW Premier, Bob Carr, was a strident opponent of the free availability of guns and was to prove one of my strongest backers. The two problem states were clearly going to be Queensland and Western Australia, both of which had Coalition governments.

For a limited number of people in rural Australia, firearm restrictions would be very hard. Mostly farmers, they clearly needed weapons for the operation of their businesses. Apart from the practical aspects involved, many deeply resented the possibility that as perfectly law-abiding citizens they should be caught up with a blanket prohibition made necessary by the actions of a madman. Then there were the numerous sporting shooter groups, dotted around the country, all of which saw what I had in mind as, at the very least, a huge pest but more menacingly a threat to their recreational activities.

I made some fascinating discoveries about gun ownership amongst my ministerial colleagues. That most mild-mannered and law-abiding Deputy Leader of the National Party, John Anderson, had a veritable arsenal. People like him were not the problem, but if we were to be taken seriously in seeking a blanket ban, he would have to give up most of his store of weapons. He did so with grace and goodwill, but that was not the case with many other dyed-in-the-wool Coalition voters, who saw what I was doing as the insensitive, kneejerk reaction of a city Liberal who did not understand country people.

Equally, however, many country people who had used guns on a daily basis from early in their lives did not understand the sense of fear and insecurity which a mass murder of the type carried out by Bryant produced amongst Australians living in our major cities, who had never held a gun. This applied particularly to urban women. My proposal certainly produced a hostile reaction in some country areas, but it also brought forth passionate approval in many other parts of the country.

From the very start I had, as PM, maintained my normal habit of walking to engagements when I was in the city, be it Sydney or any other state capital. In the days following Port Arthur, on several occasions people stopped me in the streets and, having made it plain that they had never voted for me in the past and were unlikely to do so in the future, nonetheless were emphatic that I was doing the right thing on guns and, for their children's safety, should stay with it. I spent a good deal of time talking to leaders of farming and other rural organisations, as well as Coalition colleagues in the states, in an attempt to gauge their reactions and persuade them to back tough national action. For many of them it was a painful issue. They wished to help, they knew the feeling of the nation, but it was their members and supporters who would be most directly affected. The Queensland Premier, Rob Borbidge, was a case in point. Politically it was harder for him than any other state premier, and at the cost of storing up later problems for himself, he was extremely helpful. I remained grateful for that.

The Government's position, endorsed by cabinet on 6 May, was that there should be a total prohibition on the ownership, possession, sale and importation of all automatic and semiautomatic weapons. There would be other aspects, but that was the essence. I was determined that this would not be an ambit claim. That was what we wanted. Of course we had to get the states on side. There was to be a police ministers' meeting in Canberra on 10 May.

For urban Liberals this was all relatively straightforward. For National Party MPs and rural Liberals, things were altogether different. It was going to get hard for Tim Fischer and John Anderson. They were both courageous in backing me so strongly on firearm restrictions. I never forgot. It was a prime example of the Nationals putting the good of the Coalition ahead of their own immediate political gains. It was one of the reasons why I would become impatient with those Liberals who begrudged some of the concessions I made to the Nationals on policy questions dear to them. There had to be give and take in the Coalition.

Daryl Williams, as Attorney General, chaired the police ministers' meeting. There was a lot of opposition from the Western Australian minister, Bob Weiss, who, with Russell Cooper, the Queensland Police Minister, were most resistant to the prohibition that I had in mind. I was on hand in Canberra in the expectation that a personal involvement might be necessary to get them across the line.

Williams reported to me in the early afternoon that it was all a little too difficult, and that I might have to settle for something short of what we wanted. I was determined not to do this, not only because I thought the prohibition was essential public policy, but also because of the strength of public feeling on guns. The nation had been left numb by the Bryant slaughter and it expected the newly elected Prime Minister, with a huge majority, to do something about it. The general public was not too fussed about the federal/state or constitutional niceties. To them there was a problem and the Prime Minister should fix it, particularly as he had raised the possibility that he might do so.

I met the police ministers and, through a combination of persuasion, cajolery and — always a winner with state governments — an offer by the Commonwealth to substantially fund the gun buyback, which would be needed to implement the prohibition, agreement was finally reached. The agreement included a ban on automatic and semiautomatic rifles and shotguns and a nationwide approach to registration and licensing. It covered the importation, ownership, sale, resale, transfer, possession, manufacture or use of the weapons targeted by the ban.

The senior bureaucrat advising me, Daryl Smeaton, expressed astonishment at the outcome. His advice had been that what the Government wanted was too ambitious and that I should settle for something a little less comprehensive. I felt an enormous sense of elation at what I had done. Within a few short weeks of becoming Prime Minister I had brought about a huge change in Australia's gun laws in response to an unbelievable tragedy. I had been able to use my office in a constructive and effective fashion to bring about something which the overwhelming majority of the Australian people thought was good for the country. There was an ongoing cost involved, and the pain flowing from that was to be felt within the Coalition parties, particularly the National Party. It was to reverberate for many months and feed into another completely unrelated event which had yet to break upon the Australian political scene.

On the evening of that historic meeting in Canberra I flew to Melbourne to attend the first of the three Prime Minister's Olympic dinners which I would formally host in the time that I was in the Lodge. My mood at the dinner was a mixture of exhaustion and exhilaration. It had been difficult, but we had won the right outcome, and I knew that the Government would be seen by most Australians as having put the public interest ahead of everything else. Media reaction, including from sources normally quite sceptical about me, was most complimentary. A big blow had been struck for a safer community.

If I had entertained the idea that the police ministers' meeting was the end of this matter, I was completely mistaken. As the implications of that decision began to be understood, resistance, particularly through branches of the Liberal and National parties, began to grow. I was to have several testy party room meetings when a variety of members raised objections and argued that my goal could be realised whilst at the same time granting certain exemptions for rural people generally, and sporting shooters. I took an uncompromising line, knowing only too well that once a concession was made, more would be demanded and, in the end, the whole scheme would unravel.

One proposed change involved a process called 'crimping' — the disabling of a semiautomatic weapon so that only one shot at a time could be fired without reloading. The argument was that people who had crimped their weapons should be allowed to keep them. It was claimed that the AFP thought that this could work. So I asked that the army have a look at it. Shortly afterwards Grahame Morris rang and said, 'It took the army blokes all of half an hour to reverse that crimping, boss.' I would not agree to an exemption based on crimping.

Farmers had to have access to certain weapons for their daily activities. These were defined as covering other than semiautomatic or automatic weapons. Details of that nature were finally bedded down and in a way that most people appeared to accept, and they were not seen as weakening the central thrust of the original decision.

Despite the agreement of the police ministers, it was touch and go with two of the states, especially Western Australia, as to whether all the features of that ministers' agreement would be legislated. The Commonwealth had no constitutional power beyond imports. I didn't, therefore, try to stop a newspaper story suggesting that if all of the states did not come on board, the Commonwealth might hold a referendum to obtain the power to pass laws in its own right. Given the feeling of the nation, that was a referendum which would have been carried. Thankfully, that never eventuated. I would have done it if necessary, but a lot of division would have ensued, and it all would have been on our side of politics.

The gun buyback proved to be hugely effective and despite some erosion of the national agreement, it has by and large survived. More than 700,000 guns were removed and destroyed, or one-fifth of Australia's estimated stock of firearms. The equivalent figure in the United States would have been 40 million guns.

Most importantly, gun-related homicides in Australia have declined noticeably since the introduction of the national laws. According to research from the University of Sydney released in November 2006, the prohibition has been successful. The research concluded: 'Australia's 1996 gun law reforms were followed by more than a decade free of fatal mass shootings, and accelerated declines in firearms deaths, particularly suicides. Total homicide rates followed the same pattern. Removing large numbers of rapid-firing firearms from civilians may be an effective way of reducing mass shootings, firearm homicides and firearm suicides.'[1] Separately, the Australian Institute of Criminology found that gun-related murders and suicides had fallen sharply since the 1996 moves. In 2002–03 Australia's rate of 0.27 gun-related homicides per 100,000 was one-fifteenth that of the United States. 2010 research published in the *American Journal of Law and Economics* found that our gun buyback had cut firearm suicides by 74 per cent, saving 200 lives per year.[2]

On this issue, the psychology of Americans and Australians is utterly different. Only two months after our national agreement, I hosted a dinner at Admiralty House in Sydney for Madeleine Albright, the US Secretary of State, and William Perry, the Defense Secretary, who were, with Alexander Downer and Ian McLachlan, attending the annual Australia–United States Ministerial Consultations (AUSMIN) talks in Sydney. They questioned me about these new gun laws, expressed admiration for what Australia had done, but made it clear that even amongst the more anti-gun-inclined Democrats, there was no appetite to attempt something on that scale in the United States. There was even less prospect under a Republican Administration.

In March 2008, former President George H.W. Bush hosted me at his library in College Station, Texas, before a gathering of several hundred friends and supporters, who gave me a very warm welcome. That was until I was asked to name the things of which I was intensely proud from my time as Prime Minister. I cited national gun-control laws as one of my prized achievements. This produced an audible gasp of amazement from the audience. They were good-humoured but nonetheless made their views on the subject abundantly clear.

I made one big mistake in the handling of this issue. That was to wear a bullet-proof vest when I addressed a rally of angry opponents of the measures in the Gippsland area of Victoria. The local police had received a quite explicit death threat directed against me, and both Grahame Morris and my AFP detail advised me to take no chances. My initial instinct, which I should have followed, was to reject that advice, but, it being very early days in my prime ministership, I decided to play it safe. I was wrong to have done so. We all overreacted. I felt instantly embarrassed when I saw the vest bulging inside my sports jacket during TV footage of the event. I still feel that same embarrassment to this day whenever I see the footage replayed. I have never worn a bulletproof vest on Australian soil since. I didn't feel scared when I addressed that Gippsland rally, nor indeed at any other gathering I spoke to in the whole time I was in public life. I have great faith in the essentially non-violent character of the Australian people.

The gun-control drama illustrated both the unpredictability of politics and the reality that public perceptions of a PM are often shaped by how he responds to unexpected crises. The tragedy of Port Arthur could not have been foreseen. I acted swiftly and in a manner which was compassionate to the surviving victims and the loved ones of the 35 who died.

One of those who I remained in touch with was Walter Mikac, whose wife and two small daughters were murdered by Bryant. His loss was immense, and he established the Alannah and Madeline Foundation in honour of his two little girls. He was a lovely man, and my sympathy for him demonstrated how I felt for this group of Australians who had seen the lives of those they cared for most brutally ended by a random act of violence.

Not only had I involved myself at an emotional level with the tragedy, but I used the immense authority of my newly won office to achieve a huge shift in the laws relating to guns, and in a direction most Australians supported. Many people saw me in a different light for the first, and for some, the only time. This was something that went to the basic safety of their daily lives. Maybe there is more to this man than just balancing the budget, reducing union power and strengthening our defence forces, some thought. It gave me a social dimension, above party politics, which had never before occurred to some Australians. Within just two months of becoming PM I would forever be identified with driving an effective national response to a terrible tragedy which was now part of our history. I had passed a very important character test.

23

PAULINE HANSON

The Queensland division of the Liberal Party endorsed Pauline Hanson as the Liberal Party candidate for the safe Labor-held seat of Oxley in the 1996 election. It was a Labor Party citadel and certainly not one that we felt we had any prospect of winning. Two weeks out from the election, Hanson was reported in the local Ipswich newspaper as having cast aspersions on Aboriginal people, blaming them for higher-than-average crime levels, and suggesting that they had privileged access to entitlements. These remarks were completely unacceptable, and the Queensland Liberal Party president, Bob Tucker, and state director, Jim Baron, after consultation with our federal director, Andrew Robb, Grahame Morris and me, decided that Hanson should be disendorsed. So close were we to the election that it was too late to choose another candidate or indeed to alter what was already on the ballot paper. Thus Pauline Hanson, although disendorsed as a Liberal, appeared as the Liberal Party candidate for Oxley on election day.

That would have been the end of the matter, except for the voters of Oxley. As is now part of Australian political legend, Hanson secured, at 19.3 per cent, the biggest anti-Labor swing in the nation, and won Oxley from the Labor Party. It was an amazing result. Although the general outcome in the election suggested that Hanson would have received a very big swing anyway, it is doubtful that she would have won the seat without the additional factor of her disendorsement by the Liberal Party. This, for several reasons, inflated her vote.

The swing required to wrest Oxley from Labor had been 12.6 per cent. Pauline Hanson's sacking did attract a sympathy vote. As well, her sacking drew attention to her attack on what she saw as excessive benefits for Aboriginal people. A lot of people in places such as Ipswich agreed with her. As she was no longer an official Liberal, some traditional ALP supporters felt freer to vote for her. Their usual party was on the skids, so why not. The euphoria of our massive general election win swamped a proper examination of the true ingredients of Hanson's remarkable victory.

Given the Coalition's huge majority, Pauline Hanson for several months drew little attention. She greeted me in a friendly enough manner whenever we came across each other in the halls of Parliament House. She did not strike me as a person who was about to have a big impact on Australian politics. This changed quite dramatically on 10 September 1996, when Pauline Hanson delivered her maiden speech.

The speech was full of economic populism and old-fashioned protectionism. One could disagree with many of the points she made without branding them as in any way extreme or prejudiced. She called for the abolition of the Aboriginal and Torres Strait Islander Commission (ATSIC). She was ahead of her time on that. Eight years later that became the policy of both the Coalition and the ALP. Back in 1988 the Coalition had opposed the formation of ATSIC.

There were two claims Hanson made in her maiden speech which attracted all of the attention. She said that a form of reverse racism applied to the application of Indigenous policy. She rejected outright the proposition that Aborigines were the most disadvantaged group in our society. Hanson delivered a broadside against special programs of all kinds for Indigenous Australians, including those flowing from the Mabo case.

Her most incendiary allegation was, 'I believe we are in danger of being swamped by Asians.'[1] She said that Asian migrants did not assimilate, formed their own ghettos and had their own religion and culture. Hanson also called for the abolition of multiculturalism.

I found it interesting to read her speech again, 13 years after it had been first delivered. Doing so confirmed in me the belief that my reaction to it, criticised as it was, had been correct. There was little doubt that Hanson echoed community sentiment with her attacks on multiculturalism, ATSIC and separatist policies for black and white Australians, and blanket condemnation of political correctness. Equally, though, her unwillingness to accept that Indigenous Australians were the most disadvantaged group in our midst was as inaccurate then as, sadly, it remains the truth today.

Her remarks about Asian immigration were irresponsible and

inflammatory. Asian immigration had risen, but alarmist and inaccurate talk that Australia was being flooded with Asians risked stoking old-fashioned and unwanted prejudice. The bulk of the evidence from the 13 years which have passed since Hanson's speech has been that Asians have joined the mainstream of Australian society quite freely.

Pauline Hanson would have struck a chord with most Australians by saying that we should all be one society, with disadvantage within that society being addressed effectively. She quoted some views of Sir Paul Hasluck from 1955 in support of her claims. Hanson then made the truly extraordinary assertion that in 1955 white Australians enjoyed privileges over Aboriginals, whereas 41 years later it was the other way around. She based her claims of modern-day black privilege on the existence of special benefits available only for Indigenous Australians. She made no allowance for the fact that these benefits were there precisely because of Indigenous disadvantage and nothing else.

Hanson's mistake was to argue that there was no disadvantage rather than to attack the benefits as a way of reducing the disadvantage. She would then have been on much surer ground. Australians then and now all agree that there is profound Aboriginal disadvantage. We disagree on how best it should be tackled.

The immediate issue posed by Hanson's speech was not the accuracy of her two provocative comments — they were clearly both wrong for the reasons I have given — but how to respond. My instinct from the beginning was that there should not be an overreaction.

Pauline Hanson should be corrected, but I felt she should not be made a martyr. The more people attacked her, the more supporters she would attract and the greater would be the publicity given to her views. On *A Current Affair* on 25 September, I was asked whether I thought that Australia was in danger of being swamped by Asians, the very words Hanson had used. My reply was, 'No, I don't believe that. We have a non-discriminatory immigration policy in this country.' Twice more during the interview, Ray Martin asked if I thought that there was a problem with the level of Asian immigration. I said there was not.

Interviewed by Alan Jones on 30 September I said, 'I don't agree with [Hanson] when she implied that Aborigines as a group are not disadvantaged; I think they are.' In that same interview I went on to say, 'Now, I want justice for the Aboriginal people. I did not oppose the Mabo decision, I thought it was, in itself, a very justifiable decision but I think the way the Keating Government did it, the way Robert Tickner handled the situation, was quite wrong.' The day before, interviewed again by Ray Martin, largely about Pauline Hanson, I said, 'We badly treated our Aboriginal people, shamefully treated them, and we must remedy that by helping them now to have a brighter future.'

These remarks of mine were clearly at odds with what Pauline Hanson had said in her maiden speech. I had stated my position but because I had not launched the all-out verbal assault on Hanson urged on me by the ALP, many journalists and by some Liberals such as Jeff Kennett, it was alleged I had gone 'soft' on her and was not showing 'leadership'. My approach was deliberate. So was that of our opponents, who saw the potential to divide the Coalition side of politics on the issue. That was their objective.

The truth, and this was something which I felt from the very beginning, was that Pauline Hanson was something of a metaphor for a group of Australians, most of whom did not have a racist bone in their bodies, who believed that in different ways they had been passed over, left out or generally short-changed by the pace and the intensity of economic and social change which Australia had undergone over the previous 10 to 15 years. Although Pauline Hanson's most controversial remarks were about Asian immigration and Aboriginal welfare, her general pitch, subsequent to her maiden speech, was to identify very strongly with traditional Australian values.

She literally, as well as figuratively, wrapped herself in the Australian flag. She assumed the demeanour of an Aussie battler. She was a single mother who had run a fish and chip shop in Ipswich. She spoke in a faltering manner on occasions, which only added to her popular appeal; many Australians who had not completed a tertiary education were increasingly suspicious of slick, public relations oratory and wanted to be spoken to directly in a language they felt they could understand. She argued for strong defences, friendship with our traditional allies as well as protection for Australian industry and, amongst other things, attacked the Coalition Government's gun laws.

To my mind, the Australian media, with a few notable exceptions such as the Sydney radio talkback host Alan Jones, completely overreacted to Pauline Hanson. Wide sections of the media, particularly Fairfax journalists and the ABC, saw a golden opportunity to attack me for not hitting Hanson hard enough. The huge media coverage of Pauline Hanson within Australia stimulated extensive and often lurid coverage in Asia. It always will. That is why Australian journalists have a responsibility in such matters to contemplate the impact of sensationalism.

Paul Kelly, editor at large for the *Australian*, regarded as Australia's foremost political author, allowed himself to become caught up with the Hanson hysteria. I leave aside what he wrote at the time. Comments in his recent book, *The March of Patriots*, enable me to make my point. In that book Kelly claimed that the speech I made to the Queensland Liberal Party on 22 September 1996 gave Pauline Hanson momentum. It was an unjustified claim. Kelly said that I had signalled sympathy for Hanson and contempt for her critics. I didn't even mention Hanson in the speech. What I did point out was that, following our election, some of the political correctness of the Keating era had gone. I had railed against some of the McCarthyist smear tactics of the Keating Government whenever the Liberals disagreed with an Indigenous policy of that administration. It was a highly political speech at a Liberal Party convention, just six months after a huge election win, and in a state where the Coalition had scored its greatest triumph — fancy that!

The message which the Keating Government's smear tactics generated was encapsulated in a cartoon which had appeared in the *Age* at the height of the native-title debate several years before we won office, which depicted Peter Reith and me both on horseback, shooting Aborigines. The caption read, 'The Second Dispossession'. It was outrageous. Our opposition to the Keating agenda on native title had been enough to bring forth this kind of vitriol. In writing this book I reread my Queensland speech. In it I made direct reference to that *Age* cartoon immediately after the remarks to which Kelly had referred as giving Hanson momentum. I had the McCarthyist tactics of the Keating Government in mind, not Pauline Hanson, when I said, 'The pall of censorship on certain issues has been lifted.'

In my Queensland speech I entered an important caveat. I said, 'That freedom of speech carries with it a responsibility on all those who exercise that freedom to do so in a moderate and tolerant fashion and not to convert the new-found freedom, if I may put it that way, into a vehicle for using needlessly insensitive and intolerant language.'

Hanson appealed very strongly to many traditional National Party supporters. Thus she became an electoral gift to the Labor Party. Shrewd heads in the Labor Party knew that most of her support would be from amongst those who had voted for the Coalition at the 1996 election. There may have been a few Hanson supporters in places such as the Hunter Valley of New South Wales — and indeed in her home patch of Ipswich — of a normally Labor hue, but by and large she attracted the support of people who had voted for the Coalition in droves just six months earlier.

As a consequence, Labor could attack Hanson with impunity, build the issue as much as possible and call on me and other members of the Liberal Party to denounce her and, in time of course, to place her behind Labor on our how-to-vote recommendations. Unfortunately this tactic from Labor was mimicked by some in the Liberal Party. Jeff Kennett saw himself as the great Liberal friend of multiculturalism, and therefore as a natural-born opponent of Pauline Hanson. Never reluctant to jump in and say things which he thought I should be saying, he ran the Hanson issue as hard as he could.

Peter Costello and, to some degree, Alexander Downer and even Tim Fischer went harder than I did in denouncing Hanson. I had wanted a final decision on Liberal Party preferences to be put off until closer to the election. Peter Costello announced in an interview on the *Sunday* program on 10 May 1998 that Hanson would be placed last on the ballot paper in his electorate of Higgins.

Newspapers in Asian countries ran prominent stories about Pauline Hanson. Our critics in Australia knew this and it provided added incentive for the anti-Hanson crusade to be kept at fever pitch. Pauline Hanson had no policy substance. She championed ludicrous propositions such as a flat-rate spending tax. I knew that as time passed she would be forced to declare her policies and that this would ultimately erode the support which she had gathered in the community. I also knew that many of the people who were endeared to her would deeply resent being labelled racist. It was a situation where people had only wanted to listen to certain things which she had said, but ignore the rest.

For the Prime Minister, and a Liberal one at that, to launch a full-frontal assault on Pauline Hanson with the sort of language some of my critics were demanding would have been quite counterproductive. It would have given her even greater status. Amongst other considerations, I wanted to retain the support of those former Coalition voters who were supportive of some of the things being said by Pauline Hanson.

It is hard to know what impact the guns issue had on boosting Hanson's support. Pauline Hanson would have made her controversial speech and gathered a lot of the support which she did irrespective of the national gun-control laws. However, many traditional National Party supporters had been unsettled by the laws; some of them felt betrayed by our actions. Others, having waited many years for a Coalition Government and finding that their economic conditions had not improved overnight, sought what appeared, on the surface, to be a more radical alternative in Hanson.

Even though the adverse press Australia was receiving in Asian countries was as much the result of the political campaign against Hanson in Australia as the remarks she herself had originally made, it was nonetheless damaging to our interests in those countries. For that reason I decided to deal in a more formal set-piece way with the Hanson issue, through an address to the Australia–Asia Society in Sydney on 8 May 1997.

In that speech I said, 'She is wrong when she suggests that Aboriginals are not disadvantaged. She is wrong when she says that Australia is in danger of being swamped with Asians. She is wrong to seek scapegoats for society's problems. She is wrong when she denigrates foreign investment, because its withdrawal would cost Australian jobs. She is wrong when she claims that Australia is headed for civil war.' I said that her political campaign had been based on fear and instability, and did not offer positive solutions.

Many of those who had previously attacked me praised this speech, although declaring that it should have been delivered six months earlier. In fact the substance of my denunciation of her policies in the speech had all been contained in comments I had made months earlier, both in the press and in parliament.

The remarkable feature of that speech was that I had not broken any new ground with its contents, yet it received wide praise from erstwhile critics. Perhaps the crucial difference had been the symbolism of giving the speech to a group committed to strong Asia-Australia ties. In my May 1997 speech I warned against labelling people who were taken with Pauline Hanson as bigoted, narrow-minded and racist. I said that a few no doubt were; most, however, were not. Nor did I retreat from what I had said at the Queensland Liberal Convention in September 1996 about the repudiation of political correctness, represented by the Coalition's 1996 win.

Going to the nub of her broad appeal, which was not racist, I said, 'Rather, she echoes concerns about the pace of change and the pressures that parts of our community are under. These concerns, as distinct from her responses, deserve the most sensitive understanding, and the Government is committed to giving them a serious and effective response. She also echoes long-smouldering resentments about attitudes which have been imposed upon the majority of the Australian community without that majority feeling it has even had an opportunity of debating those issues.'

Pauline Hanson, or One Nation, eventually ran out of puff and was seen as having no answer for Australia's challenges of the late 1990s and subsequent years. This was not before her movement garnered just on a million votes in the 1998 election, most of which had come from former Coalition voters, as well as contributing to the defeat of the Borbidge/Sheldon Coalition Government in Queensland earlier in the same year. Although the Coalition in Queensland had not helped itself when in office by not at least attempting to remove Queensland's optional preferential voting system, and restoring compulsory preferential voting. If that latter system had been in operation, Borbidge would very likely have survived.

One Nation also contributed to the defeat of the Court Liberal Government in Western Australia in 2001, but only because the Liberals' abandonment of the Regional Forest agreement I had signed with Richard Court drove disenchanted blue-collar timber workers into the arms of Pauline Hanson.

Indirectly Pauline Hanson added to the complacency which helped cost Kim Beazley any prospect of winning the 2001 federal election. The former Opposition leader falsely imagined that the big two-party-preferred swing to Labor in 1998 represented the first stage of Labor returning to favour amongst Australian voters. As a result he wrongly assumed that Labor could essentially coast to victory in 2001 off the back of discontent with the introduction of the GST. It was famously reported that he told his caucus late in 2000 that the opposition would 'surf to victory' because of discontent with the GST. He was completely mistaken in his assessment. 1998 did not presage the rebirth of federal Labor. Rather, it was a one-off phenomenon partly caused by the Pauline Hanson factor. There is more on this in Chapter 27.

Could the impact of Hanson have been less if I had attacked her more strongly and openly immediately after her maiden speech? I think not. Pauline Hanson was an accident, but accidents constantly happen in politics. A more vigorous response from me would have intensified the frustrations felt by those Australians to whom she gave a voice, and gratuitously alienated them from me — and for what purpose, other than the political benefit of the ALP? Those frustrations were bound to surface at some point and, coming as they did from many citizens whose natural political bent was Coalition rather than Labor, it would have been foolish in the extreme for me to have treated them with the contempt urged upon me by my many critics.

24

THE FOUNDATION
BUDGET

Peter Costello's first budget, delivered on 20 August 1996, was the most important of all the budgets delivered during our almost 12 years in government. It was a very tough budget, but entirely appropriate for the circumstances. It was the best and bravest in 25 years, and demonstrated to the Australian electorate that we were serious about economic reform and determined to take Australia off the path of deficit and debt. It helped ensure that the Australian economy would not be engulfed by the Asian downturn two years later.

The Treasurer announced a reduction in the underlying deficit of approximately $4 billion and some $7.2 billion over two years. He foreshadowed that the budget would be balanced over the term of the Coalition's first three years as a government. Its foundation stone was an actual cut in spending in real terms. It did not just slow the rate of expenditure growth. It achieved a real fall in outlays, which was no mean feat at a time when the Australian economy was only just beginning to gather strength. It contained major structural reforms in many areas, including employment programs, gave full effect to election commitments, and placed significant limits on growth areas in health expenditure.

The budget delivered our election promise relating to family tax measures as well as major reforms in childcare, aged care and superannuation. We also established the flagship Natural Heritage Trust (NHT). One of its controversial items was the introduction of a 15 per cent superannuation surcharge, which hit high income earners. This was a very unpopular decision amongst many Coalition supporters. I accept particular responsibility for this change. Given many of the other expenditure cuts, in areas such as education and employment services, where a major reform involving privatisation of the employment services system was introduced, I felt that for the sake of overall balance there needed to be something to which higher income earners made a contribution.

My judgement on this was to some degree validated when the Sydney *Daily Telegraph* with its budget headline described the Coalition's first financial blueprint as a 'Fair go for middle Australia'.[1] That was the view Peter Costello and I took of the budget. We had tackled the deficit problem head-on, and that budget of 1996 laid the groundwork for years of successful economic management.

With the passage of time it was easy to forget the contribution that budget made to setting up the economic achievements of the Howard Government. Although the budget of 2007 was, according to polls, judged the most popular budget ever, I have no doubt that in straight economic terms the budget of 1996 was the best delivered by the Coalition.

Financial commentators widely applauded the budget. They saw in it a determination by the new government to tackle the nation's problems and halt the growth of Commonwealth debt my Government had inherited, which peaked at $96 billion.

After this budget was brought down the Australian people were in no doubt that they had a government which was serious about responsible economic management, and would take the right decisions for the future of the country, even if some of those decisions were very unpopular. That was the Government they hoped they had elected.

On budget eve we implemented our promise to give the RBA independent authority to set interest rates. It strengthened our economic credentials. The economic theory underpinning independence of the central bank to set interest rates is that by removing that function from the political arm of government, anti-inflationary expectations are enhanced. Markets, and therefore wage-setters, pay more regard to the inflationary consequences of wage settlements when they know that interest rates are set by the central bank, and not by the Government.

Having experienced the old system under the Fraser Government, and having watched and listened as Paul Keating boasted of having the Reserve

Bank in his pocket, I thought the change made a lot of sense. That is not to say that I agreed with every interest-rate decision taken by the Reserve Bank in my time as Prime Minister.

The decision to grant the RBA independence coincided with Bernie Fraser's retirement as governor. His replacement, Ian Macfarlane, had been deputy to Fraser and served in that position for ten years, until he was succeeded by Glenn Stevens in September 2006.

Macfarlane was the stand-out economic official in the lifetime of my Government. His advice and sense of balance was far superior to that of anybody else who provided economic advice to us. He showed remarkable calm when the Australian dollar was under enormous pressure at various stages over the term of his governorship. He knew that central bank independence should be exercised calmly and pragmatically.

The Government also introduced its Charter of Budget Honesty. This was to prevent in the future what had happened in the 1996 campaign, when both Keating and Beazley had falsely asserted that the budget was in surplus when they knew it was in deficit. Under the charter, which was enshrined in legislation, once an election was called the secretaries of the Treasury and the Department of Finance were to publish a snapshot of the national books, telling the public exactly where the budget stood in relation to its revenues and expenditure and the size of the deficit or surplus. It was a very big reform, placing a discipline on the Government as well as on the opposition.

In addition, we commissioned two important inquiries in our early months. The first of them, led by Bob Officer, was effectively an audit of the functions of the Commonwealth, which produced some challenging recommendations, not all of which the Government took up. The other inquiry was led by Stan Wallis, the former managing director of Amcor, and was asked to scrutinise the operation of the financial system. It was something of an update of the Campbell Inquiry. Its principal recommendation was to create a new regulatory agency called the Australian Prudential Regulatory Authority, which took over certain supervisory functions from the RBA, as well as the surveillance of smaller financial companies.

The regulatory system covering Australian financial institutions, which by common accord has worked remarkably well, is essentially a product of the Wallis Inquiry. In talking up the strength of the Australian banking system in the wake of the global financial crisis, both Kevin Rudd and Wayne Swan were noticeably silent on the contribution to that stability made by the Wallis Inquiry, and the supervisory structure it either confirmed or recommended.

The 1996 budget was the first of 12 delivered by Peter Costello, a record for an Australian Treasurer. Peter was not only the nation's longest-serving Treasurer, he was, in my judgement, the best-ever Treasurer. He brought high intelligence and fine rhetorical skills to the task. His question-time performances constantly demoralised the opposition with both factual rebuttal and humorous attacks. Peter could be uproariously funny, and frequently lifted the spirits of the Coalition. He mastered the intense detail of the Treasury portfolio in an impressive fashion.

Just before the 1996 budget, the Coalition received an unexpected bonus with the defection of the ALP senator from Queensland Mal Colston. The Labor Party had reneged on an earlier understanding that he would become Deputy President of the Senate. It had become something of a convention that the opposition would fill this position, with the Senate President naturally coming from government ranks. Colston was outraged at this betrayal and, having been in the Senate for some years and with his party only newly in opposition, no doubt thought that his one opportunity for preferment, courtesy of the ALP, had suddenly and unfairly disappeared. So he turned to the Coalition. He enquired whether government senators would support him for the deputy presidency. I raised no objection to this. There was no deal made about Colston voting for government legislation in return for his installation as Deputy President.

Nonetheless, we entertained the hope that he would back the Government on some important issues. He did vote for most of the budget legislation, and joined Brian Harradine in voting against a destructive ALP amendment to the New Schools Policy Bill.

Later his voting performance was more mixed. He sank our 1998 attempt to sell the remainder of Telstra; seven more years would elapse before this goal was achieved.

The ALP turned on him with fury and hatred. He was a Labor rat, pursued with a vicious campaign of bile and abuse. Even when he was diagnosed with a serious illness there was no let-up. He later faced allegations of rorting his travel allowances and was forced to quit as Deputy President.

In opposition, I had spoken frequently about raising ministerial standards. After becoming Prime Minister, my department presented me with a formal codification of previous practice in relation to ministers' holdings of shares etc. This document largely put in writing what had been followed by a number of previous governments. I released the document as it seemed a thoroughly commonsense statement of obvious principles. Little did I realise at the time that it would cause considerable embarrassment, and for a number of my new ministers terminate their careers.

One of the requirements of the code was that ministers should avoid taking any decisions affecting companies in which they held shares, so as to avoid the appearance of a conflict of interest. Unfortunately this stipulation snared Jim Short, the assistant Treasurer, and Brian Gibson, parliamentary Secretary to the Treasurer, in October 1996. Jim Short held $50,000 worth of shares in the ANZ Bank, and in September had approved an operating licence for an ANZ Bank subsidiary. Brian Gibson had owned some Boral shares, and before the sale of them had been completed, he approved a declaration in favour of a Boral subsidiary. At the time Gibson made the decision, he erroneously believed that the sale of the shares he had owned had been completed.

Short and Gibson had been but two among thousands of small shareholders in the two companies concerned, and the decisions which each of them took could in no way have enhanced their share values. It was inconceivable that either of them had the remotest thought of personal enhancement when they made the relevant decisions. They had, from inexperience, overlooked the fact that they held shares in corporations affected by their decisions. It was sadly the case that in both instances they had technically breached the ministerial code, and I had to accept their resignations. I felt sorry at the time for both of them, and to this day I feel that they paid a heavy price for an oversight that involved no skerrick of personal gain or malfeasance.

These resignations really upset me, and I saw them as the first big setback for the Government. We took an awful bath in the media. They occurred on the eve of an unexpected by-election in the Penrith-based seat of Lindsay in western Sydney.

This was the seat that had been won by the RAAF legal officer, Jackie Kelly. Jackie was a young, attractive Olympic rower who had been born in New Zealand. Therein lay the problem. Apparently she had not fully renounced her New Zealand citizenship before the election. There had also been some questions raised about whether she had resigned in time from the RAAF so as to avoid the 'office of profit under the Crown' prohibition.

On 11 September the Court of Disputed Returns had found against Kelly and ruled that the election in the division of Lindsay was void and she would need to face a new election in that electorate. I thought it was a huge setback and worried about our prospects of holding the seat.

Jackie Kelly handled the situation extremely well, immediately taking a part-time job as a waitress in a local coffee shop and attending to the citizenship matter in preparation for the by-election. In a few short months she had established a higher-than-ever profile in the electorate, but many of us had our doubts, given the history of the seat, that she would retain it. Ross Free, the former ALP member, was chosen again as the Labor candidate, and as the by-election occurred in the wake of the resignations of Short and Gibson, and also the first budget of the new government, which had cut spending savagely and introduced a number of quite unpopular measures, I thought that we would probably lose the seat in the by-election.

To my great delight not only did Jackie Kelly hold Lindsay but she increased her majority by 4–5 per cent. It was obvious that the people of Lindsay were irked about the by-election. For them the ministerial resignations hadn't even touched the sides. Another factor in their decision was that, having seen a little bit of Jackie Kelly, they thought that she was the kind of fighter that a battler electorate like Lindsay needed.

Our first year in government ended with a startling decision from the High Court of Australia on native title, to which I will return shortly. That notwithstanding, it had been ten months of considerable achievement in which the economic direction of the nation had been changed, the style of government substantially altered, and a path set for a greater level of national self-belief and international respect.

For me it had been a deeply satisfying journey. After long years in parliament, marked at first by occasions of real success serving in a government led by another person, then the turbulent and frustrating 13 years of opposition, I finally had full control of the affairs of Australia's Government. I had not sought to exercise this authority capriciously or arrogantly, but in a cooperative fashion with colleagues, although recognising that, at the end of the day, I was ultimately responsible for all of the major decisions and the central direction of the Government. Much progress had been made in a short period of time.

The Howard Government had been an activist and reforming one. I was always seized of the possibility that the Government might not last very long. It was natural caution. Therefore I was resolved from the start not to waste time or put off hard decisions. It is always easier to do the unpalatable things at the beginning. The electorate cuts a government less slack as time passes. Looking over our first ten months, my Government had been intensely busy and had made its mark. Not everyone liked what we had done, but we had made a difference and in particular had laid the groundwork for a decade of continuous economic growth through repairing the budget and reforming industrial relations. More was to come in our second year.

25

THE CHALLENGE OF
INDIGENOUS POLICY

If ever a portfolio required a combination of idealism and pragmatism it was Indigenous Affairs, long the political graveyard of ministers who failed to understand the importance of that mixture. For my Indigenous Affairs Minister I chose the 63-year-old Brisbane general surgeon Senator John Herron. A former president of the Liberal Party in Queensland, father of ten, devout Catholic, dedicated humanitarian but hard-headed pragmatist, John Herron seemed to me to fit the bill.

I had a theory that one should avoid appointing somebody from Sydney or Melbourne to this position. The guilt syndrome was far too strong in those cities. By contrast, people from Queensland and Western Australia had a more pragmatic view about Aboriginal issues. They were not insensitive but they understood that one should, where possible, avoid the perception of special privileges for Indigenous Australians, as this frequently aggravated less well-off people from the rest of the Australian community, who felt that a special deal was being done for people whose social position was little different from their own. The other reality was that most Australians who lived in places such as Sydney and Melbourne never came into contact with Aboriginal people on a daily basis, whereas people from Queensland, the Northern Territory and Western Australia more commonly did.

Whatever the logic, I decided on John Herron. He leaped at the opportunity and came to the task with impeccable professional and personal qualifications. I had heard a lot of lofty speeches in the parliament, particularly from Labor members, about the need to help the less privileged in our community, most especially Aboriginal people. John Herron had practised what others had preached. For eight weeks in 1994, John had volunteered his services to operate on the victims of the Rwandan massacre. He applied his considerable surgical skills to helping humanity in the most wretched of circumstances. I spoke to him after he had returned from Rwanda. As a hardened surgeon of more than 30 years' practice, he had plainly been deeply affected by his Rwandan experience. To him it was using his professional skills to help suffering people. I thought a man like this, with such experience and heart, was the right person for Indigenous Affairs.

I did not have a politically correct approach to Aboriginal issues. I did not believe in separate development for the Indigenous people of Australia. It remains my opinion that the best way of helping Indigenous Australians is to include them within the mainstream of the Australian community and endeavour, as far as possible, to ensure that they share the bounty of our prosperous nation. They were the most disadvantaged group within our society, had suffered discrimination and prejudice in the past and were entitled to far greater opportunities in the fields of health, education, employment and housing than they had previously received.

I had always resisted the notion of a treaty. Whatever the legal niceties may have been, the concept of a treaty being made by different groups of people within the same nation seemed quite alien to me. The One Australia concept which I had articulated as part of the Future Directions manifesto of 1988 saw Aboriginal and other Australians as being together citizens of one nation. The idea that one section of the Australian community should, in any way, be governed by different laws than those that applied to the rest of the community was unacceptable.

The High Court's decision in the Mabo case, in 1992, had been a landmark change in the law affecting Indigenous people, because it found that native title, or continuing Aboriginal ownership of land, could exist where the land in question had never been included in a crown grant. As most property in urban areas of Australia was freehold title and therefore the subject of an original crown grant, Mabo was of largely academic interest to city dwellers. It was different in the country, where there were many leasehold titles; numerous pastoralists and miners were unsettled by the Mabo decision.

The Keating Government, with Democrat support, had secured passage of the Native Title Act in 1993, which sought to clarify aspects of the law enunciated by the High Court, as well as establishing a procedure to handle the claims which would inevitably arise as a result of the court's finding that native title could exist. The Coalition had voted against the Native Title Bill because it did not adequately protect the position of pastoralists and miners.

The concerns of pastoralists and miners were mollified to some degree by a recital to the Native Title Act which asserted that the grant of a pastoral lease had extinguished native title. This did not have the force of law, but was an operating principle for almost three years until the surprise decision of the High Court of Australia in the Wik case, late in 1996.

ATSIC, the elected Indigenous body, had been established during my first tenure as Opposition leader. The Coalition had then voted against ATSIC, believing that control of Aboriginal affairs should remain within an ordinary department of government. Speaking in the House of Representatives on 11 April 1989, I said of the ATSIC proposal, 'The ATSIC legislation strikes at the heart of the unity of the Australian people. In the name of righting the wrongs done against Aboriginal people, the legislation adopts the misguided notion of believing that if one creates a parliament within the Australian community for Aboriginal people, one will solve and meet all of those problems.' ATSIC proved a failure and in 2004, under Mark Latham's leadership, the Labor Party supported my Government's abolition of ATSIC.

Before he was elected prime minister, Bob Hawke had promised to introduce national land rights legislation. Partly under pressure from Brian Burke, the Labor Premier of Western Australia, Hawke moved away from this commitment. Hawke had also, by this time as PM, promised in June 1988 to 'reach a proper and lasting reconciliation through a pact or treaty'.[1] As Opposition leader, I said that the Coalition would never support a treaty. In its place, and with opposition support, Hawke established the Council for Aboriginal Reconciliation under the chairmanship of Pat Dodson. The remit of this body was to embark on a program of consultation in the broader Australian community, with a view to agreeing on a basis for lasting reconciliation between Indigenous and other Australians by the centenary of Federation in January 2001.

It was a lofty goal, and very difficult to attain because of the fundamental chasm between the rights agenda of most of the Indigenous leadership and the Labor Party on the one hand and, on the other, those like myself who saw the path ahead as one which brought Indigenous people into the mainstream of the Australian community. The council nonetheless realised a good deal and helped embed the notion of reconciliation within the psyche of many Australians. I would constantly talk of practical reconciliation, a concept which embraced the totality of policies in individual areas designed to help Indigenous people.

The former Labor Government, late in its time in office, established the inquiry led by the former High Court Judge Sir Ronald Wilson into the so-called Stolen Generation, or the removal of Aboriginal children from their parents. This would become one of the most emotional and controversial aspects of Indigenous policy and the foundation of the push for a formal apology, ultimately given by the Rudd Government shortly after its election.

Indigenous policy did not figure prominently in the 12 months that I had led the opposition before winning government, except for the controversy surrounding attempts by the Keating Government, which ultimately failed, to block the construction of the Hindmarsh Island Bridge in South Australia because a sacred Aboriginal site was involved, with the added twist that it was a place where 'secret women's business' was conducted, and that it was offensive to Indigenous people for men to know anything about it. To most Australians the whole saga was absurd, and drained away sympathy for legitimate Aboriginal grievances.

From the early weeks of my Government it was very clear that virtually all of the Aboriginal leadership shared the Labor view of Indigenous affairs, which was overwhelmingly about the rights of Indigenous people; symbolic gestures and commitments in furtherance of those rights assumed far greater significance than anything else. The Dodson brothers, Pat and Mick, typified this approach. Noel Pearson had developed a close relationship with Paul Keating and he was, in the wake of the Wik decision, to become a fierce critic of the Coalition until some years later when he provided some of the best advice my Government received in the whole area.

Pat Dodson was the chairman of the Council for Aboriginal Reconciliation and Lois (now Lowitja) O'Donoghue, another constant critic of the Coalition through virtually the whole time it was in office, chaired ATSIC. The Aboriginal leadership didn't take kindly to John Herron's appointment. They rightly perceived that he would talk about responsibilities as often as he talked about rights. In one particularly caustic comment, Mick Dodson expressed his resentment that I had referred to John Herron's work in Rwanda as some kind of qualification for helping Indigenous people. It was a piece of arrogance which puzzled me, as the only point I was trying to make was that Herron's surgical work in Africa was evidence of his decency and compassion.

One of Herron's first acts as minister was to expose some financial mismanagement by ATSIC and to recommend a series of changes to bring it under tighter financial control. He met fierce resistance, not only from Aboriginal leaders but also the Labor Party, which continued a business-as-usual approach to Indigenous policy.

Just before Christmas 1996, the High Court delivered its judgement in the Wik case and, to the surprise of most, did not confirm the belief implicit in the Native Title legislation of the Keating Government, and contained in a recital (or preface) to that act: that the grant of a pastoral lease extinguished native title. It found that the rights of Indigenous owners and those granted a pastoral lease could coexist, and to the extent that those rights collided in individual cases, then the rights of the pastoral leaseholder would prevail.

This decision shocked the pastoral and mining industries, disconcerted the Government, appeared on the face of it to be unworkable, and gave fresh impetus to those within the Indigenous community and elsewhere who believed that the Native Title Act of the Keating Government had not gone far enough.

The Coalition had been elected with a promise to amend the Native Title Act, to make it more workable for farmers and miners. We did not want to scrap it, but there was inevitable suspicion of us amongst Aboriginal figures because we had voted against the act in 1993. The High Court finding in the Wik case had just made our task that much harder.

The Wik decision had given native-title claimants more leverage than they had expected. There was no way that they were going to surrender any of this, particularly as they knew that the Government did not have the numbers in the Senate to pass amending legislation. The ALP and the Democrats would give us no assistance with amending legislation. I decided that the Government should try and negotiate an outcome with all of the interested parties, and that I would involve myself heavily in those negotiations.

The Wik decision caused internal problems for the Coalition. Understandably, farmers were very upset that ambiguity now existed in relation to the operation of pastoral leases. This was reflected through the National Party and some Liberal members of parliament. Some agitated for tough amending legislation and, if necessary, a double dissolution to resolve the issue. I never entertained for a moment having a double dissolution. With the Wik decision under their belt, Indigenous leaders became more strident. Noel Pearson, later to become more reasonable, was no exception. I knew that part of a successful negotiation would be to engage him. He had a superior technical understanding of native title legislation. We had some polite discussions, but it was obvious that he was in no mood to concede anything. He did not have to. The High Court's decision had been an unexpected bonus, and he knew as well as anyone else that the Coalition would not be able to get legislation through the Senate restoring what had been previously believed: namely, that the grant of a pastoral lease had extinguished native title.

I commenced the negotiation process thinking that it would be seen as a virtue to widely consult and listen to all parties. This was only partly correct. What had been needed was a short period of intensive negotiations followed by a clear-cut set of proposals on which legislation would be based.

By the time I produced the well-known ten-point plan to deal with the consequences of the Wik decision, the Liberal and National parties had passed through several months of appearing divided and indecisive about native title. This had a bad impact on many of our traditional supporters in rural areas who, bewildered by the Wik decision, had wanted a speedy and clear government response. It was hard to persuade them that life was not as simple as that. We simply couldn't do what we might have wanted to because we lacked the numbers in the Senate.

On 17 May 1997, Tim Fischer and I addressed a rally, largely of farmers, at Longreach in Central Queensland to explain our Wik plan. The turnout was big and, despite media reporting to the contrary, I found the atmosphere relatively understanding.

Predictably the Labor Party and the Australian Democrats opposed a large part of the ten-point plan. The Independent Senator Brian Harradine was more flexible, although he was unwilling to support everything in our outline. The inevitable compromise was finally reached in some frantic personal discussions with him. He was sympathetic to the Indigenous position and had no desire to see a double dissolution fought on native-title issues, but was broadly supportive of the Government.

I liked Brian Harradine a lot. One always had a good idea where Harradine stood on important questions. Despite the transparency of his position on so many issues, on the particular detail of legislation he was a wily negotiator who kept both sides guessing until the very end. He employed this tactic to the full during the Wik negotiations.

It would be more than a year before the Wik legislation, embodying most of the ten-point plan, finally passed the Senate on Wednesday 8 July 1998. The debate on these amendments had been the longest in the Senate on any one measure since Federation. Their most valuable features were the removal of uncertainties regarding action since the Native Title Act had been passed and restrictions on capricious native-title claims. It wasn't an entirely satisfactory outcome; it was a good deal less than what many of our strong rural supporters might have expected when the Government changed. In the circumstances, however, it was a reasonable solution given the unexpected High Court decision in the Wik case.

The political cost to the Coalition had been marked. By the middle of 1997, we had fallen behind the Labor Party in the opinion polls. The apparent drift on the native-title issue had played a big part in this. The Pauline Hanson factor, dealt with earlier, came into the mix; her simplistic slogans made our life harder.

I made things worse for myself when speaking at a reconciliation meeting in Melbourne on 26 May 1997. I knew this meeting would be hard and though I intended to recognise symbolic sensitivities I was determined to avoid the abjectly apologetic language so often used by members of the Labor Party and others. The audience was overwhelmingly Indigenous, and when I commenced my remarks many of them had stood and turned their backs on me, a symbolic act of contempt for a speaker.

In my speech I said:

> At the same time we need to acknowledge openly that the treatment accorded to many Indigenous Australians over a significant period of European settlement represents the most blemished chapter in our history. Clearly there were injustices done and no-one should obscure or minimise them. We need to acknowledge as a nation what European settlement has meant for the first Australians, the Aboriginal and Torres Strait Islander people, and in particular the assault on their traditions and the discrimination and violence they endured over many decades.

I mentioned the forthcoming tabling of the Stolen Children, or *Bringing Them Home*, report and said that it would neither be summarily rejected nor uncritically embraced. I did, however, say this: 'Personally, I feel deep sorrow for those of my fellow Australians who suffered injustices under the practices of past generations towards Indigenous people. Equally I am sorry for the hurt and trauma many people here today may continue to feel as a consequence of those practices.'

I cautioned against depicting Australia's history since 1788 as little more than a disgraceful record of imperialism, exploitation and racism. I said, 'Such a portrayal is a gross distortion and deliberately neglects the overall story of great Australian achievement that is there in our history to be told, and such an approach will be repudiated by the overwhelming majority of Australians who are proud of what this country has achieved although inevitably acknowledging the blemishes in its past history.'

In summary I said that Australians of the current generation should not be required to accept blame for past policies over which they had no control. However, we should acknowledge past wrongs and realise that they continue to cause pain and commit to remedy disadvantage, now and in the future.

So moderate did my remarks turn out to be that, on hearing them, many actually turned around to face me and sat down. When I got to the portion of my speech dealing with the Government's response to the Wik decision, there were some noisy interjections from a section of the audience close to me. Foolishly, I responded by shouting over the interjections, appearing to lose control. It looked very bad on television and thus became an enduring image, negative for me, on Indigenous issues. My critics were delighted, as the episode played strongly to the view that I was at permanent loggerheads with Indigenous Australians.

Regrettably, this totally obliterated what I felt had been a very balanced presentation on the whole Indigenous issue. The views I outlined that day continued to guide my Government's policy for its next decade in office.

These remarks echoed the sentiments of mainstream Australia. Such has been the hysteria of this debate that I doubt that more than a tiny fraction of Australians know that as far back as May 1997 I had expressed my personal sorrow for past injustices against Indigenous Australians.

The continuing problem for us, and worse still for Indigenous Australia, was that until the aftermath of the 2004 election, almost eight years later, the bulk of Australia's Aboriginal leadership was unwilling to accept our legitimacy, and refused to deal with us except on the basis of the Government accepting their agenda. That did massive damage to the Indigenous cause.

Then there was the *Bringing Them Home* report of the Human Rights Commission Inquiry, chaired by Sir Ronald Wilson, tabled in federal parliament on 26 May 1997. Amongst other things, it described as 'an act of genocide' the practices of past governments in removing some Indigenous children from their parents. As well as funding for Indigenous agencies and the payment of reparations, all parliaments in Australia were asked to offer formal apologies and officially acknowledge the responsibility of their predecessors for the laws, policies and practices of forcible removal.

From very early in my prime ministership, I made it known that I was not all that sympathetic to the inquiry and that I had a fundamental difficulty with the notion of later generations passing judgement on the deeds of earlier generations, not according to the values of earlier generations but according to those of current generations. It is very easy to apologise for the mistakes of your predecessors. It is a lot harder to apologise for your own and, as a consequence, real-time apologies are a lot rarer than the other type. I would never embrace the artificiality of a formal apology for the simple reason that the only person or government which can give an effective apology is the original perpetrator.

On 22 April 1996, a bare seven weeks after the Government's election to office, I had seen Mick Dodson, the Social Justice Commissioner, about the inquiry. I told Dodson that I could not give a commitment about future funding of the inquiry, and that there was a question in my mind over its long-term value. I said to him that I understood the intensity of feeling on the subject, but even people of goodwill may form the judgement that there was not a lot to be gained from an expensive inquiry on a long-past policy. I told him directly that my newly elected Government did not have the same attitude on this issue as its predecessor.

On 8 October 1996, in answering a question in the house I said that the removal practices which were the subject of the inquiry were quite unacceptable by contemporary standards and caused great trauma to those affected. I said that it was always hard to impose the standards of today on the conduct of earlier years. I added that despite the criticism it would attract, it also had to be said that some of those involved in the implementation of those past practices believed that what they were doing was right.

I saw Mick Dodson and Sir Ronald Wilson on 17 October and maintained the attitude I had expressed to Dodson in April and had explained to parliament a week earlier. They were unhappy, but intended to finish their inquiry in response to the terms of reference given by the Keating Government. They had wanted more money for the inquiry, but the Government was reluctant to agree to this.

When the report was tabled, I was sympathetic to a number of its recommendations but was unwilling to support a formal apology for the actions of past governments. I had strong doubts about the intellectual rigour of a lot of the report. No attempt appeared to have been made, systematically, to gather evidence from people still alive who had been involved in administering the practices covered by the report. They were very elderly but nonetheless some wanted to participate. Those who conducted the inquiry decided that any person who had provided evidence of their removal should not be cross-examined on their testimony or their evidence challenged. The justification for this was that given the trauma witnesses had experienced, they would be at risk of further trauma. This meant that the report was written almost entirely on the evidence presented from one side.

State governments, including a number of Coalition ones, were quick to offer formal apologies as recommended by the report. The Beazley opposition in Canberra wanted the same thing done by the federal government, but we resisted this. There were some members of the parliamentary party who agitated for a formal apology, but I do not recall a single member of the cabinet arguing for one. Indeed there was considerable scepticism inside the Government about the intellectual integrity of the entire report, which reinforced the generic objection I had to an apology.

My unwillingness to give an apology represented a dividing line between many Indigenous leaders and me for the remainder of my prime ministership. In the wake of the apology given by Kevin Rudd in February 2008, a number of the former members of my Government have said that the Howard Government was mistaken in not tendering a formal apology. I do not question that they now sincerely hold that view.

Relations with the Indigenous communities' leadership, through 1997, continued to be very strained. This was particularly so with Pat Dodson. He was frequently called the 'father of reconciliation' due to his position as chairman of the reconciliation body and a certain level of charisma which he had acquired in the eyes of many Australians. Pat Dodson's views on Indigenous policy had not altered since the change of government from

Labor to Coalition. In the latter part of 1997, Dodson made what I regarded as a calculated decision not to accept reappointment as chairman of the Council for Aboriginal Reconciliation. He knew that his action would have a real impact on the Indigenous community and create further problems for my Government.

When I knew that giving effect to this decision was imminent, I invited him to the Lodge on Sunday evening, 2 November 1997 and the two of us spent an hour and a half together, alone, trying to reach a proper basis for his continuing. I wanted him to stay as chairman, but he was determined to go. I walked to the door of the Lodge with him, we shook hands, and he started off down the gravel driveway then turned around and came back and said to me, 'My position hasn't changed, but if there is anything I can do in the future to help, I will try and do so.' This last gesture reflected some recognition on his part that what he had done might be construed in a negative way by some people. He had done it nonetheless. I had tried hard to keep him, and although he would later say that he would reconsider his position, on certain conditions of course, I had to move on. The Government appointed Evelyn Scott in his place.

The 1998 election brought Aidan Ridgeway, an Indigenous Australian, into parliament as a Democrat senator from New South Wales. I got to know him well and within a few weeks of Ridgeway taking his Senate position on 1 July 1999, we were to collaborate in preparing a motion of regret to be presented to both houses of parliament. Whilst Ridgeway didn't agree with me about an apology, he accepted that I was not going to shift. Instead of standing at arm's length, he worked with me in devising a motion of sincere regret expressing feelings with which we could all agree. He brought credibility to this approach because he was the sole Aboriginal member of the Australian parliament.

The motion, carried without dissent, expressed 'deep and sincere regret that Indigenous Australians suffered injustices under the practices of past generations, and for the hurt and trauma that many Indigenous people continue to feel as a consequence of those practices'. This was not the language that Indigenous leaders wanted because it did not use the word 'apology', but to many it struck the right balance. I knew it would not satisfy the old guard of the Aboriginal leadership, the ALP or others who continued to see good Indigenous policy through the prism of separate development, with a heavy overlay of guilt and shame.

Plate 1

My parents married on 11 July 1925 at Marrickville in Sydney. They devoted their lives to the welfare and future of their four sons.

My father 'somewhere on the Western Front'. A gas attack damaged his lungs, which contributed to his death at age 59.

Plate 2

It was a short walk from home to Earlwood Primary School. Here I am aged six, sixth from the left in the third row. World War II ended the year before.

Dad's garage in 1954, just after going 'one brand'. It was at the corner of Wardell Road and Ewart Street, Dulwich Hill, Sydney. I loved working there.

Plate 3

The Canterbury Boys High School debating team of 1956 (second from the left, front row). Debating gave the priceless discipline of marshalling arguments.

I played in the CBHS Second XI in 1956 (second from the right, front row). Captain Ian Sharpe, on my right, later a professor of economics, was a good leg spinner.

Plate 4

Before a family wedding early in 1955. Dad's health was failing; he died nine months later. The Howard brothers (from left to right): Stan, John, Bob and Wal.

With Mum at my law graduation early in 1961. My hearing problem made university quite taxing. It also meant I could not go to the bar.

Plate 5

A safe federal seat: Janette and I show elation after the Liberals picked me for Bennelong in December 1973. It was a marathon day.

Plate 6

Our wedding day at
St Peter's, Watsons
Bay, 4 April 1971.

A polling booth at Gladesville Public School on election day, October 1980.
Fraser's retreat on taxation would later disappoint me.

Plate 7

This family photo was taken after Richard's birth in September 1980.
Melanie, looking cute, is aged six. I am holding Tim, approaching three.

Plate 8

Late 1975 with Melanie and Janette on the front lawn of our Wollstonecraft home, the scene of many news conferences in the 1970s and '80s.

Family photos from the 1980s. Weekends were filled with the children's activities. There was always sport. I loved reading to them as well.

Plate 9

I became leader of the Liberal Party in September 1985 in amazing circumstances. The euphoria soon faded.

The Liberal campaign launch for the election of 1987 struck a real chord, but 'Joh for PM' made victory impossible. We didn't pick up enough speed to win.

Plate 10

Janette and I on election night 1987. Despite a 1 per cent swing to us, Hawke won four seats.

On the verandah at Wollstonecraft in 1988. Future Directions was launched later that year. It was a clear statement of my philosophical beliefs.

Plate 11

On the eve of the 1996 election, enjoying one of many family holidays at Hawks Nest. During a beach walk, the idea came to me for the Natural Heritage Trust policy from Telstra sale proceeds.

Plate 12

Election night, March 1996 — victory at last!

Watching Lleyton Hewitt's US Open victory in the lounge room of the
Australian ambassador's residence, Washington, 9 September 2001.

Plate 13

With Richard, Tim and Janette, paying respects at Ground Zero, New York, January 2002. The raw emotion was still strong.

After my victory speech in Sydney on election night 2004. It was the Coalition's fourth straight win. Unexpectedly, we won control of the Senate.

Plate 14

A proud father with his daughter: Melanie at her graduation from Sydney University, May 1996. All of my children took law degrees.

About to give away Melanie on her wedding day, September 2003.

Plate 15

With George
and Laura Bush
on the verandah
of the White
House before an
official dinner,
May 2006.

Intervarsity fencer Janette brandishes Cromwell's sword in the 'long room'
at Chequers. Cherie Blair and I admire her thrust but keep our distance.

Plate 16

With Melanie and my grandson, Angus, after voting on election day 2007.

Conceding defeat on election night 2007, with Richard, Janette, Tim and his future wife, Sarah. My Government left a stronger, prouder and more prosperous Australia.

Following Pat Dodson's withdrawal, Evelyn Scott, a dignified and capable woman, became chairman of the council. She proved a gracious and effective chairman, who at the time of the concluding stages of the council's work in 2000 exposed the male domination of Indigenous policy and, by implication, the stifling of female opinion. Along with the historian Jackie Huggins and the WA magistrate Dr Sue Gordon, who I appointed to chair the National Indigenous Council in 2005, I found Evelyn Scott the most impressive female Indigenous leader in my time as Prime Minister.

The legislation setting up the Council for Aboriginal Reconciliation appointed May 2000 as a completion date for its work. There was to be a huge gathering at the Opera House in Sydney, and an agreed reconciliation document was to be ceremonially handed to the Governor-General. Inevitably agreement could not be reached on the terms of the document. The two big sticking points were the apology and a push for recognition of customary law in cases dealing with Indigenous Australians. In the end a document containing the views of the council, including on those two issues, was handed over.

I chose to ignore the differences when I spoke to the gathering. Most of those there were unsympathetic, and because I did not say what they wanted I was heckled. As it was in Sydney, much of the organising had been done by the NSW Government. Its officials wore stickers calling for a treaty. To my knowledge, having a treaty was not formal ALP policy at either a federal or state level.

The next day probably 200,000 people walked across Sydney Harbour Bridge to show their support for reconciliation. Kim Beazley walked, as did John Herron and Philip Ruddock. I did not. Bob Hawke and Malcolm Fraser walked and both attacked me for not doing so. I had decided some weeks earlier that I would not participate.

We had discussed the bridge walk in cabinet, with some colleagues arguing that we should all walk. There was divided opinion on this; I said that I would not be walking and it was loosely agreed that Herron and Ruddock should take part. Later that year there was a similar walk in Melbourne. Peter Costello and a number of Victorian ministers took part. This had also been raised in cabinet. I had no objection to their participation. Inevitably the press drew comparisons between my non-participation, and Costello walking. I was not greatly troubled by that.

*   *   *

The Coalition's big win in the October 2004 election shifted the attitudes of Aboriginal leaders such as Pat Dodson. A major meeting took place at Port Douglas on 26–27 November 2004 at which a cross-section of the Aboriginal leadership agreed to seek a new and better understanding with my Government on Indigenous issues. After eight years and four election victories, the old guard had finally accepted the legitimacy of the Howard Government. After the meeting Pat Dodson said, 'We want to re-open the dialogue with the Prime Minister.'[2] I welcomed that but reflected that in turning his back on my entreaties, seven years earlier, not to give up the chairmanship of the Council for Aboriginal Reconciliation, it had been Pat Dodson, unarguably at that time the most influential Indigenous leader in the nation, who had turned his back on dialogue with the Prime Minister of the day.

Noel Pearson, who by this time had become an increasingly powerful force in the Indigenous firmament, had clearly influenced the likes of Dodson and others. Chairman of the Cape York Land Council, Pearson scorned passive welfare, stressed the imperative of Indigenous self-reliance and was impatient with those in his own community who saw Indigenous advancement purely in terms of treaties and statements of rights. He understood the need for Aboriginal Australians to become part of the mainstream of the nation.

A week later Michael Long, the popular and talented Essendon footballer, completed his long walk from his home in Melbourne to Canberra to draw attention to Indigenous disadvantage. I happily saw Michael, who was accompanied by Pat Dodson. It was a positive meeting.

There had been a tectonic movement in attitudes. It was tempting to think that years had been wasted, and to some degree that was right. But it was more complicated. For a generation, almost the dominant thought stream about Indigenous Affairs in Australia had been that of separate development. To challenge that in any way, as I had begun to do from the start of my prime ministership, was to be accused of wanting to return to paternalism and even racism.

So much of the debate had been conducted against a background of guilt and shame, with little attention being paid to the responsibilities of individuals within Aboriginal communities. It was a one-way application of the rights agenda. By simply opposing the Keating Government's approach to native title, Liberals were accused of racism and intolerance. Even Noel Pearson, who in time would have more influence on me and other Coalition figures than any other Aboriginal leader when it came to Indigenous policy, would call Liberals 'racist scum'.[3] He said this in angry response to the Wik plan on 31 October 1997. If ever there were a policy area which matched the metaphor of a slow-turning ocean liner, it was Indigenous Affairs.

Our last year in government finally saw a paradigm change. It was as if the dam had finally burst and much of the approach which had held sway for a generation or more was swept away. The catalyst for this was the report into child abuse in the Northern Territory entitled 'Little Children Are Sacred', and the historic intervention in the Territory launched by my Government in response to the appalling failure of the Territory Government to provide even the most basic protection to the children of the Territory.

I was transfixed by an exchange on Radio National, on successive mornings — 20 and 21 June 2007 — between Pearson and Tom Calma, the Social Justice Commissioner and very much an Indigenous leader in the old-guard mould. Calma attacked the suspension of the Racial Discrimination Act, part of the intervention, and generally maintained the rights agenda approach, totally misreading public feeling that the issue at stake was protecting little children. If that required putting aside the act, then so be it. Pearson took Calma apart; in so doing, he spoke for mainstream Australia as well as many in his own community.

The symbolism as well as the practical meaning of this cannot be overstated. Here was the man who by then had become the most respected Indigenous leader in the nation as well as enjoying widening support in his own community, backing a Howard Government action which enabled the quarantining of welfare payments. He also backed setting aside the permit system, which had allowed Indigenous people to block access to even public areas by other Australians.

Through the intervention, the Commonwealth took over Indigenous Affairs in the Territory. A taskforce chaired by WA magistrate Sue Gordon, a respected Aboriginal figure in her profession and state, and under the executive control of Major General David Chalmers, who had headed the army's mercy mission to Aceh in Indonesia, after the tsunami, in 2005, was given the responsibility of implementing the intervention plan. There was massive public support, with a sense that at long last action had been taken to fix fundamental problems of law and order and health within Indigenous communities.

Mal Brough, as the responsible minister, handled the intervention with real skill. His defeat in 2007 was a great loss to the Liberal Party and the parliament. He had the right style for dealing with Indigenous issues, being sympathetic but possessed of a direct, plain-speaking manner. His army training had given him a mix of authority and mateship. Three years on, Brough remains the person most publicly identified with the intervention, but it would not have happened without the expectation of Pearson's understanding, and the knowledge that he would reject the 'rights at any price' approach of the old guard such as Tom Calma. That was a defining change. The ocean liner had finally completed its turn.

In July 2007, shortly after the intervention had been announced, Mal Brough and I dined at the Lodge with Noel Pearson and Sue Gordon. There had been many dinners and other functions at the Lodge involving Indigenous leaders and me as PM. This one was different, because for the first time I felt that there was a real meeting of minds about what had to be done to improve the condition of Indigenous people in Australia. So many of the previous gatherings had been exercises in political circling. Pearson and Gordon did not agree with me on everything, but we shared the view that the way ahead must involve Indigenous Australians having full access to the basic entitlements of mainstream Australian society. One of those was protection of children from abuse. This meant that the separate development policies of a generation had to be abandoned.

Noel Pearson and I had grown to respect each other. I admired his intellect, his writings and his courage in espousing the need for individual responsibility on the part of Indigenous Australians. Successfully, he combined this with a patent pride in and passion for his Aboriginal identity.

Following a lengthy meeting in Sydney in September 2007, he wrote a detailed letter to me on 17 September which displayed his acute understanding both of Australian history and what had been wrong with the republican push of the late 1990s. He correctly analysed that Paul Keating and others were mistaken to base their advocacy of a republic on a repudiation of our British inheritance. Pearson wanted a republic, but rightly argued that if it were to ever come about it had to be on the basis of affirming our British inheritance and not repudiating it. He felt that I was the one political leader who could carry conservative Australia towards a republic on that basis, as well as enlisting conservative opinion to support a new preamble. 'Preamble' is the description given to the historical and aspirational words at the beginning of our Constitution.

I was at one with Pearson on the preamble and the wisdom of shifting from a welfare state to an opportunity state. My Government's policies had always been designed to encourage individual effort ahead of welfare dependency. But I did not want a republic, and told him that nothing would change my mind on that subject.

Noel Pearson was an Aboriginal leader with whom I could talk not only about Indigenous issues but, of equal importance, issues which affected all of us as Australians. This was the secret of Pearson's appeal to the wider public. He spoke from the heart in a unifying manner about our daily lives and the national condition, but in a manner which did not sell his own people short.

When I proposed, in a speech to the Sydney Institute on 11 October 2007, a referendum for a new preamble to our Constitution which would acknowledge the first Australians, I was ridiculed for having come too late with such ideas. In retrospect, of course, I had; the Coalition was on its way to electoral defeat, although Kevin Rudd said that he agreed with my proposition for a new preamble.

The reality, however, was that it would have been premature for a proposition of this kind to have been put much earlier. The ocean liner was still completing its turn. In 1999 I had proposed a new preamble, in conjunction with the republican vote, which fully and appropriately honoured the first Australians. But because it had come from me, whose legitimacy was still not accepted by the Indigenous old guard, they turned their backs on it. A great deal more time would need to pass and a change of heart would be required before the issue could usefully be revisited.

Kevin Rudd promised during his campaign to deliver an apology if elected, but it was not a big talking point in his election pitch. It was not mentioned during Labor's policy launch. The apology was delivered with great expressions of media and apparent public support. How deep that public support was will never be known — newly elected governments carry the public with them on such symbolic issues.

Several days before the apology was given, Noel Pearson wrote of being 'convulsed' by the contradictions involved. In a column in the *Australian* on 12 February 2008 he said, 'The 1997 report of Ronald Wilson and Mick Dodson is not a rigorous history of the removal of Aboriginal children and the breaking up of families. It is a report advocating justice. But it does not represent a defensible history.' He wrote further:

The truth is the removal of Aboriginal children and the breaking up of Aboriginal families is a history of complexity and great variety. People were stolen, people were rescued; people were brought in chains, people were brought by their parents; mixed blood children were in danger from their tribal stepfathers, while others were loved and treated as their own; people were in danger from whites, and people were protected by whites. The motivations and actions of those whites involved in this history — governments and missions — ranged from cruel to caring, malign to loving, well-intentioned to evil.[4]

Later Noel Pearson praised the impact of the formal apology on Indigenous communities.

26

ON THE WATERFRONT

The most bitterly fought domestic issue of my whole time as Prime Minister was waterfront reform in 1998. It was violent, divisive and produced ugliness of a type absent from other intensely debated changes. AFP sources told me that the violence by demonstrators against the Workplace Relations Minister, Peter Reith, was far worse than directed against any other member of the Government, myself included. But it was worth the effort, as the Australian waterfront emerged profoundly more efficient.

A lot was at stake; Australia's wharves were notoriously inefficient. Rogue behaviour on the waterfront was almost part of the popular culture. At the 1983 Economic Summit, Charlie Fitzgibbon, federal secretary of the Waterside Workers' Federation (WWF), now the Maritime Union of Australia (MUA), told the story of a lady in Mackay who was asked by the local police to leave her home because a cyclone was coming. Her reply was, 'You needn't worry, the wharfies won't unload it.'[1] Apocryphal or otherwise, and amusing as it was, the story tapped a sentiment in the community.

Reform of the waterfront had been at the heart of Coalition transport and industrial relations policies for many years. Our policy for the 1996 election noted that crane loading rates were at the same abysmal level as obtained when the Hawke Government's so-called reform process started. Yet that process had cost waterfront users and taxpayers $420 million. It quoted one operator rating Melbourne as only 39.9 per cent as efficient as Antwerp and only 66 per cent as efficient as Auckland.

That policy promised that the Australian waterfront would be brought into line with international competitive standards. It demanded an end to compulsory unionism; operators were to be given power to manage their own enterprises; the monopoly stranglehold of the MUA was to be terminated.

The rorts and inefficiencies on the wharves damaged our export performance. To illustrate, in 1997 working days lost in stevedoring per thousand employees was 12 times the national average. Australia had 2 per cent of world trade, but 25 per cent of dock disputations. Container movements per hour were 17.6, abysmal by world standards. Despite this 'the wharfies' had remained untouchable.

This was due in part to the well-earned reputation for militancy of the waterfront unions. It was also because successive reform attempts by different governments always took place within the traditional tripartite process — government, business and unions — with the criterion for a successful outcome being agreement between the three parties, not greater productivity on the waterfront. The Crawford Inquiry, commissioned by the Fraser Government, and the Waterfront Industry Reform Authority (WIRA), established by the Hawke Government, were prime examples of this approach. The goal of these inquiries was to moderate an outcome which all parties could live with, not confront the restrictive practices which were the core of the problem. This suited the MUA; its leaders were tough and patient negotiators.

There was a cycle of mistrust. Governments felt that in any confrontation with the unions, once the shoe pinched, business would fold and sue for peace. Likewise, business knew from past experience that once a stand-off on the waterfront caused general dislocation in the economy, there would be pressure from the Government to settle the dispute so 'the nation could get back to work'. The MUA sensed this mutual mistrust and cynically and brilliantly exploited it.

The Workplace Relations reforms put through the parliament by Peter Reith in 1996 were very important to the course of the waterfront dispute. Paradoxically, the basis of the MUA application to the Federal Court in April 1998 to have the workforce of Patrick, the stevedoring company, reinstated was the Freedom of Association provisions of Reith's Workplace Relations Act. That act restored the secondary-boycott sections to the Trade Practices Act, and this was to prove pivotal to a successful outcome to the waterfront dispute in April–May 1998.

After its election, the Government commissioned ACIL Economics to advise it on waterfront reform. Its confidential report of October 1997 contained a telling analysis of the forces which had been at work during earlier attempts to achieve waterfront reform. It found that initially there had been some improvements following the much-lauded agreement in 1989 negotiated through WIRA, which heavily involved the PM, Bob Hawke, albeit at the considerable cost mentioned earlier. This, regrettably, did not last. According to ACIL, not only did the rate of cargo handling fall, but the remaining workforce benefited substantially in terms and conditions; thus the benefits of reform had not flowed principally to trade participants via such things as reduced prices and greater reliability, which had been the original intention.

In ACIL's opinion, the MUA retreated from offering concessions because of both perceived weakness on the part of the Hawke Government and political credit later earned through its energetic support of the re-election of the Keating Government in 1993. At a crucial stage of the 1989 negotiations, the WWF (later MUA) secretary, Tas Bull, deduced that Hawke would not insist on union concessions, so he toughened his stance. Having strongly supported the ALP in 1993, the WWF no longer felt obliged to honour any commitment to the WIRA process. Not only did it feel it had earned its political keep, but it is widely believed that the Industrial Relations Minister, Laurie Brereton, prevailed on the Australian Industrial Relations Commission (AIRC), at the behest of the WWF, to reverse an intended authorisation of some dismissals of employees at Darling Harbour caught up in an industrial dispute.

Perceptions of this kind were widely held in the industry; little wonder therefore that few believed that any government might be serious about real reform. Also the AIRC was not seen as much interested in waterfront reform. To add to this the secondary-boycott provisions had languished within the remit of the AIRC for some years and had only recently been restored to the Trade Practices Act, courtesy of the Workplace Relations Act of 1996.

I was conscious of this legacy, and the psychological ascendency enjoyed by the MUA, when my Government was elected. From early on I had discussions with John Sharp, the Transport Minister, and Peter Reith about the need to develop a strategic plan to reform the waterfront. Fortunately both Sharp and Reith were determined to achieve reform. They were of a different stripe from many previous ministers in this area. They knew what the problem was and were committed to finding a solution.

Part of that plan was to give negotiation a chance, notwithstanding the long, failed history of which we were all painfully aware. Accordingly, Peter

Reith held some four or five meetings with the leadership of the MUA, ACTU officials also being in attendance. Reith visited the various port facilities accompanied by MUA officials. He put to them the desirability of reaching the Government's productivity goal of 25 container movements per hour (against the then level of 17.6). He was bluntly told that this was unrealistic and unattainable. The union movement sent a clear message that it was not for turning. It no doubt calculated that my Government would go the way of previous government flesh on this subject. The important point is that Reith tried the path of negotiation. If the MUA had been more responsive, the course of history on the waterfront would have been different.

It was idle to pretend that a big change on the Australian waterfront could be achieved without a potentially explosive face-off with the MUA. The consensus approach had been tried ad nauseam in the past. No one wanted a major strike, and I readily understood the distaste many employers felt for any kind of action that would produce a nationwide stoppage. On the other hand, I had grown tired over the years of receiving lectures from business figures about the need for the Government to stand up to union militancy on the waterfront, only to witness those same lecturers running for cover when the possibility of firm action threatened, however temporarily, their companies' livelihoods.

I also knew that to achieve the outcome the Government wanted, there must be a carefully built public campaign reinforcing in the minds of Australians the case for reform on the waterfront. Poor performance on the waterfront was an economic reality. There was a disposition amongst people to believe this, but it had to be reinforced. That was one of the reasons why we commissioned the detailed investigation and strategy outline from the economic consultant ACIL.

The Productivity Commission released two reports on 28 April 1997 which provided strong factual support for reform. One found that poor performance, especially delays and unreliability, imposed significant costs on exporters and importers. The other report indicated that the workplace arrangements on the Australian waterfront were complex, inflexible and prescriptive; they added weight to the arguments in favour of reform. The Productivity Commission found that charges were higher and services less reliable on Australian wharves than overseas ones.

For a reform initiative to have good prospects of success, it was essential that the Government talk on a regular basis with those involved in the industry, particularly the two stevedoring companies, Patrick and P&O. The only way in which reform could be achieved was to break the grip of the MUA on work practices on the Australian waterfront. The stevedoring companies had intimate knowledge of those practices.

Commonsense told us that properly trained non-union employees would be essential to the successful implementation of a reform strategy. In any confrontation, the existing union workforce would inevitably stop working, and replacement labour would be required to keep the wharves going, otherwise the country could be held to ransom. The MUA knew this, and that is why it and its supporters reacted with such hostility to suggestions that an alternative workforce should be trained. The plan struck directly at the monopoly it held on the supply of labour for the waterfront. That was the essence of its power.

A key part of the solution to the waterfront problem was a waterfront employer willing to take on the unions. The Government found that employer in the person of Chris Corrigan, the managing director of Patrick. Corrigan agreed with the Government, not only about the need to reform the waterfront but what reform entailed. He knew that the past process had failed and that at some point, after a carefully prepared plan had been implemented, a confrontation with the MUA would occur.

From the beginning we knew that the confrontation, when it came, would be difficult; indeed unpleasant and ugly. For decades the unions had been able to bluff governments and employers out of a defining moment on the waterfront. The threat of industrial stoppages and union anarchy on our wharves was always strong enough to overcome the desire for reform. The dispute, when it ultimately came in the first half of 1998, was to demonstrate that there were still many within the ranks of employers, and even Coalition governments around Australia, who baulked at taking on the union movement to achieve the outcome they all thought desirable in the long-term interest of the Australian economy.

Another essential item of a reform strategy was government help with redundancies. Reform would entail a reduction in the stevedoring workforce and neither P&O nor Patrick would be able or willing to meet the cost involved. In mid-December 1997 Peter Reith announced that the Government would support, financially, reform-related redundancies. Preparations began immediately to give effect to this decision, so that when matters came to a climax the following April the Government was able to move instantly on redundancies, and this proved crucial in achieving the historic changes on the waterfront.

Peter Reith and I met Chris Corrigan in my office in Canberra during the latter half of 1997. Corrigan outlined the action which he believed would be necessary on his company's behalf if reform were to be realised. He was careful, providing little detail. I told him that the Government would support what he had in mind, provided that at all times it was within the law. When he had left, I was not certain that he would initiate reform.

On 23 September 1997, the affairs of the Patrick group of companies were reorganised. This involved returning to shareholders what was deemed to be surplus capital, action that was to attract fierce criticism when the dispute reached its climax in April 1998. The essence of the reorganisation was that the capital left in the business was enough to keep it going only if the workforce met its obligations under enterprise agreements between the union and the employing company. If this did not occur then the company could be placed in administration, which in turn would justify the dismissal of the workforce.

The reorganisation reflected Corrigan's belief that in any industrial relations situation, both labour and capital had obligations. Labour had an obligation to make services available in accordance with agreements, thus contributing to the realisation of a reasonable profit. Capital should be available to support the operation in achieving that profitability. It was therefore fair to argue that, in any given situation, excess capital should be taken away and used elsewhere.

The MUA attacked Patrick for not informing the union or the workforce of the restructuring. Corrigan's retort was that as the restructuring did not alter the obligations of the employees under their employment agreements, there was no onus on the company, under the Stevedoring Industry Act, to provide details of the restructuring. The employees and the MUA did not become aware of the restructuring until 8 April 1998.

The restructuring would in time facilitate the action taken by Patrick to terminate the employment of its workforce on 7 April 1998, but only because the workforce had not met its commitments under the enterprise agreements. If it had, then the company would not have gone into administration, and there would have been no basis on which to retrench the workers. This was the position which Corrigan consistently maintained.

The counter to this from the union was that Corrigan had taken a lot of money out of the company. Corrigan replied that if the workforce had fulfilled its obligations, then the company would have traded with sufficient profitability to remain out of administration. Corrigan's position is supported in the Report to Creditors dated 16 May 1998, written by Grant Thornton. It said, '… the companies could expect to earn reasonable profits under the labour supply agreements on the basis that the enterprise agreements negotiated could have been fully implemented'.[2] To use Corrigan's words in an address to the Sydney Institute in 2000, '… the companies were viable, they were not shells waiting to crack. It was the fact that the employees and their union reneged on the Enterprise Agreements that had been negotiated that brought the companies down. That fact is frequently and conveniently overlooked but it's there as large as life in the Report to Creditors dated 16 May 1998.'[3]

It was always asserted by Corrigan that the rearrangement of September 1997 was a sensible corporate restructuring which, amongst other things, effectively removed excess capital in the labour-employing companies. In that same address to the Sydney Institute, he put his powerful argument in these terms:

> First, it's apparently quite acceptable for employees to withdraw their resources, namely labour, from a company and in the process send it into insolvency but it's not acceptable for directors to withdraw capital resources which may, because of subsequent events beyond their control, contribute to the same result. What an amazing set of double standards. I have always believed it was one of a director's duties to protect and manage shareholders' capital. Apparently not — it's a one-way street. If you put capital in, you cannot take it out without the risk of being judged to have contributed to possible insolvency …
>
> Secondly, had the capital not been withdrawn and had work practices continued as they were, not as they had been negotiated, I estimate that those Companies would be facing insolvency about now in any event. The $40 million of capital would have been expended. The companies would be in administration. The workers would have no jobs.[4]

To many people Corrigan had advanced a technical, legal defence of what was an asset-stripping operation. That argument had emotional appeal, yet there was compelling logic to Corrigan's case. His key point was that if the union had kept its end of the bargain, the company would have made enough money to have remained out of administration.

The problem he had in winning acceptance of his line was that the restructuring occurred in the build-up to the events of April 1998. It plainly facilitated the plan he implemented at that time, and was open to the rather superficial allegation of a conspiracy. Yet the facts, when viewed in the cold light of day, indicated that there was a lot of validity in what Corrigan asserted. In effect, the union adopted the attitude that no matter how outrageous its behaviour might be, money should always be available to keep the company going, thus ensuring continuity of employment for its members. Corrigan's position was that the only money that would be available was the amount needed to keep the company profitable, provided that the members fulfilled their side of the bargain. He had a strong case but it was not widely accepted at the time.

In his 2000 address Corrigan pointed out that if extra money had been left in the company and it had survived until the year 2000, before going into administration, then the generous redundancy arrangements put in place by the federal government in April 1998 would not have been available for the workers retrenched in 2000, as a consequence of the company falling into administration. Clearly this would have been bad for the workers.

Debate over the ethics or otherwise of the restructuring reflected the cultural division in the Australian community on industrial relations issues. It was never going to be possible to persuade the union movement or large sections of the Australian workforce that commitment to a profitable enterprise was a two-way street. Investors had responsibilities to behave in an upfront fashion and to be reasonable in their commitments of capital. Equally the workforce had an obligation to stick to its commitments and to play its part in securing the profitability of the enterprise. For many Australians, including me, the Australian waterfront had seen a consistent repudiation by the MUA of its obligation to play its part in maintaining the profitability of enterprises which employed its members.

Although there had been detailed discussions with Patrick, and the Government believed that the company was disposed to take steps to secure waterfront reform, it was by no means certain that this would finally happen. Corrigan played his cards close to his chest.

When news broke late in 1997 that a workforce, largely composed of former or currently serving army personnel, was being trained in Dubai, this was the first that, to my knowledge, anyone in the Government had known of it. Reith said at a press conference that he had been personally told by the two stevedoring companies that it was also news to them. It was true that Patrick had not been directly involved, but Corrigan was certainly aware of the Dubai operation and he believes that one of the consultants hired by the Government (not Reith's staff) would also have been aware.

There was uproar in the media when the Dubai story emerged. Dubai sounded a rather exotic and conspiratorial location for the training of an alternative workforce. Due to the pressure of all the attendant publicity, including the threat of an international union ban on ports in Dubai, the Government of the United Arab Emirates withdrew permission for the training to take place, and that part of the exercise ended. Dubai told me that Corrigan was serious about reform. As he observed, a well-trained alternative workforce was critical to any successful reform plan.

Subsequently, Patrick leased a section of its Webb Dock in Melbourne to the stevedoring company PCS, formed by the NFF, and training of a non-union workforce commenced there early in 1998. Many of those who had begun training in Dubai continued their training at Webb Dock.

Hostility to the alternative workforce continued, even though the training was out in the open and in Australia. The MUA wanted no alternative workforce available. They knew that a trained non-union workforce threatened the continuation of the cosy, unproductive arrangements that obtained on the Australian waterfront.

The MUA took industrial action against Patrick in response to the training under way at Webb Dock. Patrick retaliated, seeking injunctions and court orders. In turn, the MUA sought a court order that Patrick would not terminate the employment of its unionised workforce.

Matters were coming to a head. The hearing of the union application was set for 8 April, two days before Good Friday. Late in the evening of 7 April 1998, Patrick activated the termination clauses of the restructuring arrangement. The companies, then in administration, dismissed the unionised workforce. Security guards were sent into the Patrick docks, accompanied by the much-reported balaclava-clad individuals and dogs. Security measures were justified. It looked bad but given the unionised workforce had been retrenched, it was hard to conceive that it could be otherwise. Patrick immediately placed the non-unionised workforce at its Sydney terminal, Port Botany, and sought to continue operating the container terminal with a new workforce.

It was a drama-charged event which immediately grabbed the attention of the nation's media. This was the long-anticipated showdown on the wharves. I felt the frisson of knowing a pivotal moment had arrived in Australia's industrial relations history.

The MUA went to the Federal Court immediately and obtained a stay of the dismissals from Mr Justice North. The hearing was to take place immediately after Easter. North found in favour of the union. He said that there was an arguable case that Patrick had engaged in a conspiracy to breach the freedom-of-association provisions of the Workplace Relations Act because the workers had been retrenched on account of their membership of the MUA. He ordered the restoration of the status quo ante, pending full litigation of the matter. This meant that Patrick had to take back the MUA workforce. Justice North completely ignored the argument that the restrictive practices of the workforce had contributed to the insolvency of the company which, in turn, had triggered the appointment of administrators and therefore the dismissal of the workforce.

On appeal, the Full Bench of the Federal Court said that North's decision had been free of 'appealable error'. The matter then ended up in the High Court of Australia. Although the High Court confirmed the decision of the Federal Court in relation to the freedom-of-association issue, there was one important variation. The High Court said that an order for reinstatement would place an unreasonable burden on administrators, almost certainly obliging them to carry on business whilst the company was insolvent. That would be in clear breach of the Corporations Law.

This crucial proviso from the High Court effectively resolved the dispute by forcing the MUA to the ultimate compromise. Patrick accepted the return of an MUA workforce, but at roughly half its original size and conditional on the elimination of numerous restrictive work practices and a more productivity-based remuneration system. The June 1988 deal between Patrick and the MUA included increased casual employment/contracting out, smaller work crews, longer regular hours, and company control over rostering and productivity bonuses for faster loading.

The MUA may have remained a major player on the Australian waterfront but it had to surrender the age-old work practices which contributed to the appalling inefficiencies at Australian ports. Attendant litigation, including conspiracy suits against the federal government, Patrick and the NFF, were abandoned. Another part of the settlement was an expectation from the MUA that action against it under section 45D of the Trade Practices Act would be abandoned by the Australian Competition and Consumer Commission (ACCC). Acting independently, the ACCC decided, in its own time, to do just that.

Due to careful preparation, the Government had been able to give effect to its redundancy proposals through introducing the relevant legislation into parliament immediately Patrick took action. The redundancy legislation played a key role in resolving the dispute once the High Court found as it did. This had been spelled out on 24 April when Peter Shergold, the secretary of Reith's department, wrote to the Patrick administrators saying, 'Funds will be made available to facilitate the payment of redundancy only in circumstances that contribute to genuine waterfront reform. The objective is to reduce overmanning, eliminate inefficient work practices and create genuine competition on Australian wharves.' The MUA was caught in a bind. Many of its members wanted the redundancies, but they would only be available if the MUA agreed to the improvements in productivity insisted upon by the Government.

After the dust had settled it was beyond argument that the Australian waterfront had changed forever. It had become more efficient, and within a few years the productivity levels of Australian ports were the equal of, or in advance of, other developed countries. That was the historic achievement. The MUA had retained a place in the waterfront sun, but in a greatly diminished capacity.

A gratifying personal footnote to the dispute was the mutual trust which emerged between Chris Corrigan and John Coombs (the boss and increasingly fatherly face) of the MUA. Although worlds apart in philosophy they came to respect each other.

Although the dispute was milder in Western Australia and Queensland, the Coalition governments in those states gave strong support. By contrast, the Kennett Government in Victoria, where the dispute was intense, proved unsupportive at crucial times. It did not provide enough encouragement to the Victoria Police to guarantee the safe passage of people willing to work at the Melbourne docks. There was a total failure of the Victorian authorities to enforce a wide-ranging order from Mr Justice Beach of the Victorian Supreme Court. This failure gave reality to the declaration of Bill Kelty, the secretary of the ACTU, that the order of His Honour would be ignored. That was because the union movement did not like the court's ruling.

The weekend of Easter 1998 was especially difficult. The MUA workforce had been retrenched by Patrick, and the non-union labour was endeavouring to go in but faced a huge picket line at the ports in Melbourne. A massive port shutdown threatened. If that were to happen, damage would be done to the reform cause.

Reith rang and briefed me on the problem emerging with the Melbourne picket line. He correctly surmised that the Victoria Police were doing very little to assist people in going through the line. The police simply said they did not have enough officers. I felt that they were not getting sufficient support and encouragement from their employer, the Victorian Government. I telephoned Kennett on Saturday morning and put to him strongly the need for support, pointing out that this was a really crucial moment in workplace relations. I reminded him that we had all wanted waterfront reform for many years. I felt that I was appealing to a kindred spirit. He, after all, had championed industrial relations reform in his own state and much to his credit had stared down massive union protests. In so many ways he was an impressive reformist premier.

His response disappointed me. He pointed out the difficulties of mounting a police operation, citing the large number of people on the picket line and how, above all else, peace and order had to be maintained. Jeff Kennett had regularly, but unfairly, criticised my Government for not being sufficiently reformist. I, therefore, might have expected his enthusiastic backing over waterfront reform. I was mistaken.

Peter Reith deserves immense praise for his role in the waterfront dispute. John Sharp had begun the process in partnership with Reith. Unfortunately Sharp was obliged to resign from the ministry late in 1997 and increasingly all of the responsibility was carried by Reith. Peter Reith was subjected to enormous pressure. He never lost his cool. He endured constant ridicule and criticism from many sections of the press. He and his family received threats of physical violence and needed a very strong AFP protection detail for months.

He maintained his sense of direction, even when there were setbacks. I was open in my support for what Reith was doing and supported him through thick and thin. Some of his senior colleagues went a little quiet when the going got tough.

He came to see me at Kirribilli House one night, late in April 1998. He had been genuinely shocked, as had other members of the Government, with the decisions of the Federal Court following the dismissal of the Patrick workforce. Our legal advice was that the procedure adopted by Patrick was perfectly legal. We were therefore quite amazed at the direction taken by Mr Justice North. Fortunately the pragmatic decision of the High Court paved the way for a sensible resolution.

During our Kirribilli House discussion, Peter accepted that the dispute had not gone precisely in the manner that he had expected or advised that it would. He felt at the time that the tide of public opinion had turned against the Government. He laid out various options as to how the Government might handle the matter from then on. One of them was for him to fall on his sword.

I would have none of this option. To start with, he had displayed consistent political courage on this issue. He had held his hand in the flame. No government can predict how courts will rule on contentious issues which have political consequences. We didn't like the decision of Mr Justice North, but we accepted it. It was part of the legal framework in which everyone had to operate.

Also Reith's legislation of 1996 had been fundamental to achieving waterfront reform. Without Australian workplace agreements, created by the 1996 act; without Section 45D of the Trade Practices Act, the restoration of which was a feature of the 1996 bill; without the obligations to fulfil contractual obligations imposed by the 1996 bill, it is hard to believe that the historic turnaround on the waterfront in 1998 would have been possible.

An even more important reason for dismissing Reith's resignation option was that for him to have resigned would have been an admission of failure by the Government. Second only to me, Peter Reith was identified with the cause of industrial relations reform. Reform of the waterfront had been long sought by our side of politics. His instincts on the issue were right. His policy direction was the only feasible one, in all of the circumstances. The preparatory work which Reith and Sharp had done had been first-class. The discussion and cooperation with Patrick, the other stevedoring companies and the NFF had been both necessary and proper.

Reith had worked his way through a difficult public policy maze. If he had gone, his departure would have been cheered by the Government's opponents and interpreted as a failure of both will and policy in relation to something that we had wanted to achieve for many years.

Chris Corrigan, the boss of the stevedore company Patrick, showed the gumption and fortitude always needed from a business leader, if genuine reform of the waterfront were to be achieved.

To many true believers in private enterprise, Chris Corrigan had become something of an iconic figure. Never an establishment type, he was treated with a certain disdain by some in the business community, yet those in the broader community who believed strongly in economic reform greatly admired his strength and tenacity.

Over the years I have had numerous private discussions with business-men and women in Australia. Most of them, in different ways, have agreed on the need for key reforms. Only a limited number have been willing to match their private exhortations and rhetoric with equivalent public stances. Corrigan was an outstanding example of a man who had been willing to do this. He was very much a loner in the Australian business community, who had a certain contempt for the frequent equivocations of some industry associations, especially on industrial relations issues.

Without his courage and strength, waterfront reform would not have been achieved. If it had been left to the British-owned P&O, the inefficiencies we had more than a decade ago would still be there. During the 1998 dispute, the British-based chief of P&O, Lord Jeffery Sterling, was in regular contact with me. He was polite, encouraging and full of praise for what the Government was doing. Yet his company was not at the sharp end of the reform push. That responsibility was left to Chris Corrigan. There were a number of excuses from P&O. One of them was that the workplace relations legislation in Australia was inadequate. Corrigan did not find the legislation inadequate; nor should have P&O.

The NFF, under the leadership of Donald McGauchie, also played a courageous role in the dispute. The historic inefficiency of the Australian waterfront had done great damage over the years to our rural exporters. They, more than most, deserved a more efficient waterfront. As for the rest of the Australian business community, it can be said that they wanted waterfront reform yet were extremely pleased that the Government, Chris Corrigan and the NFF were prepared to take the risks and bear the hostility of the union movement and a fickle media when heavy weather was encountered.

The most poorly treated group in the whole dispute were the non-union employees of PCS, the NFF-backed labour-hire company. They were encouraged to sign up in the belief that there would be plenty of work opportunities for a non-union workforce on the waterfront. The unexpected turn of events before the courts meant that the upshot of the dispute would be the re-engagement by Patrick of a significantly reduced number of MUA members as employees. There was no room, therefore, for the PCS employees. They were blackguarded by the unionists in the MUA and abandoned by the NFF, although some did find jobs on the waterfront. Having not been directly involved in their recruitment, it was not the responsibility of the Government to look after them. That did not mean I was free of guilt for what had happened to them and I felt that the NFF displayed a certain indifference to their fate. They were entitled to feel that they had been used and abandoned.

Who won the dispute? The answer to that must clearly be — Australian productivity. Prior to the reforms of the early part of 1998, container movements per hour on the Australian waterfront were 17.6. Following the reforms in the wake of the dispute, that level rose to 27.5 in 2003 and has remained there ever since, despite the huge reduction in manning levels. Pre-1998 the level was well below the Organisation for Economic Cooperation and Development (OECD) average. It is now higher.

The MUA remains the only union on the Australian waterfront, although there is still some non-union labour employed. To that extent, the union movement can argue that it successfully resisted the attempt to break its monopoly on the employment of waterfront labour. Yet the price it paid for retaining that monopoly was very high. The permanent workforce has been close to halved. Many of the old and odious work practices have been eliminated, productivity levels are markedly higher and waterfront remuneration more in line with community averages.

In 2002 Access Economics wrote: 'On virtually all measures in this study, Australia is at, close to, or superior to world best practice.'[5] That represented a remarkable turnaround and a total vindication of the policies adopted by the Government. In the September quarter 2008, the national crane rate productivity remained at the world-ranking level of 27.5 containers per hour. The vessel-working rate (a measure of labour productivity) increased from about 21 containers per hour in 1998 to 30 in 2000, 35 in 2005 and 2006 and just over 40 by December 2008.

The waterfront dispute had been tough and brutal. But a huge reform had been achieved. The Government had had plenty of critics throughout the dispute but the long-term gains were unarguable. Australia would, in very short order, have a world-competitive waterfront. The rorts and excesses of the past ought never return, and the reformist credentials of the Government had been demonstrated beyond doubt.

27

THE HOLY GRAIL OF TAX REFORM

When he was Treasurer in the short-lived Government of Billy McMahon in 1972, Bill Snedden established an inquiry to examine Australia's taxation system and make recommendations as to how it might be reformed. That was almost a quarter of century before the election of my Government in 1996.

Ken Asprey QC, who headed the inquiry, reported in 1975 at a time when the Whitlam Government had entered its death throes. Essentially, he said that Australia relied far too heavily on personal income tax as a source of revenue, should introduce a broad-based value-added tax, reduce personal income tax rates, embrace a capital gains tax and make sundry other changes.

Whilst many people might have argued on the detail, Asprey's main recommendations made sense. Australia had high rates of personal income tax, and over the years the point at which the top marginal rate of tax applied had become progressively lower. In 1955 it cut in at approximately 19 times average weekly earnings. By 1975 this had fallen to 5.5 times average weekly earnings. By the middle of the 1980s it had fallen to 1.8 times. In the 1970s and '80s, the double-taxation curse was the impact of a progressive personal income tax system at a time of continuing high levels of inflation, which repeatedly pushed taxpayers into higher tax-paying brackets.

One of the first things I did as Treasurer was to take legislation through federal parliament abolishing all federal death duties. It followed the abolition of such duties in Queensland. Other states followed suit, and before long Australia was a death- and gift-duty-free country. This was a big and popular reform, but further narrowed the tax base, serving to highlight yet again the need for comprehensive tax reform.

The Fightback! experience had left the Liberal and National parties very gun shy when it came to fundamental taxation reform of the type which so many knew was needed: the introduction of a broad-based indirect tax coupled with significant reductions in personal income tax.

After the defeat of the Coalition in 1993, we accepted that the Australian people, having voted to return Paul Keating, had wanted major tax reform taken off the agenda at least for the time being. We had no plans to introduce an indirect tax during our first term in government. In 1995, I had used the strong language of 'never ever' to kill off the goods and services tax (GST) as an issue for the coming election. We had no secret plans for a GST and I knew that if that were to ever change I would need a specific mandate to bring it about.

That is where the matter rested for some two years. Despite the appallingly large debt the Keating Government had left behind, the Coalition had not drifted back to the idea that a solution would lie in having a GST. For myself, I had never intellectually abandoned the belief that Australia needed basic taxation reform and I knew that this, if it were to occur, would have to include the introduction of a broad-based indirect, or goods and services tax. I had watched the changes in New Zealand and earlier in the United Kingdom, and did not imagine that Australia could, indefinitely, remain as heavily reliant on personal income tax as a source of revenue.

There were also the imbalances in the Commonwealth–state financial relationship. Every federal government had grappled with this. It was no different for us. Despite there being only one Labor Government at a state and territory level when I became Prime Minister, it was not long before the states began to blame their financial woes on the Commonwealth.

As 1997 progressed, it became clear that the Government, for a variety of reasons, had lost momentum. Part of the problem had been the expectations created by the cracking pace of our early months. In less than a year we had begun implementing our plan to bring the budget back into balance; had delivered on our family tax promises; had implemented major workplace relations reforms; had revolutionised the approach to helping Australians find a job; had privatised one-third of Telstra and established the NHT and had also moved in many other areas to implement non-economic commitments.

Still, the sense was that despite all of this, given the huge majority we had, still more should be undertaken. I did not need a lot of persuading that the Government had to maintain the momentum of reform otherwise the public would begin to become restless. Having spent so many years of frustration in opposition, it was not my natural condition to remain on idle in government.

At the time of the 1997 budget, I had some general discussions with Tim Fischer and Peter Costello about the need for tax reform. Shortly after that budget, I said on the Sunday morning Channel 7 program *Face to Face* that the issue of fundamental taxation reform would have to be addressed at some time. I reaffirmed our commitment regarding a GST during our first term in office, and although I did not specifically allude to a GST being introduced at a later date, the possibility was left open, by implication. I had put my toe in the water and my comments attracted considerable media interest.

It took a bout of viral pneumonia which hospitalised me for a week in the excellent facilities of the Mater Private Hospital in Crows' Nest in Sydney, and a further convalescence of two weeks at Kirribilli House, to really crystallise my thinking on the issue of taxation reform. When I returned to work in July of 1997, I called a cabinet meeting to discuss the issue. By then the speculation had grown and my colleagues were anything but unprepared for the discussion. I had worked out in my own mind some principles which would govern our approach. I presented them to my colleagues for discussion and endorsement. They were:

- There should be no increase in the overall tax burden
- Any new taxation system should involve major reductions in personal income tax, with special regard for the taxation treatment of families
- Consideration should be given to a broad-based indirect tax to replace some or all of the existing indirect taxes
- There should be appropriate compensation for those deserving of special consideration
- Reform of Commonwealth–state financial relations must be addressed.

It was clear from these principles where our reform plan was headed. Prior to making a public announcement I convened a telephone hook-up of the chairmen of all of the Coalition backbench policy committees to seek their reaction to and approval of the announcement being made without a special party meeting. There was overwhelming support for the approach that we were taking. I also telephoned all of the state premiers to inform them of the planned reform. I announced the Government's intentions on 13 August 1997.

Taxation reform was a large piece of unfinished economic business for our country. It was something that I had believed in for a long time, and I felt enthusiastic that we were now going down a difficult but most desirable path towards further strengthening our economy. Some journalists, in particular Michelle Grattan of the Melbourne *Age*, poked fun at my reference to tax reform being a 'great adventure'. Perhaps it was a strangely colourful phrase for something as drear as taxation reform, but using the expression illustrated my strong commitment to what we hoped to achieve.

I was again doing what I relished most in politics: campaigning for a much-needed reform.

I said that any changes would not take effect until after the next election and, as a consequence, any major taxation alterations would be the centrepiece of the economic debate in the next election campaign. This rendered nonsensical those arguments from the Labor Party that I was being dishonourable in advocating taxation reform when I had previously ruled out a GST. Those critics conveniently overlooked the fact that I was giving the electorate the opportunity to reject the Government if it did not like our taxation proposals. Surely a political party is entitled to change its position on a major policy issue without being accused of bad faith, if it submits the change for adjudication at an election?

Debate on taxation reform had occurred fitfully in Australia over some 15 to 20 years. It was not a new issue. Experience had told me, however, that if ever it were going to be achieved, it had to be delivered by an incumbent government, in a strong political position and in the early stages of its time in office. The Howard Government in 1997 met those criteria.

The enthusiasm of the backbench for taxation reform gave me great heart. Marginal seat-holders realised that the 1998 election had to be fought on different issues from those in 1996. They saw taxation reform as a cause to fight for, something positive to advocate for the future benefit of the country.

As Treasurer, Peter Costello assumed the daily burden of putting together a detailed proposal for taxation reform. He did an outstanding job. A taxation taskforce was established headed by Treasury, with representatives from my department, the Australian Taxation Office, the Treasurer's office and the Cabinet Policy Unit. We conferred regularly about the shape of the reform. As weeks turned to months, Costello successively brought to cabinet Powerpoint presentations on various aspects of the reform plan.

There was not much doubt from the beginning that the rate for the GST would be 10 per cent. Both Peter and I felt that 15 per cent, which had been the Fightback! level, was too high and that anything less than 10 per cent would immediately invite the suspicion that it would be increased to 10 per cent not long after its introduction. We both wanted a rate which remained unchanged indefinitely.

Peter Costello and I were also keen that as many as possible of other indirect taxes at both a state and federal level should be removed. First and foremost was the removal of the antiquated and inequitable wholesale sales tax, which applied to a limited number of goods, did not apply to services and heavily discriminated against manufacturers and exporters. There should also be a major revamping of the business taxation system. Good preparatory work with the business community meant that credible figures such as John Ralph, later Commonwealth Bank chairman, were active in promoting reform. He and others would raise the money to fund television advertisements which strongly put the case for taxation reform when the detailed plan was released almost a year later.

Ralph and his colleagues had also reached out to welfare groups and, although the policy when released was not applauded by those groups, it was not completely condemned. We had learned from the mistakes of the past. In putting together the policy details, the Government went to great lengths to cushion the impact on low-income people. The compensation arrangements for pensioners initially were fair, and they were made more generous in the course of later negotiations with minor parties and Independents in the Senate.

A critical point was reached in decisions on the personal income tax rates, when cabinet agreed to the abolition of the tax rebate on savings, introduced only a year earlier, and the use of the proceeds of that decision to fund a tax rate of 30 per cent for some 80 per cent of taxpayers. To be able to say that 80 per cent of taxpayers would pay no more than 30 cents in the dollar on their last dollar of income became a powerful selling point for the policy when it was released.

Late in the preparation of the final tax plan, I asked that a rate of 7.5 per cent, rather than 10 per cent, be examined. When something as complex as this huge reform is under consideration, all manner of options are looked at. After putting the proposition to Peter Costello and his obtaining advice on it, I did not pursue it any further. It was no more than an option I wanted examined. Peter and I worked together in close professional association in preparing the plan for a new tax system. We both believed in it and we both had a lot at stake in ensuring that the right outcome was achieved. He impressed with his technical mastery of the subject.

The final plan was huge in its scope. It involved the introduction of the 10 per cent GST with only minimal exemptions for such things as health and childcare services. It covered food and stipulated that all of the proceeds of the GST would be funnelled to the states. In this fashion it became also a major structural reform to Commonwealth–state financial relations. The states now had the growth tax they had long craved. In return for obtaining the proceeds of the GST, the states agreed to abolish a large number, but not all, of their own taxes such as the bank account debits tax, the financial institutions duty and stamp duty on share transactions. The wholesale sales tax was to be abolished. Payroll tax was left untouched, which was unfortunate, but to abolish it would have meant a GST rate of at least 12.5 per cent. Major changes to business taxation were also canvassed, including a reduction in the corporate rate to 30 per cent. This reduction became part of the Government's overall tax reform program.

At my insistence it was also agreed that we would introduce a 30 per cent tax rebate for private health insurance. The earlier means-tested and more limited tax rebate had not worked, and I was concerned that unless we went the extra distance, private health insurance would continue to languish.

There were also major changes to the Family Tax Benefit arrangements. We combined a number of payments, including the family allowance and the family tax initiative, and in their updated versions they became Family Tax Benefit A, which went to all eligible families with children under 16, and Family Tax Benefit B, which in addition went to single-income families.

Released on 13 August 1998, A New Tax System (ANTS) was a sweeping reform. We laid out all of the details, including tax rates and cameos for different income groups. I knew at the time that it would be the basis of our re-election pitch, and that subject to a reasonably satisfactory launch, I would call an election within a matter of weeks. The launch received a very positive reaction from commentators and the media generally. The Labor

Party came out strongly against it, and the Australian Democrats, whilst expressing broad support for tax reform, including the introduction of a GST, opposed the GST applying to food. Crucially Senator Harradine was noncommittal.

There seemed no point in delaying the election, as the battlelines had been drawn. After watching the Wallabies complete a clean sweep against the All Blacks for the Bledisloe Cup on the Saturday night, I flew to Canberra on Sunday, 30 August, and called the election for 3 October 1998. We were provoking the gods — going to an election promising a new tax. Many thought that we were crazy. One was Kerry Packer, who just a few weeks before the release of the tax plan had rung me to say that a GST was a totally stupid idea. He said that no amount of personal tax cuts would mollify the public, which would resent paying a new tax. We were behind in the polls, and the ALP would run a populist scare campaign. It was so 'courageous' it would have made Sir Humphrey proud.

The election campaign was overwhelmingly dominated by debate on our taxation reform plan. Campaigning for a detailed taxation policy with all of the minute impacts on individuals having been spelled out was a hazardous undertaking. Both Peter Costello and I lived with the daily fear that, no matter how well prepared we might be, we would stumble on some small technicality which would be blown out of all proportion in the hothouse of the campaign. Both of us remained haunted by the birthday cake experience of John Hewson in 1993. Although there were some glitches, we managed to avoid major stumbles and emerge from the campaign with the details of the tax plan holding together extremely well. Peter Costello and his department had done a superb job in delivering a plan which was bulletproof. For something as complicated as taxation reform that was a notable achievement.

There was no way that we were going to preserve our 1996 majority. The polls remained against us throughout the campaign, but with such a big majority it seemed inconceivable that the Labor Party could make us a one-term government. Yet the final Newspoll, released the day before the election, showed a two-party-preferred vote for the ALP of 53 per cent against 47 per cent for the Coalition. If repeated on election day, that would produce a catastrophic outcome for me and my colleagues. In the space of just under three years, a thumping majority of 45 seats would have evaporated in the face of a Labor Party which had not even attempted the process of renewal and reconstruction following the rout of March 1996. As

I hosted a thank you dinner for my staff at the Stamford Plaza Hotel in North Ryde, I tried to boost their spirits by saying we had been a reformist government which had courageously taken political risks to give Australia a better future. I felt very nervous.

I respected Beazley. He had done a good job as Opposition Leader, representing experience and continuity. His colleagues liked him, and he had the right personality to hold the party together immediately after a big defeat. He had been Keating's Deputy Prime Minister but escaped much of the odium attached to my predecessor. His knowledge of foreign affairs and defence meant that he could speak with authority in these areas. All up, he gave the ALP immediate respectability in opposition and, because of his experience, the capacity to look and sound that the Labor Party, after a very short time in opposition, was once again ready for government.

That appearance hid a deeper reality. Any party which suffers the kind of defeat that the Labor Party did in 1996 needs a thorough examination so that the reasons are fully understood. Labor never engaged in this exercise and was seduced by some of the easy pickings of early opposition, such as the problems we encountered following the Wik decision, ministerial resignations over non-compliance with the conduct code and, most importantly, knee-jerk reaction to the GST, which led the Labor Party to believe that we had potentially committed political suicide by embracing it.

The real gift to the Labor Party, which ultimately proved quite illusory and would lead it to a complacent second term in opposition, was Pauline Hanson and One Nation. As well as the GST, Pauline Hanson and One Nation contributed significantly to our big loss of seats in 1998.

Election day 1998 was extremely tense for me. Pre-election polling had been very bad. As always, I toured Bennelong polling booths. I met the Unity Party candidate, who was of Chinese descent, who tackled me on a variety of subjects. He said my stance on Pauline Hanson meant that I was unsympathetic to citizens of Asian background. Labor workers were buoyant, believing that I was facing humiliating rejection.

At Gladesville Public School I shook hands with a One Nation helper who wished me luck and told me that he had always voted for me in Bennelong. I enquired why, therefore, he was handing out tickets for Pauline Hanson, to which he replied that he had been attracted to some of her views but nonetheless hoped that I would be returned as Prime

Minister. I then asked him to give his preference vote in Bennelong to me ahead of the Labor candidate, and in defiance of the preference clearly shown for the Labor Party on the One Nation how-to-vote ticket. His reply was a rather lame comment that he really had to follow the preference advice of his party. This man's attitude exemplified why we lost more ground in the 1998 election than might otherwise have been expected.

As close family and some staff gathered at Kirribilli House to watch the election results, I was not optimistic about the outcome. This pessimism was confirmed when at 6.41 pm Lynton Crosby phoned through the results of the party's exit poll. It showed 53 per cent for Labor and 47 per cent for the Coalition on a two-party-preferred basis, exactly the same as the final published Newspoll. In the Green Room in Kirribilli House, I briefed Janette and our three children on the poll outcome, telling them that I believed we were going to lose.

Grahame and Bronwyn Morris joined me in the study, with my children coming and going as the results came through. The early ones mirrored the bleak prediction of the exit poll, as we limped through the first hour of counting. Then, with a substantial percentage of the vote counted in Fran Bailey's electorate, Grahame Morris spotted a trend in McEwen: she was hanging on; McEwen was a highly marginal Victorian seat won by Bailey in 1990 only to be lost in 1993, but regained in 1996. Shouting, 'Go, Fran', Grahame declared that if she could hang on, then we might survive after all. She did hang on, and we did ultimately survive, but it was to be another hour, at least, before I believed this.

As things began to stabilise I wandered into the dining room at Kirribilli House to join others who were watching the ABC coverage, just in time to see Antony Green, whose statistical analysis was always very good, declare that he thought the Coalition would win by some 10 to 12 seats. That proved to be remarkably close to the mark.

We had copped a huge swing, and the Labor Party on a two-party-preferred basis had outpolled us. 'Gladesville man' had done terrible damage to the Coalition vote. This was the real bonus for the Labor Party, which led the ALP to a lazy second term in opposition.

As previously stated, Pauline Hanson and One Nation, as well as the GST, caused our big loss of seats in 1998. There had been miracle gains in 1996, such as the electorates later held by Kevin Rudd and Wayne Swan in Brisbane. They would obviously revert back to the ALP absent the landslide of 1996. The next layer of Labor gains in 1998 were really seats like Stirling in Western Australia, which fell to Labor because One Nation took votes predominantly from the Coalition parties and did not return a large enough portion of them to our candidates through preferences. Between 1996 and 1998 the Coalition primary vote Australia-wide fell by 7.7 per cent, just short of the Hanson vote of 8.43 per cent in 1998. Yet only 53.66 per cent of that One Nation vote was returned to the Liberal and National parties via preferences. The ALP primary vote increased by only 1.35 per cent in 1998 compared with 1996.

Over the days ahead I would pay tribute to our marginal seat-holders, many of them women, such as the three in Adelaide — Trish Worth, Christine Gallus and Trish Draper — all of whom survived. Danna Vale increased her majority in Hughes, and Jackie Kelly had a solid win in Lindsay. Fran Bailey, of course, hung on in McEwen. The blokes also did their part in marginal spots, but the contribution of the women was quite remarkable. I would not have survived as Prime Minister without their marginal-seat-campaigning skills. They were the Golden Girls of 1998.

Before going to the Wentworth Hotel, I watched Beazley's triumphal address in Western Australia. He had done extremely well, reclaiming many seats Labor had lost less than three years earlier. He looked and sounded like a man who believed he was now only one election away from moving into the Lodge.

Politically, I had had a near-death experience. Although the polls were bad right through the campaign, it was not until the last few days that I began to focus on the real possibility of losing. It had seemed impossible several weeks out, given the size of our majority and the fact that we had only been in government for less than three years. Yet we had been a controversial government, had done an enormous amount in changing the direction of the country and had proposed something which no previous Australian Government had attempted: we sought re-election with a policy of introducing a new tax.

Having, on election night, gone from believing that we would lose to the elation of hanging on, I felt quite light-headed as I was driven with my family to make my victory speech at the Wentworth Hotel. I felt very different from what I had some two-and-a-half years earlier. I was conscious of the large number of seats which had been lost, and that many good people would be leaving us, but in politics a win is a win. I had not given a lot of thought to what I might say and on the way in I felt I should throw forward to something of a noneconomic kind. We had campaigned almost exclusively on economic issues.

My election-night speech, therefore, included a commitment to achieve genuine reconciliation between Australians and Indigenous Australians by 2001, the centenary of Federation. It had come from nowhere. Most of my followers and colleagues were quite surprised that I had raised the issue. They never saw this as being a 'John Howard issue'. Regrettably, too many of them held the view that reconciliation was about a rights agenda. At that stage, the concept of practical reconciliation was struggling to gain traction.

I wanted to promote it as I sensed that many Australians saw reconciliation as I did: including Aboriginal people in the mainstream of the community.

Although this commitment raised eyebrows, it did not dominate news coverage of the challenges which lay ahead for the newly elected government. We had won, despite promising a new tax, and the general view was that it was an extraordinary achievement, even though we had shed much electoral blood in the process.

From the outset Beazley made it plain that the Labor Party would not respect the mandate on tax reform given to us by the Australian people. That was its attitude regarding all of the major issues for which the Coalition campaigned in 1996, 1998 and 2001. In 1998, we could not have been more explicit on tax reform. We hadn't campaigned in general terms. We had laid out in minute detail all of the elements of our tax plans and had taken a huge risk that the Australian public would reject it and succumb to Labor's fear tactics.

Having toiled for months to put together a complex plan, and having won an election despite the burden of advocating a new tax, we still faced huge obstacles before laws were implemented giving effect to our taxation proposals. Although Labor was total negativity from start to finish, the Australian Democrats were a mixed bag. During the campaign they said they favoured taxation reform with a GST, yet were opposed to it applying to food and some other items.

Neither Peter Costello nor I wanted to exempt food from the GST. We were both steadfastly of the view that when it came to indirect taxation, the maxim must always be, the broader the base the lower the rate. As few exemptions as possible remained our goal, and we could see no logical reason to exclude food, provided that the compensation arrangements were adequate — and we believed that they were.

Except on one issue, the private health insurance rebate, the powerful Independent Brian Harradine was the great unknown. With his help, the 30 per cent tax rebate went through the Senate, in the teeth of ALP opposition, shortly after the election. It proved most successful. As to the rest of the tax plan, he had not given an indication either way during the election campaign. I remained moderately optimistic, without there being anything on which to base that optimism. We did provide a further sweetener to the compensation arrangements for low-income earners and pensioners, which we hoped would be attractive to him. I had a long and cordial discussion with him, and he gave a similar attentive ear to Peter Costello. It was all to no avail. On 14 May 1999, in the Senate, Brian Harradine uttered those memorable and decisive words, 'I cannot.'

Harradine's rejection of the GST was an immense disappointment. We had risked all and won an election being utterly candid with the Australian people about our plans, yet we could not get those plans through the Senate in the form in which they had received the support of the Australian people. As an exercise in representative democracy, it seemed unfair, but such feelings had no currency when it came to gathering the votes in parliament to secure passage of legislation.

Peter Costello was in the Philippines when Harradine lowered the boom on the GST. I spoke to him and we both lamented the outcome. I knew then the only alternative was to negotiate with the Democrats, and realised that this would mean agreeing to exempt food. That is something I found hard to accept, given that it would create anomalies in our new tax plan and because of my feeling that it was outrageous for the Senate to ignore the mandate of the Australian people for a policy laid out in complete detail.

Over the next few days many leading business figures, such as Frank Lowy and James Packer, personally urged that we negotiate with the Australian Democrats. They didn't want food exempted either but they felt that it was too big a price to pay to let the whole plan collapse. The Coalition had a choice. It could either settle for some 85 per cent of what the Australian people had supported or accept that serious taxation reform was dead indefinitely.

At a cabinet meeting in Longreach shortly afterwards, there was an overwhelming view that we should negotiate an acceptable compromise with the Democrats, knowing full well that we would have to give ground on food and also other items. Peter Costello was still abroad, but I knew from earlier discussions that he would be unhappy about making changes to the policy we had taken to the people; so was I. Realistically though, we had no alternative if we were to salvage the bulk of a reform plan vital to the national interest, and in which we had invested so much political capital.

If the whole plan fell to ground, then not only would tax reform be off the agenda indefinitely, but also the Government would suffer huge political damage. It, and most particularly its leader, would be seen as ineffective on a central economic policy. As is always the case when a government is damaged, the person suffering the biggest injury is the Leader of the Government.

The correct thing was to have Peter Costello conduct the initial discussions with the Australian Democrats. This occurred and, predictably, no progress was made. The Democrats said that there was no way they would support the tax plan without food being excluded. There were requests on other items as well. Peter Costello told them that exempting food was off the table.

The Democrats prepared to launch their campaign against the tax plan. I telephoned Meg Lees and asked that her campaign be deferred until after there had been a further meeting, this time involving me.

The first of the resumed discussions took place in the cabinet room in Melbourne. I knew that to get anywhere we had to give the Democrats something. There was no way they were simply going to change their minds, having been so vehemently opposed to aspects of the policy during the election campaign. Also, we needed to create the right atmosphere, and that involved making them feel they were being taken seriously. One of the best ways for an incumbent government to do that is to invite the people with whom it is negotiating into the place where the Government itself meets — the cabinet room.

I was conscious of the importance of these negotiations as I knew that if they failed, the Government would take an enormous amount of water. Meg Lees was accompanied by Andrew Murray, as well as her advisors John Cherry, who would later become a senator, and John Schumann, the Red Gum singer who had run Alexander Downer to a close result in his Adelaide seat of Mayo. The Treasurer and I were accompanied by our senior private office advisors, including, for my part, Arthur Sinodinos and my economic advisor, Peter Crone.

Perhaps he resented my leading the negotiations, but Peter Costello's body language, from the very beginning, was that of a reluctant participant. I ignored it, and was determined to treat the Democrats with courtesy and attention. I wanted something from them, and it was important for the Government I led that I got it. Although it was to be some time before I finally agreed that food would be excluded, I accepted that, at the end of the day, this would happen. My tactic was to dispose of the less contentious issues at the beginning so that we could focus in detail on the more difficult propositions. These negotiations went on for several weeks, shifting from Melbourne back to Canberra, and gradually our areas of difference were whittled away.

In the process we had to agree to a number of things I disliked intensely. One was a complicated arrangement for diesel excise rebates which involved different rates according to the size of vehicles. This was in order to meet environmental objections from the Democrats with regard to large trucks in city localities. We also had to give in to the Democrats concerning the taxation of books. This had been a symbolic matter for them for a long time.

The final outcome predictably involved exempting fresh food from the GST as well as significantly reduced thresholds at which the higher rate of taxation would apply. Fortunately we were able to hang onto tax rates whereby some 80 per cent of taxpayers paid no more than 30 cents in the dollar on any dollar of their income. Nonetheless we were saddled with an outcome where the top marginal rate applied at $60,000 a year instead of the $75,000 a year on which we had campaigned. That figure itself was still very low by world standards, but $60,000 was absurdly so.

Despite my regrets about certain things we were obliged to accept, I was elated when agreement was finally achieved. I found in Meg Lees a person of integrity, and the sense of trust that we established with each other was the major reason why the negotiations were successful. Meg Lees and I disagreed on a lot of issues. She would oppose our commitment in Iraq and felt that I was not sufficiently committed to the environment, but she was someone with whom I could not only do business but whose word could be believed. The frequently used TV images of Meg Lees and me shaking hands after the GST deal was made showed two people who trusted each other, and were well pleased with the outcome of an important and lengthy negotiation.

She showed enormous courage in negotiating the taxation compromise with my Government. In the process, she unsettled her party, and almost certainly cost herself its leadership and ultimately, therefore, her place in the Senate. Yet she could legitimately be seen as someone who facilitated one of the historic economic reforms of a generation, on terms satisfactory to her. In supporting the Government, Meg Lees and the majority of her colleagues alienated Natasha Stott Despoja and Andrew Bartlett, both of whom voted against the taxation package in the Senate. Meg Lees was well aware of their disaffection during our negotiations, but it did not deter her. Andrew Murray was also of inestimable assistance. He shared her view that Australia needed a better taxation system.

We announced the successful outcome on Friday, 28 May 1999, and I felt enormous relief to have concluded that compact with the Democrats. Although a lot of detailed haggling lay ahead and the legislation had to be piloted through the parliament, it would take an extraordinary series of events and a massive loss of goodwill for the deal to fall over. Without my personally leading the Government's negotiations, an understanding with the Democrats would not have been concluded.

I don't think that Peter Costello was entirely happy with the outcome. A few days later, when we were all back in Canberra, he made some remarks at a gathering, in full knowledge that the media were there, poking fun at some of the anomalies which emerged from the exclusion of food. We all knew that there were anomalies. That was why we had not wanted to exclude food. But in order to obtain the support of the Democrats, food had to go, and I could not quite understand the point of deriding an agreement that we had worked so hard to bring to fruition.

The tax plan passed into law on 29 June 1999. This was an historic achievement. At long last major taxation reform, built around the principles outlined in the Asprey Report almost 25 years earlier, had finally been legislated. This was a vindication of our determination to be a reformist government. I also felt well satisfied in our ability to negotiate a reasonable compromise with the Democrats in order to get our legislation through. All governments must negotiate and compromise. No government can roll all before it, and the Howard Government was no exception.

There would be some teething troubles, which I deal with in separate chapters, but the first stage of the great tax adventure had been successful. Of all the big economic reforms since 1980, taxation reform was the most complex and had the potential to cause the most dislocation. Legislation to bring it about had now been passed. All of this had been realised by the Coalition despite carping opposition and negativity from the ALP, which would continue unrelentingly for the next two-and-a-half years. Although the challenge of implementation lay ahead, the achievement to date was something of which we were entitled to feel exceedingly proud.

28

WE STILL WANT YOU, MA'AM — THE REPUBLICAN DEBATE

On the evening of Sunday, 7 November 1999, Janette and I attended the opening of the Fox Studios at Centennial Park in Sydney. It was the day after the Australian people had voted against their country becoming a republic. The timing was a touch uncomfortable. The News Limited papers had campaigned with unrestrained vigour for a republic. Rupert and Wendi Murdoch were there. Rupert had been a long-declared supporter of an Australian republic.

Not that any of our News Limited hosts lacked grace and courtesy. The ever-polite David Armstrong, Editor-in-Chief of the *Australian*, congratulated me on the outcome of the referendum. I had no intention of gloating. The issue had been disposed of, and I wanted to return to the ongoing affairs of government. Moreover, it was not in my interest to have longstanding antagonisms with News Limited editors, or indeed editors of any newspapers.

I was happy at the outcome. The previous night had been a good one, with the referendum result being capped by the Wallabies winning the World Rugby Cup. I had never wanted an Australian republic. I see the value of a continuing historical connection with the second-oldest institution in Western civilisation. In addition, all of my conservative instincts told me that there was nothing to be gained by changing a structure of government which had played a big part in the incredible stability of the Australian constitutional and political system.

There was an additional, and sharper, political and indeed cultural reason why I was glad the referendum had been defeated. Although it had been toned down during the referendum campaign, the underlying theme of so much of the republican drive was that republicans were better Australians than monarchists.

Malcolm Turnbull, who had led the republican campaign, made the oft-repeated comment on referendum night that whatever else I might be remembered for I would certainly be remembered as 'the Prime Minister who broke this nation's heart'.[1] That comment didn't bother me then, and hasn't at any time since.

A year or two after the referendum, Lynton Crosby, the federal director of the Liberal Party, told me that Malcolm Turnbull wanted to rejoin the Liberal Party and become an active member. He would not, however, seek to do this if I had any objection. Apparently Malcolm was a little sensitive then as to what he had said on the night of the referendum. I told Lynton that I had absolutely no problem with Turnbull coming back. In fact I would welcome it.

There were many staunch Liberals who were also republican. I did not want support or opposition to a republic to be a criterion for Liberal Party membership.

Although there had always been many 'eventual republicans' in Australia, there was no support of any consequence for a change from within the political mainstream until November 1975. Whitlam's dismissal turned many latent Labor republicans into more active ones, even though the events of November 1975 demonstrated that the Governor-General was effectively Australia's Head of State.

Despite November 1975 illustrating that the prerogative powers of the crown were fully vested in the Governor-General, it was a fine legal argument. The political reality was that the dismissal of Gough Whitlam had produced an emotional reaction amongst many Labor people against the constitutional monarchy, because Whitlam had been sacked by the Queen's man.

Malcolm Fraser joined the republican cause in the lead-up to the referendum although he gave no inkling of any such tendency during his prime ministership. Whilst he was at the Lodge he was every bit the perfect constitutional monarchist. He was the last Australian prime minister to accept membership of the Privy Council. The Queen also made him a Companion of Honour. Such things were entirely appropriate at the time.

Bob Hawke was an 'eventual republican' but he understood the affection of the Australian people for the Queen. When prime minister he did not push the issue. On national identity matters, he understood the mood of Australians much better than did his successor. When his Government officially made 'Advance Australia Fair' our national anthem in April 1984, he specifically rejected any link between that decision and a change to the Australian flag.

Hawke's view was that things should stay as they were for so long as the Queen remained on the throne. He campaigned for the republic in 1999, and I am sure that he voted yes. I doubt that he was much perturbed by the outcome.

Paul Keating, of course, took a completely different approach. Strangely though, I was never able to find much evidence that Keating was particularly vocal on the subject before he became prime minister. I don't suggest that his support for a republic or for a change in the Australian flag were anything other than genuinely held views. Nonetheless, it was politically advantageous, within his own party, for him to take the positions which he did on these issues.

He had narrowly wrested the leadership from Hawke, and much bad blood remained amongst party followers. He was very much a one-dimensional person whose sole preoccupation had been the economy, during his years as Treasurer. The republican issue provided a diversion from some of the economic challenges at the time. Moreover, his stance was appealing to many Labor intellectuals, academics and inner-urban elites, who were so influential in Labor Party branches.

In the 1996 election campaign I had promised that, if elected, the Coalition would hold a constitutional convention to consider the republican issue. If that convention produced a consensus for a particular republican model, then that model would be put to a referendum.

On 4 February 1997 I announced arrangements for the constitutional convention to be held in Old Parliament House in February 1998. It was to comprise 152 delegates, of which half would be elected and the other half appointed. The appointed delegates were to include leaders and senior people of both the Government and opposition in the federal parliament as well as representatives of state governments and oppositions. For the remaining appointed delegates, I was keen to have a mixture of people, both background-wise and with regard to their likely views on the issue.

Having appointed delegates meant that, amongst other things, young Australians as well as Indigenous Australians would be assured of a genuine say at the convention. The younger delegates made an impressive contribution. One of them, Julian Leeser, produced one of the best lines of the convention when he described the republican push as the 'the zenith of a generation who value style over substance, to whom touchy-feely, kumbaya motherhood notions are more important than results'.[2] Julian later became the Executive Director of the Menzies Research Centre.

The ballot for the elected delegates, conducted by the Australian Electoral Commission (AEC), was a first, because it was a postal ballot involving a general franchise. It was voluntary, and the participation rate was 45.3 per cent. The Australian Republican Movement (ARM), led by Malcolm Turnbull, and Australians for a Constitutional Monarchy (ACM), led by David Flint and Lloyd Waddy, ran teams in each state. The direct-election republicans (those who wanted the President chosen by a popular vote of all Australians), who played such a crucial role in muddying the waters amongst those who wanted a republic, did well in the ballot. Amongst their number elected were Ted Mack, Clem Jones and Tim Costello. Mack had been the Independent federal MP for North Sydney, Jones was a Queensland Labor identity who had served as Brisbane's Lord Mayor, and Costello was a prominent Baptist minister and brother of the Treasurer. Later, when it had been decided that a direct-election model would not be submitted to the people, these three people went their different ways. Tim Costello threw in his lot with the other republicans; Mack and Jones campaigned for a no vote. Predictably ARM candidates polled the most votes, followed by candidates of the ACM. The republicans were the early frontrunners.

Polls continued to show majority support for a change, although it was never overwhelming. With the exception of prominent talkback radio hosts such as Alan Jones, most of the media was energetically campaigning for change. Fairfax and News Limited papers as well as the ABC were strongly pro-republican.

Supporting a republic was the fashionable attitude to have. Although it was a system of government up for adjudication, not attitudes to either the Queen or members of her family, the personal conduct of some members of the royal family over preceding years — which had provided much media fodder — was something that played into the public mood.

My opposition to a republic was well known. Liberal MPs were to have a free vote on the issue, and I was sure that the National Party would adopt a similar stance. Kim Beazley pretended that the parliamentary Labor Party would allow a free vote. It was hard to see much evidence of that in practice. They all seemed to be spruiking the republican cause. In any event, the ALP's platform had been amended in 1991 to incorporate a commitment to an Australian republic.

One brave Labor soul on the subject had been Graeme Campbell, by then the Independent member for Kalgoorlie. Campbell had lost his ALP endorsement before the 1996 election but had won despite this. Prior to that election he had, amongst other things, dissented from Keating's pro-republican push. Campbell's sacking by the Labor Party (not over the republic) was politically inept and cost the party his seat. It was a stark illustration of the straitjacket Keating's cultural agenda had imposed on his own party.

At a very senior level the Liberal Party was quite divided. In the republican camp there were to be three of the four members of the leadership group: Peter Costello, Robert Hill and Richard Alston. Peter Reith was a direct-election republican. In time he became a vocal opponent of the proposition put to the people that the Head of State should be chosen by a two-thirds majority of the Commonwealth parliament. Alexander Downer was the most prominent anti-republican outside the leadership group. As the debate progressed, Nick Minchin and Tony Abbott became both articulate and well-recognised advocates of the status quo.

In the early '90s Peter Costello had opposed a republic. I am sure that his change of heart was quite genuine, but it had potential political advantage for him. By the time of the convention, republicanism was a lot more fashionable than being a supporter of the monarchy. If the republican proposition had been carried in 1999, my position as Prime Minister would have been weakened. Although there was a free vote for Liberal parliamentarians, the reality would have been that on a fundamental constitutional issue the Liberal Prime Minister of the day would have been seen as out of step with public opinion.

To the intense disappointment of our critics, differences at the top of the Liberal Party caused no acrimony. We were determined not to allow our conflicting opinions on the republic to damage in any way the unity of the Government. Throughout the campaign Costello and I continued our close working relationship as Prime Minister and Treasurer. The Australian people quite respected the fact that the Liberal Party could be mature and disciplined enough to allow its two most senior figures to have different views but still preserve the cohesion of the Government.

Those senior liberals, both in parliament and the party organisation, who wanted a republic, knew that, in the final analysis, my personal opposition to a republic would carry a lot of weight in the electorate. Some tried to persuade me to change my position.

Tony Staley, the federal president of the Liberal Party, saw me at Kirribilli House in the middle of 1999 to discuss a range of subjects. During our discussion he put the proposition to me that, at some point, there would be a republic in Australia. His argument was that the Liberal Party would win the verdict of history if it were to preside over Australia becoming a republic at the centenary of Federation on 1 January 2001. He argued that I could win a special place in Australian history if I were to support a change to a republic for the centenary.

I understood fully what Tony was getting at. He was one of those Liberals who believed in a republic, and because of that belief saw benefit in the Liberal Party being associated with it. He also knew that the prospects of the republican cause succeeding were not very bright whilst the Liberal Prime Minister of the day remained in the other camp. I told Staley that I could not possibly change my position as I didn't believe in a republic.

The constitutional convention, held at the Old Parliament House on 2 and 13 February 1998, was a special experience. It was quite unlike any other political gathering in the lifetime experience of those attending.

The debates in the old parliamentary chamber were cordial and the contributions generally of a very high quality. Behind the scenes there was plenty of rancour, especially between the ARM and those who wanted a directly elected president. There was quite a chasm within Labor ranks on this latter issue. State Labor leaders such as Peter Beattie of Queensland and Geoff Gallop of Western Australia were direct-election people. By contrast, Bob Carr was a minimalist republican who barracked for the ARM position.

The majority of prominent Liberal MPs who participated either supported the minimalist approach to a republic or the so-called McGarvie model. Peter Costello and Jeff Kennett both supported the McGarvie model. When the litmus-test vote for or against a republic, in principle, was taken, only Richard Court, Liberal Premier of Western Australia, and Rob Borbidge, National Party Premier of Queensland, amongst Coalition state and territory government or opposition leaders supported the monarchy.

The McGarvie model was named after its author, the former Victorian Governor Richard McGarvie. Its essence was that the republican Head of State would be chosen by a panel of former judges or vice-regal identities. The selection process would be seen as above politics. A minimum of change would be involved. It attracted a lot of support in Liberal ranks; David Kemp, as well as Costello and Kennett, backed it.

It was attractive to some conservative but minimalist republicans. It may have been appealing, academically, but would have fallen at the first hurdle with public opinion. People would have regarded the selection process as elitist. Australians who wanted a republic either desired their elected representatives to choose the Head of State or, increasingly, directly vote for that person. They would have had no truck with a system which handed that power over to a group of people they had either never heard of or long since forgotten.

I had deliberately appointed two prominent churchmen as delegates: Archbishop (now Cardinal) George Pell and Archbishop Peter Hollingworth. Pell came out strongly for a republic, and in the process of calling for firm leadership from the Liberal Party on the issue was probably having a bit of a dig at me. Hollingworth did not in the end take sides. I have long admired Pell. In an age of temporising, moral equivalence and political correctness, the bluntness of his adherence to what he sees as proper Catholic values is refreshing.

There was a brief but lively clash between Geoffrey Blainey and Neville Wran. Blainey had observed that some people had criticised the Governor-General, Sir William Deane, for 'combining the twin roles of Governor-General and shadow minister for social welfare'.[5] Neville Wran overreacted by calling Blainey's comments a 'shameful attack' on Deane. It was a touch rich coming from Wran, given the ferocity of Labor attacks on Governors-General, both before and since.

Those who earned the greatest credit for having stuck to principle were the representatives of Australians for a Constitutional Monarchy (ACM). Led by Lloyd Waddy and David Flint, they refused to compromise their stance. They argued that they had been elected to defend the place of the constitutional monarchy, and that was what they intended to do without playing games. They didn't have an easy brief, as most of the press ridiculed their position throughout the convention, salivating at any embarrassment for the monarchist cause.

Opening the Convention I said:

> Never before has this historic chamber received such a wonderfully diverse group of Australians. Our moment in history is privileged. Our responsibility is great. Our common bond is Australia's future. It is a vastly different gathering from one of a hundred years ago. There were no Indigenous Australians at the convention of 1898; it was an all-male gathering; the names were overwhelmingly Anglo-Celtic; and I am sure that no delegate was aged under 25.

I endeavoured to crystallise the central issue of the debate and to put my own position very simply, in the following terms:

> In my view, the only argument of substance in favour of an Australian republic is that the symbolism of Australia sharing its legal Head of State with a number of other nations is no longer appropriate. As a matter of law, Elizabeth II is Queen of Australia. As a matter of undisputed constitutional convention, the Governor-General has become Australia's effective Head of State. Ultimately, it will be for the Australian people alone in their wisdom to resolve this theoretical conflict between our history and present-day constitutional reality — to decide whether removing the symbolism which many see as inappropriate in the present arrangement counts more than the stability and inherent strength of the existing order.
>
> I oppose Australia becoming a republic, because I do not believe that the alternatives so far canvassed will deliver a better system of government than the one we have at present.

I told the delegates that if a consensus behind a particular republican proposal came out of the convention, that proposal would be put to the Australian people in time for an Australian republic, if it won public support, to be inaugurated on 1 January 2001 — the centenary of Federation. I hoped the convention would speak with sufficient clarity to remove the need for a plebiscite, presenting a range of republican alternatives. I made it clear that on all issues of substance, members of the Liberal Party would have a free vote. In every way, therefore, I had kept faith with the promise I had made before the 1996 election. Much as I personally opposed a republic, I laid down a course of action which could ultimately produce an Australian republic by 1 January 2001.

Once the convention was under way, it was quickly apparent that although a majority of delegates supported a republic, there was deep division in their ranks and Turnbull and his cohorts would need to make concessions to those who wanted the president to be directly elected, if they were to remain within the republican camp.

So a hybrid was devised, deliberately designed by the ARM to enlist the support of direct-election republicans. In the process it fell, not between two stools but, indeed, amongst several. Under this compromise, a committee of 32 people, comprised of 16 nominated by the prime minister and 16 from state and territory parliaments, were to propose a shortlist of candidates for the presidency to the prime minister. He or she was, in turn, to place a candidate before the parliament.

There was no obligation on the prime minister to nominate someone from the shortlist. It was a completely artificial public-consultation process, having only the illusion of public involvement. In practice it would have diminished the pool of people currently available for appointment as Governor-General. Many prominent citizens would not have involved themselves in the shortlisting process through fear of public knowledge of their rejection.

It was also legitimate to argue, as I did, that the president in the proposed republic would have less security of tenure than does the Governor-General. Under the ARM's proposal, the president could be summarily dismissed by the prime minister by written notice at any time without reason or appeal. The requirement that the House of Representatives approve the dismissal added little to the security of tenure of the putative president. No government party would repudiate their own prime minister's actions. Even if it did, that would not reinstate the president. The removal would have been final and absolute.

No Australian Governor-General has been dismissed from office. Any such action by a future prime minister would almost certainly be for a political reason and therefore highly controversial. It would be seen to directly involve the monarch in a political dispute, which would act as a constraint on any prime minister because legally only the monarch can revoke a Governor-General's appointment. Although the monarch would be bound to accept her prime minister's advice, the very requirement of such advice, together with the formal consideration by her and the time taken, however short this might be, could act as a valuable additional check against completely arbitrary removal.

Malcolm Turnbull and his followers did the deal with the direct-election republicans because they needed their votes. After the event, however, some of them sought to shift the blame to me and other supporters of the status quo.

In the end, 89 out of 152 delegates voted for a republic in principle. An overwhelming majority of delegates voted in support of a recommendation to me, as Prime Minister, that I put the ARM's hybrid model for a republic to a referendum.

There was much elation from republicans, such as Neville Wran, Janet Holmes à Court and Malcolm Turnbull, at the end of the convention when I committed the Government to holding a referendum on that hybrid republican model. They were ecstatic. They felt that they had been given the opportunity to win a republic from the Australian people. It was obvious from their reaction that they believed that I had been fair to them, and they had gained from the convention all that they might have expected.

I felt when the convention ended that I had come to terms with the republican issue. It was always going to be a difficult one for me because of the stance I had taken. It suited many agendas to typecast me as too conservative and out of touch. I was not going to opportunistically change my position. Yet I knew that there were growing numbers of republicans, at that stage, within the Liberal Party.

My embracing a course of action which enabled the Australian people to vote on the issue, notwithstanding my own personal opposition to a republic, had enabled me to secure some moral high ground. People knew that I was against a republic and would not through expediency change my position. They also recognised that, despite this, I had laid out a pathway for the public to vote for a republic.

I left the convention in very positive spirits. In my closing speech I said:

> His Grace the Archbishop of Melbourne said God had had a pretty good convention. Without in any way wishing to belittle the Almighty's success, I think Australia has had an even better one. This convention has demonstrated the truth of a proposition

that I have always held very dear, and that is that the things that unite us as Australians are greater than the things that divide us.

I hope that I captured the mood of all delegates by going on to say:

> What has struck me more than anything else about this convention and the whole debate is the integrity of the Australianism that has been expressed by all the delegates. I will go away from the convention an even more idealistic Australian, one with an even greater passion to allow our democracy to flourish. We will have a vote next year. The Australian people will decide the outcome of that and we will all accept the verdict of the Australian people with grace and goodwill — all of us, whatever the result may be.

On reflection, I was being overly optimistic about the willingness of all participants to accept, with grace, the outcome of the referendum. Certainly the bitterness of many of the republicans at the result of the referendum did not match the expectations I had expressed of them in February 1998.

My good friend Jean Chrétien, the Prime Minister of Canada, followed our republican debate intensely. A French Canadian from Quebec, Chrétien knew that if Australia went republican he would have to put the issue on the agenda in Canada. He had no wish to do this, because such a debate in Canada would also open up the secessionist issue for Quebec, and the whole relationship between the Central and Provincial governments in Canada. It was a can of worms for Chrétien. He was mightily relieved when the republic went down in Australia.

As it happened, the biennial Commonwealth Heads of Government Meeting (CHOGM) took place in Durban, South Africa, exactly one week after the republican vote in Australia. At the traditional Queen's reception on the first night of the conference, Jean Chrétien warmly thanked me for the result of the referendum in Australia. With a well-executed bow, he informed the Queen, 'Your loyal Australian Prime Minister has saved the monarchy in Australia. He has also done me a very good turn.' The Queen of Canada, who had known Chrétien for a long time, understood precisely what he was alluding to and was amused by her Canadian Prime Minister's gesture.

*   *   *

As well as resolving to support the compromise ARM republican model, the constitutional convention also recommended that a new preamble be inserted into the Constitution, in place of the very short one which has been there since Federation.

I did not make a specific reference to this, and therefore no government commitment was given when I closed the convention and undertook to present the issue of a republic to the people. A reason for this was that much of the debate about the proposed wording of a new preamble proceeded on the assumption that Australia would become a republic.

A new preamble would be a significant gesture towards reconciliation, and I warmed to the idea of having a preamble put to the Australian people at the same time as the republican question. The Labor Party and the republicans were quite divided on the issue of a preamble. They worried that it would add a layer of complexity to the republican question, despite the fact that the convention had come out strongly in favour of a new preamble.

In February 1999, the government joint party room endorsed proposals for a republican referendum in November of that year as well as a separate proposal in relation to a preamble. The principles to be embodied in the preamble included not only recognition of prior Indigenous occupancy of the Australian landmass, but also gender equality, references to God, democracy and also a stipulation that the preamble would not be in any way justiciable.

The poet Les Murray drafted the first rendition, which famously included a reference to mateship, and that was released for public comment on 23 March 1999. There was an avalanche of criticism of the first draft. The Labor Party came out wholeheartedly against the proposed preamble, as did Malcolm Turnbull on behalf of the ARM. They thought that a separate debate on a preamble would weaken support for a republic. At one stage it looked as if the preamble would not get through parliament.

After intense negotiation, I secured the support of the Australian Democrats for a revised preamble. Regrettably, a price I paid for their support was the exclusion of any reference to mateship. The Democrats thought that it was too blokey; I had to live with that burst of political correctness. The preamble contained a proper reference to the Indigenous peoples of our country: 'Honouring Aborigines and Torres Strait Islanders, the nation's first people, for their deep kinship with their lands and for the ancient and continuing cultures which enrich the life of our country.'

The Labor Party opposed a new preamble including these words. This demonstrated yet again the arrogant proprietorial approach the Labor Party and many of its fellow travellers on Indigenous issues took towards matters concerning reconciliation. Unless one agreed with their version of reconciliation, one was not a believer in reconciliation.

During the referendum campaign, the republicans relied heavily on a celebrity roll-out. At carefully managed intervals, prominent Australians would declare themselves as republicans. These included two former chief justices of the High Court, Sir Anthony Mason and Sir Gerard Brennan. A most important conversion was announced by Sir Zelman Cowen, a former Governor-General, who had previously declared himself against change.

Perhaps the most spectacular conversion was that of Malcolm Fraser. His joint appearance with Gough Whitlam, in which they both declared that 'it's time' for a republic, turned votes away from the republican cause. A number of Liberals who might otherwise have been sympathetic to change found great objection in this joint appearance. In the cold light of day, and after the defeat of the referendum proposal, many republicans would probably have concluded that the celebrity roll-out was a big mistake. It had served to highlight the apparently elitist nature of their campaign. I am not sure that that is what some monarchists felt at the time. They themselves were anxious to find individuals who might declare in favour of the status quo.

Andrew Robb, later a minister in my Government, organised conservative academic and business figures, such as Charles Goode, Greg Craven and Donald McGauchie, into a group called Conservatives for an Australian Head of State. This group argued that Australians should vote in favour of the model proposed, because if the referendum were defeated, a republican alternative of the future would be more radical than that on offer at the referendum. They strongly opposed the direct-election option.

There was considerable debate about the precise form of the question to be put on the republic. The final wording decided upon by the Government was as follows: 'An Act to alter the Constitution to establish the Commonwealth of Australia as a Republic with the Queen and Governor-General being replaced by a President appointed by two thirds majority of the Members of the Commonwealth Parliament.'

I was accused of pro-monarchist manipulation over this wording. Given that it reflected exactly what was being proposed, that was nonsensical. I thought that the prize for attempted manipulation was well and truly won by

Andrew Robb, who had proposed the question read as follows: 'A Bill for an Act to alter the Constitution to provide for an Australian Citizen, chosen by a two thirds majority of a joint sitting of the Federal Parliament to replace the British monarch as Australia's Head of State.' The bill when first introduced had framed the question thus: 'A Bill for an Act to alter The Constitution to establish the Commonwealth of Australia as a republic with a President chosen by a two-thirds majority of the members of the Commonwealth Parliament.' The only real change was to make it clear that the president would replace the Queen and Governor-General. That was fair enough. The final version largely echoed the recommendation of an all-party committee and, if anything, it was slightly more favourable to the republican cause than the first version.

As referendum day approached, many in the constitutional monarchy corner made common cause with the more strident direct-election republicans. Both groups wanted the referendum to go down. The latter group still wanted a republic, but a different and more radical kind of republic. This posed a dilemma for a number of my colleagues. They wanted to defeat the republic, but in the process were tempted to embrace arguments that were both trite and added to latent public contempt for politicians as a group. The slogan 'Say no to the politicians' republic' carried with it a quite explicit claim that politicians should not be entrusted with the task of choosing Australia's Head of State.

Some of my senior and pro-monarchist colleagues, such as Nick Minchin and Tony Abbott, either embraced this rhetoric or were prepared to tolerate its use by their comrades-in-arms, such was their determination to defeat the republic.

For my part I maintained an orthodox pro-monarchist position. From the outset I said I would not engage in regular commentary as I did not wish to exacerbate differences within the Coalition by too frequently joining the debate. I always knew that as the referendum approached I would become more vocal.

On 27 October 1999 I released my detailed statement. It outlined why I would vote no to the republic and also why I supported the proposed preamble. The statement took the form of a letter to my constituents. It was a full-blooded defence of the current constitutional arrangements.

In arguing for the status quo I asserted that although the monarch was the Queen of Australia under our current constitution, the Governor-General was effectively Australia's Head of State and that the only constitutional duty performed by the Queen related to the appointment of the Governor-General, which must be done on the recommendation of the prime minister.

I referred to the circumstances of 1975 and drew attention to the response on behalf of the Queen to the speaker's letter conveying the vote of no confidence in the caretaker Fraser Government. The private secretary said, inter alia, '… the Queen has no part in the decisions which the Governor-General must take in accordance with the Constitution … it would not be proper for her to intervene in person in matters which are so clearly placed within the jurisdiction of the Governor-General by the Constitution Act'.[4]

I also drew on work commissioned by the Hawke Government. A 1988 report of the Hawke Government's Constitutional Commission, of which Gough Whitlam was a member, found that 'Australia had achieved full independence as a sovereign state of the world' sometime between 1926 and the end of World War II and was so recognised by the world community.[5]

I made it clear that I was even more strongly opposed to a directly elected president than the model to be decided upon at the referendum. My position was one of support for the current constitutional arrangement. I did not want a republic and I would vote against it. In my mind any form of republic was inferior to the current arrangement.

A directly elected president would inevitably open up an alternative power centre within the Australian political structure. The active and adversarial character of Australian politics would mean that if this nation was to have an elected president, that person would 'ineluctably' assume a political persona independent of that of the prime minister. He or she would claim a separate mandate, and the very character of our constitutional arrangements would be fundamentally altered.

In the week leading up to the vote there was extensive consultation between my office and Sir Robin Janvrin, the Queen's private secretary. Janvrin and my chief of staff, Arthur Sinodinos, had to prepare for the various possible eventualities. The Queen was obviously following the debate and awaiting the outcome with great interest.

She understood the historic nature of what was occurring in Australia. I knew of her deep affection for this country and her anxiety always to do the right thing. She had been impeccable in her public comments and her demeanour, and had always made it plain that Australia's constitutional future and, therefore, its association with the monarchy, was a matter exclusively for the Australian people. That had also been the consistent position of the British Government. This was a matter for Australia and something to be resolved by Australians. That did not mean that it was not being followed keenly in Britain, given the deep and abiding ties between the two nations.

There were three possible outcomes. The first, of course, was the reaction of Her Majesty if the Australian public voted for a republic. The second was the direct alternative, where the Australian people voted to retain the constitutional monarchy. The third possible outcome was an ambiguous result, whereby a majority of the Australian population voted for a republic, but it failed to secure a majority vote in four out of the six states. The Australian Constitution requires a so-called double majority in order to amend its provisions — a majority of votes and a majority of states.

Draft statements for Her Majesty to issue were prepared to cover all three eventualities. Arthur Sinodinos and the official secretary canvassed the possibility that in the event of the referendum resulting in the adoption of a republic, Her Majesty may wish to make a televised address to the Australian people, honouring the past association and wishing Australians well in the years ahead.

Whatever the outcome, I knew, and so did Buckingham Palace, that this was an important moment in Australia's history.

For several years opinion polls had shown a marked, if not overwhelming, majority for a republic. As the referendum date drew closer, this began to change. From a high approval rate for the republic, in February 1999, the gap began to narrow so that by October of 1999, only a few weeks before the vote, the yes vote fell behind in the published opinion polls. Inevitably this produced more frenetic campaigning from republicans.

On referendum day I was reasonably hopeful of the result that I wanted. Nonetheless, the avalanche of support from News Limited and, to only a slightly lesser degree, the Fairfax papers, meant that any outcome seemed feasible. I visited polling booths in my electorate, simply to put in an appearance and to say hello to a wide range of Liberals and their friends. There were plenty of my own campaign workers manning booths for the constitutional monarchy. There were also some handing out how-to-vote-yes leaflets. They were all treated in the same fashion. There was a lot of political life ahead of me after this referendum, and the last thing I wanted was any lasting animosity within the Liberal camp.

I spent referendum night at Kirribilli House. It was apparent very early in the evening, as the first votes came in, that the republic would not be successful. The result of the referendum was a national vote of 45.1 per cent in favour of a republic and 54.9 per cent against the proposition. It was the 13th-lowest yes vote in a referendum out of the 44 questions asked in referenda since Federation. No state yielded a majority in favour of a republic. Only the ACT produced a majority in favour of change.

The preamble suffered an even more severe defeat. The yes vote for it was only 39.3 per cent. My own electorate of Bennelong voted in favour of a republic by 54.62 per cent to 45.38 per cent. On the preamble, however, there was, in Bennelong, a vote of 52.5 per cent in favour which was the highest pro-preamble vote anywhere in the country. I have still not been able to figure out how it was that my own constituents so deliberately ignored my views on the republic yet with equal deliberation, so it seemed, embraced them on the preamble. There was a lot of amusement in the fact that as well as my electorate rejecting my views on the republic, so did Kim Beazley's electorate of Brand reject his views. The electorate of Brand voted 66.31 per cent in favour of the status quo.

There was no doubt that conflict between the minimalist republicans and direct-election republicans contributed to the defeat of the republic. Many who wanted a republic, but only if the president could be directly elected, voted for the status quo in the hope that at some time in the future there would be an opportunity to vote in favour of a republic where the president was directly elected.

Before the too-hasty conclusion is drawn that a directly elected presidency is inevitable at some time in the future, a note of caution should be introduced. Many people who favoured a republic in 1999 did so on the condition that minimal change was involved. Just as not all direct-election republicans followed the path of people like Tim Costello and threw in their lot with other republicans, it would be the case that many minimalist republicans would have refused to embrace a direct-election model, thus throwing in their lot with the constitutional monarchists.

The overwhelming media support for a republic was counterproductive. Australians are independently minded people. They resent being told how to vote. So intense and comprehensive was the campaign that the unmistakable impression was created that the Australian media had united and decided that Australians should embrace a republic.

Michael Kirby, the former High Court judge and strong monarchist, clearly held that view. In delivering the Menzies Memorial Lecture at the Menzies Centre for Australian Studies at King's College, London, on 4 July 2000, he said, during a forensic analysis of the reasons for the defeat of the 1999 referendum: 'So uneven and biased was the media coverage of the referendum issues that I consider that this became part of the problem for support for the republic in Australia. It tended to reinforce opinions, especially amongst lower-income and rural electors, that this was a push by intellectual, well-off east coasters, not necessarily to be trusted by the rest of the nation.'[6]

The 'true Australian' pitch from the republicans also backfired. The monarchy and, particularly the Queen herself, had been part of the Australian landscape in the living memory of all Australians. To be told that wanting to keep the institution, for whatever reason, somehow or other defined one as a lesser Australian was, to say the least, counterintuitive and, to millions, deeply offensive. Another problem the republicans had was that their campaign was far too elitist. The pragmatism, verging on cynicism, of most Australians asserts itself in situations such as the republican debate. The fact that a given individual may be a talented sportsman or outstanding actress does not, in the eyes of the average Australian, invest that person with any superior wisdom when it comes to matters unrelated to their field of excellence. The same applies to artists, writers, judges and, indeed, former prime ministers. The egalitarian instincts of most Australians reject the notion that the views of such people carry any more weight than those of their next-door neighbour on such basic issues as a republic.

The two campaigns had contrasting styles, which worked against the republicans. The ARM-led pro-republican push had an air of the well-funded slick advertising promotion. By contrast, the no campaign had more of a battler image. Also important was the fact that, as Prime Minister, my opposition to a republic did deliver extra support to the constitutional monarchy, particularly from Coalition voters.

That having all been said, two factors in the end played a much bigger part than has been commonly recognised. As an individual, the Queen continues to enjoy enormous respect in the Australian community. If anything that respect has grown since the defeat of the referendum in 1999. As a very dignified lady, she has retained considerable affection. There is a real sense that she has done her duty in a conscientious fashion over many decades. Some Australians of an otherwise distinctive republican bent would have, in 1999, found it hard to vote for her removal as monarch. The other factor is the innate, commonsense conservatism of the Australian electorate. The argument 'If it ain't broke, don't fix it' carries a lot of weight with the mainstream of the Australian community on a whole range of issues.

Conventional wisdom amongst political commentators is that it is only a matter of time before Australia becomes a republic. I question this. The decade which has passed since the defeat of the referendum has seen an unprecedented assertion of Australia's independent action and sense of separate and distinctive identity. The liberation of East Timor, the frontal role played in the War Against Terror, the example of being better prepared to weather the economic meltdown than virtually any other Western nation, and our continued capacity to maintain close links with the United States whilst deepening our ties with Asia have sent an unambiguous message to the world. That is that in every way ours is a robustly independent and self-confident nation. Our vestigial constitutional links with the British monarchy have not inhibited these displays of Australian national virility. The early 1990s arguments of Paul Keating that Australia needed a republic and a change to its flag to better define itself in our region now seem very distant and totally irrelevant.

The Australian people had been given a vote. The issue had been fully and fairly debated and, in the end, the defeat of the referendum, which accorded with majority sentiment within the rank and file of the two Coalition parties, meant that this issue could be set aside for an indefinite period.

We could now all return in a united fashion to the ongoing challenges facing the Government. As 1999 ended, we had no conception of the challenges which would engulf the world in the next few years.

THE LIBERATION OF
EAST TIMOR

When asked to list the achievements of my prime ministership of which I am most proud, I always include the liberation of East Timor in 1999. Now years later, it stands out as one of the more noble things that Australia has done in many years. Our nation was directly responsible for the birth of a very small country whose people remain deeply grateful for what we did.

Some of the best Australian attributes were on display. Good-quality diplomatic and consular work; our willingness, in the right circumstances, to be an active and constructive member of the United Nations, and, above all, the combined military professionalism and common humanity of the men and women of the ADF. In turn those men and women were led by a commander, Major General Peter Cosgrove, who the Australian people came to know and respect as the most prominent soldier this country has produced since General Sir Thomas Blamey in the days of World War II.

Until late in 1998, East Timor was always treated as an adjunct to Australia's relations with Indonesia. The Whitlam Government wanted to maintain close ties with Indonesia and raised no meaningful objection to Indonesia's clear intention to forcibly incorporate East Timor. Later, the Fraser Government would give formal recognition to Indonesian sovereignty over East Timor. Essentially the same policy was followed by successive governments, including — initially — my own. The realpolitik of having good links with 'our nearest neighbour' meant that, with the exception of continued rumblings within the left wing of the Labor Party, both sides of politics went along with the status quo. It was not thought appropriate to question Indonesian sovereignty over East Timor.

Although Australian governments continued to express domestically, their concern about the lack of political freedom in East Timor, it was never going to become a make-or-break issue in our relations with Jakarta. There was never any serious thought given to reversing the original Whitlam policy of 1975.

Within the Australian community, however, there were more troubled thoughts about this tiny province. The left had always been intensely suspicious of the Suharto Government, given the brutal suppression of any dissent which followed the crushing of the attempted Communist coup in the 1960s. Many Australians of the World War II generation had deep affection for the Timorese people. Some had sheltered Australian soldiers from the Japanese and had paid dearly for having done so. We owed them a debt, and whenever stories emerged about alleged Indonesian brutality in East Timor, consciences would be stirred.

The Catholic Church, because of the Portuguese colonial history of East Timor, had significant links with the Timorese. In Darwin a small but lively community of East Timorese was a constant reminder of domestic resistance to Indonesian rule. Sections of the Australian media, particularly the ABC, continued to run anti-Indonesian stories about East Timor. The added incentive here was the lingering resentment about Indonesian complicity in the deaths of five Australian journalists at Balibo in 1975. Many believed that the Australian Government at the time had not been resolute enough in seeking a proper explanation for what had happened.

Between 1975 and 1999, there were 12 official visits by Australian prime ministers to Indonesia, yet in that same period there were no return visits by an Indonesian president. General Suharto, Indonesian President since the 1960s, did not visit because he did not want to endure the indignity of demonstrations against him over East Timor.

The bipartisan constant was that nothing was to get in the way of smooth relations between Australia and Indonesia; if anything, this sentiment strengthened under the Keating Government because of the PM's close personal association with President Suharto. Pragmatically, it was in Australia's interests to have a cooperative partnership with this huge nation, on our doorstep which was, culturally and in so many other ways, completely different from our own society.

Many Australians took the view that the priority for any Australian Government was to keep the peace with Jakarta. For many in the foreign affairs establishment, harmony with the Suharto Government was the real test of whether we remained 'engaged in Asia'.

Indonesia and, by extension, East Timor had always been a more internally divisive issue for the Labor Party than it was for the Coalition. Labor had been in power when Indonesia had gone through its birth pangs in 1946. The Chifley Government, with trade union backing, helped Sukarno, who became the founding president of Indonesia, and his colleagues throw off Dutch sovereignty. It was a piece of anti-colonial conduct which warmed the hearts of many Labor followers. Later the manner of Suharto's coming to power, most particularly the immediate aftermath, complicated things for many Labor stalwarts. He had brought stability to the country, but at a cost. For the Coalition, Suharto was the man who had prevented a Communist takeover of our nearest neighbour. With all his faults he was, therefore, in the balance sheet of history, someone who had done the right thing by his country and the region.

In 1985, I visited Jakarta as Deputy Leader of the Opposition and, out of historical interest, went to the late General Ahmad Yani's home. One of the generals targeted by PKI, the Indonesian Communist Party, dissident military groups and, it is believed by many, President Sukarno, he had been murdered in his own home by military dissidents. It was a moving experience, hearing of the tremendous courage he had displayed. Along with General Abdul Nasution, he had been one of the anti-Communist heroes of those tumultuous days in 1965; Nasution had escaped the same awful fate by hiding in an incinerator. There were conflicting accounts of what had actually happened. It was clear, however, that Yani and Nasution and others like them opposed increased power for the PKI. General Suharto galvanised the anti-Communist forces and became the strongman who restored order in Indonesia after the chaos of the attempted coup.

When I became Prime Minister, I had no intention of changing Australian Government policy towards East Timor. I had not thought about the issue much at all but, to the extent that I had, my view was that a continuation of good relations with Indonesia was an important foreign policy goal for Australia. In March 1996, during our handover discussion in the loungeroom of the Lodge, Keating talked at length of APEC and, in particular, his discussions with Suharto. The personal character of the relationship obviously meant a lot to him. My attitude was a pragmatic one

— East Timor was part of Indonesia, and that was how things were likely to continue.

Although it wasn't obvious then, the ground began to shift under Indonesian sovereignty over East Timor with the onset of the Asian economic meltdown. It had become increasingly apparent that, at some point, there would need to be a succession plan in Jakarta, given Suharto's advancing age. The economic crisis added to the succession pressures on the long-serving President. The Asian downturn hit Indonesia very hard. Inevitably some of the blame for this attached itself to Suharto.

Since becoming Prime Minister I had paid two bilateral visits to Jakarta. The first of these was part of my first visit overseas in 1996 as Australia's leader, which also included a visit to Japan. The second had been late in 1997, on my return from a CHOGM in Edinburgh, when I re-routed to Jakarta to announce an Australian aid package to Indonesia. It was part of our assistance to regional economies in response to the financial crisis which had hurt the region, and in particular Indonesia, so much.

I told Suharto that the crisis had punished Indonesia more than it had deserved. Peter Costello and I felt strongly that the International Monetary Fund (IMF), under pressure from the US Treasury, had, initially, been too severe with its adjustment requirements on Indonesia. We made our displeasure plain to both the Americans and the fund. They both relented.

The financial pressure on Indonesia at the time of the Asian meltdown proved to be the last straw for Suharto. Events gathered momentum in the early part of 1998 and he was replaced by the mercurial Dr B.J. Habibie, who was the Indonesian Vice-president, on 21 May 1998. It was an historic change for Indonesia. Suharto had been its military dictator for more than 30 years. Habibie had lived for a large part of the previous 25 years out of Indonesia, working for the Messerschmitt Corporation in Germany. Habibie immediately began democratising his country in stages, releasing political prisoners and removing restrictions on the press. This began a process which, three presidents later, culminated in the election, by popular vote, of Susilo Bambang Yudhoyono as Indonesian President in 2004.

Habibie's accession to the presidency of Indonesia was also to open up the prospect of a radical change in Jakarta's approach to its troubled province. Habibie's attitude to East Timor was fundamentally different from that of his predecessor. He lacked the personal attachment of Suharto and other members of Indonesia's military class to the province. To Australia, the fresh tack from Habibie meant, in the words of Alexander Downer, '… new possibilities emerged on the horizon, including the possibility that hitherto intractable issues such as the question of East Timor could finally be resolved'.[1] From very early in his presidency, Habibie was aware that Australia saw, in his elevation, a window of opportunity regarding East Timor.

Three weeks after taking over, Habibie publicly talked about a possible autonomy package for East Timor. He saw the province, because of its economic dependency, as a liability rather than an asset for his country. In June he went much further, announcing an autonomy package for East Timor, with a view to having the future of the province resolved within the processes of the somewhat moribund tripartite discussions involving Indonesia, Portugal and the United Nations, the last-mentioned having never formally accepted the Indonesian takeover of 1975.

This was a significant advance, and although it suffered from the major defect of not allowing any involvement from the East Timorese, Australia warmly welcomed the Habibie announcement, and then set about persuading the Indonesians to include the East Timorese. Alexander Downer travelled to Jakarta in July to see both Dr Ali Alatas, the Foreign Minister, and General Wiranto, the Defence Minister. With the approval of the Indonesians, Australia's Department of Foreign Affairs and Trade (DFAT) surveyed East Timorese opinion about the future of the province.

The East Timorese favoured what Downer would describe in an attachment to a letter to Alatas as 'a transitional autonomy arrangement, to be followed by a referendum or similar process after a specified period which varied from 3 to 20 years'.[2]

Jakarta was not attracted to this. The Indonesians wanted their autonomy package to be the end of the issue, but this was never going to work. Australia rightly felt that unless the East Timorese participated in decisions about their future, the mistakes of 25 years earlier would be repeated.

Despite the gulf between our respective attitudes, I drew encouragement from the fact that Habibie had a more sceptical view about East Timor's significance than his predecessor, or indeed many of the members of his Government. He felt that East Timor, increasingly, was a costly drag on the heavily stretched resources of the central government. This appreciation of Habibie's disposition played a major part in shaping the new policy we were to enunciate later in the year.

East Timor came under intense discussion when the National Security Committee (NSC) of cabinet met on 1 December 1998. Downer gave an extensive report on the altered mood in Jakarta, East Timorese opinion, as well as broader international attitudes. Most of us felt that an important time had arrived, when it would make sense to reverse longstanding Australian policy on East Timor. The key to this was that Indonesia now had a president who did not see the retention of East Timor as a symbol of national self-respect.

The NSC concluded that it was a case of seizing the day. There was a new president, with a new attitude on an old and troubling issue for many Australians; taking advantage of such opportunities to pursue change was what practical advances in foreign policy was all about. Grand designs amount to very little unless governments have the wit to grab hold of opportunities for progress when they present themselves.

The meeting agreed that I should write to Habibie urging direct negotiations with the East Timorese leadership and, importantly, the addition of a review mechanism to the autonomy package, so that at some time into the future the East Timorese could have an act of self-determination. Alexander Downer, as the meeting ended, leaned towards me and said, 'Prime Minister, this is really big.' So it was. For the first time in a generation, an Australian Government was proposing to reverse a longstanding, essentially bipartisan approach whereby East Timor's status was subservient to good relations between Canberra and Jakarta.

The terms of the letter were settled in discussions between me and the Foreign Minister. The key paragraph read, '… a decisive element of East Timorese opinion is insisting on an act of self-determination. If anything their position — with a fair degree of international support — seems to be strengthening on this'.[3]

To our great surprise, Habibie's response was to go much further than the letter had suggested. After a lengthy and momentous Indonesian cabinet meeting, Habibie announced on 27 January 1999 that Indonesia would offer the people of East Timor a clear choice between limited autonomy as part of Indonesia or immediate independence. This rocked the Indonesian military, and much of his country's foreign policy establishment. Habibie had disconcerted many in Indonesia, as well as elsewhere, with his more radical thinking. They found it very hard to accept that an Indonesian president would do anything other than maintain a total commitment to Indonesian sovereignty over East Timor.

Australia welcomed the Indonesian response. What Habibie had chosen to do accelerated the process we had sought, but the end result was what we wanted. The people of East Timor were to be given an act of self-determination.

The proposal was taken through the tripartite mincer, and on 5 May formal agreements were announced. The UN-supervised ballot was to take place on 30 August 1999.

There were divided views within Indonesia about the future of East Timor. The militia in East Timor received an increasingly free run. Sections of TNI, the Indonesian Army, turned a blind eye to their activities, with reports continuing to come through about militia violence and the apparent unwillingness of the Indonesian military to do anything to restrain it. Some of those reports claimed that elements of TNI itself were involved.

The possibility of Australian military involvement in East Timor, in some form or other, had been discussed on several occasions at the NSC. On 11 March, the NSC ordered that the 1st Brigade, based in Darwin, be brought to a state of readiness by June. This proved a prescient decision, as the unit helped form the nucleus of the very large task force that was sent to East Timor later the same year.

April saw a sharp increase in violence. In Liquica on 6 April, a pro-integration militia group attacked civilians in a churchyard. Violence continued for days. There were conflicting reports regarding the number killed and injured, but little doubt that TNI had, at the very least, stood by and allowed attacks by the militia. A complication was that the heavy Indonesian military presence in East Timor had always operated at two levels. There were the troops acting under the direct command of Jakarta and the locally raised units of the Indonesian Army and the militia. These latter two groups were often blurred. Indeed, the whole problem for months would be that the central government in Jakarta, through its local TNI operation, by a combination of deliberate indifference and, occasionally, active encouragement, allowed a situation to develop where law and order broke down.

Later in April there were more attacks, this time in Dili, with estimates of the death toll moving between 12 and 28. The escalation in violence caused me to telephone Habibie on 19 April to express my concern and remonstrate about the permissive behaviour of TNI. I suggested that we meet as soon as possible to discuss the situation.

Our meeting in Bali on 27 April would prove crucial to events leading to the separation of East Timor from Indonesia. For an hour and a half we talked alone, without any advisors or note takers. This was the key part of the Bali meeting. Habibie spoke excellent English and prided himself on being able to go through a negotiation of this length with someone whose mother tongue was English.

Habibie was deeply committed to the referendum process in East Timor. He had a contemporary view about the significance of East Timor to Indonesia, and conveyed to me that he would not regard it as a cardinal tragedy if the province were to separate from the republic.

I raised the possibility of peacekeepers going into East Timor before the referendum was held. This produced a metaphorical explosion from Habibie. There was no way that he or the Indonesian Government would support such a move. He said his position would be absolutely untenable in Jakarta if he were to agree to this. He took a more conciliatory approach to the provision of additional police, as these would be provided to the United Nations organisation and would clearly be seen as acting under UN authority. Still he was even reluctant about having more police.

After this meeting we rejoined our colleagues and had a brief and more formal meeting where it was agreed that an adequate number of police officers as advisors would be required, consistent with the agreement regarding security to be signed with the United Nations. That meant more police, which was what Australia wanted, given that Habibie would not agree to peacekeepers going in before the ballot. I came away from this meeting believing that Habibie himself had reached a realistic and pragmatic position about East Timor. He had to pay regard to sentiment within his own country, but he was plainly of the view that there was a limit to how much national effort from Indonesia should be invested in keeping East Timor.

The security situation in East Timor continued to trouble me. After the Bali meeting I wrote to the Secretary-General of the United Nations, Kofi Annan, reporting the gist of what had been discussed. I told him that Habibie would accept a UN decision to have more police, and suggested that he press strongly for up to 300 police in the UN mission. I offered substantial additional Australian police and, as well, an Australian to command the force. This post was filled ultimately by Allan Mills of the AFP, who did an outstanding job, especially during the tense and difficult days following the ballot.

Reports of militia violence continued, often accompanied by evidence of TNI indifference. Habibie would not have a bar of peacekeepers, but Australia took every opportunity to maintain pressure on Indonesia concerning security issues. When Lieutenant General Des Mueller, then Vice-chief of the ADF, visited his counterpart in Jakarta in June 1999, he underlined the concerns of both the ADF and the Government regarding the activities of the militia and the responsibilities of TNI. Likewise in July, I wrote again to Habibie and registered my concern about an attack, obviously involving militia, near Maliana in East Timor.

As I told the House of Representatives on 21 September 1999, I kept pursuing the possibility of peacekeepers being accepted. On 29 August, the day before the ballot took place, I rang Dr Habibie and discussed the general situation in East Timor and sought assurances about the safety of Australian personnel following the ballot. I again raised the possibility of international peacekeepers going in. His response was they would not be acceptable until after the transition to independence had taken place, if in fact that was what the East Timorese voted for. I rang him again only a few days later, and his attitude remained the same. Due to the deteriorating security situation in East Timor, I rang the President yet again on 6 September. He told me that he would declare martial law and that if that did not calm the situation in East Timor he would consider inviting in an international force. That is what transpired.

I told the house that, in the light of all this, those who claimed that peacekeepers could have been inserted before the ballot were out of touch with reality.

The UN-supervised referendum took place on 30 August 1999 and resulted in overwhelming support for the separation of East Timor from the Indonesian republic. The vote was 78.5 per cent in favour of full independence. This was entirely predictable, and the challenge immediately upon us was how to handle the militia-inspired eruptions that would follow the announcement of the referendum's result, to occur on 4 September.

I had realised that if the vote went in favour of complete separation, then an international force would be needed to help keep the peace and lay the groundwork for transition to independence. I also knew that Australia would not only be expected to, but should, in my view, play a major role in that peacekeeping operation. I was determined that Australia should lead the operation.

Events moved very quickly after the ballot result was announced. There was increased violence and plenty of evidence that the militia were running amok. The United Nations had established a mission in East Timor under the leadership of an Englishman, Ian Martin. It was known as UNAMET, and its main remit had been to supervise the ballot. That it had done very well. Angered by rejection of integration, pro-Indonesian forces began harassing UN personnel.

As the situation went from bad to worse, on 5 September Martin asked Australia to help relocate 200–300 non-essential UNAMET staff to Darwin. Between 6 and 14 September, 2600 people, including 1900 East Timorese, had been shifted, overwhelmingly by Australia.

Another senior UN mission was despatched to Dili and Jakarta, to investigate the situation on the ground. Its findings were damning of Indonesia. It reported that the violence could not have occurred without 'the involvement of large elements of the Indonesian military and police'.[4] The mission said that the imposition of martial law, which Habibie had sponsored as a response to the post-ballot violence, had failed.

I had already spoken to the UN head, Kofi Annan, regarding the willingness of Australia to involve herself in a peacekeeping operation, should that become necessary. I made it plain that Australia would make a substantial contribution, but wanted it understood from the very beginning that Australia expected to lead the operation. There was no way I was going to support an outcome whereby Australia provided most of the grunt, but command was given to someone from another country which itself had contributed few troops. I was quite direct with the Secretary-General on this point.

I was impressed with Annan in my dealings with him over East Timor. He was professional, candid and fully understood my own domestic political realities. As is well known, I am not an uncritical admirer of the United Nations and, on some major issues, such as Iraq, the Secretary-General and his colleagues would have totally disagreed with the approach that I took. On East Timor, however, we worked together and achieved the right outcome.

In a telephone call on 6 September, Annan formally asked me if Australia would be willing to lead an international force in East Timor. I said yes. I indicated that we could provide 2000 troops ready for deployment with 48 to 72 hours notice, and also promised that I would pursue contributions from other countries. For the next week to 10 days I lived on the phone in pursuit of both diplomatic and potential military assistance.

Whilst I was quite willing to see Australia contribute heavily to the operation, I wanted the Americans involved. It was an instinctive reaction. US involvement would send an implicit but clear deterrent signal to any in Jakarta who might have considered resisting the intervention force. Whenever the Americans had been involved in a major operation, they had always turned to Australia seeking a contribution. We had been willing to make it. It was this that I had in mind when I first spoke to Bill Clinton about the matter, also on 6 September.

Clinton was sympathetic and offered plenty of logistic and other help, but it took me back a lot when he said that America would not be able to provide any troops, or 'boots on the ground' as it was depicted at the time. He really stunned me when he spelled out, in some detail, just how stretched the American military had become. His explanation made it clear that after the end of the Cold War and the collapse of Soviet communism, resources had been taken out of Defence, and the previously unquestioned capacity of the United States to provide men and materiel whenever and wherever sought was no longer there.

Over the next few days it was obvious that our disappointed reaction had had an effect on the Americans. Alexander Downer was interviewed on CNN and expressed unhappiness with the US response. On seeing the interview Madeleine Albright telephoned Downer to complain about his tone. Downer's response was to remind Albright that whenever the Americans asked for help, Australia was there, and now, on the one occasion that the boot was on the other foot, we felt a little put out that the Americans would not reciprocate.

The insertion of peacekeepers into East Timor still remained a hugely sensitive and difficult issue. The people of East Timor may have voted for independence, but until that was formally agreed to by the relevant processes in Indonesia, the province remained part of the Indonesian republic. Therefore, peacekeepers, even under a UN flag, could not enter East Timor without Indonesia's prior approval. Indonesian national pride was acutely involved.

Many people in Jakarta had never accepted the wisdom of Habibie's initial acquiescence in the vote by the East Timorese, and he was subjected to a great deal of cross-pressuring in the days following the ballot. Added to this were the suspicions amongst some in the Indonesian power elite about Australia's role. Although the President himself was well disposed towards Australia, the same could not be said for other leading figures in Indonesian politics. In the post-ballot period, I had maintained periodic communications with Habibie, but the situation was becoming increasingly difficult for him.

My reaction in our telephone discussion, and Downer's exchange with Albright, had had an effect on Bill Clinton. Both of us were due at the imminent APEC Leaders meeting in Auckland, and on his way to that meeting, he telephoned me from Hawaii to say that the United States would provide extensive logistic and intelligence support, the necessary transport or 'lift' for any peacekeepers and, importantly, intensify diplomatic pressure on Indonesia to accept a UN-sanctioned peacekeeping operation. This last-mentioned commitment was most important, and played a significant role in finally shifting the Indonesians.

Part of this pressure was a visit to Jakarta by William Cohen, the US Defense Secretary. He warned the Indonesians against allowing conflict to break out between TNI and any UN-sanctioned peacekeeping force. Cohen also hinted that American forces were available to provide backup, if needed.

When President Clinton and I met in Auckland on 11 September, it was clear that we were singing from the same hymn sheet. He understood that we had been disappointed with his reluctance to provide any US soldiers for the peacekeeping operation. He knew, however, that the United States could compensate for that by an all-out diplomatic effort in support of what Australia wanted, and that was Indonesian acceptance of a UN-sanctioned intervention led by Australia.

My meeting with Clinton was very successful, as evident from the public comments that the two of us were working closely together. This particular meeting was another example of how the occasion of international meetings provides the opportunity for leaders to resolve issues in separate 'corridor' discussions, often quite unrelated to the formal agenda of the meeting.

It was also an example, which I was to see repeated on a number of occasions, of the willingness of US presidents, both Democrat and Republican, to take the advice of Australia when it came to matters affecting Indonesia. Many Australians make the mistake of seeing the Australian-American relationship in terms which always depict Australia as being subservient. That is wrong. America does not, for example, pretend to understand our part of the world, particularly Indonesia, all that well. On a number of occasions in later years, George W. Bush would listen to and act very deliberately on advice I offered regarding Indonesia. Bill Clinton had done that in 1999.

It all came together in Auckland. Habibie's representative at the APEC meeting, Co-ordinating Minister for Economics Ginandjar, assured me that everything was moving in the right direction, and towards the finish Downer told me that he had spoken to his counterpart, Alatas, who had just left for New York to inform the UN Security Council that Indonesia would accept a peacekeeping operation in East Timor. Finally, late on 12 September, confirmation came from Habibie himself that Indonesia would accept a peacekeeping force.

Habibie's decision was so important that I called a news conference in Auckland at 1 am on 13 September. I said, 'Most importantly, this is a great step forward for the people of East Timor because it's their welfare, their future, their safety, their freedom that this has been all about.' I said that Habibie's announcement had been consistent with what he had told me just on a week earlier, that if the calling of martial law did not stem the violence in East Timor, he would accept UN-sanctioned peacekeepers. Much hard work and many difficult negotiations lay ahead, but I felt a huge sense of relief. It was a monumental decision for Indonesia to have accepted a peacekeeping force.

Diplomatically, Australia had achieved a great deal. We had been there at the beginning, urging a change in Indonesian policy, and through all the difficulties of subsequent months I had maintained, almost to the very end, a clear channel of communication with President Habibie. Indonesia had accepted, finally, the international indignity of a UN-mandated peacekeeping force on its own territory. There was agreement for that intervention force in East Timor to be led by Australia, with forces from a number of Asian countries, and strong American support.

Meanwhile, domestic pressure was building in Australia for the Government to act immediately to help the East Timorese. To the Australian public the situation was simple. The people of East Timor had voted for independence, and in response the militia, with the tacit support of the Indonesian military, had gone on a rampage. Therefore, the Australian Government should forthwith send forces to East Timor to protect the people, with whom they deeply sympathised.

In a number of radio interviews, I was pressed directly by interviewers and also talkback callers as to why we couldn't act immediately. In a painstaking way I had to explain that, without the authority of the United Nations, for Australia to send forces would be to invade Indonesia. To many people this sounded like a legalistic cop-out. Such had become the emotional attachment to the East Timorese cause that Australians from both the left and the right of politics were urging immediate action by their Government.

With a wide-ranging resolution, the UN Security Council processes authorised the intervention on 15 September. Andrew Peacock, still our ambassador in Washington, had maintained contact with Richard Holbrooke (later President Obama's envoy on Afghanistan-Pakistan), the American diplomat who had negotiated the Bosnian peace settlement at Dayton in the mid-1990s. Holbrooke had impressed on Peacock the importance of the mandate for the peacekeeping force being as wide as possible. This was to avoid the terrible dilemma of many European soldiers who, literally, felt that they had had to stand by whilst the slaughter of Muslim men at the hands of the Bosnian Serbs in 1994 took place, simply because the UN resolution authorising their involvement was so limited. Holbrooke's advice was very valuable.

Shortly after the resolution was passed, Kofi Annan spoke to me and confirmed that Australia would be asked to lead the peacekeeping operation. It was to be called the Interfet Force, and Major General Peter Cosgrove was appointed to lead the force. I had not previously met Cosgrove, but over the months and years ahead we were to get to know each other extremely well and to this day remain good friends. This was going to be a most challenging operation for him.

All concerned knew the inevitable sensitivities of the Indonesians. Diplomatic niceties aside, the reality was that Indonesia had been humiliated by the events of recent months. The people of East Timor had voted overwhelmingly to separate from Indonesia, unrestrained violence in that province had followed this vote, and precisely because the Indonesian authorities were either unable or unwilling to stamp out the violence, the rest of the world, through the United Nations, felt it had to intervene with a large force led by a Western country, Australia.

To a lot of Indonesians this was utterly galling. Many others, however, saw it as something that should have been faced years earlier. Indonesian sensitivity, nevertheless, did make it essential that the intervention force be drawn from a wide range of sources within the region. I worked very hard to give it the appearance of a regional, rather than Western, intervention.

The Australian public overwhelmingly supported our stance. It united people on both the right and left of Australian political opinion. Kim Beazley and his Labor colleagues presented a confused picture. The Labor Party's Foreign Affairs spokesman, Laurie Brereton, argued that our policy had really been his in the first place, and continued to attack the Government for not having seen to it that peacekeepers had gone into East Timor before the ballot. In this, he ignored totally the fact that the Indonesian Government would not have accepted peacekeepers prior to the UN-supervised ballot.

Kim Beazley, endeavouring to find a reason to attack aspects of the Government's handling of the issue, sounded both carping and equivocal in the process. He was being interviewed on Perth radio station 6PR on 5 October when a strong Labor supporter rang to reprove him for not unconditionally supporting what I had done. The caller said, 'You are 100 per cent wrong on this, Kim … I can't stand John Howard, but on this sort of issue you must stick together and not be driven aside.'[5]

There was a widespread feeling in the community that the Government had really done the right thing, and had stood up for a small, emerging nation which for too long had been pushed around by a corrupt and bullying regime. There was little concern amongst those many Australians with whom I discussed this issue, that we were putting our relationship with Indonesia at risk. To most, doing the right thing by the East Timorese was what really mattered.

This was not the case, however, with some in the foreign policy elite, who always felt that they knew better than the elected members of the Australian Government. For example, Richard Woolcott, who had played a significant role in advising Whitlam in 1975, when he was the Australian Ambassador in Jakarta, would pen an article in March 2003 for the *Age* in which he criticised the intervention, largely on the grounds that it had damaged our relationship with Jakarta.

Woolcott said that if his advice had been sought, he would have urged that Australia and other countries should have exhorted Habibie to delay any independence vote for at least five years. Such an attitude perfectly illustrated how out of touch he and others were with public sentiment on East Timor. If I had done that, the Australian people would have seen it as an act of gross betrayal of the East Timorese. His approach was typical of the craven attitude of some who regarded good relations with Jakarta, irrespective of the regime in charge at the time, the cost to others or the price Australia might pay through sacrificing its own values, as the *sine qua non* of good Australian foreign policy. They could not have been more wrong.

*   *   *

Having achieved the diplomatic and political outcome we had worked for, the more sober and potentially much more difficult phase lay ahead. Australia was about to embark on its largest foreign military activity since its involvement in the Vietnam War, some 30 years earlier.

It is easy now to look back, knowing that the intervention went smoothly, and to play down the potential risks involved at the time, and the danger to which thousands of Australian military personnel were exposed. The reality was that we had no way of being certain that there would not be conflict between Australian and Indonesian soldiers. I certainly was concerned that there would be casualties, and I know how heavily that weighed on the minds of our military leaders.

I worked hard to secure the involvement of a diverse group of nations in the Australian-led force. Jenny Shipley, the Prime Minister of New Zealand, promptly committed a New Zealand battalion, and I was grateful that, when the change of government occurred, the new Labour Prime Minister, Helen Clark, confirmed New Zealand's continued participation. With 1603 troops, Thailand made the largest land forces contribution after Australia. This was significant; it gave real expression to the belief I had that it must be a genuinely regional force. Big contributions were also made by Jordan, Italy, South Korea, Canada and the Philippines. For much of an entire week I was never off the phone, talking to other leaders, soliciting commitments to the force.

The British provided a company of Gurkhas. I was disappointed at the response of Malaysia. The Malaysian military were keen to be involved, but that idea was knocked on the head by the Malaysian Prime Minister, Mahathir. He was later to make some quite absurd remarks about Australian soldiers harassing Islamic people in East Timor. I was also surprised that Singapore did not make a larger contribution. A contribution of ground troops would not have created any difficulties for Singapore, and would have recognised the closeness of our relationship. The reality still was that in Southeast Asia, Indonesia remained the 800-pound gorilla, and neighbouring countries were very reluctant to do anything that might impinge on Indonesian sensitivities.

At its peak the Australian contribution to the Interfet Force was just over 5000. Although we committed many more people to fight in South Vietnam, this time we were leading the operation. The world spotlight would be on us.

We had plenty of assistance, but the rest of the world was relying on Australian leadership and, in substantial measure, Australian soldiers to do the job. I was conscious of the historic character of the commitment.

I was also mindful of the miserable fashion in which Australia had treated soldiers returning from service in Vietnam. It remains one of the awful blemishes on the honour of this country in recent history. When I addressed federal parliament on 17 August 2006 to mark the 40th anniversary of the Battle of Long Tan, I apologised, on behalf of the Australian people, to those Vietnam veterans who had been so shabbily treated by their fellow countrymen and women when they returned.

As I moved around the country in the lead-up to the sending of our forces to East Timor, veteran after veteran who had served in Vietnam raised this issue with me and, in some cases, pleaded that I make sure that when our troops came home from East Timor, no matter what the circumstances, they were openly greeted as patriots who had done their duty by Australia. I promised them, and I promised myself, that I would make sure that this happened. It certainly did. Two major welcome-home parades occurred: one through the streets of Sydney and another poignant one through the streets of Townsville, where so many of the forces had been based. In other ways, too, their service was honoured.

There was one other matter I attended to, of direct personal concern to the troops we were sending into danger. I decided on a large increase in their special-deployment allowances. It was a very long time since we had sent people abroad to fight and, given that only a small portion of our military-aged population was involved, I felt they deserved better pay. I gave instructions that their deployment allowance be increased significantly.

I was determined to visit the troops before they left. On Sunday, 19 September 1999, Janette and I went to Lavarack Barracks in Townsville, had dinner with as many of the troops as possible, chatted to them, assuring them of the support of the nation and our belief that they were highly trained for the challenge that lay ahead. Neither of us will ever forget walking quietly through the grounds of the barracks after dinner, on a warm spring evening, and seeing small groups of NCOs and their soldiers talking intently about the task that lay ahead. Both of us were deeply affected by the realisation that some of these young people could meet death in the service of their country.

The force, led by Australia, would be working with the approval of the

Indonesian Government and, therefore, the Indonesian military to achieve a smooth handover, and the restoration of law and order. That very day Major General Cosgrove had had a productive first meeting with his Indonesian counterpart, Major General Syahnakri, but it was only a cautious beginning. What was unspoken, but well and truly understood, amongst senior ADF people and my cabinet colleagues, was that the lack of discipline over locally raised units in the militia might continue after the Interfet Force arrived. If this proved to be the case, there was a real possibility of an Australian patrol or the like being caught in an ambush and diggers being killed. That hung upon us heavily.

The following day Janette and I flew to Darwin and, as well as seeing a number of the troops who were based at Robertson Barracks and due to go to East Timor, I also had the first opportunity of meeting Peter Cosgrove. I had heard a lot about him, all of which had been favourable, and he impressed me with his direct, no-nonsense style. He filled me in on the details of his discussion with his Indonesian opposite number.

The troops went into East Timor only a week before the Rugby League Grand Final, played between the Melbourne Storm and my team, the St George Illawarra Dragons. Although the Dragons had led 14-nil at half-time, the Storm scored an upset and spectacular win, right at the end of the game. My most vivid memory from that afternoon was the emotional comments made by the Melbourne Storm captain, Glenn Lazarus, after I had presented him with the Telstra Trophy.

Before talking about the game, he asked all Australians to think of the thousands of their fellow countrymen and women who were in East Timor. It was an example of how the nation felt, and the widespread understanding that this was something different from what our country had done for many decades. Like most Australians, Glenn Lazarus worried that we might suffer casualties.

I was now conscious that I had done something quite different from anything which, for me, had gone before. If any Australian soldiers died, or were seriously wounded, it would be because of decision I had taken. It is the ultimate responsibility of a prime minister to commit the fighting forces of his country to a military operation. It puts their lives in danger. There is a near certainty that at some stage soldiers will be killed or seriously wounded. The only real question is how many. That is the grim reality, and there is no alternative to it and no way of explaining it in another fashion. It was my experience that on each of the occasions we as a nation committed forces overseas and put them in danger, my colleagues instinctively left the final decision to me. They made their thoughts known, and I am not being in any way critical of them in making this observation. I was in no doubt on each occasion as to what their views were, but in the end they accepted that, as Prime Minister, I should take the final decision. If I had on one or other occasions decided against sending the troops, they would have readily accepted that decision, even though they may have disagreed. As it happened, our views chimed on each and every occasion.

Thankfully we did not have the dreaded ambush of a patrol in the early days of the intervention, and it went with a remarkable degree of success. Cosgrove's leadership and the support of such talented colleagues as his Chief of Staff, Brigadier Mark Kelly (later a general and our Commander of Operations in the Middle East), the excellent rapport they established with the senior Indonesian leadership and also the restored UN operation under Ian Martin, the fact that the intervention force included units from a variety of countries, most particularly within the Asian region, all combined to produce the right outcome.

Cooperation with the United Nations was important. The operation was not a 'blue helmet' operation under a UN-appointed commander. It was an international force, acting under the authority of a resolution of the Security Council, but it was not a UN force. The personnel making up the force remained soldiers of their respective countries, in turn working under the overall command of an Australian general. It was a subtle, but important, difference. Later on the international force was to morph into a 'blue helmet' operation under the command of a Filipino general.

Once things had stabilised, I was keen to go to East Timor and personally thank our troops for the difficult and dangerous job they were doing, as well as meet local leaders and UN personnel. Janette and I went there for a memorable visit on 28 November 1999. This was the first time that I had come across a large number of Australian troops who had just been through, and in fact were continuing to be engaged in, a military operation. Although, miraculously, we had not suffered casualties, there had been many near-run things. Nobody really believed, when the operations started, that that would be the situation two to three months on.

I was pleased to get a full briefing from Major General Cosgrove and his senior people, and meet Ian Martin and other local leaders. I was particularly keen to meet as many soldiers as possible and this, thankfully, I was able to do during a very full day. I have always had enormous respect for Australians who wear the uniform of their country, be it a military or police one. In dealing over a long number of years with Australian military personnel, I have always found that the direct and simple approach works a treat. Australians like directness in their dealings with political leaders. It is against their character to be unduly deferential, and frankly one wouldn't want them to be, but they are respectful. Therefore it is for the political leader to break the ice and remove any awkwardness at a first meeting. When I encountered a group of military people, I simply dived into the crowd of them and began talking to one or two. This removed any barriers or awkwardness, and before long it was possible to be engaged in a continuous banter.

Whatever their individual politics might have been, the men and women I met in East Timor knew that I had been responsible for them going, that they had received plenty of strong support from the Government, and being particularly pleased with the way the operation had gone, they were very happy to tell me all about it.

It is a long tradition in the Australian military forces that irrespective of rank, every Australian soldier, sailor or airman has a right (even some see it as a duty) to complain directly to the boss if they think something is being done wrong. This does not mean that Australians lack discipline. It is just a metaphor for our egalitarian society. Recognising this, I invariably would ask troops I visited in the field, be it East Timor, Afghanistan, Iraq, the Solomon Islands or indeed anywhere else, whether they had any complaints about their equipment, their food or any other aspect of their military life in that particular engagement. I am happy to say that most responses were positive; there was one complaint about the adequacy of State of Origin TV coverage, which was rectified.

Janette and I left Dili that day feeling as if we had made contact with hundreds of Australians who had really done a magnificent job, not only in mounting an effective military operation but through all of their conduct in East Timor, displaying the character and temperament of the Australian people to the East Timorese and the broader community of Southeast Asia. The modern Australian soldier must not only be a superb fighter, but he or she must also be sympathetic towards and helpful to the local civilian population. It is sometimes a fine line to draw, but the experience I gleaned from East Timor and subsequent military engagements, during my time as Prime Minister, told me that Australians drew that line and achieved the right balance better than any others.

We had one other East Timor-related activity before Christmas 1999, and that was to attend a large Christmas gathering at the Robertson Barracks in Darwin, involving the families of many of the troops who would spend Christmas in East Timor. It is always the hardest time for service families, and Janette and I were anxious to be part of the gathering and express our thanks to the wives, husbands, children, parents and others close to those who would be absent friends on Christmas Day.

I encountered one discordant note during the flying Saturday visit to Darwin. One soldier cornered me with a complaint. He was extremely unhappy that he had not been sent to East Timor! This incident said a lot about what that engagement, and subsequent ones, meant for the great bulk of the men and women who volunteered for the ADF. They wanted to put their training to the test and be involved in military operations. They wanted combat, not because they were warlike, but because that was what they were trained to do, and it was a natural part of career fulfilment that the opportunity to serve abroad, often in danger, would be grabbed with both hands. The nation should be eternally thankful that there are men and women who feel this way. Instead of seeing it, as some do, as a manifestation of a lingering militaristic element in our makeup, we should see it as a valuable defence in a world where there is no shortage of people hostile to the values and way of life of Australia.

Australia's leadership role in East Timor won international acclaim. It brought warm praise from the Secretary-General of the United Nations. It was also seen in many parts of the world as a model for a UN-sanctioned peacekeeping operation.

This was due to the fact that Australia was geographically on the spot, with the military capacity and political stability to provide leadership when asked to do so by the United Nations. Fortunately, none of the permanent members of the Security Council had a vested interest in frustrating the will of the international community. Unlike the tortured circumstances of the Balkans, with the Russians unwilling to support a Security Council-sanctioned operation against their traditional allies the Serbians or the mindless obstructionism of the French in relation to Iraq, everyone was on side or, at the very least, indifferent when it came to East Timor.

Sergio de Mello, the deft Brazilian UN diplomat who had headed the UN High Commission for Refugees (UNHCR), took over the UN administration in East Timor following the Interfet withdrawal and did a superb job, remaining in that position until Independence two years later. He was a polished envoy who was tragically killed by al Qaeda-backed terrorists in Iraq in 2003.

The success of the operation in East Timor was a real setback for many of my regular political critics. For the Labor Party it was a huge problem. East Timor had been on the conscience of many people in the Labor Party for years, and it rankled with them that the policy change had occurred under my prime ministership. History would record the Howard Government as having reversed a quarter of a century of Australian weakness towards Jakarta in relation to East Timor.

Without question, Australia's diplomatic and military initiative on East Timor had placed strain on the always delicate relationship with our nearest neighbour, incidentally, the world's most populous Muslim nation. Nonetheless, links with Indonesia, although disturbed, remained essentially intact.

The characterisation of Indonesia as the most populous Muslim nation would have been a passing one in 1999. It was just under two years before the world was to be turned on its head by terrorists who obscenely used the Islamic religion to justify their actions. To those who continue to question the actions of my Government in relation to East Timor, I pose the hypothesis: if the events of 1999 had not occurred, and support from Australia for separation of East Timor from Indonesia had arisen several years later, how much more difficult would relations with Indonesia have been in the wake of 11 September 2001? The opportunity to do something came when it did — the Government seized it when it was there, and a further opportunity may never have occurred.

East Timor had a profound impact on my thinking about Australia's Defence preparedness. I was not alone. I realised that for a long time into the future, Australia would need to spend a lot of money on Defence. We had mounted a hugely successful operation, but launching and sustaining it had put an enormous strain on our military resources, particularly our ground forces and strategic lift assets. The decision, in March of 1999, to bring the 1st Brigade to readiness had been timely, but had the situation deteriorated, it might not have been enough.

The absence of adequate lift capacity for our forces was plain for all to see. The standout vehicle to carry our forces had been the Incat vessel constructed for civilian ferry purposes. It had worked brilliantly in East

Timor, but would that be the case in other operations? My concern on this never left me and was, some years later, directly responsible for my persuading the cabinet to invest some $4 billion in the purchase of the giant C17 transport aircraft, as well as acquiring large amphibious lift vessels. I have known since East Timor that for years into the future, one of the prime responsibilities of the ADF will be involvement in peacekeeping operations in our own region.

I was also aware that we would have to strengthen the Australian Army, not at the expense of the navy or the air force but as a commitment in its own right. This was to be realised with my Government's subsequent investment in the hardening of the army program, and most significantly in 2006 with the decision to establish two new army battalions, which would restore the army to a force level not seen since the time of the Vietnam War.

When I left office as Prime Minister I pointed with some pride to the fact that under my Government defence expenditure had risen by 47 per cent in real terms. Whilst not all of this flowed from the experience of East Timor, that involvement and what it told me about the resources available to the ADF was the beginning of a process of committing an ever-increasing amount to defence. It was the beginning of our awakening.

East Timor had a significant psychological impact on Australians. Most thought that their country had done the right thing in East Timor. They felt proud of the way in which our forces had conducted themselves, that it had been a successful operation and with virtually no casualties. They were deeply impressed by Peter Cosgrove's leadership, and he remains a popular figure in the Australian community. East Timor also accelerated the revival of Australian, particularly younger Australian, pride in our country's military history and traditions. When our troops returned from East Timor, the Australian public did not need its Prime Minister to exhort them to offer a warm welcome home. The huge turnout for the parade through the streets of Sydney on 19 April 2000 could not have been in starker contrast to the way in which so many Australian diggers returning from Vietnam were, to this country's shame, almost secreted in under the cover of darkness.

For some years, young Australians in particular had been exhibiting growing pride in what Australian soldiers had done in past conflicts. This sentiment was gathering strength in any event, but East Timor gave it a mighty boost.

30

AN EXCESS OF EXCISE — THE PRE-*TAMPA* RECOVERY

Politically, 2000 was a year of consolidation, with the extremely successful introduction of the new tax system on 1 July.

On another front, Sydney — and Australia — enjoyed some of the finest days imaginable with the September Olympic Games. Our team put in a stunning performance, and the open hospitality of the Australian people, best evidenced by the magnificent volunteers, displayed Australia to the world in a most positive fashion. At the Brunei APEC meeting in October of 2000, I was showered with unsolicited compliments regarding the Sydney Olympics.

Janette and I made the deliberate decision to attend as many Olympic events as possible to cheer on Australian competitors. It was enjoyable and popular with the competitors, as evidenced by the enthusiastic reception they gave me at the post-Games event at the Capitol Theatre. The athletes genuinely appreciated their Prime Minister so closely identifying himself with their efforts. We endeavoured to do exactly the same at the Paralympics, attending numerous events with the same level of commitment and enthusiasm.

The smooth introduction of the new tax system was a success of another kind. This new system had a lengthy bedding-down period.

The night before felt very much like Christmas Eve had seemed to me as a child; there was plenty of eager anticipation, but I didn't quite know what the following day would bring. I decided to observe the public reaction in my electorate of Bennelong, firstly going to a small shopping centre in Top Ryde, and then on to the much larger regional shopping centre, Macquarie.

I found retailers well prepared, complimentary about the change, and quite positive in describing the reaction of their customers. I stopped several groups of Saturday-morning shoppers at Macquarie Centre and asked them about the new tax system. The reaction was either one of shrug-of-the-shoulders indifference or comments to the effect that to their surprise some items were actually cheaper. The latter reflected the impact of the abolition of wholesale sales tax on certain items.

There was intense media interest in the issue. By lunchtime I was breathing easier. The evening television bulletins provided blanket coverage which, in overall terms, was quite favourable. Some days later, Laurie Oakes, the Channel Nine veteran, told me that, before writing his story, he had spoken to two of his very experienced cameramen who had been on the spot with me. They both reported a generally favourable reaction. This was an interesting reminder of how valuable an experienced cameraman can be, even to a hardened correspondent such as Oakes. These two men in particular, Mark Jessop and Doug Ferguson, have been around for a long time, are highly intelligent and good judges of public reaction.

The Labor Party was disappointed at the lack of public hostility, and contented itself by adopting Kim Beazley's phrase that it would be 'a slow burner'. It did turn out to be something of a slow burner, but the person it ended up burning most was Kim Beazley himself.

In completely thumbing its nose at the mandate given at the 1998 election for the introduction of a new tax system, the Labor Party obviously believed that it could win the next election off the back of hostility to our tax reforms. Beazley felt that all that was required was the promise of a rollback in certain areas, plus sustained criticism of the new system. He famously told his caucus towards the end of 2000 that the Labor Party would 'surf to victory' off the back of hostility to the GST.

As the early months after the introduction of the GST passed, it looked very much as if Kim Beazley could not have been more wrong. There were, however, two issues which began to eat away at the initially favourable reaction to the new tax system. One of these issues affected a vital constituency for the Coalition, small business. The other affected just about everyone, namely, the price of petrol.

The new system required all businesses to complete Business Activity Statements, monthly, quarterly or annually according to the volume of sales. For most small businesses, this meant a monthly or quarterly return. The Business Activity Statement (BAS) required the listing of sales, the calculation of GST collected and, where appropriate, a remittance of GST to the Australian Taxation Office.

From the very beginning, the BAS was too complicated. By September or October complaints were flowing in about the time consumed in preparing the BAS. Yet the Treasury resisted change, and at this stage so did the Treasurer. He took the view, mistaken in my opinion, that any change to the BAS connoted a retreat.

Australians are always sensitive to increases in the price of petrol, and although they understand that the main driver of fuel costs is the world price of oil, they are ever ready to criticise government decisions which might add to the cost of their petrol. The price of petrol rose in the months following the introduction of the GST, resulting in even greater public scrutiny of government behaviour potentially affecting petrol prices.

Naturally the GST applied to fuel sales, but the Government had pledged that the price of petrol at the bowser would not go up because cost reductions elsewhere would offset the impact of the GST on the price of petrol.

Almost all of those cost reductions were accounted for by a cut in the excise on petrol by 6.5 cents per litre. Regrettably, the small remainder flowed from a complicated calculation by Treasury that the introduction of a GST would have the effect of reducing production and other costs feeding into fuel prices.

No doubt soundly based in pure economic terms, this was a next-to-impossible concept to sell to the punters. The result was that we were never able to say, unconditionally, that the effect of the GST was fully cancelled out by an excise cut — something people could have easily understood. Thus the public had the nagging suspicion that the GST had lifted the price of petrol. Continued high bowser prices only aggravated this.

The belief that we had a lot of fat on our political bones blinded the Government to the gathering storm on petrol prices, which broke with gale force in the early months of 2001.

Although our poll lead was far from overwhelming, the Government finished 2000 in a strong political position. There was still a perception that the opposition lacked policy direction and was relying too heavily on negatives against the Government.

2001 was shaping as an intensely active year. In a symbolic sense it would be dominated by celebrations marking the centenary of the inauguration of the Commonwealth of Australia. During 2000, I had led a largely bipartisan delegation to London to mark the centenary of the passage through the British parliament of the enabling act for the Australian Constitution. This event was marred by some Labor pettiness. After originally declaring his intention of participating, Kim Beazley decided to pull out. He then spent quite a bit of time, whilst I and a number of Labor premiers and two former Labor prime ministers, Gough Whitlam and Bob Hawke, were in London, attacking the whole exercise as a junket.

I thought that this performance from Kim Beazley, and the support it received from sections of the media, was nothing short of pathetic. Whatever one's politics might have been, the centenary of the Commonwealth of Australia, and important landmarks associated with the coming together of the six colonies, was quite a moment in Australia's history. There comes a stage when point-scoring over the cost of overseas travel by political figures demeans our national self-respect.

Just before Christmas 2000 I decided on a cabinet reshuffle. Jocelyn Newman had indicated for some time her desire to retire. She had had terrible health challenges, especially from breast cancer. She had been a great minister, putting aside her real disappointment at not being given the Defence portfolio when we won in March 1996. Jocelyn had a dogged, battling style which appealed across the political divide to many people. She had, however, reached the point where she wished, quite literally, to retire and spend more time with her family in Canberra.

John Moore was the other long-serving minister to retire. We had had a troubled relationship. He was very much the mastermind of the numbers-gathering exercise which in 1989 had toppled me from the leadership. For me, however, that was a long time ago. I had given him a senior portfolio, and he had been a good minister, both in Industry and then Defence. He wanted out, but on the understanding that he would both retire from the ministry and from parliament before the next election. I should never have agreed to this and accepted the inevitability of a by-election, even in a safe seat such as Ryan, which was Moore's electorate. This error of judgement on my part only added to the problems which beset us just weeks later.

I was, however, driven by the imperative of Peter Reith needing another portfolio. He had been in Workplace Relations since the beginning of the

Government, and had accomplished all he was going to in that portfolio. Additionally, he had taken a fearful hammering over the Telecard Affair. He had foolishly lent his telecard to one of his sons, who allowed it to be misused, and a huge bill had ensued. The bill was paid, so the taxpayer was not out of pocket. Unfortunately for Peter, it was an issue relating to perks that really affronted the community.

The reshuffle involved the retirement of Jocelyn Newman from Family and Community Services and John Moore from Defence. In Newman's place I appointed Amanda Vanstone, thus restoring her to cabinet. I made Tony Abbott a cabinet minister, promoting him to fill the vacancy left by the promotion of Reith to Defence. To complete the reshuffle, I added Mal Brough and Ian Macfarlane, both Queenslanders, to the outer ministry.

Moore was as good as his word, resigning from parliament on 5 February 2001. A by-election to fill his vacated seat of Ryan was fixed for 17 March, St Patrick's Day. At the time I was not apprehensive about the Ryan by-election. A poll conducted by the party in December showed the likelihood of a Liberal victory in the seat.

Over the Christmas holiday period, however, the petrol issue had refused to go away. It was the same with the BAS. More and more men and women in small business complained to me, ministers and members of parliament about the complexity of the form they were required to fill out. This was reflected in the comments of colleagues at the first joint party meeting in 2001.

When cabinet looked at the petrol price problem, early in 2001, John Anderson argued that we should make a further excise adjustment so that the explicit excise reduction was equivalent to the impact of the GST. Both Peter Costello and I saw Anderson's point but felt that the Government should stick with the existing arrangements, believing that any change would be seen as the acknowledgement of a serious error, and would not in any event end public pressure for further excise cuts. John Anderson was right, and Peter Costello and I were wrong. I would fully realise this some weeks later.

In preparing for the general election due at the end of 2001, a lot of thought had been given to anticipating policy initiatives from Labor and, if appropriate, pre-empting them. One such area was science and technology and the associated fields of research and development. In a major statement late in January 2001 entitled Backing Australia's Ability, I announced a range of policies to support innovation, commercialisation, science and technology. It had not been hastily cobbled together, and in part reflected the views expressed to me over many months by the members of the Prime Minister's Science, Engineering and Innovation Council, which I had chaired on a regular basis since becoming Prime Minister. It caught Labor flat-footed. We needed that boost more than we realised.

Despite the many challenges we faced, there remained a generally confident air about our political position when parliament resumed early in February. This was about to be rudely shattered.

If I were to pinpoint the moment it all began to turn sour, especially on the issue of petrol, it would be Friday, 9 February 2001. I spent Thursday evening at the Lodge, at the end of a sitting week, mindful of my fortnightly interview with Neil Mitchell on 3AW the following morning. For an hour that evening I read Henry Kissinger's book entitled *Diplomacy*. Over coming weeks and months I would require plenty of that.

John Anderson had warned me during the day of a just-released report from the Auditor General which essentially said that Australian motorists had been ripped off because there had been a shortfall in the amount of fuel excise committed to road construction. It was a technical breach, caused by the failure of transport ministers from both sides of politics to table a notification in parliament. To Australian motorists, however, at a time when the level of excise on petrol was a red-hot issue, the impression conveyed was that they had been short-changed in relation to roads funding.

Coming when it did, the report was dynamite and became a big problem for the Government. It made life particularly hard for the Nationals and rural Liberals. Road funding is always a controversial issue in the bush. Although the Government had put a lot of extra money into the Roads for Recovery program, there was still a real hunger for additional spending in this area.

Murdoch papers, particularly the Sydney *Daily Telegraph*, carried the story in lurid terms. The *Australian*'s headline on 9 February was 'Drivers Short-changed $3bn'.[1] Neil Mitchell went absolutely ballistic. A balanced and intelligent interviewer, Mitchell nonetheless had strong views about the state of Australian roads and the price of petrol. He rightly saw fuel prices as a sensitive hip-pocket issue for the Australian voter and never lost an opportunity to cross-examine me on the price of petrol. I had an extremely difficult interview with him. I was quite defensive. It had come from nowhere, and I was ill-prepared to handle it.

In retrospect, it is easy to see the Auditor General's report as the spark that ignited the combustible fuel. There was latent concern and mistrust amongst Australians about the price of petrol, with the nagging sense that the Government may have diddled them when the GST was introduced. A report of this kind, particularly coming from the Auditor General, who sounded so utterly impartial, did the trick.

Meanwhile, the Liberal Party had gone through a lively process in choosing a candidate for the Ryan by-election. Michael Johnson, who later won the seat but later still lost his party membership over fund-raising issues, had been ruled ineligible by the Queensland division, thanks to a citizenship issue. The candidate ultimately chosen was the former Queensland party president Bob Tucker, the man I wanted. He was a highly successful businessman who had done a first-class job as party president in the 1996 election campaign. Subsequently, he had been ejected from the presidency through some kind of factional vengeance, which made no sense to me at all.

By early 2001, our private polling showed that the by-election was going to be extremely hard for us to win. There was not only the petrol issue but traditional Liberal voters do not like by-elections. They are far less tribal than Labor voters, and are perfectly happy to kick their own party in the shins in a by-election, with the intention of returning to their traditional allegiance when it really matters.

In the middle of the Ryan campaign came the result in Western Australia, which saw the defeat of the Court Government. The media exaggerated the federal implications of Court's defeat and Hanson's resurgence.

Despite the volume of criticism at the first joint party meeting of the year, Peter Costello was reluctant to move on the content of the BAS. On 21 February I convened a meeting in Sydney which included representatives of business organisations both large and small, the Taxation Office, Treasury, the Treasurer and me. The purpose of this meeting was to create a consensus for change in the format of the BAS.

Ian Macfarlane, the member for Groom, who had had plenty of small-business experience as a grain grower, made a valuable and practical contribution to the meeting. He had recently been appointed Minister for Small Business. After consistent pressure from me, Costello agreed on essential changes to respond to properly based criticism of the BAS. His slowness in responding was an illustration to me of his pointless stubbornness on issues where the case for flexibility and change was overwhelming. We were, after all, dealing with an essential part of our core constituency, small business.

The much harder issue was that of petrol. I concluded that we were fighting an unwinnable war on this issue. The public had it in its mind that, one way or another, the Government had cheated them on the petrol excise issue. They believed that inadequate compensation had been provided, through excise reductions, in response to the introduction of a GST on petrol.

I called a dinner meeting at the Lodge on 28 February 2001 of the leadership group of the Deputy Prime Minister, the Treasurer, Robert Hill, Richard Alston, Mark Vaile as Deputy Leader of the National Party and myself. I told them that I thought our political situation had deteriorated markedly since Christmas, and that the major problem was fuel. The public, in my opinion, believed it had been cheated by the Government and a big gesture was needed to turn things around.

There were two possible courses of action. We could cut the excise by a specific amount and/or we could abandon six-monthly indexation of petrol excise. The latter was a particularly sensitive issue. It had proved absolutely impossible to explain how, at a time when the price of crude oil was quite high, a further hike in the price of petrol, through an automatic increase in excise, could be justified.

I said that in order to repair the political damage it would be necessary to do both. We had to cut the excise by 1.5 cents per litre and, as well, abandon automatic indexation of fuel excise. Peter Costello did not like doing both. I could understand his viewpoint as Treasurer. On the other hand, we had allowed both the petrol excise and BAS issues to run on for too long, and we were trying to recover ground from a defensive position.

The very next day I made the necessary announcement. I took advantage of the change of policy to apologise to the Australian people for having misread the situation. Having decided to reverse our stance, it made no sense to soft-pedal on the scale of the change. In a joint news conference with John Anderson I said, 'Let me make it clear that I was plainly wrong in not understanding some of the concerns held by the Australian people about the price of petrol and I acknowledge that.'

Every so often the public both respects and welcomes admissions from a government that it has got things wrong. Such admissions should not be required too often, and they should only occur when the issues at stake are important. The public never believes that a government is infallible, quite the contrary. Thus occasional acknowledgements of error are refreshing.

My parliamentary colleagues welcomed the petrol excise announcement. It well and truly lanced the boil on that issue, and said to a lot of them that, as Leader of the Government, I was willing to take pragmatic decisions, owing as much to political reality as economics. The petrol decision had major revenue implications, especially the dumping of automatic half-yearly indexation. I knew this, but I also knew that our political position had eroded.

To validate the adage that 'it doesn't rain but it pours', we faced a one-off transitional glitch flowing from the new tax system. The introduction of the GST on new dwellings had the effect of dragging forward much construction activity before 1 July 2000. Thus an impact on building industry activity in the December quarter 2000 was expected, but when the figures came out, early in March, the activity collapse had been much more than anticipated. The Australian economy had actually contracted by 0.6 per cent in the December quarter.

This news rocked the country. With a huge banner headline, the *Sydney Morning Herald* declared, 'Australia hits the wall'.[2] It was obvious what had happened, and even then it seemed likely that there would be a recovery in subsequent quarters.

I was not, however, in the mood to take any chances on this. I had a brief discussion with Arthur Sinodinos as well as one or two senior economic people in my own department. I resolved that there should be an immediate doubling of the First Home Owner Grant for an initial period which would end on 31 December 2001. Peter Costello was of the same opinion and readily agreed with my proposal. I went ahead and announced it. It received widespread support and was seen as a practical response to a difficult problem.

The Ryan by-election saw a swing of 9.6 per cent against the Liberal Party, with a narrow victory for the Labor candidate, Leonie Short. The result was still in doubt on the night, but the early postal-vote count began to favour Bob Tucker and, on the Monday after the by-election, I was hopeful that he would just make it. His rally petered out, and Labor won the seat. It was a huge blow for the Liberal Party, but calm analysis explained the reason. In the last week of the campaign, I had doorknocked part of the electorate. Voter after voter welcomed me in a friendly manner, but indicated that they had no intention of voting for our candidate because they thought that the by-election was completely unnecessary. They quickly assured me that come the general election they would naturally resume their normal Liberal voting habits.

The Ryan experience taught me never again to have an unnecessary by-election. The truth is that public attitudes, especially amongst Liberal supporters, have changed a lot on by-elections. They are widely seen as a complete waste of taxpayers' money and indulgences by political parties and local members who are unwilling to fulfil commitments made to their voters.

Although badly shaken by the loss of Ryan, the party was mollified by the fact that decisive action had been taken on issues concerning my colleagues. There had been changes on petrol excise and the BAS. As well, the speedy response with the First Home Owner Grant had pleased the party room. They realised that I was not interested in dying wondering as to whether some tweaking of policy might be needed to improve our political position.

As 2001 went on, there was no shortage of drama on the economic front. In April the Australian dollar fell well below US50 cents. From an economic standpoint, this was not in itself something to be alarmed about. It nonetheless concerned people who saw the value of the Australian dollar against the American dollar as a measure of our nation's economic strength. Not long afterwards our dollar began a recovery as the impact of the 'tech wreck' in the United States began to affect the greenback.

It was an enormous reassurance to me that, in Ian Macfarlane, Australia had a Reserve Bank governor who would respond calmly in a difficult situation and resist those who believed in kneejerk reactions, such as a sharp increase in interest rates, in the hope of lifting the value of the Australian dollar. In his view, as Australia had a floating exchange rate, we should allow market mechanisms to work their way through. Part of the market mechanism involved periodic buying and selling of currencies by the central bank. This was an essential element in smoothing currency fluctuations, not a vehicle for overturning them.

Then out of the blue in May there was the Shane Stone memo. After the easy win by Labor in the Queensland state election on 17 February 2001, Shane Stone had, as federal president, met most of the Queensland senators and members to get their views on why the Coalition had done so poorly in that state poll, and generally obtain their assessments of our federal standing. He sent me what purported to be a summary of their opinions. It was a colourful document. It would have made more sense if Shane had called on me with an oral debriefing. In any event, he didn't do that. Amongst the observations he passed on was that the Government was seen increasingly as 'mean and tricky'. Regrettably, that description would keep being thrown back at us.

In its slant, the document was particularly critical of Peter Costello. After reading it, I put it aside. I did not raise it with Peter. Most of the issues canvassed were now ancient history. We had acted on petrol excise as well as the BAS. We had responded immediately to the December quarter GDP slump, and by early April there was evidence that this response had borne fruit. I forgot about the memo until its explosive publication early in May.

Laurie Oakes had obtained a copy. He ran a *Bulletin* article on its contents and, naturally enough, he made a meal of it on Channel Nine.

The revelation of this memo was both painful and extremely difficult. I did not release it or, in any way, authorise its release. Its publication was bad for the Government, bad for me and bad for Peter Costello. To the best of my knowledge, there were only ever two copies. There was the one Shane Stone sent to me and, of course, the one which Shane himself retained.

Not surprisingly, Peter Costello was furious, especially as so many of the remarks in the memo were directed towards him. He and Shane had never enjoyed a close relationship. He saw Shane as a 'Howard man'. I assured Peter that the document had not come from me. All up, it was an intensely regrettable incident, which hurt the Government. The Labor Party and the press had a lot of fun at our expense. To this day I do not know where the leak came from.

I delve more extensively into my relationship with Peter Costello in Chapter 44.

2001 was proving to be an extremely difficult year. The Labor Party had enjoyed a good polling position for some months, and commentators began to heavily discount the Coalition's prospects of winning the election at the end of the year. Early in May, Newspoll had my satisfaction rating at 31 per cent.

On 10 May 2001 a commemorative sitting of the federal parliament took place in the Victorian parliamentary chamber. It had been preceded the day before with something of a re-enactment of the famous Inauguration of the Commonwealth in the Royal Exhibition Building, so memorably captured in the marvellous Tom Roberts painting. This event was surrounded by other centenary celebrations. One of them was a full-scale Labor dinner, complete with plenty of hubris and exaggerated predictions regarding the outcome of the next federal election.

Through all of this I maintained a total focus on rebuilding the Government's political support. The Government had been a good one viewed against the fundamentals, particularly of the economy. Unemployment had fallen steadily, interest rates were lower, debt was being repaid, and in May of 2001 Peter Costello would bring down his fourth successive surplus budget.

Major taxation reform had been implemented. The once notoriously inefficient Australian waterfront now had world-class productivity levels. We had commenced the privatisation of Telstra and established a major environmental trust fund. Mutual obligation had become a cornerstone of Australia's welfare system. On the international scene, Australia had led the liberation of East Timor and restored balance to our external relations.

There was still plenty to do, but the case to be put for the Government was a compelling one. To my mind we needed to address genuine areas of concern and be willing to act decisively in so doing. That had happened in relation to petrol excise, the housing slump and the BAS.

The next area to which I turned my attention was that of older Australians. Historically, Australians over the age of 55 gave above-average support to the Coalition. Many older Australians, particularly self-funded retirees, felt nervous about the GST. On the one hand, they bought the argument that it was in the long-term interest of Australia to have taxation reform. On the other hand, however, largely being people on fixed incomes, they were apprehensive that the value of their savings would be eroded, and that there would be inadequate compensation for the impact of the introduction of a tax on most of the goods and services which they purchased.

In the months preceding the delivery of the budget in May of 2001, I had regularly put to Peter Costello the need for the budget to address these concerns. We discussed in detail what these initiatives might be, and on budget night, the Treasurer announced a suite of new policies specially directed towards older Australians.

They included significantly more generous taxation treatment as well as a liberalisation of the entitlement to the Commonwealth Health Card, regarded by older Australians as a most valuable possession. Furthermore, there was a one-off bonus of $300 for this age cohort, the first of many such one-off bonuses for particular groups.

Commentators have been critical of one-off bonuses. What they fail to realise is that one-off bonuses make far more economic sense than permanent increases in benefits. If circumstances change, then there is no ongoing commitment from the Government which has provided the one-off bonus. In this way such a practice is far more responsible.

Our spirits were lifted mightily on 6 June, with the release of the March quarter GDP figures showing growth of 1.1 per cent for the quarter. It was direct evidence that our policy change on the First Home Buyers' Grant had worked and, even more importantly, that the December negative figure had been a one-off aberration entirely due to transitional circumstances.

On the morning of 24 April Michael Ronaldson, the chief government whip, had telephoned me at 5.30 with the news that Peter Nugent, the member for Aston in Victoria, had died earlier in the morning of a heart attack. He had been with his wife at their home in Melbourne. Peter had won the seat from the sitting Labor member, John Saunderson, in the big Liberal sweep through Victoria in 1990.

Nugent had been a good local member. Although we had developed a warm personal relationship, Peter was of the 'small l' Liberal school of thought. He would not have shared my views on the republic or many aspects of Aboriginal policy. He argued against features of the 10-point plan in response to the Wik decision. Having, however, put his views in the party room, he accepted majority decisions and well and truly played the party game. He had won my respect and support. I felt the loss of him as a valued colleague and parliamentary friend.

For a short period there was speculation that his wife, Carol Nugent, might nominate for the seat. She was articulate, well liked and widely known in the electorate. In the end she decided against it and explained the reasons why in a conversation with me.

I knew that we faced a big challenge to hold the seat. The margin in 1998 had been 4.3 per cent. In a by-election that was a thin buffer. Naturally the public attitude is different when the vacancy is due to the death of a sitting member. But there had not been many by-elections in recent years and the Government felt vulnerable, given the multiple challenges it had faced during the first six months of 2001. Fortunately the Victorian division found and endorsed a first-class candidate in Chris Pearce. He came from the area, had an engaging and fully committed wife and family and had good small-business experience in computers. He really did fit the Aston bill.

As observed earlier, the quality of a candidate in a by-election is just so crucial. The media exposure is huge. A dud candidate can be hidden in a general election but in a by-election that is impossible. Chris Pearce was able to handle the media and embrace the general campaign themes remarkably speedily.

Kim Beazley was of unexpected assistance during the campaign for the Aston seat. For reasons best known to himself, he decided to allow Barry Jones to talk in general terms about his plans for science and technology. Jones had chaired a task group developing the policy. His presentation consisted of myriad interconnecting concepts held together by what was derisively called spaghetti lines. It quickly acquired the description of Noodle Nation and was a huge embarrassment for Labor.

Another gaffe came directly from Kim Beazley. A few days out from the by-election he said that he did not think Australians were overtaxed. The interview in which he made this statement was open to the interpretation that he might support higher taxation so as to fund more infrastructure investment. Such an attitude was completely out of touch with the aspirations of the people of Aston. It was quintessentially a middle Australian electorate. The people were concerned about their mortgages, their children's education and health and the wellbeing of their elderly parents. Beazley's remarks seemed a mile away from their concerns.

Although both the candidate and the Victorian Liberals had done all they could have, I approached the by-election on 14 July with considerable trepidation. That evening I attended the final match between the Wallabies and the touring British and Irish Lions at the Telstra Stadium in Sydney. The Lions had won the first Test in Brisbane, with Australia reversing that outcome in Melbourne. The Sydney game was a decider and, being an enthusiastic follower of the Wallabies, I was keen to be there. Aston, though, was very much on my mind. The first results phoned through to me by Lynton Crosby suggested that the swing against us was insufficient to lose the seat. This was tremendous news. At the close of counting that night, both the figures and the projections suggested that Chris Pearce would narrowly win the seat.

By any measure this had been an impressive result for the Coalition. Certainly there had been a swing of some 3.5 per cent against us but, in all of the circumstances, that was really quite a small movement. We had been in government for more than five years and had passed through many difficult months with a lot of controversial decisions.

I knew, and what is more I knew that Kim Beazley knew, that Labor should have taken the seat. If Labor could not, in a by-election, win a seat such as Aston, then it had limited appeal to middle Australia. If after five years our support was holding in electorates such as Aston, then we had a real prospect of hanging on when the election came at the end of the year. There was considerable latent respect for the Government.

The next day was the first episode of the ABC's Sunday-morning television program *The Insiders*. From a combination of campaigning and barracking for the Wallabies I had picked up a dose of laryngitis. Interviewed from Kirribilli House, my voice was croaky. I was, nonetheless, able to say that the Liberal Party, as a result of Aston, was 'back in the game'.

The other lesson out of Aston was for the Labor Party. Kim Beazley had hitched his star to negativity. He had now led the Labor Party for more than five years. Although he had given it early cohesion and credibility, the time had long since passed for him to declare what a future Labor Government would do. Negativity and being the nice guy worked for a number of years. By July 2001 it had begun to wear thin.

The Aston outcome was a huge tonic for the Liberal Party. It restored my colleagues' self-belief. Once again they felt that we could win at the end of the year. They had renewed faith in our message and the conviction that good policy in the end has a generous political dividend.

Within weeks our world would be turned on its head. In Australia there were the events surrounding the turning back of the *Tampa* at the end of August and, of course, there was the horror of 11 September, which introduced the 21st century to the experience of terrorism at the hands of Islamic extremists.

The very magnitude of these happenings meant that the Government's critics would seek to explain away Labor's defeat in November 2001 entirely by reference to them. It is true that the Government's position was strengthened by the stand it took to turn back the rising tide of illegal immigration. We won public support because we did the right thing in the national interest. Our swift response, alongside the Americans, to the terrorist attack of 11 September was widely supported. To the public, this was a Government willing to act decisively in a difficult situation.

That having been said, nothing can gainsay the fact that at the beginning of August 2001, the Coalition had largely resurrected its political support. For close to eight months it had responded in an intelligent, targeted fashion to legitimate areas of concern within the community. It had displayed a sensitivity which its critics claimed it lacked. All the while the Labor Party had simply assumed that it could continue to 'surf to victory' off the back of a negative attack on one of the Government's greatest reforms.

Whilst never a completely reliable guide, the published opinion polls for 2001 offered some perspective. For the first five months of the year, Newspoll showed a clear lead for Labor, with the opposition's primary-vote lead hitting 13 per cent in March. By June the Coalition had begun to reconnect. There was very little between the parties when MV *Tampa* sailed over the horizon at the end of August. My response to the *Tampa* did give the Coalition a big lift in the polls, but if the Liberal and National parties had not proved responsive to public concerns on other issues, the public verdict on *Tampa* could well have been more cynical.

The real story of 2001 was that the policy indolence of the Labor Party, coupled with the policy responsiveness of the Coalition, meant that when the remarkable events of August and September unfolded, Labor was already off balance and completely overwhelmed by them. If the Coalition had not acted on petrol, the BAS, older Australians, the temporary housing slump and other issues, its lack of political credibility could well have coloured, in particular, the public response to its dramatic handling of the asylum-seeker challenge.

The Coalition won the general election on 10 November with an increased majority. I deal again with this elsewhere. The firm line we took on border protection and the clarity and vigour of our support for the Americans in responding to the attacks of 11 September garnered wide public support. The two combined to add to an already solid base of support for the Coalition in the Australian community.

If the *Tampa* had not come into the picture and 11 September had never taken place I still believe that the Coalition would have been returned at the 2001 election. Its majority would probably have been lower.

The Australian public felt that after five years we had governed well. The economy continued to grow quite vigorously. Unemployment was down, and despite the teething problems produced by such a big structural change, taxation reform had been embraced and, ultimately supported, by the Australian people.

Added to this Labor was seen as unconvincing. There was no shortage of people willing to say that Kim Beazley was a 'good bloke'. His convictions, though, were elusive. He demonstrated this himself when, during the election campaign, his party ran television advertisements blandly stating that he stood for general improvements in health and education. The advertisements actually had him saying, 'That is what I stand for.'

It was legitimate of Beazley's critics to ask the question, why on earth have you not established that in the eyes of the Australian public after five-and-a-half years? The explanation was that Beazley and the Labor Party totally misread the 1998 election. They saw it as substantially a negative reaction to the GST, and all that was needed for them to return to power was to enjoy the political benefits of the GST being, in their eyes, a 'slow burner'. This was not only a misinterpretation of the reasons for the swing against us in 1998 but also the open-mindedness of the Australian people to an essential, although irritating, reform.

The Coalition had won the public debate on the GST. What Kim Beazley and his colleagues completely overlooked was that there had been two to three decades of debate about the desirability of changing Australia's taxation system. Finally, a government had done something about it. The Australian public discovered, despite the aggravations of implementation, that the new system, so far from being the ogre depicted by its critics, was not only beneficial but carried with it quite significant reductions in personal income tax.

It is an iron law of politics in Australia and, I suspect, in other countries, that each election is quite different. The issues that defined and shaped an earlier campaign were almost entirely irrelevant to those of a later one. It was an iron law that the Australian Labor Party in 2001 had not carefully studied.

Writing in the *Australian*, two days after the 2001 election, Paul Kelly said that through 2001 I had accomplished one of the most stunning recoveries in the nation's history. He said that a key ingredient had been my ability to penetrate and hold traditional Labor areas. Crucial to this had been the actions taken during 2001, as well as my resolute stance on asylum seekers and national security.

Kim Beazley gave up the Labor leadership after a second successive defeat. Simon Crean replaced him. Another feature of the 2001 election was the defeat of Cheryl Kernot, the former Democrats leader, who had dramatically defected to the ALP in 1997. It was also about this time that I resumed the habit of keeping a diary on major issues. There were to be plenty of them in the next six years.

31

WASHINGTON,
11 SEPTEMBER 2001

The graceful residence for the Australian ambassador in Washington, once owned by General George Patton, was the venue for a convivial barbecue late on Sunday afternoon, 9 September 2001, attended by the top echelon of the US Administration — Richard Cheney, Colin Powell, Donald Rumsfeld, two judges of the Supreme Court and several other cabinet ministers; protocol precluded the President coming. The open personal warmth on that near-perfect late-summer day testified to the intimacy of an old and durable friendship which faced the world with hope and confidence — but blissfully unaware of what was about to hit. It was the lost 'idle hill of summer', but absent the distant drummer of Housman's imagery.

Our host was Michael Thawley, newly Australia's envoy to Washington, who had taken over from Andrew Peacock. Thawley proved outstanding in the job, with other ambassadors drooling at the access he obtained. He had been my first advisor on foreign policy and defence and was a calm but aggressive thinker. Thawley's sustained counsel and help during the East Timor intervention had proved invaluable, and he remains amongst the very top flight of people who advised me as Prime Minister. He put on a good party; our principal guests lingered, with Donald and Joyce Rumsfeld having a particularly enjoyable time. Lleyton Hewitt lifted Australian spirits by taking out the US Open from Pete Sampras whilst the barbecue was in progress.

Initially, I had been mildly put out that my visit to Washington could not take place until September, rather than the more traditional time of July. It was, however, no simple matter to match the programs of the President and me. But the eventual visit had a personal bonus. In April, our son Tim had gone to London on a working holiday, and was employed there by Lehman Brothers. He had come over to see us in Washington and was staying at our hotel, which gave us a welcome opportunity to catch up.

The ostensible reason for the visit was to mark the 50th anniversary of the signing of the Australia, New Zealand and the United States (ANZUS) Treaty. I had not previously met the 43rd US President, George Bush, but had spoken to him as a candidate some nine months before the desperately close presidential election of November 2000, and early in 2001 he had telephoned me for a general discussion.

I met the new President the morning after the barbecue, Monday, 10 September. I found him direct, energetic and likable. I will have much more to say about him in Chapter 35. Bush and I attended a ceremony at the naval dockyard in Washington to honour the ANZUS Treaty. The symbolic event of the ceremony was the President passing custody to me of the bell from the USS *Canberra*. There was a spick-and-span turnout from the US military on a clear and beautiful Washington day.

He offered me a lift in his car from the dockyard to the White House for our formal discussions. Amongst those present at the discussions were the Vice-president; the Secretary of State, Condoleezza Rice; the National Security Advisor as well as senior White House officials. There was no mention of terrorism. We recommitted to the Alliance. I canvassed the possibility of a free-trade agreement, making reference to our continued unhappiness with US agricultural protection, which hurt Australian farmers. We also talked about conditions in Indonesia.

For his part, the President spoke of his desire to build a closer relationship with the Russian Federation. At that time he placed great store on the personal links he had made with Vladimir Putin. This meeting was followed by lunch.

Later that day I went to the Pentagon for a formal meeting with Donald Rumsfeld, the Defense Secretary. He has been a controversial figure, but I always liked his direct and engaged approach. He had come to Australia for the annual AUSMIN talks — involving Defence and Foreign Affairs representatives from both countries — with Colin Powell two months earlier. We had had a very enjoyable dinner at the Lodge, attended by the Chairman of the Joint Chiefs of Staff and the newly arrived US ambassador to Australia, Tom Schieffer.

That evening I dined with Rupert Murdoch at the Occidental Restaurant, immediately adjacent to the Willard Inter-Continental Hotel, where I was staying. Murdoch is always interesting company, having a capacity to remain contemporary in his thinking and never entirely predictable with his opinions. No other Australian has had a greater impact on the world business stage than Rupert Murdoch. News Limited papers had been supportive of our reform agenda, most particularly taxation and waterfront reform.

As we left the restaurant we were 'door-stopped' by a large Australian media contingent. Asked whether he thought that I deserved a third term in office, Murdoch replied, 'It doesn't matter what I think. You ask my editors.' Back in my hotel room I remarked to Janette that my meeting with Rupert Murdoch would get a big run in the Australian media the following day. I had no idea how utterly irrelevant that meeting would be to news coverage during the next 24 hours.

The 11th of September was a sparkling Washington day. As customary, I walked from the hotel up past the Vietnam Memorial alongside the large lake and turned at the Lincoln Memorial for the walk back to the hotel. It seemed just another normal and pleasant September morning in the US capital.

As I passed that very familiar television position in front of the White House fence, with the residence in the background, I took a phone call from Peter Costello, who wanted to discuss the looming receivership of Ansett. This had become a major domestic political issue and was of concern to Peter, John Anderson, and me. We were resolved that the Government would not bail out Ansett. There was growing pressure for this to happen, but there was no way we would entertain it. I knew that we would need to do something about the entitlements of retrenched workers, but a capital injection or government guarantee had to be resisted.

I had agreed to have a news conference at the hotel shortly after 9 am. Apart from incessant questions about my visit, the Australian media were keen to talk about Ansett. Shortly before the news conference was due to start, Tony O'Leary came to my hotel room to discuss issues and likely questions at the news conference.

Almost casually, he said that a plane had hit one of the towers at the World Trade Center in New York. We both thought, and I believed said to each other, that it was probably an accident. A few minutes later he came back and told me that another plane had hit the other tower of the World

Trade Center. We knew then that there had been no accident and that some planned assault on the building had occurred. I flicked on a TV set and saw the grim live coverage of the burning World Trade Center. Like millions of others, I was stunned at the terrible images.

I prefaced my news conference by acknowledging what had occurred. 'Can I just say, before I start on the domestic things, how horrified I am at what I have just heard regarding what has happened in New York. I don't know any more than anybody else but it appears to be a most horrific, awful event that will obviously entail a very big loss of life.' Those words revealed my shocked immediate reaction. This was before the third plane hit the Pentagon, at a time when people were only just beginning to focus on the motivation for the attack.

I then answered questions about both the Ansett dispute and a court decision on the *Tampa* issue. During the press conference, the third plane was driven into the Pentagon. I was informed of this at the end of the news conference by a member of my AFP detail, who told me that their Secret Service radio frequency had picked up the very loud explosion when the plane crashed into the Pentagon building.

With the news conference over, the curtains — drawn for the conference — were pulled back, and smoke could be seen rising from the direction of the Pentagon building. Events had happened so rapidly, it was hard to assimilate their real significance.

I returned to my hotel room with some of my staff. Shortly afterwards I was told by my principal private secretary, Tony Nutt, that the Secret Service wanted me to leave the hotel immediately. The head of my detail, George Edwards, came to my room and said, 'I haven't lost anyone yet and I don't intend to start today.'

I was worried about Janette and Tim, who a short while earlier had gone sightseeing. I was assured that they were okay and would be taken to the same place as me. At that stage no one knew who was responsible, or the full scale of the loss of life and property. I did not feel panic, nor did anyone around me show it. The reaction of all I spoke to that day was amazingly calm and deliberate.

Accompanied by blaring sirens and flashing lights, we were taken to what can only be described as a bunker under the Australian embassy in Pennsylvania Avenue. Janette and Tim arrived there shortly after I did.

Janette and Tim were being driven to the Jefferson Memorial when Tim saw smoke coming from the direction of the Pentagon, which lies across the Potomac River from Washington. He asked Frank Morgan, one of my AFP detail accompanying them, 'Frank, does that [pointing to the smoke on the horizon] have anything to do with what has just happened in New York?' Morgan, who had changed his radio frequency after he himself had seen the smoke, replied, 'Yes, it does. A plane has hit the Pentagon.'

They were immediately joined by a Secret Service officer who had been following in another car who said that they were off to a safe house. Their car stopped, literally, in the middle of an intersection. The Secret Service driver, Sergeant Ranican, called to an officer who was in a marked police car, 'I've got the missus of Australia with me. Where's the nearest safe house?' He was given an address and, accompanied by screeching sirens and a police escort, they headed for what turned out to be a fire station in a Washington suburb. After about half an hour they were driven to the bunker under the Australian embassy.

The bunker was a large area, and was rapidly filling with other Australians, including many businesspeople I had intended meeting later that morning. I telephoned the acting Prime Minister, John Anderson, to discuss responses in Australia. He told me that action had already been taken to provide protection for US assets and installations. The AFP had established an exclusion zone around the American embassy in Canberra, and heightened security arrangements had been put in place for the consulates in Melbourne, Sydney and Perth. There had also been increased surveillance and protection for Israeli and Jewish assets in Australia. He also briefed me on a meeting involving the security agencies to discuss first-response arrangements.

At this point, there was no way of knowing if the attacks were the first in a series to take place around the world. It was obvious that what had occurred in New York and Washington had been a planned act of terrorism. There was a legitimate fear that similar attacks would occur in places such as London, Paris, Tokyo and Rome. Australia could not be excluded. As time went by, it became apparent that there was not to be a pattern of attacks around the world. But it was some weeks after 11 September before we could be confident of that.

Tom Schieffer and his wife came to the bunker. My instinctive reaction was literally to embrace him and say, 'Tom, I am so sorry for what has happened to your country.' I had only known him for a few months but would come not only to see a lot of him but to like him immensely. He was a wonderful representative of his country in Australia at a critical period.

His personal friendship with George Bush added enormous value to his ambassadorship. They had been partners in the ownership of the Texas Rangers baseball team. They had remained very good friends. The President told me on several occasions that if I really had a problem and was not getting anywhere through the normal channels, I should 'ring Schieffer' and he would fix it.

After speaking to Tom Schieffer, I dictated a letter to the President:

> Dear Mr President.
>
> The Australian Government and people share the sense of horror experienced by your nation at today's catastrophic events and the appalling loss of life. I feel the tragedy even more keenly, being here in Washington at the moment.
>
> In the face of an attack of this magnitude, words are always inadequate in conveying sympathy and support. You can however be assured of Australia's resolute solidarity with the American people at this most tragic time.
>
> My personal thoughts and prayers are very much with those left grieved by these despicable attacks upon the American people and the American nation.

I then addressed a news conference, commencing with the reading of the letter to President Bush. I expressed the horror and revulsion of the Australian people at the events which had taken place a few hours earlier. I reported my discussion with the acting Prime Minister and the arrangements put in place in Australia.

It was a time for unconditional expressions of support and sympathy. I said:

> ... the only other thing I can say to you is really on behalf of all of the Australians here is to say to our American friends, who we love and admire so much, we really feel for you. It is a terrible day. It is a day that recalls the words used by President Roosevelt in 1941 — it is a day of infamy that an attack of this kind can be made in such an indiscriminate fashion — not upon military

assets as was the case in Pearl Harbor but upon innocent civilians: men, women and children going about their daily lives. As I say, words aren't very adequate but they are a sign that we feel for our American friends. We will stand by them, we will help them, and we will support actions they take to properly retaliate in relation to these acts of bastardry against their citizens and against what they stand for.

I meant every word. To me there had been an attack on the American way of life. As a consequence it was also an attack on our way of life, because so much of what we held dear as basic freedoms are the things that Americans also held dear as basic freedoms.

The attacks on New York and Washington on 11 September 2001 were audacious, cruel and hideously successful acts of calculated terrorism, representing the most significant assault on the American homeland since Pearl Harbor. They hit the nation's commercial heart and its capital; they claimed more lives than the Japanese assault in December 1941.

Being in Washington meant that I absorbed, immediately, the shocked disbelief, anger and all of the other emotions experienced by the American people. They were outraged by the audacity and stunned by the chilling effectiveness of the terror mission. In 24 hours the psychology of the United States was transformed. That the United States was utterly unprepared for these terrorist attacks was abundantly clear from my discussions with the President and Vice-president, the Secretary of State, the President's National Security Advisor and the Defense Secretary, during the two days before that fateful 11 September.

There was no alarm in the bunker but, from the horrifying TV pictures, a realisation that America had been attacked in a way never before experienced. There was plenty of speculation by the businessmen about travel arrangements. Given the time differences with Australia, and the rapidly imposed closure of American airspace, speculation was the only option available.

I talked to my advisors about the possible source of the attack. Michael Thawley said that first suspicions would inevitably fall on the al Qaeda terrorist network operating out of Afghanistan. It had been linked to earlier terrorist attacks on American forces and bases abroad. Like others, I was aware of its lethal intent, but never imagined it had the capacity to mount the attack carried out just a few hours earlier.

I knew that my previously planned address to a joint sitting of Congress on Wednesday, 12 September could not go ahead, but told Michael Thawley that instead I would like to visit the Capitol Building the following day, as a mark of respect to the American people.

Janette and I decided to spend the evening at the embassy residence and that afternoon decamped there with a lot of our staff and later had an informal barbecue. We were all still quite numb. It was a sombre occasion and a sad contrast to the spirited optimism felt only two days earlier. It seemed the world had irrevocably changed in 24 hours and that so many things that seemed important just a day or two earlier would no longer be issues troubling us in the months ahead.

President Bush had been listening to the reading of a group of second-graders at Emma E. Booker Elementary School, Sarasota, Florida, when the attack occurred. Bush knew of the first tower being hit when he entered the classroom. He only knew that it was an act of terrorism when his chief of staff, Andy Card, came into the classroom and whispered news of the second attack in his ear. Later Condi Rice would do likewise, telling him, 'America is under attack.' For some extraordinary reason, some of the former president's critics, such as the film-maker Michael Moore, made a big thing of the fact that Bush continued with the children for some minutes after being told of the attack. That seemed a remarkably petty reaction. Calmly completing the task at hand and not alarming the children was entirely the right response. Those few minutes with the second-graders allowed him to adjust to what he had been told.

Bush made a brief statement to the American people from the library of that school. Fox News reported Byron Mitchell, a fifth-grader present in the library, as saying, 'I learned a lot. I learned anything can happen at any given moment. That was the biggest day of my life. I wouldn't say I was in the middle of it, but I was part of it.'[1] In his simple, direct fashion, this young American had sensed the life-changing character of the attack for America.

The President was whisked away to an undisclosed location and later delivered a short television address to the nation. It was not very comprehensive, and I could understand some of the criticism which it attracted. It must be remembered, though, that the United States had no way of knowing whether or not these attacks were the beginning of a rolling terrorist assault on various parts of the United States or whether they were, as turned out to be the case, one-off but devastating outrages.

Early on Wednesday morning, Michael Thawley was in touch with the office of the Speaker of the House of Representatives, and I was invited to attend a special sitting of Congress at which resolutions condemning the attacks and expressing support for whatever response would be necessary were to be debated.

Later that morning I had the unique experience of observing a stunned but calm US legislature discussing a response to one of the most horrific events in their nation's history. Janette and I sat in the public gallery, accompanied only by Michael Thawley, his wife, Debbie, and our security detail. There would be no other people present in the gallery. The speaker graciously drew attention to our presence and described it as an expression of support and empathy with the American people. I received a standing ovation, and felt deeply moved by that reception; I was quite emotional about being able, at that time, in those circumstances to be in the capital of the United States to convey the sympathy and support of the Australian people. Tragic as the circumstances were, I felt especially privileged to be there. After the session ended, I went onto the floor of the Senate and sought out Hillary Clinton and Charles Schumer, the two New York senators, to say how I felt for them particularly, because of the attack on their city. Hillary told me that her husband, Bill, had been in Port Douglas, in Queensland, when the attack took place.

Later that day Janette and I, accompanied by Tim, attended a memorial service at the Washington National Cathedral. This cathedral has seen numerous significant services, funerals and memorials. Many of Washington's officialdom attended the service, trying in their own way to comprehend what had occurred. After the service I returned to the embassy residence for lunch and that afternoon I was to take two important phone calls.

The first was from Rich Armitage, the Deputy Secretary of State. In recent years there has been no US official more supportive of Australia, better informed about our politics and more genuinely sympathetic to our cause than Rich Armitage. An imposing, barrel-chested Vietnam War hero, Armitage has a deceptively soft and husky voice. I first met him when he was deputy to Casper Weinberger, the Defense Secretary in the Reagan Administration. We established an instant friendship. Armitage and Colin Powell were close personally. He was a neat fit as number two to the retired general.

Armitage was not in much doubt that the attack had been organised by al Qaeda, and that the nerve centre of operations had been Afghanistan. He pinpointed the significance of Pakistan, making it clear that action was being contemplated against terrorist activities in Afghanistan. He said that Pakistan would have to make a decision quickly as to whose side it was on. He said that Perves Masharaff, the President of Pakistan, would 'feel some pain from the United States to make up his mind very quickly'.

The other phone call was from Alan Greenspan, the chairman of the Federal Reserve. He was cautious in predicting the likely impact of the attacks on the markets. He said that if there were no further attacks, then the financial impact might be relatively short-lived. I was always interested in knowing Greenspan's views. A face-to-face discussion with him was a regular feature of every visit I paid to the United States whilst he was still at the Fed. He was calm and measured and certainly did not foretell financial-system calamity as a result of the attacks. He was right.

During our many discussions on both 11 and 12 September, Michael Thawley said that he thought action against Iraq would be on the agenda as a result of the attacks. He did not say that he believed Iraq was involved, nor that this was a belief of the Bush Administration.

Due to the closure of airspace, no commercial aircraft could leave the country. After discussion with Armitage and others, arrangements were made for Air Force Two to fly me and my party from Andrews Air Force Base near Washington to Hawaii. I would then join a Qantas flight from Hawaii to Sydney. It would be the first flight from US airspace since the attacks.

Before leaving for Andrews Air Force Base, I held a news conference at the ambassador's residence in which I made an important promise on behalf of Australia. I said: 'I've also indicated that Australia will provide all support that might be requested of us by the United States in relation to any action that might be taken.' I had committed Australia to assisting the United States in her retaliation against those responsible for the outrage against her citizens. I also predicted that the fight against terrorism would be with us for years into the future and that no nation, including Australia, was immune from a terrorist attack.

In making that commitment I spoke for my Government and the people of Australia. In words I would use later, this was a time for a 100 per cent ally, not a 70 or 80 per cent one. I am sure that the gratitude of the American people for the speed and unconditional character of our response remains to this day.

Our flight left Andrews Air Force Base at approximately 4.30 pm on Wednesday, 12 September. It had been a brief and drama-packed visit to the

United States. Out of the window I watched the farewelling party on the tarmac, which included Michael and Debbie Thawley, US Air Force people, embassy staff and our son Tim. I kept my eyes on Tim for as long as possible. He was to return to London; exactly when, he did not know. After what had occurred, all manner of thoughts regarding his safety flooded through me. It would have been a like experience for parents all around the world.

Suddenly the world had become very different, much more dangerous, and vulnerabilities real or imagined abounded no matter what the calm logic of the situation suggested some months down the track.

On the way back to Australia I spoke to Alexander Downer. We agreed that, subject to cabinet approval, the ANZUS Treaty should be invoked. After I completed my telephone conversation I walked to another section of the plane and informed Tom Schieffer of our intentions regarding the ANZUS Treaty. He was moved by this important gesture by Australia. I also spoke to John Anderson regarding the Ansett matter. I would have a full plate upon my return to Australia.

After clearing customs in Sydney I was immediately confronted by a group of Ansett employees. They knew of my return. Albeit in a friendly fashion, they bailed me up. I listened to what they had to say and felt a genuine sympathy for those who feared for the loss of their positions.

The Government should not rescue Ansett. We would, however, need to provide assistance with entitlements. After speaking to the Ansett employees, I boarded an aircraft for Canberra and went straight to a cabinet meeting. There were two subjects on the agenda: the terrorist attacks and Ansett.

After the meeting I held a joint news conference with John Anderson and Alexander Downer. I announced that cabinet had decided the ANZUS Treaty should be invoked in relation to the attack upon the United States. As a result, we would consult the Americans regarding responses which might be deemed appropriate to what did amount to an attack upon the metropolitan territory of the United States, in accordance with the provisions of the ANZUS Treaty. I also said it was the unanimous view of cabinet that Australia stood ready to cooperate, within the limits of its capability, in any response that the United States may regard as necessary in consultation with her allies.

On Ansett, I confirmed the Government would not accept the proposition of the Leader of the Opposition for it to fund the operation of the company for a further two weeks. We had advice that it would cost between $120 and $170 million merely to keep the company operating until the evening of the following day. An extrapolation out to the period nominated by Kim Beazley revealed that such a step would impose an unacceptable additional cost on the budget.

I had been a regular customer of Ansett in the years before I became Prime Minister. I had always found their staff polite, helpful and efficient. Regrettably the company had become the victim of poor management, some overindulgent industrial relations arrangements and a multiplicity of aircraft types, which added hugely to maintenance costs.

Although I was adamant the Government would not fund continuing operations and the management of the affairs of the company should remain in the hands of the administrator, it was made plain that the Government would guarantee the payment of all statutory entitlements. These included unpaid salary, holiday, long service leave and so on. Furthermore we would meet the cost of what could be regarded as a community standard for a redundancy payment, which was eight weeks in all. Many Ansett employees had far more generous redundancy arrangements than these. It was always a possibility that the liquidator might recover further money which could augment the amount to be guaranteed by the Government. The Government honoured in full these commitments.

Sympathy for the Americans in the wake of the terrorist attacks was very high in Australia. The appearance of George Bush on the site of the destroyed World Trade Center, just a few days after the attack, made a powerful impact. There was great resonance in his promise that those responsible for the atrocity would shortly hear from the United States.

Knowing that Australia would be involved militarily, contact began between our military people and the Americans. Before any military action could be taken, a case in international law had to be established. If the Americans had credible evidence that al Qaeda, operating out of Afghanistan, was responsible for the attack then a military strike against the terrorist organisation, and those harbouring it, would be completely justified.

On 20 September President Bush made a powerful and special State of the Union address to a joint sitting of congress. He said that all the evidence so far gathered pointed to a collection of loosely affiliated terrorist organisations known as al Qaeda being responsible for the attack. He said they were some of the murderers indicted for bombing US embassies in Tanzania and Kenya and responsible for bombing the USS *Cole*.

At this very early stage, when American anger was at a white-hot level, the President was careful to distinguish between terrorists obscenely using the Islamic religion and the mainstream of that religion's adherents. He said, 'The terrorists practise a fringe form of Islamic extremism that has been rejected by Muslim scholars and the vast majority of Muslim clerics — a fringe movement that perverts the peaceful teachings of Islam.'

He went on to say:

> I also want to speak tonight directly to Muslims throughout the world. We respect your faith. It is practised freely by many millions of Americans, and by millions more in countries that America counts as friends. Its teachings are good and peaceful, and those who commit evil in the name of Allah blaspheme the name of Allah. The terrorists are traitors to their own faith, trying, in effect, to hijack Islam itself. The enemy of America is not our many Muslim friends. It is not our many Arab friends. Our enemy is a radical network of terrorists and every government that supports them.[2]

In all subsequent speeches George Bush was careful not to conflate his unceasing attack on Islamic extremism with a general condemnation of Islam. Those who continue to argue otherwise are themselves responsible for distorting the truth. The gist of what Bush had to say about Islam then was precious little different from Barack Obama's much-heralded 2009 speech to the Muslim world in Cairo. Yet the latter address was represented as creating a new dawn in relations with Islam.

Bush made specific demands of the Taliban regime, then in charge of Afghanistan. They included the delivery to the US authorities of all leaders of al Qaeda, the release of all foreign nationals who had been unjustly imprisoned, the protection of foreign journalists, diplomats and aid workers, the immediate closure of every terrorist training camp in Afghanistan and the handing over of every terrorist and their support structure to appropriate authorities.

He also demanded that the United States be given full access to terrorist training camps so that inspections could ensure those camps were no longer operating.

These were uncompromising and non-negotiable demands. Given what had happened, they were entirely legitimate and a necessary precursor to any military action. It was a direct and emotional address, probably the best delivered by George Bush in the eight years of his presidency. He was strong but measured. He spoke with feeling and sensitivity, and yet displayed a steely determination to go after those who had murdered his fellow countrymen and women as well as the citizens of many other countries, including our own.

The Americans were meticulous in building their case. Shortly afterwards, Tom Schieffer called on me with a bundle of intelligence material which reinforced the already firmly held belief that al Qaeda was responsible for the attack. On the basis of this and other intelligence material, I was as convinced as anyone could be in the circumstances that al Qaeda was to blame and that, absent full compliance with the President's demands of 20 September, a military assault on their centre of operations in Afghanistan and, if necessary, elsewhere would be justified.

There was powerful public support for joining the Americans. The Labor Party lined up beside us. We determined that the best assistance could be provided through Special Forces and P3 surveillance aircraft to operate out of Diego Garcia, a joint British–American base in the Indian Ocean. Our naval vessels were still in the Persian Gulf helping to police the sanctions against Saddam Hussein. George Bush telephoned me on 28 September, brought me up to date with planning and thanked me for the offer of military assistance.

The time for calling the 2001 election was fast approaching. The planets had begun to align for the Coalition. The steps the Government had taken to respond to the concerns of many had begun to bear fruit. We had recovered a long way from the political nadir of the Ryan by-election, which had proved to be a St Patrick's Day massacre for the Liberal Party. All of this had occurred before the *Tampa* incident. I've dealt with this in more detail in Chapter 32.

Critics claimed otherwise, but I never argued that terrorists had deliberately sought to use the process of illegal immigration or asylum-seeking to gain entry to Australia for the purpose of carrying out terrorist activities. I did make the most obvious of points that there was always a possibility of this occurring, if Australia did not enforce a strict policy of border protection.

I called the election for 10 November, announcing this on Friday, 5 October. A few days later Richard Cheney, the US Vice-president, telephoned me to indicate that military operations would commence against the Taliban in Afghanistan within a matter of hours. I immediately announced this at a news conference, and issues relating to the war against terrorism inevitably intruded heavily into the election campaign, given our forces were involved. There were several anthrax scares, none of which proved positive, throughout the campaign and the backdrop to our electioneering was the new and still quite frightening war against terror.

The next scheduled Asia-Pacific Economic Cooperation group (APEC) meeting was for 20 and 21 October 2001 in Shanghai. In normal circumstances I might not have attended, given that an election campaign was under way. These were not normal circumstances. I knew that the issue of terrorism would be high on the agenda. It was also a big moment for China and its President, Jiang Zemin.

That APEC meeting in Shanghai in October 2001 would be the most significant international gathering to take place in China since the Communist takeover in 1949. Coming as it did just a month after the terrorist attacks in the United States, it was an important opportunity for the APEC countries to demonstrate a united effort in responding to terrorism.

There was an added personal note for me. Jiang Zemin and I had developed a close working relationship since our ice-breaking meeting in Manila, on the fringes of the 1996 APEC meeting which laid the groundwork for the productive links developed between our two countries over the ensuing five years. It would also be an opportunity for me to speak personally to George Bush concerning the war against terrorism and the military action against the Taliban in Afghanistan.

There was intense public and media interest in the APEC meeting. The meeting itself flowed smoothly. Jiang Zemin conducted the entire proceedings in English, and that included the delivery of his own leader's contribution to general debates. The Chinese impressively organised the event, and the expressions of support for the Americans were both comprehensive and convincing.

Away from the formal sessions at such gatherings there are numerous bilateral conversations. At one of these, a quite passionate Vladimir Putin spoke in scathing terms to me of the activities of Muslim separatists in Chechnya. He had strong feelings, although Russia herself could not escape some blame and responsibility for the tragic loss of life in that part of Russia.

Bush thanked me for Australia's contribution of SAS soldiers, of whom he spoke admiringly, to the military operation in Afghanistan. I am sure that he echoed the feelings of the US military. Relations between Australian and US military personnel had been close for many years, and I knew from frequent discussions with senior officers from both countries how much they enjoyed their professional cooperation.

The US-led attack in Afghanistan was both swift and successful. Within a matter of weeks the Taliban had been routed, and something of a motley collection of replacements, dominated by the Northern Alliance, assumed control in Kabul. Or, perhaps, to put it more accurately, assumed a semblance of control in Kabul.

Afghanistan, historically, has proved virtually ungovernable. It has a track record of either devouring or at the least effectively resisting invading armies. It was lost on no one that the very forces which the Americans encouraged to resist and ultimately expel the Soviet invaders in the 1980s, the Mujahedeen, went on to form the core of the al Qaeda terrorist network.

Hamid Karzai, a pro-Western figure, assumed the presidency of Afghanistan after the fall of the Taliban. An Indian-educated urbane man, Karzai was ideally suited for the international diplomatic circuit. He was the friendly, acceptable face of the new Afghanistan. Beneath the surface, however, his writ did not run all that widely in his own country. He nonetheless remains in charge nine years later and has proved more durable than his many critics allowed.

Australian troops came home from Afghanistan late in 2002. They would return several years later when, along with the forces of other countries, they re-engaged the resurgent Taliban in a protracted campaign which continues to this day. At the time of writing Australia has about 1400 personnel in that country. By September 2010, more than 20 Australians had died on active service in Afghanistan, with many more being wounded. A big increase in US forces has enabled a large NATO offensive in Helmand Province, which has made progress.

The continued military operation in Afghanistan presented yet again the awful dilemma of Western societies being engaged in such missions. Unless those operations are quick, decisive and overwhelmingly successful, domestic political support for them ultimately ebbs away and can, in certain circumstances, turn into toxic opposition. That was the lesson of Vietnam.

Australia's commitment in Afghanistan should continue to receive bipartisan support. The cause is just. It is in this country's national interest that Afghanistan never again becomes a terrorist haven.

Late 2001 and early 2002 represented the high-water mark of international support for George Bush and the United States in its response to the attacks of September 2001, and its ongoing war against terrorism. As the United States and some of its allies, including Australia, turned their attention to Iraq, the international alliance began to fragment. This is dealt with in later chapters.

My first personal contact with George Bush could barely have occurred against the background of more remarkable circumstances.

I was not to know it when I arrived in Washington on Saturday, 8 September, but the epoch-changing events of three days later were to take the alliance to new levels of intimacy. The personal relationship between the American President and me would become the closest of any between the respective heads of government of the two countries.

32

MV *TAMPA*

On Sunday, 26 August 2001, MV *Tampa* suddenly appeared on the horizon of Australian politics. What transpired over the following few days dramatically recast the debate in Australia about asylum-seekers, and the word *Tampa* became a permanent part of the Australian political lexicon.

The *Tampa* was a Norwegian-registered and flagged vessel. On that Sunday, en route from Fremantle to Singapore, the *Tampa* received an urgent request from Australian Search and Rescue, alerting it to a vessel in distress. In response, the *Tampa* diverted its course and rescued 434 potential unauthorised arrivals in international waters, from a fishing boat that had set off from Indonesia and had an Indonesian crew.

Before describing the remarkable developments which followed, some context is needed to depict accurately the mood of the Australian people at the time.

Australia is one of only about 20 countries which participate in United Nations High Commission for Refugees (UNHCR) refugee resettlement programs on an annual basis. In 2008 Australia accepted the second-largest number of refugees for resettlement in the world, taking 6500, after 56,750 by the USA. To preserve perspective, it should be borne in mind that this resettlement program only places a small proportion of the world's refugees. The great bulk of them remain in the neighbouring countries to which they have fled. This means that a heavy burden is placed on those neighbouring countries, so many of which are desperately poor. At least, however, Australia does more than many other developed countries to help relieve the refugee problem.

Australia has a long and compassionate record in accepting refugees. In the 1970s, under the Fraser Government, this country, on a per capita basis, took more Indo-Chinese refugees than any other nation on Earth. Most of them had fled the brutal Communist regime in Vietnam, which had emerged victorious from the long war in that country. Many Australians felt that we had a moral obligation to take a large number of Vietnamese refugees, because Australians had fought beside their South Vietnamese allies in the war against the Communist Vietcong. Taking the Vietnamese 'boat people', as they were to be called, was seen as something of a special case. Most of them were processed in regional holding centres offshore.

Unauthorised boat arrivals occurred spasmodically, but not at a rate which caused any real public concern. Between 1981 and 1988 no arrivals were recorded. The number began to rise again in the early '90s, but not significantly. There was a huge jump in 1999 to 3721 from just 200 in 1998. In 1992 the Keating Government had introduced mandatory detention. This followed a three-year period in which there had been a kick-up in arrivals, but nothing like the surge some years later. Initially mandatory detention covered only unauthorised arrivals. In 1994 it was extended to include all non-citizens who did not hold a valid visa. It is worth noting that most of the people in immigration detention centres in Australia during the past two decades have been visa overstayers, unauthorised air arrivals and those whose visas had been cancelled. The one exception to this was the spike which occurred between 1999 and 2002 in the number of boat arrivals. It was this marked increase in unauthorised boat arrivals which lifted public anxiety so sharply.

The figures tell a clear story. The number rose quite suddenly to 3721 in 1999, remained high at 2939 in 2000 and almost doubled to 5516 in 2001. The dramatic rise in 2001 put the issue on the front pages. Every day, so it seemed, another boat had arrived. The sheer size of our coastline led Australians to feel particularly vulnerable to the unchecked arrival of scores of boats. Visa-holders who came by air had to present valid documentation to arrive here in the first place; even if they overstayed they were not viewed in the same light as people who came here in the first instance without documentation. That is why the alarm about the rise in the number of unauthorised boat arrivals was understandable.

By July and August 2001, there was genuine concern in the Australian community about the flow of asylum-seekers. There was a growing feeling that Australia had lost control of its borders. No matter how logical the arguments the Government had employed to date might have been, there was intensifying public unease. In the process, public support for orthodox immigration and an orderly humanitarian refugee program began to erode. This was apparent to me from extensive talkback radio sessions, comments from MPs and random encounters with members of the public. Politicians are rightly exhorted to 'keep in touch' — no MP doing that would have missed the strength of community feeling.

In rescuing those 434 people, the master of the *Tampa* acted in accordance with long-established protocols designed to ensure the rescue of people in distress on the high seas.

After picking them up, at the direction of the Indonesian search and rescue authorities, the *Tampa* proceeded towards the Indonesian port of Merak, where the ship had been granted approval to dock. Likewise, the people rescued had received approval to disembark at the same port. Again the *Tampa* was acting in accordance with established maritime protocols.

The vessel carrying the 434 people had sailed from an Indonesian port. It was thus appropriate, under international law and practice, for the people rescued at sea to be returned to the country where they had originally embarked on their now sunken vessel.

It was at this point that events unexpectedly changed, and produced the extraordinary situation which led to the boarding of the *Tampa* by Australian soldiers. Realising that they were bound for Indonesia, those rescued by the *Tampa* applied duress to the ship's master, and forced him to completely alter course and head for Christmas Island.

The *Tampa* stood off Christmas Island, outside Australian territorial waters. The master of the ship was told by Immigration Department officials that he did not have permission to enter Australian waters. It was obvious that the asylum-seekers wanted to get to Australia and that the way to do that was to be taken to Christmas Island. The Government was determined that this should not occur. If this mutiny were allowed to succeed, the impression would be created that Australia was a soft touch, and people-smugglers would take careful note. Under international law those rescued should be returned to Indonesia. To make our position perfectly clear, in two separate telephone conversations Alexander Downer warned his Norwegian counterpart that the ship had no permission to enter Australian waters. In the second conversation he informed the Norwegian Foreign Minister that, if necessary, the Australian military would be used to prevent the *Tampa* violating Australian waters.

Separately, I telephoned the Norwegian Prime Minister, Mr Jens Stoltenberg, to reinforce our concern about what was occurring. He absolved himself and his Government of any responsibility, despite the fact that it was a Norwegian-registered and -flagged vessel with a Norwegian captain. He said care for those rescued at sea was entirely the responsibility of the Australian Government.

Initially the ship's captain, Arne Rinnan, agreed that he would not bring the vessel into Australian waters if medical assistance for necessitous cases was provided. We told him then, as we had previously, that Australian authorities would be able to provide medical assistance, either through use of an Australian helicopter or, if the ship's captain preferred, by permitting the lifeboat of the *Tampa* to pick up medical supplies and assistance from Christmas Island. The lifeboat was an enclosed one and was internationally certified.

The captain then indicated that he would accept the Australian offer. While the *Tampa* was standing off Christmas Island, Australian authorities conducted distance medical examinations (by radio) and concluded that there was no medical emergency on board requiring evacuation. At that stage no one had presented as a medical emergency.

Suddenly, on the morning of 29 August, the ship's captain relayed a high-priority medical distress call declaring he would proceed to Christmas Island if medical assistance were not forthcoming by 1500 hours EST. This was completely contrary to both what he had previously said, and the basis of the understanding the Australian authorities thought they had concluded with him.

Captain Rinnan was reminded of the previous advice that there was no basis for a distress call and that, in any event, the authorities were working with all possible speed to get medical supplies and a doctor to the vessel. He was again told that he did not have authority to enter Australian waters.

Despite this, the *Tampa* shortly afterwards entered the 12-nautical-mile limit of Australian territorial waters. He was then informed that all necessary steps would be taken to maintain the integrity of our borders, including territorial waters.

As a consequence of Captain Rinnan's action, the Chief of the Defence Force was authorised to order Defence personnel to board and secure the vessel, now in Australian territorial waters. At approximately 12.45 pm EST, on 29 August, the ship was secured by a unit of the Special Air Service (SAS) under the command of Lieutenant Colonel Gus Gilmore.

After the SAS had secured the vessel, Captain Rinnan provided advice which contradicted his earlier explanation for seeking to enter Australian territorial waters. His position now was that he decided to enter Australian territorial waters because a spokesman for the survivors of the Indonesian vessel had indicated that the survivors would begin jumping overboard if medical assistance was not provided quickly.

The preliminary assessment provided by the Australian Defence Force doctor (who, along with a paramedic, had gone on board with the SAS) indicated that nobody had presented as being in need of urgent medical assistance as would require their removal to the Australian mainland or to Christmas Island. Medical examinations of the asylum-seekers on board the *Tampa* continued.

Later that same day I reported to parliament on what had happened. I emphasised that our advice was that Australia was under no legal obligation to accept responsibility for the survivors of the Indonesian vessel. This was a point I had made in my discussion with the Norwegian Prime Minister, earlier in the day.

The Government's view was that the *Tampa* should resume its original voyage for the Indonesian port of Merak. We had put this to both the Norwegian Government as well as the company which owned the vessel. Neither was the least bit helpful. Both imagined that my Government would cave in to the pressure applied by the asylum-seekers through the duress they had brought to bear on Captain Rinnan.

The situation was to turn even more difficult. The Indonesian Government became quite uncooperative. President Megawati declined to take my telephone calls to discuss the matter. It was obvious that, irrespective of international legal niceties, Indonesia saw this as Australia's problem. The Indonesians were now in no mood to receive the asylum-seekers back.

My critics made much of the fact that President Megawati refused to speak to me. Given the Javanese cultural aversion to confrontation, her refusal to pick up the telephone was hardly surprising. She wanted to avoid saying no. By refusing to take my telephone call, she communicated her position without the embarrassment of a personal conversation.

Speaking to parliament, I said:

> This is a very difficult — in fact, for Australia, I think — unprecedented situation. Nobody is lacking in compassion for

genuine refugees. Nobody pretends for a moment that the circumstances from which many people flee are not very distressing. But, equally, it has to be said that, in the last 20 years, no country has been more generous to refugees than Australia. After the Indo-Chinese events of the 1970s, this country took, on a per capita basis, more Indo-Chinese refugees than any country on Earth.

We have continued to be a warm, generous recipient of refugees, but we have become increasingly concerned about the increasing flow of people into this country. Every nation has the right to effectively control its borders and to decide who comes here and under what circumstances, and Australia has no intention of surrendering or compromising that right. We have taken this action in furtherance of that view. It remains our very strong determination not to allow this vessel or its occupants, save and except humanitarian circumstances clearly demonstrated, to land in Australia, and we will take whatever action is needed — within the law, of course — to prevent that occurring.

As well as thanking the men of the SAS, I emphasised our position in relation to humanitarian medical assistance. I made it plain that the vessel returning to international waters would in no way affect our willingness, or capacity, to provide whatever humanitarian medical assistance was needed, including the transport of necessitous cases to the mainland or to Christmas Island. The Norwegians were not to be allowed to use medical emergencies as an excuse to remain in Australian waters.

What I said to parliament summarised my attitude on asylum-seeker policy. Although the circumstances of the *Tampa* had not been foreseen it became, almost immediately, a powerful symbol of our determination to regain control over the flow of people into Australia.

It was apparent after a short period of time that the Australian people strongly backed the stand my Government had taken. My actions on the *Tampa* were instinctive, driven both by application of international law and the simple principle that every nation has a right to protect its borders and decide who to admit as immigrants or refugees.

Much has been made of the declaration of mine at the Coalition's policy launch on 28 October 2001 when I said, 'We'll decide who comes to this country and the circumstances in which they come.' It was a spontaneous paraphrase of what I had told parliament. It resonated with Australians because it said directly and simply what they felt.

Some 15 minutes before I made my statement to the house, I had spoken to Kim Beazley, the Opposition leader. His reaction was cautious but supportive. He responded immediately to my statement and endorsed what the Government had done. On reflection, it would not have been credible for him to have done otherwise. He had been a member of the Keating Government which had introduced mandatory detention in 1992. Mandatory detention was part of a broader framework of policies designed to protect our borders from illegal immigration.

Later that day the Attorney General advised me that, for more abundant caution, a special Border Protection Bill should be put through parliament as soon as possible, placing beyond any argument the legal authority of what the Government had done regarding the *Tampa*. The bill, when enacted, would have express operation from 9 am on 29 August 2001, the morning the *Tampa*'s captain had called us.

It was framed broadly, sought to have effect notwithstanding any other laws to the contrary, and was not specific to the *Tampa*. The reason for the bill not being restricted to the *Tampa* was to ensure that the legislation would apply to any future situations similar to that of the *Tampa*. It was this provision which was subsequently used, more than any other, to justify the action of the Labor Party and the Democrats in blocking the legislation in the Senate.

I introduced the Border Protection Bill into parliament on the evening of 29 August, having handed a copy of it to Kim Beazley in my office shortly before dinner. It was obvious when I gave him the bill, plus a quick explanation, that he was uncomfortable. He had to make a decision as to whether or not to back it. His initial reaction was not encouraging.

I do not know what internal Labor Party processes occurred between my handing him a copy of the bill in my office, and his replying to my second-reading speech that evening. The Labor Party, whilst agreeing to urgent debate and therefore a vote on the bill, came down decisively against it.

There had been a dramatic change in Kim Beazley's rhetoric. In the afternoon he had been in strong bipartisan support, but later that evening he trenchantly attacked not only the substance of the bill but also the motives of the Government. He said that we were trying to use the bill and, therefore, the issue, as a political wedge. He said it was politically motivated. His complaint of substance was that the bill itself had sweeping provisions which could apply to any circumstance.

Beazley displayed poor judgement in his response to this bill. We faced an unprecedented situation. Beazley must have known this. There was mounting public anger about illegal immigration, and very strong support for the Government's action in relation to the *Tampa*. Beazley had realised this in giving endorsement earlier in the day.

Yet within the space of a few hours his tone had changed. He reacted in a completely different fashion in his response to the Border Protection Bill. Given that the bill sought to reinforce the legality of what had been done earlier in the day, and given also that Beazley said then that it was completely proper to use the SAS to board the *Tampa*, his response to the Border Protection Bill was inexplicable.

In the debate he said:

> What is going on here is a desperate effort, of a piece with efforts to reintroduce native title, with efforts to do native title legislation, with efforts to again put forward industrial relations legislation, all of it in the last couple of weeks of this parliament, to try to drive wedge politics and to play politics with the lives of Australians. Well, I tell you, Mr Prime Minister: we will not be in it. Whatever particular political advantage you think it gives you, we will not be in it. In the circumstances in which you have apparently made a series of errors, given the advice that has been given to you, we are prepared to consider, if it is necessary, a legislative solution to the *Tampa* problem in particular. What we are not prepared to consider for one minute is a legislative solution which claims to alter the regime that applies now, entirely on the basis of three hours' consideration in this parliament this night. This is extraordinary and we will not be going along with it.[1]

It was a remarkable turnaround. His references to native title and industrial relations represented political hysteria. We had not brought about the *Tampa* crisis. A week earlier nobody in federal parliament had heard of the *Tampa*. The issue had come like a bolt from the blue, and the Government had had to deal with it quickly and effectively.

On the face of it, the legislation was far-reaching. What we needed, however, was a piece of legislation that did give us the capacity to deal with a *Tampa*-type situation again if needed. If in fact, as Beazley had said earlier in the day, our action in relation to the *Tampa* was completely proper, then surely the opposition could have no valid objection to future action of that kind also being put beyond legal argument.

Clearly Beazley faced internal pressure on the issue. There were many in his party unhappy with the bipartisan support he had given on the *Tampa* despite the strength of public feeling. As a compensation for this, he decided to oppose the Border Protection Bill. It was typical of how he often ended up in a compromised position. He endeavoured to walk both sides of the street on issues when the Australian people clearly demanded direct, unconditional behaviour from their government. The community felt that Australia was losing control of its immigration policy, and firm action was needed to end this.

In response to Beazley's objections to the Border Protection Bill, I offered the insertion of a sunset clause of only six months. He rejected this as a compromise, further evidence of the internal pressure being applied to him. The bill passed all stages in the House of Representatives that evening, but was defeated in the Senate.

Almost immediately after the boarding of the *Tampa* by the SAS, legal action had been commenced by the Victorian Council for Civil Liberties and others seeking orders from the Federal Court that a writ of habeas corpus be issued on the grounds that the asylum-seekers had been unlawfully detained on the *Tampa*. On 11 September, Mr Justice North decided in favour of the Council for Civil Liberties in relation to the claimed unlawful detention. He ordered that the asylum-seekers be brought to mainland Australia. That is what they had wanted all along.

The Commonwealth appealed against North's decision. On 17 September the Full Bench of the Federal Court overruled North's decision and found that the asylum-seekers had not been illegally detained. They would not have to be brought to the mainland.

Fresh legislation then went through parliament, addressing issues left outstanding as a result of the court decision and some other issues related to the boarding of the *Tampa*. By then they were incidental.

The pressing problem had become what to do with the *Tampa* asylum-seekers. If they were processed through the normal mandatory detention system, that would involve them coming to the mainland, thus defeating the original purpose of the whole exercise. The Government wanted to deter people from setting out for Australia in the first place and that required sending a message that not even the processing of their refugee claims would occur in Australia. Once it became clear that Indonesia would not take any of them, a search commenced for other destinations.

A nearby location was logical, and Alexander Downer suggested Nauru. The UN would not agree to East Timor. We agreed that Peter Reith should talk to Nauru's President, Rene Harris, because of earlier contact in a previous portfolio. Reith went there immediately and within a few days had negotiated an agreement to establish an offshore processing facility on Nauru. Thus was born the Pacific Solution.

Meanwhile, Downer had also raised the issue with Simon Murdoch, the New Zealand High Commissioner in Canberra. Murdoch was a highly respected New Zealand bureaucrat who had held all the senior positions. He was likable, intelligent and strongly committed to the Trans-Tasman relationship. He was the most helpful New Zealand interlocutor I came across in my time as Prime Minister.

Murdoch spoke to Helen Clark and, to our considerable relief, she agreed that New Zealand would take 150 of the 434 asylum-seekers. This was quite a breakthrough. I rang Helen Clark to finalise the agreement and expressed my gratitude to her. Here was an example of the pragmatism of our relationship. On one interpretation Helen Clark would have been a fierce critic of what the Australian Government had done. She was an internationalist, and there were no shortage of people denouncing my Government's actions as being contrary to the spirit of what the United Nations stood for on refugees.

On the other hand, she saw the value of assisting her Anzac partner. It was a gesture from her that I would not forget. It burnished New Zealand's credentials as a humanitarian country. Also New Zealand, by reasons of geography, was never likely to become a target for people-smuggling.

HMAS *Manoora*, with appropriate military personnel, undertook the delicate transfer of the asylum-seekers from the *Tampa* to Nauru. Understandably they strongly, and in some cases violently, resisted being taken off the *Tampa*. This all occurred in the glare of heavy media coverage, much of which sought to show Australia's actions in the worst possible light.

Australia's handling of the *Tampa* was heavily criticised by the United Nations and human rights organisations. Despite the international hand-wringing, more careful observers in other countries, facing even more daunting problems with illegal immigration, thought otherwise of our stance.

I repeatedly said that for every asylum-seeker who had their refugee claim accepted, one less person who had waited patiently in a refugee camp could be admitted to Australia. Every one of the 12,000 places allocated annually in our humanitarian program taken by an asylum-seeker validly winning acceptance meant someone else was disappointed. I was not heartless towards the asylum-seekers, but there was a limit to how many refugees Australia could take. My critics gave little thought to the millions of people in refugee camps all around the world hoping their turn would come. Those critics bristled at my use of the term 'queue-jumper', but I persisted because it described, simply and accurately, what was at stake.

Deterrence had to be the core of any effective response to the surge of asylum-seekers. It had to be made crystal clear that asylum-seekers would find it hard to reach Australia, so there was no point in trying in the first place. Offshore processing in Nauru as well as Manus in Papua New Guinea was a key component, but it was reinforced by legislation, in September, which gave the minister power by regulation to excise offshore territories from our migration zone. Given the way in which various islands dotted the northern approaches to Australia, this was an effective way of intercepting asylum-seekers before they reached the mainland. Initial excisions were Christmas Island, Ashmore Island, Cartier Islands and then Cocos Islands. Most boat people arrived at these islands and, by reason of the excisions, were deemed to be outside Australia's refugee protection system. They could be taken to Nauru or Manus for processing.

The final component was the use of naval vessels and Orion aircraft, under the codename Operation Relex, to conduct surveillance and interception operations in the waters between Australia and Indonesia. The navy would meet boats on the high seas and ask them to turn around. If a boat refused, then when it reached Australia's contiguous zone (the water adjacent to our territorial waters) the navy was legally able to board a boat and return it to international waters. Part of the remit to the navy was to ensure that boats returned to the high seas were seaworthy. Also starting in September, this policy really worked, partly because of the tacit cooperation of Indonesian authorities in allowing the boats back. This followed a careful briefing from a special ADF mission to Jakarta. Wisely, little was said about Indonesia's role.

The processing of claims for refugee status on Nauru and Manus was handled by the International Organisation for Migration, at arm's length from the Government. In the meantime, we would provide proper shelter, clothing, food and medical attention for the asylum-seekers. In many respects the physical conditions in these facilities were superior to conditions in refugee camps in other parts of the world.

By the end of November asylum-seekers had stopped coming to Australia. According to figures tabled in the Senate on 27 May 2009 by the Secretary of the Department of Immigration and Citizenship, the number of unauthorised arrivals by sea had fallen from 5516 in 2001 to precisely one in 2002. It was a stunning turnaround.

These new measures, controversial and tough in the eyes of many, had been a resounding success. We had regained control over our border protection processes. Restoration of confidence in Australia's migration program had begun, and the Australian people were in full support of our actions.

The Rudd Government changed our policy by abandoning the Pacific Solution and softening the visa regime. Australia has again become an attractive target for people-smugglers. Kevin Rudd repeatedly said in his defence that a high percentage of the people on the *Tampa* ultimately made it to Australia when their refugee status was established. This missed the point entirely. The core of our policy was that we stopped the boats coming. They only returned because the Rudd Government weakened the policy.

My involvement in what became known as the Children Overboard Affair began on Sunday, 7 October when, attending a campaign event in Danna Vale's electorate of Hughes, in the Sutherland shire of Sydney, I took a phone call from Philip Ruddock, the Immigration Minister. He told me that the secretary of his department, who was a member of the People Smuggling Taskforce (which comprised senior officials from all relevant agencies and was chaired by Jane Halton, deputy secretary of the Department of Prime Minister and Cabinet [PM&C]), had informed him that during a naval interception by HMAS *Adelaide* of a vessel known as SIEV IV, asylum-seekers had thrown children overboard as part of their attempts to stop the vessel being sent back to Indonesia. I had no reason to doubt this advice. Ruddock was a reliable minister. That evening I read a report from the Taskforce, dated the same day, which had been faxed to my Kirribilli House study. In part it read: 'This [the naval interception] has been met with attempts to disable the vessel, passengers jumping into the sea and passengers throwing their children into the sea.'[2] Halton later told a PM&C inquiry that the paper sent to me, which included specific reference to 'children thrown overboard', had been cleared by every member of the taskforce before being sent. Earlier that day and after being given the advice, both Ruddock (before he had informed me) and I had spoken to the media about the incident, criticising the behaviour of the asylum-seekers.

The following day, Monday, I repeated my comments but more strongly, on both the Alan Jones and Neil Mitchell radio programs. On the latter one I said, 'It's not within my frame of comprehension that people who are genuine refugees would throw their children into the seas.'

Both Philip Ruddock and the Defence Minister, Peter Reith, also made comments that day. Reith said that there was a video of the incident which showed that children had been thrown overboard. I continued my comments during interviews on 9 October.

On 10 October, during a news conference at Ballarat, I was closely questioned regarding evidence to support the original claim. After explaining again how I had come by the advice, I said that I would seek more information. I spoke to Reith, who told me that he had photos supporting the claim. They were released that day and showed children in the water, with sailors apparently rescuing them. Reith said that there was a video, but that it was very grainy.

I then dropped the issue, not even referring to it during my campaign launch speech in Sydney on 28 October.

Children overboard effectively disappeared from the election campaign until Wednesday, 7 November, only three days before the election. That day the *Australian* carried a story quoting unnamed Christmas Islanders stating that 'naval officers' told them that the story of children being thrown overboard, during the interception by HMAS *Adelaide*, was false.

Concerned by this story, I spoke to Reith later in the day and discussed the desirability of releasing the video, irrespective of what it might show. I had not seen the video. I knew that if I did not release it, the Government would be accused of a cover-up. We agreed that one of Reith's staff, Mike Scrafton, would go to Naval Command in Sydney, which had a copy of the video, and view it. Scrafton was then to speak to me about its contents.

That night, Wednesday, 7 November, I had dinner at the Lodge with my wife and senior advisors in preparation for my final press club address the following day. The others present were Arthur Sinodinos, Tony Nutt, Paul McClintock and Tony O'Leary. I had two telephone conversations with

Scrafton that evening. The first, and lengthier one, consisted of his describing to me what was in the video. He said it was inconclusive, although it did not clearly show children being thrown overboard. After speaking to my staff and also Reith, I rang Scrafton back with instructions for the video to be released early the next day.

I received several questions at the press club on the issue. In responding, I carefully explained the circumstances which had lead to the original statements. I quoted an Office of National Assessments (ONA) report, thinking at the time that it was an independent corroborative source. That report, ONA Report 226/2001, provided to ministers, indicated that 'HMAS *Adelaide* has intercepted a boat with 187 Iraqis, including children, near Christmas Island, and escorted it to international waters where it was scuppered by its passengers ... asylum seekers wearing lifejackets jumped into the sea and children were thrown in with them. Such tactics have previously been used elsewhere, for example, "on boats intercepted by the Italian navy".'[3]

The media, especially the ABC, pursued the issue until election eve. I had two appearances on *Lateline* on 8 November, the second caused by the fact that the chief of the navy, Vice Admiral David Shackleton, had erroneously, earlier in the day, said that the navy had not advised the Government that a group of asylum-seekers threw children overboard.

Although the advice was later established as incorrect, there was no argument that the navy had originally provided that advice. Shackleton, later that day, corrected his statement. So I sought a second interview on the program.

In an unrelated incident earlier that same day, there was an explosion on another vessel carrying asylum-seekers, with the loss of two lives.

At no time before the election did I receive advice from Reith, my department or anyone else that the original information alleging that children had been thrown overboard was wrong.

Kim Jones, then Director General of ONA, advised me on 12 November, two days after the election, that ONA did not have independent information about the incident. Given the relationship of ONA to the Government, ministers were entitled to think otherwise, and that ONA's analysis had been self-generated.

Doug Kean, head of the Strategic Analysis Branch at ONA, would later tell an inquiry that ONA had relied on media reports of the issue and had placed a high level of credibility on the reports because they reflected statements of ministers. ONA had told my foreign affairs advisor, Miles Jordana, on 7 November that it was not aware of the source on which ONA had relied in compiling the report, and that it might, in part, be based on statements made by ministers. That information was not passed to me at the time.

After the election, Defence conducted an internal inquiry under the leadership of Major General Powell. At my request, Max Moore-Wilton commissioned Jenny Bryant of the Department of Prime Minister and Cabinet to conduct an inquiry as well. Both inquiries reported in January to the effect that children had not been thrown overboard on 7 October, and that the original advice saying they were had been wrong.

These reports indicated that as early as 11 October, confirmation that children had not been thrown overboard began to be passed through the Defence chain of command. There was a breakdown of communication between the Defence Department and not only its minister, Peter Reith, but also the Chief of the Defence Force, Admiral Chris Barrie, who well into February 2002 held to the position that he had not been presented with evidence to justify an alteration of the original advice that children had been thrown overboard.

It emerged that the photos to which Reith had referred, and which were published on 11 October, had been taken on 8 October, the day after the alleged throwing overboard incident. The vessel had capsized that day and the photos were of children in the water after the capsizing.

Unsurprisingly, the Labor Party pursued the issue in the Senate. The most dramatic evidence, both before the Senate Estimates Committee and a special Senate inquiry, came from Air Marshal Angus Houston, later Chief of the Defence Force. He told both hearings that as acting CDF — and on 7 November 2001 — he had telephoned Peter Reith and told him that in his view, based on an examination of the relevant material, children had not been thrown overboard, and that the original advice to ministers had been wrong. This was contrary to the view which Barrie, the CDF himself, had maintained to Reith. Interviewed for this book, Reith told me that he was not going to change his position on the children overboard story unless advised by the CDF that it was wrong. This guided Reith's approach throughout. In the discussion between Reith and Houston, it was agreed that the issue would be raised between Houston and Barrie on the latter's return to Australia within a few days — the weekend of the election.

Reith did not tell me of Angus Houston's telephone call before the election. I did not know of it until shortly before Houston was to give evidence before Senate Estimates in February 2002. He had rung Max Moore-Wilton to warn him of what he was about to say and Moore-Wilton had relayed this information to me.

The initial reaction of Admiral Barrie, in his testimony to Senate Estimates, was to maintain his original position that children had been thrown overboard.

A short time later, presumably after much internal discussion within Defence, Barrie shifted his position and also acknowledged that the original advice to ministers had been wrong. On 27 February 2002, at a news conference Admiral Barrie said, 'After speaking at considerable length on Sunday with Commander Banks, the commanding officer of HMAS *Adelaide*, I have now reached the conclusion that there is no evidence to support the claim that children were thrown overboard.'[4]

Many of the Government's critics speculated that Angus Houston had done his career prospects great damage with what proved to be embarrassing evidence for the Government before the Senate inquiry. I personally assured him, shortly afterwards, that this would not be the case. My Government appointed Angus Houston as Chief of the Defence Force with effect from 4 July 2005, following the retirement of General Peter Cosgrove.

Evidence before the Senate inquiry indicated that multiple doubts had arisen quite early inside Defence about the original story, and that within a short time senior officers in the uniform branch believed the story to be wrong. Yet at no stage did this crystallise into countermanding advice to the minister that children had not been thrown overboard until Angus Houston's call to Reith on 7 November 2001. Given that the statements by Ruddock, Reith and me early in October were based on advice from the People Smuggling Taskforce, and that the CDF maintained his original position until late in February 2002, Reith's determination not to change his position whilst the CDF held to his, although heavily criticised as politically convenient, was quite defensible.

The Secretary of the Defence Department, Allan Hawke, appeared to play a particularly passive role, especially as the CDF's overwhelming preoccupation then was Australia's military deployment in Afghanistan. It is easy to sympathise with Barrie's view that at the time children overboard was small beer. In Paul Kelly's book *The March of Patriots*, Hawke acknowledges that he was told of the mistake with the photographs on 11 October, but did not raise it with Reith.

In the course of the Senate inquiry, evidence revealed poor lines of communication, not only within sections of the Defence bureaucracy, but also and crucially, between Defence public relations and the minister's office. The erroneous belief that the photographs published on 11 October were of children having been thrown overboard put the People Smuggling Taskforce off the scent of further investigation, at precisely the time when such further investigation would have established that the original advice was wrong. Jane Halton, head of the People Smuggling Taskforce, now Secretary of the Health Department, gave evidence to this effect.

Between 10 October and 7 November 2001, I gave no thought to the children-overboard issue. I did not mention it in any speech or interview. When it was revived by the *Australian* story on 7 November, my total preoccupation was to avoid any suggestion of a cover-up by ensuring that the navy video was released, and whilst repeating the basis of my first comments in early October 2001, I took care to go no further. It was three days before the election. I had not treated children overboard as a major campaign issue, and it was unrealistic that I should have then ordered an inquiry into the affair.

Almost three years later, and on the eve of the 2004 election, Scrafton, by then employed by the Victorian Labor Government, went public with an allegation that during his telephone discussions with me on the night of 7 November he had advised that the original claims were wrong and that children had not been thrown overboard.

I strongly disputed this. The opposition majority in the Senate reconvened an inquiry in the hope of embarrassing me and the Government. Scrafton's evidence was undermined when he claimed to have had three conversations with me that evening. The Lodge telephone records were produced, which showed only two calls: one had been at 8.41 pm, lasting 9.36 minutes, and the other at 10.12 pm, lasting just 51 seconds. This was consistent with my recollection.

By February 2002, after it had been established that the advice to ministers that children had been thrown overboard was erroneous, the original claim, based on that erroneous advice, had been elevated — in the view of many — to being the major reason why the Coalition had won the 2001 election. In the eyes of electoral conspiracy theorists such as Labor's

John Faulkner, I had stolen the election through the making of the original allegations.

That was palpably absurd. The children overboard allegations played a minor role in the election campaign. They were dwarfed by the broader and defining issue of border protection. I doubt that the children overboard allegations would have shifted a single vote.

Those who voted for the Coalition due to its strong and successful border protection policies did so because we had stopped the boats coming — not because of the children overboard allegations.

Judging by the published opinion polls, the additional surge for the Liberal and National parties because of their border protection policy came hard on the heels of the *Tampa* having been turned back. That was the decisive action which shifted community perceptions.

The poll lift for the Government over border protection had begun to subside slightly by the time the children-overboard saga commenced. The *Tampa* was turned back on 29 August, but the issue did not arise until the end of the first week in October. According to Newspoll, the Coalition's peak lead, in the run-up to the election, was immediately before children overboard emerged. This contests the claims of those who assert that the incident was politically significant.

Giving the children-overboard issue prime status as the explanation for Labor's defeat, retrospectively of course, satisfied the hunger of Labor Party apparatchiks to have a plausible 'we wuz robbed' excuse to explain away the ALP's third successive election defeat.

33

THE BALI ATTACK

Any lingering thought that Australia was different, and the lucky country could escape the foul embrace of terrorism, was shattered on Saturday evening, 12 October 2002, when 88 Australians died and scores more were horribly burned and injured as two bombs planted by terrorists exploded in and adjacent to Paddy's Bar and the Sari Club, at Kuta Beach, Bali. That night the last vestiges of Australian innocence were blown away. It was the largest loss of Australian lives sustained abroad in a single peacetime incident. Inspired by Jema'ah Islamiya (JI), an Indonesian affiliate of al Qaeda, the attack was a wanton act of Islamic extremism designed to kill Westerners, especially but not only Australians.

The Bali attack was a reminder that the war against terrorism had to go on in an uncompromising and unconditional fashion. Any other course of action would be folly. Retreat would not purchase immunity from attack. That had been the experience of the past year; it had been the experience of mankind through history. It is impossible to escape the reach of terrorism by imagining that if you roll yourself into a little ball you will not be noticed, because terrorism is not dispensed according to some hierarchy of disdain; it is dispensed in an indiscriminate, evil, hateful fashion.

On the Sunday evening, at a meeting of senior advisors I had convened at the Lodge, Dennis Richardson, Director General of ASIO, in his typically blunt style, said, 'Something like this is, by definition, a failure of intelligence.' Dennis was being too hard on himself, and his and other agencies. Despite some determined, and on occasions quite disreputable attempts, of the Labor Party to establish the contrary, several inquiries came up with the same conclusion. There was no specific warning of the attack. There had been no failure of intelligence.

Nor was there to be any failure of will by the AFP, ASIO and other agencies; they bent every effort, in cooperation with their Indonesian counterparts, to bring to justice those responsible for the attack. It was in many respects the AFP's finest hour on my watch. The forensic and other help given to the Indonesians was outstanding and quite crucial in tracking down the culprits.

The attack had been designed to cause maximum carnage. Just after 11 pm on 12 October, a bomb hidden in a backpack exploded inside Paddy's Bar. It was almost certain that the person carrying the backpack was a suicide bomber. He died from the explosion. Just 10 to 15 seconds later a much more powerful bomb, close to 1000kg, which had been placed inside a white Mitsubishi van parked in front of the nearby Sari Club, was detonated by remote control. The explosion inside Paddy's Bar had attracted people to the Sari Club entrance, which increased the death and injury from the second blast. There was a third bomb, which went off in front of the US Consulate, causing minor injuries to one person.

I first learned of the attack early Sunday morning when I was telephoned by Malcolm Hazell, one of my senior advisors. The information then was sketchy, with confirmed deaths being only a few. The magnitude of the tragedy was to become increasingly apparent as the day wore on. Later in the morning I spoke to Ric Smith, a veteran diplomat, Australia's ambassador to Indonesia. He in turn was receiving his information from Ross Tysoe, our consul in Bali, who, literally, had been on the streets helping victims within minutes of the attack.

The Federal Police Commissioner, Mick Keelty, had already rung his Indonesian counterpart, General Da'i Bachtiar, to offer Australian police help in hunting down the killers. Fortuitously, the man put in charge of the Indonesian investigation, General Pastika, and Mick Keelty were friends, having met in 1993 at a police management course in Canberra. This facilitated the smooth cooperation between the police forces of the two nations. The AFP man put in charge of the Australian contingent quickly despatched to Bali was Graham Ashton, who had been AFP liaison officer in Jakarta between 1995 and 1997. He spoke Bahasa (Indonesian) and knew many senior Indonesian police extremely well.

I authorised the despatch to Bali of all available C-130 transport aircraft. Loaded with medical personnel and supplies, they were on their way within hours of the attack. In the 37 hours immediately after the attack, the RAAF would complete the total evacuation of 66 Australians and others to various hospitals in Australia. The most serious burns victims were taken to Royal Perth Hospital. In the weeks which followed, Dr Fiona Wood, later Australian of the Year, would become a household name for the work that she and her team at the Royal Perth burns unit did for the worst burns victims. Under the guidance of its administrator Dr Len Notaras, the Royal Darwin Hospital did an amazing job acting as both a treating hospital and clearing point for injured victims brought to Australia.

This rescue operation, which unquestionably saved many lives, as the Bali hospital system could not have coped with such an overwhelming emergency, was a tribute to Australian teamwork and pragmatic capacity to get something done in a hurry, when that was required. Almost all of the evacuation work was carried out by the men and women of the RAAF, assisted by army medical staff as well as civilians. Under the codename 'Operation Bali Assist', it was the largest Australian aero medical evacuation since the war in Vietnam. Later I went to Richmond Air Base, near Sydney, to personally thank the RAAF people for what they had done. Amongst many on that day, I met a new RAAF recruit who spoke with pride of how she and a group captain had worked side by side to sustain and comfort a badly injured person on the journey back to Australia. That was typical of the efforts of scores of military personnel and civilians. In its official report on the evacuation, published in the *Medical Journal of Australia* in December 2002, the ADF noted, 'The patients were mostly young, quiet and stoical. There were no complaints or unreasonable demands; on the contrary, most were concerned for their mates.'[1]

Just after 1 pm I spoke to President Megawati of Indonesia. We agreed on total cooperation between our two countries, not only in finding those responsible for this outrage which had killed so many Indonesians and Australians, but also in the ongoing fight against terrorism. I also telephoned Simon Crean, the Opposition leader, and offered him regular briefings. The Australian people would want their political leaders to stand together in responding to this shocking event.

Mid-afternoon I held a news conference in Sydney. Although there was no clear picture of numbers, I knew that the death toll would be much higher than early reports suggested. I wanted to prepare the nation for this. I sensed already that this was a horror that would tear at the emotions of my fellow Australians. It would be qualitatively different from anything we had previously experienced. In that news conference I not only expressed my compassion for those who had lost relatives and friends and displayed anger at the outrage, but began explaining what Australia proposed to do in helping the Indonesians catch those who were responsible.

This was the first of many occasions over coming days and weeks when I would seek to reassure the Australian people, badly shaken by an event which brought our nation face to face with the full evil of Islamic extremism.

Parliament met just two days after the attack, and for the best part of the next two weeks there was a suspension of the normal political combat. The grim character of what had occurred demanded nothing less. Question time was used to provide as much information as possible about the repatriation to Australia of the seriously injured; the tortuous task of identifying the dead and the return of their remains would take a lot more time and cause considerable distress to relatives and many others.

The bodies of many who had died were either burned or mutilated beyond easy recognition. The victim identification process would prove to be arduous, gruesome and, for loved ones, traumatic. Scores of close relatives had travelled to Bali immediately after the attack, grief-stricken, but anticipating that fairly quick arrangements could be made for the remains of victims to be returned to Australia. For a lot of those relatives, this was not to be. They would, sadly, have a much longer wait.

The victims' remains were in the care and control of the Indonesian authorities, and had been placed in a makeshift morgue. Identification had to follow a strict Interpol protocol which, for some remains, entailed a protracted process. This was a sensitive and difficult issue. Many victim identification experts from Australia had flown to Bali to augment the understaffed Indonesians, who were doing a praiseworthy job in the most trying of circumstances. Identification was taking place in a foreign country and in accordance with the laws and procedures of that country. I could completely understand why distraught family members did not fully appreciate this. But there had to be an absolute premium on accurate identifications.

The Interpol protocol required one of three identification methods to be used: dental records, fingerprints or DNA. As so many of the victims were young, dental records would be of little help. That generation of Australians, because of the fluoridisation of most of Australia's water supply, had been blessed with exceptionally good teeth. As a result of the badly charred nature of bodies, fingerprints were often not available. Thus, in approximately half of all cases, DNA recognition was the only available method. In turn this had to be followed painstakingly, otherwise mistakes would occur, adding to the anguish of loved ones.

I was personally advised by an expert who was on the spot, Professor Chris Griffiths, the head of the ID unit of the Department of Forensic Medicine at Westmead Hospital, that if the protocol were not followed meticulously there was a one-in-five chance of an identity error. Professor Griffiths was known to me, and I respected his counsel. Delay with the repatriation of victims' remains had begun to become an issue with some media because of the distress of relatives. Given the raw emotions of so many grief-stricken relatives and friends, this was a painful issue. I had to be sympathetic, but I could not put aside the need for prudent adherence to the Interpol protocol.

The Bali attack rocked Australia to its core. Not only was the loss of life large, but because of our links with Bali it felt almost like an attack on Australian soil. *Time* magazine would describe Bali as 'party central' for young Australians. That was right. The island was close, accessible and well within the price range of most Australians wanting a relaxing holiday. The friendly, culturally distinct Balinese people added to the attraction of the place.

Early October marked the end of the football season for those Australians who played or followed Australian Rules or either code of rugby. Many of them went to Bali to unwind at the end of a hectic season. The national recall of the Bali attack will forever include the names Coogee Dolphins, Kingsley Football Club, Sturt Australian Football Club, Forbes Rugby Club and Southport Australian Football Club. No fewer than 19 of the 88 Australians killed in the blast came from teams affiliated with these clubs.

Not all of those who lost their lives were young. The simple stone memorial to the Bali victims, located in the English garden adjacent to the House of Representatives' side of Parliament House, contains the names of a cross-section of largely carefree Australians whose lives were cut short by terrorism.

Speaking in parliament on 13 October I tried as best I could to capture the national mood in the following terms: 'For the rest of Australian history, 12 October 2002 will be counted as a day on which evil struck, with indiscriminate and indescribable savagery … This foul deed — this wicked evil act of terrorists — has not only claimed the lives of Australians but also claimed the lives of many of the innocent people of Bali, a beautiful, hitherto peaceful part of Indonesia. Bali is much loved by so many Australians.'

On Thursday I decided to go to Bali the next day. My original intention had been to delay going until the middle of the following week. A prime ministerial visit would strain resources on the ground, and I did not want this while more urgent tasks needed attention. But disquiet regarding the time involved in the identification process continued. This, together with a wish to talk to the victims' families, persuaded me that I should go earlier. I was determined to preserve the bipartisan nature of Australia's response to the attack, so I asked Simon Crean, the Opposition leader, to join me and John Anderson, the Deputy Prime Minister, on the trip to Bali. I wanted those who had lost relatives and friends to know that there was shared grief across the Australian political spectrum.

Denpasar Airport was swarming with representatives of the world's media when we arrived in Bali. I went straight to the Australian Consulate in Bali to take part in a sunset service in the grounds of the consulate, in front of a large wooden cross. Some relatives and friends of victims came to the service and I was able to talk to them afterwards. I spoke briefly at the service. This would be the first time that I was to speak to Australians who had lost loved ones in the attack, and if ever a speech from the heart were needed, this was such an occasion. During the plane journey I had thought about what I would say, especially to those who had lost so much. I was glad that I did not usually read my speeches. Especially then, I owed it to my grieving fellow Australians to look them in the eye and say what I felt. No speechwriter, however gifted, could have captured the emotions which were swirling through me that tragic but balmy evening. It was a sad moment in history for our country. While grieving for those who had been left bereaved I wanted to sound a note of defiance, saying, 'The young of Australia will always travel. They will always seek fun in distant parts. They will always reach out to the young of other nations. They will always be open, fun-loving, decent men and women.' Later I said, 'It will take a long time for these foul deeds to be seen in any kind of context. They can never be understood. They can never be excused. Australia has been affected very deeply, but the Australian spirit has not been broken. The Australian spirit will remain strong and free and open and tolerant. I know that is what all of those who lost their lives would have wanted, and I know it is what all of those who grieve for them would want.'

After spending time with relatives, I went to a full briefing from all of the Australians leading the rescue operation: police, military, medical and consular. It included Mick Keelty, Commissioner of the AFP, and Ric Smith, our ambassador. I invited Simon Crean to be there and fully participate, along with John Anderson and me. A number of decisions were taken, including repatriation arrangements for bodies which had been identified.

There had been much media comment on the temporary morgue, particularly the extensive use of ice to preserve remains in the very sultry weather, because of the absence of normal refrigeration. The media had been denied access to the morgue as close-up photographs and television coverage would have further distressed relatives. I wanted to visit the morgue, but was persuaded against this by Mick Keelty, who argued that it would prove impossible to keep the media away if I went. Later that evening, I spent some more time with relatives.

The following day I had a full-scale meeting with all of those relatives or friends who had lost loved ones in the attack. Closed to the media, it was an emotional gathering. I wanted to assure them that the Government was doing all it could to expedite the victim identification process, which was obviously tugging at the heart-strings more than anything else. After speaking in general terms and assuring the gathering of the compassion of the entire nation, I invited the experts in different areas to provide more detailed briefings.

After the meeting concluded, I stayed behind to talk to those who remained, offering as much comfort as I could on an individual basis, to scores of my fellow Australians unexpectedly bereaved by this evil terrorist attack. It was a sobering experience, which I will always remember. There was the couple from southern Sydney who showed me a photograph of their 23-year-old daughter, who had taken the full impact of the bomb explosion outside the Sari Club as she left the club with two friends. They speculated about what the girls had been discussing and tried, in their grief, to draw a little comfort from the belief that such had been the ferocity of the explosion to which their daughter had been exposed, she would have died quickly.

One of the young victims had been an Olympic rower from Tasmania. His father and twin brother had come to Bali to retrieve his body. For a young man in his early 20s, death is always hard to come to terms with. A violent, unexpected death which snuffs out the life of a young and physically fit person is incomprehensible.

As I moved from group to group during a two-hour period, I grasped how representative of the Australian nation had been the families torn apart by this terrible event. Its scars would stay indefinitely. In each case I tried to establish some personal engagement by asking very direct questions about their loved one. What had brought them to Bali? What did they know about the circumstances of their death? Were they in the Sari Club or Paddy's Bar? Instinct told me whether a spontaneous hug or merely a firm handshake was the right greeting. I left that gathering feeling deep empathy towards these grieving Australians and congealed anger towards those responsible for their losses.

For months after the attack I retained contact with some of the bereaved relatives. Some wrote letters or sent other messages and one or two telephoned me. I tried to respond as fully as possible. I knew that they were passing through intense grief and needed as much comfort as could be provided.

Before leaving Bali later that day, I visited the site of the attack accompanied by the Police Commissioner, who was able at that early stage to provide a close reconstruction of what had occurred on the night. Mick Keelty then took me to the AFP operations centre, already in full swing. There was an Australian police complement of about a dozen, who had been joined by two officers from Scotland Yard; 34 British citizens had died in the attack. The investigation was already well advanced. The professional determination of the police was deeply impressive. They were men and women with a real mission.

I had held a major news conference in Bali, early that day, during which I was closely questioned regarding the investigation then under way, as well as the possible causal link between Australia's involvement in the fight against terrorism and the Bali attack. Much of the questioning, both from the Australian as well as the international media, followed a well-trodden path. To what extent, they asked, was the attack a consequence of our steadfast participation in the fight against terrorism? I did not take a backward step with my answers.

I designated Sunday, 20 October as a national day of mourning for the victims of the Bali attack. Special church services as well as other events were held throughout the country. Janette and I attended the special service at St Paul's, Manuka, in Canberra. It was also decided that a National Act of Commemoration should be held in Parliament House, to which all relatives and close friends of victims would be asked. It was held in the Great Hall on Thursday, 24 October 2002. It was a religious service, at which Bishop Tom Frame, the senior Anglican chaplain to the ADF, presided. A makeshift altar was erected, as had been done for the special service following the attacks of 11 September. Canberra lacked a cathedral-sized church, the largest being St Christopher's Catholic Church in Manuka, which could only seat 300. Converting the Great Hall was a sensible compromise. It could hold up to 1000 people.

It was a sad and emotional occasion, but essential to a national expression of compassion and understanding. Janette and I invited all of the families and friends to the PM's suite for morning tea before the service began. John Anderson and Simon Crean and their wives joined us. The service itself was deeply moving. Family groups came forward to light candles for their murdered loved ones. The haunting sound of a lone piper, as always, stirred the emotions of us all. Both Simon Crean and I spoke. There was an Islamic contribution, in recognition of Indonesia's majority faith, as well as a Hindu component, given the religious provenance of the Balinese.

In my address I referred to what I would later call the duality of the Australian character. We could be compassionate and caring but, where necessary, as tough as tungsten. I ended my remarks by saying to the grieving relatives present, 'I hope you go from this gathering thinking that in every corner of 19½ million Australian hearts, there is a place for you and for the person you have lost.'

Tom Frame was the right person for these occasions. He was sensitive, without being maudlin. From mingling with family members as they left Parliament House, it was clear that the service had meant a lot to them.

In all the contact I had with the relatives and friends, on only one occasion was there a reference to the possibility that the Bali attack might have been because Australia was too closely identified with America in the fight against terrorism. That reference had been muted, more a question than an accusation. An Adelaide magistrate, Brian Deegan (who I had not met), whose son, Josh, had died in the attack, became the lightning rod for that line of argument. He wrote me an open letter which contained plenty of criticism of my Government's foreign policy. He directly criticised our close alliance with the United States and attacked some of the activities of ASIO. I replied promptly and publicly, being careful to show proper respect for his evident grief. Brian Deegan continued to be a periodic and public critic of the Government. In the 2004 federal election, he ran against Alexander Downer in his seat of Mayo. Some of those who had lost relatives and friends in the Bali attack may have shared Deegan's views, but I doubt that it would have been widespread.

To Islamic extremists, influenced by JI and the poisonous doctrines of al Qaeda, Bali was a symbol of what they saw as Western depravity; the alcohol, the scantily dressed women and the partying. It was all there. Therefore they felt justified in attacking the decadent Westerners. It was a way of life, as much if not more than a defined set of political opinions, which was their target. The testimony of Mukhlas Samudra and Amrozi, the principal participants in the Bali atrocity, bore this out.

The idea that Australia should wind back its opposition to terrorism because the Bali attack represented retaliation for our stance gained virtually no traction with the Australian community. There was hostility to the notion that Australia's foreign policy should be adjusted to threats from foreigners — and worse still, terrorists. The Australian people openly supported my Government's actions on both East Timor and Afghanistan, the very two actions which had won the ire of Islamic extremists. To many, this was almost a badge of honour and they were not in the mood to apologise for what their country had done.

Australians did not blame Indonesia for the Bali attack. On the contrary they sympathised with our neighbour, and especially the Balinese, for what had happened. They knew what damage had been inflicted on the Balinese economy. If one of the motives for the attack had been to drive a wedge between Australia and Indonesia, that failed totally. The post-Bali cooperation between the agencies of the two nations was a catalyst for improved relations generally.

Out of this tragedy came an inter-faith dialogue, inaugurated by Australia but enthusiastically picked up by the Indonesians and some others in the region. This involved clerics, scholars and others in the two countries coming together to better understand each other and their respective beliefs. It was a priceless antidote to the vile hatred which the terrorists had hoped to spread. The first inter-faith dialogue took place on 6–7 December 2004 at Yogyakarta, in Indonesia. It was opened by President Yudhoyono.

The Australian delegation included Cardinal George Pell as well as representatives of other Christian churches and Islamic, Jewish and Buddhist leaders.

Australia and Indonesia also signed a memorandum of understanding on security, which further cemented the already close relations between the security agencies of the two countries. This arrangement was to be replicated with other countries in the region.

The highlight of the post-Bali cooperation was, however, that between the two police forces which resulted in the capture and later conviction of those responsible for the Bali atrocity. The lasting advantage of this was that it added value to the relationship at the popular level. To the average Australian, inter-faith dialogues and security memoranda were fine, but catching those terrorists who had killed 88 other Australians was what really mattered. When this happened courtesy of a partnership with the Indonesian police, Australian regard for Indonesia rose accordingly. That was not what the terrorists had wanted.

The first real breakthrough came when the nightwatchman at a mosque reported two men having parked a motorbike outside the mosque just after the attacks. With the help of explosive residue on the bike, the link was established to the attacks, and the sale of the bike was traced to a local dealer who clearly remembered the three men who had bought it two days earlier. They had not haggled over the price; that's what made them memorable. Face-fit experts from the Victoria Police interviewed witnesses for hours and produced images of three men — Amrozi, Idris, and Ali Imron. According to those on the spot, the images turned out to be 'uncannily correct'. This was a case study in cooperation between local witnesses and foreign experts.

Pastika's patience was rewarded in relation to the Mitsubishi van. The engine and chassis numbers had been filed away, but he told his men to keep looking. They did and finally found, beneath a welded plate, a number used to register the van as a bus some 15 years earlier.

The first of the suspects, Amrozi, went on trial in May 2003. In June 2003 separate trials began for Samudra and Mukhlas. They were convicted and then executed by firing squad on 8 November 2008.

There had been the odd hair-raising glitch, such as when Ric Smith, our ambassador, found himself standing in front of bulldozers which had been directed by civic authorities to raze the wreckage of the Sari Club, just days after the attack, so as to expunge evil spirits, thus enabling tourists to safely return. It might have satisfied local folklore, but would have created a nightmare scenario for forensic experts who wanted to scour the ruined site for clues. Smith's direct action saved the day.

In the eyes of most Australians, the Indonesian justice system had prevailed. Whatever generic views may have been held about capital punishment, there was little doubt, as I said on 12 October 2007, that the Australian people would have felt let down if the sentences of death, handed down in relation to the three of them, were not carried out.

The first anniversary of the attack was an occasion which focused heavily not only on the continued grieving of relatives and friends, but also on the effective cooperation between Australia and Indonesia. A special commemoration was held in Bali which I attended, along with the senior minister, and future Indonesian President, Bambang Yudhoyono, whose passionate attack on terrorism drew admiration from those present. That day it was announced that both General Bachtiar and General Pastika would receive honorary awards in the Order of Australia in recognition of their work in bringing to justice those responsible for the Bali attacks.

Bali, October 2002 was not the last that Indonesia was to experience of terrorism, but it was the worst. There was another attack in Bali, which took four Australian lives, the attack on the Australian embassy on the eve of the 2004 election, and the 2009 bomb attack at the Marriott Hotel, where four Australians died.

The Bali tragedy brought Australia and Indonesia closer together. Citizens of our countries had died in the same attack at the hands of evil people, who were hunted down, tried and convicted, and then put to death for their crimes. The Indonesian security system, albeit with much Australian help, had been equal to the task of pursuing and punishing those who had killed 88 of our citizens. If one of the goals of the murderers had been to drive our two nations further apart, that had not happened.

34

IRAQ

Speaking to the General Assembly on 12 September 2002, George Bush not only recited Iraq's long record of defying the demands of the United Nations, but made it clear that if the United Nations did not act, the United States would. In one sentence he encapsulated the primeval fear of the Americans. 'And our greatest fear is that terrorists will find a short cut to their mad ambitions when an outlaw regime supplies them with the technologies to kill on a massive scale.'[1] Almost eight years later, President Obama echoed that primeval fear when he said, 'The greatest threat to US and global security is no longer a nuclear exchange between nations but nuclear terrorism by violent extremists.'[2] All along that was at the heart of the American anxiety about Iraq. Iraq, under Saddam, was an outlaw regime; the United States believed Iraq had weapons of mass destruction (WMDs), and feared that Saddam might supply terrorists with deadly weapons for use against America. Having experienced 9/11, who could blame Americans for thinking that the next time a hijacked plane headed for a tall building, it might contain a chemical, biological or even nuclear weapon.

Understanding that is essential to a proper appreciation of America's action against Iraq and is fundamental to an evaluation of my view that Australia did the right thing in backing the Americans. It should be the constant touchstone as I recount the events and tribulations of those turbulent months in 2002 and 2003.

Joining the Americans and the British in the military operation against Saddam Hussein in March 2003 was the most controversial foreign affairs action of my Government. Military action is always the agonising, last-resort option. Those who think that democratically elected leaders enter military conflicts lightly have no idea of the emotional and other conflicting pressures involved.

Worst of all, there is the dread of casualties. There is the near certainty of casualties in any conflict. Incredibly, Australia did not suffer battle casualties in Iraq. Most of our forces were withdrawn after the initial combat phase, but the merciful outcome of no battle casualties was due, also, to a combination of good fortune, superior training and the pre-positioning of forces, which allowed the maximum feasible time for acclimatisation.

On two earlier occasions, namely East Timor and Afghanistan, I had as Prime Minister involved the ADF in military action. Both decisions involved strong popular support, especially East Timor. Iraq was, in that sense also, much harder. Our decision to go into Iraq was against the weight of public opinion.

The most regular popular criticism was that our action increased the likelihood of a terrorist attack involving Australians. That was not our assessment, no matter how intuitive the notion was for many people. Now, seven years on, the weight of evidence remains that Australia was a target for terrorism much earlier.

Australia had first attracted critical attention from al Qaeda long before Iraq because of our action in East Timor. On 3 November 2001, Al Jazeera satellite television broadcast a message from Bin Laden in which he said that 'crusading Australian forces were on the Indonesian shores and they actually went in to separate East Timor, [which] is part of the countries of the Islamic world'.[3] The major terrorist attack claiming Australian lives was in Bali, in October 2002, five months before the invasion of Iraq.

No self-respecting nation should, in any instance, allow its foreign policy to be dictated by terrorist threats. Most Australians support this proposition but will still judge each situation in which the principle is at stake according to its merits.

The terrorist attacks of 11 September had radically changed the world in which we lived. It was a paradigm shift of historic magnitude. A new enemy, unrestrained by borders, had arrived on the international stage. That enemy was lethal and efficient. Its dagger was aimed at the heart of a way of life which would forever be ours. The terrorists were staring straight at us; no amount of metaphorical averting of our eyes would shake their resolve to injure us and punish our way of life.

Plate 17

Cutting my teeth with local street-corner campaigning in Earlwood during the early 1960s. I was working for the local MLA, Eric Willis.

Plate 18

With Phillip Lynch (left) and John Carrick, my mentor, at the cabinet swearing-in of late 1977. Doug Anthony, Tony Street and Governor-General Sir Zelman Cowen are in the background.

Malcolm Fraser and I prepare to meet state leaders at a Premiers' Conference/ Loan Council meeting, May 1981.

Plate 19

Andrew Peacock and
I shake hands early in
1983. Fault lay on both
sides in our leadership
rivalry. We are now
quite friendly.

In Canberra, 1988, with Margaret
Thatcher, Britain's greatest prime
minister since Churchill.

A confident
opposition front
bench of Fischer,
Costello, Downer
and Reith heckle
Paul Keating in
February 1995,
shortly after my
return to the
leadership.

Plate 20

The first cabinet of the Howard era, with Governor-General Sir William Deane, who had sworn us in. Costello, Downer and I would retain our original positions through till 2007.

Congratulating Peter Costello on the foundation budget, August 1996. A great budget, and he was Australia's best ever Treasurer.

Plate 21

With (on my left) Tony Nutt and
Tony O'Leary, both long-serving
and loyal advisors.

Receiving wise political counsel from
my long-time advisor and friend,
Grahame Morris.

At the United Nations with Arthur Sinodinos, my outstanding chief of staff.
Also pictured are Ashton Calvert (DFAT chief), my redoubtable PM&C head,
Max Moore-Wilton, and John Dauth (Australia's UN envoy).

Plate 22

In Townsville in 2003 with General Peter Cosgrove, who led the Timor intervention and later became Chief of the Defence Force during the Iraqi operation.

I always enjoyed meeting the men and women of the ADF. Their welfare will always be of concern to me.

With Australian troops at Baghdad Airport, March 2007. Later I met US General David Petraeus, who led the successful surge.

Plate 23

Outside the ruins of the Sari Club, Bali, October 2002. General Da'i Bachtiar is on my right. My security head, Gary Hanna, is on my left.

Inspecting the devastation of the tsunami in Aceh Province with Brigadier Chalmers, head of the Medical Taskforce, January 2005.

Plate 24

Campaigning in the bush with John Anderson, Deputy PM, close colleague and friend. We trusted each other completely.

Holding Deborah Rose Dumoo at Wadeye in the Northern Territory, 2005. 'No school, no pool' was a policy that worked a treat.

Plate 25

Carried aloft by Australia's magnificent 2000 Olympic Games team. They appreciated the constant support Janette and I gave.

With Mark Taylor and others of the victorious 1997 Ashes team. Mark dubbed me a 'cricket tragic'. We remain good friends.

Plate 26

Political life made
playing competition
cricket impossible,
but there was the
occasional breakout.

Regular morning walks
sometimes included others
— here it was Wallaby
captain George Gregan
in Canberra.

Plate 27

A light-hearted moment with Her Majesty the Queen (centre), Don McKinnon, Commonwealth Secretary-General (left), and Nigerian President Olusegun Obasanjo (right) at CHOGM, Abuja, December 2003.

Canberra, November 1996. Introducing Bill Clinton to the Speaker and Senate President. Hillary Clinton and Janette are looking on.

Plate 28

Presenting Nelson Mandela with an Honorary Award in the Order of Australia in Pretoria, South Africa, November 1999.

Hopes for Israeli–Palestinian peace were high when, with world Jewish leader Isi Leibler (right), I met Yasser Arafat in May 2000. Arafat did not deliver.

Plate 29

George Bush and I exchange views on our ponchos at the APEC meeting held in Santiago, Chile, in November 2004. We keep in close touch.

Tony Blair and I held many similar world views, especially on the threat of terrorism, even though our politics were different.

Plate 30

China's President, Jiang Zemin, and I share a joke at one of our many meetings. We had a close and productive relationship. I liked him.

Australia's trade with China grew dramatically under the leadership of Premier Wen Jiabao (pictured) and President Hu Jintao.

Plate 31

With President Susilo Bambang Yudhyono and his wife, Ani, at Batam, Indonesia, in June 2006. Our links strengthened the Australian–Indonesian bilateral relationship.

With Junichiro Koizumi, the longest-serving and most reform-minded of the Japanese prime ministers I knew. He was colourful as well.

Plate 32

Meeting Pope John Paul II at the Vatican. His strong moral leadership did much to bring down the Soviet empire.

On Sydney Harbour during APEC 2007 with Condoleezza Rice, the gifted US Secretary of State and great friend of Australia.

Joining hands with Manmohan Singh of India and Abdullah Badawi of Malaysia at the inaugural East Asia Summit meeting, December 2005.

Along with moderate Muslims around the world, who were so often targets and victims too, nations such as the United States, Britain and Australia were in this together. We were exemplars of things which Islamic extremism despised: freedom of expression, equality of men and women, freedom of religion and the core value of an individual conscience. In our history we had given these values more than passive endorsement. We had defended them repeatedly, often at a painful cost.

Supporting the United States in Afghanistan, and later in Iraq, was more than giving expression to our most important alliance relationship; it signalled a determination on our part to participate in an aggregate response to the terrorist threat. Al Qaeda, operating out of Afghanistan, had been responsible for the attacks on New York and Washington. Saddam had not been involved in September 11, but his regime was listed by the US State Department as a state sponsor of terrorism because of support for other terrorist groups. He had the potential to facilitate a future terrorist outrage.

The decision to go into Iraq was right for a variety of reasons. It was right for the Americans to do so, not only because of Iraq's continued defiance of previous UN resolutions. It was also right to act on a reasonably entertained belief that Iraq did possess WMDs. Even more importantly, it was a legitimate act of anticipatory self-defence against future terrorist facilitations by a regime which had a track record both of regional aggression and support for terrorist activities. Saddam had paid $25,000 to the family of each Palestinian suicide bomber who had carried out an attack on Israel. He had used poisoned gas against his own people as well as the Iranians.

Within hours of the attack on 11 September 2001, Michael Thawley, our ambassador in Washington, said to me that as a result of the attack, Iraq would be back on the agenda for the Americans. This was because of continued American suspicion about the willingness of Iraq to support, facilitate or promote terrorist activities by others as well as the general view in the United States that Iraq and, in particular, the removal of Saddam Hussein remained unfinished business. This was a sentiment of Democrats as well as Republicans.

It was neither unreasonable nor implausible of the Americans to believe that WMDs possessed by Iraq might, at some time in the future, be handed to a terrorist group for use against the United States or others, with horrific consequences.

The overwhelming preoccupation of the United States in the months, and indeed for several years, following the attacks of September 2001 was when and from whom might the next attack come. The attacks of 11 September had a deep and lasting impact on the American psyche. To many, they were worse than Pearl Harbor. They involved assaults on the American mainland and hit the economic and military heart of the nation.

The passage of more than nine years since those attacks has produced complacency. It is easy now to feel that past trepidation about another terrorist assault was an overreaction, although the near miss of Christmas Day 2009, involving a Detroit-bound flight, would have been a reality check. Complacency was the last description to match the mood of Americans in the wake of 11 September.

The first responsibility of any head of government is the protection of his or her country from attack. America had been violated on 11 September in an unprovoked, unjustified fashion by a ruthless enemy which had declared war on the United States and had previously been responsible for a series of deadly outrages against its citizens. There was a legitimate concern that there would be another attack. The dominant responsibility of the President of the United States, at that time, was to do all in his power to deny the enemies of the United States another opportunity to bring destruction to his country.

As the early months of 2002 passed, it became more and more obvious from the public statements of George Bush and other members of the Administration that Iraq was very much back on the American agenda. Media speculation that military action would be taken continued to grow. The case against Iraq built by the Americans and also, increasingly, the British led by Tony Blair, was that Iraq had failed to comply fully with existing resolutions of the United Nations concerning WMDs.

After the first Gulf War, UN Security Council (SC) resolution 687 required Iraq to declare and remove, destroy or render harmless her remaining WMDs and related production infrastructure under UN Special Commission (UNSCOM) or International Atomic Energy Agency (IAEA) supervision. Saddam Hussein played a cat and mouse game with both the UN weapons inspectors and the IAEA. There would be weeks of non-compliance and subterfuge behaviour by Iraq in relation to the inspections authorised under the UN resolution, only to be followed by last-minute agreements to either let inspectors in or allow them to examine hitherto prohibited areas. The suspicion was that Saddam was engaged in an elaborate game of put and take with the international community, in which he always stayed one step ahead of the UN inspectors.

According to UNSCOM, Iraq had failed to properly account for more than 30,000 special munitions for the delivery of chemical and biological agents, and up to several hundred tonnes of bulk chemical agent, including 1.5 tonnes of deadly VX nerve agent. UNSCOM could not confirm Iraq's claim to have destroyed all its artillery shells filled with chemical agent and aerial bombs for the delivery of chemical agent.

UNSCOM found no credible evidence to support Iraq's claim to have unilaterally destroyed all its biological-weapon holdings. It assessed that Iraq could have produced twice as much botulinum toxin and three times as much anthrax as it had declared.

UNSCOM noted that Iraq's industrial capacity and knowledge base had given it the ability to make large amounts of new biological agents quickly, if it wanted to. UN inspectors were unable to establish that Iraq had destroyed all the ballistic-missile warheads it had filled with chemical and biological agents. Iraq never fully accounted to UNSCOM for all its ballistic missiles and missile-related infrastructure.

Concern about Iraq's WMD potential was not only soundly based in fact, but was reinforced by Saddam's duplicitous behaviour surrounding compliance with UN resolutions. With the exception of limited access to one declared nuclear material storage facility, UN inspectors were denied access to Iraq between December 1998 and November 2002.

There was intense debate about access to the presidential palaces of Saddam's regime, as the Iraqi dictator had declared them off-limits to weapons inspectors. One of them was much larger than Buckingham Palace, a point I made in a speech to the American Chamber of Commerce in Sydney on 2 October 2002. Just 24 hours earlier Saddam had reached agreement with the UN weapons inspectors for a resumption of inspections — but the eight or nine so-called presidential sites were to be excluded from the inspections! Such was the ineffectual character of the existing SC resolutions on Iraq's WMDs.

The combination of the even closer relations we had established with the Bush Administration and the quality of Michael Thawley's representation in Washington meant that we had a direct pipeline to Administration thinking all through the first half of 2002. By mid-2002 I had formed the view that if Iraq did not satisfactorily respond to international pressure about her WMD capacity, the Americans would almost certainly take military action against her, and that Australia would need to decide whether or not to join that action.

The desire to remove Saddam was not confined to Republicans. It is widely forgotten now that in 1998 the American Congress enacted the Iraq Liberation Act, which declared that regime change in Iraq was an objective of US foreign policy. President Clinton was in the White House, and the legislation drew powerful backing from both sides of the aisle. That act reflected a bipartisan view that Iraq, with its past rogue behaviour, and WMDs — which most Americans believed she possessed — was a threat not only to her neighbours but potentially other countries, including the United States.

After 'Operation Desert Fox', when American and British forces launched air strikes against Iraq late in 1998 to enforce UN sanctions, Clinton declared, 'So long as Saddam remains in power he will remain a threat to his people, the region and the world.'[4] According to Clinton, the best way to end that threat was for Iraq to have another government.

In February of that year Clinton insisted that the world had to face facts about Saddam. He said that the world had to deal with the 'kind of threat Iraq poses ... a rogue state with weapons of mass destruction, ready to use them or provide them to terrorists ... who travel the world among us unnoticed'.[5] Those words could just as easily have been spoken by George Bush or Donald Rumsfeld.

If that was America's attitude in 1998, how much more apprehensive about Saddam must the people of the United States have been in the months following September 2001? Whereas, prior to the terrorist attacks, America's appetite for regime change in Iraq fell short of supporting a military invasion, the mood was different afterwards — and not just amongst the neo-conservatives.

In his book *The Threatening Storm*, Kenneth Pollack, national security man in the Clinton White House responsible for Iraq, records a comment from his boss, Sandy Berger, Clinton's national security advisor, that they 'had a responsibility to leave the next Administration with a viable Iraq policy, not a mess. It would be up to that Administration to decide what to do'.[6] The Clinton Administration did not regard military action against Iraq as an unthinkable option, and that was long before 9/11.

'Operation Desert Thunder', in February 1998, contemplated air strikes by the Americans and British against Saddam's WMD capacity as well as other strategic assets of the regime, because of another round of defiance of UN resolutions by Iraq. The aim of the strikes was to disrupt Saddam's ability to maintain his grip on power.

After a personal request from Bill Clinton, I had agreed to the pre-positioning, in the Middle East, of units of the SAS to support the US/UK operation. In the end the forces were not needed, as a compromise was agreed between the Iraqi leader and the United Nations. But in December 1998, 'Operation Desert Fox', involving precision air strikes, was executed due to Iraq not heeding its obligations regarding UN inspections.

The Labor Party, under Kim Beazley, endorsed my action in sending the SAS. It was common ground between the Government and the opposition that the action contemplated by the Coalition against Iraq was fully sanctioned by existing UN resolutions.

Yet now it is hard to see the qualitative difference between what was sought to be enforced in 1998 and what was sought to be enforced in 2003. That was apparently the opinion of such a well-credentialled Democrat as Richard Holbrooke. Addressing the American Enterprise Institute on 13 June 2003, the late Jeane Kirkpatrick told of a conversation she had had with Richard Holbrooke, appointed by President Obama as special envoy to Pakistan and Afghanistan. According to Kirkpatrick, Holbrooke said, 'Three times Clinton did what many Democrats are now saying Bush can't do. He did it in Bosnia in '95, in Iraq with Desert Fox in December of '98, and in Kosovo in '99. In the Balkans case he had no Security Council authority.'[7]

Certainly there was a vast difference between the scales of the respective military operations, yet the principle at stake, namely the failure of Iraq to fully comply with the United Nations' requirements regarding WMDs, was the same. In 1998 Kim Beazley was no reluctant conscript. I invited him to attend the private farewell of the SAS at Campbell Barracks in Perth. He backed what I had to say about the mission. It was a genuine bipartisan display.

The public record in the United States in 2001 and 2002 is replete with statements calling for regime change in Iraq, and not only from neo-conservatives. On 10 October 2002, the House of Representatives in Washington voted by 296 to 133 to authorise the use of military force against Iraq. The Senate resolved likewise, by 77 to 23. Many leading Democrats, including Hillary Clinton and Joe Biden, voted for the use of force. Hillary Clinton's speech was remarkable for its tone of quite strong support for the Bush approach. She showed no reluctance to put the boot into the first Bush Administration for 'leaving the Kurds and the Shi'ites, who had risen against Saddam Hussein at our urging, to Saddam's revenge'.[8] Senator Joe Biden, now Vice-president, described the resolution he would vote for as 'a march to peace and security'.[9]

Through 2002, it became apparent that if action were taken by the Americans, Tony Blair would commit British forces to fight alongside the United States. Blair, himself, became an articulate and frequent critic of Iraq. His reaction to the attacks of 11 September had been similar to mine.

The American military commenced contingency planning for an invasion of Iraq in the early part of 2002. Although they and others, including Britain and Australia, knew that the lion's share of the forces involved, if an invasion took place, would be American, they did not want to be entirely alone. They were keen to see the involvement of a limited number of other countries, of which Britain and Australia were at the top of the list. Australian officers went to Central Command at Tampa in Florida to participate in the contingency planning, although it was understood that no Australian commitment to participate had been made.

From the very beginning we knew what was in the minds of the American military. We also knew how we might contribute in the most effective manner possible and in a way that safeguarded, as best one could, the position of any Australian troops which might ultimately be committed.

In his public and private utterances, Bush always kept his options open on Iraq. That having been said, I am sure that from soon after the attacks of September 2001, his instincts would have favoured taking out Saddam's regime. This was not because he thought that Saddam had been involved in the attacks on the World Trade Center or the Pentagon, but because he believed that given Iraq's history there was far too great a risk that Iraq, under Saddam, would be involved in some way in a future assault on America. If that was his disposition, he would not have been alone. Millions of Americans would have shared his instincts; who could have blamed them?

As 2002 progressed, considerable support emerged in the United States for action against Saddam. By contrast, as time wore on, Blair's domestic political challenge on Iraq became increasingly difficult. He was, and would remain, ahead of his party on Iraq.

Tony Blair led a British Labour Government which included many with an almost childlike faith in the processes of the United Nations. To them the sine qua non of good foreign policy was always adhering to the dictates of multilateral organisations, especially the United Nations. Also there remained that lingering jealousy, on both sides of British politics, towards US foreign policy leadership.

By contrast, Blair was instinctively more pro-American than many other European leaders. He correctly believed that many Europeans took the mistaken view that America would always be there, and that no matter how many insults might be delivered and no matter how indifferent Europeans were to the United States, the friendship and support of the past could always be drawn upon.

He frequently said to me that many Europeans failed to understand that there was a latent isolationist sentiment within the United States and, if push came to shove, plenty of Americans would be perfectly happy to turn their backs on Europe.

Like me, Blair believed that there was a long struggle ahead of liberal democracies and that they had to oppose Islamic extremism, with military action where necessary and also through winning the battle of ideas between Islamic fascism and moderate, progressive Islam. As the months passed I found that, despite our formal political differences, Tony Blair's world-view in relation to issues such as terrorism was similar to my own.

I went to Washington again in July 2002. The highlight of that visit was my postponed address to a joint sitting of congress, a real honour for any visitor. It was a chance to identify the common values between Australia and the United States. I saw the invitation very much as a compliment from the United States to Australia.

In our discussions during that visit, President Bush and I were careful to avoid specifics about Australian troop commitments to a possible invasion of Iraq. He knew that close discussions were under way between the US military and their Australian counterparts. He was entitled to assume on the basis of that, and also the tenor of our discussions, that if the military option was chosen by the United States then, in all likelihood, Australia would join.

But he knew that I had not made any commitment to this effect and that for understandable political and other reasons I would keep my options open until the time when a final decision was needed. This was, in fact, his position. He and Colin Powell both made the point that no final decision had been taken and that they were continuing to pursue a diplomatic approach. The President was not optimistic that it would succeed. He cited a recent speech at West Point in which he asserted that the Cold War doctrine of containment did not work in the world of terrorist movements and failed states.

I left my discussion with the President believing that he would follow the diplomatic route and seek another UN resolution, without any real faith that it would work and that, in the end, he would take military action against Iraq. There was no way he would allow the issue of Iraq to slip onto the back burner.

Divisions were emerging between Colin Powell, Vice-president Cheney and the Defense Secretary, Donald Rumsfeld. The latter two had little patience for pursuing another UN resolution, believing it was not only postponing the inevitable but wasting valuable time. A build-up of US forces in the Middle East would not be sustainable indefinitely — particularly with the onset of the hottest part of summer.

For Australia and the United States, the push for a further resolution was not derived from legal concerns, but driven by the belief of Powell and others that the moral authority of the Coalition would be reinforced if it had been seen to have tried to obtain another SC resolution.

There was also the particular predicament of Tony Blair. He was likely to commit substantial British forces to any operation. His legal advice, at that time, was reported to be more equivocal than that given to the Australian Government. Ultimately his legal advice was similar to ours. More importantly, the growing revolt within his own Labour Party increased the political necessity for Blair to go back to the Security Council and seek a new resolution on Iraq, in the hope of placating the internationalists and the doubters.

Early in September Bush rang seeking my advice about the next steps on Iraq. I was in Brisbane to give an address to the convention of the Queensland Liberal Party. Bush told me that Colin Powell was keen that the United States return to the United Nations for a further resolution, that he, Bush, was scheduled to address the General Assembly the following week, and he would then need to outline the future path of American policy on Iraq. Bush expressed concern that any further resolution he might obtain would not be of much use. I told Bush that I agreed with Powell's line about seeking another UN resolution and that it would provide valuable domestic political help to Blair. That was the path he followed. On 12 September Bush addressed the General Assembly, foreshadowed a further resolution and laid out in plain terms previous UN failures on Iraq and was frank about US concerns regarding Saddam Hussein.

Although this new resolution was, eventually, carried unanimously, it only added incrementally to the pressure on Iraq, because it lacked a final trigger mechanism. It would remain the case that if, after the processes of this new resolution had been exhausted, Iraq was still non-compliant, there would be furious debate as to whether the existing resolutions contained enough authority for military action. It was precisely because countries such as Russia and France wanted to withhold explicit authority for an invasion that the resolution had ended up in the terms that it did.

It is easy to understand why Cheney and Rumsfeld chafed at the decision of their President to go back to the Security Council. Their prediction that not a lot more would be obtained by doing so proved correct. Yet their arguments did not allow for the political imperative of accommodating Tony Blair. Some 45,000 British troops would be committed to Iraq; an unmistakable earnest of Britain's determination to join the Americans. Bush was absolutely right to accommodate Blair's domestic political realities. He owed it to an old and close ally.

Some hope was entertained that, in the light of further evidence of Saddam's lack of compliance, it might be possible to obtain, via yet another resolution, explicit authority from the SC for military action. The dilemma for Bush was that once he had sought and obtained a fresh resolution, he had, to some extent, become a hostage to the world body. Good faith had led him into the dilemma.

The optimum time for an invasion of Iraq would be February/March 2003. The American troop build-up began in October. They and their British allies faced the twin challenges of time and weather. Iraq is impossibly hot for most of the year. It is prohibitively so from April onwards for a period of three or four months. I knew that if an invasion were to take place then it could not be later than March 2003. This had implications for Australia as well as the United States and Britain.

Our ground force commitment was likely to be limited to Special Forces for the intensive phase of any military action against Iraq. I foreshadowed this in a speech in November 2002. I also knew that if our forces were to be given every opportunity to prepare in theatre, thus minimising the likelihood of casualties, then they should be pre-positioned by early February at the latest.

An important prelude to attempts to obtain a specific invasion mandate from the Security Council was Colin Powell's special address to that body on 5 February 2003. Months later it was claimed that Powell felt he had been badly misled in relation to his speech. That always puzzled me. I could not imagine that a man in Powell's position would have delivered a speech of that kind without being fully satisfied that the claims being made in it were as carefully verified as possible. In fact Powell told me, when I saw him in Washington on 10 February, that he had sat with the CIA director, George Tenet, for three days sorting through the intelligence used in the presentation and made it clear he would not use anything that was not corroborated from multiple sources.

This speech contained the allegations regarding dual-use mobile laboratories for the production of biological weapons. It would be months before the widely held belief of Allied intelligence agencies regarding these mobile vans proved to be unfounded. Powell also used explicit intelligence, based on telephone intercepts, to demonstrate the steps taken by the Iraqi regime to hide material from weapons inspectors.

It was only at the beginning of 2003 that many Australians began focusing on the arguments for and against invading Iraq. Powell's speech therefore had a big impact on people. He was a strong, convincing figure and his presentation, so widely covered, shifted numbers of people towards the belief that Iraq did have WMDs.

Prior to Christmas 2002, the fresh inspections required under the new resolution, 1441, had commenced and, once again, the old cat and mouse game was played by the Iraqis. The chief weapons inspector, Hans Blix, a consummate Swedish diplomat and international bureaucrat, much enjoyed the pivotal role he occupied.

Almost like clockwork he produced a report which, on balance, chided the Iraqis for their lack of cooperation. This was to be followed by another report which provided a glimmer of hope and something approaching a pass mark for Saddam Hussein. This maintained the stake of the United Nations in the whole affair.

Iraq's response to the new SC resolution 1441 was inadequate. In reporting to the Security Council on 27 January, Hans Blix said, 'Iraq appears not to have come to a genuine acceptance, not even today, of the disarmament which was demanded of it.'[10] A later report from Blix struck a more optimistic tone, but inevitably pleaded for more time. There was a legitimate fear that this process would go on interminably.

Another widely reported speech, given to the Security Council on 14 February, came from Dominique de Villepin, the French Foreign Minister. An urbane, highly articulate, and somewhat anti-American figure of the soft right in French politics, de Villepin delivered a vituperative speech, full of rhetoric about disarming Iraq, but in reality a thinly veiled attack on American motives and policy. The speech dashed any hopes that the French might, in the final analysis, wave through an additional SC resolution.

De Villepin's performance produced lasting resentment from the Americans. It was not the speech of an anguished friend unable, after careful consideration of the facts, to agree with what the Americans were putting forward. It was the speech of someone intent on humiliating the Americans before a world political forum.

He further cemented his anti-American credentials with his energetic diplomatic mission in Africa and elsewhere, openly urging non-permanent members of the Security Council to oppose any new British and American resolution.

By early January 2003 the moment of truth was fast approaching. On 10 January, at a news conference, I detailed the composition of any Australian commitment to Iraq. I also foreshadowed that in the weeks ahead there would be a forward deployment of forces. In addition to the Special Forces, Australia would commit a squadron of FA18 fighters, or Hornets. We would maintain the two naval vessels enforcing UN sanctions in the Gulf, and also commit some P3 Orion surveillance aircraft and some navy clearance divers. This was a big commitment, and much larger than the force sent in 1991. From the beginning I told the Americans that if we committed forces, it would be to the invasion phase. We could not be part of any longer-term stabilisation operation. We had our own regional commitments, particularly in East Timor, and the ADF was too small to sustain a sizeable ongoing ground-force contribution in Iraq.

On 22 January, Robert Hill, the Defence Minister, announced the forward deployment of the sea transport HMAS *Kanimbla*, lead elements of a Special Forces Task Group and a Royal Australian Air Force reconnaissance team to the Middle East to allow the ADF adequate time to prepare, if military action against Iraq should come about. *Kanimbla* sailed from Sydney the next day. The vessel and her company received a rousing, but emotional send-off. The one discordant note came from Simon Crean, the Opposition leader. After wishing the troops well and expressing his hopes for their personal safety, he said bluntly that they should not be going. Whatever might have been his political feelings, it was an appalling thing to say to men and women who were about to put their lives at risk. He should have wished them well, and left it at that. He had ample opportunities, away from the farewell, to repeat his well-known objections. His judgement was abysmal and his remarks were insensitive.

I spent much of the Australia Day weekend working on the speech I planned to give to parliament as soon as it came back in February. This would need to be scripted as I knew that all of the references to intelligence, and the history of Iraq's behaviour in response to previous UN resolutions must be factually accurate. Careful checking with my department as well as Foreign Affairs and, most particularly, the Office of National Assessments (ONA), the latter being the final assessment agency of intelligence reports to the Government, was essential.

In all of my speeches I placed heavy reliance on intelligence assessments that Iraq had WMD capacity, and that capacity was at the heart of our case for military action. I was determined that the intelligence case presented was concise, factual and unemotional.

As argued earlier, there was a legitimately held fear by the United States that, given her past record, Iraq under Saddam could be involved in or facilitate a future terrorist attack on the United States. Therefore the Americans were justified in pursuing Iraq over its WMDs, especially given Iraq's years of contemptuous behaviour towards UN resolutions. Those considerations, coupled with our crucial alliance relationship with the United States, constituted the principal reasons Australia joined the action against Iraq. I did my best to articulate this in my February address to parliament, a later press club speech, and my address to the nation on 20 March.

At this stage a final decision to commit forces had not been taken. It was obvious, though, that only a last-minute and unexpected development would preclude Australia from supporting an American-led operation, if George Bush decided to mount it. Our forces were in position, following months of dialogue between the military leaderships of our two countries. The Australian contribution, numerically, would be small against the more than 150,000 American troops who would finally be committed to Iraq. Nonetheless, the symbolism as well as the reality of what the Australian force could contribute was deeply valued by our American friends.

In February George Bush invited me to come to Washington to discuss the situation. He did it to publicly demonstrate the significance he attached to consulting a key US ally and to a likely Australian contribution. As well as seeing the President and doing the other rounds in Washington, I also went to New York to see Kofi Annan.

It also made sense to go on to London and discuss the Iraqi position with Tony Blair, especially as Blair himself was still passing through a challenging domestic political time on this issue. He was determined to stare down opposition within his own party and Government, even if, in the end, he had to rely on the Conservative opposition to carry the day in the House of Commons.

I also decided, importantly, to call on President Megawati of Indonesia on my way home from London. I knew that any involvement by Australia in an operation against Iraq would raise sensitivities, to say the least, in the Muslim world. As the largest Islamic country and our nearest neighbour, it was important that Indonesia hear first-hand from me the reasons behind any Australian decision to be involved in an operation against Iraq.

It was clear from my talks in Washington that the Americans would act against Saddam, with or without a further SC resolution. President Bush wanted another resolution because he knew that it was important to his allies, such as Britain and Australia. In his assessment it was not all that important in the United States itself. Bush was hopeful that both the French and the Russians would ultimately go along with the extra resolution. That proved to be overoptimistic. Only a last-minute and total capitulation by Saddam, or a palace revolution, would remove the need for military action. Neither of us thought that likely.

Bush described the diplomatic manoeuvring over Iraq as akin to being in a mosh pit. When I told him that I would go on to New York to see both Blix and Kofi Annan, he remarked that Australia was well and truly in the mosh pit. Blix was due to make another report to the Security Control in four days' time. I pressed the Americans as to whether they thought the Blix report on 14 February would be consistent with that delivered on 27 January. Powell said that he thought it would, but in addition a little bit of movement on the Iraqi side would be reported, and more time sought. Powell proved to be spot-on.

Bush praised Powell's speech to the Security Control on 4 February. I agreed, saying that it had been a class act. Bush said that a lot of material had been 'left on the floor', on the insistence of Powell, and that he had been right to do so. I told my American interlocutors that the information about telephone intercepts had been particularly compelling. Powell replied that he had left out the names from the telephone intercepts to protect the safety of the Iraqis involved, but some had come forward to deny that they had been involved in the telephone conversations. The Americans were very confident about the intelligence they had on Iraq. It was also obvious that enormous care and effort had gone into the preparation of Powell's speech to the Security Council. Both Bush as well as Powell himself regarded the speech as the tour de force of the public presentation of the case against Iraq.

My calls in New York were interesting. I trudged through the snow piled before Kofi Annan's residence in New York. As always, he was amiable. The impression I took away was of a man who understood the inevitability of American-led military action and, without approving of it, accepted that there was some justification in the attitude of Bush and his colleagues. He was naturally opposed to action outside of a further UN mandate. He thought that the Americans and the British should give the whole process more time. Annan placed considerable stress on what would happen after the conflict, and was concerned with the notion that the Americans and not the United Nations might stay in charge. I said that if the United Nations were involved from the beginning, its post-conflict role would be more automatic. He had plenty to say about the domestic politics of the major UN players, being especially critical of Rumsfeld. Annan said that he was too abrasive. Annan's goal was, of course, preserving the central place of the United Nations.

Hans Blix called on me at the Pierre Hotel. He gave nothing away regarding Iraq's weapons position. He would be a company man to the very end. Blix would not contribute to action being taken without a new SC resolution. Deep down, he must have known that the Russians and the French were not going to agree to this. Powell had picked him in one. Blix was critical of Iraq as well as saying that it had become more forthcoming; therefore more time was needed. Blix said that Powell's presentation had been powerful, but some of his claims were 'quite shaky'; US intelligence had not revealed a 'smoking gun'. Then the United States, itself, had not made that claim. He said that the United States and Britain were basing their political decisions on intelligence that, insofar as it had been shared with the United Nations Monitoring, Verification and Inspection Commission (UNMOVIC), had not revealed much. Given that Blix must by then have realised that there would not be a further resolution from the Security Council, he needed to keep his distance from the United States and Britain.

Blix made the astonishing admission to me that Iraq would 'not have moved an inch', without the pressure of the Allied military build-up. In other words, according to the chief weapons inspector appointed by the United Nations, a resolution of the Security Council carried no weight at all. He said that the military pressure must be maintained. I saw this as remarkable because of the double standard it connoted, as well as his acceptance of the inherent impotence of SC resolutions. Blix and others were highly critical of the United States acting outside any remit of the United Nations, yet were perfectly happy to help themselves to the benefits of a massive military build-up which was an essential prelude to a military invasion they would later condemn.

I pointed out to Blix that there came a time when the build-up no longer worked, and action needed to be considered. I said that no one should underestimate the resolve of the United States and Britain to carry through with military action. Blix replied that he had emphasised to the Iraqis that it was 'five minutes to midnight', but he had not picked up a sense of desperation from them.

In Downing Street, not only did Tony Blair make plain to me his strong position, and his determination to overcome domestic opposition, he confirmed the scale of the British military contribution. He had invested much personally into his association with Bush, and the alliance between Britain and the United States. He again displayed his exasperation at the blatant anti-Americanism which existed in many parts of Europe.

I then met the head of MI6, the British Secret Intelligence Service (SIS), Sir Richard Dearlove, at the High Commissioner's residence. Dearlove was a real professional. He showed me the most recent British intelligence on Iraq's weapons. The HUMINT, or Human Intelligence sources, available to the British from Iraqi sources, appeared quite extensive. This intelligence contained references to specific discussions, as well as intercepts, fully consistent with Iraq actually having some stored weapons and active weapons programs. It was quite compelling.

Then I returned home via Jakarta. Megawati was pleased that I had chosen to include her. The atmosphere was one of cordiality — but at a distance. That was par for the course following East Timor, and not due to Iraq. She both understood and appreciated my gesture in coming. She opposed any action against Iraq outside the express authority of the United Nations under another resolution, which she must have guessed would not materialise. Megawati said that, as a friend, Indonesia hoped that Australia would not be caught up in action against Iraq.

She nonetheless said that she did not see international efforts to disarm Iraq as anti-Islamic. Her reaction pleased me. I knew that our participation alongside the Americans in Iraq would not be popular in Islamic Asia. Anything I could do to reduce concerns was well worth the effort. This was especially so with Indonesia.

Despite my resolve to join the Americans and the British if a military invasion eventuated, I continued to hope that this could be avoided. Like Bush and Blair, I wanted another SC resolution. This was not because I doubted the legal authority available under existing resolutions 687 and 1441. It was because of the extra moral and political value. If there were a further resolution, then it would be harder for the ALP to oppose our involvement, given what Crean had previously said.

By the time of my return from overseas, in the second half of February, there was still no clarity about a fresh resolution. The French and the Russians were playing their usual games on the issue. Some intelligence suggested that France would finally come on board and that Moscow would then go quiet. Chirac's public comments did not encourage that view. The Americans and the British were reluctant to present another resolution unless it had reasonable prospects of being carried.

Blix reported again to the Security Council on 14 February. This report was more positive than that of 27 January, almost predictably so. He wanted more time to complete the inspections. Iraq was being more cooperative. That sounded fine in isolation. The problem was that Iraq had had 12 years to cooperate. The United Nations itself had done nothing at all about Iraq's non-compliance for four years, from December 1998 until being prodded into action by George Bush. Despite this, the Americans now were being beaten up for wanting to bring matters to a head.

On 1 March there was a real and unexpected setback for the United States, when the Turkish parliament voted to block the deployment of American troops through Turkey. This denied the United States the chance of a second front and needlessly complicated their military plans. The Americans had complacently assumed that Turkey was in the bag, and had not invested enough diplomatic effort into mustering internal support where it mattered, amongst Turkish legislators.

The parliamentary vote was narrow, thus underlining the fact that a little more legwork would have produced a different outcome.

The French position became more galling by the day. It was by now clear that they would not support another resolution, but Chirac openly acknowledged that the presence of the American and British military force in the Middle East, in preparation for a possible invasion of Iraq, had been highly beneficial, because of the pressure it had put on Saddam.

Speaking on 10 March, Chirac said, '… if the Americans and the British had not deployed their substantial forces, it is highly probable that Iraq would not have given this more active cooperation which the inspectors were demanding'.[11] The internal inconsistency of refusing any form of ultimatum or use of military force, while acknowledging the efficacy of military pressure, did not concern Paris.

By now Iraq was completely dominating my thinking. Other issues were dealt with, but the prospect of ordering Australian forces into battle in a conflict which would be very divisive in Australia troubled me a lot. I wrote in my diary on 19 February: 'Anyone who thinks that I'm a warmonger should understand how I feel. I think about it all the time, have broken sleep and hope that a late capitulation (very unlikely) or assassination of Saddam will remove the need for military action.' As the time for a likely invasion grew closer, some continued to hope that there would be a palace revolution in Baghdad. It was a hope that proved forlorn.

On 24 February, a fresh resolution was tabled at the Security Council by the United States, Britain and Spain. The gist was that the Security Council was being asked to say that Iraq had failed to take the final opportunity afforded it by resolution 1441. That it did not go the step further of authorising action to be taken, as a consequence of that failure, showed that support within the Security Council for military action being taken was at best lukewarm. That resolution was the maximum that the Americans and British thought that they could get. Even that calculation proved, in the end, to be too optimistic.

I knew that time had just about run out. Bush had stretched the process as much as possible to accommodate Blair, who needed to demonstrate to his own parliamentary party that he had exhausted every conceivable avenue in the pursuit of another resolution. By doing that he hoped to minimise defections within the British Labour Party when the House of Commons vote was taken.

As the countdown to D-day continued, we cleared our lines on process with the Americans. On 3 March, Thawley reported on a discussion he had had that day with Paul Wolfowitz, the deputy Defense secretary, in which he conveyed the steps we required in preparation for a final government decision to join an invasion, if one were decided upon.

Writing in my diary again, on 12 March, I said: 'It is 4 am in the morning. I could not sleep — a bad, but understandable sign. The UN process has bogged down. The French appear hell-bent on a veto. The Russians are making similar noises. There is a sense in which it is all slipping away from Britain and the US. The momentum is all the other way.'

Trying to marshal votes for the fresh resolution, I telephoned three leaders whose nations had rotating seats on the Security Council. They were Perves Masharaff of Pakistan, Bertie Ahern of Ireland and Vincente Fox of Mexico. I knew that Masharaff walked a tightrope as the leader of an overwhelmingly Islamic nation. Yet he had backed the Americans after 11 September. He listened to what I had to say, but was noncommittal; being like me a cricket tragic, we also discussed the latest developments in the great game. Bertie Ahern was also non-committal. I felt that in the end Ireland would simply go with the flow.

Fox was a different kettle of fish. He was quite unsympathetic to the Americans. He even presumed to tell me that he thought that Australia would be mistaken if it joined a military invasion. I knew that George Bush had hoped to build a good relationship with his Mexican counterpart. They seemed to have a lot in common, given Fox's business background. Fox was invited to address a joint sitting of congress, within months of his taking office. Iraq was an example of such gestures not being reciprocated. Fox's attitude verged on the hostile.

There was now only the remotest possibility of another SC resolution. Again writing in my diary of 12 March, I said: 'That will make it hard and bitter in Australia. There will be legal debates and some in the parliamentary party may object if we finally decided to go it alone with the US and UK. So far the colleagues have been superb. Their loyalty, in trying times, has been remarkable. I have had some very dark moments before, but this is as hard as it gets.'

Although the cabinet, most particularly my senior National Security Committee (NSC) colleagues, unconditionally supported our stance, I had been the driving force behind the firm support we had given to the Americans. Both the party and the public saw this as something to which I had given a deep personal commitment. Recognising this, I wrote the following in my diary, again on 12 March: 'I think all of us realise that if this really does go "pear-shaped", then that would be it for me. I should take the rap, for the sake of the party's future.' In thinking this I was not being unduly pessimistic, just utterly realistic. I had put everything on the line.

Supporting George Bush over Iraq made the Australian public quite uneasy. If military action took place with Australians involved, and by then most Australians believed that that would be the case, and it was quick, with few casualties, then the public's verdict would be accepting. On the other hand, if the invasion were protracted, with greater-than-expected casualties, then the public reaction would be hostile. Understandably, I would then wear the blame.

Bush invited me to a meeting in the Azores on 16 March of leaders of those nations likely to contribute to the sharp end of the military operation. Given the travel involved, there was no point in my going and, in any event, I was needed at home. Crunch time had arrived. There was now no hope of another resolution, not even in the mild form tabled on 24 February, and the United States and Britain abandoned their SC push.

Australia was to commit forces to battle without bipartisan support. I did not like that one bit, but had no alternative.

I had contempt for Labor's position. Beazley had backed our troop deployment in 1998. This time his party had effectively tied its future action to the whims of Jacques Chirac and Vladimir Putin. The irony of this, while repeatedly I was attacked for too closely following George Bush, never occurred to the opposition or indeed much of the Australian media.

I was falsely accused of slavishly following the Americans because of my close personal friendship with the President. Yet from the stance taken by the Labor opposition, it was clear that the determinant of Labor's position would ultimately be how France and Russia might vote in the Security Council on the further resolution sought by the Americans and the British, late in February 2003. Simon Crean said that if that resolution were carried, then his party would support Australia being involved alongside the Americans.

The Labor Party, consciously or otherwise, had taken a decision, effectively, to outsource Australia's foreign policy on Iraq to the Russians and the French, both of whom agreed Iraq had WMDs but were determined to exploit their power of veto in the UN Security Council for political advantage.

Apparently it was wrong of me to base a decision to go into Iraq, partly at least, on the strength of our decades-old and crucially important American alliance, yet it was in order to allow the caprice of an SC vote by the Russians and the French to determine the policy of the Australian Labor Party.

That further resolution sought by the Americans and the British failed to materialise, thanks to the unwillingness of the French and the Russians to support it. The other veto-wielding permanent member of the Security Council, China, would not have stood in the way of the resolution if the Russians and the French had waved it through. I had divined that from talking to Li Peng, the former premier, when he came to Australia in 2002.

The political debate in Australia was not between the Coalition arguing that a military operation was justified against the Labor Party asserting that it could never be justified, but rather about the precise circumstances in which it would be justified.

Indeed, Simon Crean, the Labor leader, made it clear on several occasions that if a further resolution of the Security Council were obtained, authorising the use of force, then the Labor Party would support Australia's involvement. Typically, though, Labor said that it did not support the type of military involvement which the Government had in mind. On 15 January 2003, Crean even suggested there might be circumstances in which he would support military action, absent a further resolution of the Security Council. He said, 'The UN could find itself in circumstances in which there is very strong support, based on the evidence that Saddam Hussein still has weapons, but a UN Security Council resolution can't be passed because one of the permanent members vetoes it. In those circumstances, I'm saying that we should consider those facts at the time.'[12]

Nor was the debate in Australia about whether or not Saddam Hussein possessed WMDs. The former prime minister, Kevin Rudd, then opposition spokesman on Foreign Affairs, famously said in an address to the State Zionist Council of Victoria on 15 October 2002 that it was 'an empirical fact' that Iraq had WMDs.[13] Instead of relying on UN reports to this effect, Rudd pointed the doubters in the direction of a report of the Federation of American Scientists. This body was founded by scientists who had worked on the Manhattan Project to develop the first atomic bomb. Rudd said that they attested to what he asserted to be an unarguable fact. In that same speech he said it was also an empirical fact that Saddam was a mass murderer.

When necessary, the ADF always displayed blunt professionalism, precisely what one should expect from Australian military commanders. A short while before the final decision was taken, the CDF, General Cosgrove, and the director of the Defence Intelligence Organisation (DIO), Frank Lewinkamp, called on me in my Canberra office. For more than an hour they spelled out in much detail the possible conditions and dangers our forces might face in Iraq, including from chemical and biological weapons.

They pulled no punches. They had charts, illustrations and graphs, and all that was necessary to drive home the fact that this would be a dangerous mission. They were coldly professional, and did not, in any way, gild the lily. They had served the men and women of the ADF extremely well. When the meeting finished, the man who, ultimately, would take the decision had been left in no doubt as to what was involved.

Once it was clear that no further SC resolution would eventuate, only a matter of days would elapse before George Bush pushed the button on the invasion of Iraq. The military forces of America, Britain and Australia were in place. The men and women themselves were rearing to go. Thankfully, soldiers always are. They join armies largely in the hope of seeing active service.

The legal advice given to the Government was that there was sufficient authority under earlier UN resolutions to justify action against Iraq. That advice was tabled in parliament.

Michael Thawley kept me constantly informed of White House thinking on when and how hostilities would start. Bush decided to issue Saddam with an ultimatum on 17 March that called on Saddam and his sons to leave Iraq within 48 hours in the name of the Coalition of the Willing — the collective name to describe those supporting in different ways the US-led operation — otherwise military action would start at a time of the Coalition's choosing. The President had been fully briefed on the domestic process I had to follow and, as a result, telephoned me twice in the days preceding the start of hostilities.

Iraq rejected the ultimatum almost immediately, and Bush felt quite at liberty to give the go-ahead forthwith, and even before the time set by the ultimatum had run out.

The NSC had been meeting regularly on Iraq, but I wanted full cabinet endorsement of a final decision to commit to the invasion. I called that cabinet meeting on the evening of 17 March. George Bush had telephoned me earlier that day; it was the day of his ultimatum to Saddam. There was unanimous support for Australian forces joining the action. It was the only possible decision, given all that had gone before.

I called a special joint party meeting to tell the two parliamentary parties of the decision. It came as no surprise to them, and there was no dissent. I then called a news conference to announce the decision to the Australian public. To complete the process I presented a resolution to the House of Representatives on 20 March seeking endorsement of the Government's action. As already explained, this was not necessary, but we had nothing to fear from a parliamentary debate. The Australian people would have found it unacceptable if a debate in parliament had not taken place.

In January 2003 a poll in Fairfax newspapers had shown that support for Australia joining an invasion of Iraq, without UN approval (meaning a new and specific resolution), stood at just 6 per cent. In the face of such widespread public hesitation, the unity of the Liberal and National parties, when it came to the crunch on Iraq, was quite remarkable. In the final vote every single person in the Liberal and National parties supported the Government's position, as did the former National Party member and by then Independent, Bob Katter. The other two Independents, Peter Andren and Tony Windsor, voted with the Labor Party.

Some colleagues were uneasy. Peter Lindsay was unhappy that there had not been another UN resolution. Judi Moylan worried about the humanitarian situation in Iraq. Alexander Downer listened to her concerns, and ensured that she participated in a delegation sent to the Middle East to assess humanitarian issues. I spent time talking to both of them. I was grateful that their loyalty to the Government and acceptance of its good faith took precedence over their individual concerns.

During a cabinet meeting late in 2002, Warren Truss had said that some staunch National Party supporters were uneasy, and one of them had said to him, 'Can't we just this once not go along with the Americans?' He sounded uneasy himself. This issue had stretched the loyalties of a great many people.

I had asked a lot of them on this issue, and their steadfastness was moving. It was a splendid illustration of the camaraderie and sense of loyalty and cohesion which was a hallmark of our almost 12 years in government. When I wound up the parliamentary debate on the Iraq resolution on 20 March I expressed my profound gratitude to my colleagues for their forbearance and loyalty.

On the day hostilities commenced, there was a special church service in the chapel of the Royal Military College Duntroon. We all prayed for the safe return of our men and women. That evening I addressed the nation to explain the Government's decision. I repeated my earlier arguments about the danger posed by Iraq's possession of WMDs, in particular that such weapons might fall into the hands of terrorists.

I also stressed the alliance dimensions of our decision, in the following way:

> There's also another reason and that is our close security alliance with the United States. The Americans have helped us in the past and the United States is very important to Australia's long-term security. It is critical that we maintain the involvement of the United States in our own region, where, at present, there are real concerns about the dangerous behaviour of North Korea.
>
> The relationship between our two countries will grow more rather than less important as the years go by.
>
> A key element of our close friendship with the US and indeed with the British is our full and intimate sharing of intelligence material. In the difficult fight against the new menace of international terrorism there is nothing more crucial than timely and accurate intelligence. This is a priceless component of our relationship with our two very close allies.
>
> There is nothing comparable to be found in any other relationship — nothing more relevant indeed to the challenges of the contemporary world.

In that address I asked for tolerance towards people of Arab descent and of the Islamic faith. I said, 'Our argument is with Saddam Hussein's regime. It is certainly not with Islam. Australians of an Arab background or of the Islamic faith are a treasured part of our community. Over the weeks ahead and beyond we should all extend to them the hand of Australian mateship.'

Also, and mindful of the disgraceful treatment of many Australian soldiers when they returned from Vietnam, I said that those in the community who disagreed with my decision should vent their anger against me and the Government, not our soldiers.

As events unfolded, Australian SAS were the first Coalition forces to cross the Iraqi border and engage the Iraqi Army. Press critics of the Government's decision tried to make something of this, suggesting that our forces had jumped the gun. This was not the case. The SAS did not enter Iraq until after the Iraqis had rejected the Bush ultimatum.

George Bush rang me again on Friday, 21 March for a general discussion and also to tell of a precision air strike which, he hoped, had taken out both Saddam and his two sons. The final result was not what he had hoped for. It was clear from this telephone talk that Bush felt a sense of relief that, for good or ill, things were at long last happening. He had known for some time that this day would come but he had patiently, and against the counsel of many in his Administration, sought additional SC cover for an invasion of Iraq. He had been right to do so.

It was a Thursday in Australia when the invasion order was given, and Janette and I spent the following weekend in Canberra so I could be in constant touch with the ADF hierarchy. On Saturday evening Janette and I invited the CDF, General Peter Cosgrove, his vice-chief and the three service chiefs and their wives to the Lodge for dinner. Those five men were a deeply impressive group. They understood the inherent dangers in military action of any kind and they harboured no illusions about what may lie ahead. I felt a special bond with them. The Lodge dinner was a way of emphasising that.

The sharp end of the military offensive against Iraq was both quick and effective. After rapid progress being made in the first 10 days, there was a hiatus while US forces secured over-extended supply lines and sandstorms restricted air operations. Critics in the United States lost no time alleging that Rumsfeld had not sent enough troops for the intensive phase of the attack. He immediately refuted this, and subsequent events, which saw the end of Saddam's regime in a little over a month after the start of hostilities, vindicated Rumsfeld in relation to the attack itself. As later developments were to highlight, it was an entirely different matter when it came to the stabilisation of Iraq after Saddam had gone. It was there that the claim that the Pentagon had skimped on the number of troops committed to Iraq had more potency.

There was euphoria at the sight of the pulling down of Saddam's statue, thus symbolising the successful conclusion of the invasion phase. The ordinary people in that country were glad to see the back of him. Even in the blackest moments in the several years of chaos that predated the surge, there was no appetite for a return of the hated former dictator.

The rapid conclusion of the assault against Saddam changed public opinion in Australia. On 26 March, Newspoll said that 50 per cent of Australians supported involvement in the war, up from 25 per cent only two weeks earlier. Similar movements occurred in both the United States and Britain.

The SAS, as always, performed with much distinction, this time suppressing Scud missiles in the Western Desert. The Hornets flew the first RAAF combat missions since Vietnam and HMAS *ANZAC* provided shellfire cover for the Royal Marines when they assaulted the Al Faw Peninsula. The Australian contingent packed a real punch and was warmly welcomed by our allies.

Their mission finished, the SAS returned in May 2003, and I welcomed them back at their home base at Swanbourne in Perth on 18 May, having the day before greeted the returning HMAS *ANZAC* and *Darwin*. I had had the opportunity of seeing quite a number of our troops in Qatar, on the way back from my May visit to the United States and Britain. They had done a superb job. Likewise with the squadron of Hornets; I went to Tindal Air Base in the Northern Territory several days earlier, to welcome them home. I could tell from the comments of the pilots and others just how much they had savoured the experience.

Although Australian forces were not part of the post-invasion stabilisation effort, significantly, in May 2004 Major General Jim Molan was appointed Chief of Operations in Iraq, directly answerable to General Casey, the US Commander. Molan oversaw a force of 300,000, including 150,000 Americans, through some of the bloodiest years of sectarian violence. His appointment said a lot about his professionalism as a soldier, as well as signalling the high regard in which the ADF was held.

Although Kevin Rudd would, opportunistically, back away from his unqualified assertion that Saddam had WMDs, the truth was that both Kevin Rudd and Kim Beazley were rather restrained, early in 2003, in their criticism of my Government's decision to go into Iraq. A careful analysis of their statements showed that if the post-invasion phase had gone better for the United States and her allies, neither of them would have had much difficulty in finding themselves supporting what the Government had done.

On 18 April 2003, Beazley told the *Age*, 'I was glad to see Saddam removed, and I am hopeful it will ensure at least one problem area in weapons of mass destruction is removed.'[14] In November 2003 Rudd wrote me a long letter, after visiting Iraq, with suggestions for additional Australian involvement. He wrote, 'Now that regime change has occurred in Baghdad, it is the Opposition's view that it is now the responsibility of all people of goodwill, both in this country and beyond, to put their shoulder to the wheel in an effort to build a new Iraq.'[15] No mention there of pulling out our troops. He wanted more resources for Baghdad.

Rudd was hedging his bets. Several years later, and before the surge had begun to turn things around in Iraq, Rudd would allege that Iraq had been 'the greatest failure of national security policy since Vietnam'.[16]

George Bush was immensely grateful for our support. As a way of indicating publicly how he felt, he invited Janette and me to spend a weekend with him and Laura at the family ranch in Crawford, Texas. We were to be joined, as guests at the ranch, by Condi Rice as well as Laura's mother, Jenna Welch. It was a most enjoyable stay, which gave an added personal dimension to the already close relationship between us.

Janette and I joined the President on Air Force One at Travis Air Force Base, near San Francisco, for the flight to Texas. The three of us discussed a whole range of political issues, including the challenges as well as the benefits of having so many politicians in the one family. It was obvious from this discussion just how important the Bush clan was to the President's whole life and motivation.

The last stage of the journey was by helicopter, and during this ride Condi Rice remarked to me that George Bush and I agreed on many things. I said that one area of disagreement would have to be gun control laws, where the sort of action I had taken after Port Arthur could never even be contemplated by an American president.

She thought for a moment, and then said, 'Prime Minister, as a black girl, growing up when I did in Alabama, something my father taught me early on was how to use a gun.' It gave an entirely different perspective to the issue. Thankfully it was not something that young Australians had had to grapple with. In his book about Condoleezza Rice, *Twice as Good*, the journalist Marcus Mabry describes graphically how the black community of which the Rice family was part had, for a time, to establish their own vigilante groups to afford protection, due to the indifference of the local police.

Condi Rice is a remarkable and highly talented person. The story of her success despite the adversities which her family had to endure is quite inspiring. Of the African-Americans who have risen to very high office in recent times, none endured quite the raw brutal segregation of the Rice family in Birmingham, Alabama, in the 1950s and '60s. She belonged to a tight, loving family whose constant emphasis on the critical role of educational attainment was the key to her success.

As well as socialising there was plenty of work over the weekend. The President invited me to sit in on his daily CIA intelligence briefing, and, later on Saturday morning, we had a full bilateral discussion (which covered many topics unrelated to Iraq) followed by a joint news conference outside the well-televised Crawford barn, complete with the 'first dog', Barney. During our formal meeting Bush made it crystal clear to me and his advisors, including Bob Zoellick, the Special Trade Representative, that he wanted the free trade negotiations between our two countries finished by the end of the year.

There was a lot of resistance from within the American system to the very notion of a free trade agreement (FTA) with a developed country such as Australia. That morning in Crawford, Bush decreed that it would be otherwise with Australia. I knew then that, all things being equal, we would achieve the FTA.

After Texas I went to New York and saw Kofi Annan. We talked about the United Nations' role in Iraq. He needed a tested figure to head up the UN mission in Baghdad, and I recommended Sergio de Mello, the urbane Brazilian diplomat who had been the UN man in East Timor. Annan appointed him to the post, and a few months later he was killed in a terrorist attack on the UN headquarters in Baghdad. Whenever I think of that attack, I recall the recommendation that I gave to the Secretary General, and feel just a touch responsible.

Then it was on to London to see Tony Blair, who had just reached his 50th birthday. He was not to have much of a celebration. At the end of May, straight after visiting British troops in Iraq, Blair was confronted with the BBC report claiming that Downing Street had 'sexed up' a detail — the 'ready in 45 minutes' assertion — in the intelligence dossier published the previous September. The British Prime Minister was dogged for months by this issue, which turned into a nightmare in July 2003 with the suicide of the scientist Dr David Kelly.

A judicial inquiry, headed by Lord Justice Hutton, concluded that there was no justification to the allegation that the Blair Government probably knew that the 45-minute claim was unfounded. Hutton also concluded that the dossier containing the 45-minute claim was issued with the full approval of the British Joint Intelligence Committee, the agency having ultimate responsibility to assess the quality of intelligence material.

Despite this emphatic exculpation of the Blair Government by a respected and totally independent jurist, and the appalling behaviour of the

BBC revealed by the affair, the perception remained that Tony Blair had deliberately distorted the intelligence case over Iraq. The British press gave Blair a torrid time over Iraq.

As the weeks following the combat phase in Iraq turned into months, two issues began to haunt the Government. No WMDs were found and, worse still, violence within Iraq began to escalate. With the growing insurgency came increasing American casualties and, inexorably, support for the war in the United States began to erode, but only slowly at first. A similar pattern emerged here in Australia, but it was less intense. Most of our troops had come home.

After the regime was toppled I thought that it would only be a matter of time before some WMDs were found. I had believed the intelligence which pointed overwhelmingly to Iraq possessing at least chemical and biological weapons. I and many others were to be disappointed. After months of the most intensive search possible the Iraq Survey Group, essentially put together by the CIA, reported that it could not find stockpiles of WMDs. There was plenty of evidence of WMD programs, but no actual weaponry itself. In other words, Iraq had the know-how and the capacity to make the weapons, but no stockpiles of weapons themselves.

This gave a lethal political weapon to our opponents, and they made the most of it. In the process they ignored the fact that, prior to the military action, they too had accepted the existence of WMDs. The truest of the true believers on the Labor side had been none other than Kevin Rudd. He had boldly declared that it was 'an empirical fact'.[17] So far from feeling constrained by that assertion, he would later go on to claim that I had taken Australia to war in Iraq based on 'a lie'. The implication was that I had in some way faked the intelligence. Similar attacks were mounted against George Bush and Tony Blair.

To illustrate the force of the intelligence on which I and my colleagues, as well as Bush and Blair, had relied, I quote from the National Intelligence Assessment (NIA) of October 2002. This document, made available to the Australian Government as well as the US Administration, was declassified on 18 July 2003. It contained the following key judgements:

> We judge that Iraq has continued its weapons of mass destruction programs in defiance of UN resolutions and restrictions. Baghdad has chemical and biological weapons as

well as missiles with ranges in excess of UN restrictions; if left
unchecked, it probably will have a nuclear weapon during this
decade. (See INR alternative view at the end of the key
judgements).

We judge that we are only seeing a portion of Iraq's WMD
efforts, owing to Baghdad's vigorous denial and deception
efforts. Revelations after the Gulf War starkly demonstrate the
extensive efforts undertaken by Iraq to deny information. We
lack specific information on many key aspects of Iraq's WMD
programs.

Since inspections ended in 1998, Iraq has maintained its
chemical weapons effort, energized its missile program, and
invested more heavily in biological weapons; in the view of most
agencies, Baghdad is reconstituting its nuclear weapons
program.[18]

An NIA is a distillation of the views of all of the intelligence agencies,
including, of course, the CIA. It is the most authoritative intelligence
statement in the US system. The key judgements of October 2002 had not
been made up. They had not been invented or coerced out of officials to
satisfy political needs. They were professional conclusions which had to be
treated with the utmost seriousness.

The Bureau of Intelligence and Research (INR) is the intelligence unit of
the State Department. The alternative view of INR referred to in the
judgements related to the claim that Saddam had tried to source uranium
from Niger. The State Department believed that this claim had no
foundation. Using entirely different intelligence sources, the British SIS
(MI6) believed that Iraq had approached Niger for uranium. My reference
to this issue, in one of my speeches, was based on the British advice, not the
American. Subsequent parliamentary inquiries in Britain have concluded
that this intelligence was correct.

The language of the NIA was sharp and direct. The agencies did not
hedge their bets. The stark language of the key judgements presented a
strong intelligence basis for the decision to take out Saddam.

Nonetheless, as time wore on, and no stockpiles of WMDs were found,
the embarrassment became intense. The mounting violence only made
matters worse. In time it would become the more nagging problem. Failure
to find WMDs was an acute problem but if, in other respects, the post-

invasion period had gone well, with a relatively smooth pathway to a more democratic future being in prospect, failure on the WMD front would have been less damaging.

The frustration for the United States, and especially George Bush, on Iraq lay not in the original decision, nor in the military operation. That decision was right and the military phase was well executed, with low casualties on both sides. The real failure of American policy over Iraq lay in the breakdown of the post-invasion arrangements.

It is difficult to escape the conclusion that more troops had been needed to keep order in the post-invasion phase. This mistake was compounded by the decision to disband the Iraqi Army. That army, minus its senior Ba'athist leadership, could well have been deployed to help maintain order in the wake of Saddam's removal.

The post-invasion chaos and the failure to find stockpiles of WMDs led to a decline in public support for the Iraqi operation in Australia.

This mattered tremendously in both the United States and Britain, due to the large ongoing troop presence from those countries, especially the Americans, who sustained painfully high casualties over four years. Over 4000 Americans have died in Iraq.

Nonetheless, the accusations of faking intelligence were hurled thick and fast at me. The claim that I had lied about or deliberately manufactured intelligence was palpably absurd, deeply offensive to the intelligence agencies and in no way supported by the parliamentary and other inquiries, conducted later in 2003, into the pre-war intelligence. I believed the intelligence assessments; so did George Bush and Tony Blair. We were not presented with proof beyond a reasonable doubt. That never happens with intelligence. ONA said in its submission to the parliamentary inquiry, 'ONA said in a report of 31 January 2003 that there is a wealth of intelligence on Saddam's WMD activities, but it paints a circumstantial picture that is conclusive overall rather than resting on a single piece of irrefutable evidence.'[19]

The DIO, which provided regular reports as well, largely agreed with the substance of ONA's assessments, although its language was sometimes more qualified. Still, taking as its foundation the track record of non-disclosure, obfuscation and downright deception by Iraq, DIO, in its submission to the same inquiry said, '... DIO consistently assessed that Iraq probably retained a WMD capability — even if that capability had been degraded over time. DIO also assessed that Iraq maintained both an intent and capability to recommence a wider WMD program should circumstances permit it to do so.'[20]

These statements, made months after the invasion, and when it was increasingly apparent that WMD stockpiles would not be found, scarcely support the criticism that there was insufficient evidence before the Government that Iraq had WMDs, let alone the more disgraceful allegations of dishonesty and manufactured intelligence.

As well as the parliamentary review, there was an inquiry conducted by Phillip Flood, a former secretary of the Department of Foreign Affairs and Trade (DFAT). Amongst other things, he found 'no evidence of politicisation of the assessments on Iraq either overt or perceived' or that 'any analyst or manager was the subject of either direct or implied pressure to come to a particular judgement on Iraq for policy reasons or to bolster the case for war'.[21]

Flood went on to say that assessments 'reflected reasonably the available evidence and used intelligence sources with appropriate caution'. He said that the obverse conclusion, that Iraq had no WMDs, 'would have been a much more difficult conclusion to substantiate'.[22]

Late in 2003 Mark Latham, who had attacked George Bush over Iraq and more generally, surprisingly defeated Kim Beazley for the leadership of the ALP to succeed Simon Crean, who had been pressured to go. Given Latham's volatile temperament it was only a matter of time before he got himself into trouble over Iraq. This happened on 22 March 2004, when he told Radio 2UE in Sydney that if he won the election he would bring the troops 'home by Christmas'.[23] This was a sign of bad judgement on a delicate issue. He, and others in the Labor Party, failed to realise that many Australians who opposed our going into Iraq nonetheless were of the view that having gone there, we should stay and complete the job. They did not want us to cut and run.

With the failure to find WMDs, and the mounting violence inside Iraq, the issue began to become a negative for the Government. The political question was how much of a negative? A growing number of Australians were reaching the conclusion that it had been a mistake to have gone in, but that did not mean that they favoured pulling out before the job was finished.

The centre-right government in Spain was spectacularly defeated on 14 March 2004, several days after a horrific attack by an al Qaeda-inspired terrorist group on a train in Madrid which killed 191 people. Under Jose Maria Asnar, that government had supported the invasion. Many argued the train attack was a reprisal for Spain's support of Bush, and the election result punishment of the defeated government for having backed the Americans.

The latter proposition was more problematic. Despite signs that the attack carried an al Qaeda imprint (within hours of the attack the director general of ONA had informed me that he believed that, at the very least, it had been inspired by al Qaeda), the Spanish Government tried to blame the attack on the Basque separatist group Eta, which had been engaged in a long-running terror campaign designed to win autonomy for the Basque region of Spain.

The Spanish public did not buy the Eta argument. They thought that their government was being manipulative. Also, it did not help that Asnar himself, who had been the architect of Spain's Iraq policy, was retiring at the election. The impression was created that the Spanish Government was walking away from its Iraq policy.

The defeat of the Spanish Government had an unexpected and most regrettable consequence in Australia, involving the federal police commissioner Mick Keelty. Interviewed on Channel Nine shortly after the Madrid attack, Keelty said if it turned out that the Madrid attack was the work of Islamic extremists, then 'it's more likely to be linked to the position that Spain and others took on issues such as Iraq'.[24] That comment directly challenged the view of the Government that involvement in Iraq had not lifted the likelihood of terrorist attacks in Australia. For Spain read Australia. The commissioner knew our position. He was not commenting operationally. The ranking terrorism advisor in Australia was Dennis Richardson, head of ASIO, who shared the Government's view.

When it became known that Arthur Sinodinos, at my request, had telephoned Keelty to discuss the handling of the issue, the media came in hot pursuit. I was accused of heavying the commissioner on an issue vital to Australia's security. The public liked Keelty, and over the next two weeks there was a wave of support for him. He contemplated resignation, but after a long discussion I persuaded him to stay at his post. That was a huge relief, as he had done splendid work in many areas, and we enjoyed a positive relationship. In different ways the AFP had prospered under the Howard Government. I was quite distressed to have been seen at odds, publicly, with a man I both liked and respected. But he had been out of line. It was not his patch; he was not possessed of information denied to others and, importantly, he had never expressed a different view on Iraq from that of the Government to either his minister or me.

That much of the media support for the commissioner was really a proxy attack on me was made clear four years later, when it turned savagely and unfairly on Keelty over the Haneef Affair.

Iraq continued to echo in the political ears of governments which had contributed to the Coalition. The result in Spain had unnerved a lot of people. My Government would face an election in a few months, ahead of either the United States or Britain. There was intense interest in both countries about what would happen in the Australian election.

On the night of the 2004 election George Bush and Tony Blair rang to congratulate me on winning. I took both of their phone calls whilst I was still at the Wentworth Hotel in Sydney, where I had gone to deliver my victory speech. In fact I had only just finished my speech when the Bush phone call came through. He was genuinely excited about my win. Not only was there full-blooded centre-right partisanship in his reaction, but our close personal relationship gave the moment a special edge. To cap it all he would have his moment of truth with the American people in just under a month. If I had lost, that would have fed directly into the US campaign and could have acted as a real circuit-breaker for his opponent, John Kerry, who was campaigning hard against Bush's policy on Iraq. Bush was ecstatic. He saw my win as a good omen.

Blair was a little more restrained, but only by degrees. He was after all meant to be barracking for the other side. He fully absorbed the significance of what had happened, as had Bush. Iraq had not been an impediment for me, therefore it might not be for them, despite the fact that their nations' respective involvements had been greater than had been Australia's.

Bush went on to win the 2004 presidential election quite comfortably. When I rang to congratulate him, his first words were, 'John, I've fought my last election campaign.' It was a reminder of the different character of a presidential system, with term limits, when compared with a parliamentary system. He knew then that he would retire from the White House on 20 January 2008.

During the election campaign in Australia I had been asked, several times, the routine question as to whether or not more troops would be sent to Iraq. I had replied in the negative, as that accurately reflected the fact that the Americans had not asked for more, and the issue simply had not come up within the Government.

In mid-November, however, the issue did arise. The Japanese had an engineering detachment doing reconstruction work in Al Muthanna Province in southern Iraq. Security had been provided for them by Dutch troops. They were going home, which created a problem. Without force protection, the Japanese engineers would need to be withdrawn, which obviously neither the British (who had overall responsibility for the southern section of Iraq), nor the Americans, wanted.

At a military level our Coalition partners said that they would like us to supply the 500 or so soldiers needed to plug the gap. Bush would not ask me directly for help, feeling that that would go against our original understanding that our involvement of combat troops would be limited to the initial invasion phase. The Japanese wanted us involved. After a good deal of discussion, the NSC decided to provide the troops. Blair and Junichiro Koizumi, the Japanese Prime Minister, both made formal requests of me.

I saw this decision as important in building a strategic dimension to our longstanding economic partnership with Japan. It was this deployment which paved the way for the historic Joint Declaration on Security Cooperation I was to sign with the Japanese Prime Minister, Shinzo Abe, in 2007. The fact that the soldiers were being sent to guard Japanese engineers helped win acceptance of the decision from the Australian public. We had come a long way from World War II. Japan had become, to most Australians, a key partner, economically and now strategically.

Earlier in this chapter, I touched on the proper context in which to assess America's decision to go into Iraq. The other requirement for a more balanced appreciation of US, British and Australian policy on Iraq is to understand just how much pain and difficulty the Iraqis have endured to establish some kind of democratic structure in their country. At a national level there have already been four separate sets of elections. The first was to vote in a Transitional National Assembly. The second was to approve a new constitution, in which 80 per cent of the electorate voted. The third was in December 2005, to elect a new parliament. Another full parliamentary poll took place in March 2010, with a turnout slightly higher than that which elected Barack Obama. In addition, there have been provincial elections. These were held in January 2009 in 14 of Iraq's 18 provinces.

Millions of Iraqis have voted, despite intimidation involving death threats, murder and other acts of violence designed to frustrate the emergence of democracy. That the Iraqis have endured all of this and persisted with embracing their form of democracy means that the democratic ideal has more long-term appeal in that country than many of George Bush's critics want to admit.

These elections have been carried out in the glare of international inspection. By and large they have passed the test of authenticity and transparency. The contrast between what occurred in Iraq from 2005 to 2010 and the disgraceful sham of the 2009 election in Iran could not be more pronounced.

It will be a long time before there is a settled historical verdict on Iraq. Much will depend on that country's future internal stability and interaction with other Middle Eastern states. If Iraq consolidates into a functioning democracy, a lot will have been achieved. Given its natural resources (largely oil), and a well-educated population, it has much potential. The crucial determinant will be the extent to which Sunnis, Shi'ites and Kurds can live together as Iraqis.

America and her allies were justified in taking out Saddam's regime. There was a proper legal basis, flowing from the unrequited resolutions of the UN Security Council. Given the wholly understandable concern of the Americans, after 11 September 2001, that there would be another attack, Saddam's past record, and the reasonably entertained belief that he had WMDs, meant that leaving him be was too great a risk for the United States to take.

In the prelude to March 2003, I and my colleagues carefully argued the case that Saddam had WMDs. Never far beneath the surface was, however, the alliance dimension of the decision. As I have already written, Americans do fret about how they are seen around the world. The image of Americans as arrogant, gun-toting individuals who are insensitive to foreign opinion has never been particularly accurate. Americans felt especially vulnerable after 11 September. There was a latent feeling amongst many that a mistake had been made in 1991 in not finishing off Saddam, after the liberation of Kuwait.

Australia's emphatically supportive reaction, in the wake of the terrorist attacks, lifted our relationship to a new and higher level. Americans, as well as their President, were touched by our support. For the citizens of such a powerful country, Americans have always had a surprising sense of isolation, verging on a feeling of unpopularity. Thus, open support coming from Australia, with which they have long felt an affinity, because of our common settler and new world histories, was especially welcome.

In May 2003, after the combat phase of the war in Iraq was over, I attended a baseball game at Yankee Stadium in New York. My presence was acknowledged; I received a standing ovation from the crowd and was deeply moved by a short on-field ceremony honouring recent war dead, which involved parading the flags of our two nations as well as the Marine Flag. That crowd of sports-mad New Yorkers knew who their nation's friends were. At the game, I was interviewed by a cable-TV sports channel. The presenter had been provided with that wonderful old photograph taken in the early 1930s of Babe Ruth and Don Bradman during the latter's visit to the USA. He showed it on the screen and we talked about the significance of these two lengendary figures to their respective countries.

Just as the United States had gratefully accepted allies in striking against the Taliban in Afghanistan, so it was that she would be seeking allies in any invasion of Iraq. It was almost instinctive that the US would look to nations such as Britain and Australia for support. We had been together before on so many occasions. The added dimension this time was that Islamic fanaticism viewed as anathema the open, liberal pluralistic societies of which the United States, Britain and Australia were so emblematic.

From the start George Bush knew that going into Iraq would be controversial, no matter how strong the feeling to do so might be in the United States. It would be a world away from the relatively simple task his father had faced in putting together the alliance to expel Saddam from Kuwait. There an orthodox invasion of the old-fashioned kind had occurred. Saddam's army had rolled across the border and taken Kuwait. It would have been impossible for the United Nations to have stood by and done nothing.

Iraq in 2003 was entirely different. There had been no conventional aggression to which all could point. Rather the case against Iraq rested on cumulative acts of non-compliance with United Nations resolutions, a track record of condoning and supporting acts of terrorism, as well as compelling evidence that Iraq had WMD stockpiles. The other overwhelming difference from 1991 was that in 2001 America felt vulnerable and genuinely scared that there would be another assault by terrorists.

In all of these circumstances I found it inconceivable, given our shared history and values, that we would not stand beside the Americans. To baulk at that decision, purely on the basis that the Security Council had not passed another resolution — especially when it had not been deemed necessary in 1998, when similar action was contemplated — seemed to me to be cloaking unwillingness to confront the substance of the issue with a thin and legalistic veneer.

My attitude has not changed.

35

GEORGE BUSH

My close personal friendship with George Walker Bush, the 43rd President of the United States, attracted great attention in my time at the Lodge. We were closer friends than any other two occupants of the leadership positions we once respectively held. We remain in regular contact. We have seen each other and dined together with our wives on a number of occasions since both being out of office. Janette and I have been to the home they established in the suburbs of Dallas, Texas, after leaving the White House. It is a genuine friendship. We enjoy each other's company.

That authority on friendships Dr Samuel Johnson said that one never has to explain them. That ought to be as true of presidents and prime ministers as it is of others, but my experience has been that it is not. If an association between heads of government becomes a friendship, as was the case with me and Bush, then there seems to be a lot of explaining to do.

I was in office for almost 12 years and thus had the opportunity of many associations with fellow leaders. Most of them did not progress beyond the stage of professional cordiality, either through infrequency of meetings or departure from office or, in some instances, not finding much to talk about except the business at hand. At our only meeting, Joseph Estrada, the Philippines President, nodded off.

Others became closer, reaching a certain level of friendship. Into that category I would place Susilo Bambang Yudhoyono of Indonesia, Jiang Zemin of China, Helen Clark of New Zealand, Jean Chrétien, the former prime minister of Canada, as well as his successor but one, Stephen Harper.

In Harper's case I was the one who departed the scene. We only shared office for some 18 months, but became quite friendly. We were philosophically aligned, and in that short time I addressed a sitting of the Canadian parliament and Harper a joint sitting in Canberra, the only Canadian prime minister to do so. We remain in touch.

I have written elsewhere of my relationship with Helen Clark. We are different people with different perspectives on life. Our common desire to keep relations between our countries as close as possible produced an amiable relationship when we were both in government. I write in Chapter 38 of my friendship with Jiang Zemin.

Susilo Bambang Yudhoyono, the President of Indonesia, is easy to like. His instincts towards Australia are naturally warm and friendly. We first connected when he was a senior minister in Megawati's Government. A progressive Muslim, he understood the threat that extremism posed to his country as well as to the reputation of his faith. He knew that the terrorists had to be actively hunted down and removed from society. I was delighted when he was elected president in 2004. We became good friends during the time that we led our respective governments. The legacy of that friendship is to be found in the continuing good relations between Indonesia and Australia.

A common passion for cricket was a bond between Perves Masharaff, the former president of Pakistan, and me. I liked him a lot and we visited each other's country when in office. Australia's loss of the Ashes in 2005 coincided with a large UN meeting in New York. At the formal reception I congratulated Tony Blair on England's win. Masharaff saw us together and came over, saying to me, 'John, we will avenge you.' Pakistan's cricket team was as good as their President's word. Later that year Pakistan defeated the touring Englishmen. Masharaff and his wife were progressive Muslims, who strongly supported an improved place for women in Pakistani society.

My last conversation, as PM, with Masharaff was early in November 2007. He was by then deep in the constitutional stand-off following his dismissal of the chief justice of Pakistan. As a friend, I said that his action against the judiciary was not something that I could possibly defend. It did not in any way involve Australia, but as someone who liked him, I felt I owed him the candour of my views.

He never sought the presidency, but I found Colin Powell an impressive and engaging man, gregarious and good-humoured. He called to see me only a few months after my election, and we spent two hours one Saturday morning at Kirribilli House talking extensively about a range of international issues as well as his experience in the American military. I knew from that meeting that he would never be a candidate for the US presidency, although filling another high position was not out of the question.

I asked him why the Coalition forces had not gone on to Baghdad in 1991 and finished off Saddam Hussein. My strongest recollection of his response was Powell saying that Coalition forces would have found it morally repugnant to pursue the Iraqi Army, which by then was so shattered and vulnerable that heavy losses would have been inflicted on a defenceless foe. It was a soldier's explanation rather than the rationale of a politician. He sounded sincere.

Close though these relationships were, they did not match the intensity of my interactions with both George Bush and Tony Blair. The shared adversity of what we did together, especially over Iraq, created a natural bond.

The former British prime minister was a polished public presenter, widely respected in Australia, even by many who strongly opposed his support for the invasion of Iraq. I always found the embarrassment of the Australian Labor Party regarding Blair as quite exquisite. Here was their man, a highly successful Labour leader, agreeing with the approach of George Bush and me on the most controversial foreign policy issue of the day. When Labor furiously attacked Bush and me over Iraq, there was never a mention of Blair. Our opponents just didn't quite know how to handle this. And it was not as if Blair soft-pedalled his position on Iraq. He was always full-on with what he both said and did.

His address to a joint sitting of the Australian parliament on 27 March 2006 led to feet shuffling from some Labor members. He was uncompromising in his attacks on terrorism and made no apologies for Britain's staunch support of Bush's Iraqi policy. Speaking of both Iraq and Afghanistan, he declared, 'We must not hesitate in the face of a battle utterly decisive as to whether the values we believe in triumph or fail.'[1] He could not have been plainer. Blair drew a more enthusiastic response from our side than he did from our opponents.

Bush and I came from the same side of politics. I don't want to overvalue this, but it can matter in how a relationship starts. I had a natural sympathy for George Bush from the beginning, not only because he was a Republican and the son of his father, whom so many Australians liked. He was also not Al Gore. Gore had stood in for Clinton at the APEC meeting in Kuala Lumpur in 1998, and had appeared to me, and, I suspect, many others, as arrogant and overbearing.

The tense and protracted ballot count in the disputed election of 2000 guaranteed an even greater sense of satisfaction with the outcome and interest in the victor, when it was finally resolved. Whilst publicly neutral, privately I had wanted Bush to win. There was a small personal element in it because of his mother and father. I had first met them both, 18 years earlier, when they had represented their country at Battle of the Coral Sea celebrations in Australia in 1982. I sat next to Barbara Bush at an official dinner. The wife and mother, respectively, of two future presidents is a forceful, eminently likeable woman. Her candour is both genuine and endearing. Her son has his mother's bluntness, in spades, and his father's whimsical sense of humour.

In 1986, George Bush, the older, received me in his Vice-presidential capacity when I went to Washington as Leader of the Opposition. Twelve years later we met again on the Royal Melbourne Golf Course, when, as spectators we followed some of the contestants in the President's Cup competition, won on that occasion by the Rest of the World team captained by Australia's own Peter Thomson. We talked a lot about American politics and the possibility of his son seeking the Republican nomination. The younger Bush had just been re-elected as Governor of Texas. The older Bush exhibited huge pride in the prospect of his son also going into the White House. Although it would have been against his nature ever to have said it, there must have been a sense in which the father was hoping that the son would at least have that extra four years in the White House which Bill Clinton's victory of 1992 had denied him.

Always alive to the future, Michael Thawley, who became Australia's ambassador in Washington early in 2000, established contact with Condi Rice, who had joined the Bush team before he won the Republican nomination. Methodically Michael built the relationship with her. Coincidentally, my regularly seeing Dick Cheney, whenever he came to Australia on Halliburton business (he was CEO of the company), meant that another valuable link existed when he was nominated as Bush's running mate. An overarching rule of politics is constant networking. The frequency of international travel means there is always somebody in town who wants to see you. Unless one has finally and utterly left public life, you always try and fit in as many calls as possible. I enjoyed seeing Cheney, but I had no idea when he started coming that he would in a few years' time be Vice-president.

I spoke to Bush by phone when he was still Governor of Texas, and after he had secured his party's nomination for the presidency. That was our only contact before he became president. The prolonged 2000 presidential ballot drama meant that the normal round of congratulatory phone calls of a newly elected president did not take place. Bush had a rushed transition. As a result we did not speak to each other as president and prime minister until early in February, two weeks after his inauguration.

That discussion occurred one day after the death of Don Bradman. Well briefed, Bush referred to this event at the beginning of our discussion; responding competitively, I said that Babe Ruth had been the Don Bradman of the United States. Apart from appreciating his courtesy and punctuality — his National Security Advisor, Condoleezza Rice, had come onto the telephone five minutes before our conversation was due to take place to apologise for the fact that he might be a few minutes late as he was finishing off a meeting with a congressional delegation — I had not formed any opinion of him.

I had no occasion to speak to him again until those momentous days in September 2001. My impressions, on meeting George Bush in person for the very first time on Monday, 10 September 2001, were all positive. He was friendly, courteous, well briefed, and fully understood the historic warmth of the relationship; he gave every indication that he would make the requisite time commitment as befitted a friendship as old and as close as that between our two nations.

On our first day together, which included the impressive Naval Dockyard ceremony to mark the 50th anniversary of the signing of the ANZUS treaty, Bush and I spent some four hours together.

At every stage Bush was unhurried and relaxed. His mind was on our talks. He did not pretend to be an expert on Australia, but he knew a lot about our country. There was nothing artificial in his reactions. He was well across his brief and spoke easily and definitively on each subject in our discussions. He impressed me as a highly intelligent man with a well-organised mind. He had little patience for intellectual pretensions and did not waste his time airing his knowledge on subjects irrelevant to the topic under notice. He was self-confident, but, so far from being arrogant, I detected at our first meeting a tendency to humorous self-deprecation. I would experience a lot of this likeable character trait over the years ahead.

Back in my hotel, after my dinner with Rupert Murdoch, I reflected that, when added to the turnout at the ambassador's barbecue the previous day, and the meetings I had had with Colin Powell and Donald Rumsfeld, the latter at the Pentagon, after my discussion and lunch with the President, I was entitled to feel that not only was the alliance in good shape but that our American friends had gone out of their way to make me feel welcome. And, at that stage, there was an address to a joint sitting of congress still to come. Such a reception went way beyond the normal courtesies extended to visitors to Washington, even from the ever-cordial Americans. This had been driven from the top. At this early stage in his presidency, and only hours before events which would change the world in our lifetimes and drive our nations even closer together, the President of the United States had signalled that he placed a premium on his and his country's links with Australia.

This is a crucial understanding. There has been far too great a readiness on the part of commentators to see the closeness of my relationship with George Bush exclusively in terms of September 11 and its aftermath, with the implication that without it the relationship would not have received any special emphasis from Bush himself. The truth is that the President had decided to lift the relationship several notches, quite independently of the terrorist attacks. It was coincidence, and nothing else, that this occurred on the very eve of those attacks.

Why was this so? Some of the explanation lies in the personality of the President himself and some was due to his world-view. Although George Bush was far less of the unilateralist than his critics claimed, he correctly believed that we still lived in a world of nation states. He always had more faith in cooperative effort between like-minded nations than in the processes of multilateral movements or organisations. Dismissed by its critics as American arrogance, this approach had the history of the 1990s on its side.

The United Nations stood by or, worse still, ignored the Rwandan slaughter. Its Kosovo mandate had been so limited that NATO forces helplessly watched the Bosnian Serbs systematically kill thousands of Muslim men, in what many described as Europe's worst ethnically driven atrocity since the Holocaust. In 1999 NATO countries properly ignored the Security Council's impotence (due to a threatened Russian veto) to bomb

Serbia, thus finally breaking the Milosevic regime. In strict legal terms, there had been less authority in international law for this action than that of the Coalition of the Willing when it invaded Iraq in 2003.

Then there had been the dilemma of the first Gulf War in 1991. The President's father had assembled a mighty coalition to speedily eject Saddam Hussein from Kuwait. Yet he had stopped short of rolling on to Baghdad and removing the hated Iraqi dictator altogether. Constrained by the limitations of a UN mandate which only extended to the liberation of Kuwait, George H.W. Bush would, in the eyes of many, particularly Americans, be seen to have only half completed the job. The Shi'ite population of southern Iraq felt betrayed, having risen against Saddam in the expectation of getting American help, only to be bitterly disappointed when it did not come. Even worse was the belief that the limitations imposed on Saddam at the end of the first Gulf War regarding the use of his forces permitted activation of enough of them which were needed to re-assert his authority over the Shi'ia and Kurds, then in revolt.

Throughout his presidency George Bush talked of his freedom agenda. He believed that the greatest benefit that the United States could bring to the world was to use its immense power to spread political freedoms to those many countries which did not have it.

His raison d'être was expanding freedom; if that could be realised with cooperation through bodies such as the United Nations, then all well and good. If, by contrast, that were not forthcoming he would look to kindred spirits amongst other nations in pursuing his freedom agenda. He was not prepared to surrender to the United Nations the ultimate authority to determine international right or wrong or the circumstances in which the use of force by nations might be justified, especially when the use of that force might result in large numbers of people gaining their freedom.

To many this was defiance of the international rule of law and a repudiation of the lofty ideals on which the United Nations had been founded. The world had put its faith in international order as an alternative to the horrors of two catastrophic wars. The rule of law, applied universally, would save the world from such disasters in the future. What was needed was for all nations, powerful and weak alike, to play by the rules and submit themselves absolutely to the adjudication of the United Nations.

There was another view, which I shared. Few credible historians would argue that the existence of the United Nations in the 1930s — or, more precisely, the old League of Nations, with greater authority and with the United States as a member — would have stopped World War II. Rather it was the failure of nations such as Britain, France and the United States to stand up to Hitler in the 1930s that emboldened the Germans. If a coalition of the willing had resisted Hitler when he re-occupied the Rhineland, the course of world history could have been very different. The enduring lesson from the 1930s was the folly of appeasement, not the need for new procedural architecture for the international world order, desirable though that may have been in its own right.

Moreover, improvement though it may have been on the League of Nations, the United Nations was anything but an ideal arbiter of the disputes of nations. Its permanent veto-wielding members reflected a by-gone power structure, with Europe massively over-represented. For all of its existence, many of its member states have not had democratically elected governments. That has not prevented them sitting in judgement on some of the world's oldest continuing democratic states.

George Bush never saw multilateralism as an end in itself. His goal was the expansion of democracy. By contrast, the international centre-left and some Europeans and Americans of the centre-right put much of their faith in international organisations.

Bush also disturbed the so-called realists within his own Republican ranks. Gathered around such figures as Brent Scowcroft, it included many who had been close to his father. Henry Kissinger by instinct was a realist, although on Iraq, which provoked public criticism from them, he held his peace, displaying loyalty to Bush. In 2008 Kissinger would say that even though he supported the 2003 invasion of Iraq, the Bush Administration had rested too much of the case for invasion on the supposed existence of WMDs. Kissinger also argued that there had been too few American troops in the invasion and that the Iraqi Army should not have been disbanded.

The realists had little faith in multilateral institutions. On that point they shared Bush's attitude, and that of the so-called neo-conservatives such as Paul Wolfowitz, close to Bush. The realist view was that the world was too complex and dangerous a place for powerful democracies (meaning in practical terms the United States) to proactively impose their will on other nations in the name of spreading freedom. Rogue states should be contained. The United States should stop short of trying to topple rogue regimes, acting only to repel open aggression, as had happened when Iraq invaded Kuwait in 1991. The weakness of this argument was that the threat posed by rogue states possessing WMDs, was not of the border-crossing variety, and therefore a different approach might be needed.

Republicans and Democrats alike had been impressed by our initiative in East Timor. It might have been UN-sanctioned, but it was Australian leadership which pulled things together. Against this background, and Australia being a longstanding ally, Bush may well have thought that I would lend a receptive ear to his freedom agenda.

Bush instinctively liked Australia. Then most Americans do. To some it is the common pioneer experience; both were settler and immigrant societies. Many Americans remain deeply appreciative of the fact that Australia has fought beside the United States in every major conflict in which she has been involved, since America entered World War I in 1917.

Many Americans and Australians alike overstate the similarities between our two peoples. We are close, but there are real and important differences. Our senses of humour sharply diverge. Americans are often thrown by Australian irony. In many parts of the country Americans are more formal than many Australians expect. Australian over-familiarity can sometimes jar. My experience has been that the similarities are more evident amongst Texans and Californians, less so amongst northeasterners.

George Bush was infinitely curious about differences, as well as similarities, between the US and Australian political systems. In 2006, at the end of an official visit to Washington, during a private dinner in the family quarters of the White House, he told me that he proposed announcing the appointment of John Roberts as Chief Justice of the United States the very next day. He enquired about the procedure for appointing judges in Australia, and when I told him they were entirely executive decisions, without any requirement for parliamentary approval, he expressed wistful envy for such a system.

The most perplexing characteristic, to me, about George Bush was the big difference between his persuasive, well-informed, attentive and charming presence in private and his often stilted and unpersuasive presentation style in public. He was not good on television, which made his communication task all the greater. In relation to Iraq he faced vocal hostility to his policy from the start, and this would grow almost exponentially as time went by. Therefore cogent and compelling arguments, directly communicated, were at a premium.

Bush's limitations here compounded a reality, common to all American presidents. Their job specifications required them to propound and declare, but not to argue and persuade. In this there is a marked difference from prime ministers in a Westminster system, such as Tony Blair and me. The adversarial parliamentary environment, so often derided by those who experienced it, at least required its principal participants to argue their case and often on a daily basis. I can testify, from long experience, that nothing compelled me quite like preparing for question time to crystallise in my own mind the reasons why my Government had adopted a particular policy. That was a priceless discipline. The absence of it as well as the infrequency of presidential press conferences means that no American president is ever subjected to such a discipline.

In the environment of a hotly contested policy decision, such as involvement in military conflict, American presidents are both less disposed and less well prepared to argue their case regularly and persistently. They don't appear repeatedly on talkback radio; they don't appear as frequently as do Australian PMs on television talk shows.

Bill Clinton was a good speech maker, but mainly of the grand-occasion variety such as at political conventions or State of the Union addresses. Even his superior media skills — to those of George Bush — would not have more effectively carried the day on an issue like Iraq, simply because American presidents don't see their role as involving day-to-day advocacy of the type regularly engaged in by Westminster PMs. They mistakenly think that much of the legwork can be done by others. This attitude completely misunderstands the attitude of the modern electorate towards the responsibilities of their leaders. In their minds, the man at the top made all the big decisions (and they are right about that), and they want to hear from him as to why he made those decisions.

George Bush recognised his communications shortcomings. He was much better in one-on-one TV interviews than in press conferences. I thought that he should have done lots more of the former, as they allowed the warmth and candour of his personality to come through.

Bush was interested in people, their lives and families, and what drove them. He was curious about history and widely read on that subject. His religious faith was evident, but in no way overbearing or sanctimonious. Immediately before our Friday evening meal during our weekend visit to the Bush ranch in Crawford in May 2003, the President invited all present — about a dozen — to join hands while he said grace. It seemed the most natural thing in the world for him to do, but it was carried off in such a way that any non-believer in the group would not have felt uncomfortable. He was frank about having given up drinking and seemed at ease with his subsequent more disciplined way of life.

Although highly intelligent, he had no pretensions to being an intellectual. In fact a lack of pretension was a Bush hallmark. He dealt in principles and broad concepts. This infuriated the liberal elite in the United States, who adopted a condescending attitude to anything which they saw to be conservative populism. For many of them, national politics was a far too serious and complicated area to be left to ordinary people.

To so many Australians, whose only acquaintance with Bush was the nightly TV news grab, he was a brash Texan who sometimes mangled words. They were never exposed to a person who had easy conversational skills, genuinely listening to what other people said to him.

Socially engaging, he worked a room effortlessly. Neil Mitchell, the Melbourne radio journalist, was one of my guests at the Lodge barbecue in October 2003 honouring George Bush. He told me afterwards that, measured by responsiveness in a brief personal encounter, Bush was amongst the most impressive political figures he had met. Mitchell wrote glowingly of his encounter with Bush several days later in the *Herald Sun*.

How strange therefore, that the relaxed, engaging and personable interlocutor, in the flesh, became taut and tense on television. It was something that he understood only too well. Sometimes he joked about it. As so much of modern politics is bound up in the quality of electronic media presentation, the communication deficit suffered by George Bush affected his presidency.

I have already mentioned that he frequently engaged in self-deprecation. Asked once why he called me 'a man of steel', he replied that he had simply drawn on 'my extensive vocabulary'.[2] To use an Australian expression, he did not take himself too seriously. The fact that his religious faith was not something that he frequently thrust into conversation added to the authenticity of the man. When Janette and I travelled with him for two hours, en route to his ranch in Crawford, Texas in 2003, on Air Force One, we realised just how central his family, and not just Laura and their twin daughters, was to his entire life. He spoke to us with genuine feeling and affection about the whole Bush clan.

George Bush displayed intense loyalty to people who stuck by him or who shared his values and belief system. Likewise he did not take kindly to those who let him down. He never forgot the way in which the German Chancellor, Gerhard Schroeder, who promised support over Iraq, backed off once the domestic going got tough. His continued regard for Tony Blair was due in no small part to the fact that Blair persisted in supporting Bush on Iraq despite tremendous domestic political opposition and personal hostility, which endures to this day. To him that was the mark of a true friend and political ally.

His affection for Junichiro Koizumi, the Japanese Prime Minister, and Alvaro Uribe, the President of Colombia, who was awarded the Presidential Medal of Freedom, along with Tony Blair and me, were examples of the Bush gratitude towards world leaders who had stuck by him over hard issues or shared his values. Koizumi had kept military engineers in Iraq despite domestic disquiet. Uribe had waged a courageous fight against the drug barons in his country. Bush detested the drug trade; Colombia was the source of over 90 per cent of the cocaine entering the United States and a significant source of the heroin on American streets.

His loyalty to me was plentiful. The better-known examples were his warm personal remarks as well as the Medal of Freedom, the latter being so much a compliment to Australia. Less well known was the fact that the four nights he spent in Sydney during APEC 2007 was the longest period he spent in a foreign city during his entire presidency. It was in part a personal gesture to me. He knew that the particular gathering was the most important Australia had ever hosted. He wished to fully honour that fact. This was despite crucial military testimony being given in Washington at that time concerning Iraq.

My being out of office during his last year in the White House did not affect our relationship. He hosted a dinner for me and several members of my family when I went to Washington in March 2008 to receive the Irving Kristol Award from the American Enterprise Institute. In discussing contemporary issues, our old intimacy continued over that dinner.

He asked me about Kevin Rudd, who he was to meet for the first time as Prime Minister in just over a week. I said that Rudd was pro-American and, therefore, unlike at least one previous Labor leader. I remarked, 'He'll stick by the alliance.' I said nothing critical of Rudd, and gained the distinct impression that Bush would welcome my successor with warmth and cordiality. That is exactly what happened. The new Australian PM was given every courtesy, including a full-scale news conference. They joked about the similarities between Texas and Queensland. The generosity of the welcome

Rudd received from Bush made all the more reprehensible the dishonest briefing which occurred, at the Australian end, following Rudd's telephone conversation with Bush, late in 2008, concerning the G20. That briefing falsely asserted that, in his discussion with Rudd, the American President had shown ignorance of what the G20 was. It was a disgraceful way to treat a man who had shown him much courtesy and, even more importantly, was a true friend of Australia.

George Bush had an open, sunny style with people. We, and our wives, dined together in old Saigon (now Ho Chi Minh City), after the 2006 APEC meeting in Hanoi. The restaurant had endured a huge security operation, but the owner was delighted to have us, providing a private room. After dinner we left through the main part of the restaurant, which still had plenty of diners. Bush stopped to greet most of them, displaying that uncanny knack which some politicians have of knowing who in a crowded room wants to meet you — and who doesn't. Most of them that night did, including a group of Australians who wanted photographs with both of us. He did the rounds of the place with just the right mix of friendliness and dignity. The owner literally beamed. It was copybook retail politics, yet he wasn't at home seeking to impress potential voters. The truth was he did that because he enjoyed meeting people; he did it everywhere, in a natural, spontaneous fashion. It was the same when he came to Australia for APEC in 2007. It was never too much trouble for him to respond to requests for photographs.

The presidency of George Bush will be defined largely by history's judgement of his response to the terrorist menace which hit the world without warning on 11 September 2001. We are a long way short of that judgement. Part of the calculus will be the extent to which the presumably different approach of Barack Obama is seen to be more successful than that of Bush. I say 'presumably' in relation to Obama, because he was elected as a change agent although, in relation to fighting terrorism, it is by no means obvious as yet where he differs in substance, as distinct from rhetoric, from George Bush.

In one area Obama can only hope to match Bush, but not exceed him. That is in defending the homeland from another attack. I have already written of how preoccupied the American people were with the possibility of another terrorist attack in the weeks and months, even several years, which followed 11 September. George Bush rightly saw it as his overriding task to stop this happening. In this he was spectacularly successful. Against all the expectations which came after the original attack a further one did not eventuate. With the passage of time this began to be taken for granted, yet it had not been by pure chance. The myriad security and other steps taken by Bush to buttress the homeland paid dividends. For his efforts Bush was routinely accused of violating individual rights. I am sure that on occasions this did happen, but the question to be put is, was that violation justified by the dividend of no further attacks? Most Americans would answer positively. Yet as time went by they would give their President diminishing credit for his role in keeping the country safe.

Iraq has been something of a case study of George Bush. He went after Saddam because he wanted to pre-empt the Iraqi dictator's capacity to facilitate further terrorist attacks, and also he believed that he could create a new democracy in the Middle East. There was plenty of domestic backing for his action, which was to be later condemned as reckless and provocative when things went sour after the invasion had been completed.

At the beginning of 2007, when the Iraqi operation seemed to have reached a stalemate, with American casualties continuing to mount at a painful rate, Bush, against almost all advice, decided on the surge, which, under the direction of General David Petraeus, proved to be remarkably effective. Bush held his nerve. Although he understood that the three years which followed the invasion had been a near disaster for the United States and had damaged his own credibility, he had not averted his eyes from the original objective — Iraq as a functioning democracy. He knew that to reject the surge would cement Iraq in history as an American failure; a successful surge could bring events back on track for the original objective.

36

BLUE COLLARS AND GREEN SLEEVES — LATHAM'S IMPLOSION

At 4.50 pm on Tuesday, 31 August 2004, I wandered to the window of my Canberra office and stared at the artificial waterfall in the courtyard. I had just 10 minutes to take a decision which was to prove fateful to the outcome of the election on 9 October, called by me only two days earlier.

I had to decide whether or not to include expenditure of $830 million over four years in the commitments of the Government to appear in the pre-election economic statement (PEFO), issued by the secretaries of Treasury and the Department of Finance, under the Charter of Budget Honesty. The PEFO had to be issued within 10 days of the beginning of the caretaker period for the 2004 election, which was to start at 5 pm Eastern Standard Time on that very same day, 31 August.

The caretaker period was a longstanding Westminster convention, whereby, in the weeks immediately before an election, the incumbent government took no policy decisions and made no appointments without the consent of the opposition. The logic was obvious. If the government changed, the new government should not be burdened with decisions taken during the very time that the people were deciding which government they would have.

A government could decide on new spending and/or taxation measures after the election had been called and before the caretaker period started, but details of any such decision would appear in the PEFO.

There was advantage for a government announcing, and including in the PEFO, a new decision, rather than making it an election promise. This was because the cost of the decision was taken into account by Treasury and Finance in calculating the size of the surplus (or deficit) notionally available for campaign promises. Although the size of that surplus constrained the commitments of both sides, there was normally more restraint on an opposition, because in good economic times — and that was the case in 2004 — an opposition always had a harder task in establishing economic credibility.

The $830 million was the total cost of a program to remove, completely, all remaining old-growth forests in Tasmania from future logging. The plan involved repudiation of the Regional Forest Agreement (RFA), concluded with the Tasmanian Government in November 1997, and the loss of hundreds of jobs in the timber industry. The impact on small communities heavily dependent on forestry would be significant. Compensation was to be generous, with assistance in tourism and plantation reafforestation. To its protagonists, and there were quite a few, it was a big bold environmental initiative which would dramatically reposition the Coalition on the environment, win votes on the mainland of Australia and, because of the generosity of the proposed compensation, not damage the Government in Tasmanian electorates. To them it was win-win.

The Opposition leader, Mark Latham, had been sending strong signals all year that for the election he would do something big on old-growth forests. Complete with leather jacket, and accompanied by Greens Leader Bob Brown, he had stood on an old tree stump in a Tasmanian forest. They had both gazed into the distance. As far as the eye could see there was a steady flow of Green preferences to the Labor Party.

Saving old-growth forests was still the iconic green issue. It was a classic case of elite urban opinion being ingratiated at the expense, potentially, of other people's jobs in faraway parts of the country. In any event, they could get other jobs in new-growth industries like tourism, so everyone came out on top, according to this view. The difficulties involved in retraining a 50-year-old timber worker for something entirely different rarely occurred to tertiary-educated city dwellers.

More than in many other policy areas, the environment was susceptible to the politics of symbolism. Feel-good politics were at a premium here. Saving whales and preserving endangered species, whilst meritorious in themselves, returned a doubly handsome dividend in the realm of the warm inner glow. When it came to the aspirations of environmentalists, old-growth forests were of the same genre. The big difference was that there was a cost on the other side. Saving whales did not involve Australian jobs. Saving old-growth forests might well do so. The Labor Party was to learn that to its electoral expense at the election of 2004.

Although we had worn away at Latham's credibility by the time the election was called, I was by no means certain that we would win. For that reason a surprise initiative on the environment on my part had been a live option for weeks. It was obvious that if we were to go big in this area, it would be with old-growth forests. That meant the Tasmanian old-growth forests.

Most of my senior colleagues and staff favoured embracing the $830 million plan. One exception was the minister responsible for forests, Senator Ian McDonald, who was from North Queensland. He thought that the policy document was good but that the politics were all wrong. He was right.

As it was likely that any major environmental initiative would involve Tasmania's old-growth forests, there was heavy traffic into my office from the various interest groups, including the Forestry Division of the Construction, Foresty, Mining and Energy Union (CFMEU). Arthur Sinodinos and I had several discussions with its president, Michael O'Connor, who was a likeable man and an effective advocate for his cause.

If it were to go with the Tasmanian option, the Government could either announce it before release of the PEFO or at some time during the campaign, as an election promise. The first approach would have given old-growth forests a huge profile in the campaign. Was that really what the Government wanted though? Weren't economic management and national security the Coalition strong suits?

As I gazed at that waterfall, my instinct told me that to go with the supergreen option in Tasmania would be to betray the 'Howard battlers' in timber communities there and elsewhere. How could I explain to them such a sudden policy reversal? For eight years I had been a Prime Minister who had put jobs ahead of pandering to noisy minority groups for political advantage. Now I was chasing Green preferences in the leafy suburbs of Sydney and Melbourne. That would have been an oversimplification and not completely accurate, but it is how they would have felt. That was the real reason why I did not put that $830 million in the PEFO.

Although I didn't see it that way at the time, my rejection of the upfront embrace of the old-growth option meant that it would not be the policy of the Coalition at any time during the election campaign. Looking back, the alternatives were either to go a deep shade of green right at the beginning or stay true to my instincts and wait for Mark Latham to stumble on the issue.

Latham and I played a cat and mouse game. On 3 September, campaigning for Larry Anthony in Murwillumbah, I said that I was in favour of preserving old-growth forests, but not at the expense of throwing timber workers on the unemployment scrapheap. My response kept open the possibility that the Coalition would move on old-growth forests, but it gave my opponent no clue as to how or when. That is exactly what I wanted. I suspected all along that the ALP leader had done a deal with Bob Brown to lock in Green preferences, and that at some point he would have to commit himself publicly. His position was relatively easy for me to read, but the reverse was not the case. Latham had no real idea of what I would do; nor, in fact, did anyone else. I decided to play my cards close to my chest and wait out Latham. It was a test of nerves.

By Sunday, 3 October, just six days before polling, Latham had, as I predicted, run out of time. His nerve broke and the next day he suddenly altered his travel plans and headed for Tasmania to announce a plan to buy out the old-growth forests and implement the full green agenda. Bob Brown had got his way. In fact, he had had his way for quite a long time on this issue; only now it was to be out in the open.

The Opposition leader could not have handled this issue more clumsily. He had completely ignored the Labor Premier of Tasmania, Paul Lennon, who was a passionate supporter of the timber industry and its workers. A former union official, Lennon's first and last loyalty was to the men and women of an industry which had been crucial to the Tasmanian economy for decades. Lennon was not given the details of the Latham takeover until they met the next day in Hobart. He was livid at what he was told. Workers in the industry, who had rallied outside Lennon's office, were ignored, literally, as Latham snuck out the back door and headed for the airport and a speedy return to the mainland.

The Latham plan was based on a commitment to end all further logging in Tasmania's old-growth forests. There were plenty of promises about new industries, plantation reafforestation, and the immense potential of the tourism industry in the island state. All of that was of cold comfort to those in the industry, both workers and small business operators.

Within hours of Latham's policy statement there was an angry reaction from union and Labor people. Although Michelle O'Byrne and Sid

Sidebottom, the Labor MPs for Bass and Braddon, the two Tasmanian electorates most directly affected, held their tongues, Dick 'Grizzly' Adams, a former timber worker himself and MP for the adjoining seat of Lyons, let fly against his own leader's policy. Although he remained tight-lipped, Lennon's opinion was widely known. The politics of this issue had been comprehensively bungled by Latham and were now savagely biting Labor.

In the final days of the campaign this was manna from heaven for the Coalition, but our own position had to be carefully handled. We had to state a policy, and that policy could not completely ignore old-growth forests. Yet, obviously, it had to stop short of locking up all of the old-growth areas with the lethal implications that had for jobs. It was here that the constant dialogue between my office and the several interest groups over previous months proved invaluable. We were in a position to pull together a policy likely to win wide acceptance. I had a well-developed idea of what that policy would be when I flew to Launceston the following day.

The industry and unions had organised a big rally in City Park, Launceston, and many of those attending had drifted to the nearby Albert Hall to hear speeches from industry and union leaders. Everyone knew that I was in town and they naturally wanted to hear from me about the Government's policy. They were angry with Latham, but that did not mean that they would automatically endorse me and the Coalition.

I met industry and union leaders as well as representatives of the timber communities for an hour or more at the Grand Chancellor Hotel, Launceston, which was within easy walking distance of the Albert Hall. At that meeting I settled on a policy that I would announce to the public meeting at the nearby hall. As I walked to the Albert Hall I felt nervous, even though I knew that what I would announce was infinitely more palatable than what they had heard from the Labor Party.

The next hour was one of the more remarkable in my political life. It was the most adrenaline-charged moment of the 2004 campaign for me, and the impact of that meeting reverberated around the nation. The hall was overflowing with some 2000 people when I arrived. They were noisy, some were well lubricated and, above all else, wanted to hear directly and without humbug from me about our plans affecting their futures.

When I rose to speak I came straight to the point. I did not start by attacking the Labor Party. They knew that they didn't like its policy on Tasmanian forests, but now they wanted to hear from me about what we would do. I said that my Government would honour the RFA. This struck an instant chord. The RFA had provided stability to the industry. It enshrined long-term commitments from both federal and state governments. These agreements were seen as pragmatic compromises between the various competing interests. Latham had been extremely foolish to repudiate the Tasmanian RFA. He had repudiated stability.

I then said that a re-elected Coalition Government would add 170,000 hectares to the current reserve system. That was a win for the environment, but a long way short of the job-destroying lock-up proposed by Latham. A large number of individual initiatives my office had worked out with the industry, when added to the preservation of the RFA, meant that our policy was overwhelmingly a pro-jobs one. When I finished my speech I received thunderous applause. I left the stage and plunged into the crowd, giving my security detail a minor heart attack. Burly tattooed timber workers hugged me and declared that I had a better understanding of their position than the party they normally supported; family groups told me that whole communities of hundreds of people would be devastated if old growth logging were halted altogether; others declared that they liked the forests too but there had to be a balance.

Television coverage of this meeting and the aftermath dominated news bulletins that evening and into the following day. It was a magical public relations boost for the Liberal and National parties. The image was of a Labor heartland embracing a Liberal Prime Minister. It didn't get any better than that. Writing in the *Australian* on 8 October, Ken Hall, a self-styled lifelong Labor supporter, said, 'I have come to believe that John Howard is the best leader to represent the timber workers of Tasmania ... On Wednesday, I went to a protest in Launceston to hear Howard's pitch to timber workers. I expected to hear the worst. But I quickly learned that he is the right man in the right place at the right time. It was a great relief to hear him say that he will maintain the RFA. This means having the continued confidence to go on building our family business for the long term.'[1] His comments symbolised the colossal political miscalculation Mark Latham had made.

Latham paid a high price for his misguided policy five days later. Bass and Braddon both swung heavily into the Liberal camp. There was a swing against Dick Adams, but as his margin was bigger, he survived. His outspoken public stance against Latham's policy also helped. The ramifications were felt in other timber electorates on the mainland, such as MacMillan in Victoria and Eden-Monaro in New South Wales. Even in urban areas where the Labor policy was meant to have significant appeal, Latham's announcement had come too late in the campaign to appear convincing to swingers interested in the environment. It had proved much harder to wear a green sleeve with a blue collar than Mark Latham ever imagined.

This remarkable component of the 2004 campaign had reminded me yet again that when faced with a difficult decision, always trust your instincts. I am so glad that as I stared at that waterfall I allowed my instincts to win out.

The Coalition won the 2004 election with an increased majority of 24 seats, but, before then, it had been a rollercoaster time for the Liberal and National parties. The unexpected election of Mark Latham at the end of 2003 had unsettled the Government. Late in that year, Simon Crean had been tapped on the shoulder and became the first leader of the ALP, since World War II, to be denied the chance of leading his party to an election. Crean had never been convincing, and his demise was no surprise to me. Most of us in the Coalition had thought that the ALP would go with the safe option of bringing back Kim Beazley, but Latham won in an upset by just two votes.

Latham started well; the Canberra press gallery liked him. They had had almost eight years of me and that was more than enough for a lot of them. They were prepared to give him a good run, overlooking many of his shortcomings. For example, when he delayed the US free trade agreement with the totally fallacious claim that it would make pharmaceuticals dearer in Australia, that was lauded as good politics, not irresponsibly playing with the national interest, which it was.

Latham was openly hostile to George Bush. He had called him one of the most dangerous and incompetent presidents ever. President Bush had had a perfectly cordial meeting with Simon Crean when he had come to Canberra in October 2003, but it was difficult to imagine that occurring with Latham. After Bush had delivered his speech to the October joint sitting, I took him around the floor of the house, and introduced him to as many MPs as possible, including, of course, Labor ones. They were mostly friendly, some more than others. I made a point of introducing him to Latham. Bush enjoyed the encounter; Latham averted his eyes. The American President won that body language encounter hands down.

Unpredictable, Latham sometimes wrong-footed the Government. He built a convincing narrative of the boy who had grown up in a housing commission estate in Green Valley, in the western suburbs of Sydney, losing his father at an early age, going on to university and caring for his widowed mother. He made great play of the 22-year age gap between us yet, as time went by, Mark Latham, for all his protestations of modernity, would reveal old-fashioned class prejudices and attitudes increasingly out of place in contemporary Australia. He thought of Australia, particularly Sydney, as composed of 'insiders' and 'outsiders', roughly equivalent to the North Shore on the one hand, and Sydney's west on the other. His class bitterness spilled into Labor's policy on private schools, with a hit list of so-called wealthy schools which would lose funding under a Latham Labor Government. It frightened many private-school parents who were anything but wealthy. Latham failed to understand just how aspirational middle Australia had become.

On 22 March 2004, speaking to Mike Carlton on Sydney Radio 2UE, Latham declared that, if he won the election, he would hope to have Australian troops 'home by Christmas'.[2] It was a careless, ill-disciplined comment which immediately called into question his judgement more generally.

It raised more questions than it answered. For instance, to which troops was he referring? Was it all of our forces? Did it include the naval vessels in the Gulf which had been acting under direct UN mandate for years? Did it include the detachment guarding our embassy in Baghdad? If so, who would look after our diplomats — the Americans?

Bit by bit, over the months ahead, Latham answered these questions after a fashion, but the damage had been done. The incident raised doubts in people's minds about his fitness for the Lodge. It was something of a turning point for him. Until then he had enjoyed a charmed existence, with many in the Canberra press corps cheering him on.

On the eve of the 2004 election the children overboard affair resurfaced in the circumstances described in Chapter 32, and as no stockpiles of WMDs had been found in Iraq, my critics gave ever-increasing voice to the claim that I was untrustworthy. I decided to take this head-on by running my campaign on the theme of trust. Announcing the election for 9 October 2004, I asked a series of rhetorical questions. Who do you trust to keep interest rates low? Who do you trust to keep the budget in surplus? And so it went on. It was an effective approach which worked because it was based on reality. We had managed the economy well, and I had found a pithy way of telling people that. Latham never found an answer and, as the campaign progressed, doubts about him grew.

There was a tinge of personal aggression in his style which bothered people, particularly some women. His infamous bullying handshake with me, three days out from the poll, may have shifted votes. I knew it was coming, because he had done the same thing before the start of our Leaders' debate at the beginning of the campaign, but it had not been properly captured on camera and therefore was not televised. The latter one was well and truly captured. Weeks after the election, NSW Premier Morris Iemma told me that his wife, Santina, when attending a children's birthday party near their home in Beverly Hills, the day after the election, could not find a single woman at the party who had voted for Latham. Beverly Hills, an inner suburb of Sydney, was anything but staunch Liberal territory.

Mark Latham's amazingly rapid implosion after the 2004 election stunned us all. It certainly disappointed many in the media. There had been much sentiment that 'Latham became an alternative Prime Minister during the campaign'. A spectacular example of this had been Geoffrey Barker of the *Australian Financial Review*. Writing on the day of the election he said, 'Win or lose Mark Latham is the future of political Labor. A win will cement his place in Labor history as the man who crashed through to end the long Howard government incumbency. A loss will be judged an impressive first tilt at high office yet to be attained.' That was only the half of it. Barker went on to say, '[Latham] made himself the emotional representative of many Australians, giving them hope for a (slightly) easier and better quality life. That is the key to political success.'[3]

Most thought that Latham would have about a year from the election defeat in which to present an effective alternative to the Coalition. Labor had no stomach for another leadership stoush. Beazley, the obvious alternative to Latham, clearly thought that he would have at least this time up his sleeve before the opportunity of taking over from Latham arose. Latham's sudden resignation on 18 January 2005 meant that Kim Beazley had to step up to the crease earlier than anticipated. He had not appeared all that well through much of 2004 and I don't think that his health was fully restored when he resumed the top job.

From Kevin Rudd down, Labor figures began to ridicule Latham, but many of them, admittedly not including Rudd, made him Labor Leader. One who remained conspicuously silent was Julia Gillard, formerly a close Latham supporter.

Latham's clumsy handling of the old-growth forest issue in 2004 illustrated a dilemma the Labor Party faced during the Coalition's time in office, namely that its active party membership, especially in inner-city areas, was increasingly at odds with its hitherto traditional support base, particularly on issues such as asylum-seeker policy and the environment. Tension of this type was apprehended years earlier by the late Kim Beazley senior, with his memorable cry from the heart, 'When I joined the Labor Party it contained the cream of the working class, now it has the dregs of the middle class.'

Large swathes of traditional Labor voters supported the Coalition in 1996, 2001 and 2004. The 'Howard battler' liked the economic security my Government delivered, was socially conservative, strongly supported our policy on asylum-seekers and was suspicious of policies which satiated environmental prejudices at the expense of other people's jobs. He or she felt great pride in the Australian achievement. The Coalition also suffered from 'base bleeding', although less so. It was apparent in 2007 on ratifying Kyoto. But the gulf between party activists and traditional supporters never opened up as much for the Liberals as it did for the ALP.

37

THE HUMAN DIVIDEND

Social policy reform and progress were the quiet but impressive achievers of the Howard Government. Economic management and national security were such major preoccupations of the Government that there was less focus on other areas.

Yet the accomplishments on the social front were formidable. Tangible symbols of those were the reduction to 3.9 per cent in the unemployment level, a 33-year low, and the equitable, as well as efficient, distribution of the fruits of economic growth. Work by the Organisation for Economic Cooperation and Development (OECD) showed that the distribution of social benefits in Australia was so progressive — and the level of taxes paid by the poor so low — that Australia distributed more to the poorest 20 per cent of the population than virtually any other developed country.

Before we won office in March 1996, I had delivered guarantees about the social security safety net and the maintenance of Medicare but, in addition, I had foreshadowed more emphasis on individual choice in social and educational services.

As Prime Minister, I frequently reminded Australians that good economic policy was not an end in itself; that economic changes made no sense unless there was a human dividend. The clearest human dividend was, undeniably, reduced unemployment, so important to enhancing human dignity and making inroads into poverty.

Australia's 33-year low in unemployment, delivered by my Government, was largely attributable to strong economic growth. Specific changes to labour market policy, the introduction of work for the dole, coupled with a broader preference for work over welfare, also played a part. WorkChoices accelerated the fall in unemployment, because it made some who were without work more employable.

I wanted to change the culture of welfare dependency, as much as was consistent with fairness to the genuinely underprivileged. I did not want a social welfare system as harsh as that in many parts of the United States. A constant theme of mine was that Australia had struck the right balance between the laissez-faire insensitivity of the Americans, and the paternalistic approach of so many European countries. I always opposed the introduction of any time limit on the payment of unemployment benefits. Some people found it impossible, no matter how hard they tried, to find a job. Those people were entitled to continued support, so long as they met their community obligations through work for the dole or related activities.

Another goal of mine was to involve the charitable organisations of Australia, mainly religious, not only in the provision of services but also the giving of advice to the Government. Nobody understands better than a Salvation Army officer just how hard life can be for those in poverty. In addition, they know better than anyone in politics or the bureaucracy the value of the charitable dollar.

That time-honoured Liberal principle of choice was applied wherever practicable. Private health insurance was withering on the vine when we came to government. The limited private health insurance rebate introduced in 1996 failed. It was the introduction of a non-means-tested 30 per cent rebate, as part of the New Taxation System, which did the trick. Very quickly, the percentage of the population covered privately rose from somewhere near 34 per cent to approximately 44 per cent, where it has remained ever since.

Abolishing Labor's restrictive new schools policy led to rapid growth of low-fee independent schools. As a consequence some 34 per cent of Australian children in primary and secondary education are now in non-government schools. There is no country in the world which has embraced freedom of choice in education more faithfully than Australia.

Finally, and importantly, my Government rebalanced the taxation system towards a greater recognition that it costs money to bear and raise children. It had long been my view that a taxation system which did not recognise this adequately was without social vision. To me taxation fairness for families has never been a welfare issue. Debate on this rages today with the inaccurate and socially purblind description of family tax payments as 'middle-class welfare'. I return to that subject later in this chapter.

We also acted, in various ways, to encourage more philanthropy in Australia. A body called Community–Business Partnerships, chaired by me and including leading and generous business figures such as the late Richard Pratt, David Gonski and Rob Gerard, devised ways of bringing about that cultural change. Largely from David Gonski's recommendations there were changes to the tax laws which contributed to a lift in charitable donations. Between 1997 and 2005 there was a 58 per cent increase in real terms in donations.

In 1996, in a world first, we effectively privatised employment services by abolishing the Commonwealth Employment Service (CES) and replacing it with the Job Network, where potential providers bid for contracts to provide services to the unemployed. They were remunerated on the basis of positions filled. A striking feature of this new system was the entry into it of agencies associated with some of the major religious charities, including Anglicare, Wesley Central Mission and the Salvation Army. There were also quite a number of for-profit private providers; some of them were extremely successful.

It has been an innovative and significant reform. On an anecdotal basis, both employers and employees preferred it to the old CES. Certainly its operation coincided with unemployment steadily falling to a 33-year low. There was residual hostility from public sector unions and the ACTU, but the Rudd Government retained the system, although under the cloak of a major review and a rebadging exercise.

I always believed in work for the dole. It seemed to me perfectly fair that an able-bodied person receiving unemployment benefits should be required to do an appropriate amount of work in return for those benefits. Whenever I had raised the issue in earlier years, I would be told that it was not practical and, in any event, it would be a breach of our obligations under the International Labour Organisation conventions.

In February 1997, I resurrected the issue and said that for people who had been out of work for six months, the Government would examine introducing some kind of work for the dole system on a pilot basis. I said, 'What I've got in mind is to pilot both voluntary and compulsory schemes in regional and rural areas of Australia where there are high levels of unemployment.' The reaction was predictable. Speaking for the Labor Party, Martin Ferguson said that it was 'a Mickey Mouse scheme'. The ACTU threw up its arms in disgust, as did some, but not all, welfare groups.

The reaction of the public was totally different. Some of the most enthusiastic support for work for the dole came from lower- to middle-income working people who resented unemployment benefits being paid to people who did not try at all hard to find work.

The scheme altered community attitudes. The Labor Party's opposition weakened, although many within the broader labour movement still remain bitterly opposed to it. I will therefore be surprised if any ALP government dumps it.

To me, the right balance is a relatively regulation-free hiring and firing system for staff, supported by a fair unemployment benefit which can last indefinitely, provided the recipient gives something back in return for the benefit and continues actively to seek work.

The problem with the European approach (except Britain) is that the severity of unfair dismissal laws, and associated termination requirements, reduce the hiring propensities of firms. To many, it is not worth the risk, given the cost involved, in letting someone go who is unsatisfactory. As a consequence, firms hire fewer people. This problem does not exist with the Americans. They, however, have an unemployment benefit system which can result in people being without any means of support. Regrettably, this does tip some unemployed Americans into crime.

Illicit drug-taking and the high youth suicide rate troubled me.

I did not need any encouragement to embrace a zero-tolerance approach to illicit drugs. I had no patience with the argument that because tobacco and alcohol were legal, then the logical thing was to legalise marijuana use. Of course we could never eliminate the consumption of tobacco and alcohol, although Australia has done a better job than most countries in curbing cigarette smoking. I refused to accept the argument that a tough and effective policy could not make inroads on such terrible habits as heroin and cocaine taking.

Major Brian Watters of the Salvation Army had attracted me with his uncomplicated views on drug abuse. A special body called the Australian National Council on Drugs was established, and I appointed Brian Watters as its chairman, with Mick Palmer, the AFP commissioner, as deputy chairman. Most police advice, both federally and state, was that progress could be made only if there were sufficient commitment from governments and adequate funds.

The council advised on the implementation of the National Illicit Drugs Strategy, which I had launched in November 1997. Very quickly financial backing for this strategy from the Commonwealth grew to $600 million. It tackled the problem in three areas, augmenting or cooperating with what the states were doing: more resources for law enforcement, additional education about the consequences of drug abuse and, importantly, more money for rehabilitation services. I had been struck by the frequency of talk-back callers relating their desperate experiences as parents in failing to find sufficient rehabilitation support for their drug-dependent children.

The diversionary strategy was highly successful. In cooperation with the states, we established a regime whereby a person caught up, for the first time, in the criminal justice system because of drug use would be told that he or she could agree to undergo an extensive course of rehabilitation and, if so, no further action would be taken. If this offer were not taken up then that person would continue to be dealt with through the criminal justice system.

There were some Liberals, and even more members of the Labor Party, who joined the then fashionable stampede to decriminalise marijuana use. They still flirted with the now totally discredited theory that marijuana was a harmless recreational drug. The linkages between marijuana and chronic depression and/or schizophrenia are now clear. That was not so obviously the case in 1998. Jeff Kennett encouraged debate at that time. He is now firmly against decriminalisation.

The Government also provided generous financial support for a youth suicide prevention program, under the leadership of Dr Ian Webster. The unexpected, and usually unexplained, suicide of a child is about the most confronting and traumatic experience that any parent could have. As a member of parliament some of the most moving discussions I had were with constituents in exactly this situation.

To reach back over one's life and interaction with a son or a daughter, desperately trying to pinpoint the moment or occasions when the wrong thing was done which may have triggered an ultimately tragic act, must be painful beyond belief. Yet that experience was the nightmare of far too many Australian parents. In so many cases, drug addiction was the core of the problem.

For those who dismissed the value of investment in programs confronting drug abuse or the high youth suicide rate, the figures are a persuasive answer. The heroin death toll in 1998 was 927, in 1999, 1116; by 2005 it had declined to 374. Critics will say that it was all due to a shortage of heroin. There was a reduction in supply, but that was not the only explanation. The Tough on Drugs campaign, and not least the effort made to encourage parents to talk to their children directly about drug issues, had had a real impact.

I attended many launches of individual Tough on Drugs programs with Brian Watters. Brian would finish his short speech at a launch by referring to a forthcoming event such as Easter, Mother's Day, Father's Day or Christmas, and then simply say that, as a result of the Tough on Drugs strategy, there would be a specific additional number of young Australians spending that occasion with their families than would otherwise have been the case. Those present were left in no doubt about what was at stake in fighting drug addiction.

In 1996 the suicide rate amongst young males, particularly those living in rural areas, was one of the highest in the world. According to Australian Bureau of Statistics (ABS)-sourced statistics, the suicide rate for both males and females declined by 37 per cent between 1998 and 2007. The most remarkable improvement had been amongst young males, where a 50 per cent fall was recorded between 1997 and 2007. I have written about the issues of suicide and drug abuse together because of weighty evidence that the two are causally related.

The high youth suicide rate bothered many young Australians. For each of the last seven or eight years as Prime Minister I, along with the Leader of the Opposition, would attend a conference in Parliament House which brought together young men and women from all around Australia to talk about personal beliefs and the values of our society.

I spoke about my own values, spiritual beliefs and what meaning I found in life. On quite a number of occasions the question was asked of me, why did I think the youth suicide rate in Australia was so high. It was not an easy question to answer. The high suicide rate clearly troubled those young people. I replied that one of the reasons was that we no longer lived in a society governed by absolutes. Everything in life had become relative. Taking one's life had been, years ago, one of those taboo, or absolutely unthinkable, acts, which only the most completely desperate contemplated. Perhaps society's steady descent into relativism was one of the explanations why suicide, especially amongst the young, had become more common.

*　　*　　*

Recently the term 'middle-class welfare' has been used, pejoratively, to attack payments and tax concessions to people whom the critics believe should not be receiving them. The use of the term 'welfare' is dishonest, because the payments under attack are not true welfare or income-support payments; rather, they are measures to change individual behaviour in pursuit of good public policy or, in the case of Family Tax Benefits, recognise the cost of something society regards as vital — the bearing and raising of children. By contrast, the unemployment benefit is a true welfare payment, because it gives the recipient a basic level of financial support to keep him or her from poverty.

The universal 30 per cent private health insurance rebate is frequently attacked as middle-class welfare. It is not a welfare payment. The welfare component of the health system in Australia is the financial support for consultations with a GP and free public hospital treatment available under Medicare.

The private health insurance rebate is an incentive for people to take out private health insurance, so that the private hospital usage it supports will carry some of the load that would otherwise be carried by the public hospital system. If the incentive is withdrawn, or too heavily means-tested, then there will be a decline in the number of people being insured, which in turn will push more people into the public hospital system at an increased cost to the taxpayer. That would be a bad public policy outcome.

For many years companies in Australia have been provided with tax and other incentives to invest more heavily in research and development. It is beneficial, economically, to have such investment and, therefore, incentives through the tax or payments system to induce more of that investment is good public policy. By analogy, means-testing the private health insurance rebate would be the equivalent of denying research and development tax concessions to highly profitable companies.

The middle-class welfare argument becomes even more illogical in the case of tax benefits for the cost of having children. It also raises the issue of horizontal equity in our taxation system.

It is sound public policy to ensure that taxpayers who carry heavier family responsibilities than other taxpayers, at the same level of income, should receive some support through the taxation system for carrying those responsibilities. Is it really fair that a couple earning a combined income of $80,000 a year should be treated in exactly the same fashion, through the taxation system, as a couple earning the same amount but supporting two or three children? It is equally legitimate to ask the same question of couples on much higher incomes, particularly as we still have a strongly progressive taxation system.

To me, the answer to the question must properly be no. Surely it is in the national interest to encourage childbearing, to help with the cost of raising children and also to recognise the contribution made to society by those who care and provide for others out of their incomes?

That used to be a widely accepted belief in Australia. Many of those who currently attack Family Tax Benefits as middle-class welfare completely overlook the fact that, until 1987, the principal method of assisting Australian parents with the cost of raising their children was non-means-tested.

Over the years there have been many changes in the ways in which governments have sought to help families, and much complexity added, largely due to means-testing. Perceived gains on the equity front have been at the cost of heavy losses on the simplicity front.

When I became PM I wanted the tax treatment of families with dependent children to be made more generous and also extra tax breaks given to single-income families in recognition of the entire income they sacrificed when a parent stayed at home full-time to look after a child. Our 1996 policy gave increased tax-free thresholds for each child and significantly boosted the threshold for single-income households. Subsequent Family Tax Benefits continued to reflect these priorities.

In 2001 NATSEM, the National Centre for Social and Economic Modelling at the University of Canberra, released research which compared the disposable incomes of a range of families in 1996 with their situation in March 2001. It showed that at every level, there had been an increase in the disposable incomes of those families. In particular the relative positions of sole parents and single-income families had increased quite dramatically. It was irrefutable evidence that my policy goals for families had been achieved. The finding in relation to sole-parent families demonstrated that I had kept faith with my 1995 Australian Council of Social Service (ACOSS) speech promise that a Howard Government would protect the more vulnerable in society.

In 2002, departmental analysis threw up figures which formed an instructive backdrop to our examination of policies influencing the work/family balance and, in particular, the issue of paid parental leave. At that point 22 per cent of couples with dependent children were single-

494 / The Howard Government

income families — a greater proportion, in fact, than the number of couple families with children where both parents were in full-time work. The largest group, at 27 per cent, was that of one parent working full-time and the other part-time. The remainder of families with dependent children were either sole-parent families or those where the parent or parents were unemployed. In 2009, the single-income cohort was 27 per cent, the two full-time earners' was 22 per cent and one full-time/one part-time was 36 per cent. There was plenty of media and interest-group pressure for universal paid parental leave. The Sex Discrimination commissioner and feminist groups gave it iconic status; failure to adopt it meant that the Government was unsympathetic to the aspirations of modern women.

The deeper we delved into the parental leave issue, the more problematic it became. Any system which involved compulsion on business generally to provide paid parental leave would not be supported by my Government as, amongst other things, it would be manifestly unfair to small business. It would also disadvantage many women contemplating having children by reducing their attractiveness to potential employers.

Something like 45 per cent of the workforce enjoyed some kind of parental leave. It was widespread in the public service, and many large corporations had quite generous schemes. The Government should not reduce incentives for this to continue.

A further consideration was that of equitable treatment of all mothers of newborn children, irrespective of their work choices. I, and many of my colleagues, remained firmly of the view that the decision of a mother, or indeed a father, of a newborn baby to remain at home full-time for an indefinite period to look after that child should receive the same degree of respect, and financial recognition, as the decision of a parent to return to the full-time or part-time workforce as quickly as possible after the birth of the child.

Perhaps it results from the mistaken belief that only quite wealthy families opt to have one parent stay at home that there is almost blanket insensitivity to the fact that when that choice is made, the financial sacrifice by the family is usually greater than the cost of childcaring arrangements when both parents stay in the workforce. An entire income is given up. A large number of low-income families really struggle to achieve their desire to have one parent at home while a child is very young.

In putting together the details of a scheme, we found the potential for anomalies when parents, as they inevitably would, changed their minds about care arrangements after the birth of a child. How would one treat a declared stay-at-home mother who decides to re-enter the workforce? Conversely what of the mother who at the time the child was born intended to return to work, thus taking advantage of a paid maternity leave scheme, and then changes her mind and wants to remain at home indefinitely?

Given difficult experiences with recovering overpayments of family tax benefits, I was determined not to have a parental leave system which gave rise to that. Of even more importance, I wanted fair treatment of both stay-at-home and workforce-bound parents.

For these reasons my Government decided in 2004 not to have a separate paid parental leave system. Instead we elected to have a more generous, and new, baby bonus scheme. Its official title was Maternity Payment. The new baby bonus incorporated earlier schemes. It was set at $3000 in 2004 for each newborn baby, with increments of $1000 each in 2006 and 2008. At its 2008 level of $5000 it was broadly equivalent to 12 or 13 weeks' leave at the federal minimum wage. Financial conditions permitting, it could be made more generous.

The payment of a non-means-tested lump sum meant far less administrative complexity, no definitional problems and unarguably all mothers were being treated equally, whether they were returning to work or staying at home.

The Rudd Government scheme, intended to operate from 1 January 2011, would pay 18 weeks at the federal minimum wage. It discriminates against stay-at-home parents (who remain eligible for the baby bonus), and does so quite deliberately. The Families Minister, Jenny Macklin, boasted to this effect when she said in her speech introducing the legislation that 85 per cent of families would be about $2000 better off if they took paid parental leave. The policy announced by Tony Abbott was more generous and, as a consequence, discriminates even more heavily against stay-at-home parents.

I thought again of the estimable welfare organisations when I reflected on how the operation of the Family Law Act might be improved. For a long time I had imagined that, in some way, their marriage guidance and relationship activities could be more effectively involved in both holding marriages together as well as providing comfort and practical help when they fell apart. My social welfare advisor, John Perrin, put me into contact with a Sydney lawyer called Patrick Parkinson.

The two of us, ably assisted by Senator Kay Patterson, the Minister for Family and Community Services, developed the concept of Family Relationship Centres. Then to be fully funded by the Government, tenders for them were, in the main, picked up by the major religious groups through their existing marriage guidance and family relationship units. When a couple with children separate, a custody matter cannot be taken to court unless a genuine attempt has been made to resolve any differences through dispute resolution, using either a Family Relationship Centre or other registered dispute resolution provider. The role of the centre is to achieve, if possible, a total and non-litigious resolution of outstanding custody (now called parenting) issues between couples before they go to court. Because of their community focus and the variety of services offered, they act as non-judgemental shock absorbers for many couples during the early, difficult time following a separation. The 65 centres planned by the Howard Government are fully operational.

Many of my Coalition colleagues felt that the divorce laws had become unfair in their operation against fathers. Amongst the changes produced in 2005 was the introduction into the law of the presumption of joint responsibility, which did not, incidentally, mean that children must spend equal amounts of time with each of their separated parents, only that courts should be more accommodating to the interests of non-custodial parents. It was a long-overdue change which afforded proper understanding of the anguish and feeling of exclusion experienced by many fathers at the hands of Australia's divorce laws. There is pressure to reverse some of the changes. If that occurs, many will be surprised at the backlash it generates.

The advice that John Perrin gave me in relation to these changes was his last contribution to better social policy in Australia. He died on 21 May 2006. At his moving memorial service at the Wesley National Memorial Church in Canberra, I reflected on just how faithful he had been to the values of a practical Christian life. A humorous, intelligent and engaging man, John had both applied his convictions and used his abilities, in the fortunate position in which he found himself, to bring about beneficial changes for his fellow Australians.

Finally, of course, reference must be made to the way in which the Government I led not only retained but measurably strengthened Medicare. When my Government was defeated on 24 November 2007, the level of bulk-billing in Australia for ordinary GP consultations was 78.2 per cent.

It was an even higher figure for older Australians and children under 16. It had been a long time since the ALP could mount any kind of argument that the Coalition had allowed bulk billing to languish. In addition, the Medicare Safety Net, whereby 80 per cent of the cost of out-of-hospital services, over and above GP consultations, in excess of quite generous thresholds for families and individuals, provided remarkable security and peace of mind to Australians in relation to their healthcare costs.

The Medicare Safety Net has been the most significant improvement to the entire Medicare system since its introduction in 1984. Yet the ALP voted against its introduction.

The area of continuing concern remained the public hospital system, which was the responsibility of the state governments, although the federal government has a vital funding role. Support for bulk billing and the Medicare Safety Net had given real substance to the commitment I made some 12 years earlier that a Coalition Government would not only retain but build on Medicare. Coupled with the way in which we had revitalised private health insurance, it meant that the Coalition Government had an impressive record in strengthening our national health system. There was much substance in Tony Abbott's frequent question-time refrain that 'The Howard Government is the best friend that Medicare has ever had.'

Australia's health system, with all its faults, which are many, is better than any other around the world. On talkback radio I often said that if the battler were to get ill, it was better that he do so in Bankstown or Broadmeadows than in Brooklyn or Brixton. Political infighting, especially at a state level, denigrates our health services and the professionals who staff them far too much. I do not believe that a federal bureaucracy would run hospitals more efficiently than do state ones. However, devolved local control would bring a vast improvement. Australia should work to restore local hospital board control over our many public hospitals. It was Coalition policy in 2007. Tony Abbott has made it so again. We must maintain and, where possible, bolster the partnership between public and private hospitals. Our public hospitals need more beds and fewer bureaucrats.

38

SHAKESPEARE IN
MANDARIN

Of all the events I was involved with which had a foreign policy connotation, nothing came anywhere near the symbolism of two days in October 2003, when, successively the presidents of the United States and the People's Republic of China addressed joint sittings of the two houses of the Australian parliament. There was both coincidence and deliberation about these events.

Two American presidents, George Herbert Walker Bush and Bill Clinton, had previously addressed joint sittings. In 2003, Hu Jintao became the first Chinese President to be extended that honour. It was a mark of the importance I attached to the relationship with China. The symbolism was powerful. In one unmistakable gesture, Australia was telling the world it was possible, simultaneously, to have close relations with both the United States and China.

That did not mean that we treated the two nations equally. The United States will always be the more important partner, and more intimate friend, for Australia. Our shared history, values and security interests guarantee this. The fact that our relationship with the Americans became even warmer during the time of my Government made it that much easier, rather than more difficult, for us to build a friendly, pragmatic association with the Chinese.

This is where my critics were completely wrong. They argued, and some still do, that the closer you get to the Americans, the harder it becomes to get along with the Chinese. What they refused to accept was that the Chinese saw no incongruity in our having a close relationship with the Americans. To them, barring a military showdown with the United States over, say, Taiwan, our US alliance was no impediment. Many Chinese saw it as an asset. Others respected the fidelity displayed by Australia to our American friends. It was evidence that we were a dependable, reliable people with whom to have an association.

At another time and in other circumstances, having the two addresses following each other would have generated sensitivity. An American president less confident of the intimacy of the relationship between his country and ours might have wondered about the apparent equal billing being given to the Chinese. For their part, the Chinese may have expected a stand-alone focus for such an important occasion. It was precisely because we had unambiguously strengthened the American relationship, whilst pursuing a pragmatic, and to that point highly beneficial, improvement in our relations with China, that the two events were able to take place in such a smooth manner.

Some antecedents illustrated the vastly different cultures of the two countries. George Bush had spoken to me about his forthcoming visit and his address to the joint sitting whilst we were at the APEC meeting in Bangkok, just over a week before he was due in Australia. He asked me what sort of a reception he would get. I said it would be supportive from both the Government and the opposition, although in the case of the latter it might, due to such issues as Iraq, be a little more subdued. I said to him that there could be an outburst from a minor party. I told him there was 'a Green called Brown' who might be noisy. He laughed at the play on words and said, 'Thanks for the warning.' American politicians are frequently fascinated by the robust parliamentary system practised in both Britain and Australia.

The Green called Brown did interject. Bush handled it with aplomb, responding, 'Isn't free speech great?', and drew a resounding burst of applause in the process. This incident, however, set off alarm bells for the Chinese. They were despairing at the prospect of a recurrence of the Brown interjection when President Hu Jintao spoke the following day. There were numerous communications between the Chinese embassy and the speaker's office as well as my own. I made it clear that although we hoped for an incident-free address, there was no way that we could guarantee it and that naturally, as a member of the parliament, Senator Brown was entitled to be in the chamber. He would be dealt with in accordance with the Special

Standing Orders adopted for the joint sitting, but only if he became unduly disruptive. The anxiety of the Chinese to avoid any appearance of an affront to their President contrasted sharply with the willingness of President Bush to embrace the hurly-burly of a political exchange.

The Chinese displayed the same sensitivity over the official luncheon following their President's address. As had been the case with President Bush, we offered a luncheon in the Great Hall, to which all members of parliament would be invited as of right. The Chinese knocked this back in favour of a function at the Hyatt Hotel in Canberra that evening, to which selected people were invited. In this way Brown's attendance was avoided. I fully understood what they were up to with the Hyatt reception. Having made the point about Brown's rights in the parliamentary chamber, I saw no point in going further. In any event it was a Chinese call. They were not obliged to have a full parliamentary lunch.

Quite a number of Chinese Australians were invited to the evening dinner. Some of them I knew well, and they asked to meet the President. At an appropriate time I motioned them over to the table where we were both sitting. I introduced them and as they were chatting amiably we were suddenly surrounded by a large number of Chinese security personnel. They were not used to this kind of informal access to their leader. I smiled at them benignly.

In every way, it had been quite an achievement having these two addresses one after the other. It had underlined a great duality in our foreign policy. It had been achieved without any apparent self-consciousness about the equal billing from either leader. In the process, as well, we had been reminded of the continuing gulf between Australia and the United States on the one hand, and China on the other, when it came to openness and freedom of speech.

The Chinese were chuffed at what had happened, despite the sensitivities of their officialdom. They knew that Hu Jintao had become the first foreigner other than the US President to address a joint sitting of the two houses of parliament. He even achieved that honour in advance of a British prime minister. Equally, I knew that the courtesy extended to him would be long remembered, and be seen by the Chinese as a real gesture of friendship and a mark of the importance I personally attached to the relationship between our two countries.

Strengthening the US alliance was an instinctive given, so far as I was concerned. When I became Prime Minister I did not believe that the alliance was in disrepair or anything other than our most important bilateral relationship. Rather, I believed that it had become somewhat stale and needed revitalisation.

Relations between the Howard Government and China got off to a rocky start. The Taiwan Straits flare-up in 1996, involving both the United States and China displaying military might in those waters, caught Australia unprepared. Quite properly, we supported the Clinton Administration's position, but did it in a way which probably exacerbated Chinese sensitivities. Then there was the axing of the Development Import Finance Facility (DIFF) Scheme as part of the necessary cost savings in our first budget. It was a concessionary finance program benefiting developing Asian countries, including China.

Things went from bad to worse with the relationship; many developments came about through no fault of ours. We were fully within our rights in attacking a Chinese nuclear test in June. It was unreasonable of the Chinese to expect us to ban the pro-independence mayor of Taipei City from coming to Australia to attend an Asian cities summit in Brisbane. To cap it off, the Chinese bitterly resented a visit to Taiwan by John Anderson as Minister for Primary Industries, even though the visit was fully in accord with the One China policy, as well as the final indignity, so it seemed, of my seeing the Dalai Lama. The relationship virtually went into deep freeze in August/September of 1996. The Chinese placed a ban on visits to China by Australian ministers.

It was essential to find a way of drawing a line under what had happened and in a sense start again. I had the opportunity of doing this at the APEC meeting in Manila in November 1996, when I could have my first opportunity to talk face to face with the Chinese President, Jiang Zemin. Jiang as leader received mixed reviews. Some commentaries suggested that he lacked substance. Other, more, astute commentary gave him credit for being quite a cagey survivor. All of my experience with him suggested that the latter version was, overwhelmingly, the more accurate one. Jiang Zemin was amongst the more astute and fascinating and genuinely interesting leaders that I met.

My attitude was we should take the opportunity presented by the APEC meeting to put the relationship on a sensible footing. We should neither pretend there was an emotional content to the relationship, nor ignore the potential of building on the practical links that already existed and could be expanded in the future. For me there would be none of those rhetorical references to special relationships. China and Australia had vastly different histories. China was an authoritarian nation. By contrast, Australia was one of the longest continuous liberal democracies in the world. With a population of more than one billion people, China dwarfed Australia. On the other hand, the precious resources exports of Australia were of enormous potential benefit to a growing Chinese economy.

Chinese Australians were making a lively contribution to the development of modern Australia. Already in Australia's largest city, Sydney, dialects of Chinese were the most widely spoken foreign language. There was much on which to build, provided both China and Australia adopted a commonsense approach.

I went to that meeting determined to focus on the things that we had in common and to put aside those things that could never be resolved between our two nations. With human rights in China, I favoured a formal dialogue between the two countries, thus avoiding the annual ritual of the United Nations passing a resolution condemning human rights abuses in China, without any likelihood of future action.

It has long been my view that eventually there will be a collision within China between her economic liberalism and her political authoritarianism. China's political system will undergo change, but such a change is unlikely for decades. Meanwhile, China will continue to grow economically, and it is in the national interest of Australia that we take advantage of that growth, without conceding ground on issues that are important to the values of our country.

I rate the meeting I had with President Jiang Zemin in Manila on 25 November 1996 as about as important a meeting I held with any foreign leader in the time that I was Prime Minister.

The President stated the obvious when he said at the outset that the relationship between Australia and China depended on the efforts we both put into it. I told Jiang Zemin that I was personally committed, as was my Government, to building closer relations between the two countries. I said that there would be differences in emphasis because of the differences between our societies. I told the President that Australia would like to see China as a member of the World Trade Organisation (WTO). I further said that I saw participation by China in the region as a force for stability and important for the region. I reiterated the longstanding One China policy of Australia.

I made it clear to the Chinese President that the alliance between Australia and the United States was deeply rooted in history and not in any way directed against China. It was designed to promote our security, not undermine the security of any other nation. I felt that Jiang understood this, even though he did not say so.

Jiang made the point that he was quite familiar with both Bob Hawke and Paul Keating and that it was, therefore, beneficial to get acquainted with me. He expressed appreciation for the remarks I had made about China's membership of the WTO. The President talked extensively and rather defensively about Tibet.

Importantly, towards the end of the discussion, the President extended an invitation to me to visit China. I accepted this invitation and indicated that I would very much like to visit China again. I said I would like to visit in the first half of 1997, if that were possible.

As the meeting ended I told the President that I would like to see China and Australia go into the next century in peace and cooperation, respecting our different cultural heritages and political standpoints. I said I did not believe in lecturing others any more than we liked receiving lectures ourselves.

Encouragingly, as we walked out of the meeting, the President said to me in English, 'Face to face is much better, isn't it?' In my later news conference, I said that I had told the President that 'Australia and China had some very basic differences so far as our political systems were concerned', but that we should focus on pursuing the mutual interests that we had. I made it clear that I wanted to focus on commonsense practical aspects of the relationship. I felt that the meeting had the effect of placing a floor under the relationship, and that the rebuilding process could now start.

I would visit China over Easter of 1997, and fully understood the importance of the trip. I decided to take a broad-based business delegation to emphasise to the Chinese the importance I placed on economic links. The delegation included Hugh Morgan of Western Mining; Charles Goode, Chairman of ANZ; Lachlan Murdoch; David Murray of the Commonwealth Bank; Lewis Ting of Ernst and Young; and Russell Madigan, one of the icons of the Australian mining industry. It was a heavyweight delegation and told the Chinese that we were serious about the relationship and that the core of that relationship was mutual commercial interest. The visit in 1997 was positive. It built on the progress made at my meeting with Jiang Zemin in November 1996.

The visit also gave me the first opportunity to meet Li Peng. Long regarded as the architect of the suppression of the student uprising in

Tiananmen Square, he was the hard man of Chinese politics. As Premier he exerted enormous influence. It was with him that I raised, specifically, the concept of a human rights dialogue as a possible substitute for Australia deciding each year whether or not to support an anti-Chinese resolution at the United Nations on the issue of human rights.

There was also discussion concerning the growing importance of liquefied natural gas (LNG) as an energy source for China. Li Peng struck me as a tough, uncompromising operator who would have had no hesitation in brutally suppressing dissent. The time devoted by Li Peng and the intensity of the dialogue reflected the fact that the Chinese were taking the visit seriously, and that a corner had been turned in the relationship.

My visit to Shanghai revealed just how much that city had changed in the 12 years that had passed since I had last been there in 1985. At that time, Mao suits and bicycles predominated. Twelve years on it was almost the complete reverse, so extensive had been the modernisation.

I had an amusing experience with my Chinese security detail. The first morning I was in Shanghai, they accompanied me on my morning walk, all decked out in business suits. They obviously thought this early-morning walk of mine was a bit of a stroll. When they discovered otherwise, they turned up the next morning replete in tracksuits ready for a more energetic workout. The walks on both mornings took me through a park in Shanghai filled with mainly elderly Chinese doing their Tai Chi or ballroom dancing accompanied by music from old gramophone players.

While in Shanghai I attended an Easter Day church service, where I ran into Newt Gingrich and his wife.

It was during this visit that I got to know and almost inevitably like Jiang Zemin. He was a fascinating character. His conversational English was quite good, although his fluency in Russian was, allegedly, superior. He was of an age that he had spent time during his early working life in the old Soviet Union. He was an engineer.

Jiang was a lover of Western music, literature and movies. He had quite an extensive knowledge of composers such as Beethoven and a passionate interest in Shakespeare. When he discovered that Janette had been a high school English teacher, his eyes lit up and, from then on, exchanges about Shakespeare between the two of them became a feature of any meetings. Janette told me that she felt that meeting Jiang Zemin represented something of a Shakespearean examination. From time to time he would quote something from Shakespeare and ask her the name of the play containing the quotation.

Jiang's fascination with old Hollywood and other Western movies was demonstrated at the Shanghai APEC meeting in 2001. At the conclusion of the cultural presentation, at the gala dinner, the host ensemble gathered on the stage to the tune of 'Auld Lang Syne', which intrigued Janette and me no end. When we asked Jiang about this later he replied, 'Remember the ending of *Waterloo Bridge* when "Auld Lang Syne" was played?', indicating that this was the reason for the tune's inclusion in the cultural presentation. *Waterloo Bridge* was a 1940 movie starring Robert Taylor and Vivien Leigh.

I grew to like Jiang a lot. The personal relationship we began to build over that Easter visit made a material contribution to the energy the bilateral relationship enjoyed over subsequent years.

I also met Zhu Rongji. He was the presumptive Premier and a person dedicated to further liberalisation of the Chinese economy. He visited Australia not long after my visit to China and played a key role, by then as Premier, in the negotiations in 2002 over an LNG contract, to which I will refer a little later.

After the Easter 1997 visit, the relationship between our two countries gathered momentum, with trade growing at a rapid rate. Between 1996 and 2006, Australian exports to China were to increase by a staggering 626 per cent or an average annual rate of 18 per cent. In that latter year China became Australia's largest export destination. It was one of those happy conjunctions of the availability of natural resources required by the hungry needs of an expanding economy.

It would, however, be a mistake to assume that it was all serendipitous. There were features of Australia as a supplier which made her attractive to the Chinese.

During Zhu's visit to Australia in May 1997, he disavowed an article in the *China Daily* and told me that his government did not view Australia's alliance with the United States as a threat. Such a statement, unexceptional today, was quite groundbreaking then. The Chinese had understood and absorbed the message on this issue which I had delivered to Jiang at our Manila meeting in November 1996.

As time went by the effective relationship established with China began to be noticed by others, including the Americans. In mid-1999 I saw Bill Clinton in Washington. It was not long after a particularly unsuccessful visit to the United States by the Chinese Premier Zhu Rongji. Through whatever combination of poor preparation and misunderstood agendas, the visit had been a public relations disaster. Zhu had got the impression that the Americans remained hostile to China's application for membership of the WTO. This bothered Clinton, and he asked me, during our meeting at the White House, to tell the Chinese that America really wanted them in the WTO. He said, 'They will listen to you because you get on well with them.' I was only too happy to respond to the President's request. It was Australian policy to welcome China into the WTO.

I tracked the Premier down in London and had a 30-minute conversation with him, entirely in English. His English was particularly fluent and it struck me at the time just how globalised our world had become. Here was the Australian Prime Minister conducting a 30-minute conversation with the Chinese Premier, fluent in English, he himself being in London. I think I conveyed the message to him. The significance of this incident was that the Australian way of dealing with the Chinese had won attention.

Jiang Zemin himself visited Australia in 1999. It was a visit which consolidated earlier gains and included a luncheon at Admiralty House to which I invited all of the state premiers. In different ways, they all had interests in Chinese investment and trade. It was a further sign of the strengthening of the relationship.

The November 2000 APEC meeting held in Brunei was Bill Clinton's last participation, as President, in that gathering. The meeting took place whilst the outcome of the presidential election between George Bush and Al Gore was still being contested. That impasse was a topic of constant social discussion amongst leaders.

At the formal luncheon, I felt that something should be said about Clinton's contribution to APEC. I had acquired some years of seniority, even though I had only been attending since 1996. I therefore presumed to speak on behalf of all the leaders in thanking Clinton and his country for its contribution to APEC and wishing him well for the future. Quite spontaneously, my remarks were seconded by Jiang Zemin, who spoke with equal warmth about Clinton's contribution. For those who are interested in symbolism, there was an element of that in what I have just described. There was acceptance of Australia as an appropriate spokesman for APEC participants, recognition of the American contribution, and a willingness by the Chinese to be associated with it. The Taiwan Straits tensions of early 1996 seemed a long time ago.

I felt pleased that this was the case. Whilst I always knew that, come a showdown between China and the United States, Australia would align itself with the United States, it was overwhelmingly in our interests to prevent any such occurrence in the future. As Prime Minister I used every opportunity to encourage the Americans, the Chinese and the Taiwanese to keep the temperature as low as possible over Taiwan.

In the end some pragmatic accommodation will be reached between the People's Republic and Taiwan. The passage of time has seen a growing rapprochement. The return of the Kuomintang as the government party in Taiwan means calmer relations with Beijing. I believe that at some time in the next 10 or 20 years, an understanding akin to that now existing between the People's Republic and Hong Kong will be arrived at with Taiwan. I was strengthened in that belief after a visit to Taiwan early in 2010, which included a lengthy meeting with President Ma.

In 2002 the prospect of Australia participating in a huge natural gas sale contract with Guangdong Province in China emerged. The North West Shelf Consortium was in competition with a number of other suppliers for a $25 billion contract over more than 20 years. It was a very valuable potential contract in its own right. It was also a precursor to other contracts. Hitherto China had tended to source its natural gas from the Middle East. It was now on the lookout for alternative sources of supply. Australian companies had to be in there. At that time it was still a buyers' market for LNG.

Discussions had been going on for some time. Ultimately the real competition was between the North West Shelf Consortium and a 'green fields' partnership between BP and the Indonesian Government in relation to the Tangguh fields, in Indonesia.

It was a commercial negotiation. In the end it would be driven by price, reliability and all the other factors that normally influenced decisions of this kind. Yet given that it was a sale of a large, natural resource commodity to a Chinese province, government involvement, on both sides, could not be ignored. No matter what our own culture on these things was, Asian governments expected governments of other countries to be actively involved in advocating the cause of their nation's enterprises.

Towards the end of the negotiations I thought that it was important to lobby personally on behalf of the Australian consortium.

I had kept in close contact with both the consortium and the Australian embassy in Beijing. Our ambassador, David Irvine, had done an excellent job in assisting the North West Shelf Consortium and liaising with the Chinese authorities. At a time seen as propitious by both the consortium and the embassy, I went to China to discuss the issue with both Zhu Rongji and Jiang Zemin. Although Premier Zhu had a more hands-on involvement, Jiang's opinions would be quite crucial in the end.

I had a lengthy and detailed discussion with Zhu and gained the distinct impression that he wanted the Australian group to get the contract. The Chinese valued our reliability. To buy from an Australian consortium would represent a quite significant diversification of supply sources. That is what the Chinese wanted. I suspect that they regarded the alternative as potentially less predictable than would be the case with the Australian offer.

Notwithstanding his broadly favourable disposition towards Australia, Zhu was a tough bargainer. He made it plain at our meeting that some further movement on price was needed. I took away the impression that if that were forthcoming then the contract would be ours. I directly and immediately conveyed this to the consortium. Acknowledging that it was a commercial decision, I ensured that they were aware of my assessment that the Chinese wanted the contract to go to Australia and that, provided some attempt were made to meet their further requirements regarding price, it could fall the right way.

Zhu had a good sense of humour. He said that John Prescott, Deputy PM of Britain, had been in town lobbying for BP. Zhu had joked that Prescott was bound to lose as Britain had only sent the Deputy PM, whereas Australia had sent its PM. Prescott had retorted that Tony Blair would be on the next flight if necessary.

I saw Zhu Rongji in Beijing. I then flew to Chongqing in central-western China to see Jiang Zemin. He was impressed by the fact that I had made the effort to follow him to another part of China. Both Jiang Zemin and Zhu Rongji made great play of the fact that in the end it was a matter for the local authorities to decide. I knew that was theoretically the case. I also knew that their favourable disposition would in the end be quite crucial. That turned out to be so and the consortium won the contract. It was an historic resource win for Australia. It was worth $20–25 billion in export income and was then Australia's largest-ever export deal. It was for the supply of 3 million tonnes of LNG per year for 25 years.

Winning the LNG contract was the culmination of a remarkable transformation in a relationship in just five years. In early 1997 it would not have been thought likely that such a deal could have been clinched. It had been a whole-of-government effort aided by the professionalism of two fine ambassadors to Beijing, Ric Smith and David Irvine. In the process we had established a method of dealing with the Chinese, and a government-to-government relationship that was qualitatively different from that of the Americans. In the process we had not alienated Washington. Indeed, the special depth of our Washington links had meant that differentiating the product in dealing with China had not raised any hackles.

Although trade between China and Australia had grown exponentially over a short period of time, it seemed the logical next step to commence negotiations for a free trade agreement (FTA). Bilateral FTAs had become the flavour of the month as a result of the totally failed multilateral trade talks in Seattle in 2002, followed by the tortuous and slow progress in reviving multilateral trade talks in the so-called Doha Round.

I understood why it was the next thing to do, but I always had a nagging suspicion that, by embarking down the path of such a negotiation, we were creating an objective which we did not really need to realise. It was always going to be hard to get agricultural concessions from the Chinese. They in turn would want more manufacturing concessions than Australian industry would want its government to make. Negotiations continue to this day.

This was a good example of when process and form displace substance. The truth was, and remains, that Australian and Chinese trade relations will be quite remarkable whether or not there is an FTA. If the negotiations ceased tomorrow and were never resumed, China would remain the most valuable customer imaginable.

Despite the enormous strides made on the trade front and the very pragmatic government-to-government relations of the past decade, there were periodic examples not only of Chinese naïvety in dealing with Australia, but also examples of the vast cultural gap between the two nations. The latter served to remind us of the limitations in the relationship.

The Dalai Lama came to Australia in 1996. I had not met him before and naturally was pleased when he called on me. He is a colourful, charismatic religious leader. There is worldwide sympathy for the people of Tibet, and it was unthinkable that I should do other than see him. Beijing was most put out that I saw him. He came again to Australia in 2007. On this occasion I was less committed to seeing him, but all of that changed as a result of the attitude of the Chinese.

A spokesman for the Chinese Foreign Ministry made it clear that relations between our two countries would be damaged if I saw the Dalai Lama. That meant, of course, that I would have to see him and I did. The Chinese did not seem to understand the impact of such a clumsy threat, and just how counterproductive it could really be.

The same insensitivity was on display when a Mr Chen Yonglin, an employee of the Chinese consulate in Sydney, sought political asylum in Australia. The Chinese Foreign Ministry and China's most capable ambassador to Canberra, Madame Fu, made strenuous representations to the effect that Mr Chen should be returned to China. The Government carefully pointed out that we had a well-established procedure for dealing with applications for political asylum and that Mr Chen was entitled to the potential benefits of this procedure. Once again the Chinese rather clumsily made it known that relations would be affected if Mr Chen were granted political asylum.

He was granted political asylum. We heard no more from the Chinese on the subject, and there was no visible impact on relations between our two countries.

Both of these incidents illustrated a sharply different cultural approach to what could be described as the national dignity or sense of propriety of a nation. Perhaps the Chinese way is that it is part of the preservation of national self-respect that the desired outcome must be stated, irrespective of whether stating that outcome will have a counterproductive impact.

I had experienced an earlier example of Chinese attitudes on such issues in May 2002. In Beijing for the visit principally bound up with the LNG negotiations, I was invited to address a meeting of the cadres of the Chinese Communist Party, having been told that I was the first-ever leader of a Western political party to have received such an invitation.

It was an enthralling experience to address hundreds of dyed-in-the-wool party people. I spoke forcefully about the mutual respect between our two societies despite our different political systems. During question time I was told by a questioner that visits to Australia by the Dalai Lama were bad news for the bilateral relationship, because the Dalai Lama was engaged in wicked activities under the cover of religion.

In my reply I referred to the result of the referendum in Australia in 1951, when the Menzies Government proposal to amend the Constitution to ban the Communist Party was defeated. My argument was that this was a splendid example of how a democratic nation such as Australia was tolerant enough to allow the continued legal operation of a political party totally opposed to the democratic order.

If it was good enough for Australians to tolerate the continuation of the Communist Party as a legal entity, it ought to be good enough for the Chinese to tolerate the leader of a friendly country not only allowing the Dalai Lama to visit but also seeing him. The audience reaction was cold, so my analogy did not work. The criterion brought by the Chinese to behaviour of this kind was quite different from ours and no amount of arguing by Western analogy would get me anywhere.

Following the Rudd Government's Defence White Paper, which dwelt heavily on China's military growth, there has been much debate about the extent to which China constitutes a military threat to Australia. In the short-to-medium term there is no feasible threat to Australia or indeed to other countries in the region — except, of course, Taiwan — from China. That country's preoccupation is economic growth and social stabilisation. It has a strong sense of its own importance in the region, but does not harbour territorial ambitions, at present.

The Chinese know that they can influence outcomes in the Asia-Pacific region. When Chinese interests are not directly affected, they are more than likely to display pragmatic indifference. This was the case with Chinese attitudes to Iraq, detailed in Chapter 34.

Increasingly there were differences in the character of Australia's responses to China and those of the United States. In a major speech in New York, when attending a special session of the United Nations in September 2005, I said that China's growth was not only good for China but also good for the world. These remarks were warmly received by the Chinese and from time to time played back to me in subsequent discussions with Chinese leaders. From about this stage onwards, Chinese leaders began to omit the previously obligatory references to a One China policy during discussions with me.

On a bilateral visit to the United States in July 2005, President Bush and I were asked the same question about China at our joint news conference, and gave noticeably different responses. The President observed that Australia effectively had its own way of handling the Chinese. I agreed with this assessment and pointed out that one of the bases of our links with

China was a fundamental understanding by the Chinese of just how important the American alliance was to Australia.

None of these comments should be taken to mean that I have a gentle and benign attitude towards China's great power ambitions. I am sure that Beijing will get to them at some point. That is why I believed that one of the shrewdest foreign policy thrusts of the Bush Administration was to encourage the development of the trilateral security dialogue between the United States, Japan and Australia. The possibility of extending it to include India, thus creating a quadrilateral dialogue, was raised during the Bush presidency.

The real impact of that strategic dialogue was that it was an unexceptionable way of providing a democratic counterbalance to China. I experienced sensitivity towards China amongst nations in Southeast Asia. Therefore anything which represented a democratic riposte would be, however quietly, welcomed by some of the smaller nations in our region.

It was a mistake for the Rudd Government, so early in its term of government, to rule out the inclusion of India in an expanded and quadrilateral security dialogue. The clumsiness of this was intensified by the Foreign Minister, Stephen Smith, making the announcement ruling out Indian participation whilst standing side by side with the Chinese Foreign Minister.

China can exercise a mesmerising effect on some, distorting their judgement. Bob Hawke has described Deng's decision in 1978 to open up China to the outside world and move it towards a market economy as the single most important decision taken by any national leader in the 20th century — a big call — and a sign of the hypnotic effect that can be exerted by the Middle Kingdom. In August 1980, as Treasurer, I instructed that Australia's vote on the Interim Committee of the International Monetary Fund (IMF) be cast against an attempt then under way to credit Taiwan's gold deposits at the fund to the Beijing Government. Almost all of Taiwan's gold had been accumulated since the Communist takeover in 1949, and Beijing had no right to it. I thought the proposal was international financial brigandry. I saw no need to consult the PM about my decision, but when he learned of it, Fraser rang in anger and said that he would investigate having the decision reversed. It was too late for that — the IMF vote had already been taken and came out narrowly in Taiwan's favour. This was another case of an Australian leader being just a little too enthralled by China.

39

ASIA FIRST,
NOT ASIA ONLY

For more than 40 years, every serious political leader in Australia has been committed to the belief that close engagement and collaboration with our Asian neighbours was critical to Australia's future. The difference which Paul Keating brought to this bipartisan understanding was his laboured, and contentious, narrative about the Australian identity which implied that, in some way, Australia had to show an overt preference for our links with Asia over our ties with traditional allies such as the United States and Britain, especially the latter.

In a phrase which I would use frequently as Prime Minister, I did not believe that Australia had to choose between her geography and her history. It was one of the signal triumphs of Australian foreign policy under the Howard Government that simultaneously, over a period of more than a decade, Australia built even closer relations with our Asian neighbours whilst reasserting the traditional intimacy of our links with Washington and London. It was always possible to do both, if one wished to.

Uniquely, Australia is a product of Western civilisation, closely allied to the United States, but located cheek by jowl with the nations of Asia. Both history and geography have given us a rare opportunity; why should we be so foolish as to think that we must choose between the two?

Whether Australia should become a republic or change the design of our flag are exclusively domestic matters, irrelevant to the rest of the world. Although both Paul Keating and I said this, I believed it. By contrast, he did not. In an interview on the *Sunday* program on 26 March 1992, John Dawkins, the Labor Treasurer, cited the presence of the Union Jack in the corner of Australia's flag as important to whether Australia related to Asia as an independent country. In that interview he said, 'The point about Australia is that we've never gone through the catharsis of breaking those links and therefore being able to establish new and permanent and firmer links in the region in which we live.'[1] This was the Treasurer saying directly that in order to get on in Asia we had to break links with Britain. He argued that we had to choose.

It was juvenile stuff. Ten years later when involved in the negotiations for the huge natural gas deal with the Chinese President and Premier, my main negotiating rival was Britain's Deputy PM, John Prescott, who was advocating BP's proposal. I can assure John Dawkins that Union Jacks, small or large, didn't come into it.

I came to office sharing the views of my four predecessors that close links, at every realistic level, with the nations of Asia were fundamental to Australia's future. Addressing the National Press Club for the last time as Opposition leader, on 28 February 1996, I said that Indonesia would be the first country that I visited as prime minister.

Paul Keating's error with Indonesia was to define the relationship too heavily in terms of his personal relationship with President Suharto. I didn't predict Suharto's demise in 1998 or the rapid and remarkable transformation of Indonesia from a military autocracy to the third-largest democracy in the world. Nevertheless, when change did come rapidly and unexpectedly in Indonesia, my more detached association with Suharto meant that Australia was able to adjust and, over time, influence other events more effectively.

In the first weeks of office Alexander Downer arranged for me to see Mahathir, the prickly Malaysian PM, in Brisbane as the latter travelled en route back to Malaysia from New Zealand. It was a useful meeting. He spoke quite personally about his associations with both Hawke and Keating. He retained a lingering resentment about Hawke's criticism of the execution of the two convicted Australian drug couriers, Barlow and Chambers. He also had a different, more narrowly East Asian vision for regional cooperation in Asia — one which sought to exclude Australia and the United States. The meeting restored normal transmission in diplomatic relations between Australia and Malaysia. Fortunately, the people-to-people links and business investment, particularly from Australia in Malaysia, had remained strong, despite the freeze at head-of-government level. This evidenced the lasting impact of the education opportunities for Asians under the Colombo Plan. There were a larger proportion of Malaysian alumni from universities in Australia than from any other country. This was a Menzies legacy.

My relations with Mahathir remained good until 1998. I had accepted an invitation to visit Malaysia in February that year. Due to the Government's decision to respond to Bill Clinton's request that we send SAS units to the Middle East to support American and British action under 'Operation Desert Fox', I decided, at the last minute, to cancel the visit. I felt that I should not be out of the country when it was announced that Australian troops would go overseas, potentially into combat. That was the right decision, domestically. I am equally certain, however, that Mahathir was particularly offended. This would have been all the more so given that the troops were being committed to a conflict with another Muslim country. Mahathir was openly critical of our later involvement in Iraq. He also made wild, and untruthful, allegations about the behaviour of Australian troops the following year in East Timor.

Mahathir was incensed at the critical comments I made about the way in which Anwar, his former deputy and heir apparent, on whom Mahathir had savagely turned, had been treated by the Malaysian police and judicial system.

The normal transmission re-established in Brisbane in March 1996, having broken down, was never restored whilst Mahathir remained Prime Minister. Other heads of government found him difficult. His successor, Abdullah Badawi, and I saw a lot of each other whilst Badawi was Deputy Prime Minister. When he assumed the top job we exchanged visits and generally saw to it that at a head-of-government level the historic warmth between our two nations was maintained.

I had arranged to have my first overseas visit, to Indonesia and Japan, in July 1996. Janette being diagnosed with cancer and needing to undergo a major operation later that month, I put off that travel until September. Early visits in a new prime minister's term have symbolic implications; Indonesia was our nearest neighbour, and Japan had for years been our closest partner in the Asian region, so my priorities were right.

Japan had just installed a new Prime Minister, Ryutaro Hashimoto, and the bilateral links were strong. The major challenge was to keep it that way and, as time went by, to reassure the Japanese that we were not flirting too much with the new suitor, China.

Kevin Rudd made a big mistake ignoring Japan during his first overseas visit, particularly as that visit included a stop in China. As a former Australian diplomat, he must be aware that status, face and form matter a good deal in Asian countries, not least Japan. Anyone who cared to listen knew how offended the Japanese had been at this treatment, given the long loyalty of Japan as a customer of Australia, dating back to the late 1950s.

I had met Suharto on several earlier occasions before becoming PM. He had always been a willing interlocutor with senior Australian politicians and had readily agreed to see me, firstly as Treasurer in the Fraser Government and later as both Deputy Leader and Leader of the Opposition.

This visit took place within the old paradigm. East Timor was to be mentioned, but we were not to obsess about it. It was still a highly sensitive topic with the Indonesian leadership. I travelled from the airport to my Jakarta accommodation with the Indonesian Foreign Minister, the wily and experienced Ali Alatas. We identified subjects which might come up at our meeting. He stressed the continuing prickliness about East Timor. The continuation of warm relations between Canberra and Jakarta came first. The tone I sought was businesslike rather than effusive.

The subtext of that first meeting between Suharto and me was that of Indonesia as a nation performing strongly and willing to have good relations with Australia, provided that Australia accepted the character of the Indonesian Government, and that sensitivities such as East Timor were dealt with in an appropriate manner. If so, everything would be fine.

I dwell on the psychology of that meeting because it was the last occasion on which a meeting between the heads of government of the two countries was conducted in such an atmosphere. A year later, when I saw Suharto again, on my way home from a Commonwealth Heads of Government Meeting (CHOGM) in Edinburgh, Indonesia was in financial crisis, having been battered by the Asian economic meltdown. I came to Jakarta to announce Australian assistance as part of an international bail-out of the Indonesian economy. These economic events dramatically changed Indonesia, the dynamic in the relationship between Australia and our nearest neighbour and, most importantly, ultimately led to Suharto's removal as president.

During the election campaign Paul Keating had said that Asian leaders would not deal with me as prime minister. Even for someone way behind in the polls, predictions of that kind are always quite foolish.

Nonetheless, some Australian commentators were intent on that Keating prophecy being fulfilled. My every word was analysed. There was a particular brouhaha over the fact that in my speech at the official banquet in my honour in Jakarta I said, 'Neither do I see Australia as a bridge between Asia and the West, as is sometimes suggested.' These words were followed by others which put them in proper context, yet for several days the press wrote of a 'blunder'. There was also comment over the fact that words I uttered during a speech did not appear in the prepared text of the speech issued to the media. It seemed an utterly inconsequential preoccupation. The Australian media were quickly to learn that I rarely read speeches, let alone read them word for word.

Suharto was grateful for Australia's help in 1997, but he must have known that the sands were shifting rapidly. Within months of my visit, an era in his country ended, and he was replaced by the excitable, voluble and quite unpredictable B.J. Habibie. My relationship with Habibie was almost totally consumed by the focus on East Timor, dealt with extensively in Chapter 29.

Unexpectedly Habibie was succeeded by Abdurrahman Wahid, known as Gus Dur, an almost totally blind, highly intelligent, Baghdad-educated, Muslim former cleric and scholar. He was the most fluent English speaker of the five Indonesian presidents with whom I dealt (they were all good). Wahid could imitate the Australian accent, having a standard joke that a person should always go to Australia either yesterday or tomorrow. It should never be 'today', thus playing on the broad Australian pronunciation of 'today', which sounded like 'to die'.

He was an inveterate traveller, and finally the long drought in visits to Australia by Indonesian presidents was broken when Wahid came to Canberra in June 2001. The last visit had been that of Suharto in 1975. During Wahid's presidency, our relations with Indonesia trod water. Although our exchanges were polite, there was no real energy. The anti-Australian feeling arising from our role in East Timor lingered.

Indonesia's fledgling democracy passed its real test in July 2001 with the transfer of power from Wahid to his Vice-president, Megawati Sukarnoputri (the daughter of the first president of the Indonesian republic, Sukarno). The National Assembly voted unanimously to end Wahid's tenure after Wahid had tried to retain power by declaring a state of emergency and purporting to dissolve parliament. The armed forces, the Supreme Court and the People's Consultative Assembly all rejected him. They pledged support for the due process newly established after Suharto's departure. It was a significant event; a change of Indonesian president had occurred with virtually no bloodshed or social unrest. Whatever else might be said about the country, this was a promising sign.

Megawati's major appeal was her patrimony. She did not prove to be an energetic reformer and, in time, greatly disappointed her supporters. Her presidency covered two highly charged events involving Australia: the *Tampa* incident and the terrorist attacks in Bali which killed 88 Australians.

Megawati and I spoke to each other more frequently by telephone and, in the wake of the attack, had a common reference point for many of our discussions. We agreed on practical anti-terrorism measures, and cooperation to fight people-smuggling improved. Although improved, the relationship was still held at a distance.

It was the arrival of Dr H. Susilo Bambang Yudhoyono (SBY) on the Indonesian political scene, and the close relationship I established with him, which proved the catalyst for the more intense friendship of today. A former general in the Indonesian Armed Forces, SBY was Megawati's coordinating Minister for Political and Security Affairs. A Muslim who detested terrorism and understood the need to fight it at every turn, SBY knew the challenge Indonesia faced on both the economic and security fronts. He is a likeable, engaging man.

He represented his President at the commemoration of the first anniversary of the Bali attack on 12 October 2003. He made a passionate speech denouncing terrorism. By then speculation had begun that he would be a candidate for the presidency of Indonesia when a popular ballot for that post was held the following year. His speech was a rallying call to the mainstream of Muslim Indonesia to fight terrorism. He concluded his speech quoting from the Koran, 'Take not life, which Allah hath made sacred, except by way of justice and law: thus doth he command you, that ye may learn wisdom.'[2]

SBY easily won the run-off presidential ballot against Megawati on 20 September 2004, obtaining 60.6 per cent of the valid vote. He was the first-ever Indonesian president elected by popular vote in a truly democratic ballot. It was a landmark for his country. It was also good news for Australia as SBY had genuine warmth towards our country. At the time of his election, one of his sons was studying at Edith Cowan University in Western Australia.

SBY's inauguration as President was scheduled for 20 October 2004, only a few weeks after my re-election as Prime Minister on 9 October. On impulse I indicated that I would attend the inauguration. There had not been an expectation that the inauguration would be an occasion for representation at a head-of-government level, rather at the more understated ambassadorial level. Once my intentions were known, other heads of government from neighbouring countries also decided to go.

Impulse-driven or otherwise, my decision to go plainly touched SBY. To me it was a most important occasion. By dint of the ballot which elected SBY, Indonesia had become the third-largest functioning democracy in the world. He was a man with whom Australia could have not only friendly but highly productive relations. He believed in democracy, the importance of economic growth and foreign investment, and was instinctively pro-Australian. He also wanted to resume better relations with the United States.

SBY also understood that as a moderate Muslim with strong anti-terrorist instincts he carried a heavy responsibility, not only in his own country but in the world Islamic community. I wanted our relations at a head-of-government level to start in a positive way.

After the inauguration ceremony SBY held a brief meeting with visiting heads of government. I assumed the role of spokesman on behalf of all present in congratulating SBY and assuring him and his country of our goodwill and desire to assist. Of itself, that was highly symbolic. The difficult days of late 1999 were firmly behind us.

Just a few months later the overwhelming tragedy of the Boxing Day tsunami which ravaged Indonesia more than any other nation brought our two countries closer together. An estimated 300,000 Indonesians died and countless millions were made homeless. The first physical relief for Indonesians came from units of the Australian military and those of the United States.

Australia's response was more generous than that of any other country. It included, at $1 billion, our nation's largest-ever aid package for a specific country. At every level of society, there was an outpouring of support and concern from Australians for what had happened in Indonesia. Our medical assistance teams in Aceh did heroic work. Australian Army engineers were heavily involved in the sweat, dirt and grime of the rescue effort.

I formally announced Australia's aid package at a donors' conference convened by SBY in Jakarta on 5–7 January 2005. I had telephoned SBY immediately news of the tsunami came through, offering all the assistance Australia could reasonably muster. I was the first foreign leader to call him, and we remained in constant contact until I saw him in person at the donors' conference.

SBY knew in advance what I planned to announce. His greeting was warm, emotional and that of someone who was reaching out to a friend at a time of genuine need. There was nothing symbolic or artificial about Australia's assistance. It was a lot of money, and we both agreed that it should be spent under careful supervision over a measured period so that the maximum benefit could be derived by the Indonesian people.

Out of this terrible natural disaster the opportunity had been taken to help in a thoroughly practical way, thus drawing the two nations even closer together. Australia is building 200 schools across 20 Indonesian provinces. In the space of six months, two deliberate acts of mine helped bridge a wide gulf which had existed for some years.

By the end of 2005 the bilateral relationship with Indonesia had become stronger than at any time in recent memory. The difference with past episodes was that it was built on the surer foundation of it being between two democracies.

It would never be a trouble-free association. Instances of young Australians ensnared in the tough anti-drug laws of Indonesia, as exemplified by the case of Schapelle Corby, although difficult, were never going to derail the association.

As I was at pains to point out on numerous occasions, Asian countries have tough, anti-drug criminal laws. Young Australians who trafficked or dealt in any way with drugs did so at their own peril in Indonesia, Singapore, Malaysia or Thailand. On a number of occasions I literally begged young Australians not to risk their lives and liberty by transgressing the anti-drug codes of neighbouring countries.

As a further sign of warmer relations, Indonesia proved to be a friend at court in Australia's successful bid to be part of an East Asia summit, comprised of the Association of South-East Asian Nations (ASEAN) countries (Indonesia, Malaysia, Singapore, Thailand, the Philippines, Laos, Burma, Brunei, Cambodia and Vietnam) plus Japan, China, India and Korea. Australia and New Zealand wanted the group expanded to include our two nations. China was lukewarm. We received crucial help from both Japan and Indonesia, and without it we would not have won inclusion in the group.

Early in 2006, when all but one of 43 West Papuan refugees were granted asylum through Australia's independent assessment process, real tension entered the Indonesian relationship. SBY had telephoned and assured me that the West Papuans would be treated well, if they were returned, and no doubt assumed that I would see to it that this happened. In responding to Indonesian resentment about the asylum decision, the Government overreacted and introduced a measure to change the law designed to ensure that all similar asylum-seekers would, in future, have their claims assessed offshore, thus providing a powerful deterrent.

Some government MPs saw this as breaching agreed changes to our asylum-seeker policy, and when it was apparent that it would be voted down in the Senate, I scrapped the bill.

In retrospect, the claim could be made that we had tried too hard to placate the Indonesians, but there was a lot at stake. The success of our border protection policy from late 2001 onwards had depended, in part, on Indonesia's willingness both to discourage people-smuggling from its shores and also accept the return of boats intercepted by Australian naval vessels. We did not want that disturbed.

It was clear from a positive meeting that SBY and I had at Batam in June that the relationship remained in good fettle. It would, nonetheless, always be a complicated one which needed constant attention.

Closer to home the Anzac relationship needed revitalisation; Australians must stop taking it for granted, and the regular pattern of testy relations between Australian and New Zealand PMs should not return. Fraser and Muldoon did not get on, Hawke and Lange sparred regularly and the relationship between Bolger and Keating ended in acrimony over airline policy.

Starting with Jim Bolger, for a brief period with Jenny Shipley and then for eight years with Helen Clark, I tried in a balanced way to change some of that.

Helen Clark never forgot the courtesy I displayed to her when she visited Canberra in 1996, when she was Opposition leader with an approval rating below 10 per cent. It paid dividends later. Despite our considerable differences on political philosophy, we were able to work together in close and constructive harmony. On more than one occasion, we were each able to help the other out of a difficult situation. If there had been less personal trust between us, this cooperation would not have occurred.

Kevin Rudd also worked closely with his New Zealand counterparts. I hope that this continues. It makes enormous sense. We are two closely linked nations with a rich and entwined history in a remote part of the world. We should make a point of getting on with each other. That is what our respective peoples expect of their leaders.

After the crucial meeting with President Jiang Zemin of China in November 1996, I accepted his invitation to visit China, and this took place over Easter of 1997. It was thus the situation that I had visited Japan, Indonesia and China before undertaking a visit to either the United States or Britain, although Bill Clinton had paid a prearranged visit to Australia in November 1996. My travel schedule had not been deliberately planned that way, nor was it entirely accidental. The assumption was that I was a pro-American Anglophile. I didn't mind that description, because it was largely true, but I put relations with our Asian neighbours front and centre of our foreign policy.

In July 1997 I went to Washington, saw Bill Clinton and did the usual rounds of both Washington and New York. Then I went on to London and called on the only recently elected Tony Blair. He had defeated John Major just two months earlier and I am not sure that he was really ready for a visit from a centre-right Commonwealth Prime Minister. For two people who as time went by were to become quite close in the common struggle against terrorism, our first meeting was a little strained. He himself would say later that he found me rather understated. For my part, I wondered what his core beliefs were. He was certainly enjoying a wave of popularity. By coincidence, we both ended up on the floor of the London Stock Exchange at the same time. He received a delirious reception.

We had a slightly difficult discussion about climate change. Coincidentally, on the way over on a Qantas flight, I had watched the British film *Brassed Off*. It told the story of a band from a mining town in Yorkshire winning a national competition in London's Albert Hall. When accepting the award, the band leader launched a tirade against the Thatcher Government's policy of closing down uneconomic coal mines. When I saw Tony Blair he remarked, with pride, that Britain would easily meet the targets contemplated by Kyoto because of the closure of so many coal mines. Naturally he didn't acknowledge that many of the pit closures had been vehemently opposed by the Labour Party, as well as the trade union movement.

This exchange intensified my belief that the Kyoto agreement had been Eurocentric. Adopting a starting point for measurement of emissions of 1990 was accommodating for the Europeans. Not only did it capture the benefits of pit closures in the United Kingdom, it also embraced the emissions reductions benefits of the extensive de-industrialisation of Eastern Europe, following the collapse of the Soviet bloc from 1989 onwards.

Just three months later, I returned to the United Kingdom to attend the Edinburgh CHOGM. This found Tony Blair and me working together quite collaboratively, and I regarded this meeting as the beginning of an association, indeed friendship, between the two of us which has lasted to this day. He chaired the meeting with flair and style. I met Nelson Mandela for the first time at the Edinburgh CHOGM. He had a magnetic personality and it was impossible not to respect the personal generosity of a man who could be so forgiving towards people who had kept him in captivity for 27 years.

Membership of the Commonwealth is a legacy phenomenon for Australia. Yet it does bring us an association with nations, especially in Africa, with whom we might otherwise have little relationship. The Commonwealth link can mean quite a good deal when certain bilateral issues arise. To me it always had two facets. Firstly there was the almost separate historical association with Britain, New Zealand and Canada. This could loosely be described as the 'old Commonwealth'. The other considerable merit in the organisation was the African connection.

In my time as Prime Minister, the Commonwealth's greatest challenge and one on which, I am sorry to say, it failed absolutely was that of Zimbabwe. To be fair to other members of the Commonwealth, the real Zimbabwean story has been the failure of Southern African countries to impose any discipline on Robert Mugabe.

It is a measure of the failure of the international political system that this man remains President of his sad, economically devastated nation. His personal avarice and contempt for any semblance of justice and democracy has brought forth worldwide condemnation. Yet he is still there. The reason that he is still there is a legacy of the white-versus-black struggle in Southern Africa. Mugabe had been a brother-in-arms in the struggle against apartheid, and gratitude towards him was understandable. But when that gratitude translated into a complete refusal to acknowledge the terrible damage he had inflicted on his overwhelmingly black population, it lost both reason and moral justification.

Pressure against Mugabe reached a point of controversy at the CHOGM in Coolum in Queensland early in 2002. Commonwealth and other observers reported extensive electoral fraud and abuse in the recent elections in Zimbabwe. Mugabe's party had corrupted the electoral process. Intimidation and cheating had been widespread.

There had been a hands-off approach to him from leaders of most Southern African countries, and this took Zimbabwe into stalemate territory. The Commonwealth could not move without the active involvement of Southern African countries, especially the most powerful one, South Africa.

The Coolum CHOGM established a troika to handle the Zimbabwean issue, with me as chairman. President Obasanjo of Nigeria and Thabo Mbeki of South Africa were the other two members. We met in London in March 2002 and, in a straightforward way, agreed that Zimbabwe must be suspended from the Commonwealth. That sent a public rebuke, without that rebuke really meaning anything. The practical consequences of suspension were simply that Zimbabwe could not attend meetings of the group's heads of government or other bodies. Given the other preoccupations of Robert Mugabe, this was hardly going to trouble his scorers.

The London outcome, seen as something of a mini-triumph for the Commonwealth, had merely bought time. The more important task was to apply pressure on Mugabe to hold a fair and fraud-free ballot. It was clear to me after the London meeting that there were three positions within the Commonwealth on Zimbabwe, represented by the three members of the troika.

I spoke for countries such as Britain, New Zealand, Canada and the Caribbean states. Obasanjo spoke for northern and East African opinion. He was troubled by what had happened in Zimbabwe but was wary of putting too much pressure on Mbeki.

For his part, Mbeki gave all sorts of soothing reassurances about 'talking to Robert' or 'understanding Robert's position'. When the crunch came, he would simply declare Mugabe a no-go zone. Agreeing on a suspension had been easy. Reaching a consensus on the next step proved to be impossible.

It was decided in London that both Mbeki and Obasanjo, particularly the former, would talk to Mugabe and it was intended that we would meet again. Months went by, and it was obvious that not much had been done to take the matter forward. I suggested another meeting, and this was set for Abuja, the Nigerian capital, on 23 September.

After refuelling at the beautiful Seychelles Islands, my aircraft continued on its journey to the Nigerian capital. I then received a message from President Mbeki, informing me that he had decided that he would not attend the Abuja meeting, that it was a complete waste of time and that, in effect, he and others should be left alone to continue their discussions with Mugabe.

This was an astonishing communication. I immediately instructed our High Commissioner in Pretoria to convey in the appropriate terms my displeasure at what the South African President was proposing to do. He was to tell the South Africans that his non-attendance would be insulting, as I was already on my way. He ran the risk of doing real damage to the relationship between Australia and South Africa. It was a strong, but justified, response. Mbeki turned up at the Abuja meeting.

Mbeki's approach was dispiriting. As the most prominent Southern African leader, he had the power to bring about change in Zimbabwe. If he had pressured Mugabe to go, or accept arrangements for a proper ballot, either of those outcomes could have been achieved. The moral authority of the South African President demanding reasonable standards would have put the issue beyond doubt. Yet this did not happen. The troika never met again, and Mugabe continued in office. His nation continued its downward spiral, with the bleak achievement of an inflation rate of 100,000 per cent in February 2008. Many white farmers had their properties stolen, violence increased and Mugabe's security forces continued to suppress political opponents.

I was not alone in my concerns. Helen Clark was equally vitriolic in her condemnation of Mugabe. She exhibited the same frustration, along with Tony Blair, at the attitude of the Southern African countries.

Incredibly enough, come the CHOGM in Abuja in December 2003, the issue was no further advanced. Zimbabwe had become an even more tragic, failed state. The chairman of this CHOGM, Obasanjo of Nigeria, formed a small group to discuss Zimbabwe, chaired by P.J. Patterson, the Prime Minister of Jamaica. It included Mbeki and Jean Chrétien, the Canadian Prime Minister, and me. Within a few minutes of the meeting starting, Mbeki and I had a heated exchange. Attitudes had not altered, Zimbabwe was still forbidden territory, and Mugabe would not experience any pressure from the Commonwealth to mend his behaviour.

A power-sharing arrangement has now been instituted in Zimbabwe with Mugabe's long-time opponent Morgan Tsvangirai serving as Prime Minister. Tsvangirai, who has suffered several family tragedies, has displayed immense courage. Another figure in that government deserving of praise is David Coltart, its only white member.

Although power-sharing has led to some improvement, it is very much a second-best solution resulting from the unwillingness of neighbouring countries to stand up to Mugabe, who still controls the security apparatus. Zimbabwe was just about the most demoralising foreign affairs issue that I touched in my time as Prime Minister.

The intervention in East Timor illustrated our capacity to play a larger role for good in our immediate region. That was later manifested in the Australian-led Regional Assistance Mission (RAMSI) of July 2003, which restored law and order and delivered better governance to the Solomon Islands. RAMSI, which involved several Pacific Island states as well as Australia, New Zealand and Papua New Guinea, was the culmination of a paradigm shift in Australian policy towards those states. From a refusal to intervene and an aid policy attaching few strings, Australia in 2003 began to insist on reduced corruption, better economic management and improved criminal justice as conditions of ongoing aid, as well as of any police and military intervention which might be requested.

Led by Australia, RAMSI showed not only the Solomon Islands but also other small island countries that their neighbours cared about their future. Named in pidgin 'Operation Helpen Fren', the intervention force began arriving in Honiara on 25 July 2003. It was immensely popular in both Australia and the Solomons. Australians felt that this part of the world was our responsibility.

Nick Warner, a highly experienced DFAT officer, headed the mission. He had something of the derring-do about him. One of his more difficult jobs would be in Iraq, where he was at the forefront of attempts to prise back Douglas Wood, a freewheeling Australian businessman taken hostage by terrorists. Amazingly, and only with vital help from the Americans and the Iraqis, he pulled it off. Warner did a first-class job in the Solomon Islands. My Government later made him Secretary of the Department of Defence. Still later, the Rudd Government appointed him Director-General of the Australian Secret Intelligence Service (ASIS). I am sure that he is in his element there.

I received an extremely friendly welcome from the local people, when I went to Honiara on 25 August to see our troops, police and departmental officials, as well as members of the Solomon Islands Government. Hundreds lined the streets to cheer, with children holding up a banner reading, 'Thank you Uncle Howard'. The biggest problem that Warner encountered was from the local politicians.

Solomon Islanders loved RAMSI, because the army and police quickly restored law and order, brought the gangs to heel, and helped deliver a proper criminal justice system. When, however, the implications for many members of the Islands' legislature of RAMSI's insistence on better governance began to be felt, there was resistance. Regrettably, corruption was widespread. It was often just a question of degree. Sir Allen Kemakeza' s government had originally invited us in; there were successive changes of government, including an interregnum under Manasseh Sogavare, who was anti-Australian and also wanted RAMSI gutted. Fortunately, later PMs backed RAMSI.

Remembrance of wartime friendships was deepest in Australia for the 'fuzzy-wuzzy angels', of New Guinea, who gave such vital help to Australian soldiers in their struggle against the Japanese. There was a special bond, as well as the obligation of a former colonial power, but they constantly rubbed against corruption and governance issues through my entire prime ministership, culminating in my strained relations with Michael Somare over the Julian Moti Affair. Moti faced an outstanding arrest warrant in Australia, and a Defence board of inquiry in Port Moresby found that Somare had acted improperly regarding the use of a military aircraft to fly Moti to the Solomon Islands, where the PM, Sogavare, wished to make him Attorney General. Long years in power frequently result in abuse of the trappings of office. As developing countries go, Papua New Guinea has more to work with than most and should be doing better. The remedy lies within.

Speaking at the launch of the Lowy Institute on 31 March 2005, I said, 'Australia has no greater friend in Asia than Japan.' The ties we now have with our one-time enemy are a tribute to the people of both countries. It has been a genuinely productive relationship for Australia.

The most impressive of the five Japanese PMs with whom I dealt was Junichiro Koizumi, who held the post between April 2001 and September 2006; that was a long time by Japanese standards. Quite different from most

Japanese prime ministers, he was flamboyant, reform-minded and determined that he, and not the bureaucrats, would govern Japan. This was quite a task; the power of the bureaucrats in Tokyo is legendary. Koizumi also wanted to break the grip of entrenched interests on the dominant Liberal Democratic Party (LDP), which maintained a stranglehold on Japanese politics until its heavy defeat in August 2009. The scale of that defeat demonstrated just how right Koizumi had been in his push for change within the party.

In supporting privatisation of the Japanese Post Office, he challenged the orthodoxy of the LDP. Campaigning on this issue, he won the 2005 election, bringing into parliament a clutch of new MPs, dubbed 'Koizumi's children'. They shared his ideas on economic reform. During my congratulatory phone call, he said that he would need to retire in two years, because that was what the rules of the LDP required. I told him that having just won an election with an increased majority, he was powerful enough to change those rules and should do so. He gave me the impression that he would not do this.

As I expected, Koizumi did retire in September 2006. He was replaced by Shinzo Abe. A quiet, thoughtful man, he lasted just under a year in the job and hosted my last visit to Tokyo as Prime Minister. There was an unexpected glitch involving an Australian citizen, formerly of the Dutch East Indies (now Indonesia). She had given evidence to a congressional hearing in the United States of being abused by Japanese soldiers as part of the shameful 'comfort women' deeds in World War II. Responding to a question, Abe gave a somewhat ambiguous answer, which showed the continuing problem many Japanese have about the past.

Unless resolved, this issue would cloud our forthcoming meeting. After a message to Abe's office, he stated publicly how much he condemned the behaviour in question. I was thus able to welcome his comments, when speaking to the media, before my formal talks with the Japanese Prime Minister.

Abe and his wife attended the APEC meeting in Sydney in September 2007. He joined George Bush and me, together with our respective Foreign Ministers, at a full-scale meeting of the Trilateral Security Dialogue during the APEC meeting period. Only days after his return from that meeting, Abe was replaced by Yasuo Fukuda, the 71-year-old Finance Minister, in the role of prime minister.

*   *   *

Bilateral free trade agreements (FTAs) were often more important with countries where there was no natural trade relationship such as existed with Japan. Singapore and Thailand were two examples. After three years of negotiations, agreement was reached for an FTA between Australia and Singapore on 17 February 2003. This became the first bilateral FTA signed by Australia since the 1983 Closer Economic Relations Trade Agreement with New Zealand. It was particularly valuable for Australia in the areas of services, intellectual property, investment, and competition policy.

In July 2004 Australia and Thailand signed their bilateral FTA. There was also an agreement struck in relation to working holidays. Australia gained valuable new access for dairy products, wine and motor vehicles. Fortuitously, my bilateral meeting with Thaksin Shinawatra, the Prime Minister of Thailand, at the Bangkok APEC meeting the previous October was the catalyst for a breakthrough in the negotiations. Officials had reached a deadlock. Both of us were keen for a speedy resolution, particularly Thaksin, the host of the APEC meeting. Quite spontaneously he told his officials to go away and resolve outstanding issues with my advisors. That is exactly what happened. Without that particular meeting, the FTA would have never been achieved. Thaksin and I enjoyed a good relationship. He was democratically elected as PM and his unjustified removal was the root cause of Thailand's recent disturbances.

Occasionally, in the many discussions I had with world leaders, one would use a phrase which captured the essence of a relationship. That happened during my second visit to India as PM, in March 2006. My Indian counterpart, Manmohan Singh, said to me, 'We have a lot in common, but we haven't had much to do with each other.' It was so true. My visit in 2006 went a good distance towards changing that.

I had been to India as PM in 2000, but our relationship then was still very much in the 'history and cricket' paradigm. The common British connection had brought us together in both world wars, and we were linked by language and law. Of course cricket, about which Indians were passionate, meant that names such as Bradman, Border and Waugh were by far the best-known of all the Australian ones in India. Immigration flows to Australia were rising, as were student numbers. Yet the relationship lacked commercial energy; there was nothing like the complementarities of our trade with Japan and China. India looked elsewhere for resource needs.

Australia had never had an extensive political dialogue with India, in part a legacy of India's decades of non-alignment during the years of the Cold War when, paradoxically, democratic India more often than not sided with the dictatorial Soviet Union against the United States. Singh acknowledged this in our discussions. We interacted as Commonwealth partners, but the relationship had nothing of the intensity of those we had with nations in Southeast Asia.

A combined government/commercial effort was needed to achieve change, so I invited a top-notch business group to accompany me in 2006. It included John Ellis-Flint, Santos managing director; the trucking magnate Lindsay Fox; and Charles Goode, ANZ Bank chairman. As well I was joined by Glyn Davis, Vice-chancellor of Melbourne University, to emphasise the growing potential of the education market.

Providentially, there was a commodity which had the potential to give momentum to the commercial and political relationship: that was uranium. In 2006 India had a growing appetite for energy, flowing from an expanding economy and a desire to move to cleaner energy sources. Nuclear power was on the agenda. She was keen to buy Australian uranium.

Just a few days before I arrived, George Bush had completed a visit to India which had opened a new phase in relations between his country and India. Bush had promised to help India achieve her nuclear ambitions. Part of the Bush foreign policy in Asia was to build links with the deep-seated democracies of the region; it was the perfect counter-poise to China. The US President's journey had a big impact on Singh. He told me that, seeing the visit as a real turning point in links between the two countries. He was in the mood to savour associations with fellow democracies.

Singh raised the possibility of uranium sales from Australia to India almost from the moment I arrived. We hit it off personally, and talked freely about the past low-key nature of our links. It was during such a discussion that he made the comment which left a lasting impression on me. I wanted Australian uranium sold to India. I knew that under existing policy this could not happen, because India was not a signatory to the Nuclear Non-Proliferation Treaty, and the policy banned sales to non-signatory states. A way around that policy would need to be found.

Both Alexander Downer and his department were wary about changing the policy. I understood the concerns, but this was a big prize. India was going for nuclear power and would obtain the uranium she needed. India had an excellent non-proliferation record. Why should Australia pass up such a commercial and political opening? In addition I did not believe that we could sustain, indefinitely, selling uranium to China and Russia but not sell it to India, simply on the grounds that those other two countries had signed the treaty and India had not.

I set in train a process which would have resulted in a change in policy to the benefit of India, if the Coalition had been returned at the 2007 election. It would have involved arrangements containing the same practical safeguards as were provided under the treaty, which India could never sign because of her possession of nuclear weapons. Regrettably the Rudd Government refused to help India, being determined to maintain the strict letter of the treaty's stipulations and lacking the desire or imagination to find another way forward. This is a major foreign policy mistake and is profoundly disappointing to India. It is quite a roadblock to better relations between the two nations.

A WONDER DOWN UNDER

On 18 March 2004 the *Economist* published an article about the Australian economy, 'A Wonder Down Under'. Although complimentary, it questioned whether the booming conditions of our economy could be sustained, given the bubble in house prices. It need not have worried. Thanks in no small measure to the firmer monetary policy of the RBA governor, Ian Macfarlane, in 2002–03, home prices did not collapse. The 'wonder down under' went on to sail through the biggest challenge to the world economy for many decades.

There is agreement, across the political divide, on at least one thing. The Australian economy has survived remarkably well from the world financial plunge. It deserved the description, given by many in 2009, of the strongest-performing economy in the OECD area. Always unwilling to give any credit to the Howard Government, which on one occasion he described as 'indolent' with economic management, Kevin Rudd regularly claimed that the sole reason Australia performed so well was the spending stimulus his Government injected into the Australian economy in 2008 and 2009. At the very least, the jury is still out on whether or not that stimulus should have been so large.

Australia entered the global financial crisis, which began in 2008, in a superb fiscal state. Its budget was in surplus to the tune of at least 1.5 per cent of GDP. There was no net Commonwealth debt. Speaking to alumni of Sydney University on 15 May 2008, the governor of the Reserve Bank, Glenn Stevens, said, 'But there would be very few countries, if any, which would not envy Australia's fiscal position. The capacity to respond, if need be, to developments in the future is virtually without peer. This seems light years from the situation in the 1970s.'[1]

Mark the date of this speech, 15 May 2008. Four months later the global financial maelstrom hit with all its fury. The prescience of the governor's speech had been remarkable. The robust fiscal health of the Australian economy made it possible for the Rudd Government to embrace a large fiscal stimulus which still left Australia with impressively low debt and deficits. The big bank balance left by the Howard Government enabled Kevin Rudd and Wayne Swan to look good.

Australian banks survived infinitely better than those in the United States and Europe. At the Davos meeting in Switzerland early in 2009, the Deputy Prime Minister, Julia Gillard, was positively lyrical about Australian banks. She said:

> And we come to this new challenge with many remarkable strengths; Australia has strong financial institutions. Of the 11 banks around the world that are rated AA and above, four of them are Australian. Australia has a AAA foreign currency rating. We have open and competitive markets backed up by a world-class financial and prudential regulatory system — indeed given the flaws exposed by the global financial crisis in financial and prudential regulation, I would say our system is even better than world-class.[2]

This was a remarkable, if unintended, compliment to the economic prudence of the Howard Government. The regulatory system of which Gillard spoke in such glowing terms was that established by the former government. Inherited fiscal rectitude and a stable, well-supervised banking system proved to be the guardian angels of the Australian economy as it passed through the perils of the recent international financial crisis. No objective analysis can conclude otherwise.

Australia's stimulus package was big by world standards. According to the OECD, Australia's stimulus package, as a proportion of GDP, was of a similar size to that of the United States, and much greater than that of Britain or other major European economies. It was dwarfed only by the boost given in China. I thought that the stimulus was far too large. However, those who argue that it was the right size should, at least, acknowledge that it was made possible by Australia being in such a solid fiscal position when the process of stimulating the economy commenced.

Although Kevin Rudd gave most of the credit for our economic deliverance to the stimulus package, he did acknowledge the impact on the economy of large reductions in interest rates. Once again the starting point was relevant. Interest rates in Australia were higher than in most other countries, largely because our economy was growing more firmly than in other parts of the world. Also, interest rates were higher in Australia because, being fully independent, the Reserve Bank adjusted interest rates according to its judgement about the performance of the Australian economy. The RBA used that independence to run tighter monetary policy than many other central banks. Those interest rate adjustments were not always politically palatable.

In the final stages of the 2007 election campaign I had developed a mantra, obviously too late, which best encapsulated what my Government had achieved. I said that Australia was a 'stronger, prouder and more prosperous nation in 2007 than it had been in March of 1996'.

This mantra covered the totality of the Government's record in office. Nowhere was it more accurate than in relation to our economic management. Australians felt legitimate pride in the virility of the Australian economy; by any benchmark Australia was a more prosperous nation than it had been in 1996.

Bringing the budget back into surplus, a foundation objective of my Government, not only had economic virtue in its own right, but also immense confidence dividends. In his book *In an Uncertain World*, Robert Rubin, Bill Clinton's highly regarded Treasury secretary, wrote, '... the US Budget deficit had become the symbol of the Government's inability to manage its own affairs — and of society's inability to cope with economic challenges more generally ... The view that fiscal discipline was being restored contributed to lower interest rates and increased confidence, and that led to more spending and investment which in turn led to job creation, lower unemployment rates and increased productivity'.[3] That assessment neatly fitted the Australian experience.

The prosperity was broadly based. Whilst it was true that the Australian rich had got richer, they had not done so at the expense of the poor. Many surveys revealed that the lower-income groups, particularly families, had not fallen behind in the wake of the growing wealth of the more affluent in our community. This had been no accident. It was the result of a policy deliberately and consistently applied.

As explored in Chapter 37, it was a cardinal value of my prime ministership that good economic management should never be regarded as an end in itself. The ends were always the human dividends. The greatest human dividend of all was on display in February 2008, when the unemployment rate in Australia dipped below 4 per cent for the first time in 33 years. There could be no better demonstration that one of the great human goals of our years in government had been achieved.

The Rudd Government made two paltry attempts to denigrate the economic record of the Howard years. The first was to allege, shortly after it came to government, that the inflation genie was out of the bottle. That false claim was given an outing for a few months and then promptly abandoned, as it lacked any credibility.

Assertions that my Government had been 'warned' about a serious inflationary problem were without foundation.

Another attempt was made to smear our record on the night of the 2009 budget when Australia heard it had a structural deficit. A structural deficit arises when, after subtracting temporary surges in revenue or expenditure, the ongoing situation is one of deficit rather than surplus.

Treasury had never told either the former Treasurer or me that Australia was in structural deficit or likely to be so. Perhaps this was because the Treasury itself, during our time in office at least, held the view that undertaking calculations about the structural state of the budget was an inherently unreliable analytical exercise.

In the *Economic Roundup* in autumn 2005, Benjamin Ford, from the Macroeconomic Policy Division of the Treasury, wrote, 'Significant assumptions about the economy's potential output level and the cyclical sensitivity of revenues are required to calculate estimates of the structural fiscal position. The arbitrariness of these assumptions limits the usefulness of structural fiscal indicators as a guide for policy in the short term. For these reasons, official estimates of the structural balance are not published by the Australian government. However, measures produced by both the IMF and OECD suggest a structural improvement of Australia's fiscal position over the past few years.'[4]

Not only did Ford's article explain why Treasury had never done structural calculations, but observed that according to both the IMF and the OECD, Australia's structural budget position had improved over several years up to 2005.

Yet in 2009 Treasury argued that its estimate of the structural deficit now used a different approach than that of the IMF and OECD — how convenient for my critics! Given that the Treasury had not previously attempted an analysis of the structural surplus or deficit, had not warned my Government of the alleged deterioration, which it was now claiming started in 2002–03, and the IMF and OECD held contrary views, one is entitled to conclude that the Treasury was being less than fully objective on this occasion.

In response to a question from a Liberal senator later in 2009, the Treasury said that because of big changes to the structure of the economy, it was inappropriate to stretch its 2009 budget-night structural deficit analysis back to 1971 as requested by the senator. Instead it provided an answer based on the structural deficit analyses of the IMF and OECD, both of which suggested that the budget had remained in structural surplus until the end of the Coalition's time in government. Even the Treasury itself had begun to get cold feet about its structural deficit argument.

On top of this, having run the line before the election in 2007 that Australia had to prepare for life after the resources boom, Kevin Rudd later happily endorsed the view that the China surge could last for years into the future.

The real key to the economic success of the Howard Government was the close working partnership between Peter Costello as Treasurer and me. Since the election there have been some claims, particularly in Peter Hartcher's book *To the Bitter End*, suggesting ongoing trench warfare between the two of us regarding economic policy, for a substantial period of my Government.

Those claims are wrong. For the entire 11 years and eight months of the Howard Government, Peter Costello and I worked together in close professional harmony in managing the economy. The powerful evidence for this was the enduring strength of the economy over that time, and how that has carried Australia through the challenges of 2008–09.

Costello and I agreed on all of the main economic issues. We both believed in balancing the budget and eliminating debt. We both believed in a better tax deal for Australian families. We were both strong supporters of labour market reform and privatisation of Telstra. Both of us believed in policies which shifted people from welfare and back into work. We both supported central bank independence. Although there were some disagreements about detail along the way, we both promoted taxation reform.

There were inevitably some differences, but not on the really major issues of government economic policy. That is the crucial point. Having got the budget back into balance, there was no way that either of us wanted to return to deficit. We even agreed that the desirable size for future surpluses should be at least 1 per cent of GDP.

If the fundamentals of the relationship between a prime minister and a treasurer are sound, then there is no reason why, from time to time, there should not be differences between them on particular policies. No two people will think exactly alike. It is the role of the treasurer always to argue for expenditure restraint. It is the responsibility of the prime minister, at various times, to determine that some additional expenditure in certain areas is necessary. Peter Costello and I argued, on occasions, over particular levels of expenditure. That was a normal and proper part of the process. The important thing to remember is that all of the decisions relating to expenditure were taken within the guiding principle that the budget should remain in surplus.

Unless a treasurer has the support of his prime minister on the fundamentals, then he is crippled. The dynamic of the cabinet process is that the backing of the prime minister is essential to winning approval of any economic change or reform which involves a measure of short- or longer-term political pain. Having held both positions in my career, I am better placed than most to understand that reality. In a professional sense, my relationship with Peter Costello was closer and more enduring than that of any other prime minister/treasurer combination in recent history.

Costello and I had essentially the same economic philosophy. We would agree, in the lead-up to a budget, that the order of priorities was to ensure that there was adequate investment in important areas such as Health, Education, Infrastructure and, importantly for me, Defence. Again, after allowing for an appropriate surplus, any excess should be devoted towards taxation relief, either by way of Family Tax Benefit enhancements or reductions in rates of tax or alterations in tax thresholds. It was an orderly process and its logic was compelling.

Chapter 24 is dedicated to the subject of Peter Costello's first budget in 1996, which was crucial to the Government's later success. It set the standard, and it was a gold standard. After that budget of August 1996, the atmosphere was of a government in charge which was serious about reform. Major reforms had already been implemented, and the fiscal turn-around of that first budget further consolidated what had been a very active first six months for the new government.

The pattern had been set for the rest of our time in government. Expenditure restraint in subsequent budgets did not match that of the first budget, but it was always sufficient to ensure that we delivered a budget surplus (or very close to it on one occasion). The commitment of the Treasurer and me to balancing the budget became a key foundation stone of both our economic recovery and enduring economic strength. It became accepted wisdom that we would never go into deficit.

The early return of the budget to surplus and the continuing health of the Australian economy, which in turn produced falling unemployment and rising tax revenues, provided the Government with more fiscal flexibility. It was possible to spend more without being economically irresponsible. The proper measure of whether or not government expenditure is excessive is not its nominal growth, rather its share as a proportion of GDP, or national wealth. A bigger economy can responsibly accommodate greater expenditure. Like so many other things, its relative size is the fundamental benchmark.

Those critics who have claimed that my Government spent too much have overlooked several factors. As a proportion of GDP, Commonwealth Government spending during my Government's term in office actually fell from 26.2 per cent to 24 per cent. When the Howard Government left office, Australia had the third-lowest level of general government outlays (including the states) in the OECD, at 36 per cent; slightly lower even than in the United States and Japan and significantly lower than the average in Europe.

Some would reply that it should have fallen further, and that my Government had been the beneficiary of a rapidly growing economy. That in turn overlooked other considerations. If the economy had not been growing strongly, then inevitably government expenditures sensitive to the economy would have been larger (unemployment benefits, for example), and the size of the surplus may well have been lower so as to stabilise the economy. This in turn would have affected discretionary expenditure decisions, given the Government's determination to keep the budget in surplus.

It was also the case that some of the good health of the Australian economy flowed from the confidence impact on the business community and overseas investors in particular, knowing that Australia was in the hands of a government determined to get out of deficit, pay off debt and keep the budget in surplus. At a time when this was far from a universal economic credo, the confidence impact should not be underestimated.

My Government maintained fiscal discipline through a time when large additional spending was required for both Defence and intelligence activities. From 1999, the demand for extra resources in these areas was without precedent in a period of more than 30 years. The terrorist threat which confronted the world from 11 September 2001 onward increased, quite dramatically, the pressure for these extra resources.

Importantly too, the distinction between spending and taxation has become totally artificial in certain areas. For example, Family Tax Benefits appear on the spending side of the budget, despite their origin being tax breaks for children.

I learned, during a meeting of the Expenditure Review Committee (ERC), that all of the money put aside from the budget to fund the 30 per cent rebate for private health insurance was classified as an outlay. This included the cost to revenue of the admittedly small percentage (about 7 per cent) of people who claimed the rebate in their tax return, rather than request that it be paid to the private health insurer. The explanation I was given when I queried this practice was that 'from an accounting point of view it was simpler'.

In similar vein Treasury and Finance treat any tax credit that is made refundable — that is, it will be paid even if someone did not have a tax liability — as an expenditure item, and it appears on the outlays side of the budget. Refundable imputation credits, the refund of the excess of the company tax paid on a dividend over the taxpayer's own rate of tax, are shown in the budget as an expenditure item. It would be hard to find a single self-funded retiree in Australia receiving an imputation credit who treated it other than for what it was: a refund of an over-payment of tax. It is not a government hand-out, and assuredly not middle-class welfare.

In many ways, the goal throughout our time in government was to remove, progressively, the speed limits on the growth of the Australian economy, by increasing its flexibility and enhancing the supply-side factors that are fundamental to our productive capacity. The Australian economy had been no stranger to periods of strong economic growth; the problem had always been its durability. In the past such growth could not be sustained because it would inevitably come up against rigidities or bottlenecks in the economy affecting the capacity, or supply side, of the economy, causing inflationary and balance-of-payment pressures which had to be met by lifting interest rates and contracting the economy. The description 'boom or bust' accurately captured the character of the Australian economy on earlier occasions. It did boom in the 1950s and '60s. That boom took place behind a protective wall, and in a world that disappeared, never to return.

The Australian economy came face to face in the 1970s with the need to change fundamentally, not only to recover from the affliction of stagflation but also build the basis of sustainable growth in the years that were to follow.

Australian policy makers were forced to embrace far-reaching change in areas of which I have written; namely financial market deregulation, labour market changes, taxation reform, privatisation and tariff reform. The domestic political story of Australia in the past 30 years has, largely, been the response of leaders to that challenge.

I have not included fiscal consolidation or balanced budgets in that group of reforms. That is because balancing the budget is in part a product of the functioning of the real economy, and it was the impact of policies in the areas which I have mentioned that improved the functioning of the real economy with beneficial consequences for the budget. This is not to diminish the great significance of those early and hard budget cuts which returned the national books to the black. Fiscal consolidation eased, considerably, pressure on interest rates and reduced the risk premium in AU$ denominated assets.

The difficulty faced by the Fraser Government as well as the Labor Party, then in opposition, was the reluctance of a generation of politicians who had learned their craft and formed their ideas in the more protected environment of the Menzies/McEwen period of economic management in Australia to change their approach to economic policy.

Their attitude had been barely surprising. The 1950s and '60s were, collectively, a comfortably long period of considerable prosperity and extremely low unemployment. Most Australians under the age of 45 with whom I have discussed the subject found it difficult to accept that at the change to the Whitlam Government in the 1972 election, Australia's unemployment rate was less than 2 per cent.

Both sides of politics have played a positive role, in government, in bringing about the major reforms, of which I have written. Therein lies a crucial distinction. I have deliberately said 'in government'. Only one side of politics, the Coalition side, has played a positive role in bringing about reforms in opposition. Political parties have obligations in both government and opposition. Policy work in opposition can be influential as well as rewarding.

The notable economic reforms of the past three decades in Australia comprised the unopposed reforms of the Hawke/Keating period and the opposed reforms of the Howard Government. There is no artificiality about such a distinction. In modern combative politics, the readiness of an opposition to support a serious reform not only smooths its passage through the parliament but removes much of its controversial nature.

Financial deregulation, especially floating the dollar, and tariff reductions were the two really praiseworthy reforms of Labor in power. The Coalition indemnified the Labor Party politically in respect of both. Hawke and Keating had no stronger supporter than me in further dismantling regulation of the financial system. A fear campaign aimed at blue-collar Labor voters when the ALP decided to cut tariffs would have been absolutely lethal, if the Coalition had embraced it. Instead the Coalition backed tariff reform.

These bipartisan gestures were never reciprocated after the Howard Government came to power even when, in the case of the GST, we had received the most explicit mandate ever from the Australian people for a major reform. Labor not only opposed taxation reform, but labour market changes and, incredibly, privatisation of Telstra, ignoring the fact that our support in opposition had facilitated Keating's privatisation of the Commonwealth Bank.

Taxation reform, centred on the introduction of a goods and services tax, had been a long-overdue reform. Before it came about, however, the Australian economy was to come through a challenge which gave an early sign of its gathering strengths. That was the Asian economic downturn of 1997–98.

Both Peter Costello and I were concerned as the contagion ripped through Asia that it would spread to Australia. There were many institutional reasons why this should not have been so. Our banks were stable with a balanced regulatory environment. My Government had sent an unambiguous message to markets, both financial and otherwise, that we would run a disciplined fiscal policy. We had begun in earnest the task of industrial relations reform. In 1997 I signalled that we would tread the long path of taxation reform. We had eschewed an interventionist approach with industry policy. There was no crony capitalism in Australia. All of these things meant that the Australian Government was seen in the rest of the world as being serious about economic reform.

That being said, the flexible exchange rate then enjoyed by Australia played a crucial role in our avoiding the impact of the Asian economic downturn. An economic adjustment, as a consequence of the downturn, was unavoidable. That adjustment was taken on the exchange rate. The value of the Australian dollar fell. Wisely the Reserve Bank kept its nerve by not lifting interest rates, and we rode through the Asian economic decline virtually unscathed. Not only was Australia largely to avoid the effects of the downturn, it was able to play a major role in helping nations in our region recover.

Australia and Japan were the only individual countries to provide supplementary help to that of the IMF to help nations in Asia adjust to the impact of the downturn. Our assistance packages to Thailand, Korea and Indonesia were not only important signs of the capacity of the Australian economy, but they demonstrated our credentials as an economic partner in the region. Their psychological value was great, if not greater, than their economic assistance. Australia felt assertive enough to lobby hard with both the Americans and the IMF to ease the stringency of the adjustment measures imposed on Indonesia. A nation feeling less confident about its gathering economic strength would not have done what Australia did in response to the Asian economic downturn.

In office the Government took only two major tariff decisions. They related to the motor vehicle industry and the textile, clothing and footwear sector. Tariffs were on a downward path and had reached a level where, with a floating exchange rate, a further change in the nominal tariff level was of lesser significance. The downward movement continued under my Government, although not at the rate sought by the Productivity Commission and the Treasurer. Despite Labor having cut tariffs in Government and been supported by the opposition, the Beazley-led opposition took the opportunistic approach of calling for a freeze on further tariff cuts.

As we approached the turn of the century and the dawn of a new millennium, two aberrations appeared on the Australian economic scene. It was impossible to know whether the first of them, the Year 2000 (Y2K) scare, was an aberration or a real threat. My instinct was that it was an aberration, but like others I felt we had to treat it seriously, spend a lot of money preparing as best we could and hope that the computers would not switch off and planes fall out of the sky. Thankfully, that turned out to be the case.

The other aberration was the growing belief on the part of some economists, certain foreign investors with interests at stake and quite a few opportunistic doubters that Australia was an 'old' economy. Their argument was that with its heavy reliance on the mining industry and the lack of an indigenous information technology (IT) industry, Australia was increasingly seen as an old economy.

In retrospect it was an astonishing proposition which highlighted a reality. The reality was that by the beginning of 2001 the mining industry was not yet seen as the generous benefactor of the Australian economy. What is now called the China boom was certainly not there in 2001, and did not arrive in earnest until two years later. That, of itself, is an important item in the economic narrative of my years as Prime Minister.

Critics have constantly said that it was all made easy for Peter Costello and me because we had the boom in China. The truth is that much of the heavy economic lifting had been done before the China boom arrived. We had restored the budget to balance; we had introduced a new taxation system; we had fixed up the waterfront and gone a long way down the path of industrial relations reform. The privatisation of Telstra was still a work in progress, due to the unyielding obstructionism of the Labor Party and others in the Senate. That criticism merely disclosed a serious lack of wisdom on the part of those who made it.

The old-economy argument levelled against Australia reflected a mindset which wrongly assumed that an industry that had been around for a long time was all beef and little brain. As a simplistic consequence, the conclusion was drawn that the Australian economy had little future because of its heavy reliance on both agriculture and mining. A companion to this argument was that Australia needed an indigenous IT industry; that unless we generated our own know-how in this area, we did not have a future. Once again, this was an extraordinary proposition and gainsayed the reality that whether technology was home-grown or imported, provided it was available, it could transform the operation of a firm and a whole industry.

Much of this rather fatuous economic nonsense emanated from the World Economic Forum (WEF) which was held in Melbourne in September 2000. These wrongly held views that Australia was an old economy played a part in the decline of the Australian dollar late in 2000, which continued into 2001, when it hit a low of US47.73 cents on 3 April. The early part of 2001, and particularly March, was a hard month for economic management. There was news that the economy had contracted 0.6 per cent in the December quarter; unemployment rose; there was a 15.4 per cent plunge in the Westpac–Melbourne Institute index of consumer sentiment for March, and this was on top of continued public unhappiness about the price of petrol. The further slide in the dollar pushed up the price of petrol and risked cancelling out the benefit of the excise reduction I had announced only a short time earlier. My respect for Ian Macfarlane as governor of the Reserve Bank was further reinforced during this time. As had been the case in the teeth of the Asian downturn, he held his nerve on interest rates.

Despite the problems, I was convinced that the fundamentals of our economic management were correct. I did not have to wait long for confirmation of that belief.

The pricking of the so-called high-tech bubble in the United States in the first half of 2001 had a big impact on perceptions of the Australian economy. Having sunk to below US50 cents, the dollar began a strong recovery. Interest rates in the United States were cut as it appeared that its economy was heading for a mini-recession. Thus the interest rate differential between the two currencies widened, which assisted the rally of the Australian dollar. By the middle of the year, perceptions about the economy had fully recovered. The belief that Australia had operated an old economy was seen as quite nonsensical. The 'tech wreck' in the United States had brought many people back to earth. We had been on the right course in Australia and the soundness of the fundamentals of our economy re-emerged.

That first half of 2001 would be the last period in which the Australian economy would face particular difficulties in the time that my Government remained in office. The next almost seven years were to be ones of continued economic growth and, most importantly, progressive falls in the level of unemployment. This time marked, in effect, the half-way point in the life of the Howard Government. Unemployment, when the government had been elected in March 1996, stood at 8.2 per cent. By March 2001 it stood at 6.5 per cent. In February 2008, just after the Government's defeat, it had nudged down to 3.9 per cent.

With some of the unavoidable dislocations associated with the introduction of the GST now behind us, the Australian economy had the right settings for an acceleration of economic growth. We were now in a better position than ever before to remove some of those speed limits on our national growth.

The hard decisions which put us in a position to grow at a faster rate were to have a fairly early reward. It was within a year or two that the beneficial effects of the China boom began to be felt by the Australian economy as our sales to that country accelerated. Between January 2004 and January 2009 the value of Australia's merchandise exports to China quadrupled. As if to dramatise the arrival of China as a major contributor to our economic growth, early in 2002 the North West Shelf Consortium would sign the $25 billion contract for the export of LNG to the Guangdong Province in China which I have detailed elsewhere.

The terrorist attacks of 11 September 2001 changed our security environment dramatically. They also added new priorities to our economic planning. Large increases in defence, intelligence, border security and related security expenditures became a constant feature of Commonwealth budgets after 2001. That Australia was able to accommodate these additional demands, yet keep the budget in surplus and for five successive years further reduce income tax, became a testament to the strength the Australian economy had acquired.

In the 2002 budget Peter Costello released the inaugural inter-generational report which, incidentally, had been a stipulation of the Charter of Budget Honesty. For the first time, an Australian Government explained to the Australian public the impact of demographic changes, such as an ageing population, and what that meant to future budgets and the spending and taxing priorities of future governments, both federal and state. It was a far-reaching document and initiated a long-overdue national debate.

With the final repayment of the debt we inherited now in prospect, the Coalition was able to turn its attention to the debt-free future. One of the commitments made in the 2004 election campaign was to establish an Intergenerational Fund, and in his 2005 budget speech Peter Costello announced the establishment of the more appropriately named Future Fund. David Murray, the highly respected former managing director of the Commonwealth Bank, was appointed chairman of the guardians of the fund. Given an independent mandate to invest within prudent but sufficiently flexible guidelines, the fund had at its disposal the growing accumulation of surpluses from successive budgets. Its remit was to meet the superannuation liabilities of retiring commonwealth public servants, including a large number of defence personnel. As well as accumulated surpluses, the proceeds of the sale of the remainder of Telstra were also paid into the fund. When the Government left office in November 2007, the assets of the fund stood at some $61 billion.

The comparison was stark. When I became Prime Minister, the Commonwealth net debt was $96 billion. When I left office on 24 November 2007, not only had that net debt been liquidated, but the Future Fund had been established and it was worth $61 billion. Australia was well and truly ready for that rainy day.

The introduction of a GST, that historic reform of our taxation system, involved the largest income tax cut in Australia's history. But the Government did not cease cutting income tax in 2000. In its last five budgets, up to and including the budget of 2007, the Treasurer announced reductions in personal income tax. In the seven years that went by after the introduction of a new taxation system, the commitment to taxation reform never wavered.

It always puzzled me that there was constant criticism that the Government had not done enough on the tax reform front. In theory, of course, no government ever does enough when it comes to cutting tax. Expectations always run well ahead of reality and capacity. Tax cuts announced in the Coalition's last budget meant that a low-income earner eligible for the low-income tax offset would not pay any tax until his or her annual income exceeded $11,000. More than 80 per cent of taxpayers would face a top marginal rate of 30 per cent or less across the four-year period commencing on 1 July 2007. The top rate would apply to only approximately 2 per cent of taxpayers. In his 2007 budget speech Peter Costello said that in 1996 the top marginal rate — which was higher than it was in 2007 — applied from $50,000. If that threshold had merely been indexed, it would have stood below $68,000 by 1 July 2008. Under the changes announced by the Treasurer in that speech, the threshold would in fact be at $180,000, as at 1 July 2008. Claims that the Government had gone to sleep on taxation reform after 2000 were totally unjustified.

To those who saw my Government as obsessed with economics, to the detriment of the human condition, I had something to say. In my Australia Day address on 25 January 2006, entitled 'A Sense of Balance: The Australian

Achievement in 2006', I said that the achievement was higher, rarer and more precious than was commonly supposed. I reminded my audience that the Economist Intelligent Unit released a ranking of life in major cities around the world. It found that of the 12 most liveable cities on Earth five of them were in Australia. Of the top dozen, almost half were in one country, this country, with only one-third of 1 per cent of the world's population. It evoked what to my mind was the secret of Australia's enviable success — our sense of balance. I went on to say that 15 years before, Australia's income per capita had fallen to 19th in the developed world. By 2006 it had recovered to be the eighth-highest. Total household disposable income had grown in real terms by more than one-third over the previous decade, and over the same period real private-sector wealth per capita had more than doubled.

It was the broader measures of our national wellbeing that were even more striking. At the beginning of 2006, Australia ranked number three, out of 177 countries, on the UN Human Development Index, which took account of achievements in education enrolment, adult literacy levels, per capita GDP and life expectancy. A report the previous year on Australian social attitudes found that Australians were much more confident in the economy than they had been 10 years earlier. Eighty per cent of people surveyed said that they were now proud of Australia's economic achievements.

I argued that the economic management of the previous 10 years had given Australia a government — generically speaking — which was lean but not mean. As a share of GDP, Australia, at the beginning of 2006, had the second-lowest level of general government outlays in the OECD. Our elimination of net government debt compared with average government debt across the OECD of approximately 50 per cent of GDP.

Yet the real achievement was that we had been able to score these high economic marks without leaving behind the most vulnerable members in our society. Nothing could more powerfully refute the allegations that we had governed for the rich to the detriment of the poor. This condition was the very antithesis of the 'brutopia' which Kevin Rudd was to claim only a few months later that I had created in Australia.

This was reinforced in an OECD report, dated 7 January 2010, which found that Australia, whilst spending less on welfare, provided better protection against poverty, especially for families, than most other OECD countries. That was a double riposte to the Howard Government's critics. It was a put-down to those who said that we had wasted money on welfare handouts and rebuked those who claimed we had been hard-hearted.

41

OUR WARM, DRY LAND

Australian politics has had some perfect storms. In my time, none exceeded the perfect storm which crashed onto the environmental debate in October–November 2006, dramatically recasting the politics of global warming within Australia.

The climate-change debate had simmered for some time. It was a complicated issue, but there was a strengthening belief in the community that mankind had contributed to the growth of greenhouse gas emissions and that something had to be done. Most published scientific work supported this conclusion. A symbolic act seemed the perfect answer, and ratifying the Kyoto Protocol satisfied the desire to 'do something'. That there was no immediate cost involved made the action even more attractive.

Although Australia had fully participated in all the climate-change conferences and had met her emission growth obligations under the Kyoto Protocol, my Government had refused to ratify the protocol. This was because we thought it bad for Australia to do so unless and until the major polluters were subject to its conditions. The United States had flatly refused to ratify. This was the attitude of both Democrats and Republicans. The United States Senate on 25 July 1997 voted 95–0 that the USA should not adhere to any protocol which did not bind developing countries as well as developed ones, or would result in serious harm to the US economy. This meant that there was never any real possibility that Washington would give Kyoto a tick. This is worth emphasising, particularly as so much of the blame for the anti-Kyoto stance of the United States has been sheeted home to George Bush. In turn the anti-ratification stance of my Government was falsely depicted as blindly following a prejudice peculiar to George Bush. Hostility towards Kyoto has been a bipartisan constant in US politics for many years, the former Vice-president notwithstanding. Nothing has changed with the Obama Administration. Like his Democrat predecessor, Bill Clinton, Barack Obama will not submit his country to any international deal which does not also bind developing nations. That was made clear by the Americans at Copenhagen in December 2009.

China was an adherent to Kyoto, but was not subject to the same conditions as would apply to developed countries such as Australia. That meant that if Australia ratified, industries with high emissions, if established in Australia, would carry a higher cost penalty than would be the case if those same industries were set up in China or Indonesia. It would stand to reason, therefore, that investment in those industries would flow from Australia to other countries. That is why my Government saw ratifying Kyoto as being potentially damaging both to jobs and industry. Rudd's ratification came so late in the cycle that there is insufficient time for the negative consequences to show up before the current phase of Kyoto ends.

Even though there was a valid reason for not ratifying, it did not win acceptance, because 'doing something' about the environment had entered the popular culture. Whenever the Government said that we were meeting our obligations under the protocol, the reply was, if we were meeting the obligations, why not ratify?

Another logical argument against ratification was that the Kyoto Protocol was rapidly becoming obsolete, and the nations of the world should plan for an understanding post-Kyoto, which would include countries such as the United States and China on the same basis as all others. As if to demonstrate that in politics timing can be everything, the need for a world agreement beyond Kyoto was precisely the argument advanced by the Rudd Government at the chaotic and failed Copenhagen Summit.

To listen to Penny Wong, the Climate Change Minister, say again and again at Copenhagen that Kyoto needed to be replaced by a new agreement which bound China and the United States, and to know that this had been the self-same argument that I used to no political effect just two years earlier, was to feel acute political frustration. In the election campaign of 2007, Kevin Rudd held out ratification of Kyoto as Australia's contribution to saving the planet. By the Copenhagen meeting in December 2009, salvation was elsewhere; Kyoto had to be replaced by a more comprehensive world agreement. That was an argument I had first advanced in November 2006, right in the middle of the perfect storm.

By the second half of 2006 the climate-change debate remained a lively one; it was one that the Coalition was not winning, but it was not really prominent in the public's mind. That was until the perfect storm broke.

In the space of several weeks, commencing in October 2006, four separate events came together to push the climate-change concerns of the Australian community to higher levels than ever before. In Victoria the bushfire season started early; the drought affecting large areas of eastern Australia lingered on. So concerned had I been about the impact of the drought on the Murray-Darling River system that I called a meeting of premiers for Melbourne Cup Day, November 2006, to discuss emergency measures to help communities cope with the water shortage.

From outside Australia came the contributions of Al Gore, the former Vice-president of the United States, and Sir Nicholas Stern, a former chief economist at the IMF. Gore's movie *An Inconvenient Truth* was a slick production and had an enormous impact on the millions of moviegoers around the world who viewed it. He came to Australia to promote the film, giving added impetus to the message he was conveying. My close friendship with his old nemesis, George Bush, gave him a further incentive to make his point in our country.

Stern's contribution, through a specially commissioned report for the British Labour Government of Tony Blair, was more cerebral. The executive summary said, '… the scientific evidence is now overwhelming: climate change presents very serious global risks and it demands an urgent global response'.[1] The analysis offered by Stern was beguilingly simple and seductively cheap.

He argued that the economic costs of not acting would be much greater than those of acting. He estimated that if a wide range of risks and impacts were taken into account, then the estimates of damage could go from a conservative one of 5 per cent of global GDP each year to 20 per cent of GDP each year. In contrast, he argued, reducing greenhouse gas emissions to avoid the worst repercussions of climate change could be limited to about 1 per cent of global GDP each year.

An argument in those terms was irresistible. If it was as cheap and simple as that, why on earth didn't every government, including the Howard Government, grab it with both hands?

Later analyses asserted that Stern's reasoning was based on flawed assumptions, particularly in relation to the discount rate, a standard economic methodology which measures future benefits against present costs. Nigel Lawson, Chancellor of the Exchequer in the Thatcher Government, delivered a particularly trenchant criticism of Stern in his book on the global warming issue, entitled *An Appeal to Reason*. Lawson's broadside was that the discount rate employed by Stern was much too low. He cited a range of eminent academic economists who shared that opinion. This was a crucial point because, as Lawson rightly surmised, 'And it has been demonstrated that with a higher, more normal discount rate, the argument for radical action over global warming now, on conventional cost-benefit calculations, collapses completely.'[2]

These four events coincided and dramatically increased the focus on global warming in Australia. The problem for the Coalition was that, because of its longstanding support for the simplistic solution of ratifying Kyoto, the Labor Party was regarded as more committed to taking decisive action against climate change than was the Coalition.

I concluded that the Government would need to shift its position on climate change. I nonetheless remained opposed to ratifying the Kyoto Protocol. There were, however, two important new policy attitudes struck by the Government. The first was to say that Australia would be part of a 'new Kyoto', provided that any new treaty included all of the world's major emitters. This was the argument repeated almost ad nauseam by the Rudd Government at Copenhagen. We also needed to examine the establishment of an emissions trading system (ETS).

Sentiment had been gradually shifting within the business sector. Service industries had begun to sign up to the climate-change agenda. Some firms saw new business in the emissions trading world; others believed a lot of the science; yet still others felt that an ETS was inevitable and business should be in on the ground floor, influencing its design. Business minds were also concentrated by the threats of certain states to establish their own ETSs, which would have created an administrative nightmare for companies. If there had to be a scheme, a national one would be much more acceptable.

Speaking to the Business Council of Australia (BCA) in Sydney on 13 November 2006, I announced that the Government would establish a joint government/industry taskforce to give advice on the form which an ETS, both domestically and internationally, might take. I said that any system which might be established should make an effective contribution to the greenhouse gas challenge, but not in a way which did disproportionate or unfair damage to the Australian economy or our vital industries. I stressed the importance of our fossil fuel industries as well as the need to keep the nuclear power option on the table. I also acknowledged a role for renewable energy sources, always recognising that their contribution to base-load power generation would be limited.

The taskforce could hardly have been more high-powered. Chaired by Dr Peter Shergold, the secretary of my department, it included the heads of Treasury, Foreign Affairs and Trade, the Environment Department and the Department of Industry. Amongst those from business came Margaret Jackson, chairman of Qantas; Peter Coates of the coal producer Xstrata; and John Stewart, boss of the National Australia Bank. This group would work in close professional collaboration for several months and, in May, produced what became known as the Shergold Report.

Cabinet was advised on 4 December 2006 that without new measures, Australia would be 109 over 1990 levels against the target of 108, under the Kyoto benchmarks. Although barely a slippage to speak of, the Government decided at that meeting to phase out incandescent lights from 2009–10 and replace them with high-efficiency compact fluorescent light bulbs. This was a practical step which could have a measurable impact. Another practical policy was our Global Initiative on Forests and Climate, announced in March 2007, under which $200 million was committed to reducing forest clearing in countries such as Indonesia.

At a meeting of the federal council of the Liberal Party on 3 June 2007, I outlined the framework of an ETS that the Government would work towards. It largely reflected the recommendations of the Shergold Report. In designing the ETS, the Government would take into account global developments; Australia would not run ahead of the rest of the world; and the ETS would also ensure that the competitiveness of our trade-exposed industries would be preserved.

There was a sharp difference between the Coalition and Labor on nuclear power. Nuclear power was part of the solution to the global warming challenge. It was an impeccably clean source of energy; the modern experience was that nuclear power generation was extremely safe; many other nations had successfully adapted it for use in electricity generation (80 per cent of electricity in France came from nuclear power) and, very importantly, Australia had close to 40 per cent of the world's readily exploitable reserves of uranium.

It is hypocritical of any Australian government to happily allow sales of Australian uranium abroad but ban the nuclear industry in Australia because, allegedly, it is not safe.

For decades, as a residue of both the Cold War and the nuclear power plant accidents at Chernobyl in the old Soviet Union and Three Mile Island in the United States, there had been implanted in the minds of most Australians a dread of the use of nuclear power. Yet the passage of time had made the use of nuclear energy infinitely safer, and I detected a change in the Australian community, accelerated no doubt by the dawning realisation that here was a clean source of energy generation, which over time would become economic.

On 6 June 2006 I had established a Prime Ministerial Taskforce to review uranium mining, processing and the contribution of nuclear energy in Australia. This group was chaired by Ziggy Switkowski, then the head of the Australian Nuclear Science and Technology Organisation (ANSTO), and included Professor George Dracoulis, an eminent nuclear physicist, and Professor Warwick McKibbin, who was not only a first-class economist and member of the board of the RBA but also widely recognised as having a deep understanding of the economics of energy and issues relating to climate change.

The inquiry reported, late in December 2006, that nuclear power was a practical option for part of Australia's electricity production. Switkowski found that it would take time for nuclear power to become economic, but it would become more so once a price was put on carbon, which would be a consequence of an ETS. The Rudd Government's refusal to countenance the nuclear power option seemed based on nothing more than remnant ideology.

Whilst I am an agnostic rather than a sceptic on climate change, instinctively I doubt many of the more alarming predictions. What makes me suspicious are the constant declarations from the climate-change enthusiasts that the science is all in, the debate is over and no further objections to received wisdom will even be considered. First principles teach us that no debate is ever concluded, and it can never be said of a scientifically contestable proposition that all the science is in. For many, it has become a substitute religion. Most of the mass media has boarded the climate-change train; arguments to the contrary are dismissed as extremist.

Moral bullying has been employed to silence those who question the conventional wisdom. The chaos at Copenhagen, and mistakes discovered in the work of the International Climate Change Partnership (ICCP) have shaken the edifice, but it will not be easily toppled.

From 1 April 2001, Australia had a mandatory renewable energy target scheme. This required electricity traders to obtain a certain proportion of their output from renewable sources such as wind and solar energy. The initial target was just 2 per cent. It was from a review of this scheme that the Energy green paper of 2004 emerged, with its core commitment to rely heavily on developing new technology as the principal method of tackling greenhouse gas emissions. The key conclusion was that, recognising Australia's enormous energy endowments, the goal should be to protect and enhance this asset whilst searching for ways to reduce the greenhouse gas emissions coming from exploitation of Australia's energy resources. It made no sense to hobble such an enormous natural advantage. No other country in the world would have done so. For the life of me, I could not see why Australia should.

The centrepiece of this strategy was the establishment of a Low Emissions Technology fund. The Government would provide initially $500 million to this fund, which in turn would leverage at least $1 billion in private-sector investment to develop and demonstrate low-emissions technology. Australia had decided to go for technology as a way of contributing to the reduction in greenhouse gas emissions.

The green paper followed, which said that Australia needed both renewable and other energy sources; the choice should be between high- and low-emissions outcomes, not renewable and other sources. In launching the paper, I made it plain that for the foreseeable future, coal, oil and gas would meet the bulk of our energy needs.

The paper had this to say on emissions trading: 'Australia will not impose significant new economy wide costs, such as emissions trading, in its greenhouse response at this stage. Such action is premature, in the absence of effective longer term global action on climate change, and given Australia is on track to meet its Kyoto 108 percent target. Pursuing this path in advance of an effective global response would harm Australia's competitiveness and growth with no certain global climate change benefits.'[3] Six years later nothing has transpired to shake the commonsense of that statement.

The big shift in the political climate, late in 2006, resulted in the Howard Government developing a framework for an ETS earlier than originally intended; the commencement and operation of such a scheme was, however, to be influenced by what the rest of the world did.

With its emphasis on technology, Australia was anything but out of step with world opinion. In Sydney in January 2006, the first meeting of the Asia Pacific Partnership for Clean Development and Climate took place. It brought together Australia, the United States, China, Japan, India and Korea. Canada was welcomed as the seventh member at the October 2007 meeting. This was an important grouping. It included the United States and other major emitters who were not adherents to the Kyoto Protocol. The common thread was an emphasis on developing a technological response to the greenhouse gas problem. In the spirit of this grouping, Australia and China signed a clean energy partnership in October 2006.

The most positive response to the greenhouse gas challenge over the next decade or two will be a technological one. Low-emissions technology, including carbon storage and sequestration, and the development of nuclear power by those countries not now employing it, are together far more likely to bring about an early reduction in the rate of growth of greenhouse gas emissions than anything else. Technology is universal. National and regional differences will always colour the usefulness of ETSs, however economical, logical and rational they may seem.

Until late 2009 there appeared to be strong public support in Australia for an ETS, albeit with lively debate about its structure. The unexpected change in the leadership of the federal Opposition, with Tony Abbott being elected with a commitment to oppose the Rudd Government's ETS bill, dramatically changed the scene. Further complicating the picture was the total collapse of the Copenhagen Summit. These two events have already had major consequences. Kevin Rudd decided to postpone the ETS for at least three years, and this commenced a sequence of events which led to his downfall as PM. Ratifyng Kyoto in December 2007 was feel-good politics at its best. Persuading the public to accept an ETS proved much harder.

Concern about climate change may have gone off the chart, but during my final three years as Prime Minister, water was the most immediate environmental issue that Australia faced. Years of successive drought had crippled our farm sector and brought the mighty Murray-Darling River system to its knees. To the climate-change true believers the drought was simply another facet of what was happening to our planet. To others, however, it was history repeating itself. The worst drought in Australia since European settlement had been the Federation drought of the early 1900s. Those old enough to remember knew that the first 50 years of the 20th century in eastern Australia had been particularly dry. The second half of that century had been much wetter.

After the 2001 election John Anderson, Deputy Prime Minister, fifth-generation wheat grower and passionate believer in the survival of rural Australia as an integral part of our nation, had begun campaigning strongly for reform of water policy. Reminding me of the dimension of the challenge, John would point out that Australia had 5 per cent of the world's landmass but only 1 per cent of the river and water basin run-off.

It was a daunting problem for a federal government. All the power was with the states. The only thing the Commonwealth had was large amounts of money; the states were always conscious of this. Water entitlements to farmers were handed out by state governments. Most water consumed in Australia was used in country areas. According to the advice of the Murray-Darling Basin Commission at the time, rural consumption was 80 per cent, urban 12 per cent and the rest 8 per cent.

The Murray-Darling River system encapsulated the dilemma of water policy in Australia. Unless something fundamental changed, Adelaide could face a threat to the adequacy of its drinking water in less than 20 years. For decades, governments from both sides of politics in New South Wales had issued far too many water entitlements, thus depleting river flows. Victoria had run a more disciplined water system. Queensland had been less indulgent than New South Wales, but it also issued too many licences. The basin commission was a hybrid organisation with limited power, and a monument to the unwillingness of parochial state governments to cede something so obviously national to the Commonwealth Government. Rivers pay no regard to state borders. The Great Artesin Basin lies beneath four states and territories.

Recognising this, John Anderson began a patient campaign. He talked on a one-on-one basis to his counterparts in the various state governments, and eventually, at a meeting of the Council of Australian Governments (COAG) on 29 August 2003, agreement was reached for a national water policy, which involved acceptance of an important principle: water entitlements should be invested with the characteristics of property rights. They should become tradable, even across state borders. Called the National

Water Initiative, this was a huge step forward and a tribute to Anderson's persistence. He has received little praise for what was genuine cooperative federalism. John Anderson, typically, gave some credit to his NSW Labor counterpart, Craig Knowles, for agreement being reached. John would later tell me that this was partly due to the fact that, in his pre-political life, Knowles had been a property valuer and thus understood the need to treat water entitlements as property rights and put a value on them, if progress towards a rational system were to be achieved.

Part of the water initiative was the establishment of a National Water Commission whose tasks included advice on the allocation of a $2 billion water fund established by the federal government for investment in water use and conservation projects, largely put forward by the states, on a shared funding basis.

As the grip of the drought tightened, consequences of the over-allocations of water entitlements became more acute. At some point it would become necessary for the over-allocations to be returned. The problem was that none of the states was willing to invest the money needed to buy back the entitlements.

This became the genesis of the policy which I began devising, in discussion with Malcolm Turnbull, at the end of 2006 and presented by me in a speech to the National Press Club in Parliament House on 25 January 2007, as the Murray-Darling Rescue Plan.

The plan involved the Commonwealth spending some $10 billion over a period of years, essentially doing two things. It would fully fund the buyback of water entitlements by the states, even though the states themselves had been reckless in their allocation of those rights. It would also fund a program to line and pipe the irrigation channels of the Murray-Darling. This would dramatically reduce evaporation and lead to millions of litres of water being conserved. There was also money to fund water conservation projects on individual farms.

In return for this enormous sum of money and the assumption by the Commonwealth of a financial responsibility which had been incurred by the states, they were asked to refer their powers over regulating water usage within the Murray-Darling River system to the Commonwealth. The fragmented state regulatory approach had failed; consistent national regulation was needed. I thought that, in agreeing to pick up the entire price tag for buying back the over-allocations, the Commonwealth was making a generous offer.

If this offer had been made at the commencement of a new term of my Government, the states would have all agreed to it. It was obvious from their immediate response that they were taken by surprise at the scale of the Commonwealth offer, and sorely tempted to accept it. The problem was that it was an election year. The Coalition had been in power federally for 11 years, and Labor was desperate to get rid of us. In the end Labor tribalism took precedence over the national interest, even on such a life-and-death issue for Australia as water.

The states were a fascinating study with their responses. Morris Iemma from New South Wales responded in a positive fashion from the word go. This was understandable. His state would be the greatest beneficiary, as New South Wales had been responsible more than any other state for reckless over-allocations. Peter Beattie was reasonably accommodating. Mike Rann huffed and puffed about a different way of doing it, but knew in the end it was a good deal for South Australia.

To discuss the plan, I convened a meeting of relevant premiers as well as the Chief Minister of the Australian Capital Territory in Canberra for 8 February for what was a preliminary gathering which reconvened on 23 February. It was obvious from this discussion that New South Wales, Queensland and South Australia (with some haggling) would come on board, as would the Australian Capital Territory. The problem proved to be Victoria.

On 23 February, after my discussion with them as a group, I allowed the premiers to discuss the matter alone. When I returned to the cabinet room, Peter Beattie (who I liked to deal with) indicated on behalf of all of them that three states, namely New South Wales, Queensland and South Australia, plus the Australian Capital Territory, were agreeable, but that Victoria had a problem. I asked to see the Victorian Premier, Steve Bracks, alone. In this meeting he said to me, 'John, I need more time to shift my people. I will ultimately come to the party on this but I just need a bit more time.' I took him at his word. The statement at the end of the whole meeting indicated that progress had been made and hopes were reasonably high. Of concern, though, public comments later made by Bracks were starkly at odds with the private indication he had given me.

Victoria would never honour the private understanding I had reached with Bracks. Malcolm Turnbull, the responsible minister, had numerous discussions with the Victorians. It is true that the Victorian farmers were critical of aspects of the Commonwealth plan. It was also true that it did not suit the national political interests of the ALP for my plan to win acceptance.

It was bold and imaginative. To have won acceptance of something as sweeping as this would have been a real plus for the Coalition in the lead-up to the election. To this day I remain convinced that, on this occasion, the Commonwealth was the victim of a good cop/bad cop routine put together by the premiers out of tribal loyalty to their federal colleagues; there was scant regard for the interests of the Murray-Darling River system. In frustration my Government introduced legislation to implement as much of my national plan as was possible under existing constitutional power. It fell short of what the national interest required but was approved by parliament on 17 August.

The issue remains unresolved. In recent months there has been litigation threatened between the states. The Murray-Darling will likely enjoy some respite due to the heavy rains of 2010 in Queensland and northern New South Wales, but this can only be temporary. Australia needs a national system. At some point the federal government will need to seek constitutional power at a referendum to assert control over the Murray-Darling basin. This is a classic example of failed cooperative federalism. My sense is that the people of the Murray-Darling basin states would vote to give power to the national government. They understand the logic of this vital river system belonging to the entire nation and not remaining under fragmented state control.

Australia is now a long way from the global warming debate of 2007. The Labor Government went into full retreat from what the former PM called 'the great moral challenge of our time'. People are turning against the ETS; the ALP lazily assumed that negative attacks on the Coalition would be enough to win public endorsement of its ETS without the need to explain its complexity. It should not be surprised at changed public attitudes.

Equally, the world should not have been surprised at the stance of China during the recent gathering in Copenhagen. It should never have been left to the meeting itself to confirm that China is not willing to accept the same disciplines as the developed world. The United States in particular must have known that China would take the position she did. It surprised me that the Americans had apparently made no attempt to engage both China and India well before Copenhagen and, knowing their likely responses, work to adjust expectations accordingly. It was poor diplomacy. Surely the Obama Administration realises that we still live in a world of nation states. When it comes to the crunch on really big issues, multilateralism usually falls short.

42

BILLY GETS A JOB, BUT WHO CARES?

The Australian system of compulsory conciliation and arbitration, like Australian Rules football, was indigenous. We may have inherited the British craft union system, but our forebears did not give Australia the legally clothed industrial relations system established with Federation. It was the Commonwealth Conciliation and Arbitration *Court* that was inaugurated in 1904.

Then retired as prime minister, Sir Robert Menzies told an American audience in 1967, 'The system of compulsory arbitration has, on the whole, worked well in Australia, largely because the judges and commissioners have been regarded by the general public as impartial.'[1] He went on to say, 'It is my own considered opinion that most thoughtful people in Australia would not want the great issues of pay and hours of work, with their tremendous economic implications, dealt with by a political auction at a federal election.' Those comments revealed an almost reverential attitude to arbitral tribunals; they still retained the aura of courts. The suggestion that pay and hours of work were above politics sounds otherworldly. Yet his remarks were close to the sentiment of the times.

Until the Coalition, then in opposition, began to change its policy in the mid-1980s, both sides of politics supported conciliation and arbitration, accepted a union monopoly of the bargaining process and unions having legal privileges. Enormous energy went into trying to persuade the Australian Industrial Relations Commission (AIRC) to deliver different wage judgements, without the central role of the commission in that wage-setting process ever being questioned. My action as Minister for Business and Consumer Affairs in outlawing secondary boycotts by unions removed a major union privilege, and was something of an exception. But it was achieved through changing the competition, and not the industrial relations, law.

Earlier I have written of how the wages explosion of 1981–82 highlighted the need for a less centralised wage fixation system. It was this that I had in mind as shadow Treasurer when I told the National Press Club on 31 August 1983 that it was time to turn Mr Justice Higgins on his head. Higgins delivered the Harvester and Broken Hill judgements of the Conciliation Court in the first decade of Federation, and these were the foundation stones of centralised wage fixing.

I had also witnessed the misrepresentation of the Metal Trades agreement by the Labor Party and the ACTU as an early exercise in decentralised wage fixation. As the agreement had caused immense economic distress through higher unemployment, it suited them politically to argue that way.

That claim was wrong, because at no time during the events surrounding the agreement did the commission or, indeed, the Government embrace decentralised wage fixation. There was no talk of enterprise bargaining; no watering down of the award system; no alternative workplace contracts were provided; and there was no suggestion that in any way the union monopoly of the bargaining process should be weakened. Centralised wage fixation and comparative wage justice were well and truly alive in 1981 and '82, and their operation played a material role in the devastatingly high unemployment which occurred at that time. That is why Paul Keating thought that George Campbell had lots of dead men around his neck.

The December 1983 floating of the Australian dollar increased the pressure on the durability of the wage fixation system. Exposing Australia's currency to the fluctuations of world currency markets would highlight internal rigidities within the Australian economy. Deregulation externally called for matching deregulation internally.

Whatever logic there was behind this view, it struggled to gain support in the post-1983 election period. The newly elected Labor Government, led by a popular Prime Minister in Bob Hawke, the ACTU, those sections of the business community which swallowed the Labor Party line on the real meaning of the 1981–82 wages breakout, most academics and a significant section of the Liberal and National Parties continued to support the old system. There were, however, some encouraging dissenters.

From very early in the 1980s, the farmers, the miners and small business groups became increasingly frustrated with the centralised system. For farmers and miners their attitudes reflected the experience of having to compete on world markets. They well understood that, to a large extent, centralised wage fixing had become the handmaiden of tariff protection. The one complemented the other. As exporters, the farmers and miners saw wage increases through the centralised system, made possible by high tariffs, as inimical to their longer-term interests. The disenchantment of small business reflected the fact that industrial relations in Australia had always involved two worlds. There had always been a small number of large companies employing big workforces, most of which were either fully or heavily unionised. Then there were the rest, comprising thousands of small- and medium-sized firms whose workforces were largely non-unionised.

To smaller enterprises it was increasingly unfair that their industrial relations should continue to be governed by a system custom-built for large companies employing heavily unionised workforces.

In the mid-1980s the climate of the industrial relations debate was changed by three separate events. The first was the successful common law suit by the Dollar Sweets Company to obtain remedies against a union which effectively had placed a blackban on its business. Michael Kroger, later the president of the Victorian division of the Liberal Party, was the company's solicitor and he briefed Peter Costello as one of the counsel in the case. This legal action was a significant breakthrough, using common law powers which the industrial relations hierarchy had never believed were available.

In the Mudginberri dispute, the National Farmers' Federation (NFF), then ably led by Ian McLachlan, strongly supported an abattoir in the Northern Territory which was kept operational through the use of workplace contracts in defiance of heavy union picketing. The Mudginberri dispute would never have been resolved in the way it was without the use of section 45D of the Trade Practices Act, resulting in very large penalties being imposed on the union by the Federal Court.

The third separate dispute was that involving the provision of power in Southeast Queensland. The Bjelke-Petersen Government succeeded in employing many of its power workers on contracts and, in the process, scored a decisive victory over the power unions. At one stage in the dispute, the ACTU president, Simon Crean, actually pleaded with the Queensland Government to resume negotiations as he feared for the future of the award system in that industry. The Hawke Government attempted by legislation to override the actions of the Queensland Government, but this proved unsuccessful. At one stage in the Queensland dispute, the use of sections 45D and E of the Trade Practices Act was threatened.

Neil Brown, Deputy Leader of the Opposition and shadow Minister for Industrial Relations, launched the long-awaited Coalition industrial relations policy in April 1986. For the first time, the Coalition unequivocally promised that employees would have the right, if they so chose, to leave the award system and sign a workplace contract which could embody all the terms and conditions of their employment. It would not be necessary for that contract to be approved by the commission or for a union to be involved, unless the employees wished it so. The policy stipulated that a person employed under a voluntary contract had to be paid at least the hourly rate for ordinary hours of work specified in the relevant award. To the extent that these contracts were silent on other conditions of employment, then the award stipulations continued to prevail. If, however, the agreement went on to canvass such issues as penalty rates and overtime loadings, then whatever the contract said would override the award.

Although the operation of these agreements was limited at that time to workplaces employing fewer than 50 people, it was, in relation to that category of workplaces, a radical and innovative policy. In respect of them, it went much further than the 1996 industrial relations reforms. The 50-employee ceiling was removed in the policy taken to the 1987 election.

The early 1990s saw public and media support for the Coalition's industrial relations approach reach its highest peak yet. A widespread view had developed that the system did need basic change; that the Government was confused; and that industrial relations reform was an idea whose time had truly arrived. In July 1992 a Newspoll showed that 64 per cent of respondents believed that individual workers should have the right, if they so chose, to negotiate directly with their own employer without the intervention of a union.

Even within the then current system, change, albeit at a glacial pace, was occurring. Late in 1991 the commission established an enterprise-bargaining principle which went a big way towards meeting the wishes of the Government and the ACTU. In 1992 the Keating Government amended the Industrial Relations Act to bring into play its own version of enterprise bargaining. In substance, this was that any agreement struck between an employer or group of employers on the one hand, and a union on the other hand, could, provided it met certain criteria, be submitted to the AIRC for virtually rubber stamp approval. There was no reference to agreements not involving unions, and no provision for direct negotiation between workers and their employers without the insertion of a union.

After the 1993 election Paul Keating said that his government would extend workplace bargaining to the non-union sector. In reality, the 1993 Industrial Relations Reform Act fell well short of this commitment. Rather than further freeing the labour market, this act introduced more rigidity.

Most perniciously, the 1993 act introduced new and unreasonable unfair dismissal rules which shifted the onus of proof heavily against the employer. They became a further disincentive for small business to take on more staff. The 1993 act also gutted the former secondary-boycott provisions in the Trade Practices Act, and restored unions to a privileged position under the law. This was done by removing the secondary-boycott law from the Trade Practices Act and placing it in the hands of the AIRC.

Under the 1993 act a workplace contract in the non-union sector, described as an 'enterprise flexibility agreement', could only be negotiated if its starting point was the totality of the existing award, it was approved by the AIRC, and any union having coverage in the area was given a full opportunity of opposing ratification of the agreement before the commission. This last-mentioned stipulation applied even if none of the employees covered by the agreement belonged to the union in question. This proviso, in particular, meant that in practice few employers would bother to go down the path of seeking an enterprise flexibility agreement in the first place.

By the time the act was amended by Peter Reith as minister in the Howard Government, a bare 261 agreements covering just 23,200 employees had been concluded. Keating's alleged new world of bargaining freedom was a mirage. Direct agreement-making was still held in contempt. In November 1995, the AIRC belled the cat on Keating's so-called reforms by endorsing a 1994 judgement in another case that 'the establishment of conditions of employment at an enterprise level through a system of individual contracts ... is one at variance with our system of industrial relations, a system which, since its inception, has been based on collective processes as the means of providing terms and conditions of employment at the workplace'.[2] The industrial relations umpire had given Mr Keating out.

In industrial relations folklore Labor-style, the 1993 act, together with the 1992 changes, have enjoyed a wholly undeserved status as the true beginning of enterprise bargaining in Australia. Rather, the 1993 act especially was a classic sell-out to the trade union movement for the massive support given the Labor Government during the 1993 campaign. In a burst of candour, Jenny George, assistant secretary of the ACTU, later Labor MP for Throsby, dismissed employer concerns about the new act by saying that employers should understand who had won the election.

It would take the Workplace Relations Act of 1996 of the Howard Government to entrench individual contracts, remove the union monopoly on the bargaining process, restore section 45D to the Trade Practices Act and bring more balance to our industrial relations system.

Through these years of change, commitment to widespread industrial relations reform united all sections of the Liberal Party; likewise the Nationals. There was wider instinctive support for workplace changes than for even taxation reform. When Kevin Andrews presented the final version of the workplace relations legislation, known as WorkChoices, to the joint party room on 1 November 2005, there were no objections. In retrospect this may seem remarkable, and although it is true that various iterations of the legislation had been discussed in detail with colleagues prior to that date, it was, nonetheless, significant that this historic bill received such overwhelming backing.

The conventional wisdom now is that WorkChoices went too far and was a major, if not the major, reason why we lost in 2007. If that is a valid retrospective, then as party leader, I must accept the principal responsibility for such as error of judgement. It was nonetheless a mistake embraced with eyes wide open by the entire party room.

The emphatic attitude of Coalition members in 2005 was that, having unexpectedly won control of the Senate at the 2004 election, the opportunity to further advance industrial relations reform should not be squandered, and that the system should be made even more flexible.

As well as mainstream reforms to the workplace relations system, the Government had a specific policy response to the anarchy in the building and construction industry, as well as special legislation in the Government's last term dealing with independent contractors.

Terence Cole QC, a former highly respected judge of the NSW Supreme Court, headed a Royal Commission which found there was widespread thuggery, intimidation and, on occasions, criminal behaviour within the building and construction industry. The Government heeded his recommendation and established the Australian Building and Construction Industry Authority, with particularly strong powers to bring the industry back within the normal law and order of the nation. In its short life, the authority brought huge improvements to the industry, especially in Melbourne and Perth, notorious killing fields for militants in the sector. A sharp reduction in strikes and stoppages, as well as improved productivity, bore testament to this. The Rudd Government weakened this body, and it remains ALP policy to remove it altogether.

There was also legislation protecting the status of independent contractors. Unions and the Labor Party had long cast covetous eyes on them. In different ways, they fantasised about bringing independent contractors within some broad definition of employer and employee. Independent contractors comprise some of the most fiercely entrepreneurial small businessmen and women in the country, and not surprisingly they regularly sought both support and, where possible, legislative protection from the Coalition Government.

The mainstream reforms of 1996 and 2005, as well as the initiatives in the specific areas mentioned, had the common goals of removing monopoly union power and lifting economic productivity, so as to boost employment and real wages. There was abundant evidence that this happened. More broadly there was the goal of removing unnecessary third-party intervention from the conduct of industrial relations, be it from the Government, the commission or indeed anywhere else. When I outlined the WorkChoices reforms to parliament in May 2005, I concluded by saying, 'The era of the select few making decisions for the many in industrial relations is over.'

The 1996 legislation produced the historic reform establishing Australian Workplace Agreements (AWAs). For the first time the negotiation of an individual employment contract, directly between an employee and employer, was a legislated option. The terms of that contract could be largely what the two parties wanted. The big proviso was that the employee's pay and benefits under the contact had to be no less in value than what he or she would have received under the relevant award (the no-disadvantage test). This change effectively ended the union monopoly on the bargaining process. The Coalition never wanted to take unions out of the bargaining game, only to end their monopoly.

AWAs operated for over 11 years. They were widely used in the mining industry as well as in recreation and hospitality; their uptake in other parts of the economy had been steadily rising. They did not supplant awards; they were a further option available to employers and employees.

But because their introduction did end the union monopoly on the bargaining process, AWAs remained objects of continuing hostility from both the union movement and the Labor Party.

The first legislative act of the newly elected Rudd Government in the industrial relations area was to prohibit the conclusion of any new AWAs. That legislation preceded action on any other industrial relations front. The priority for Labor was the restoration of union power. It took precedence over alleged protection of workers' rights, productivity issues and the new framework to administer the changed industrial relations landscape.

Due to the unwillingness of the Coalition, newly in opposition, to attack the Government on industrial relations, this priority, given by the Rudd Government to serving the interests of union power in relation to AWAs, went by largely unnoticed. There were few protests from the business community, ever anxious to cosy up to a newly elected Labor Government.

Generically, our 2004 election policy on industrial relations had promised more reform and increased flexibility. There was a commitment to 'pursue changes to take the unfair dismissal laws burden off the back of small business and protect small business from redundancy payments'.[3]

The 2004 policy also promised implementation of the Cole Commission's recommendations, with which I have just dealt, and we also promised that a re-elected Coalition Government would introduce an independent contractors bill, designed to protect and enhance the freedom to contract and to encourage independent contracting as a desirable small business arrangement. There were sundry other enhancements of existing legislation promised, but no other major proposals.

I did not expect that the Coalition would win control of the Senate at the 2004 election. To my total surprise, the Coalition won a fourth Senate seat in Queensland, and the Family First senator, Steve Fielding, was elected in Victoria. In Queensland, the final senator elected was not, as popular legend has it, the National Party's Barnaby Joyce. Rather it was the third person on the separate Liberal Senate team, Russell Trood. There was plenty of irony in this. As a long-time Coalitionist, and as someone who had criticised the Queensland Liberal Party for breaking the joint Senate ticket arrangement in that state in 1980, I acknowledge that if there had been a joint Senate ticket in Queensland at the 2004 election, the Coalition would not have won four Senate seats in that state.

The separate, and energetic, campaign run by the National Party candidate Barnaby Joyce, together with a tight flow of preferences from him to the Liberal Party, as well as the preferences of a number of small, right-of-centre groups, delivered that final Senate spot to the Liberal Party.

Some claimed that winning control of the Senate, via the Queensland outcome, was a poisoned chalice for the Coalition, because it encouraged it to go too far with potentially unpopular industrial relations legislation. I always gave that idea short shrift. The Coalition deserved to be judged by the electorate according to what it did in government, and nothing else.

Knowing that the Coalition would have a majority in the Senate, I turned my mind to possible further industrial relations reforms. It was common ground that we should move on unfair dismissals. This had been a bugbear of small business for many years. There was wide public understanding that a particularly disruptive employee in a small enterprise could be destructive, not only to the owner, but also the other employees, and that change here was warranted. Changing the unfair dismissal laws was in our election policy; we had a clear mandate to act.

There would also be little difficulty in securing passage of the special legislation regarding the building and construction industry as well as the Independent Contractors Act. Apart from fierce union opposition, these had broad support. They had been extensively debated for a number of years. The Coalition's position was well known and on their own or together they would certainly not be deal breakers with the electorate.

The big question concerned further industrial relations reform, beyond unfair dismissals, as the Coalition had been given a once-in-a-lifetime opportunity to further mould the industrial relations framework of Australia. The Senate victory in 2004 was a one-off event; if the window of opportunity were not availed of then, that opportunity would not come again in the political lifetime of those who led the Government.

The overwhelming view within the Government was that it should take advantage of the unexpected majority it gained in the Senate to press ahead with further industrial relations reform. The collective attitude of the Coalition was that history would deem us policy cowards if we did not make further workplace relations changes. And by this I mean going beyond what was promulgated before the 2004 poll.

Business groups all wanted change, with some being much more radical than others. The IMF and OECD waded in, with the latter recommending that Australia cut the level of minimum wages, which were the second-highest in the developed world. The Government had no intention of doing this. Such steps have theoretical economic merit, and can boost employment because not only do they make the unemployed more employable, they also allow firms to retain more staff in a downturn. The problem is that when the starting point is a high minimum wage, any reductions are seen as harsh on the low-paid, thus violating the egalitarian ethos of Australia.

On 14 February, during an interview on the Channel Seven *Sunrise* program, Peter Costello argued that there was a once-in-a-generation opportunity to enhance individual contracts, to cut down on arbitral matters, to try and get wages linked to productivity improvements and enhance profitability. He also saw the opportunity to get ease-of-entry, ease-of-exit into employment situations, and to give flexibility in relation to hours and improve opportunities for part-time work.

The Government's thinking began to take shape. We would act on unfair dismissals. In an important area, though, I thought that we should go further than previously envisaged. Although no employee number had been specified in our election policy, the assumption was that the restrictions would be scrapped for firms employing fewer than 20 people — that having been the number specified in our previous failed attempts to get amendments through the Senate without it being appreciated that if this figure were a headcount, then many small businesses would miss out because of their large number of part-timers and casuals.

This was really driven home to me during a luncheon I attended on the Sunshine Coast, early in 2005. Most of those present were motel proprietors, restaurateurs or small property developers. They attacked the notion of the ceiling being 20. One after the other they pointed out that in their own businesses, which they all regarded as relatively small, they employed full-time, casual and part-time employees well in excess of 20. Most of them said that the Government changes, if limited to a firm of 20 employees, would be of no benefit to them.

That group had made a convincing point to me. Australia had far more casual employees and many more part-time workers in the growth sectors of the economy, particularly in the service sector. We needed to revise our thinking about what constituted a small business.

Personally, I had long believed in a national industrial relations system. More than ever, Australia was a single national economy. The flow of citizens between states increased continually, and the fewer discrepancies in such things as employment rules, educational opportunities and trade qualifications, the better. Sensing that change was in the air, state Labor governments and unions began mobilising against a national system, with threats of a High Court challenge. It's not that they objected so much to a national system, rather it was what they thought would be my national system.

In the past the Labor Party had been more vocal about the need for a national system than had the Coalition. An exception to this had been the Kennett Government in Victoria, which handed over its industrial relations powers to the Commonwealth. Speaking from opposition, the Liberal leader in New South Wales, John Brogden, said on 11 April 2005 that, if elected, the Coalition would refer its industrial relations powers to the Commonwealth. This was not a universal Coalition view. The leader of the Liberal Party in Western Australia, Matt Birney, came out against his state vacating the arena. Likewise there were dissenting sentiments coming from the National Party in Queensland and the Liberal Party in South Australia.

Speaking to the Menzies Research Centre, also on 11 April 2005, I argued for a national system in the following terms: 'In this area the goal is to free the individual, and not to trample on the states. We have no desire at all to take over functions that have been properly discharged by the states and the territories.' My argument was that in contrast to industrial relations at a federal level, where union power had been reduced, with individual freedoms enhanced, state industrial relations systems went in the opposite direction. To impose the federal order on the states was to free the individual and to extend the winding back of monopoly union power.

I agreed, at the request of Bob Hawke, to see Greg Combet, secretary of the ACTU, to discuss industrial relations changes. He and his ACTU colleague George Wright had an amicable discussion lasting more than an hour with me and Arthur Sinodinos in my Sydney office. The striking feature of the discussion was that Combet spent most of the time trying to persuade me to the view that if a majority of people in a particular enterprise voted in favour of a collective agreement then that collective agreement should be imposed on all workers at the enterprise, even those who had voted in favour of individual agreements. Neither of us shifted ground.

Combet argued that whilst employment conditions were robust at that time, if there were a downturn then people could be adversely affected by a freer system. There was no simple answer to this, as I pointed out. Having more rigid conditions in employment might well advantage people who retained their jobs, but those same rigidities could well, in turn, lead to more people losing their jobs in a downturn than would otherwise be the case. This highlighted the abiding conflict in industrial relations between the interests of the unemployed and those fortunate enough to have and retain jobs.

Cabinet agreed to act on unfair dismissals. Kevin Andrews argued against my proposed limit of 100. Others argued for a compromise between 100 and 20. In the end cabinet accepted my view that we should go the extra distance. Most went along with the concept of a national industrial relations system. Kevin Andrews successfully championed a new Fair Pay Commission to replace the wage-setting role of the Industrial Relations Commission. He wanted it modelled on a body with a similar name in the United Kingdom, with strict criteria guaranteeing a balanced outcome.

The most difficult and, as it turned out, most crucial area was that relating to minimum conditions. In the final result cabinet decided to abolish the old no-disadvantage test established in 1996 and replace it with what was called a new Australian Fair Pay and Conditions Standard. It was also decided to simplify the making of employment contracts.

This standard was to be based on minimum wages as set by the Australian Fair Pay Commission (and which were to be reflected in awards), and the guaranteed minimum conditions of employment as set out in legislation. Those conditions were to be for annual leave, personal leave, parental leave (including maternity leave) and a maximum number of ordinary working hours.

The important difference between the new Fair Pay and Conditions Standard and the old no-disadvantage test was that penalty rates and overtime loadings were no longer absolutely guaranteed as part of a person's pay package. In political terms, this proved to be a bad mistake.

Under the no-disadvantage test, a person's remuneration under an AWA could never be less than the aggregate value of what that person would have received under the relevant award. In calculating that aggregate value, regard had to be paid to that person's entitlement to penalty rates and overtime loadings under the relevant award. That particular stipulation was missing from the new Fair Pay and Conditions Standard. What the new standard guaranteed was the hourly rate, drawn from the relevant award, plus the minimum conditions relating to annual leave, parental leave and so on. It did not include penalty rates and overtime loadings.

The law when enacted stipulated that if the AWA was silent on the issues of penalty rates, leave loadings and the like, then the provisions of the relevant award regarding these entitlements would operate. This meant that an agreement could specifically exclude entitlements to penalty rates and leave loadings. It is my belief that fear and concern regarding the progressive exclusion of penalty rates and leave loadings did more political damage to the Government than any other issue flowing from WorkChoices.

The economic case for the change was compelling. It provided much greater flexibility. It was built on the default proviso that penalty rates and leave loadings would apply unless expressly excluded. Most importantly, however, it provided an opportunity for people not in the workforce to enter employment — albeit at lower rates, in some instances, than might otherwise be the case, but that lower rate would inevitably mean the difference between the person remaining on the dole or getting his or her first job opportunity. Once again we saw in operation that abiding conflict between the marginal employment opportunity for the unemployed and the guaranteed working conditions for the majority who are in work.

All evidence suggests that the new laws did accelerate the already downward path in Australia's unemployment rate. It fell just under 4 per cent in February 2008, the final proof of just how effective our industrial relations changes, particularly WorkChoices, had been in generating new jobs.

The phenomenon I have just described was particularly at work in the restaurant and hospitality industry. This industry is awash with part-time and casual employees. Much of the business is done in the evenings and at weekends. As a consequence, the greater flexibility available to employees regarding penalty rates and leave loadings meant a larger number of employment opportunities being available.

From an economic policy standpoint, the change was desirable. Our economy was inexorably moving in the direction of a 24-hour day, seven-days-a-week economy. The service sector was an increasing proportion of the aggregate economy. With the desire of the community for less rigidity in their daily life, casual and part-time work was also growing. Changed family lifestyles meant changed family shopping patterns.

People wanted the opportunity to shop virtually at any hour. They did not, however, like the idea of paying higher prices for the same goods and services purchased at certain hours of the day as opposed to others. Yet inevitably that would prove to be the case unless more freedom operated in relation to penalty rates and overtime loadings.

There was a further and generic argument in favour of the change. The reforms were being introduced when the economy was operating very vibrantly. The bargaining position of Australian workers had rarely been better. Real wages were continuing to grow, and employers frequently voiced their concerns about labour shortages. The first half of 2005 — and indeed the following two to three years — was an employees' labour market, the like of which I had not previously seen. If ever there had been a time to introduce more flexibility into the system, this was it.

Those were the arguments which finally persuaded the Government to make that crucial change. The political consequences were nonetheless quite real. In 1996 I had been able to give 'a rock solid guarantee' that no person would be worse off under a contract than would have been the case if he or she had remained under an award. 'You can't get less, but you can get more', had been the mantra then. I could not in all honesty give that same guarantee in 2005. I knew there would be cases of some people, at the margin, being employed without penalty rates or overtime; but in the overwhelming bulk of those cases, the person concerned would have gone from the dole queue to his or her first job. Manifestly that person would have been better off.

The Labor Party frequently asked me to give the 'rock solid' guarantee. My regular response was that 'my guarantee is my record'. I would then point to the impressive lift in real wages under my Government, declining levels of unemployment and generally buoyant economic conditions.

The Government did not seek to hide the change which had been made. When the legislation finally passed through the parliament late in 2005, the explanatory booklet included many cameos. One cameo, which I insisted be inserted in the booklet, spoke of 'Billy'. He had been on unemployment benefits since leaving school. He had got his first job, without penalty rates or overtime, in a retail store. He was much better off than he would have been if he had remained on the dole. Yet plainly he was not paid penalty rates or leave loadings. I don't think anybody could objectively argue that it would have been better for Billy to have remained on the dole than be employed without penalty rates and overtime loadings. Yet that inevitably would have been the consequence for some people if the change we launched in 2005 had not been made.

Our final position on the major changes represented a broad consensus within the cabinet. Kevin Andrews was uneasy about the 100 ceiling for unfair dismissals. He wanted it to be much lower. Tony Abbott expressed general concern about making too many changes. Peter Costello supported the changes but thought that the complexity of the award system was a real problem. We decided, late in the piece, to include a commitment to award simplification.

The time which elapsed between my statement to the parliament on 16 May and the legislation itself, in November 2005, was too long. We allowed time for a fear campaign to gather momentum. Until the final technical details of the legislation had been completed, it was impossible to refute each and every allegation, no matter how false such allegations might prove to be.

Yet through this period, the overwhelming view of the parliamentary party remained both positive and optimistic. In one way or another, we all believed in these reforms. They attuned with our philosophy. They would further wind back monopoly union power; they would further promote direct agreement-making between employers and employees; they would be warmly welcomed by small business; and they would contribute to a further reduction in unemployment.

The attitude of most colleagues was that these benefits in the long run would blunt any short-term unpopularity flowing from the changes or the impact of any fear campaign mounted by the unions. We all believed, myself included, that the continued buoyant state of the Australian economy further reducing unemployment and sustaining high real wages would be answer enough to the doomsayers of the ACTU and the Labor Party.

Both the unions and state Labor governments behaved as if the whole issue were a life-and-death battle for the future of the union movement. On 19 June, the ACTU launched its flagship ad — an emotional and effective one — depicting a mother being threatened with dismissal if she did not turn up at work at short notice, even though she had no one to care for her children. This would not have been allowed under our proposed changes; the circumstances depicted in the ad would have constituted an unlawful termination because it disregarded the mother's family responsibilities.

Even though the misrepresentation was pointed out immediately by Kevin Andrews, our problem was that the public knew that we were making big changes — we had said so. Therefore it was easy for the ACTU to persuade people that they would be hurt by the changes, even if there were no factual basis for most of the allegations being made.

As well as drawing criticism from the ACTU, the Labor Party and many academics, our proposed changes also drew flak from spokesmen for major Christian denominations. On 10 July the Anglican Primate joined other Church leaders, including Archbishop George Pell, in expressing concerns, especially the possibility of the minimum wage falling in real value. The new Fair Pay Commission did not cut minimum wages. The Anglican Archbishop of Sydney issued a statement arguing that changes in workplace relations must not be taken lightly, as they would affect families. He didn't specifically attack the proposals, but raised concerns. It all added to the sense in the community that our changes could be bad for families.

The Government received support from the IMF and, in a general fashion, from the governor of the Reserve Bank, Ian Macfarlane, who said that industrial relations reforms to date had allowed the economy to run faster without generating inflation. The Business Council would, later in the year, launch a television campaign lauding the benefits to the economy of a number of economic reforms and stressing the desirability of still more industrial relations reform.

Such support as the Government was able to garner was puny against the campaign of fear and misrepresentation launched by our opponents. Yet, despite this, most of our colleagues remained committed in their determination to see the reforms through. Their reasoning was that this was the first year in a three-year term. It was a big and necessary reform. In the past when large reforms had been introduced, such as the GST, the Government had gone through bad times politically, but as the fearmongering abated and the reality of the new laws proved different from what our critics predicted, the Government's standing improved.

The other unspoken reality was that if the Government had done very little by way of industrial relations changes it would, by the middle of 2005, have been beset with mounting criticism from economic commentators, the business community and certainly from within its own ranks that it lacked the bottle for further economic reform.

The reforms were good policy. After eight years in office, with control of the Senate, a thriving economy, falling unemployment and an apparently dispirited opposition, the Coalition would not have been easily forgiven if, in the face of all this, it had baulked at the changes for fear of the political consequences.

Media responses and those of serious political commentators were overwhelmingly favourable, endorsing the view that the Government would have failed the test of political will if it had not opted for significant reform. The respected commentator and author Paul Kelly said of the changes, 'This is the final saga in the 1980s project to remake Australia's economy.' Kelly said that in opposing the changes, Kim Beazley and the Labor Party were trapped on the wrong side of history. He went on: 'Howard's package is a declaration that Australia's egalitarianism does not depend upon wage regulation but should be achieved via the tax-transfer system ... It is the model Australia needs for the globalised age, and a model that Labor, at some stage, must embrace.'[4] The *Australian* editorialised in support of the measures, saying that in opposing them Kim Beazley was 'plain wrong'.[5] The newspaper said that the reforms had not gone far enough. The *Daily Telegraph* said, 'The Prime Minister's package is the basis for a new and productive era in the way the nation works.'[6]

From the Fairfax stable the *Financial Review* was full of praise, the *Sydney Morning Herald* mildly supportive, and the *Age*, normally more left-of-centre, raised a series of questions, rather than launching an all-out attack. The most critical paper of note was the *Courier-Mail*.

Both the Business Council of Australia (BCA) and the Australian Chamber of Commerce and Industry (ACCI) said the changes had not gone far enough, as did Des Moore, former deputy secretary of the Treasury and economic commentator. He said the package was 'a dud'. Naturally, the unions attacked the changes, as did Labor spokesmen.

In summary, independent responses were predominantly supportive, and, where critical, it was on the grounds that not enough change was in prospect. There would have been a caustic response to a less ambitious set of measures. As for falling behind in the polls, that had occurred before and we had recovered, especially when the Government held its nerve on something really important. This was all part of the collective political memory of the Coalition as we worked our way through 2005. Yet for six months, the poll news for the Coalition had been bracing. Most believed that our slump was due to the unpopularity of WorkChoices.

*　　*　　*

The membership of the Fair Pay Commission was finalised on 17 March 2006. Chaired by the respected Melbourne economist Professor Ian Harper, it was as balanced a group as could be practically put together. Kevin Andrews made several attempts to obtain the services of well-known union figures, with a number saying privately they would be happy to serve but because of pressure from the broader union movement they simply could not accept the Government's invitation. One of the members, Hugh Armstrong, had a strong union background. Judith Sloane, a free-market economist, provided what might be termed economic rigour from the right; Patrick McClure, the former chief executive of Mission Australia, would bring welfare compassion and plenty of commonsense. Mike O'Hagan, the owner of a successful furniture removal business, MiniMovers, would bring extensive small- to medium-sized business experience. It was a top-class team.

The first decision of the commission, on 26 October 2006, gave increases larger than expected and immediately blunted a likely union attack. So far from the minimum wage being cut, as some had feared, it had been lifted to a level that probably would not have been delivered by the Industrial Relations Commission, which had been replaced by the Fair Pay Commission as the arbiter of the wage.

Most of the bill's major provisions came into operation on 27 March 2006. The continued delay in the legislation actually taking effect, and thus the opportunity being available for a lot of the fearmongering to be disabused, did not help the Government. Delay with such complicated legislation was unavoidable. The Rudd Government's new workplace relations system was not fully operational until July 2010, two-and-a-half years after that government took office.

The most formidable challenge the Government faced in this war of attrition was the united front of the federal opposition, the ACTU, the state Labour Councils and by then eight state and territory Labor governments. State Labor governments were only too ready to run advertising campaigns, commission reports, establish committees of inquiry and generally weigh in heavily against the Government's changes.

As well, the states mounted a full High Court challenge against the validity of the legislation, which was heard in May 2006. The Victorian Labor Government, though, resisted pressure to reclaim the industrial relations authority ceded to the Commonwealth by Jeff Kennett.

With different strategies, state Labor governments legislated, purportedly, to protect state employees from the alleged evils of WorkChoices, in most cases only adding to protections already available. In the political drama at the time, they did, however, keep WorkChoices and its claimed negative effects before the public eye.

A real headache for the Government was Senate Estimates hearings. In May 2006 the Office of the Employment Advocate told a Senate Estimates hearing that of a sample of 4 per cent of all AWAs filed under WorkChoices, 16 per cent excluded all protected award conditions, and 22 per cent didn't provide for a pay rise over their term. As was so often the case with such answers, the media coverage did not tell the full story. For example, it did not address the issue of whether or not the protected award conditions (penalty rates, leave loadings, etc), when absent, were compensated for in the overall wage payment. The scale of the changes was such that there was an almost limitless availability of individual stories, appearing negative on the surface at least, to be told about the new laws.

Generic good news about falling unemployment, rising real wages and a continued boom in the Australian economy had become so commonplace and taken for granted that it could not match the coverage of individual cases involving people who claimed to have been hurt by the new laws.

Almost all of the attacks came from people who said the legislation had gone too far. Occasionally flak came from the opposite direction. In December 2005, Ray Evans, president of the H.R. Nicholls Society, a group formed in 1986 to campaign for a freer labour market, wrote an article for the *Australian*, attacking me for not having gone far enough.

In his column Evans said that so far from my Government turning Mr Justice Higgins 'on his head', the learned judge had turned me on my head. Evans said that we should legislate to cut the minimum wage in the name of reducing unemployment and that, as far as possible, we should throw industrial relations to the operation of the common law. He attacked the award system and the continuing role of the Industrial Relations Commission. His attitude was politically unrealistic, as no government could possibly embrace such a radical agenda.

Senator Nick Minchin, the Leader of the Government in the Senate, hurt the Government when, in March 2006, he apologised to an H.R. Nicholls Society dinner because the Government's WorkChoices laws had not gone further. He said, 'We do need to seek a mandate from the Australian people at the next election for another wave of industrial relations reform.' He said that these new reforms should target what Minchin called 'the whole edifice', including awards and the Industrial Relations Commission.[7]

Unbeknown to Minchin his speech had been recorded and was played, shortly afterwards, to the mass audience of the ABC Radio program *AM*. He had been naïve, had broken very directly with the principle of cabinet solidarity and, worst of all, had played into the hands of the Labor Party. It reinforced a Labor argument that the Coalition had secret plans to reduce protection for Australian workers.

The sudden rising against Beazley late in November 2006 was to change the Australian political landscape, and I analyse this elsewhere. Beazley's replacement, Kevin Rudd, maintained the lines of Beazley's attack on WorkChoices.

By the end of 2006 it was becoming increasingly apparent that unless the business community retaliated with a well-funded hard-hitting campaign in support of WorkChoices, then the public relations debate would be won by the union movement and the Labor Party. Government-funded publicity campaigns could explain new laws but not make the sharp political points so essential in rebutting the union onslaught.

Both the BCA and the ACCI did run valuable campaigns. They were hampered, however, by the reluctance of many companies to contribute financially. The challenge for the Coalition government and also supporters of WorkChoices in the general community was that the circumstances required an emotional rebuttal of union distortions, including an all-out assault on excessive union power, and a passionate espousal of policies designed to reduce unemployment. This meant lots of companies providing large amounts of money to fund a heavy advertising campaign.

Employers were usually reluctant to take this additional step. They argued they had to live with whichever government was in power. The weakness, on this occasion, of that argument was that at long last a government had legislated in a fashion which many of them had advocated for decades. What is more, the profit share was at a record level and there were fewer industrial disputes than at any time since before World War I. Yet when it came to the crunch, most of them were unwilling to chance their arm in support of that government. They wanted it both ways. The hard-hitting 2010 mining industry campaign against the Rudd Government's Super Profits Tax was just what the doctor would have ordered regarding WorkChoices.

At least the BCA and elements of the ACCI were prepared to sponsor a campaign. Many other employer groups and individual companies, despite benefiting enormously from the industrial relations reforms of more than a decade from the Coalition, refused to commit any resources and adopted pious neutrality towards a political debate which would define for many decades to come the shape of industrial relations in Australia.

The 2007 election would be historic for workplace relations in Australia. If the Coalition were returned, our changes would be cemented, never to be overturned by a future Labor Government. The less regulated system would be so entrenched that it would be too disruptive to upend it. By contrast, a Labor win would see these vital reforms rolled back. That has happened. Julia Gillard's changes have taken us back to the rigidities of the 1980s. For the first time in a generation, a major economic reform has been reversed. It will be a while before the consequences are felt, but in time they surely will be. The impact of that will be dire for our economy.

These were themes which I hammered repeatedly. There was furious private assent right across the business spectrum, but it was never matched with enough public passion. The one exception seemed to be Western Australia, where I found a deeper realisation of what was at stake than in any other part of the country.

In many respects the most disappointing of all of the employer groups was, surprisingly, the NFF. Long before other groups came out in support of industrial relations reform, the farmers' body had been advocating it. Farmers had been huge beneficiaries of waterfront reform and they, more than most, were people who needed a fair and more open industrial relations system. In 2003 the NFF had called for the abolition of the no-disadvantage test. In framing the 2005 legislation, the Government went through a lot of legal hoops to protect the position of the farmers who, not in the main being corporations, were not picked up by the national scheme.

Back in the 1980s, when Ian McLachlan led the farmers, a large fighting fund had been amassed. I, and many others, thought that this fund was available to support causes for the future wellbeing of farmers. In fact money had been raised at the very time when industrial relations disputes such as Mudginberri were in the public eye.

On several occasions in 2007, I directly approached David Crombie, the president of the NFF, asking that the fighting fund be used to support an industrial relations structure which had been so helpful to the farmers. Ian McLachlan remained a trustee of the fund, so I lobbied him as well.

The NFF did run some TV advertisements, consisting of comments to camera by its president. One of them praised workplace flexibility, urging a continuation of workplace reforms. It was bland and lacked any punch or emotion. The NFF had entered the lists but only just. Such an approach had no impact in a rhetorical battle which had reached fever pitch towards the end of 2007.

The verdict must be that the union movement demonstrated the courage of its convictions. Its members had been prepared to contribute vast amounts of money to fund a most effective campaign. The campaign was often dishonest, excessively emotional and, in the long run, because of its political success will have done damage to the Australian economy. That the business community was unwilling to match this campaign, not with dishonesty, but full-on advocacy of the benefits of our changes, implicates sections of that community in the ultimate responsibility that must be carried for the damage that the reversal of WorkChoices and other industrial relations changes of the Howard Government will finally represent for the Australian economy.

Despite reassuring legal advice about the ambit of the Corporations Power, I remained apprehensive about the outcome of the challenge of the Australian states to the High Court. David Bennett QC, the extremely able Commonwealth Solicitor General, had told me after completion of the case that he was confident that the validity of the legislation would be upheld — by a margin of 5 to 2 in favour of the legislation. His advice proved stunningly accurate. This was a load off my mind. It was not going to stop the unions or the Labor Party campaigning against the legislation. However, if the High Court had gone in the opposite direction, that would have delivered a mortal blow to the Government's authority on such a contentious piece of legislation.

Despite its resources, the Government was fighting a lone political battle, with even the popular culture being conscripted to the union/ALP cause. The Nine Network program *McLeod's Daughters* featured a scene where a WorkChoices AWA was offered, reducing pay, resulting in the character quitting his employment.

So in August I appointed Joe Hockey as minister assisting Kevin Andrews on industrial relations, because I believed he needed assistance in a defining political battle. Andrews had an excellent grasp of the details of the legislation, and had done a first-class job in steering it through parliament, but different styles of media presentation were needed in response to the all-out assault from the other side.

The anecdotal evidence, particularly from MPs in marginal seats, suggested no great public resentment against WorkChoices. I regularly telephoned our marginal seatholders asking about their experiences with the legislation. To a man and a woman virtually, they said that few people raised particular cases with their offices, and the general advice I continued to receive was that because the legislation was good policy, and was contributing to an accelerating decline in unemployment, we should stick it out and that eventually public opinion would come around.

Nonetheless, specific public polling on WorkChoices continued to be bad. For example, on 26 March 2007 an A.C. Nielsen opinion poll said that 59 per cent of voters nationally, including 25 per cent of Coalition voters, opposed the WorkChoices changes. As evidence of the carpet-bombing character of the anti-WorkChoices campaign, the Victorian Government, on 27 March 2007, released a negative report on the effects of WorkChoices. Two days later Senator Fielding, of Family First, introduced a Private Member's Bill aimed at restoring certain conditions allegedly removed by WorkChoices.

From the time he took over as Labor leader in December 2006, Kevin Rudd took his party to a big lead in the polls. That lead never faltered from then until the election just on 12 months later. It is now obvious in retrospect that Rudd coming to the leadership brought about a sea change in political attitudes across the nation.

Elsewhere I will deal with the Coalition's declining political fortunes during its last year in office.

Rudd and Gillard set about emphasising the differences between Labor and the Coalition on industrial relations, although their pitch was not all that different from what Kim Beazley's had been. Yet they seemed to have more impact. Perhaps because Beazley lacked overall acceptance, the electorate had not taken his commitments seriously.

Our internal qualitative research was mixed. Some of it showed a generalised fear, not based on actual experience, but rather on what 'other people have told us'. Other research data suggested that some concerns were subsiding and that the public could see the benefit of a number of the WorkChoices changes, particularly in the area of unfair dismissals.

I spent Easter 2007 at the Lodge with most of my family, and during the break, carefully digested three separate sets of research material. The first lot was from our regular pollsters, Crosby/Textor. To provide further views, two other polling firms with which the Liberal Party had done business over the years were asked to contribute.

The message from this material was that although WorkChoices was not exercising the minds of voters on a daily basis, there was an underlying fear that the changes made could work against the position of average wage- and salary-earners. The depressing reality from this and all other research was that the contribution made by industrial relations changes to lower unemployment meant nothing to the voting public. The individual citizen was interested in unemployment only to the extent that it affected him or her or their family. If unemployment was not rising, and that was certainly the case in 2007, then it was not seen as any kind of threat to the bulk of the Australian workforce. Therefore the human benefit of WorkChoices — still lower unemployment — was of no political value at all to the Coalition.

As Easter ended I knew that the Government had to do something to soften the perceptions of WorkChoices. I didn't like this. I knew that it was good policy and, objectively assessed, it was not unfair to the Australian workforce. The cumulative impact of our industrial relations changes over more than a decade had proved highly beneficial to individual workers, as well as the Australian economy as a whole.

What was needed was the restoration of something akin to the old no-disadvantage test. Cabinet met in Brisbane on 24 April 2007, and there was overwhelming support for a change in policy. There was near unanimity in the view that the deepest area of public concern was the possible loss of penalty rates and overtime loadings. Employees regarded these payments as an integral part of the weekly pay package. With a booming economy, there were plenty of opportunities to work overtime or at weekends. The extra money received for this work was not seen as some kind of one-off bonus but rather the properly expected reward for a good worker in benign economic conditions. People had borrowed money on the strength of the aggregate wage package including penalty rates and overtime loadings. Any suggestion that they might be at risk was seen as a direct threat to a worker's standard of living.

We decided to fight back by introducing a fairness test. For any future AWA with a remuneration of $75,000 a year or less which modified or removed any of the so-called protected award conditions (eg, penalty rates and overtime loadings), the total salary under the agreement should at least equal what the remuneration would have been if those protected award conditions had not been removed. We had decided to restore the old no-disadvantage test, under a different name.

I strove hard to give this new announcement every amount of political exposure. Working from my office in Melbourne, on the night of 3 May I telephoned more than a dozen senior journalists and commentators around Australia, briefing them for their papers the following day with the details of the changes.

In doing this I hoped to put the changes in context. I wanted them to be seen as a response to people's concerns, yet not a wholesale retreat from industrial relations changes. I had also telephoned the leaders of key industry organisations. Some were disappointed with the change, yet others were quite supportive. All of them understood the political challenge the Government faced. Peter Costello and I had agreed that it would be a good idea for the changes to be out and at least initially understood before the budget was brought down just on a week later.

Press coverage of the changes was comprehensive and fair. But, as time went by, it became clear that the changes had had little effect on public opinion. Despite the positive reaction to the budget, the Government continued to languish badly in the opinion polls.

The changes involved in the Fairness Test allowed the Government to run an extensive information campaign about the legislation. Although there were many hard-hitting things that could be said in a government-funded campaign, such a campaign could not include the direct political material so essential at that stage of the electoral cycle. This is where the absence of a really well-funded business campaign was keenly felt.

Sections of the media remained obsessed with WorkChoices. As late as the last week of the campaign, Channel Seven ran a story about the options which had been presented to the Government two years earlier about possible changes to the Workplace Relations Act.

One of the options was obviously to have gone further than we ultimately did with WorkChoices. The fact that we had specifically rejected this more radical path and, in any event, through the Fairness Test, had overturned one of the biggest changes in WorkChoices, was utterly irrelevant to the author of the Channel Seven story. What was presented to the Australian people in that news report was that the Government had considered even more draconian changes to workplace relations law. The subliminal message was that, if re-elected, the Coalition might just revive that more drastic option. The ACTU could not have written a better script.

We were never able to get clear air on WorkChoices. The attacks came from every direction. No matter how good the economic news was, and it continued to be so, individual hard-luck stories or allegations of unfairness always attracted far more media coverage. They were easy stories. Good economic news had become pathetically boring and uninteresting. To use that old cliché, we had become victims of our own success in managing the Australian economy.

Elsewhere in the book I have written of both the polling evidence and the field evidence I accumulated throughout my political life of the attitudes of the voting public. I obtained my field evidence on WorkChoices on 9 October 2007 when I visited the Williamstown Dockyard near Melbourne for the signing ceremony for the first of the RAN's amphibious ships, to be built by Tennix.

There were more than 1000 people present, most of whom would have worked on the construction of the ship. They gave a friendly response to my short speech and to me personally as I moved through the crowd after my speech. I then came head to head with field evidence 2007.

An amiable man in blue overalls and in his middle 30s engaged me in quite friendly discussion about his work. He then said, 'John, what about this WorkChoices business?' He said that he had voted for me at the previous election. I asked him whether he had been affected by the new industrial relations changes. He said that his position was perfectly okay and his pay and conditions were not in any way under question. 'But I hear around the place that other people might be affected. Are you sure it is all going to be okay?' he said. I gave him that assurance, pointing out that changes which made the economy run better helped everyone.

I left that conversation feeling quite uneasy. I reckon that man voted Labor on 24 November, not because he was angry with me. In fact he displayed genuine warmth and friendliness, but the cumulative effect of the union/Labor Party campaign had instilled in him the belief that his working conditions might, in the future, be threatened by WorkChoices. He epitomised the sort of problem we encountered from the time we introduced our changes. Those changes were good policy. They helped many unemployed people into work; they were beneficial for the economy overall, but there was a severe political downside. The contribution of that downside to our election defeat is something that I will analyse in more detail later in the book.

43

SHOPPING CENTRES, BOARDROOMS AND DRESSING ROOMS

So much of this story of mine has been a narrative of my actions as a politician, within the political institutions of Australia or the rest of the world. Cabinet meetings, parliamentary question time, Liberal Party gatherings of all different kinds, bilateral meetings with other leaders, Commonwealth and UN meetings and APEC councils — the list is endless. They have in common that they are political gatherings, of political decision-makers of various kinds. Participation in them is the meat and vegetables of a senior politician's life, particularly that of a PM.

Being an effective PM of Australia compels scrupulous attendance and informed involvement at, and in, such gatherings. Much of what I have written in this book is the story of what went on, or was decided, at these myriad meetings. After all, they shaped the economic and diplomatic direction of our country for more than a decade.

There were other meetings, though, and far more numerous ones, which often only involved one politician — and that was me — when I came face to face with a cross-section of the people of Australia, to whom I was accountable and whose best interests I was sworn to advance. These encounters took place in an endless variety of places. Many were organised encounters, some gatherings were small, others large. Necessarily, some were one on one.

Many were random. Most were polite and friendly, even when the political message I was delivering was deeply unpopular. Some were heart-wrenching.

When I left politics, I received thousands of letters and other messages. I replied to them all. In those responses I said that of all the experiences I had had, none would be more memorable than the wonderfully open and positive spirit I encountered amongst Australians from all walks of life. More than anything else, that experience sustained and refreshed me through the challenges, reversals and pressure of my years in the Lodge. I never tired of meeting other Australians. I never will.

These other meetings, shared experiences or chance encounters, I hope gave me the wisdom to take the right decisions at all of those political meetings, which I, along with other elected representatives of the public, attended.

Being successful requires a politician always to 'be in touch'. Part of keeping in touch is closely following what is said in the media. I don't believe those politicians who say they don't read the papers. It is impossible to do your job properly without knowing what the press is saying. It is arrogant beyond belief to completely ignore what is being said in the media. It is always a question of balance. Never be deterred by the media from a course you are convinced is right, but don't be so conceited as to think the attitude of the media is irrelevant. It isn't. As PM I would frequently say that there were three institutions which truly guarded freedom in Australia: our competitive parliamentary system, an incorruptible judiciary, and a free, robust press. I will pit them any time against a Bill of Rights, which would reduce the power of citizens to control their own lives by handing political decision-making authority to judges.

I used talkback radio more than any other PM because it was the most effective way of getting across an unfiltered message.

An hour can be spent doing a Canberra press conference, yet what appears on the TV that night, on the radio or in the newspapers is entirely at the discretion of journalists or news editors and might bear little or no relation to the central purpose of the news conference. At the very least the talkback radio audience hears your message directly, and many of those audiences are very large. I still did the press conferences; it's just that I did the talkback as well as a form of communications insurance.

Working journalists as a class have progressive, centre-left political views. This applies especially to those in the federal parliamentary press gallery, who report exclusively on national politics. Many of them have signed up to the climate-alarm agenda; they were overwhelmingly republican 10 years ago — so much so that their bias hurt the cause they supported. They strongly supported the giving of an apology to Aboriginal Australians, and thought that I was too hard on asylum-seekers. A lot of them thought my social values were too conservative.

The bulk of them, however, generally support economically rational responses. A prime example of this was the willingness of most journalists to give the Government a fair hearing on the GST, despite Labor's spoiling tactics.

Many talkback radio hosts — Alan Jones, Neil Mitchell, Ray Hadley and previously John Laws — don't fit any stereotype. Often contrarian, they can take a more conservative stance, and to much effect. Jones had a big impact on the republican debate in Sydney. He had an even bigger impact on the global warming debate late in 2009, especially on attitudes amongst Liberal supporters. Too many Canberra journalists take a patronising attitude towards talkback radio presenters. My experience has been that both their intelligence and detailed knowledge of individual subjects match that of their colleagues in the national capital. Pity help any MP who agrees to be interviewed by Alan Jones on a subject that interests Jones if he or she has not done their homework.

The Australian public has a great capacity to filter out some of the bias when it is displayed by journalists. It happened with the republican issue. It is happening with the global warming debate.

The net of all this is that the media is a critical part of the equation for a senior political figure, particularly a PM. He must deal with them, and on a civil basis. That doesn't mean that he won't have favourites, but he shouldn't ignore the adversaries either. The politics of Kerry O'Brien, presenter of the ABC's *7.30 Report*, were a mile away from mine. Yet I appeared regularly on his program, because it was a serious current affairs presentation; he had usually done his homework, and the show was widely watched by other politicians and journalists.

Other PMs and senior ministers have had fixed groups of businessmen from which they have drawn economic and business advice. This approach has often worked, but it was not one that I tried. I wanted to avoid going to the same people all of the time, preferring to consult as widely as possible. Given the importance of small business to the Coalition, a wide network was essential.

*　　*　　*

The ubiquitous boardroom lunch was an indispensable part of the keeping-in-touch process. The economic success of Australia in the past 15 to 20 years owes so much to the energy and skill of our men and women of business. They have been an integral part of our success story. They have proved adaptable and innovative. They have been praiseworthy wealth creators, and without them the Australian economic story would have been utterly different.

I have watched some businessmen transition from apostles of industries demanding high protection to effective players in the new export culture which developed following the dismantling of protection. I think here of John Uhrig. When I first encountered him, he ran Simpson Pope, a white goods manufacturer. This was in an industry which historically had argued for continued tariff protection. Uhrig was a supporter of lowering tariffs and opening up our economy. He demonstrated his versatility through his effective chairmanship of both Conzinc Riotinto Australia (CRA), now Rio Tinto, and Westpac. Some, such as Hugh Morgan, joined the intellectual debate, arguing over long periods of time for reform and restructuring of the economy. Running a successful company by day and arguing for change and innovation by night can be a powerful combination.

As a cohort, business leaders were usually advocates of the reform agenda my Government wanted to pursue. This was certainly so in relation to taxation reform. At critical stages of the IR debate, we could have done with a few more bodies on the line; a few more like Chris Corrigan would have been of much assistance in the workplace relations debate during our last year in office.

I never met a more astute businessman than Kerry Packer. His intuition was legendary and he had the common touch. It was a rare achievement for the richest man in Australia also to speak for a sizeable chunk of the population. He did this when he told a Senate inquiry in 1991 that the public was not so impressed with the job the Government was doing with their taxes that people were queuing up to donate extra.

No one has gone near him in understanding the mood and tastes of Australian television audiences. Packer's impact on sport, especially cricket, has been immense. Once again he displayed a rare instinct in detecting what the sporting public would warm to.

Frank Lowy and Arvi Parbo personified a distinct part of the Australian achievement. They came to Australia from war-ravaged Europe after 1945, embraced this country with a passion and went on to make a lasting contribution to Australia. Some of Frank's family died in the Holocaust.

He went first to Palestine, where he fought in the Israeli Army against the Arabs in the 1948 War of Independence, then settled in Australia and, with the late John Saunders, built the Westfield shopping centre empire. Not only is it vast, but now it is the largest shopping mall chain in the USA.

Over the years that we have been friends I have always valued Frank's advice and opinions. As was Kerry Packer, he is always worth listening to. Frank Lowy has also pursued a sporting passion; in his case, soccer. At the age of 79 he is leading the push for Australia to host the 2022 World Cup.

Arvi Parbo is a splendid example of the migrant-boy-makes-good story. Born in Estonia in 1926, Parbo went to Germany for a time after the war and then came to Australia, speaking virtually no English. A mining engineer by training, he helped build Western Mining into one of the pre-eminent mining houses of our country. The expansion of that company, involving major discoveries as well as astute investments, was a metaphor for the growth of the mining industry, now so important to our economy, in the 1970s and '80s. In 1989 Sir Arvi Parbo became chairman of BHP, then 'the Big Australian'.

As well as his business interests, Arvi Parbo maintained a lively interest in public affairs, never forgetting the brutal treatment of his native Estonia by the Soviets. He treasured the freedom Australia had given him and took opportunities to tell his fellow citizens not to take it for granted.

John Ralph, former boss of CRA, former chairman of the Commonwealth Bank, once deputy chairman of Telstra and president of the BCA, was as regular a business advisor as any that I had in my political life. He was a shining example of how success in business and ethics are not mutually exclusive. John Ralph was tough and uncompromising in his business judgements, but always straight.

He was a relentless proponent of industrial relations reforms. He put his beliefs to work within CRA, with considerable success. In 1992 he spent some hours in my Sydney office, when I was opposition spokesman on Industrial Relations, accompanied by the boss of his company's New Zealand subsidiary, explaining the enterprise-based reforms which the company had achieved in that country. John Ralph worked tirelessly to pull together a business coalition in support of tax reform in 1997–98.

Australians' love of sport is widely perceived and properly based. It is part of our national cement. No horse race in the world stops a nation the way the Melbourne Cup does. The AFL Grand Final, or what many describe as simply 'the last Saturday in September', grips the southern states of Australia with fervour. Cricket retains pride of place as our national game, with the Boxing Day Test, traditionally held in Melbourne, having a special place in our sporting calendar.

Melburnians must be the most conscientious sports fans in the world. For many years Melbourne held the record for a crowd attending a cricket Test match, although that has probably been surpassed by attendance at Eden Gardens in Kolkata, India. It also does for a rugby union match in Australia, despite the city being the home of Australian Rules football. Our grounds are as good as, or usually better than, others in the world, not only for size but also facilities and spectator comfort.

Many foreigners are baffled that a nation of just 21 million people boasts four football codes. Only in the past 25 years has football become more national in character, predominantly through Australian Rules securing a foothold in Sydney and Brisbane. I'm not sure that the two rugby codes have been as successful in their reciprocal penetration of the southern states.

Although it is not national, Australian Rules, like cricket, spans every demographic where it is played and followed. Historically the other three codes suffered from sectional tags. League was the working-class game, union was heavily identified with private schools, and soccer was seen as the ethnic game. In different ways those three codes have thrown off this typecasting.

Having a natural interest in sport, I did not have any trouble in embracing that part of the job. Australians expect their prime minister to take an interest in sport and to identify with our national teams and champions. Janette and I hurled ourselves into barracking for Australia and Australians at the Sydney Olympics. We attended every event we could get to. Instead of the public seeing this as an indulgence, it was precisely what they had wanted. This was a big moment for our nation, and my job was to cheer for Australia. For many smaller sports, almost totally reliant on volunteers and with no source of funds other than competing for a share of government allocations, Olympic and Commonwealth games provide a place in the sun. Their hardworking supporters appreciate the recognition.

There are, however, traps for players, old and young. Australian sports fans know their favourite games backwards. They pride themselves on it. As a result they can spot a phoney a mile off, particularly if that person happens to be a PM or other public figure. From the start I resolved to avoid this trap by recognising, and asking my staff to recognise, that whilst I was well versed in a number of sports, particularly those which I had played, there were some that I was a lot less familiar with, and I should not pretend otherwise.

Australian Rules was the big challenge, if I could put it that way. It was the one code of football I had not played as a young person. I broadly understood the rules, but having grown up in Sydney at a time when there was no Rules to speak of there, and the divide between the codes was quite sharp, I was still unfamiliar with the game.

Several of my colleagues said that the way to fix this was to adopt a Melbourne club. More than one suggested Carlton; Menzies and Fraser had both been Carlton men. I decided not to do this, as I sensed it would seem artificial.

Instead I would attend games and events as appropriate, acknowledge my absence of background in the game, but pay proper respect to its place in the sporting psyche of our country. Followers of the code knew my background and would not have been taken in by what were essentially gimmicks, designed to ingratiate. There was no shortage of people willing to further educate me about the game whenever I was attending an event, a regular AFL game, or a Grand Final. Two wonderful people and former accomplished players, John Kennedy and the late Ron Evans, were the successive presidents of the AFL for almost the whole of the time that I served as PM. Over the years they added enormously to my knowledge and, therefore, my enjoyment of Australian Rules.

The North Melbourne Grand Final Breakfast, always held on the morning of the Grand Final, is the most amazing event of its kind in Australia. The top table represents a cross-section of our nation and is testament to the reach of the game to every part of the community in those parts of Australia where it is widely played. It is always addressed by the PM and the Leader of the Opposition. I attended every one of those breakfasts during the 16 years that I held those two positions, with the exception of 2003, when it was the day of my daughter's wedding in Sydney.

Poor Tony O'Leary, the head of my press office and a South Australian, was an avid Rules follower. For some years after I became PM, he would prepare detailed notes for my Grand Final Breakfast speech, replete with references to past Grand Finals, no doubt familiar to keen followers of the code. I never used this material. I just didn't feel comfortable doing so as I had no personal recall of, or familiarity with, the events I would be talking about. I always kept these speeches short, opting to speak about how important sport was in the life of Australians. I apologised to Tony for not referring to his work, and after a while he gave up.

My passion for cricket was well known to Australians long before I became PM. It was Mark Taylor who christened me a 'cricket tragic', and the expression really caught on. It was during a speech of his at a *Daily Telegraph* lunch, which I attended to mark his remarkable innings of 334 not out at Peshawar in Pakistan in October 1998. I had rung Mark the morning after his innings to congratulate him, and it was then that he told me he would retire so as to share with Sir Donald Bradman the honour of the highest Test score by an Australian. Matthew Hayden would surpass them both when he scored 380 against Zimbabwe in Perth in 2003.

If there is such a thing, the senior sporting post in Australia is captain of the Australian cricket team. It is our one truly national game. I formed a close link with the three men who held the captaincy during my time in the Lodge: Mark Taylor, Steve Waugh and Ricky Ponting. I had also got to know Allan Border well from my earlier contacts with the team. He had a tough row to hoe, as he led the team through a period when other cricketing nations were strong, and our team was not always at or near the top.

I occasionally joked about how being captain of the cricket team was the most or equal most important job in the nation. It was a mark of my respect for the game as well as a piece of self-deprecation. Australians don't like their PM taking himself too seriously. Most saw my remark for what it was, although the odd utterly humourless journalist took me to task for saying what I had.

Each of these four Australian captains brought different qualities to the leadership. Two of them, Taylor and Waugh, had to endure periods when critics said their form with the bat was not good enough any more. Both answered the critics: Taylor with his memorable innings of 334, and Waugh with his superb 102 at the Sydney Cricket Ground against England in January 2003. That innings was one of the highlights of my watching cricket in recent years. His autobiography was as good a sporting book as I have read, and I was delighted to launch it for him.

Ponting's form over such a sustained period means that the question should be asked: since Bradman has there been a better Australian batsman? Certainly none of the others played the hook shot as well as he does. He feels keenly the two Ashes losses under his captaincy, and I can understand his desire to lead the team once more to England. I hope that it happens.

I still believe very much in role models in sport. In cricket it would be hard to go beyond Adam Gilchrist. He was an unbelievable player, always entertaining and seeming to have all the time in the world to play his shots. On top of that his willingness to walk when he knew that he was out was a breath of fresh air. We are ferociously competitive as a sporting country and should remain so, but we can keep the sportsmanship as well. The most eloquent advocates for this are champions like 'Gillie' who walk.

Both codes of rugby attract me. Rugby league is built around the NRL club competition and the titanic State of Origin clashes. I have followed the St George-Illawarra Dragons for years. I have been in many dressing rooms over the years, celebrating and commiserating. The most devastated dressing room I have been in, without question, was that of the Dragons after their 1999 Grand Final loss to the Storm. St George had led 14–0 at half-time, but it all went to custard after that, and Melbourne just got home at the last minute. Not a word was spoken. The players, coach and club leaders were numb. This was gloomier than a Queensland dressing room after losing a State of Origin to New South Wales, and that sets a high benchmark in post-match despair, and gloomier than the Wallabies' room after the World Cup loss to England in 2003.

When I was young, the really big clashes in rugby league, apart from club Grand Finals, were the Tests between Great Britain and Australia. They were fairly evenly matched then and they were muscular encounters, to say the least. The gap has widened since, and Australia has been regularly dominant in what passes for an international contest in rugby league. State of Origin games have become the big representative fixtures on the league calendar.

I never took sides in these matches. State rivalries leave me cold. Besides that, I have a dirty little secret when it comes to NRL clubs. I am a passionate Dragons supporter, but my default choice if the Dragons are out is the Broncos. I was delighted when the Broncos beat the Storm in 2006, having never quite got over 1999. I arrived in the Broncos' dressing room just ahead of the victorious 13. Shane Webcke, who had played his last game that night, arrived first. I greeted him by saying, 'What a way to retire from the game.' He replied, 'Just like five straight election wins.' The Grand Final was played only weeks after I had announced that I would lead the Coalition at the 2007 election. I liked his spirit.

The Wallabies played in three World Cup competitions in my time as PM. I followed their fortunes intently, and developed a close bond with many members of the team as well as those running the game. After the

1999 World Cup win I held a reception for the team in Parliament House, and then invited the team plus wives and girlfriends to the Lodge for a very memorable dinner. Rugby union had reached a pinnacle in Australia at that time. At that dinner we had not only the team plus others but also the William Webb Ellis Trophy (the World Cup), the Bledisloe Cup (Australia and New Zealand) and the Cook Cup (Australia and England). The cups were all drunk from. Things could not be any better for Australian rugby.

The members of that victorious 1999 team were an impressive bunch. They were champions, had lots of fun and represented their country with considerable dignity. John Eales, the captain, was another fine sporting role model. He played the game hard and to great effect; many rate him the best-ever Wallaby. To use that old, but relevant, cliché, they were all good ambassadors of the game.

In the same vein, Pat Rafter had been an exemplar of sportsmanship and generosity of spirit in tennis. George Gregan, who succeeded Eales as captain of the Wallabies, also brought credit to Australian rugby. He led Australia in defence of the World Cup when Australia hosted the competition in 2003. As the games in 2003 progressed, many gave Australia little chance of making the final, let alone retaining the trophy, won in 1999. I went to London in the middle of the competition for the dedication of the Australian War Memorial at Hyde Park Corner on Remembrance Day. Tony Blair, whose football passions were much tied up with soccer, asked me how I thought the World Cup would end up. I replied, 'Tony, the way things are going at present, I regret to inform you that the final is likely to be between France and New Zealand.' It was a fair comment on form at that stage, but I could not have been more wrong.

The following weekend I saw Australia defeat New Zealand in one of our best-ever performances in rugby, and the next night I watched England defeat France on a soggy ground. So Tony Blair was entitled to write me off as a rugby sage. The final saw Jonny Wilkinson break Australian hearts with a deft field goal in extra time. The Australian dressing room afterwards was disappointed but not devastated. Our team had not expected to reach the final. Their PM was pretty devastated, and apparently it showed when I presented the trophy to Martin Johnson, the English captain.

A few weeks later I chatted informally to the Queen just before the start of the Abuja Commonwealth Summit in Nigeria. She complimented me on how well Australia had hosted the World Cup, and remarked that I had not looked happy when I presented Johnson with the Webb Ellis trophy.

I simply replied, 'Ma'am, I was not.' I may support the monarchy and respect Australia's British heritage, but it really hurt to hand over that wonderful cup to an English captain.

I tried hard to support all Australian national sporting teams and was assisted in this by Janette. She was a keen soccer follower and we got to as many representative games as possible in that code. We had much pleasure in hosting the Socceroos to a reception at Kirribilli House following their impressive showing in the 2006 World Cup. She was also a conscientious patron of the Australian women's hockey team. She developed a real friendship with them. After she ceased being patron, she still kept in touch and received a warm and well-deserved reception from them after we watched them defeat Holland at the Beijing Olympics in 2008.

The mind can play tricks when one encounters the children of former sporting greats, now deceased, who bear a striking physical resemblance to their famous parents. This happened to me when I agreed to inaugurate the Racing Hall of Fame in Melbourne some years ago. I was not a regular racegoer, but as a boy I had listened to the ABC Radio coverage of races, and was familiar with the famous jockeys of that era: Billy Cook, Neville Selwood and, of course, Darby Munro. Munro, long since dead, was one of the inaugural inductees in the Hall of Fame. I had seen many photos of him and knew what he looked like. The inductees, or those accepting in their place, were asked to walk down a long carpet towards me and the head of racing in Australia to accept their awards. Darby Munro's son was there to accept the award in honour of his father. The physical resemblance was extraordinary. As he walked towards me, I said to myself, 'Darby Munro's dead, isn't he?' It was quite an uncanny experience.

It's something of a tradition for some Australians to boo a PM when he walks onto the field to present a trophy or the like. The extent of it can be a wider sign. I had copped it from a section of the crowd at several NRL Grand Finals in the late 1990s. At the 2001 Grand Final, on the eve of the election, I was struck by the absence of hostility. It proved to be a good omen.

Throughout my political career and especially in the time that I held a leadership role, I sought constant personal contact with voters, beyond what was involved in meeting constituents to discuss their concerns or attending functions to which I had been invited. I liked doing street walks and, being very well known, walking through a shopping centre was no chore. People recognised me and most wanted, at least, to say hello. Many proffered a view, others asked questions, and many simply wished me well. Others of course made it plain they did not support me. Only a few abused me.

These experiences were something of a barometer of what the public was thinking. I never felt that the Liberal Party should dump its pollster and rely on my gut feeling from street walks, but I always paid regard to what I called field evidence. I have referred to it elsewhere. It was instructive in the 2007 election. I walked through Tuggerah shopping centre on the Central Coast of New South Wales, three days out from the election, accompanied by Jim Lloyd and Ken Ticehurst, the two Liberal MPs for the adjoining seats of Robertson and Dobell. It was hard going. People weren't hostile, just uninterested. I gained the impression that some of them had simply moved on from me and my Government. Both seats swung to the ALP.

By contrast, two days earlier I had walked through Cannington shopping centre in Perth. It was in the electorate of Swan. The reception was really enthusiastic and warm. People wanted to talk, were definite about their opinions, and sufficient were enthusiastic about the Liberals to really buoy me. Steve Irons, the Liberal Party candidate, won Swan from Labor at the election. As has been the case on earlier occasions, Western Australia voted quite differently from the rest of Australia on 24 November 2007.

Certain personal encounters were reminders of the immense sadness experienced by some in life. Late in 2005, whilst visiting Pakistan, I went to a mountainous area of Kashmir to see an Australian Army medical team helping the victims of the terrible earthquake which had hit the region. I was introduced to local people who were either being treated at their improvised hospital or were helping to treat the injured. One of the latter was a woman doctor from a village some distance up the mountainside. She had lost her husband and two children in the earthquake, yet had volunteered her services to help care for survivors. Her strength and compassion were remarkable.

I doubt that I had a more heartbreaking meeting in my whole time as PM than the one I had at my electorate office in Gladesville on 15 November 2005 with the mother of Nguyen Tuong Van, a Vietnamese-Australian who was awaiting execution in Singapore for drug offences. I had already raised the issue directly with Lee Hsien Leung, my Singaporean counterpart, after a formal appeal for clemency to the President of Singapore had failed. I knew that this poor lady's son would die very soon on the gallows. The Singaporeans are extremely tough on these issues, and notwithstanding my good personal relations with Lee, he was not going to relent. In an earlier discussion, at the CHOGM in Valetta, Malta, he had explained the rationale of his country's policy on drug offences. He firmly believed that the hard line taken both against Singapore's own citizens and foreigners had worked.

If every young Australian — and most of them are young — foolishly contemplating being a drug courier from an Asian country could have been in my Gladesville office that November day, and witnessed the unrelieved anguish of that heartbroken mother, they might think twice before doing something which could land their own mother in a similar predicament. Mrs Kim Van Nguyen and her children had been refugees accepted by Australia in the 1970s. Her other son had been in trouble with drugs as well. It was said that the son held in Singapore had agreed to carry drugs to earn money to pay off his brother's debts.

It was difficult to imagine a sadder situation for a mother. I didn't pretend that I could save her son. I couldn't. For close to an hour I offered her what comfort that I could by listening to what she had to say, assuring her that I would continue to pursue the issue with the Singaporean Government, but not in any way holding out hope that I could be successful. I embraced her when she left as I had on her arrival, and at various times when she broke down during our discussion. I was her PM and she was begging me for help, which I was powerless to provide. All I could do was show compassion and concern as a human being and a father for her tragic situation. I hope that I was equal to the task.

Her son was hanged in Changi Gaol, Singapore, on the morning of 2 December 2005.

44

THE LEADERSHIP

If certain events had been handled differently, Peter Costello, following my retirement, would have become Leader of the Liberal Party and, as a consequence, Prime Minister towards the end of 2006. He would have done the job well; whether or not he would have won in 2007, we will never know. The focus of this chapter is the leadership issue and why a transition late in 2006 did not take place. All I can do is to tell the story from my perspective; readers will make their own judgements.

It is central to a proper understanding of the leadership dynamic within the Liberal Party to recognise that the Government was not regularly plagued by leadership debate. For most of the time that we held office, the issue simply did not arise.

When leadership tensions did arise, neither Peter Costello nor I allowed them to affect our strong professional partnership. At no stage did leadership issues disrupt the proper functioning of the Government.

Following the lead of our respective chiefs of staff, Arthur Sinodinos (and later Tony Nutt) and Phil Gaetjens, our staff worked together for the good of the Government. Personal relations between them remained positive; so much so that David Gazard, a senior media advisor of mine in my early years as Prime Minister, later became a senior advisor to Peter Costello. He stayed with the former Treasurer until the 2007 election.

Likewise, Nigel Bailey, once a key economic advisor on Costello's staff, became my chief economic advisor in 2006. Niki Savva, a senior advisor to the Treasurer for a number of years, joined the Cabinet Policy Unit in 2007, thus working very closely with my office.

*   *   *

I was not removed as Liberal leader in favour of Peter Costello because the great majority of Liberal senators and MPs never wanted that to happen. Politics is relentlessly driven by the laws of arithmetic. If a political party thinks that its electoral arithmetic will be boosted by a leadership change, it will make that change, irrespective of the circumstances. In 1991 the ALP removed Bob Hawke, its most successful leader, because it thought it would have a better chance of winning the next election with another leader, Paul Keating. Sentiment and gratitude for past favours played no part in it, just as sentiment and gratitude for his past work in rebuilding the credibility of the ALP, after the wreckage of 1975, had not stopped that party from replacing Bill Hayden with Hawke on the eve of the 1983 election, in order to strengthen its electoral prospects. Most dramatically of all, Labor, in June 2010, removed Kevin Rudd in favour of Julia Gillard because it thought she would be more likely to win the forthcoming election. For the first time since Federation, an election-winning PM had been denied the opportunity of completing his first term.

If at any time during my prime ministership the federal parliamentary Liberal Party had concluded that Costello had a better chance than I did of winning an election, it would have removed me in his favour. Peter Costello would have sensed the change in sentiment, and would have moved against me. That would not have been wrong or disloyal. It had not been disloyal of Rudd to challenge Beazley, nor had it been disloyal of me to work to regain the leadership of the Liberal Party in 1994–95 when Alexander Downer's position became increasingly unsustainable. Likewise, Julia Gillard displayed no disloyalty in accepting the draft of her party.

Nobody has an entitlement to lead a political party. There is no code of fairness which ultimately drives the members of a party to choose one person over another. If there had been, then the ALP would never have replaced Hayden with Hawke in 1983. If ever a person had earned the right to lead his party to what looked like a winnable election, it was Bill Hayden. He was the one credible senior ALP figure who had come out of the chaotic Whitlam years. He made his party economically respectable again. Yet his party pushed him aside and, in the process, broke his heart by installing Bob Hawke in his place. His plaintive invocation of 'the drover's dog', to describe his assessment of Labor's electoral prospects, meant nothing to a party determined to leave no stone unturned in its quest to oust the Fraser Government.

I thought that it was unfair of the Liberal Party to throw me out of the leadership in 1989 after all that I had been through in fighting both the ALP and the madness of Bjelke-Petersen in 1987. Fairness didn't come into it. When we lost in 1990, I thought that I was entitled to another go, and that surely the defeat in 1990 demonstrated how mistaken the party had been to cast me aside in 1989. Yet Liberals decided that their future lay with someone else. Again in 1993, issues of entitlement and fairness did not enter the equation. The Liberal Party was not willing to reach back to a former leader.

When the party turned to me in January 1995, it was not out of a sense of fairness — that it had been wrong to remove me six years earlier — or a feeling that I was entitled to the position of leader. It was because the majority of my colleagues had by then concluded that I had a better chance than anyone else of taking the Coalition to victory. Once again, the relentless laws of political arithmetic had driven a decision.

Peter Costello was never entitled to the leadership of the Liberal Party. He had a right to challenge for it, and freedom to hope that I would retire and he would succeed me, but it was not an entitlement. It is, and always has been, the unique gift of the party room, conferred on the person regarded as most likely to lead the party to victory at the next election.

Since the election in 2007 Peter Costello has said on several occasions that he did not challenge me because that would have put the party through too much turmoil and disunity. Whilst I have never doubted Peter's concern for the party, his statements represented ex post facto rationalisation and nothing else. If he had had the numbers, he would have used them; of that I am certain.

Prior to our defeat in November 2007, Costello's only path to the prime ministership was through my retirement. For reasons I will explain, his own conduct helped to remove this as an option at the very time that I was contemplating it. There was, of course, another path to the prime ministership subsequently open to Peter Costello. He could have stayed in politics for the long haul after our defeat in 2007, thus keeping alive the opportunity, as Opposition Leader, to pursue the prime ministership. I accept that history has been against governments being voted out after only one term, but at the age of only 52 when he resigned from parliament in October 2009, Peter Costello had years of political life left in him. He was not forced to go; his party would have been delighted if he had stayed and made himself available for whatever role he might have thought suitable. I was 56 when I was elected Prime Minister; Bob Menzies was 55 when he commenced his 16 years in the Lodge; Gough Whitlam was 56 when he won the prime ministership.

Peter wanted to emulate a predecessor in Higgins, Harold Holt, and come to the leadership whilst the Coalition was still in power. It was an understandable aspiration. The transfer of the Liberal leadership, in office, from Menzies to Holt has had no real parallel since Federation. Barton's assumption of a seat on the High Court in 1903, with Deakin replacing him, went close, but was not comparable, as Barton remained active in public life. On all other occasions, changes in the leadership of the incumbent government were the result of death, ill-health or the serving leader being forced out.

Costello had a remarkably smooth ride in his early political years. He won the first preselection which he contested, defeating a sitting Liberal MP, the late Roger Shipton, for the safe seat of Higgins. He entered parliament in 1990, and just four years later became Deputy Leader to Alexander Downer in May 1994, when that duo replaced John Hewson and Michael Wooldridge. Costello did not even face a vote for the deputy's position. When Downer defeated Hewson, Wooldridge pulled out and Costello was elected unopposed, although he had lost a contested ballot against Wooldridge for that post in 1993. For the next 13½ years there were no leadership ballots in the party. I replaced Downer unopposed in January 1995, and from then until our loss in November 2007, Peter Costello and I retained our positions without challenge.

My Liberal colleagues did not want me back as their leader after our loss under John Hewson, in 1993. Their attitude had not altered when, towards the middle of 1994, they realised that it was pointless for Hewson to stay as leader. They opted for the 'dream team' of Downer and Costello. The description of generational change was applied to them. It wasn't really; Downer was only five years younger than Hewson, and had entered parliament three years earlier — anything but a 'generation'. The term was code for saying that the Liberals definitely did not wish to go back to Howard.

In 1994 Liberal MPs went for Downer because he had done well as the shadow Treasurer. There was respect for Costello's ability, but Downer seemed more battle-hardened. In addition, some of the so-called moderates, especially from South Australia, who had given up on Hewson, saw Costello as too hardline for their liking.

I have already dealt with the much-commented-upon meeting of Costello, Ian McLachlan and me on 5 December 1994. Peter Costello never mentioned that meeting to me until July 2006, almost 12 years later, and only then in the wake of stories regarding the meeting having appeared in the newspapers of the previous Sunday.

There were two isolated incidents, though, involving the leadership. The first was late in July 1998, when Peter Costello confirmed during a radio interview that he had been approached about seeking the leadership by colleagues. He denied any intention to challenge and said that I had his support. I spoke to Costello about it and, on the basis of his response, I decided to simply bat the issue away.

The other incident was my ill-disciplined interview with Philip Clark on 2GB on 26 July, my birthday, in 2000. It was a real lapse and I should never have said what I did. At that time I had absolutely no intention of retiring, had not contemplated it, and had simply stated the obvious: that at some time I would go. I said, speaking of the period after the 2001 election, 'I'll then be in my 63rd or 64th year, and you start to ask yourself and that's fair enough. And nothing is forever. And I don't have the view that I am so indispensable and so important and so vital that, you know, the Liberal Party will be bereft without me — that is an arrogant view. By the same token … I have very good health and I am applying myself to the job very effectively and I am enjoying it.'

Some of my senior colleagues were justifiably angry with this comment, as I had gratuitously injected some uncertainty into perceptions of the Government at a time when it was travelling well. We had just successfully introduced the GST. Costello never mentioned the Philip Clark interview to me or sought in any way to draw implications from it in talking to me.

Relations between Peter Costello and me were badly strained by the leaking of the Shane Stone memo in May 2001. He reacted angrily to its contents, understandably feeling that as the memo was more critical of him than me or anyone else, it must have been leaked to damage him. He was openly furious with Stone. I don't think that their relationship ever recovered. Peter did not use any of the discussions I had with him over the leaked memo to raise the broader leadership issue.

My foolishness on the Philip Clark program meant that the future leadership of the Government would be an issue in the 2001 election campaign. Kim Beazley saw to that. It wasn't a big issue though. Given the dominant role I had played in driving the Government's response to the threat of terrorism as well as the asylum-seeker issue, not many Australians thought that I would be leaving the Lodge any time soon.

The new but unspoken reality in the leadership equation was that the sudden arrival of national security as a dominant political issue, which was destined to grow even further in 2002, meant that the case for my being replaced by Costello in the near term was significantly weakened. The public strongly endorsed my handling of the *Tampa* incident, and border protection generally, as well as the aftermath of 11 September. The Australian people did not want me to go. The public judged that I was the safe pair of hands in a time of unexpected turbulence. I am sure that Liberal MPs sensed this sentiment.

When asked about the leadership, my reply was that I would give consideration to my future about the time of my 64th birthday, which was in 2003. I should never have put myself or the Government in this position, but having been ill-disciplined with my remarks, I had fixed an artificial deadline for saying something about my future. Journalists and others drew a circle around 26 July 2003, my 64th birthday, as the time when I would indicate a possible retirement. There were many jocular references to the famous Beatles song 'When I'm Sixty-Four'.

Costello did not raise the leadership after the 2001 election. The Government had increased its majority and there was a widespread belief that national security had been a big factor in our impressive win. As our third term progressed, there was no agitation of any kind from within the parliamentary party for a change in leadership. They had no wish to alter a winning formula. There was general acceptance that if I succumbed to the hypothetical bus, then Peter would take my place.

Peter Costello not raising the leadership with me after our return at the 2001 election could well have been due simply to his accepting at face value what I had said publicly: that I would consider my position at the time of my 64th birthday. The dominance of national security would only intensify as 2002 wore on, with all the implications that had for the leadership dynamic within the Liberal Party. There was the tragic attack in Bali, claiming the lives of so many Australians; there was also the growing likelihood of a showdown with Iraq and the strong likelihood of Australian troops being directly involved. It must have been the instinctive view of most Liberal MPs that this was no time to be changing prime ministers or even talking about it.

That certainly seemed to be the view of the Australian public. I took a call from a young mother during a talkback session on a Perth radio station on 23 October 2002. Her name was Beverly. She told me that she had never been so fearful for her future and that of her family, and pleaded with me not to retire. She said, 'I have no confidence in somebody else.'[1]

Peter Costello was widely admired within the Liberal Party for the job he had done as Treasurer. Now, however, economic management had to share top billing with defence and national security. Inevitably this reinforced the view that most of the colleagues had of keeping the status quo at the top.

Late in February 2003 I initiated a discussion with Peter Costello about the future, in which I repeated my public position that I would assess the situation in the middle of the year. I went to some lengths to make it clear to Peter that he should not assume that I would decide to go. My diary entry of 26 February 2003 said, in part, 'I raised the leadership issue and told him that I had not made up my mind. I said several times that there was no guarantee that I would go.' I told him that it was the views of colleagues that mattered most. He never seemed very receptive to this notion. His rather elitist dismissal of what his fellow MPs thought on a whole range of issues was one of the main reasons why the widespread respect for Costello's abilities within the parliamentary party never translated into enthusiastic support for him as party leader. Peter is not a good listener. His colleagues knew that. They had experienced it first-hand. In this discussion, Peter Costello made no reference to my meeting with him and Ian McLachlan back in December 1994.

This conversation occurred on the eve of the invasion of Iraq. Peter Costello backed the decision to go into Iraq. We both understood that if things went badly for Australia in Iraq then the public would want a head and that head would have to be mine. In committing units of the ADF to the Coalition of the Willing, a great risk was being taken. I diarised that if Iraq had gone wrong (meaning significant casualties) then I would have fallen on my sword and taken the blame for the whole government. I would have resigned the prime ministership. Iraq did not go badly for Australia. The men and women of the ADF did an exemplary job and mercifully suffered no battle casualties.

As the middle of 2003, and my 64th birthday, approached I received frequent signals from colleagues, some direct, others through the chief government whip, Jim Lloyd, that I should stay on and lead the party to the next general election. That was also the view of the party organisation. Peter had a core group of supporters amongst Liberal MPs, probably 15 to 20 out of more than 100 colleagues. That was not the basis for a serious challenge. His only hope was for me to decide to go.

My decision to stay was quite an easy one. It was what the public, the Liberal Party and all of my senior cabinet colleagues, except Costello himself, wanted. I was physically very fit and had plenty of enthusiasm for the responsibilities of the job. On 2 June 2003, I saw Peter Costello in my Canberra office and told him of my decision. He should not have been surprised yet he affected to be, both privately and, later, publicly. I had given plenty of warning of my likely decision when we discussed the issue in February. He did not raise the discussion involving Ian McLachlan nine years earlier, in December 1994, nor allege that I had broken an undertaking to hand over the leadership.

I told the party meeting the next day of my decision. It was warmly received. It was what the majority of my colleagues wanted.

Peter Costello displayed public disappointment at my decision. In doing so he missed the point with his colleagues. Most of them were happy with my decision. It had been welcomed in the party room and also, quietly, by the National Party. He would have done himself a greater service if he had taken the decision a little more in his stride. Costello said that in future he would assert his right, as Deputy Leader, to speak more frequently on a broader range of issues. I said immediately that this was his right as Deputy Leader.

A diary entry I made on 8 June 2003 reads, 'He argued during our hour-long discussion last Monday morning that the Party's best interests would be served by a transition now. Future events could prove that he was right. There was, however, overwhelming support in the parliamentary party for me to stay. There has been a very positive reaction to the decision.'

The issue of leadership slipped from the radar screen. When I had told the party room in July 2003 that I would stay I said that I would continue to lead the Liberal Party for so long as it wished me to, and if it was in the best interests of the party that I did so. From then on, when asked about the issue, that was my comfortable response. That should always have been my public position because it directly reflected the true position.

I called the 2004 election on 29 August. During an interview the following day, Peter Costello was pressed to rule out a leadership challenge if the Government were re-elected. He answered as best he could, given that I never expected him to categorically rule out a challenge. We had scheduled a joint news conference in Canberra that same day. Anxious to kill off the leadership issue for the campaign, I raised the matter directly with Costello before the news conference. I stressed how important it was that the leadership matter not dog us in the campaign; that I understood his desire to lead the party; that this would probably be my last election and that it was better that he succeed me in government.

Using more direct language than he had earlier, Peter Costello deflected the leadership issue at our news conference. It always seemed to me that my deputy's best response on the leadership was to endorse my own language. He could simply say that I should remain leader for so long as the party wanted me to and that it was in the best interests of the party that I continue. If, in the future, he did launch a challenge, he would have been testing whether or not the Liberal Party wanted me to stay and self-evidently declaring that, in his opinion, it was no longer in the party's interests that I remain as leader.

The size of our win in 2004 surprised me. It further strengthened my hold on the leadership of the Liberal Party. Peter Costello said nothing to me about the leadership matter. Life in the Coalition resumed its normal settled and stable pattern. Within weeks Mark Latham had self-combusted and Kim Beazley, minus his avuncularity, was back. He acknowledged that he was prolix, but I knew that nothing had changed when he declared that 'henceforth simplicity will be my talisman'.

2004 had been a remarkable victory, particularly winning control of the Senate. I had now led the Coalition to four straight election wins. I would be 68 by the time of the next election. Healthy though I was, and much and all as I was stimulated by the job, I knew that I had to retire at some point. If I stayed and fought yet another election, and were successful, that would take me to 70 before I might properly step down. I thought that would be staying too long and tempting fate. Shattered the ALP might be after our increased majority in October 2004, but politics was always volatile.

Janette and I kicked the issue around, and I concluded that it would be in the party's best interests, all things being equal, if I retired before the 2007 election, giving my successor, who I assumed would be Peter Costello, plenty of time to establish himself. From early 2005 this became my working assumption; it was not set in cement — nothing like that ever could be — but it was to remain my working assumption until blown apart by the events of July 2006.

I didn't tell Peter Costello or any other colleagues. There was no need to. Apart from anything else, it would have found its way into the media, and my authority would have been undermined, with immediate calls for me to name the date of my departure. Some would have called on me to go quickly. For myself I felt that I would need to leave my successor at least a year in the saddle before facing the people. That would mean a retirement before Christmas 2006.

Peter Costello failed to understand the impact of the 2004 result on leadership dynamics within the Liberal Party. By winning again, I had become the most successful election winner for the Liberal Party since Menzies. For a proud political party that meant a lot. With each successive election victory, more people came into parliament who felt that they owed their success to me as leader. To them, talk of entitlement to inherit the leadership, coming from Peter's barrackers, sounded discordant.

The leadership dynamic post-2004 meant that Peter Costello had two available options. The first and most sensible one was that he could simply accept the obvious and wait until I chose to retire. That was the Harold Holt approach, which Peter cited but would not emulate. Having won four successive elections, the great bulk of the party wanted me to stay as long as possible, and would react angrily to pressure applied or deadlines imposed by Peter or his acolytes. The other alternative was to plan and endeavour to execute a challenge. That was his right. He was entitled to openly confront the Liberals with a choice between him and me.

Regrettably he chose neither of these options. Instead he entered the grey area of both advocating himself and having others, on his behalf, argue the case for an orderly transition. Notional deadlines were set, after which unspecified action would be taken. The implication always was that if I did not go by the appointed time then he would challenge. Peter thought that he was entitled to the leadership. This cut no ice with Liberal MPs. They didn't want the status quo changed. They respected his ability, revelled in his rhetorical skills in question time but, by an overwhelming margin, wanted him to stay as Treasurer in the Howard Government.

If Costello had chosen the first option and recognised that in no way would I be pressured out of the leadership, he would have become PM towards the end of 2006. There would have been no regular briefing of the press about deadlines, and importantly he would have handled the December 1994 story in mid-2006 differently. There may not even have been such a story.

In electing to approach the leadership as he did, Peter Costello completely misread both my temperament and my personality. Having worked closely with me for a decade it surprised me that he imagined I would succumb to the sort of rank amateur pressure placed on me through media briefings and the like. Those who understood me realised how counterproductive such a tack would become.

The Canberra press gallery had a natural obsession with the leadership issue. Every answer I gave about a forthcoming event which might be more than a few months away was scoured for clues about my future. When I announced that Sydney would be the venue for the 2007 APEC meeting, I was promptly asked who would host the meeting. I replied that the host would naturally be the PM of Australia. So the game went on. Questions, originally designed as trick ones, became so predictable that they were easy to handle.

I still don't know how to categorise the question Steve Lewis, of the *Australian*, asked me in Athens about my capacity to beat Kim Beazley again. My response became the foundation of the so-called Athens declaration, which caused Peter Costello to hit the roof. It was during a sit-down interview with two print journalists from Australia, Steve Lewis and Malcolm Farr. Many of the questions were about the leadership. I joked about the trickiness of their questions. I would later be accused of exhibiting hubris because in answer to a question from Malcolm Farr as to what jobs I might seek in a post-PM life, I said, 'I'm not planning on going anywhere.' That answer was not only literally correct, but I also knew that even to answer a question about my life beyond politics would be to invite a headline like 'Howard Ponders Life After the Lodge'. The journalists knew that also; that's why one of them asked the question.

Towards the end of the interview, focus shifted to Kim Beazley, who had not been back in the job for long. I said that I did not treat him lightly. Steve Lewis then asked, 'You reckon you could best him three times?' Taking the question as a hypothetical one, which, given the way it was phrased, I was entitled to do, I replied, 'Yes. I hope so. Try.' Lewis followed with another question, 'You like the challenge?' There was nothing hypothetical about that; I replied, 'There're those curly ones again.'

The journalists present believed that they had a huge story. According to them, I had made a declaration that I would stay and lead the Liberals to the 2007 election. I had done no such thing. I don't know how else I was expected to answer the question about beating Kim Beazley. It had, after all, been hypothetical. My press secretary, David Luff, warned me that the journalists would take a baseball bat to my replies. He was right. It became a big story. Given Luffy's assessment, I rang Peter Costello to warn him of the story. He already knew about it from my office and was not ready to accept my assurances that my responses carried no implications for the leadership issue. He seemed only too happy to act the wounded deputy rather than see things in a different light. Perhaps he thought that the bigger the drama the better for him.

The media was close to united in its opinion that my Athens interview represented a declaration that I intended to stay and fight another election. My belief that it was nothing more than fending off suggestions that I had decided to go found little support. For example the *Australian*, in an editorial on 2 May 2005, dismissed as 'nonsense' my interpretation of the Athens interview. It said that I had 'challenged [my] own deputy to come and take the leadership or go away'.[2] I should not have been surprised at this; leadership tensions within a political party are the stuff of wonderful yarns for the regular political correspondents.

Typical of the 'deadline' tactic adopted by Peter Costello and his backers was a story in the *Age* of 4 May 2005. Written by Michael Gordon and Misha Schubert, it stated that Costello would not stay on as my deputy or Treasurer beyond early the following year. According to 'well-placed sources' the option of me contesting another election with Peter Costello as deputy was not viable. The 'Costello forces' spoke of following the Keating path when he challenged Bob Hawke. The first challenge would fail, but he would get it the second time. An unnamed source said, 'Howard needs to understand that there will be a transition this term — the only question is whether it will be smooth or messy.'[3] This story had been carefully and deliberately briefed. It was a world away from what Harold Holt had done.

In his memoirs Peter Costello confirmed what I had suspected, that he took my call about the Athens interview whilst having dinner with a group of journalists in Melbourne, all from the *Age* newspaper. They were Misha Schubert and Michael Gordon, the author of the 'deadline' story on 4 May, Shaun Carney and Jason Koutsoukis. Peter Costello wrote that the purpose of the dinner had been to improve relations between the Government and that newspaper. Given that the dinner was just a few days before the Schubert 'deadline' story appeared, I am entitled to assume that some other things were discussed at the dinner as well.

The leadership issue remained a latent theme in the stories of regular columnists. Given the time I had already served in the job, it would have in any event, but the regular stimulation it received from sources guaranteed that. The 'deadline' of autumn 2006 was still there, but did not trouble me. My working assumption about departing some time towards Christmas 2006 had not changed, and I did not think that Costello would mount a challenge, as there was negligible support for that within the party.

Politically, 2005 ended on a note of achievement for the Coalition. We had secured passage through the Senate of the sale of the final tranche of Telstra, our additional workplace reforms and, right at the end, a prohibition on compulsory student unionism. I was proud that at long last my Government had been able to keep faith on something which went to the fundamental Liberal value of freedom of association.

The first half of 2006 saw the lifting of the 'deadline' of autumn 2006, the time by which I was meant to have indicated when I would retire. Writing in the *Sydney Morning Herald* on 22 April 2006, Louise Dodson said, 'But now they [Costello's supporters] acknowledge the leadership decision is Mr Howard's to make whenever he chooses. Mr Costello has no plans to challenge for the leadership.'[4] She wrote in the same comment story that I could wait until January (2007) before I made up my mind on a leadership handover. This, she asserted, was in substitution for the previous 'deadline' of May 2006.

It was quite plain that Peter Costello would never mount a challenge because there were insufficient supporters in the Liberal Party to make it credible. There had also been a half-hearted realisation that setting deadlines was counterproductive, as my failure to respond to them merely underlined how little support there was for him to mount a challenge. Yet, having abandoned, in the first half of 2006, the deadline strategy, my deputy and his close spear-carriers never completely saw the wisdom of genuinely allowing me the freedom to go at a time of my choosing; his inept handling of the December 1994 story in July demonstrated this.

Tony Blair had come to Australia in March 2006 to attend the Commonwealth Games in Melbourne and then go to Canberra to address a joint sitting of parliament, the first British PM to have been extended that honour. He and his wife, Cherie, flew with Janette and me on the VIP jet from Melbourne to Canberra on 27 March, and during the flight we had an intriguing discussion about leadership transition issues. Blair remarked that, unlike him, I had not nominated in advance an intention to retire at a particular time in the future. Prior to the 2005 election in Britain, Blair had said that if Labour won that election he would stand down in favour of Gordon Brown during the subsequent term. He rather ruefully reflected that it had probably been a mistake, as it had made him a lame duck.

Blair then turned to my position and said, 'They [the ALP] are all waiting to see what you do. They think that Beazley can beat Costello.' The implication was that there continued to be doubts in Labor ranks that Beazley could beat me. I had no reason to believe that this was other than a perfectly honest comment from the British PM. We were good friends and he would not have indulged in any partisan political game playing.

March 2006 marked the 10th anniversary of the election of the Howard Government. It would also mark a first in Australian politics. For a whole decade, the same three people had occupied the posts of Prime Minister, Treasurer and Foreign Minister. More than anything else, this symbolised the stability and unity of the Government.

The events marking the Government's 10 years in office were deliberately low-key, and were accompanied by surprisingly little comment about the leadership issue. Contrary to claims made later, no colleagues approached me with suggestions that 10 years had been enough and now was the time to go.

In May 2006 I went on an official visit to the USA, and then on to Canada and Ireland. Due to the absence of Mark Vaile, the Deputy Prime Minister, from Australia during the same period Peter Costello was acting PM for a few days and performed well in the job, drawing praise from a number of commentators, as well as public compliments from several of his colleagues. On reflection this stint in the top job should have been an ideal prelude to an orderly transition later in the year. It was not to be.

Well into 2006, opposition to Costello replacing me began to emerge from within senior Liberal ranks. Brendan Nelson, then the Defence Minister, and I returned together from the funeral of Private Jake Kovco at Sale in Victoria on 2 May 2006. Kovco had died while off-duty in Iraq. During the flight Nelson said that he was strongly opposed to Costello becoming Liberal leader, that he hoped I would stay at the helm, and that if I were to go he would consider standing against Costello himself. He detailed several incidents involving what he saw as contemptuous behaviour by my deputy towards him.

Separately Alexander Downer strongly urged me to stay. During a conversation towards the middle of that year he had said, 'Look, John, there's no reason why you can't go on doing this job into your 70s. You're still very fit. I don't know that I could work with Costello as PM. Stop thinking about retirement.' Mal Brough had also told me that he did not want me to go, expressing doubts about Costello's electoral appeal. Mal had extensive rugby league links in Queensland, and quoted the opinions of some identities in the game in aid of his assessment that I still had much electoral appeal. I had a lot of respect for Brough. He had won a new and marginal seat in 1996, and his knockabout style brought him into contact with swathes of middle Australia.

Then there was Malcolm Turnbull. He and Costello did not like each other, and that mutual disdain has continued. Costello thought that Turnbull was a carpetbagger with no deep loyalty to the Liberal cause. He had publicly opposed Turnbull's preselection bid for Wentworth in 2004. He was needlessly sensitive to Turnbull when the latter entered parliament. Turnbull was never a threat to Costello as my successor. Costello would have wiped the floor with him in any leadership ballot, in Government or in opposition. As a mark of his needless sensitivity, Costello had totally overreacted when Turnbull produced a plan to reform the tax system. Instead of welcoming the initiative and promising to examine it, Costello publicly ridiculed the plan and its author, and privately complained to me, suggesting that something be done to discipline Turnbull. That was absurd as Turnbull had a perfect right to put forward ideas.

In mid-2006 Turnbull gave Arthur Sinodinos a detailed account of a long discussion he had had with Costello at Turnbull's home in Sydney about the future of the Government, Costello's impatience with my not having retired and how he had carried the Government. Turnbull wanted it to be made known to me that on the basis of this encounter and other considerations, he was adamantly against Costello becoming leader, and that he hoped I stayed on as PM. Not long after, in a personal discussion, Turnbull confirmed to me the substance of what he had told Arthur.

My reading of the mood of the party was that colleagues really hoped I would stay, and I felt I could leave a final decision on my future until the end of the year. There would be pressure as year's end approached, as it was commonly accepted if I did retire, my successor should be given at least 12 months to cut his own mustard.

The leadership was not constantly on my mind. There were several pieces of unfinished business before me: the High Court adjudication on

WorkChoices — the states had challenged the validity of our reliance on the Corporations power — and finally resolving Telstra — two very significant matters which went to the heart of reform causes I had championed since becoming PM. However, the working assumption that I would retire before the next election had not changed.

That is, it had not changed until the Glenn Milne story in News Limited papers on Sunday, 9 July 2006. Under a *Sunday Telegraph* headline, 'PM Broke His Secret Deal', the story said that at the December 1994 meeting involving Ian McLachlan, I had said that I would hand over the prime ministership to Costello after two terms. Although the headline carried the word 'deal', the story itself did not say that Costello had agreed to support my replacing Downer, an essential element if there had been a deal. McLachlan had made a note of his recollection of the meeting and kept it in his wallet.

This was not a chance story. In February 2008, after the Government's defeat, Peter Costello acknowledged on the ABC's *Four Corners* that McLachlan had telephoned asking if he, Costello, had any objection to McLachlan confirming to Milne the substance of the story, which would guarantee that it would appear. Costello had no such objection, nor did he give advance warning of the story to me or my office. That came from Milne himself to David Luff, my press secretary, after it had been put to bed.

Peter was happy for the story to appear — at the time — despite the fact that almost 12 years had elapsed since the meeting, and that he had never over that period raised the meeting with me or alleged that I had broken my word. Revealingly, in a comment piece Milne said, 'The leak is designed to force Howard's hand.'[5] It did, but not in the way Peter must have wanted.

When asked about the story the next day I simply said that there had been no deal about the leadership. In retrospect, it was probably a mistake not to have spoken to Costello about the issue before either of us said anything to the media. Though, given my instinctive belief that Costello had wanted the story to run, I doubt that anything I might have said to him would have made any difference. He had cast his bread upon the waters. He hoped that the drama surrounding the 12-year-old story would shake things up about the leadership, and to his advantage.

That calculation proved disastrously wrong. The reaction of Liberal MPs, apart from a few Costello activists, was one of both astonishment and irritation. The near-universal comment was, 'For goodness' sake, that was 12 years ago. We've won four elections since then. Why bring it up?' If the story had been the spontaneous product of investigative journalism, then it had been within Costello's gift to kill it off. All he had to do was give his version of what had happened in December 1994 but say it was a long time ago, the Coalition had won four elections since then and what transpired at that meeting in 1994 had no relevance for the current situation of the Government. He could have reiterated his desire to lead the party, but said that the time of my departure was entirely up to me. That response, with honour, would have ended the story. The fact that Peter did not handle it that way suggested that he hoped the story would shift the dynamic of the leadership issue in his favour. It certainly had an impact, and a decisive one, on the leadership, and in a way that destroyed Peter Costello's hopes of my retiring before the 2007 election.

Even those who completely accepted his version of events and wanted me gone and Costello in the Lodge as soon as possible realised that his handling of the issue had hurt him. Christopher Pyne, a close Costello activist, telephoned me, acknowledged Costello had mishandled the issue and said that Peter wished to continue working with me in his role as Treasurer. He had no need of such advocacy. It was my wish that Peter stay in his job. Other colleagues, strong Costello people, spoke to Tony Nutt, telling him that although they wanted Costello as PM one day, he had bungled things, and I had to stay on and fight the next election.

The incident brought urgency back to the leadership issue. Discussion quickly shifted from who said what 12 years earlier to who do we want as leader? This was the last thing that Peter Costello should have desired. It meant that suddenly the pressure was on me to make it known, quickly, whether or not I would lead the party to another election. Before this, my future was something which could wait until a time close to Christmas. Now, courtesy of the Milne story, and the way in which it had been handled by Peter Costello, both of us would be forced to declare our hands almost immediately. Within only four days, an *Australian* editorial called on me to declare my leadership intentions.

Don Argus, chairman of BHP-Billiton and doyen of the Melbourne business community, telephoned me and said, 'I hope that you're not thinking of going. Nobody down here thinks you should be leaving the reservation any time soon.' A few days later Ron Walker, the party's veteran fund-raiser and Victorian activist, called. My diary entry records Walker having told me of a lunch he had had the previous day with four leading members of the Melbourne business community (Hugh Morgan; John

McFarlane, CEO of the ANZ Bank; Robert de Crespigny, a leading mining industry figure; and Laurie Cox, a former chairman of the Australian Stock Exchange) at which, according to Walker, there was scathing criticism of Costello's behaviour.

Nobody, however, cut to the core of the issue quite like the respected Melbourne journalist Neil Mitchell. Writing in his weekly column in the *Herald Sun*, he described Costello's performance as 'petulant, arrogant and indulgent'. He said that Costello had 'wounded a government that was not in serious trouble and significantly damaged any hope he has of realising what he seems to believe is his God-given right to ascension'. Mitchell went on to say, 'Howard is one of the most successful conservative leaders in history. He has been elected four times by the people as Prime Minister. His popularity remains high. His government is not a shambles, at least not until now.' He continued, 'But here we have his deputy and some of his backbenchers telling him to get out, not because of public clamour or scandal but because of this immature whining that "it is my turn".'[6]

The party and the public had turned against Costello over this issue. Even the Canberra press gallery, never my greatest cheer squad, judged him harshly. The published polls had me way ahead of him as preferred Liberal leader, and as well continued to give me a big lead over Beazley, whereas Costello was behind the Labor leader in a head-to-head contest, according to a Newspoll conducted a week after the December 1994 story broke. This was consistent with the results of that popularity measurement over the preceding few years, except for a poll in April 2006 which had Costello ahead of Beazley. The irony for my deputy could well have been that he badly misread public sentiment on an issue just as the public was beginning to warm towards him.

Pressure mounted on me to declare my position. Parliament was due to meet after the winter recess on 8 August. I knew that if I had not said anything about my future by then, the leadership would be the only game in town, and that would damage the Government.

I had to make a decision there and then. There was little doubt that the decision had to be that I would stay and fight another election. Contrary to so much of what has been written about my decision to stay, I had genuinely mixed feelings about it. The Government had been in power for a long time; seeking a fifth term was tempting fate; only Menzies had done it, and he had profited from the momentous and bitter split in the ALP. There was nothing like that on the horizon for me.

If I stayed and won again, I would be a hero. If I lost, many would brand me the stubborn old bloke who stayed too long, denying Costello his rightful inheritance by preventing generational change. These were thoughts that I committed to my diary at the time. It was a hard decision. It was the wrong time and the wrong set of circumstances in which to make it. Yet I had no alternative. Putting it off was not an option. The Government would bleed profusely if I remained silent.

It was a tragedy for the Government that it had reached this sorry state of affairs. The fact that I had to make the decision then meant, inevitably, that the decision had to be that I would stay. To have gone in the wake of the Milne story about the December 1994 meeting would have had history recording that I had been forced out by the revelation of a broken deal, no matter how untrue that might have been. I was never going to allow that to happen. Compounding this powerful constraint on my retiring at that time was overwhelming evidence that my colleagues and the voting public both wanted me to stay. That attitude had only been reinforced by what the publication of the December 1994 story had set in train.

If this drama had not occurred or had been effectively cauterised, there would have been little pressure on me to say anything about my future until the approach to Christmas. In those circumstances I would have gone then, allowing Peter Costello a full year within which to make his own mark as PM; that, however, was not to be.

At the end of July I decided to announce, by way of a letter to my Liberal colleagues followed by public confirmation, that I had decided to stay and lead the Coalition to another election. I had consulted widely within the party and it was obvious that the overwhelming majority wanted me to stay as leader. They also wanted Peter Costello to remain where he was. I rang Peter on Sunday, 30 July to tell him of my decision, and how I intended to announce it. I recorded a diary entry of this conversation and some of my other thoughts on the issue. Peter told me that my decision was the wrong one for the Liberal Party, that the letter I proposed sending to our colleagues could easily have been written by Menzies when he was contemplating his future, and that MPs, particularly senior ones, never tell the leader their true feelings. He said that I might not end up facing Beazley at the next election.

I reminded him that in 1991, six of Bob Hawke's most senior colleagues had gone to him and said it was in the ALP's best interests that he stand down. That was not the mood of the Liberal Party in July 2006. I made the point several times that there was wide support for me staying.

Although he reserved his position regarding a response to my commitment to stay, I did not believe that he would either challenge for the leadership or resign and go to the backbench. There was no serious support for a challenge. He must have known that. To simply resign and retire to the backbench would be seen as purely self-serving. Peter said that he would inform me of his response after thinking of it overnight. His observation to me that it would be difficult to go through the next election campaign with the current leadership arrangement did not suggest to me that he was about to jump ship.

Although I was relieved a decision had been made, I felt no joy about it. As I sat in my Kirribilli House study, signing my letter to each of more than 100 Liberal colleagues, I felt quite reflective. This was not what I had either expected or hoped for. This was not an unpressured decision about my future. I had that nagging feeling that the decision was being taken in the wrong circumstances, although in those circumstances I had no doubt that the decision I was about to announce was not only the right one but also the one that Liberal MPs and the public wanted. All my instincts told me that the next election would be extremely hard to win.

I flew to Innisfail in far north Queensland the next day to talk to local people about how they were handling recovery from the cyclone which had hit earlier in the year. The Commonwealth had provided massive aid, which totalled in the end about $230 million. It was there in tropical dress, no jacket and no tie, that I made my announcement. It was in Bob Katter's electorate. Peter had rung me earlier to say that he would stay on as Deputy Leader and Treasurer. That did not surprise, and I thanked him for his decision. I spoke warmly of him in my own comments. I told the assembled journalists that it was the emphatic wish of the parliamentary party that the current leadership team of me as leader and Peter as deputy should stay in place and lead it to the next election.

In the space of three weeks, the whole leadership issue had been disposed of in a way that I had never expected. Instead of an unhurried decision at the end of the year, with all pointers being that I would go, Peter's inept handling of the December 1994 story incident had created a situation where I had no alternative but to announce when I did that I would stay.

Since then I have occasionally tried to play devil's advocate with my decision. If I had said nothing about the leadership before parliament resumed, both Peter and I would have been relentlessly pursued about it every question time. Would I give a promise to stay and fight the next election? Costello would have been asked repeatedly about a challenge. MPs would have been constantly drilled by the press. The less disciplined ones would have given plenty of quotable quotes. It would have been the dominant political story for weeks. Before long there would have been calls for me to make my future intentions plain in the interests of the Liberal Party. Pressure for that from some media had started early. The Government's political position would have eroded rapidly. That course of action was simply not a viable option.

The early December putsch which replaced Kim Beazley with Kevin Rudd and immediately lifted Labor's stocks presented, some months later, another exit option for me. Under Rudd the ALP shot ahead in the polls, and as this trend consolidated, my departure then would not have been linked to the December 1994 story, but simply seen as a pragmatic recognition of the fact that a new leader from Labor required a different one from the Liberals.

The main problem with this option was that Rudd's arrival had further intensified sentiment in the party for me to continue as leader. Colleagues thought that only I had the experience to handle this new, unexpected challenge. The other drawback was that it would have dramatically enhanced the perception of Rudd as a world-beater. After only several months into the job he would have scared Australia's second-longest-serving PM into retirement, after that PM had declared only months earlier that he would lead his party to the next election. I thought about it, but concluded that it was not a viable option, either. The reality was that, as I knew when I reluctantly made my announcement the previous July, I was committed to fight the next election as PM, irrespective of the circumstances. It was long past the time when I could decide that I would retire in advance of the next poll. In any event the view was held early in Rudd's time as leader that the tide would eventually turn, and the more so if I stayed at the helm.

The polls, both public and private, provided unrelieved gloom for the Coalition for the first seven months of 2007. What small rays of hope that did appear occasionally, extinguished themselves quickly. Separate polls in my Bennelong electorate showed that, consistent with the general swing against the Coalition in the generic polls, I would lose my seat. Labor's Bennelong candidate was the well-known former ABC presenter Maxine McKew. When late in 2006 she had announced on the *Lateline* program that she was leaving the broadcaster, I speculated to my wife, 'She's going to run in Bennelong.' By the end of July I had concluded that if the polls were to turn around, that would not happen until the election had been called, and voters were faced with making a real choice. I drew a small amount of comfort only from the experience of 2004, when the polls did move more firmly our way once the campaign had started.

Throughout this period there had been, to my knowledge, no serious debate within the party about the leadership. It was regarded as having been firmly settled the previous year. There was virtually no press speculation either.

Then, in successive months, Peter Costello was involved in incidents that produced the impression of a government which was unravelling. He must have known that the biography of me written by Wayne Errington and Peter Van Onselen would be published prior to the 2007 election. This did not prevent him making severe criticisms of my record as Treasurer to the authors of the book. Not stopping there, he called into question my commitment to economic rationalism, and even industrial relations reform. The book was published late in July 2007. The timing could not have been worse. When I raised the comments with Costello, he reacted with embarrassment. He mumbled something to the effect that he had only been trying to help. I felt it unnecessary to make the point that his remarks could hardly qualify as helpful. This was appalling conduct on his part. The fact that we were so close to the election and our moment of political truth meant that I suppressed the deep anger I felt.

Then, in the middle of August 2007, little more than three months before a probable election date, a story broke regarding what Peter Costello had allegedly said about the leadership issue during a meal with three journalists at the Waters Edge Canberra restaurant on 2 June 2005. It was common ground that those attending were Costello, his press advisor David Alexander, Tony Wright of the *Age*, Michael Brissenden of the ABC's *7.30 Report* and Paul Daley of the *Bulletin*. Costello and Alexander claimed that the discussion was an off-the-record one, meaning that what was said should not be divulged, even on a non-attributable basis. The journalists disputed this, claiming it was background, thus allowing use of the information transmitted during the dinner, but without attribution. They claimed that, the day after the dinner, Alexander had rung them and pleaded that the comments of the Treasurer be treated as off-the-record.

For a long time at least, it was treated as an off-the-record discussion and no reports of the dinner emerged. Approximately a year later, Daley alluded to it, but in a way that did not attract much attention. He was more specific in a *Bulletin* column on 7 August, where he alleged that Peter Costello had told them that I could not win the election, but he could.

When questioned, Peter Costello denied the Daley story. This denial provoked both Brissenden and Wright into going public with their detailed and similar accounts of what they claim Costello had said. They both asserted that as Costello had denied what they had heard him say, they were justified in breaching the confidentiality of the discussion.

Perhaps a fine piece of journalistic ethics turned on the matter, but what concerned me were the bad headlines. Under a heading of 'He Can't Win. I Can', Tony Wright told the readers of the *Age* his version of the dinner in 2005. It was that Costello had set a deadline of April 2006 for me to hand the leadership to him, and that if that did not happen he would challenge, and if, as anticipated, that did not succeed he would go the backbench and 'carp' at my leadership and 'destroy it'. He said that he was prepared to do this because 'He [Howard] will lose the election. He can't win. I can. We can, but he can't.'[7]

Costello publicly denied the alleged comments with a dismissive response that he did not know where journalists got these stories. Both Wright and Brissenden claimed to have a common note of the discussion. In addition, both the timing of the dinner and the alleged remarks about my having an April 2006 'deadline' within which to retire were consistent with briefings which had so obviously been given on other occasions about what I supposedly had to do to avoid a challenge. The whole story hurt Costello within the party but, most importantly, added yet again to the impression of the crumbling of a once united and impregnable government, particularly at the top. At no stage did Peter Costello seek me out privately to deny the story. Given the long association we had had, this suggested to me that it was true.

In the light of these incidents, the constant mantra of an unceasingly loyal deputy had worn thin. That aside, the two incidents were bad for the Government. They would not have endeared Peter Costello to those of his colleagues who held marginal seats and faced the fight of their electoral lives.

*   *   *

In August 2007, Malcolm Turnbull raised our difficult political position with me. He said he had been kept awake the previous night worrying that I might lose my seat at the election. He said that would be a terrible end to such a wonderful career. I expressed a rather more philosophical view about it, pointing out that given its marginal character, it was inevitable that Bennelong should be at risk. We also discussed the position in his own seat, which on 2004 figures was even more precarious than Bennelong. He was nervous about Wentworth, an electorate which was unrepresentative of middle Australia, and would have contained many people who opposed my stance on border protection, Iraq and aspects of Indigenous policy. Turnbull suggested that I consider resigning the leadership. This was different from the Malcolm Turnbull of a year earlier, who had been passionate that I should stay.

APEC was scheduled to meet in Sydney on 2–9 September. On 4 September there was another depressing Newspoll, showing Labor ahead by an astonishing 59–41 on a two-party-preferred basis. Later that morning Alexander Downer called to see me in my Sydney office and we had the frankest possible discussion on the political scene. I said that I had to face the reality that the Government was headed for defeat and that part of the outcome would be my losing Bennelong. We agreed that nothing the Government had done had shifted public sentiment and that voters had plainly decided to get rid of us.

Downer said that he had noticed a hardening of attitudes amongst people in both Adelaide and Melbourne the previous weekend. He reported that people were saying that they were 'over John Howard'. No particular policy issue was mentioned by my colleague.

I then said to Downer, 'Do you think it would help if I went? Could Costello do better than I could? Perhaps a new leader would upset Rudd and turn things around?' Downer's response was that he did not know but it might be worth a try. I said that I wanted to know the attitude of cabinet colleagues. I gave him authority to call them together during APEC events, as most of them would be in Sydney.

I told Downer that I would not leave in circumstances of cowardly flight. In no way would I countenance the appearance of going because I was afraid of defeat. If, however, my cabinet colleagues were strongly of the view that they had a better chance of winning under Costello — he was the only possible alternative — and made that plain to me, then I would go. But they had to publicly 'own' the request.

Downer did as I asked and assembled most of the ministers in cabinet on Thursday, 6 September at the Quay Grand Apartments in Sydney. Having spoken to a good number of those who were present, I am satisfied of a number of things. Downer told them of my pessimism about both the election outcome and my own seat. They were genuinely shocked by this. The majority of them did not think that the Government could win under my leadership but were unconvinced that it would be any better under Costello, although some believed he would have a better chance. Several of those present related 'war stories' of their dealings with the Treasurer; there was little enthusiasm for him. Downer encouraged ministers to speak to me direct with their views.

Downer saw me the next evening at Kirribilli House, Janette also being present. He reported on the meeting. I asked whether the cabinet would be willing to 'own' a request to me to stand aside. He replied that there was absolutely no support for this. They would not do it. They felt they would suffer in their electorates if they were seen to be pushing me out. My response was that if they were not prepared to publicly ask me to go, then a resignation by me would look like cowardice. I would rather go down fighting than desert on the eve of the battle. Downer pleaded with me to talk to them as they were quite depressed.

Naturally Costello had not been at the meeting; nor had Nick Minchin, Tony Abbott or Mal Brough. Downer had obviously discussed the issue with Costello, as it subsequently emerged that part of the understanding amongst quite a few colleagues was that if Costello were to replace me, then Downer would become Deputy Leader and, presumably, Treasurer. Mal Brough was not part of such an understanding, rather angrily telling me the following week that he would not support Downer as deputy.

At this stage news of the ministers' meeting had not seeped out, but it was only a matter of time before it did. I discussed the whole issue with my own family over the weekend. Janette and my three children were adamant that I should not look as if I were running from an electoral fight. Their attitude was that I should only give up the leadership if publicly requested to do so by my senior colleagues. That was my attitude as well. We agreed that I should not put the party through a ballot if that public request were to come. I doubted that it would. I was right.

This all occurred during APEC. We returned to parliament the following Tuesday, with an address from the Canadian PM, Stephen Harper, to a joint sitting, returning the compliment paid to me the previous year. News of the Downer-led discussion had begun to get around. Some of the coverage portrayed certain ministers as plotting against me. That was not right, as I had inaugurated the whole discussion in the first place. The next day I had a meeting with Costello and Abbott at which it was agreed that I would announce that if the Coalition were returned at the election, I would stand down midway through the next term. I subsequently told a meeting of Liberal MPs that I did not feel any of my ministers had been disloyal and that I would retire during the next term, if we won. That evening I appeared on the *7.30 Report* and announced my conditional retirement plans. It was a poor performance on my part as I sounded defensive and indecisive. Several ministers, including Downer and Minchin, had gone on the media earlier in the day and killed the idea that I was going. It had been a messy few days.

I had made a serious mistake in asking that Downer sound out the cabinet members. The continued bad political news had affected my judgement. In retrospect, the idea of changing the leader in those circumstances, that close to the election, was preposterous. There was never any prospect that my cabinet colleagues would publicly request me to resign. The majority of the parliamentary party members still wanted me to lead them to the election, despite our dire electoral position.

Joe Hockey and Mal Brough had both rung me over the weekend and said they believed I should stand down. Neither really pushed the issue, and I had the distinct impression that both were getting on the record for the sake of posterity. I did not hold it against either and respected their candour. They were the only ones.

Apart from Andrew Robb calling to see me at the Lodge on Sunday night a week later to inform me that he would start lobbying the next day amongst MPs to organise a request that I go, the whole issue fizzled out. The next Newspoll, the following Tuesday, was better than the one which had helped distort my judgement. It was only 55–45 against us! Robb argued that he was driven to do what he foreshadowed because I had said I would only stay for part of the next term, if we won. His logic was that I should commit to staying on into my 72nd year. That was not sustainable. Robb believed that my declaration had made me a lame duck. He said that if voters knew I was going, come what may, many would think it a good idea to accelerate that process in the name of having a change of government anyway. The British experience, where Tony Blair had said he would retire after the election and well into his new term, had not stopped the British Labour Party from winning the 2005 election quite comfortably. In any event, the Robb initiative went nowhere.

If the leadership were to have changed during what proved to be our last term, the time for that was in 2006. For the reasons I have explained, that did not happen. From then on, the die had been cast and, barring a spontaneous rising against me (à la Kevin Rudd in June 2010), with a public request for me to depart, to which I would have willingly acceded, the leadership should not have been canvassed again.

45

THE TIDE RUNS OUT

My favourite subject at Sydney University Law School was the Law of Evidence. It went to the heart of disputes between the recollections of people about certain events important to them and to the testing of those recollections in court. In 1960, when I did the subject, my year had a magnificent lecturer, Len Badham QC.

Badham taught us that human recollection is inherently frail, the more so with the distance of time. Therefore contemporaneous evidence, however given or recorded, is always the most reliable. I have occasionally remembered his commonsense counsel as I have reflected over the past three years about events during my Government's last year in office and the reasons for our sharp change of political fortunes. Fortuitously, my habit of making diary notes on various occasions has enabled me to compare how I felt about certain issues several years ago, as compared with how they rate now.

On 8 November 2006, just over 12 months before the Government lost office, I entered a note in my diary which revealed my innermost concerns for my Government, and is worth quoting in full:

> A very bad day; interest rates rose by 0.25 per cent. This is the 4th increase since the election. If there is another one next year we will be in a heap of trouble. I did my best but this is really quite damaging. It will eat away at our economic credibility. Coming on top of the past two weeks of seeming to be on the back foot over climate change and also the continuing bad situation in Iraq

the political climate has become quite hard. Yet the 12 or so benchmark polls and the published ones don't, as yet, show a systemic fall in our vote. But I do have the feeling that we are 'running on empty' and that sooner or later something will give.

As an unvarnished reflection, it was interesting for the subjects it mentioned, as well as for those it did not touch. Interest rates and climate change were cited, but not workplace relations. Iraq rated because the situation there was so bad in late 2006; this was before the surge, and the opposition had really hammered away at it in parliament. Early November 2006 was right in the middle of the perfect storm on climate change.

Interest-rate increases bothered me politically. My fears about interest rates were more than realised the following year. They went up again in August and also, most damagingly, in the middle of November 2007 — two weeks before the election. Given the strong campaign I had run on interest rates in 2004, any rise would be used heavily by the opposition, particularly against me.

The reasons why governments are voted out of office are usually more prosaic than either politicians or commentators wish to admit. There is rarely one single reason, although the longer a government has been in power, the desire for change becomes an increasingly potent consideration.

Naturally Beazley had to step in when Latham resigned unexpectedly, on 18 January 2005, but he was far from ready. He had wanted more time out of the limelight. And I don't think that his health had fully recovered. There was warmth but not much excitement about Beazley's return. Given the way in which he had departed, the Labor Party wanted to forget the whole Latham exercise. So did some of his more enthusiastic media backers.

It was obvious from the outset that Beazley's minders had convinced him that he had to be more belligerent towards me. There was to be no more Mr Nice Guy. Almost literally, Kim Beazley began to snarl across the parliamentary table at me, and referring to me as 'Howard', not Prime Minister or Mr Howard. It didn't work; worse still, he didn't look comfortable when he said it. On 31 October 2005, to mark 20 years of Beazley being in parliament I decided that I would make special mention of that fact. As a normal courtesy I had forewarned Beazley of my intention to do so. I made a short and friendly speech, praising his contribution to Labor, mentioning his father and remarking on his service to his constituents. I felt that it had been the right thing to do. To my surprise, Beazley did not reply personally. He delegated that task to his deputy, Jenny Macklin. It was quite pathetic. Nobody was the least bit interested in what Macklin had to say about Beazley. I had paid him a compliment which he deserved, and he should have replied direct. Tone-deaf minders had taken over.

Even worse had been Beazley's decision, several months earlier, to vote against the tax cuts in the 2005 budget. With confected indignation, he denounced them as favouring the rich, which was ludicrous given that the lion's share of earlier reductions had favoured low- and middle-income earners. The principal result of the personal tax cuts delivered by the New Taxation System in 2000 had been to leave at least 80 per cent of taxpayers with a marginal tax rate of no more than 30 per cent, which was a beneficial reform for low- and middle-income earners. The 2005 budget proposed tax cuts in the 2005–06 year for all taxpayers; in 2006–07 the proposal was to lift the thresholds at which the top two rates applied. That change was long overdue. The low levels at which our top rates cut in had a negative impact on incentives to work harder. All that filtered through to the public was that Kim Beazley had voted against tax cuts. In the end he capitulated, looking faintly ridiculous, and with many in his own ranks muttering darkly about his lack of judgement.

He never really recovered from this gross error of judgement. There was some early enthusiasm about his return to the leadership, the feeling being that Labor had made a terrible mistake with Latham (which it had) and was now back on track, with Beazley making things competitive. In an April 2005 Newspoll, his satisfaction rating hit 52 per cent; by mid-July, two months after the budget, it had slumped to the low 30s. It ended 2005 at 36 per cent and well in negative territory, with more disapproving than approving of his stewardship. The experiment with an angrier Kim had not worked.

Beazley's poor personal performance through much of 2005 had been masked by the Coalition's difficulties with WorkChoices. By the end of the year we were behind in the polls, although that had not produced any widespread concern. As had been the case when we brought in tax reform, we were going through the process of introducing a major change, and it was only natural that in the early stages there would be public disquiet; in time that would subside. Long years in government had given my colleagues the capacity to experience extended periods of bad polls without panicking. It was a valuable asset.

Policy-wise, 2006 was dominated by the debate about industrial relations and the sale of the remaining public shareholding in Telstra. As a negative issue, the Australian Wheat Board (AWB) scandal was an irritant for the Government. We had established a Judicial Inquiry with the powers of a Royal Commission. Downer, Vaile and I had appeared, under oath, and although the affair attracted heavy press interest and enabled Kevin Rudd to obtain mountains of coverage as the chief opposition attack dog, it was not something that would bring the Government down. We had not done anything wrong. There had been no cover-up. As soon as I had got wind of concern from the Volcker Inquiry, established by the United Nations under the leadership of the former and highly respected Chairman of the Federal Reserve, that AWB might have been dragging its feet in responding to that inquiry, I had given firm instructions that there should be maximum cooperation and transparency. The Cole Inquiry was set up by the Government in direct response to the Volcker findings. Australia went further than any other country in responding to those findings. The Cole Inquiry found no wrongdoing on the part of any government ministers, and that AWB Limited had deliberately misled both the Australian Government and the United Nations. Cole's findings directly repudiated Kevin Rudd's allegations that I had deliberately lied over aspects of the issue.

2006 saw the most innovative policy from the Treasury area in our whole time in government, the superannuation reforms announced by Peter Costello in the 2006 budget. They included the removal of all tax on superannuation payments from taxed contributions, and a significant simplification of the entire superannuation structure. These reforms were widely welcomed. They were accompanied by a major liberalisation of the assets test for the aged pension. Given the way in which the global financial plunge of 2008 ravaged the retirement incomes of many Australians, these 2006 changes provided a valuable buffer for older Australians.

For all of its famed intellectual resources, and they were formidable, the Treasury produced few really inspiring new policy ideas during our time in government, or certainly not ones of which I was made aware. Big changes such as the GST had been around for a long time and were finally brought to fruition when the requisite political will came into play. The independence of the Reserve Bank and the Charter of Budget Honesty were both pre-election promises, way back in 1996. I don't diminish the fine technical work of the Treasury in the design features of big policy reform, such as taxation. It was impressive and indispensable to the final product.

But the big ideas never seemed to come from there in the first place. Perhaps it was because new ideas often involved spending money, therefore Treasury's attitude was no new ideas.

The Commonwealth Treasury does not always oppose spending money. According to numerous reports which have never been disputed, Ken Henry, the current Treasury secretary, told the Rudd Government when the world financial plunge hit in September 2008, to 'Go hard, go early and go households', with lots of new spending. That advice led to the biggest discrete federal spending splurge in my lifetime. Presumably it was judged that the huge fiscal injection of late 2008 and early 2009 was justified by the circumstances.

There were times between 1996 and 2007 when spending extra money in areas such as Health, Education and welfare reform were fully justified. Yet the Treasury usually saw its role as resisting the spending, rather than playing a leading role in designing the best way in which the extra resources should be used. Welfare to work reforms, work/family balance policy and the major health changes of 2003 and 2004 are leading examples of where the policy drive came from elsewhere than the Treasury.

When I recorded my thoughts about the Government in my diary on 8 November 2006, I had no idea that Kim Beazley's days as Labor leader were numbered. I was aware of the personal dislike of Kevin Rudd in ALP ranks, believed the opposition would not make the left-wing Julia Gillard leader, and assumed that the genuine affection for Beazley within Labor ranks as well as his vast experience would sustain him.

He certainly needed sustenance. He had had a number of lapses, two of which were quite embarrassing, indicative of a man heavily affected by the pressure of the job. In August, he mistook comments of the Reserve Bank governor Ian Macfarlane for those of Ian McFarlane, the Industry and Resources Minister, and, in error, attacked the central bank boss. Worse still, in November, when Belinda Emmett, the popular wife of the TV host Rove McManus, died at the tragically early age of 32, Beazley, on the morning of her funeral, extended his condolences to 'Karl Rove' (George Bush's principal political advisor). The name confusion was excruciating. It was impossible not to feel sorry for Beazley.

I was in Kuala Lumpur on a visit to Malaysia when, on Friday, 1 December, speaking to my Canberra office by telephone, Ben Mitchell, one of my press secretaries, said, 'Rudd has just been to see Beazley and told him he is mounting a challenge. Beazley has called a meeting next week. Rudd and Gillard are in it together.' Speculation had been there, but this development surprised me. The night before, Brian Loughnane, the federal director, had given me the results of a further series of benchmark polls in marginal seats. Not every one of them was marvellous, but we were still in a winning position. That was all about to change.

I sensed that Beazley's fate was sealed when I saw Michael Forshaw, a right-wing ALP senator from New South Wales, say on TV, 'I'm voting for Kevin Rudd, but with a heavy heart, because I think Kim Beazley deserves great tribute, great admiration from the party. I hope that he will understand the decision of many people who have supported him in the past, still respect him, but we have to move on.'[1] He was a NSW Labor Party machine man, pure and simple. Beazley's solid NSW support base had eroded. Rudd's big spruikers in New South Wales were John Robertson, head of Unions NSW, and Mark Arbib, the general secretary of the ALP's NSW branch, later a senator and junior government minister.

These alliances, and the deal he had made with Julia Gillard for her to replace Jenny Macklin as Deputy Leader, were the decisive elements in Rudd's 49 to 39 victory over Beazley on Monday, 4 December. It was an immensely sad day for Kim Beazley. Not only did he lose the leadership, but that day his brother died suddenly in Perth. I made sure that there was a VIP jet available to fly him home to his grieving parents.

The day of the ballot, an A.C. Nielsen poll, published in the *Sydney Morning Herald* and the *Age*, showed Labor ahead of the Coalition by 56 to 44 on a two-party-preferred basis, with a 12 per cent primary vote for the Greens. Beazley was then still leader, although, when most of the interviews for the poll were conducted, there would have been full knowledge of the upcoming leadership vote. That was as big a lead as Labor had had all year. I was still miles ahead of Beazley on the preferred PM measure, and the Green vote remained high. These suggested that doubts about Beazley were suppressing the ALP vote. The Green vote eased somewhat once Rudd replaced Beazley, with Labor's primary vote jumping to about 47 per cent, and staying in that region in every subsequent Newspoll and A.C. Nielsen survey until right on the eve of the election.

The Rudd–Gillard team transformed the political scene. New leadership teams always do, especially against a government which had by then been in power for almost 11 years. Rudd's strategy was simple: he would run as a younger version of me and without what he argued were the rough edges of issues such as WorkChoices and our refusal to ratify Kyoto. There was widespread press interest in the duo, and they got off to a flying start. The first Newspoll after Rudd's elevation had Labor leading the Coalition 55 to 45 on a two-party-preferred basis, and the opposition never looked back from there. By March, Rudd led me by 10 points on the preferred PM measurement; the last between Beazley and me had given me a margin of 30 points. In the middle of March 2007, Labor's two-party-preferred lead was an astonishing 61–39, according to Newspoll.

Rudd's election surprised me. I had thought that his style would grate too much with ALP members who didn't appreciate being lectured to on a regular basis. I obviously underestimated their sense of despair with Kim Beazley.

It was obvious from the published polling and our own internal research that Rudd and Gillard presented a huge challenge. For the first time in more than a decade the Labor Party had momentum. Rudd was energetic, and presented well in a clear, cut-through fashion. This was not what I had expected, and I knew that I faced the fight of my life.

As I pondered the year ahead over the Christmas/New Year break, first at Kirribilli and then briefly at Cable Beach, near Broome in Western Australia, I thought a lot about the composition of the cabinet. The reshuffle I decided on involved my seeking Amanda Vanstone's resignation, not an easy conversation; she had been Australia's longest-serving female cabinet minister and had been part of my ministerial team from the outset in 1996. Nonetheless, I felt that Immigration needed a new person at the helm. Amanda was impressive on broad policy and concepts, not so committed to detail and paper shifting — an essential part of that portfolio. A little while later she was appointed Australia's ambassador to Italy.

I promoted Malcolm Turnbull straight into cabinet as Minister for the Environment and Water Resources. It was a punt but a justified one. Turnbull had done well as a parliamentary secretary for Water. He had flair, and I thought that in a year in which the media would be obsessed with the environment and climate change, he would do a better job than Ian Campbell, the Environment Minister. I shifted him to Human Services, still in the cabinet.

I respected Kevin Andrews and I had no desire to demote him, so I made him Immigration Minister in place of Amanda Vanstone. He was disappointed but accepted the change and handled a tricky job well. The other cabinet change, and an important one, was to promote Joe Hockey into Workplace Relations and add him to cabinet. Hockey was a good media performer. He had gathered a lot of publicity from his joint appearances on the *Sunrise* program with Kevin Rudd. He came from Sydney, the nation's major media outlet, and that would help give the post more exposure. It was a difficult, but necessary, reshuffle.

This was the last significant ministerial reshuffle I would have. On the subject of reshuffles, it is worth noting that old habits amongst critics always die hard. Throughout the time I was Prime Minister, there was an express or implied criticism that the so-called moderates or 'small l' Liberals were unfairly treated by me when it came to ministerial preferment. It was a false charge. I only have to list the names of Hill, Ruddock, Nelson, Vanstone, Hockey, Turnbull, Patterson, Wooldridge, Fahey, Williams, Brandis and Brough to refute this allegation.

All of them, in one way or another, identified with the progressive side of the party on the quite rare occasions when such labels were an issue. I honoured the broad church that our party was. That is one reason why we were so successful for so long.

Although I knew how hard it had now become, I was by no means defeatist, nor were my colleagues. We had all been here before — or sort of. Mark Latham had started well, not as well as Rudd, but enough to unnerve us for a while. Then he had stumbled, and gradually we had worn him down, only to go on and win the 2004 election with an increased majority. In the early phase of Rudd's leadership, it was believed that the same pattern would be repeated with him.

We were all imbued with the belief that the public would not throw us out against the background of such a powerful economy. Colleagues continued to report that there was no general hostility towards the Government and that my personal stocks with voters remained high. Given the polls, we concluded that despite the people being happy with the Government, they were excited with the possibility of change.

Our internal research highlighted an emerging problem. Australians thought that we had run the economy well and saw the Coalition as far superior economically to the Labor Party, but, ominously, had begun to take the strength of the economy for granted. There was an increasing tendency to attribute the healthy domestic economy to the strength of the global economy, especially China. Such an attitude, if it were to take hold, would reduce the risk of a switch to Labor. Unsurprisingly, we set out to highlight

Labor's past failures on the economy, especially high interest rates and as well the potential influence of trade union bosses on a future Labor Government.

I was determined that the Government would continue to take major decisions and not be spooked into timidity by Labor's new-found poll ascendency. If the Coalition became too defensive, the public would sense that it had lost its nerve and certainly vote it from office. We also had to work hard to solve issues which really aggravated sections of the electorate for no long-term policy gain and where no important principle was at stake. I called them 'barnacles'.

The prime example of a barnacle was the time it had taken for the Americans to bring David Hicks to trial. Most Australians suspected that Hicks was at least guilty of the things to which he ultimately pleaded guilty. They had little sympathy for him, but he should have his day in court. The fact that a lot of the delay was due to major constitutional challenges against the military commissions which were intended to try detainees such as Hicks went through to the keeper with most Australians. The longer the wait dragged on, the harder it became to stop supporters of Hicks building him into some kind of martyr.

At every level we had pressured the Americans to bring Hicks to trial. I spoke to George Bush about it at the APEC meeting in Hanoi the previous November, and again in February 2007, stressing the domestic political problems for my Government. Just a few days later the Vice-president, Richard Cheney, arrived in Australia. I pressed him hard on Hicks. He told me that Hicks was 'at the head of the queue'. They had got the message.

On 30 March the US Defense Department announced that Hicks had been convicted of giving material support to terrorism. Hicks admitted to 35 facts that supported the charge. These included training at multiple al Qaeda camps in Afghanistan and joining fighters at Kandahar Airport and frontline forces in Konduz after the terrorist attacks of 11 September.

We then turned our attention to the 2007 budget, with both Peter Costello and me realising that this could be the last Coalition budget for some years. The nation's fiscal position was enviable, so a popular budget would be fully consistent with sound economic policy. There needed to be a heavy emphasis on tertiary education, because a highly educated workforce was critical to our future. There was a $5 billion tertiary education fund as well as further taxation relief, for the fifth year in a row. There were also vouchers for parents of children who had not met the national literacy and numeracy benchmarks, as well as generous measures to aid the professional development of teachers. There were one-off payments to retired Australians and, yet again, special bonus payments to carers.

The budget received a rapturous reception. It touched as many bases as one could possibly hope for. Ross Gittins of the *Sydney Morning Herald*, often a harsh critic of the Government, said, '… as pre-election budgets go this one's not bad. As you would expect, there are a lot of giveaways, but their total cost is not sufficient to put pressure on interest rates.'[2] He said that the budget was about investing in the future. Terry McCrann said that the budget posed no threat to interest rates. Polling found that it was the best-received budget ever. Yet, incredibly, it had not lifted our support. The Government was completely flattened by the finding of the first voting-intention Newspoll after the budget that Labor led the Coalition on a two-party-preferred basis by 60 per cent to 40 per cent. Our political fortunes remained in the doldrums.

The Liberal and National parties faced a perplexing situation. For close to five months the Labor Party had held a commanding poll lead, enough to give it a really big win if replicated at the polling booths. Nothing we had done in response seemed to work. We had delivered a popular and widely applauded budget. The public and the boffins both liked it. There was good long-term policy in the document. The fairness test had been introduced to remove the perception of harshness from our workplace changes. The Hicks issue had been resolved. We had launched a huge water initiative, although some of the states were playing games on this. We had bitten the bullet on emissions trading, with the Shergold Report released on 1 June rapidly being turned into clear policy. This was the agenda of an active government, still policy-confident and by no means spent and exhausted after 11 years of power.

My colleagues remained remarkably sanguine about it all. I am sure that most of them thought that I would pull a rabbit out of the hat. Sensing this air of unreality I deliberately dramatised the serious political challenge we faced by telling a joint party meeting on 22 May that we faced 'annihilation' if the opinion polls were fulfilled at the election. I knew that would receive a big press run. It sure did. It was a rudimentary approach, but I was anxious to shake any remaining complacency out of my colleagues. We had been in power for so long that the majority of them had never known opposition. Of the Coalition MPs and senators of the 41st parliament, only 46 had been elected before we came to power in 1996, compared with 81 elected since 1996.

It was to Alexander Downer that I spoke most candidly about our political position. His theory was that the prolonged drought had depressed people, and that once it rained again our electoral fortunes would turn around. It was an interesting take but I didn't believe it.

Early in 2007 I had formed a small political tactics group, to meet over dinner at the Lodge, which would regularly assess our political position. As well as me it comprised Mark Vaile, Peter Costello, Alexander Downer, Nick Minchin and Mal Brough. I added Brough both because I saw him as good potential talent and because he was from Queensland, a state which would loom large as the year wore on. I did not have a monopoly on wisdom when it came to solving our problems, and I thought that a small group such as this would encourage the frankest of discussions including, where necessary, an analysis of my own performance.

There was very little disagreement within this group; there was no push, for example, to ratify Kyoto; no pressure to change policy on Iraq; and endorsement of our embracing the framework of an emissions trading system. Knowing just how tough the political climate had become, I wanted to create maximum opportunities for senior colleagues to question the direction in which we were heading, if that was their wont. The group of five added another, more intimate forum in which that might happen.

When the election neared, this group debated the major options to be put in the 2007 campaign. We opted for the big tax reduction package announced by Costello and me right at the commencement of campaigning. At one stage, I had canvassed extensive tax breaks for savings as the centrepiece of the campaign pitch. In the end I decided that across-the-board tax relief should be supported because of its simplicity and consistency with previous Liberal and National Party policy.

From the moment he took the leadership of the Labor Party, Kevin Rudd had a Teflon quality. There were several instances where he was let off the hook by the media. In 2007 he wanted the timing of a dawn service which he was attending at the Long Tan Memorial in Vietnam altered so as to accommodate the program scheduling of the Seven Network, and then pleaded ignorance, despite the clear involvement of his staff. Similar conduct by one of my ministers, let alone me, would have drawn withering press abuse. He escaped largely unscathed.

The same could be said of his association with Brian Burke, the former, highly controversial Labor Premier of Western Australia. Burke had been referred to several times in WA's Criminal Justice Commission, and declared persona non grata by his own party in the west. Rudd had attended a dinner with Burke, which he initially denied. At that time he was campaigning hard for the leadership. When sprung, he pretended that he had simply gone along as the guest of his WA colleague Graeme Edwards, who was a long-time associate of Burke's. That, also, was later disproved, with the release of email traffic suggesting that the context of Rudd's contact with Burke was indeed Rudd's future.

Rather than hurting Rudd, it ended up terminating Senator Ian Campbell's ministerial career. Campbell, a West Australian, was the Minister for Human Services. When news of Rudd attending the Burke dinner surfaced, we decided to hit the ALP leader very hard. Peter Costello attacked Rudd in parliament, saying that anyone who dealt with Burke was morally and politically compromised. Then it emerged that Ian Campbell had seen Burke several months earlier, in his former capacity as Minister for the Environment. In other circumstances that would not have mattered, as the contact had been innocent and predated some of the more recent allegations against Burke.

Unfortunately, Campbell told no one of his meeting with Burke. He must have realised the potential embarrassment if that meeting became public, which it surely would once Costello elevated the attack on Rudd. The press had become aware of the meeting by the following day, and knowing that it would break as a big story the day after, Campbell then told my office about it. Politically, Campbell had been wrong not telling us of the Burke encounter and allowing Costello and others to go out and attack Burke, only to be left high and dry when the meeting with Burke was revealed.

I indicated to Campbell the next day that he should resign. He did so with little demur. He knew that he had let us down politically. It was a tough price to pay, but the stakes were high. Here was an opportunity to dent Rudd's credibility and our attack had been derailed because of his failure to tell us of the Burke meeting. I felt sorry for Campbell, but there was no option.

The public seemed unshaken in its desire to have a new government. The economy powered ahead, with unemployment continuing to fall. But there was a growing disconnection between these two indicators and the public mood. Despite the aggregate strength of the economy, it was the relative position of citizens that mattered. Most Australians paying off their homes in 2007 would have borrowed to buy their homes when interest rates were lower than they were in 2007. Their relative position had deteriorated. The fact that rates had been much higher years earlier cut no ice with them. Petrol prices were higher, which added to the squeeze on many families. The drought had affected food prices, as had rises in food costs around the world.

There were logical explanations for all of these things and little blame could be sheeted home to the Howard Government, but that did not diminish the growing sense amongst a lot of Australians that, 'This economy of ours might be going gangbusters, but I'm getting squeezed a lot and need help.' Rudd exploited this mood with fraudulent gimmicks such as Grocery Watch, which he cynically abandoned after about a year into government. Our problem was longevity. The longer we were there, the less likely it was that the public would see a risk in change. In any event the people seemed more and more of the view that the economy practically ran itself or was driven by external factors.

In this climate the Coalition's best line of attack had to be that there was a risk to the steady management of the Australian economy in electing the Labor Party. Surveys always showed that economic management was our prime asset. This, though, was not enough. People might think we could run the economy better, but this did not automatically mean that they thought Labor would be incompetent economic managers. We had to elevate in the mind of the public that there was a risk in electing Rudd. This was best done by emphasising trade union influence on a future Labor Government.

Rudd knew this was his vulnerability, so he played down union links, even pretending not to know the name of the union to which he belonged. Given his career background, he was the least easily typecast as a servant of the union movement of all of Labor's recent leaders. Despite this there were times when the union factor began to work against Labor. The draft industrial relations policy produced by the Labor Party conference in April 2007 was much too radical, and after an outcry from the business community and fierce criticism from the Coalition, Rudd forced Gillard to water it down.

Militant building unions, especially in Victoria and Western Australia, worried Rudd. The ugly faces of union militancy in building were Kevin Reynolds and Joe McDonald, both from Western Australia. McDonald had been caught on camera threatening people on a building site. Sensing a problem Rudd prevailed on the WA branch of the Labor Party to suspend McDonald's party membership. He also said that a Labor Government would retain the Australian Building and Construction Commission (ABCC) until 2010, when it would be absorbed into Fair Work Australia, the umbrella agency it was intended would run industrial relations under a Labor Government. Rudd and Gillard kept attacking unlawful behaviour in the building industry and repeating the mantra that they would have 'a tough cop on the beat'. In government, Rudd and Gillard weakened the ABCC in advance of its proposed disappearance into Fair Work Australia.

Such was the hunger of Labor MPs, party officials and leading union figures for the return of a federal Labor Government that they all fell into line when confronted with any union militancy which might prove unpopular with voters. They all knew that the Howard Government was far from unpopular, and that the desire for change could easily disappear if the public sensed that was a risk in opting for Labor. Their collective discipline meant that Rudd could get away with superficial assurances and contrived toughness whenever confronted by union excesses.

The unions were particularly well disciplined. Greg Combet, the ACTU secretary, knew what was at stake for his movement. If the Coalition won again, the industrial relations landscape would be changed forever. The transformation of the previous decade would be consolidated; the possibility of some future Labor Government restoring the privileged position the unions once occupied would be virtually non-existent.

Combet showed a far more sophisticated appreciation of the historic importance of the 2007 poll for industrial relations than did most business leaders in Australia. Although they supported the open and more balanced workplace system we had put in place, they failed to realise the obverse of the Combet nightmare, despite my repeated public warnings. If the Coalition lost, and the perception was that the loss had been due to its industrial relations policies, then for a long time into the future no Coalition opposition would be willing to campaign too hard for industrial relations reform. That certainly proved to be the case.

Despite the continuing poll gloom, the Coalition kept its policy nerve. The announcement in June of an emissions trading system was followed within weeks by the dramatic intervention in the Northern Territory, which overturned 30 years of failed Indigenous policy based on the doctrine of separate development. My Government intervened because the Territory Government had failed to provide the most basic of all services to Aboriginal children in the Territory, namely protection from child abuse. That matter is explored in Chapter 25.

Awkward news intruded. Inflation for the June quarter at 1.2 per cent was higher than expected. My heart sank when I heard it in the Perth studio of the ABC, as I knew immediately that with the economy growing so firmly the RBA would lift interest rates at its monthly meeting in two weeks' time. The cold political reality was that another rate hike in August 2007 made it five rate increases in all since the 2004 election. It hurt us a lot. We dared not contemplate it at the time, but worse was to come.

Other awkward news was the decision of the AFP to abandon altogether any action against Mohamed Haneef, the Indian doctor employed in a Queensland hospital and detained on suspicion of a link with a terrorist attack in Glasgow, Scotland. Even though Haneef had been released, Kevin Andrews cancelled his visa and the man returned to India. The detention and charging of Haneef had occurred independently of the Government. The AFP had acted on the advice of the Director of Public Prosecutions (DPP), who later admitted that the advice given had been faulty. Even though Andrews had adequate reason on character grounds to cancel the visa, the Government was heavily attacked for trying to exploit fear of terrorism for political gain. The AFP's decision to abandon the case against Haneef bolstered, however unfairly, that attack on the Government.

On Monday, 6 August there was a highly damaging leak of research analysis prepared on 21 June by Crosby/Textor, the firm comprising Lynton Crosby, the former Liberal federal director, and Mark Textor, who had done our polling for close to 15 years. I did not know of its existence until word of the pending publication of the leaked material reached my press office. It was highly critical of me, and could not have been leaked at a worse time. Its disclosure was calculated to cause maximum injury to the Liberal Party, and me in particular. The *Daily Telegraph*, to whom the material was leaked, made merry with it.

I was both angry and mystified about what had happened. In my time as PM, research material had not leaked like this. This had been designed to really wound me and the Government, and it did. With an election due in approximately three months, I had to put the incident behind me, particularly as Mark Textor, who was a good pollster, would continue to do our tracking and focus group research up to and including the campaign.

APEC met in Sydney in the first week of September; it was the most prestigious gathering of world leaders ever to come to Australia. All of the heads of government of APEC turned up, with the final communiqué —

called the Sydney Declaration — containing a commitment from developing and developed nations alike to move forward on climate change. APEC was neutral for domestic politics. I had expected nothing else. Rudd won points for being able to speak Mandarin in public at the official luncheon for the Chinese President.

The captains and the kings having departed, all attention turned to the forthcoming election. The sensible option was to hold the election in November, and I ultimately decided on 24 November. There was no particular magic about this date. Given that the Coalition continued to trail the ALP in all of the polls, it made sense to give ourselves the maximum time, consistent with the election being held comfortably before Christmas.

It emerged, from a comparison of the polls on the day with those before the election, that the Coalition had made up a lot of ground during the campaign. Could the gap have been closed even more, so that the Liberal and National parties might have hung on? The answer must be in the negative, absent a calamitous mistake by the Labor opposition which might have cast real doubt on its ability to govern. Given its discipline since Rudd had taken over, that was not going to happen to the ALP.

In my opinion the Australian people were contemplating a change of government from as far back as the middle of 2006. But they had no real confidence in Beazley. If he had remained Leader, the ALP would not have won the election. The 'It's time' factor, which I believe was the principal reason for our defeat, would not have overwhelmed their reservations about Beazley. After all, Rudd did not win in a landslide. His 2007 victory was the narrowest win producing a change of government since Whitlam's in 1972. It fell well short of Hawke's win in 1983, and was nothing like Fraser's margin in 1975 or mine in 1996.

Although the Coalition clawed back Labor's big poll lead during the campaign, it was dogged by the interest-rate issue and a series of individual incidents which all combined to rob us of any real momentum after the first week. We got off to a good start with our commitment to wholesale further tax relief, easily paid for out of the prospective surpluses across the forward estimates. This promise totally blindsided the Labor Party. We had grabbed the agenda. For five days Labor was silent, eventually matching our proposal except for some of the top-end cuts. Rudd redirected the money needed for these towards a rebate for laptop computers for all school students. Many already had them, but it played well, with his best line of the campaign being, I think, his description of the laptop as 'the toolbox of the 21st century'.

Rudd was judged to have won the leaders debate. The published polls gave the Coalition little comfort. Any hope that once the real thing had arrived, the public might flood back to the devil they knew quickly disappeared. Our internal research was not much different, although on one occasion the aggregate of the track had us just ahead. Nothing suggested that we do other than hammer away on the economy and hope that Rudd or one of his foot soldiers would blunder.

Peter Garrett, shadow minister for the Environment, obliged — twice. During an *AM* radio interview, he said that Australia should commit to binding emissions reduction targets in advance of agreement from other nations to do likewise. I pounced on this and Rudd was forced later that day to overrule Garrett. Soon afterwards, Steve Price of Radio 2UE reported that, in an airport conversation, Garrett, when pinned on the difference between his pro-environmental rhetoric and Labor's actual policies, had said, 'Once we get in, we'll just change it all.'[3] This was dynamite and threw the ALP onto the defensive.

Regrettably, just a few days before, the *Weekend Financial Review* had carried a story, which was true, that Malcolm Turnbull had argued in cabinet for ratification of Kyoto. The timing of the piece was atrocious. It meant that full pressure could not be applied to Garrett on an issue of straight hypocrisy. In one fell swoop, public attention was back on the Coalition's refusal to ratify Kyoto, with the added bonus for Rudd that he could argue that even the Environment Minister in the Government disagreed with the Prime Minister. Try as we did, the attack on Garrett fizzled out.

On 24 October came the body blow. The CPI figure for the September quarter produced an underlying inflation rate of 0.9 of 1 per cent. The headline rate was lower, but it was the underlying rate which drove interest-rate decisions. The tipping point for a rate rise was seen as 0.7 of 1 per cent. At or below that meant there would be no movement in rates. Given the commentary which had been allowed to develop, the RBA must either lift rates by 0.25 per cent at its November meeting, an action with unmistakable political implications, or risk being accused of acting politically by not lifting rates. Inevitably the bank lifted rates on 6 November, just 18 days before the election.

This catch-22 had arisen because the bank had ignored the implied understanding which had existed between the Government and the bank, since full RBA independence in 1996, that the RBA saw to it that it kept out of the crossfire during election campaigns. There had been no rate increases in the 12 months before the 2004 election.

It could not seriously be suggested that the bank lacked independence. After all, it had already lifted rates in August, just three months from the election. It would have been well within its capacity and in no way compromising of its independence to have made it known, with its inimitable smoke signals, that in the absence of a serious spike in inflation (which the November figure clearly was not), rates were on hold until the beginning of 2008.

The markets would have understood, and no damage would have been done to monetary policy. After all, the case for a hike in November 2007 was marginal. If the increase in the underlying rate had been 0.7 and not 0.9, rates would not have changed. Monetary policy is anything but that precise. The other measurements of inflation in the September quarter figures had been more benign. So far from preserving its aloofness from the political fray, the RBA had run the risk of being seen to enter the lists against the Government by lifting rates so close to the election.

I don't claim that the rate increase in November cost the Coalition the election. However, from the moment the September quarter CPI was released, both the prospect and then the reality of the increase coloured reporting of the economic aspects of the campaign. It diverted attention from other features of the campaign which may have been more favourable to the Coalition.

Being on the defensive, as the Liberal and National parties were for most of the campaign, magnified setbacks such as Tony Abbott's shocking day when not only was he late for his debate with the shadow Health minister, Nicola Roxon, but worse than that, he foolishly impugned the motives of Bernie Banton (now deceased), the frequent spokesman for James Hardie employees affected by asbestos.

I started the last week of the campaign, on 17 November, in Perth, where the reception was warm and the results, a week later, the best in the country, with the net gain of a seat in Western Australia. On Monday afternoon I called to see Matt Price, the gifted *Australian* columnist, stricken with cancer and surrounded by his adoring family. We chatted for 40 minutes or so about politics and sport. He displayed humbling courage and cheerfulness. Matt's life was ebbing away; I only faced an election. It reminded me of life's priorities. Sadly, he died just six days later at the age of only 44. He was a real loss to the profession of journalism.

Having spent five weeks treading water, some of the polls suddenly began to tighten. Galaxy came back to 52–48, still against, but a vast improvement on earlier surveys. Newspoll also began to shift. Just maybe there was a glimmer of hope. Then on Wednesday another hammer blow. Some Liberals, including Gary Clarke, Jackie Kelly's husband, had been caught distributing bogus leaflets in the electorate of Lindsay, falsely claiming ALP support for the Bali attack and attributed to a fake allegedly Muslim organisation. It was outrageous, and contained an unjustified slur on the ALP. Those responsible were expelled from the NSW division of the party, and everything possible was done to disown this stupidity.

Karen Chijoff was the Liberal candidate for Lindsay, Kelly having opted to retire. Chijoff's husband had been involved with Gary Clarke in organising the fake leaflets. Their marriage later broke up. I felt sorry for Karen. She had worked hard in difficult circumstances and deserved better than this monumental stupidity. Jackie Kelly made matters worse by trying, during an interview on *AM*, to excuse what had happened as some kind of 'Chaser prank'! I was staggered when I heard this. The incident received extensive and damaging coverage on Thursday, the day of my final press club appearance.

My speech there was strong, and I brought together the themes of my campaign. It was to no avail. The press were only interested in Lindsay. If any last-minute rally were under way, the lunacy in Lindsay well and truly put paid to it.

I never stopped. I left Canberra after the press club for a last-minute swing through Queensland, travelling first to the suburbs of Brisbane, greeting Thursday-night shoppers, and then on to Cairns, to campaign for Charlie McKillop, Liberal candidate for Leichhardt. She had replaced Warren Entsch, an extremely popular local member who had decided to pull out for family reasons. Charlie tried hard but was out of her depth. It was plain that without Entsch, we had no hope of holding Leichhardt.

Then it was on to Townsville and Peter Lindsay, the indefatigable member for Herbert. Peter had held the seat since 1996. He stayed on to fight the 2007 election, and as parliamentary secretary for Defence he had intimate links with the huge Defence community in Herbert, clustered around the famous Lavarack Army Barracks. I am glad that he stayed; without him the Liberal Party would have lost Herbert. My final campaign stop was in Rockhampton, where I helped both the Liberal and National candidates in the new seat of Flynn. Labor won the seat, but that was something of an aberration. It is a natural Coalition seat.

I entertained some hope, based on the movement back to us shown by Newspoll and Galaxy, that there could be a late rally which might put us over the line. Our younger son, Richard, who had been working in the United States for some years, had come back for the last week of the campaign. He travelled with us through the final few days and was the source of much cheer and amusement. He had enjoyed all the electoral triumphs of the past decade and, much as he wished it would be otherwise, he had prepared for a loss on the coming Saturday, whilst working to the very end to stop it happening. Together we composed the slogan 'Stronger, prouder, more prosperous'. I was immensely lucky to have three children who cheered me on always and supported my career to the very limit. They were affectionate, helpful and ever loyal. It's not easy being the children of a prime minister; they wore it with pride and dignity, and I will forever love them for it.

Election day, 24 November 2007, was a lovely summer day in Sydney. I had my customary morning walk, followed by hordes of press people. I thought that it was probably my last day as PM, but still held out a small amount of hope, based once again on that poll shift earlier in the week.

Having been a member of the House of Representatives for 33 years and 6 months, which made me the 12th-longest-serving MP out of the more than 1100 who have been elected since Federation, I had a good sense of the mood of the electorate, simply from moving around, talking to people on polling booths and observing their body language. By mid-afternoon I sensed that the Government was gone and that I would probably lose Bennelong. Too many eyes were averted. There were the two middle-aged women at Denistone East who simply said, 'No thanks, Mr Howard'. There was the veteran at Putney School who was handing out Labor tickets because we had not agreed to a particular recognition for a form of service in Korea. It was a different mood from that of the two previous elections.

There was no special mystery about my vulnerability in Bennelong. Progressive redistributions plus some demographic changes had made it a marginal seat. My majority was 4.1 per cent, having had a further 0.6 of 1 per cent shaved from my previous margin by the 2006 redistribution. I no longer had any blue-ribbon areas such as Hunters Hill, which had been removed after the 1998 election. Bennelong was a radically different seat from the one I won way back in 1974. As well as the boundary alterations, demographic changes were working against the Liberal Party, with more students, fewer retired citizens and an Asian community with volatile voting habits.

There was also the myth of the local member's personal vote. Vanity encourages long-serving MPs in metropolitan seats to believe that they have large personal votes. When it is remembered that the true definition of a personal vote is the support of a person who, if you were not the candidate, would invariably vote for other than your party, that vote is nowhere near as high as many imagine. I didn't have a large personal vote in Bennelong; if anything, as PM I probably drew more flak than if I had been an ordinary MP.

The swing against me in Bennelong was the average pro-Labor swing in New South Wales. To be precise, it was 5.3 per cent. The statewide average was 5.1 per cent. I lost a marginal seat.

We gathered again at Kirribilli House to await the outcome. As well as my close staff, Tony Nutt, David Luff, Aileen Weisner and Tony O'Leary, Grahame Morris and Arthur Sinodinos and their wives joined us. The exit polls predicted an ALP win. We calmly accepted the outcome. By 8.30 it was all over, even though the polling booths in WA had not closed. At about 9.30 pm I rang Kevin Rudd, congratulated him and discussed transition arrangements. Peter Costello phoned. I told him that I would make my concession speech shortly and would say that I thought he should assume the leadership of the Liberal Party. He replied that he was not sure he would take it on and intended to discuss it further with family and friends. Having other things on my mind, I did not think much more about Peter and the leadership. I was genuinely surprised when he walked away from the leadership the next day. As events were to prove, I had wrongly assumed that politics was so much part of his being that he could not walk away whilst the possibility of the ultimate prize was still there.

My concession speech and the time I spent with supporters afterwards was an emotional hour and a half. I was determined to remain calm, remembering that I had revelled in four previous victories at the same hotel. More importantly, disappointment is part of life's experience, and I knew that the keen loss Janette and my three children felt would be easier for them if I handled it well.

Although given with immense regret, my concession speech was really quite easy. I congratulated Kevin Rudd and the ALP, accepted full responsibility for the defeat, told the Australian people what a privilege it had been to serve as their PM, thanked the Liberal Party for all it had done for me, and expressed remorse at the loss of so many fine colleagues. My final thanks were to my staff and, of course, my family.

That was it. That was how I ended more than 33 years in parliament and just short of 12 years as PM. There was nothing more to say at that time. I declined all requests for valedictory speeches and interviews. Later there were some generous tribute dinners, but by then political life had moved on and they took place in the context of the new battle between the Rudd Government and the Coalition led by Brendan Nelson.

The following morning I went on my normal walk, accompanied by an army of press people, which included a few strays who had come along for the ghoulish pleasure of watching me the day after my loss. I disappointed them and kept up my usual pace. Later that morning, Janette and I attended Holy Communion at the local Anglican church in Lavender Bay. If we had won the election, we would have done the same thing. By these actions I was saying in my own way that I fully accepted what had happened; it disappointed me, but that was the democratic process. For me and my family, life would go on, and it would continue to be a good life.

The following Tuesday I returned to Canberra for some farewells and a big pack-up. I said goodbye to my department properly. Peter Shergold, the secretary of PM&C, assembled them all and thanked me. I then spoke and thanked them for their professionalism over more than 11 years. I meant it. We had developed a respectful relationship. I suspected that approximately 60 to 70 per cent of them would have voted Labor three days earlier. They were not especially hostile to me, but Canberra is a Labor town. If the ALP still has a tribe, as distinct from supporters, it is the tertiary-educated salaried professionals of the public service. They are thick on the ground in Canberra. That having been said, the employees of my department had, by and large, behaved in a truly professional fashion during my time.

Janette and I invited all members of the ministry and the parliamentary secretaries to lunch at the Lodge on Tuesday so I could say my thanks. Most, but not all, were able to come and, despite the emotional let-down we all felt, it was an important occasion. Together we had produced a government of remarkable reform and achievement; even at this very early stage, we had to commence defending our legacy.

Another important farewell was a call at Russell Hill to say thank you and goodbye to the leadership of the ADF. They were all there, and I was genuinely moved by their gesture: the CDF, Air Chief Marshal Angus Houston, presented me with a wonderful replica of an Australian soldier carrying a wounded comrade. Simply entitled 'The Digger', it bore the inscription, 'To John Howard Prime Minister — For your leadership and genuine concern for the wellbeing of the soldiers, sailors and airmen of the Australian Defence Force'. That replica sits in a prominent place in my office and always will. In my time as PM I grew extremely close to the ADF. I went out of my way to back our service personnel. Their welfare will always be in my prayers.

We vacated the Lodge on Friday and, before returning to Sydney, formally called on the Governor-General to say goodbye to him for the last time as PM. It was more than a constitutional formality. Michael Jeffery had given years of military and vice-regal service to Australia; he and his wife, Marlena, were gracious and distinguished occupants of Yarralumla. My resignation was to take effect the following Monday. The day before, Janette and I invited Kevin Rudd and his wife, Thérèse, to the Lodge for afternoon tea and a 'house handover'. Media coverage of this event conveyed the impression of the orderly and civil transfer of power which is the hallmark of a mature democracy.

Why did we lose, particularly given the very robust economy? The desire for change, and a belief that with Kevin Rudd leading the ALP it was safe to do so, was the main reason. It is difficult for a national government to remain in office for much longer than a decade, unless the opposition is dysfunctional. Saturation press coverage limits the shelf life of all modern political leaders. I had been the dominant face of the Liberal side of politics for more than 20 years, even longer than the period of my prime ministership.

The mood of the electorate in November 2007 was akin to that of a reader who had reached the end of an interesting, but rather long, book. He puts it aside feeling satisfied with what he had read, but in the mood for something different.

Although the overall economy was vibrant, cost-of-living pressures were being felt everywhere. Most Australians paying off their homes were facing higher interest rate payments than several years earlier. Petrol was much dearer. As some columnists put it, there was a difference between the 'measured' economy and the 'felt' economy.

I was reminded of this in a humorous fashion at the end of 2008 by a friend. He said to me, 'John, I'm much better off than I was when you were there. My interest rates have come down and my petrol's cheaper.' Our conversation occurred after the RBA had sharply cut rates in 2008, and the financial plunge had sent fuel prices tumbling. He may not have been as sanguine in the middle of 2010.

The fear campaign on WorkChoices, especially concerning penalty rates, hurt us badly. Our refusal to ratify Kyoto fed the perception that the Coalition was unwilling to do enough on climate change and at a time when the public was really exercised on the issue.

Would we have won if I had retired in 2006 and Peter Costello had been prime minister? The only correct answer to that is that we will never know. We can only speculate. My speculation is that Peter leading us would not have changed the outcome. The desire for change relates to governments. British Labour changed from Blair to Brown, but still lost. On all the big issues, such as economic management and national security, Costello and I were as one. His style would have been different from mine, but the policy substance of the Government would have been the same. His social views were not much at variance from mine. Despite what has been written by others, I do not recall him ever advocating a formal apology to the so-called Stolen Generation.

Given the stance he had consistently taken over the years on industrial relations changes, Peter Costello could not, credibly, have taken a softer position in that area to mine.

Whether the mere fact of change and the different style Costello might have brought would have increased our vote was at least debatable. For the last 12 months of our time in office, my personal approval ratings were well ahead of the Coalition vote, some evidence at least for the proposition that I was not dragging the Coalition down.

Given the doleful tidings of the opinion polls — both public and private — for 12 months, going down in the election was no surprise. That did not, however, remove the loss and disappointment I felt and the concern I had for each of my defeated colleagues. I telephoned them all, offering commiserations and chatting about their plans for the future.

Some of them would endeavour to return at the next election; others had non-political intentions; none expressed bitterness. The common theme, in some cases through the pain of deep disappointment, was that they were proud to have been part of a government which had achieved so much for Australia.

Long years in government — which had been our good fortune — are of little avail unless the power and opportunity it brings are put to good purpose. Over almost 12 years we had done that in every area of Commonwealth Government responsibility. Australia was indeed a stronger, prouder and more prosperous nation than it had been in March 1996. That undisputed legacy was to gather strength over the ensuing few years.

*　　*　　*

Will the new Gillard Government last? The only answer is that no one knows. Menzies had exactly the same majority in 1961, but his troops were all Liberals and Nationals (then Country Party), not the cosmopolitan collection which gave Gillard a lifeline to the Lodge.

History will offer her no comfort. The last time something like this happened — in 1940 — there were two changes of Prime Minister — first from Menzies to Fadden and then from Fadden to Curtin — before another election took place.

Rob Oakeshott's opportunism should cost him dearly when he next faces electoral judgement. Tony Windsor apparently believes that good government is achieved if the 43rd parliament lasts three years, not by what the government does during that parliament. Bob Katter emerged with honour. He objectively assessed the benefits on offer for his electorate and kept faith with his political values.

By the narrowest possible margin Tony Abbott fell short of upending more than 100 years of political history in Australia. Scullin's first-term loss is distinguishable as it was in the middle of the Great Depression when incumbent governments were especially vulnerable. By contrast the Australian economy was in world-class condition when the people voted on 21 August 2010. This should have virtually guaranteed the return of the Labor Government. That the ALP did not win in its own right will always bear testament to the poor political judgement of the federal Labor MPs who consented to the removal of Kevin Rudd as PM.

Kevin Rudd would have led the ALP to a clear victory if he had still been PM. It was a colossal blunder by Labor to dump him. He had not been a particularly good PM; he had little policy substance; he was increasingly perplexing the public with his verbose style of communication; and he treated his colleagues in an arrogant way — an elemental failure for a political leader in egalitarian Australia. He would, however, have brought one great virtue to the election campaign for the ALP. Rudd would have been able to deliver an uncomplicated re-election message — that his Government had saved Australia from a recession. It would have been a false and fiercely contested claim, but it would have been direct, unconditional and decisive.

It was never possible for Gillard to claim, convincingly, that the ALP had saved the nation from recession, because that required her to rationalise the execution of the man who led the rescue operation. Rudd, according to Gillard, had to go because under him the Government had 'lost its way'. That invited the unanswerable retort: how could a government which had lost its way have saved Australia from recession?

Gillard compounded this problem by calling the election much too soon. A poll late in October would have given her two precious months in which to gain traction from incumbency and, importantly, draw some of the poison from within Labor's rank and file over Rudd's downfall, especially in Queensland.

The foregoing is written from the perspective of ALP errors. Some of them were unforced, such as the ludicrously early poll. Others were a direct result of the dramatic change in the dynamic of Australian politics when Tony Abbott, unexpectedly, became Leader of the Opposition early in December 2009. Abbott won the leadership on a policy principle — opposition to the ETS. Malcolm Turnbull lost his leadership because he did not try hard enough to hold his party together on the issue. Joe Hockey failed to win the leadership — despite strong evidence at one point that he was the favoured compromise candidate — because of his foolish decision to offer Liberal MPs a free vote on the ETS. It was a mainstream economic issue, thus requiring any leadership aspirant to have a clear attitude, one way or the other.

Rudd and Abbott could not have presented a sharper contrast. Abbott was direct and authentic, Rudd wordy and process-driven. As a result, the PM lost his nerve on climate change and passed up the opportunity of a double dissolution, which he would have won. He then completed his capitulation by deferring the ETS for several years. So the 'great moral challenge' (always a ludicrous description) had become just another malleable policy. It was his biggest single mistake, from which committed Labor and swinging voters concluded that he didn't really have strong convictions about anything. That began his poll slide, which ultimately brought about his replacement by Gillard.

Just as Rudd had lost his nerve on the ETS, his colleagues lost theirs over his popularity. All leaders have poll slumps. In both 1998 and 2001 my approval rating, in Newspoll, fell as low as 28 per cent. The lowest Rudd's score ever went was 36 per cent. Moreover his narrowest lead on the preferred Prime Minister measurement was 9 per cent, whereas in both of the years mentioned I fell behind on that measurement, and on a number of occasions.

Rudd was astonishingly friendless when the knock on the door came, a consequence of his bad people skills. Yet he was like that when they made him leader and he won the 2007 election. Those Labor MPs who now blame the faction leaders for this historic political setback for the ALP, which Gillard's deal with the independents narrowly prevented from being a disaster, are themselves collectively to blame. In the Australian political system, it is the MPs alone who vote for the leader, Labor or Liberal. If Labor MPs believed the factional heavies, their judgement was abysmal; if they were bullied into it through fear of losing their endorsements, they were cowards. Either way they were the guilty men and women.

Gillard's campaign was shrill and negative, relying much too heavily on demonising Tony Abbott. The ALP underestimated Abbott, as epitomised by Bob Hawke's statement that although he was 'a good bloke' he was 'as mad as a cut snake'.[4] How foolish that assessment appears now. The claim that Abbott would bring back WorkChoices lacked credibility. As explained earlier, Abbott was never a zealot about industrial relations changes.

Tony Abbott deserves hero status amongst Liberals. His high intelligence and superb discipline in the campaign confounded his many patronising critics. No other person leading the party could have achieved what he did.

He may have secured the Liberal leadership by just one vote, but he quickly pulled his party together and dealt in such a way with his National Party allies that the Coalition remained impressively united. One of his great strengths is his consultative style. He is a good listener; he understands the ambitions of others as well as striving to realise his own. When he suffers a poll slump, as he surely will, there will be no shortage of colleagues prepared to stand by him. His conduct will accrue loyalty.

The Greens polled well, partly by courtesy of Labor voters unhappy with the ALP's shillyshallying on climate change and its opportunistic shift on asylum-seekers. These were protest votes and not lasting gains for the Greens. There was a similar phenomenon in 1990 when the Democrats increased their numbers in the Senate to eight. Twenty years later, the Democrats have gone completely from federal parliament. For some years after 1 July 2011, however, the Greens will have the balance of power in the Senate. This bodes ill for any long-term economic reforms.

Its alliance with the Greens means that, at best, the new Gillard Government will tread water on reform.

46

REFLECTIONS

Any person who has ever been in public life for as long as I was and experienced the opportunities that I did has no excuse for personal regrets. I believed in all of the major decisions of my Government. There were execution errors, many I have acknowledged, but the policy content I always felt to be in the national interest. Those reforms or causes in which I believed I either achieved or promoted or, to the limit of my ability, attempted to do that.

That was because I stuck to the core political values I brought with me to parliament in 1974. Compromise is a necessary political tool, but conviction is the mother of success in politics. If that proposition is doubted, ponder the words of the British author John O'Sullivan in his book *The Pope, the President and the Prime Minister*, written about Pope John Paul II, Ronald Reagan and Margaret Thatcher, and which traced those periods in the careers of those three leaders when their values were out of fashion. It memorably records the fact that, at one stage, none of them was gaining traction: 'Put simply Wojtyla was too Catholic, Margaret Thatcher too conservative and Reagan too American.'[1]

Ultimately, their values did gain traction, were widely accepted within their constituencies, and profound change for the world ensued. The contribution they made together to the collapse of Soviet imperialism — the most significant political development since World War II — cannot be questioned. If Ronald Reagan had followed the dictates of moral relativism urged upon him by his many critics, the course of world history in recent decades would have been profoundly different. When he brought his simple values of freedom and individual liberty to his dealings with the Soviets, many within the left liberal intelligentsia shuffled their feet in embarrassment. They couldn't believe it when Ronald Reagan called on Mikhail Gorbachev to 'tear down this wall'. Reagan certainly meant it, and his approach prevailed.

The policy attitudes I struck in government were a patent reflection of my basic political credo. My belief in the maximum degree of individual freedom meant that my Government always gave high priority to personal taxation relief, believing that people were better judges than governments of how to spend their money. It drove my support for parental choice in education, as well as my continuing belief in the worth of private health insurance. My passion for the role of small business made me a natural opponent of the unfair dismissal laws of the Keating Government. It also informed my attitude to secondary boycotts by unions, which were often used against small- and medium-sized firms. My belief in a self-reliant but fair society found expression in the Howard Government's preference for work over welfare and work for the dole, but also the maintenance of a strong safety net for those who genuinely needed help.

My Burkean conservatism meant I would oppose Australia becoming a republic or adopting a Bill of Rights which would pass authority from parliament to unelected judges. My instinctive belief that shared values and history create the strongest bonds between nations meant that I would want, in government, to maintain close links with traditional allies such as the United States and Great Britain as well as deepening our ties with regional neighbours.

I brought a philosophical road map to government. It was bitterly opposed by some but, for a long time, supported by more. Both supporters and critics knew what I stood for. In its broadest iteration, that road map was one of economic liberalism and social conservatism. That duality was no politically convenient contrivance. I believed in it. From the late 1970s onwards, Australia needed major economic reforms to set it up for a transformed world economic environment. Those reforms had to be built on freedom and openness, not regulation and protection. That meant a lot of change, some of it quite bewildering. The more an individual's world of work and business changed, the more he or she would seek continuity and reassurance in other aspects of life. That is why social conservatism complemented rather than mocked economic liberalism.

To me the Liberal Party of Australia has always been the custodian of both the conservative and classical liberal traditions in the Australian polity.

That is its special strength. It does best when it demonstrates that duality; it should be wary of those individuals or groups who parade the view that only one of those two philosophical thought streams represents 'true' Australian Liberalism.

My stance on asylum-seekers, anti-terrorism laws and Pauline Hanson were depicted by critics as at odds with the 'true' Liberal attitudes of the party's founder, Robert Menzies. This displayed little knowledge of Australian political history and also ignored the important injunction that 'context is everything'.

Let me illustrate. Menzies' 1951 attempt to ban the Communist Party, involving, as it did, a partial reversal of the onus of proof, was a deeper violation of the personal political liberties of some Australians than anything comprised in the anti-terrorism laws of the Howard Government. Those 1951 actions were justified by Menzies and his colleagues as a legitimate response to the worldwide threat of communism; many thought that World War III would be upon us in a few short years.

In 1961 a meeting of Commonwealth prime ministers refused, effectively, to re-admit South Africa to the Commonwealth after that country voted to become a republic, not because of that decision but due to the racially based apartheid system then applied in South Africa. Menzies was appalled at the decision, declaring, 'For myself, I am deeply troubled.'[2] He attached supreme importance to the principle of non-interference in the internal affairs of member states of the Commonwealth. Also, the fact that the South African Government was staunchly anti-Communist would not have gone unnoticed. His concern on those issues took precedence over his distaste for apartheid. Other issues aside, neither of those Menzies approaches would today be seen as of the 'small l' liberal genre.

It is a great honour to hold the highest elected office in a democracy. One consequence of that honour is to accept that history will and should judge you entirely on what you have said and done when in office. No amount of ex post facto rationalisation, confessing or rejection of previously held views can alter that reality. I am somewhat cynical towards those who, after leaving office, self-indulgently parade a change of heart on a controversial issue, to the applause of former critics but without regard to the impact such a changed attitude might have on those affected by the repudiation of the decision taken in office. No better example exists than Robert McNamara's recantation over the Vietnam War. It may have made the Defense Secretary in the Kennedy and Johnson administrations feel better, but I doubt that it helped the thousands who had lost loved ones in a conflict he ordered them into.

In the past 40 years, both the ALP and the Liberal Party have ceased to be mass political movements. Changed family lifestyles work against meeting attendances during evenings and weekends. Today's generations are not the joiners of earlier years, and the impact of this goes beyond political parties. Reduced and less-representative membership has made political parties more susceptible to internal group control of the candidate-selection process. ALP head offices regularly treat branch members with contempt in relation to preselections. Some Liberal Party factions are nothing more than preselection cooperatives. As a result, far too many new MPs, especially at a state level, have had no working-life experience outside a political or union office. It is becoming increasingly difficult for the talented outsider to win party favour. The Liberal Party should fully embrace the branch plebiscite system for candidate selection. This is likely to deliver a more representative bunch of future candidates.

The most overworked cliché about Australia's future is that our best years lie ahead. Whether or not that proves to be the case depends, entirely, on the attitudes and values of future generations. If the next generation is as successful in managing economic change, whilst preserving social harmony, as was the last then we should be optimistic. Part of the Australian achievement is that, in a generation, attitudes to work, competitiveness and the interdependency of trade between nations have permanently changed for the better.

No respected Asian leader of the future would feel able to say, as Lee Kuan Yew did in the early 1980s, that Australia ran the risk of becoming 'the poor white trash of Asia'. The mutuality of our trade with Japan and China has played a major educative role in this. Earlier generations largely saw such countries as sources of cheap imports and, therefore, a threat to Australian jobs. By contrast, the current generation knows that maintaining a booming resource trade with North Asia is crucial to Australia's economic future.

A key determinant of our economic future will be Australia's willingness to persist with economic change and reform, and to resist any regression to protectionism and over-regulation in the totally mistaken belief that the global financial plunge of 2008 represented a failure of market capitalism.

Economic reform is like competing in a footrace towards an ever-receding finishing line. The race is never won, but one dare not stop otherwise competitors will surge past. For 25 years or more, Australia has done well in that footrace. Whether or not those competitors will surge past in the future depends entirely on our willingness to regain interest in economic reform. In recent years, reform has stagnated in Australia; in one area — the labour market — it has gone backwards.

Despite the much-trumpeted return of Keynesianism in the wake of the global financial crisis, the lasting economic development of the past 30 years has been that tens of millions of people were lifted from poverty by the twin forces of globalisation and market capitalism. Government intervention played a subsidiary role. The ongoing debate is about the mechanics of that market system, not the benefits of the system itself. In the process, the centre of gravity of the world's middle class began to shift to Asia. By 2030, it is likely that the majority of the world's middle class will live in Australia's region of the world.

Economic strength is only part of our future. Cultural and national self-belief will be the armour plate of a successful and confident Australia for the remainder of this century. We have prospered to date because of who we are and where we have come from, not in spite of that. The Australian achievement has many facets; by far the most significant has been the transplanting to our island continent of Western civilisation tempered by the egalitarian and cooperative habits necessarily embraced by a small population living in a vast country. The circumstances of history allowed us to cast aside the class divisions and rigidities of our cultural inheritance but keep its civilisation.

Australia wins respect in the world when we display who we are and not what self-appointed cultural dieticians would want us to become. Multiculturalism is not our national cement. Rather it is the Australian achievement, which has many components. One of them has been, successfully, to absorb millions of people from numerous lands into the mainstream of our nation.

The past 30 years has seen a revival of interest in Australian history, not least our military history. In the 1970s there was genuine concern that interest in Anzac Day would decline; no such thoughts are now entertained. The sight of thousands of young Australians draped in the national flag visiting Gallipoli or the Western Front may offend some of the politically correct, but it warms the hearts of mainstream Australia.

I will not forget Anzac Day 2005, which included participation in the Lone Pine Service on Anzac Cove. I was greeted with spontaneous warmth at that service by thousands of my fellow countrymen and women, not as someone they all agreed with politically but as the PM of their country — there to share their pride and gratitude for something done which would be forever special to all of us as Australians.

We should keep our faith in the efficacy of liberal democracy. The United States will remain the most powerful nation in the world for many reasons, not least of which is that she is a conspicuous exemplar of liberal democracy. Just as predictions 20 to 30 years ago that Japan would surpass America proved wrong, so it will be proven the case with claims that China will outpace the United States. The growth of China has been good for China and good for the world, not least Australia, but she has challenges of demography and limitations on property rights which will bulk as ever-larger problems in the future. China will grow old before she grows rich. Beyond this lies the ultimate Chinese dénouement, between her economic liberalism and political authoritarianism. India carries many burdens, including some poisonous religious rivalries, but does not face the frightening demographic future of China. Being the largest democracy in the world, India does not face a Chinese-style dénouement. By the end of this century, India could well be more powerful economically and politically than China.

In continuing our long tradition of being a good international citizen, Australians must remember that we still live in a world of nation states and that for the foreseeable future it will be cooperation between like-minded nations which will solve the most difficult problems. Likewise, we should be wary of giving unqualified assent to the dictates of multilateral bodies whose rules are written sometimes by majorities which include nations neither believing in nor practising the rule of law.

I had a fortunate life in politics and will always feel deep gratitude towards the Liberal Party for its immense loyalty and forbearance. To my parents, members of Australia's greatest generation, who gave me the values and determination which I took into politics, and to my wife and children, who sustained me with love and constant support through a long political career, I owe the greatest debt.

APPENDIX

Memorandum of Advice to incoming Conservative Government in Britain, prepared by John Stone, Treasurey Secretary, in 1979.

THE UK ECONOMIC SITUATION: WHAT IS TO BE DONE?

To address the question 'What is to be done?' one must first address the question 'What is wrong?'

Clearly, a **great many** things are wrong
- first and foremost, the UK public sector has swollen beyond belief
- the nationalistion of the 'commanding heights' of the economy has contributed to that, but
- more basically, the problem resides in the Welfare State, rampant.

Necessarily, therefore, the overall burden of taxation is too high
- and its effects are exacerbated by the **structure** of the taxation system
- which, although ostensibly directed at the 'fat cats', in practice results not (or not so much) in levies falling on genuinely well-to-do but rather on the middle classes
- so that, literally, people in that category are increasingly disposed to 'vote with their feet' by taking their skills, their energies and, not least, their attitudes towards their society, elsewhere.

Meanwhile, **union power** has become a threat not merely to economic stability
- but to civil liberties and the very concept of the role [sic] of law upon which the British society has been founded and of which it has been for so long such a noteable exemplar
- as to which, note for example the several writings of Paul Johnson.

The 'monopoly power' of labour has now far outrun what, 50 years ago, was seen in Western Societies as the then threat to them – the 'monopoly power' of capital.

But whereas in most industrial countries today one finds laws (more or less effective) against the latter, we find no such laws against the former

- and indeed, noteable instances of laws positively favouring labour against capital
- such as the present position of the Law of Tort, 'closed shop' provisions and so on.

This naked power of labour has in recent years increasingly manifested itself in a senseless push for ever-rising money wage rates
- with consequences for inflation, the balance of payments (and hence the exchange rate)
- and with the consequences to be anticipated in such circumstances for business uncertainty and investment
- not to mention unemployment.

With a Budget basically unhinged (i.e. a large and continuing Public Sector Borrowing Requirement) and wage pressures of this kind, inflation has become endemic
- and **expectations**, both of consumers and of businessmen, have adjusted accordingly
- with characteristically deplorable results

In very recent times, some valiant attempts have been made to yoke in the consequences of these phenomena by the application of broadly 'monetarist' policies
- which have been pursued with some courage by Mr Healey in particular
- but a single instrument of policy – no matter how appropriately directed – can hardly prevail when under the pressure of so many other adverse forces.

WHAT IS TO BE DONE?
First, a point about timing.

A new Government would be well advised to go in hard at the outset.
- at any rate in those areas where its writ plainly runs
- that is to say, in those areas of policy (the budget and monetary policy) where it still holds the effective levers of power
- by contrast, a new Government will be very unwise to get itself immediately into a situation of confrontation with trade union power which it cannot win
- because the blow to authority which such a situation necessarily entails (cf. the Heath confrontation with the coal miners in 1974) is likely to be fatal to the Government's policies more widely.

Secondly, a point about expectations.

At all costs, a new Government succeeding to such a depressing inheritance should avoid like the plague the kind of rosy optimism which, one notes, is implicit in the London Stock Exchange's response to the election announcement.
- for any well-directed set of policies must, in the circumstances of Britain today, smack much more of 'blood, sweat and tears' than of the kind of rosy optimism which political parties like to generate and which the more unthinking among their supporters are only too happy to believe.
- at any rate, until rude reality comes upon them.

From this aspect, therefore, a clear and early prescription for any new Government would be to make a sober and necessarily stark statement about the '5 years hard slog' which lies before the Government and the country.

That way, expectations can perhaps be harnessed in such a way as to work in support of the policies that will be necessary, rather than against them
- and there can be no subsequent cries of outrage about the people having been misled.

Returning to the first point about going in hard at the outset
- clearly the first place to do so is in the area of fiscal policy.

Details cannot be adumbrated here but
- a vigorous clamp-down on numbers of people in Whitehall should have a place in any initial package
- far better to **abolish** spending programs than simply to whittle away at them across the board (there is a remarkable capacity within bureaucracies and backbenches to re-fertilize and bring again to lusty growth even programs which have been heavily pruned but not abolished)
- there will be a great need to turn a deaf ear to the manifold sirens who will aver that expenditure cuts should be appropriately 'discriminating' (e.g. as between capital and current expenditures, programmes for the 'deserving' rather than the 'undeserving' and so on)
- the key point being that when one has a cutting job of this magnitude to do, the only practical course is to cut wherever and as hard as one can.

Moreover, while holding out the further **prospect** of tax reductions (for both individuals and the business sector) it would be wise to concentrate the results of one's expenditure cuts in the first instance on hacking away at the PSBR
- without which the conduct of a firm monetary policy (which will be fundamental) will be so much the more difficult

- in short, the temptation of easy popularity through tax cuts will need to be eschewed in the short run in order that they may be more effectively (and more permanently) pursued in the somewhat longer run.

Two particular types of expenditure programs may be singled out for specific mention, namely
- so-called 'job creation' schemes; and
- so-call 'industry policy' subventions
- the former being effectively a costly method of 'shuffling the pack of unemployed'
- while the latter merely serve to prop up industries which, in the long run, have little chance of staying propped up and which, by definition, are restraining the growth of overall productivity and the rise in real incomes which, in the end, is what successful economic (political) policy is all about.

In the area of **monetary policy** what is needed is an even more full-blooded application of the kind of policies which, as noted above the present Government has recently been following.

Such a policy will necessarily entail
- a sustained downward pressure upon the rate of price increases
- a sustained refusal to validate (through the monetary system) any excessive rate of money wage increases
- the acceptance, particularly at the outset, that this will almost inevitably mean a sharp rise in unemployment (because it will take trade unions some time to accept that **that**, in the end, is the consequence of their wage pressures).

It should be taken for granted that exchange rate policy will continue to reflect the degree of flexibility which has characterised it in recent years
- but with a disposition (within reason) to hold the rate perhaps a shade higher than it might 'naturally' settle at with a view to backing up through that channel also the more general thrust of anti-inflationary policies.

As to the basic problem of trade union power, that is not a problem which will yield to instant remedies
- but rather one which is best 'chipped away at' over time and within the context of a labour market which (within the context of the foregoing) is increasingly less receptive to the wilder flights of union militancy.

However, some things can be done

- the removal wherever possible of legal provisions which presently serve to bolster and magnify trade union power
- government support, wherever practicable, for resistance by individual employers to particular 'stand-over tactics'
- a clear brake upon the 'pace-setting' proclivities of the public sector itself (including the nationalised industries) and so on.

CAN IT BE DONE?

I understand that Mrs Thatcher has said that the forthcoming election will be Britain's 'last chance' to turn its back upon the steady downward slide which has led it to the brink of the precipice now confronting it.

- **If** she is right in that regard, there must equally be a real question as to whether **any** government now elected can put in place (and **maintain**) the range of policies necessary to effect that eleventh hour turnaround.
- Whatever the answer to that question may be, it can be safely asserted that there will be no way out through attempts to choose 'soft options' or through policies of so-called 'gradualism'.
- Whether or not policies of the other kind – i.e., of the kind broadly set out above – will in the end be confirmed by the British people, only time will tell.

Perhaps therefore the **final point** to be made is that in such a situation as will confront a new Government it will be as well for that Government to face the possibility that it may enjoy (sic) only one term of office

- and that an essential part of the climate of **expectations** which it will have to strive to produce, will be that it proposed to 'see things through' for a full 5 years irrespective of the state of the opinion polls!

In short, with its feet once embarked on the foregoing roads, there can be no turning back.

NOTES

PART 1: Early Life and the Fraser Government

Chapter 1: The Source

1 Les Carlyon, *The Great War*, Pan Macmillan, Sydney, 2006.
2 Tony Wright, 'Howard's coming home of the heart', *Age*, 30 April 2000.

Chapter 5: 'The Only Game in Town'

1 Based on interviews with Ainslie Gotto and Ian Hancock, Gorton's biographer; they are both emphatically of the view that he would have voted against a republic.
2 Gough Whitlam, 'It's Time For Leadership', Blacktown Civic Centre, 13 November 1972; see www.australian politics.com, viewed 12 August 2010.

Chapter 7: The Honourable Member for Bennelong

1 Frank Crean MP, Treasurer, Second Reading (Budget Speech), Appropriation Bill (No. 1) 1974–75, Australia, House of Representatives, *Debates*, 17 September 1974, p. 1276.

Chapter 8: Fraser Takes Over

1 Philip Ayres, *Malcolm Fraser: A Biography*, Mandarin, Port Melbourne, 1989, p. 245.

Chapter 9: The Dismissal

1 'Nothing will save the Governor-General', *Age*, 5 November 2005.

Chapter 11: 'May I Speak to the Treasurer?'

1 J.O. Stone, Secretary to the Treasury, memo to Malcolm Fraser, Prime Minister of Australia, 3 April 1979.
2 P.W. McCabe & D.J. Lafranchi, *Report of inspectors appointed to investigate the particular affairs of Navillus Pty Ltd and 922 other companies*, Victorian Parliament, Melbourne, 1982.

Chapter 12: 'Your Indirect Tax Is Dead, Cobber'

1 Michelle Grattan, 'PM puts taxation changes in doubt', *Age*, 10 February 1981.

Chapter 13: Fooled by Flinders

1 Paul Keating MP, shadow Treasurer, 'Mr Howard and Foreign Bank Entry', press statement, 26 January 1983.
2 'Bob Hawke talks to Richard Carleton', *Nationwide*, ABC Television, broadcast 3 February 1983.

PART 2: The Opposition Years

Chapter 14: Peacock vs Howard

1 Kerry Coyle, 'Peacock, Howard returned', *Canberra Times*, 8 December 1984.

Chapter 16: Joh for PM

1 H. Brown, 'Premier to set national political agenda', *Australian*, 3 November 1986.
2 M. Taylor, 'Hinze claims Peacock would be better leader', *Australian*, 3 November 1986.
3 S. Rous, 'Wagga goes wild as Joh gets political', *Courier Mail*, 2 February 1987.
4 P. Davey, *The Nationals: the Progressive, Country, and National Party in New South Wales 1919–2006*, Federation Press, Annandale, 2006, p. 288.
5 John Howard MP, Leader of the Opposition, news release by the Coalition, Canberra, 28 April 1987.

Chapter 18: The 'Unlosable' Election

1 Australia, House of Representatives, *Debates*, 5 November 1992, p. 2733.
2 The Hon. Paul Keating, Prime Minister of Australia, election victory speech, Bankstown Sports Club, 13 March 1993.

Chapter 19: Lazarus Has His Triple Bypass

1   Greg Sheridan, '"I was wrong on Asians", says Howard', *Weekend Australian*, 7–8 January 1995.

PART 3: Prime Minister

Chapter 22: Seizing the Day on Guns

1   P. Alpers, K. Agho & S. Chapman, 'Australia's 1996 gun law reforms: Faster falls in firearm deaths, firearm suicides, and a decade without mass shootings', *Injury Prevention*, no. 12, 2006.
2   Peter Martin, 'Howard's gun legacy — 200 lives saved a year', *Sydney Morning Herald*, 30 August 2010.

Chapter 23: Pauline Hanson

1   Pauline Hanson MP, maiden speech, 10 September 1996.

Chapter 24: The Foundation Budget

1   Brett de Vine & Malcolm Farr, 'Fair go for middle Australia', *Daily Telegraph*, 21 August 1996.

Chapter 25: The Challenge of Indigenous Policy

1   B. Hawke, *The Hawke Memoirs*, William Heinemann, Port Melbourne, 1994, p. 435.
2   Paul Kelly, 'Black leaders offer new accord', *Weekend Australian*, 4 December 2004.
3   'Special Minister of State responds to criticisms from church groups over the native title legislation', ABC Radio, broadcast on 5 November 1997.
4   Noel Pearson, 'When words aren't enough', *Australian*, 12 February 2008.

Chapter 26: On the Waterfront

1   M. Steketee, 'A time to embrace, a time to speak', *Sydney Morning Herald*, 13 April 1983.
2   Grant Thornton, *Report to Creditors — Patrick Companies under Administration*, 16 May 1998.
3   Chris Corrigan et al., 'The Battle for Australia's Waterfront', address to The Sydney Institute, 27 June 2000.
4   *Ibid.*
5   Access Economics Pty Ltd in conjunction with Maunsell Australia Pty Ltd, *Benchmarking Technology on the Australian Waterfront: Implications for Agricultural Exports Publication No. 02/116*, a report for the Rural Industries Research and Development Corporation, August 2002.

Chapter 28: We Still Want You, Ma'am — the Republican Debate

1   Tony Stephens, 'The day democracy rained on a sunny boy's parade', *Sydney Morning Herald*, 8 November 1999.
2   Constitutional Convention, Old Parliament House, Canberra, transcript of proceedings (Day 7), 10 February 1998.
3   Constitutional Convention, Old Parliament House, Canberra, transcript of proceedings (Day 3), 4 February 1998.
4   Sir John Kerr, *Matters for Judgement*, Macmillan, South Melbourne & Artarmon, 1978, pp. 374–75.
5   *Final Report of the Constitutional Commission*, Australian Government Publishing Service, Canberra, 1988.
6   Michael Kirby, 'A Centenary Reflection on the Australian Constitution: the Republic Referendum 1999', Menzies Memorial Lecture, King's College, London, 4 July 2000.

Chapter 29: The Liberation of East Timor

1   Alexander Downer, 'East Timor — Looking Back on 1999', *Australian Journal of International Affairs*, Vol. 54, No. 1, 2000: 5–10.
2   Letter from Alexander Downer MP, Australian Minister for Foreign Affairs, to HE Ali Alatas SH, Minister for Foreign Affairs, Republic of Indonesia, 1998.
3   Letter from the Hon. John Howard, Prime Minister of Australia, to H Dr B.J. Habibie, President, Republic of Indonesia, 19 December 1998.
4   United Nations, *Report of the Security Council Mission to Jakarta and Dili, 8–12 September 1999*.
5   'Opposition leader discusses East Timor', Radio 6PR, broadcast on 5 October 1999.

Chapter 30: An Excess of Excise — the Pre-Tampa Recovery

1   Ian Henderson, 'Drivers short-changed $3bn', *Australian*, 9 February 2001.
2   Laura Tingle, 'Australia hits the wall', *Sydney Morning Herald*, 8 March 2001.

Chapter 31: Washington, 11 September 2001

1   'Florida Schoolchildren Recall Their Moments with President Bush on Sept. 11', *Fox News*, 7 September 2006, www.foxnews.com/story/0,2933,212775,00.html (accessed 25 March, 2010).

2   George W. Bush, Address to a Joint Session of Congress and the American People, 20 September 2001, the White House, Washington, D.C.

Chapter 32: MV *Tampa*

1   Australia, House of Representatives 2001, *Debates* (Hansard, 29 August 2001), p. 30570.
2   People Smuggling Taskforce, *Options For Handling Unauthorised Arrivals: Christmas Island Boat*, Canberra, 7 October 2001.
3   The Hon. John Howard, Prime Minister of Australia, National Press Club, Canberra, 8 November 2001.
4   'Admiral sails away from "children overboard" view', *The 7.30 Report*, ABC Television, broadcast 27 February 2002.

Chapter 33: The Bali Attack

1   'Operation Bali Assist: The Australian Defence Force response to the Bali bombing', the *Medical Journal of Australia*, vol. 177, 2/16 December 2002; 620–23.

Chapter 34: Iraq

1   President George W. Bush, address to the United Nations General Assembly, New York, 23 September 2002, Office of the Press Secretary, United States Capitol, Washington, D.C.
2   President Barack Obama, statement on the release of Nuclear Posture Review, 6 April 2010, Office of the Press Secretary, the White House.
3   'Bin Laden rails against Crusaders and UN', *BBC News*, 3 November 2001, http://news.bbc.co.uk/2/hi/world/monitoring/media_reports/1636782.stm (accessed 26 March 2010).
4   William J. Clinton, Remarks of the President on Iraq, The White House, Washington, D.C., Office of the Press Secretary, 19 December 1998.
5   William J. Clinton, Remarks by the President on Iraq to Pentagon Personnel, Office of the Press Secretary, 17 February 1998.
6   Kenneth Pollack, *The Threatening Storm: The Case for Invading Iraq*, Random House, New York, p. 102.
7   Jean Kirkpatrick, 'Legitimate War: The Case of Iraq', American Enterprise Institute Friday Forum, 13 June 2003.
8   Floor speech of Senator Hillary Rodham Clinton on S.J. Res. 45, A Resolution to Authorize the Use of United States Armed Forces Against Iraq, 10 October 2002.
9   Floor speech of Senator Joseph Biden on S.J. Res. 45, A Resolution to Authorize the Use of United States Armed Forces Against Iraq, 10 October 2002.
10   Hans Blix, *Chief UN Weapons Inspector Hans Blix's report to the UN on Iraq*, United Nations, New York, 27 January 2003.
11   James Graf & Bruce Crumley, 'France Is Not a Pacifist Country', *Time Magazine*, 16 February 2003.
12   Simon Crean MP, Leader of the Opposition, transcript of doorstop interview, Melbourne, 15 January 2003.
13   Kevin Rudd MP, shadow minister for Foreign Affairs, keynote address to the State Zionist Council Annual Assembly, 15 October 2002.
14   Tony Parkinson, 'The thoughts of Beazley now', *Age*, 18 April 2003.
15   Letter from Kevin Rudd MP, shadow minister for Foreign Affairs, to the Hon. John Howard, Prime Minister of Australia, 17 November 2003.
16   Lincoln Wright, 'Proof Rudd approved of Iraq war', *Daily Telegraph*, 12 August 2007.
17   *Ibid.*
18   United States of America, *National Intelligence Estimate: Iraq's Continuing Programs for Weapons of Mass Destruction*, National Intelligence Council, October 2002.
19   Parliamentary Joint Committee ASIO, ASIS and DSD, *Inquiry into Intelligence on Iraq's Weapons of Mass Destruction*, 15 September 2003, quoting an ONA assessment of 31 January 2003.
20   *Report of the Inquiry into Australian Intelligence Agencies*, Australian Government Publishing Service, Canberra, July 2004.
21   *Report of the Inquiry into Australian Intelligence Agencies* (Flood Report), Commonwealth of Australia, 2004, reproduced by permission.
22   *Ibid.*
23   'Opposition Leader discusses Newspoll; AFP Commissioner; troops in Iraq; and Alexander Downer', Radio 2UE, broadcast on 22 March 2004.
24   Mick Keelty, AFP Commissioner, *Sunday*, Nine Network, transcript of broadcast, 14 March 2004.

Chapter 35: George Bush

1   Rt Hon. Tony Blair, Prime Minister of the United Kingdom, address to the House of Representatives, 27 March 2006.
2   President George W. Bush, 'The Howard Years', ABC Television, transcript of broadcast, 1 December 2008.

Chapter 36: Blue Collars and Green Sleeves — Latham's Implosion

1   Ken Hall, 'Latham betrays workers', *Australian*, 8 October 2004.
2   'Opposition Leader discusses Newspoll; AFP Commissioner; troops in Iraq; and Alexander Downer', Radio 2UE, broadcast on 22 March 2004.
3   Geoffrey Barker, 'A dual destiny', *Australian Financial Review*, 9 October 2004.

Chapter 39: Asia First, Not Asia Only

1   The Hon. John Dawkins MP, Treasurer, *Sunday*, Nine Network, transcript of broadcast, 26 March 1992.
2   Dr H. Susilo Bambang Yudhoyono, 'Bali remembered' [edited version of speech by the President of the Republic of Indonesia], *Age*, 13 October 2003.

Chapter 40: A Wonder Down Under

1   Glenn Stevens, Address to the Inaugural Faculty of Economics and Business Alumni Dinner, The University of Sydney, Sydney, 15 May 2008.
2   Julia Gillard MP, Deputy Prime Minister, Address to the Australian Reception, World Economic Forum, Davos, Switzerland, 29 January 2009.
3   Robert Rubin & Jacob Weisberg, *In an Uncertain World: Tough Choices from Wall Street to Washington*, Random House, New York, 2003, p. 122.
4   Department of the Treasury, *Economic Roundup*, Autumn 2005, Australian Government Publishing Service, Canberra, 2005, reproduced by permission.

Chapter 41: Our Warm, Dry Land

1   Nicholas Stern (dir.), *The Stern Review Report: The Economics of Climate Change*, HM Treasury, London, 30 October 2006.
2   Nigel Lawson, *An Appeal to Reason: A Cool Look at Global Warming*, Duckworth Overlook, London, 2008, p. 83.
3   Department of Prime Minister and Cabinet, *Securing Australia's Energy Future*, Australian Government Publishing Service, Canberra, 2004.

Chapter 42: Billy Gets a Job, but Who Cares?

1   Sir Robert Menzies, *Central Power in the Australian Commonwealth*, Cassell, Sydney, 1967, p. 130.
2   Australian Industrial Relations Commission (AIRC) (1994), *Aluminium Industry CRA [Comalco] Bell Bay Case, Full Bench Decision*, Print No. L7449.
3   Liberal Party of Australia, 'A stronger economy, a stronger Australia, flexibility and productivity in the work place: the key to jobs'. Howard Government election policy, 2004.
4   Paul Kelly, 'Milestone on quest for reform', *Australian*, 27 May 2005.
5   'A big win for all the workers', *Australian*, 27 May 2005.
6   'A new way of working', *Daily Telegraph*, 27 May 2005.
7   'Finance Minister addresses H.R. Nicholls Society on industrial relations reform', ABC Radio, broadcast on 8 March 2006.

Chapter 44: The Leadership

1   'Prime Minister discusses Bali bombings; Premiers' meeting; handguns; APEC; and medical indemnity', Radio 6PR, broadcast on 23 October 2002.
2   'Costello stays on a slow boil', *Australian*, 2 May 2005.
3   Michael Gordon & Misha Schubert, 'Costello backers set deadline', *Age*, 4 May 2005.
4   Louise Dodson, 'The rubbery deadline still taunting Costello', *Sydney Morning Herald*, 22 April 2006.
5   Glenn Milne, 'At last, a 12-year secret is revealed', *Sunday Telegraph*, 9 July 2006.
6   Neil Mitchell, 'After his latest petulant outburst ... He's on the nose', *Herald-Sun*, 13 July 2006.
7   Tony Wright, 'He can't win. I can: The Year: 2005, The Pretender: Peter Costello, The Strategy: Destroy Howard', *Age*, 15 August 2007.

Chapter 45: The Tide Runs Out

1   'Labor ahead no matter who leads: poll', *ABC News Online*, 3 December 2006, www.abc.net.au/news/newsitems/200612/s1802994.htm (accessed 31 March 2010).
2   Ross Gittins, 'Good politics has met good economics', *Sydney Morning Herald*, 9 May 2007.
3   Steve Price, 'Peter Garrett's gaffe was no simple joke', *Sunday Telegraph*, 4 November 2007.
4   Rosanne Barrett, 'Former leaders suck publicity oxygen from current party heads', *Australian*, 14 August 2010.

Chapter 46: Reflections

1   John O'Sullivan, *The President, the Pope, and the Prime Minister*, Regnery Publishing, Inc., Washington, 2006, p. 2.
2   Sir Robert Menzies, *Afternoon Light: Some memories of men and events*, Cassell, Melbourne, 1967, p. 215.

AUTHOR'S NOTE

No person can have the political career I did without continued support and counsel from staff and advisors. I owe the many who fall into this group special gratitude. They are entitled to share the success publicly attributed to me.

For nine years of my prime ministership Arthur Sinodinos gave outstanding leadership to my office as my chief of staff. Arthur had an endearing sense of humour. He was policy driven but politically savvy — a crucial combination in such a role. Universally respected by my staff and my parliamentary colleagues, Arthur was a trusted sounding board on the multitude of complex issues which come the way of a PM's office. He also enjoyed the respect and confidence of the public service, which added greatly to the harmony between the political and administrative arms of the Government. Likewise he was a point of easy access and reference for many in the business sector. They were comfortable dealing with him if they could not speak to me. His knowledge and candour minimised the inevitable misunderstandings which arise in communications between business and government. A gifted economist, Arthur Sinodinos began as a cadet with the Commonwealth Treasury and in his post-Canberra life has been successful in pursuing a banking career.

The partnership between Arthur and my principal private secretary, Tony Nutt, was a key ingredient in the unity and smooth functioning of my office. Tony's political science and Liberal Party staff experience meant that they neatly complemented each other. Tony's corporate knowledge was priceless in dealing with party issues. I joked often that he knew 'where all the Liberal bodies are buried'. He had a deep understanding of Australian and world political history, and loved the hurly-burly of political combat. Tony's sharp grasp of parliamentary procedure and capacity for detailed research was invaluable in the political battles of attrition which come the way of all governments. Tony gave great service as chief of staff during our last difficult year in government. Currently director of the Victorian division, Tony Nutt is the most gifted professional employee of the Liberal Party anywhere in Australia.

References to Grahame Morris appear regularly during the book. It is no exaggeration to say he has devoted much of his working life to the Liberal cause and to me in particular as the standard bearer of that cause. He was on my staff during my first and difficult turn-out as Opposition leader, came across from Downer's staff in 1995 and was with me in my early prime ministerial years. He always gave earthy political advice, and it was mostly correct. We remained in regular contact after he left my office. He and his wife, Bronwyn, spent every election night with us from 1996 onwards. We remain close friends.

Barbara Williams worked a total of 18 years for me as my personal assistant, commencing when I became Minister for Business and Consumer Affairs and continuing through various positions until my removal as Opposition leader in May 1989. She returned to that role when I became PM and stayed until 2002. Barbara was efficient, loyal and possessed of remarkable contacts, so indispensable in such a position. Her service to the Liberal cause and to me was exceptional. Suzanne Kasprzak assumed that role after Barbara left and did it well and enthusiastically.

For eight years Peter Crone was my economic advisor, and a talented person in that role. He was steady, thoughtful and balanced in his advice as well as his assessments of departmental views. To have both Peter and Arthur, who liked to keep his hand in on economic issues, meant I was well served in this crucial policy area. Peter rejoined the private sector in 2006 and was replaced by a highly skilled former Treasury economist, Nigel Bailey. He knew the political dimension well, having worked on Peter Costello's staff for some years. He also had a stint as Treasury man at the Australian Embassy in Washington.

I write elsewhere in the book of John Perrin, who died prematurely in 2006 and was my social policy advisor for nine years. His advice was important in securing the improvements delivered by my Government in this immensely important policy area. His technical grasp of issues as well as a strong policy compass made him a first-class advisor. Perry Sperling followed John in that role, and likewise brought immense policy depth, thus ensuring that an effective social vision remained a prominent part of the Government's public face.

Michael Thawley, of whom I write elsewhere, was my first international advisor and later, importantly, ambassador in Washington. David Ritchie (later our ambassador in Jakarta during the 2004 bomb attack), Miles Jordana, Peter Varghese (now high commissioner to India), Paul O'Sullivan (for a time head of ASIO, now high commissioner to New Zealand), and Nick Warner (later secretary of Defence, now head of ASIS), followed Michael in that role. They filled that position through years of intense policy debates and controversies. All brought foreign-policy skills and experience to my office. The final occupant of the post was Andrew Shearer, who has left the government service and flies something of a centre-right foreign policy flag at the Lowy Institute. He remains a frequent sounding board of mine on foreign policy.

Two of my former policy advisors have pursued federal political careers. Jamie Briggs is now the Liberal MP for Mayo, having succeeded Alexander Downer in that seat. He was my advisor for three years on industrial relations and related industry matters. Joshua Frydenberg is now the Liberal MP for Kooyong, Robert Menzies' old seat. Both Jamie and Joshua were bright advisors. At a state level, Barry O'Farrell, who worked for me when Opposition leader in the 1980s, is currently NSW Opposition leader and, I hope, the next Premier of that state. One of his colleagues is Anthony Roberts, the state MP for Lane Cove; he worked for a number of years in my electorate office.

Complicated anti-terrorist legislation featured heavily after 11 September 2001, making it essential that I had immediate, high-quality legal advice at hand in my office. For a time Josh Frydenberg filled this role, and after the 2004 election Simone Burford, who was an excellent lawyer, took over the responsibility. She shone in the position, having a great capacity to distil the legal essence of an issue into intelligible language.

What I called the 'paper flow' between me and my department — ensuring that departmental submissions were dealt with in a timely fashion — was handled by several people over the years, most particularly Stephen Brady, who is now the Governor-General's official secretary, and Malcolm Hazell, previously official secretary to two former occupants of that position. I frequently dubbed Malcolm my royal and ecclesiastical advisor; part of his role was to maintain liaison, when necessary, with Government House and Buckingham Palace. They both did their jobs with skill and discretion.

There was no more hardworking and loyal staffer than Tony O'Leary, a highly experienced journalist who was the head of my press office for the whole period of my prime ministership. He was astute, had a good news sense, rarely gave me bad advice and maintained good relations with the gallery, while usually knowing what its members were up to. Willie Herron, whose natural openness and straight-dealing style made her popular with journalists, was a well-loved staffer, particularly by another staffer, Patrick Coleman, who married her. They now have four children. Ben Mitchell and David Luff (affectionately known as 'Luffy'), were a duo who worked effectively with Tony O'Leary. David Luff, a former *Daily Telegraph* man, had a good knockabout news sense. Based in Sydney, he travelled back and forth to Canberra with me. I spent a lot of time with David and found him an excellent media advisor. He became a regular on my early-morning walks. We enjoyed each other's company.

Aileen Wiessner filled a special role in my office. With me from March 1996 onwards, she kept in touch with backbench Liberal MPs and kept a constant finger on the pulse of marginal seat opinion. Aileen understood better than most what influenced swing voters; her advice was always candid and direct. Gerry Wheeler was something of a keeper of the conservative flame in my office. He was a passionate anti-republican. Gerry and I high-fived after the referendum went down.

The Cabinet Policy Unit (CPU), which I established in 1996, was led by three people in my time as PM: Michael L'Estrange, Paul McClintock and Peter Conran — all extremely able, but in different ways. I have written elsewhere of the careers of both Michael and Paul, who have both achieved so much in their professional lives. L'Estrange served as high commissioner in London during times of intense cooperation with Britain in the fight against terrorism, and then I appointed him secretary of the department of Foreign Affairs and Trade. Paul McClintock has resumed a busy and successful commercial career. Peter Conran had variously worked for the Northern Territory and Western Australian Governments, before joining my staff before the 2004 election. After that election he took over the CPU. One of his great assets was to understand and interpret likely state responses to Commonwealth ideas. He was a poacher-turned-gamekeeper, only to turn back again. He is now director general of the department of Premier and Cabinet in Western Australia.

One speech writer I had as PM was John Kunkel. I disliked reading speeches. Less than 10 per cent of the speeches I made as PM were scripted. In my last three years as PM, I found in John Kunkel, who joined the CPU in 2004, someone who grasped the type of language I was comfortable with and was able, after much workshopping between us, to craft some really good speeches. As well as being a good economist, John shared my interest in history and the ebb and flow of the cultural debate. I especially recall working with him in March 2005 on my speech launching the Lowy Institute, which enunciated the broad themes of my foreign policy views.

Two other people were responsible for me looking better on television than I sometimes deserved. They were Carol Robertson and Susan Bruce. They successively headed my group of 'advancers': staff members who visited venues in advance of me to check logistics. They and their colleagues were always friendly and obliging and won over countless citizens who may have been just a little sceptical about this visiting PM.

Many of my former policy advisors have provided helpful comments on chapter drafts of this book. Those comments have sharpened the book's presentation.

Two businessmen, Bob Mansfield and Fergus Ryan, filled consultancies and gave good advice regarding investment projects. Geoffrey Cousins also provided valuable public relations advice.

A security detail from the Australian Federal Police is a fixed part of the daily life of an Australian PM. A close personal protection unit spends a lot of time with the person they are looking after. I was able to establish good personal relations with the various members of my team over almost 12 years. Three efficient and highly professional men, Michael Casey, Blen Rowley and Gary Hanna, headed up my detail during that time. I trusted them completely. My family and I remain deeply grateful for the unobtrusive and reassuring security they and their teams provided. Their teams included at various stages David Capper, Ben McIntyre, James Bareham, Peter Bassett, John Blandford, Andrew Bailey, Terry McCarthy, Ron Learmonth, Bill Townsend, Annie Brooks, Frank Morgan, Richard Kelland, Michael Jackson, Chris Collingwood, Philippa Cottam, Bruce Hayward, Mark McIntyre, Steven Martin, Michael Howard, John Collins, Bevan Moroney, Phil McInerney, Alan Paterson, Graham Leaver, Clinton Wright, Michael Dainer, Nye Konig, Ross Casella, Richard Breiner, Andrew Bailey, Gary Mills and Adam McCormack.

Officers from state police forces also provided regular protection. They included Andrew Slattery, Mark Hargreaves, Christopher Reardon, Susan Bielby, Christopher Reeves, Timothy Holt, Kevin Toohey, Rod Brown, Geoff Chiddy and John Hodge.

In the mobile phone era, discreet and utterly trustworthy drivers are essential. I was very lucky to have Mario Bartolic, an ever friendly and obliging man, as my

Sydney driver for most of the time that I was Prime Minister. His Canberra counterpart, Dan Radovanovic, was equally reliable and helpful. They were both excellent drivers and I thank both for their service, as well as Greg Wright and the late Wayne Patterson, who drove for me in Sydney in the early years. From earlier times I record my thanks to Bob Jenkins and Tony Barry.

Wonderful staff at Kirribilli House and the Lodge, particularly our great KH chef, Adam Thomas, looked after us so well. Others included the Lodge chef, Stuart Heddle, and Mary Quinn (Canderle), Sally Stocker, Ian Spencer, Trina Barrie, Sharon Dominick-Gill and Brenda Shearwood.

Keeping my constituents well looked after was the task of my hardworking electorate staff, led by Kay Long who was my electorate secretary for 16 years. Scottish-born, possessed of a good sense of humour and immaculate spelling and stenographic skills, she was a popular figure in the local community. My electorate assistants, Jenny Stearn and Sam Kursar (who was in charge of the electorate office for the last 18 months), had caring and conscientious manners with constituents, and did terrific jobs in those roles. During the last and difficult year, when my seat of Bennelong was vulnerable, Chris Stone obligingly assumed responsibility for much of the campaign liaison effort. It was a tough assignment, which he tackled with dedication.

From earlier years I thank Geoff Hodgkinson, my chief of staff when I was Treasurer, and Gerard Henderson, who filled that role during my time as both Deputy Leader and then Leader of the Opposition. They both worked hard and gave intelligent counsel. Nicole Feeley ran my office effectively during our last year in opposition. She was chief of staff at the beginning of my time as Prime Minister. I have written elsewhere of John Hewson's valuable contribution.

Among the many other people who worked for me and helped from the time I entered parliament in 1974, I would like to particularly thank John Griffin, Anthony Benscher, Catherine Murphy, Brett Cox, Hellen Georgopoulos, Jamie Fox, Alastair McLean, Peter Langhorne, Andrew Kefford, Marnie Gaffney, Gary Dawson, Adam Connolly, Niki Savva, Gavin Jackman, Bill Hogan, Terrie Ryan, Rebecca Rough, Kate Hogg, Kay Gilchrist, Natalie Jarrett, Nicole Chant, Kylie Jacobson, Katherine McFarlane, Stephen Copeman, Dominique James, Sue Cox, Vanessa Kimpton, Danielle Collins (nee Kerr), Michelle Perry, David Gazard, Jodie Doodt, Tim James, David Elliott and Stephen Galilee.

Many others worked on my staff in the various positions I held in my career. They include Fiona McKenna, Jan Saunders, Jenny Hungerford, Mark Veyret, Liz McCabe, Peggy Hailstone, Sue Fife, Bill Kerley, Tim Stewart, Chris Jordan, Martin Riordan, Adele May, Kay Vollett, Kerry Bamford, Dick White, Jackie Jurd, David Pigott, Joan Linklater, Richard Turnley, Pat Hutchinson, Jon Powis, Greg Bright, Suzanne Johannsen, Lucille Kerslake, Susan Kay, Helen Blake, Anita Simmons, Mary McKeown, Charmain Lorch, Jacquelin Chalker, Kerry Warner, Nikki Storey, Kaylie Stuart, Jenny Anderson, Terry Crane, Allison Brown, Samantha Lindsay, Alex Staples, Carolyn Ireland, Katrina

Edwards, Scott Bolitho, Suzanne Ferguson, Kimberly Hopkins, Gary Dawson, Sarah Casey, Kirsty Haylock, Diane Balke, Kathryn Muldoon, Rebecca Roberts, Kate McQuestin, Carolyn Jack, Andrew Hirst, Kathryn McFarlane, Rhys Turner, Katrina Tesoreiro, Kristin May, Raelene Green, Trish Tragear, Jodie Williams, Sarah Considine, Victoria Davies, Helen Schloss, Sheila Duncan-Mullaney, Lousie Mulcahy, Erika Cevallos, Andrew Hale, Sue Hollins, Georgina Jassonos, Natalie Todd, Leonie Stewart, Vanessa Kimpton, Elizabeth O'Rourke, Fiona Brown, Genevieve Hughes, Mondana Scott, Lee-Anne Dean, Robin Lewis-Quinn, Julie Roberts, Tim Moore, Chantal Sydenham, Clair Dace, Estee Fiebiger, Tony Rutherford, Bronwyn Morris, John Burston, Darren Brown, Jamie Fox, Peter Langhorne, Jenny Howse, Mark Henderson, Stephanie Collins, David Quilty, Peter Jennings, Emma Heales, Mark Baker, Jo-Anne Ashley, Christopher Pearson, Maxine Sells, John Robertson, Marina Kislitsa, Di Perry, Sue Nixon, Kim Logan, Carolyn Pascoe, Kilner Mason, David Stevens, David Piggott, Paula Matthewson, Fiona Brown and (the late) Gerri Ashmore.

I fought six elections as Leader of the Liberal Party: 1987, 1996, 1998, 2001, 2004 and 2007. Four federal directors of the party worked with me in those campaigns, starting with Tony Eggleton in 1987, who commenced his association with Liberal leaders when he was Menzies' press secretary just before his retirement, and became a familiar face to Australians as principal spokesman for the Government and the Holt family in the frantic hours and then days which followed Harold Holt's disappearance in December 1967. Tony was ever calm and always ready with sensible political advice.

Good advice also came from his successors: Andrew Robb in the 1996 campaign, Lynton Crosby in 1998 and 2001 and Brian Loughnane in 2004 and 2007. They were all devoted servants of the Liberal cause and worked closely and cooperatively with my staff in all of the campaigns. Different in style and temperament, I enjoyed working with each of them.

Tony Staley was federal president of the Liberal Party when I won government, having worked assiduously for my return as Leader. He had a good political brain and has given years of effort to our cause. Shane Stone then occupied the position for seven years. He was an active president whose Darwin residency brought a different and helpful perspective to certain issues. We developed a close relationship. Chris McDiven, previously NSW president, held the post during our last challenging months in government.

Over the years hundreds, if not several thousands, of Liberal supporters assisted my many campaigns to win the seat of Bennelong. I cannot name them all. I have mentioned Chris Stone's liaison work; to that should be added my expressions of gratitude to my 2007 campaign director, Rod Bosman; conference president, Michael Beinke; and secretary, Gloria Martin whose unflinching loyalty is of the stuff of any successful volunteer organisation. I remain humbled that so many worked so hard to help me win public office. A special thank you is owed to those who ran my earlier campaigns stretching back more than 30 years. They were Andrew Davis, Bert

Richards, the late Philip King, Donald Magarey, Tony Scotford, Michael Murray, Victor Moran, Ian Hardwick, Stephen Sim, Stephen Peoples and Peter Bardos. Dick White, for years an electorate assistant, gave invaluable support in numerous campaigns.

There is another person, not ever on my staff, who I want to mention. Tony Clark, a close friend and regular golfing partner, gave remarkable support to me before and after I became PM. A gifted and successful accountant, he was a prodigious fundraiser, regular sounding board and always able to provide timely and frank advice when the Government encountered heavy weather. He was the epitome of a true believer. I remain grateful for his deep friendship and loyalty. Likewise Malcolm Irving, former banker and company director, businessman Michael Crouch, a most successful Australian manufacturer, and Paul Ramsay were people who remained supporters through the hard times as well as the good ones.

Our close personal friends Donald and Janet McDonald shared the rollercoaster political ride of the past 25 years. Contributors to the community in their own special ways, Donald as chairman of the ABC for 10 years following a distinguished career as director of the Australian Opera, and Janet in many charities and particularly the fight against breast cancer; they remained constant in their friendship and support.

Finally I thank my present staff; they have done so much to help in the compilation of this book. My tireless research assistant, Troy Daniel, has spent countless weeks and months, unquestionably the equivalent of several PhD theses, digging and fossicking for material from my own records, archives, journals and other publications. His efforts have been invaluable, and without them the enterprise would not have been possible. Ruth Gibson and Sally Murphy, my two personal assistants, have not only typed various versions of the manuscript but as long-time Coalition staffers, their corporate knowledge has either corrected or placed in better context some of my intended utterances. I am much in the debt of Troy, Ruth and Sally for their dedication and also my driver, Stuart Stephens, for ferrying transcripts and photographs to and from my publisher.

Shirley Sullivan of the National Archives and Janet Wilson of the Parliamentary Library have willingly provided helpful responses to the many requests made of them in the course of the book's compilation. I thank both of them for their invaluable assistance.

I have really enjoyed working with the HarperCollins team on this book, especially Anne Reilly, my editor. That is not to diminish the great work of others, including the CEO, Michael Moynahan, Shona Martyn, Christine Farmer, Jim Demetriou, Amruta Slee, Sandy Weir, Jennifer Blau and Ian Hancock, who played a valuable fact-checking role. Alan Walker produced a very fine index. I also thank the many others who contributed expertise in proofreading, typesetting, fact-checking, production, marketing, promotion and sales.

CREDITS

Pictures
AAP Image/Jason Weeding: plate 22 (top)
AFP photo: plate 13 (top)
Andrew Taylor/Fairfaxphotos: plate 22 (bottom)
Auspic: plate 1 (bottom); plate 2 (top); plate 2 (bottom); plate 3 (bottom); plate 4 (bottom); plate 8 (bottom left); plate 8 (bottom right); plate 9 (top); plate 10 (top); plate 13 (bottom); plate 14 (bottom); plate 15 (top); plate 16 (bottom); plate 17; plate 19 (middle); plate 19 (bottom); plate 21 (bottom); plate 22 (middle); plate 23 (bottom); plate 24 (top); plate 25 (bottom); plate 26 (bottom); plate 27 (top); plate 28 (top); plate 29 (top); plate 30 (top); plate 30 (bottom); plate 32 (top); plate 32 (bottom)
Australian Women's Weekly: plate 10 (bottom); plate 11
Channel 7: plate 25 (top left)
Dean Lewins/Reuters/Picturemedia: plate 23 (top)
Fairfaxphotos: plate 7
The British Government: plate 15 (bottom); plate 29 (bottom)
J.W. Howard private library: plate 1 (top); plate 4 (top); plate 8 (top); plate 21 (top right)
John Hearder Studio: plate 6 (top)
Kevin Berry/Fairfaxphotos: plate 5
Lisa Maree Williams/GettyImages: plate 16 (top)
Mike Bowers: plate 14 (top); plate 20 (top); plate 20 (bottom)
National Archives of Australia: A6135, K22/12/77/33: plate 18 (top)
Newspix/News Ltd: plate 3 (top); plate 18 (bottom); plate 19 (top); plate 25 (top right)
    Newspix/News Ltd/Phil Blenkinsop: plate 9 (bottom)
Newspix/News Ltd/John Feder: plate 12 (bottom) and plate 21 (top left)
Newspix/News Ltd/Bruce Howard: plate 26 (top)
Newspix/News Ltd/Michael Jones: plate 12 (top)
Newspix/News Ltd/Lyndon Mechielsen: plate 24 (bottom)
Prime Minister's Office, Tokyo, Japanese Government: plate 31 (bottom)
The White House: plate 27 (bottom); plate 32 (middle).

Text
The Treasury, Australian Government, Economic Roundup Autumn 2005, Canberra, 15 June 2005, copyright Commonwealth of Australia, reproduced by permission.
Philip Flood AO, Report of the Inquiry into Australian Intelligence Agencies, Canberra, July 2004, copyright Commonwealth of Australia, reproduced by permission.
Department of Foreign Affairs and Trade, East Timor in Transition 1998–2000: An Australian Policy Challenge, Canberra, 2002, copyright Commonwealth of Australia, reproduced by permission.
Tony Wright, 'Howard's coming home of the heart', Age, 30 April, 2000, © Tony Wright, National Affairs Editor, Age, reproduced by permission.

The author and publisher have made all reasonable attempts to locate and acknowledge owners of copyright material. If you believe you have further information in relation to copyright material, please contact the publishers.

INDEX

business, 590
Commonwealth relations, 524
East Timor, 351
foreign policy, 520, 526
Howard Government
relations, **521–22**
Howard's friendship with
Clark, 462–63
Mahathir in, 514
refugees and asylum-seekers,
402
sport, 595
tax reform, 303
Newcastle, NSW, 50
Newman, Jocelyn, 237, 362–63
news. *see* media
news conferences. *see* media
News Limited, 317, 320, 332, 378,
614
newsagents, 20
Newtown, NSW, 9
NFF. *see* National Farmers
Federation
Nguyen Kim Van, 598
Nguyen Tuong Van, 597–98
NHT. *see* Natural Heritage Trust
NIA. *see* National Intelligence
Assessment
Nicholls Society. *see* H.R. Nicholls
Society
Niger, 453
Nigeria, 524–25, 595, Plate 27
Nixon, Peter, 56, 92, 95, 99, 105,
117, 132, 160
Nock & Kirby's (department
store), 8
North, Anthony Max (Justice),
296, 299, 401
North America
Australian links, 233
see also Canada; United States
North Korea, 447
North Ryde, NSW, 309
North Shore, NSW, 201, 483
North Sydney (federal electorate,
NSW), 52, 66, 320
North West Shelf Consortium,
507–8, 545
Northern Ireland, 41
Northern Territory, 149, 169–70,
204, 270, 283–84, 639, Plate
24. *see also* Mudginberri
abbatoir dispute
Norway, 393, 395–98
Notaras, Len, 413
Nuclear Disarmament Party
(NDP), 147
Nuclear Non-Proliferation Treaty,
530–31
nuclear power, 530, 552–53, 555
nuclear weapons, 147–48, 423,
427, 501, 531. *see also* Iraq
Nugent, Carol, 371

Nugent, Peter, 371
Nutt, Tony, 379, 405, 599, 615,
646, 668, Plate 21

O
Oakes, Laurie, 116, 218, 360, 369
Oakeshott, Rob, 650
oath of allegiance, 240
Obama, Barack, 349, 388, 423,
429, 458, 474, 549, 559
Obasanjo, Olusegun, 524–25,
Plate 27
O'Brien, Kerry, 194, 202, 223,
588
O'Byrne, Michelle, 479–80
O'Connor, Michael, 478
O'Donoghue, Lowitja (Lois), 273
OECD. *see* Organisation for
Economic Cooperation and
Development
Office of National Assessments
(ONA), 238, 406–7, 436, 454,
456
Office of the Employment
Advocate, 578
Officer, Bob, 267
official residences. *see* Admiralty
House, Sydney; Kirribilli
House; Prime Minister's
Lodge
O'Hagan, Mike, 577
oil, 359, 554
oil prices, 54–55, 107, 122, 361,
366. *see also* petrol prices
old growth forests. *see* forest
policy
older Australians, 143–45, 370,
374, 497, 545, 629, 635, 645
O'Leary, Tony, 220, 378, 405,
592–93, 646, 670, Plate 21
Olympic Games, 251, 267, 417
1956 Melbourne, 18
2000 Sydney, 359, 591, Plate
25
2008 Beijing, 596
ONA. *see* Office of National
Assessments
'One Australia' (Howard
speeches), 173, 271. *see also*
multiculturalism
One China policy, 501–2, 511
One Nation (Hanson movement),
262, 309–11
One Nation (Keating statement,
1992), 189–90, 201
one-off payments. *see* bonuses
OPEC. *see* oil prices
opinion polls. *see* polls
Opposition
caretaker periods, 476–77
Opposition, ALP in. *see* Australian
Labor Party (ALP) in
opposition

Opposition, Coalition in
elections. *see* elections
(Federal)
Victoria, 177, 180
see also shadow ministers
Opposition, Coalition in (before
1949)
East Timor, 338
Menzies as leader, 8, 79, 139
Opposition, Coalition in
(1972–75)
1975 crisis and dismissal,
82–85, 88–89
Fraser as leader, 70, 78, 84,
87
Gair Affair, 64
Howard as MP, 48, 71–72
Howard as whip, 78–79
non-parliamentary work, 79
policies, 54, 65–67, 70, 72, 78,
108
Senate (1975), 83
Snedden as leader, 56, 76
Opposition, Coalition in
(1983–96), 94, **137–228**, 560
Brown as deputy leader, 563
Coalition split (1987), 139,
155, **160–67**, 170–71
Downer as leader, 204–5, 210,
212
Downer's shadow cabinet,
204, 210
economic reform, 126, 541
Hewson as leader, 193
Howard as deputy leader, 338,
516
Howard as leader, 118, 145,
152–54, 178, 188, 212–13,
219–20, 222, 227–28,
272–73, 465, 514, 516,
Plate 19
Howard as manager of
business, 197
Howard as shadow minister,
181–82, 185
Howard in, 48, 136, 228, 266,
268, 304
Indigenous policy, 272–73
industrial relations, 136, 287,
565
Keating's attacks on, 189–90
leadership. *see* Liberal Party of
Australia leadership
older Australians, 370
policies (1980s), 177
policies (1990s), 186–97, 205,
212, 215, 218–27. *see also*
Fightback!
republican debate, 217–18
shadow cabinet, 210
tax policy, 160
waterfront reform, 287
whips, 206